T0040339

The Silver Age of Comic Books took place between 1956 and approximately 1970 and was the second major era of American comics. This period saw the deepening of the mythos of different characters and the DC Universe itself, as well as an increasing number of horror, crime, and romance titles. One of those crime comics was *Detective Comics*, which had first featured Batman in issue #27 (May 1939). Batman headlined almost every issue of *Detective Comics* from then on, and the

Silver Age saw the introduction of notable Batman supporting characters such as Barbara Gordon's Batgirl (May 1964). The Bronze Age of Comics ran though the early 1970s into the mid '80s, revitalizing Batman as a more brooding and dark hero, an interpretation of the character that has lasted to present day. This collection contains *Detective Comics* covers from issues #301 to #600, celebrating the Batman story arcs of the Silver and Bronze eras and the beginning of the Modern Age.

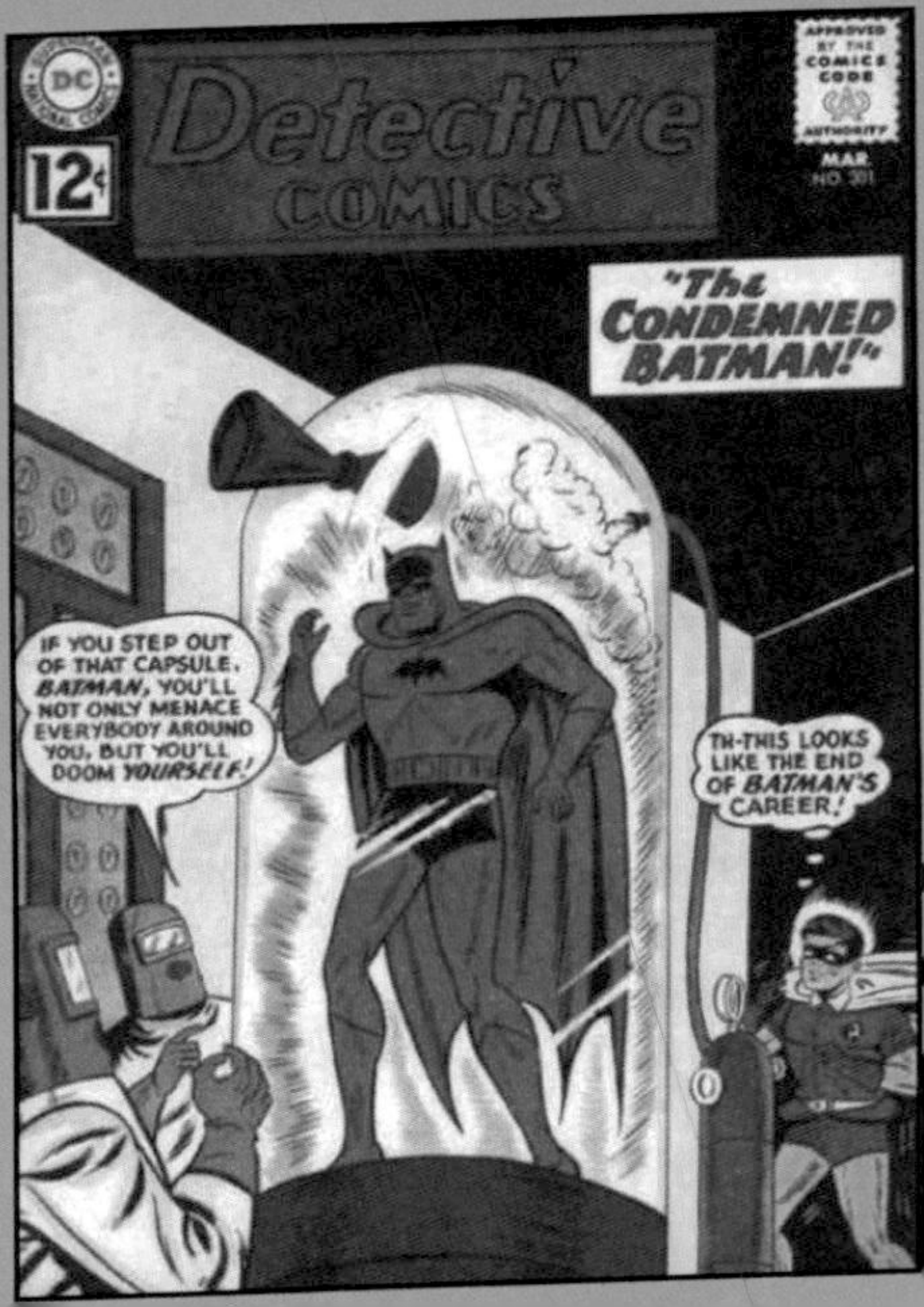
DC
12¢
Detective COMICS
APPROVED BY THE COMICS CODE AUTHORITY
MAR
NO. 301
"The CONDEMNED BATMAN!"
IF YOU STEP OUT OF THAT CAPSULE, BATMAN, YOU'LL NOT ONLY MENACE EVERYBODY AROUND YOU, BUT YOU'LL DOOM YOURSELF!
TH-THIS LOOKS LIKE THE END OF BATMAN'S CAREER!

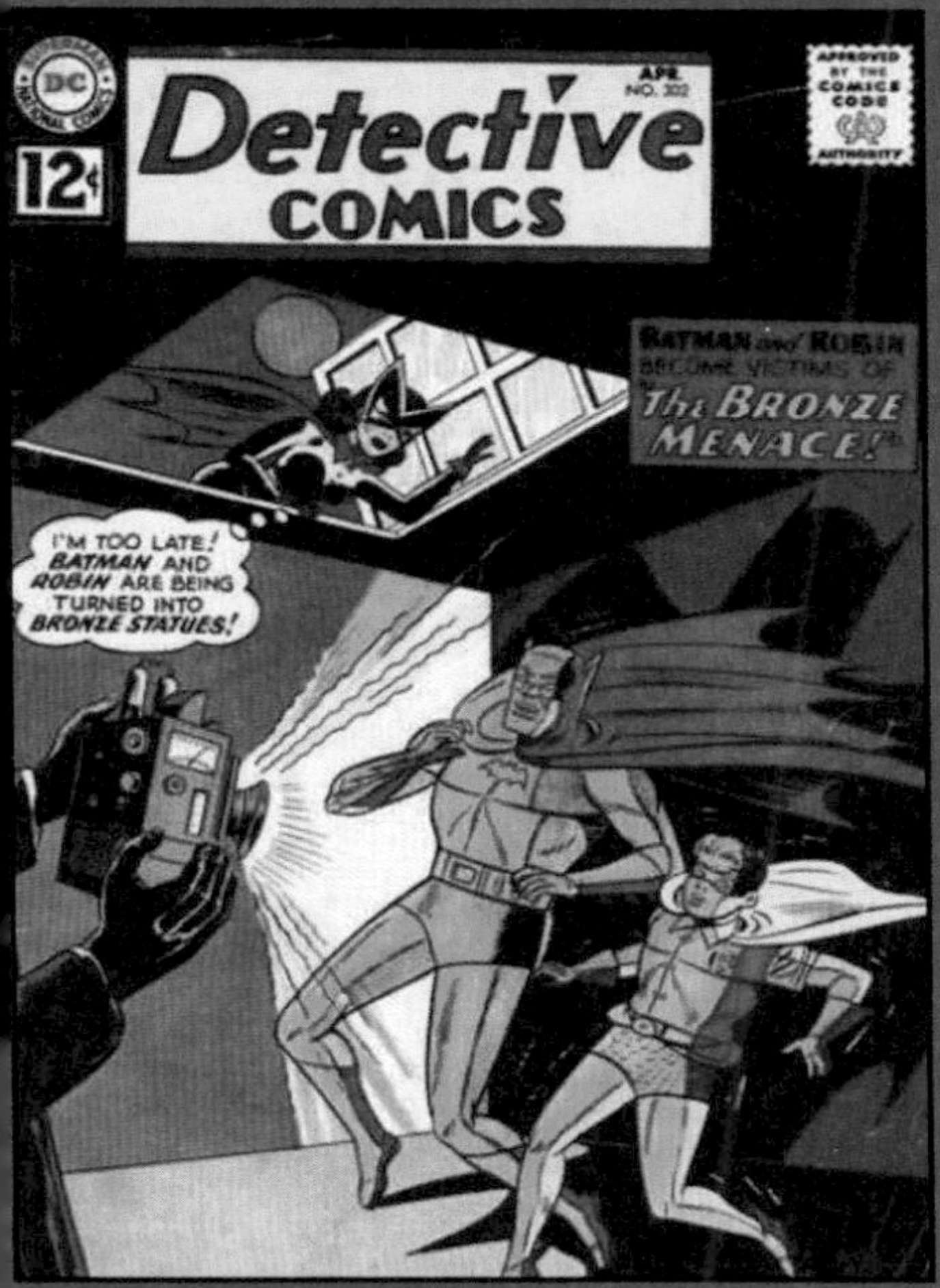
DC
12¢
Detective
COMICS
APR.
NO. 302
APPROVED BY THE COMICS CODE AUTHORITY
BATMAN and ROBIN BECOME VICTIMS OF The BRONZE MENACE!
I'M TOO LATE! BATMAN AND ROBIN ARE BEING TURNED INTO BRONZE STATUES!

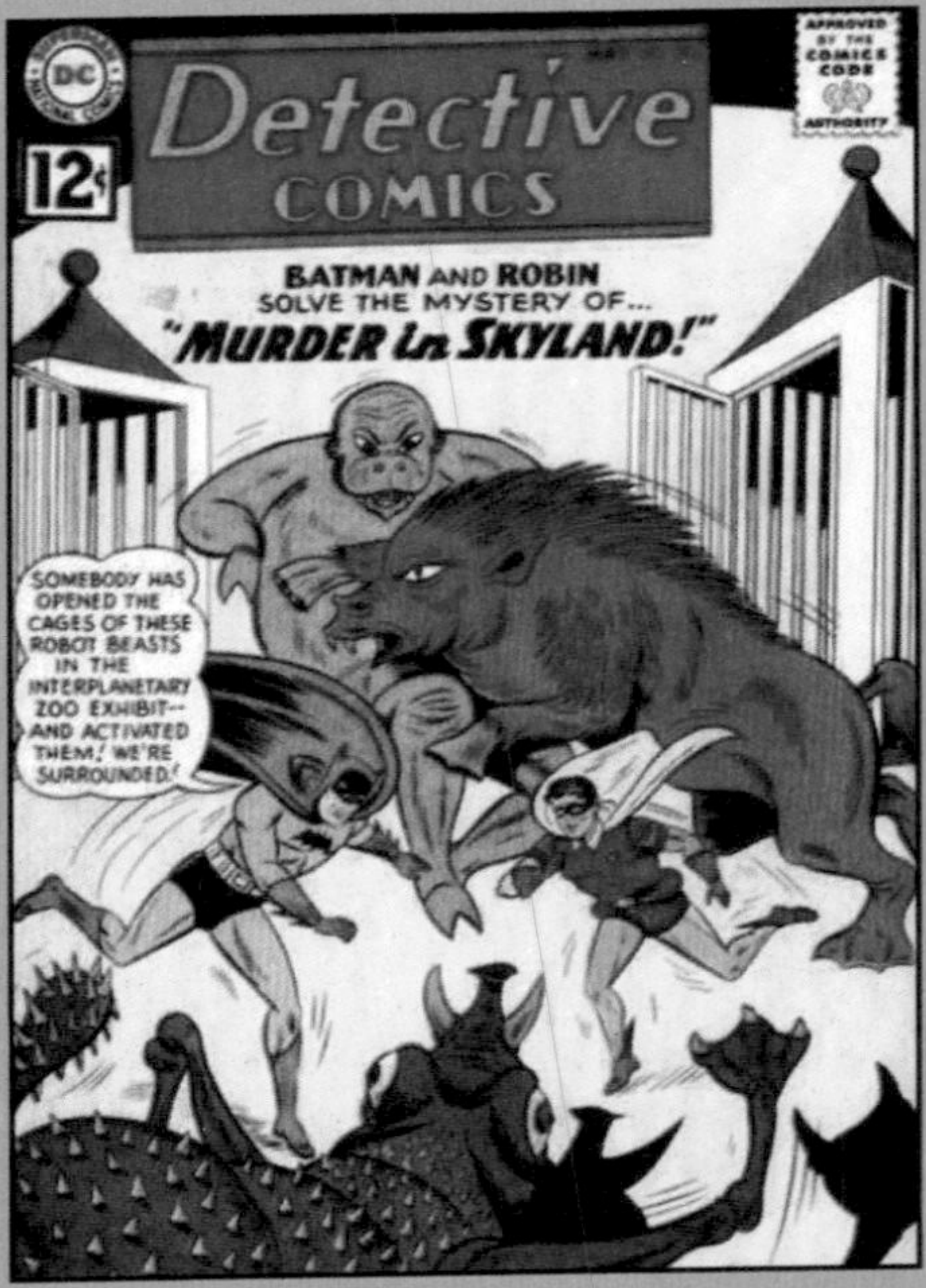
DC
12¢
Detective
COMICS
APPROVED BY THE COMICS CODE AUTHORITY
BATMAN AND ROBIN
SOLVE THE MYSTERY OF...
"MURDER IN SKYLAND!"
SOMEBODY HAS OPENED THE CAGES OF THESE ROBOT BEASTS IN THE INTERPLANETARY ZOO EXHIBIT-- AND ACTIVATED THEM! WE'RE SURROUNDED!

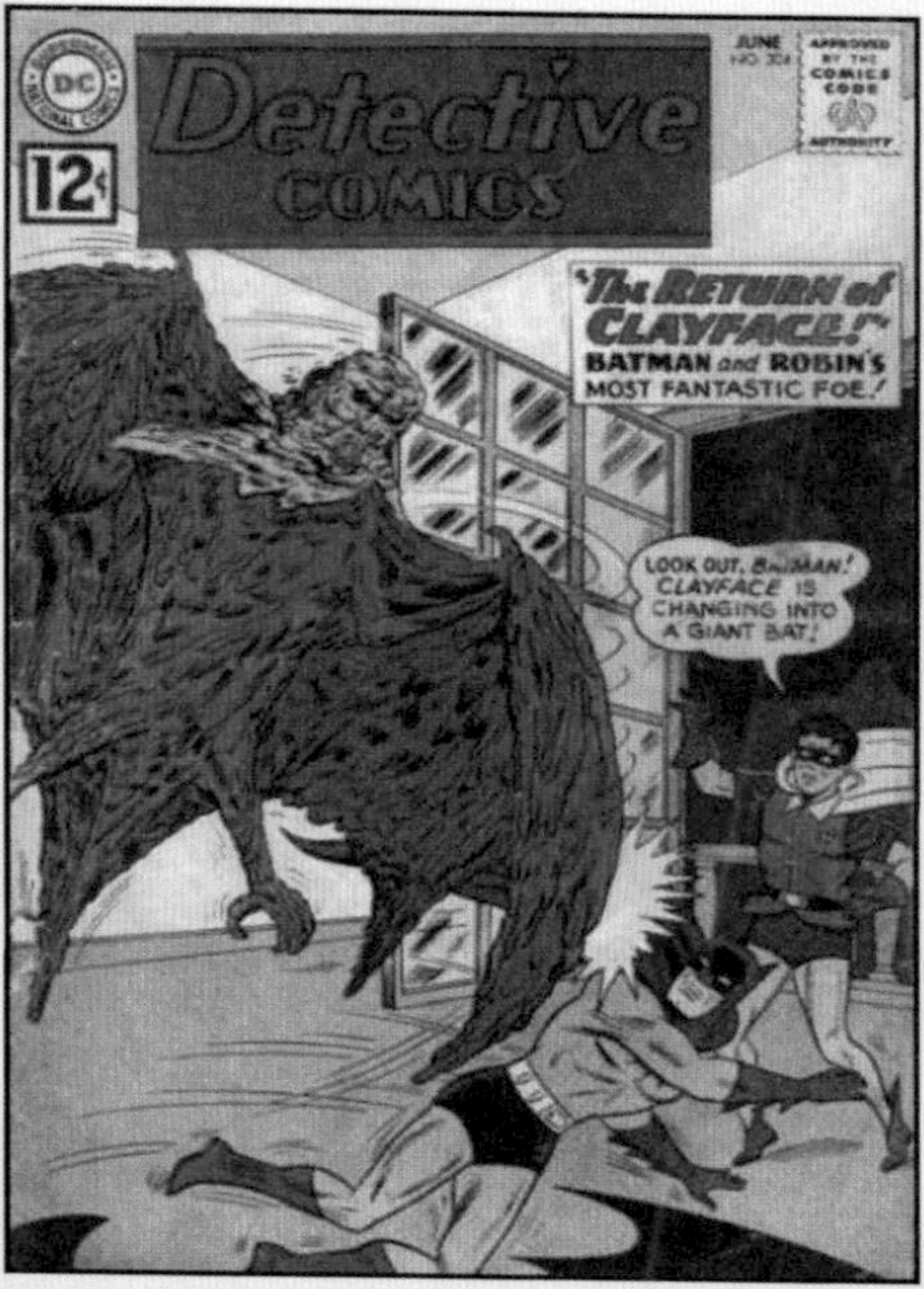
DC
12¢
Detective
COMICS
JUNE
NO. 326
APPROVED BY THE COMICS CODE AUTHORITY
"The RETURN of CLAYFACE!"
BATMAN and ROBIN'S MOST FANTASTIC FOE!
LOOK OUT, BATMAN! CLAYFACE IS CHANGING INTO A GIANT BAT!

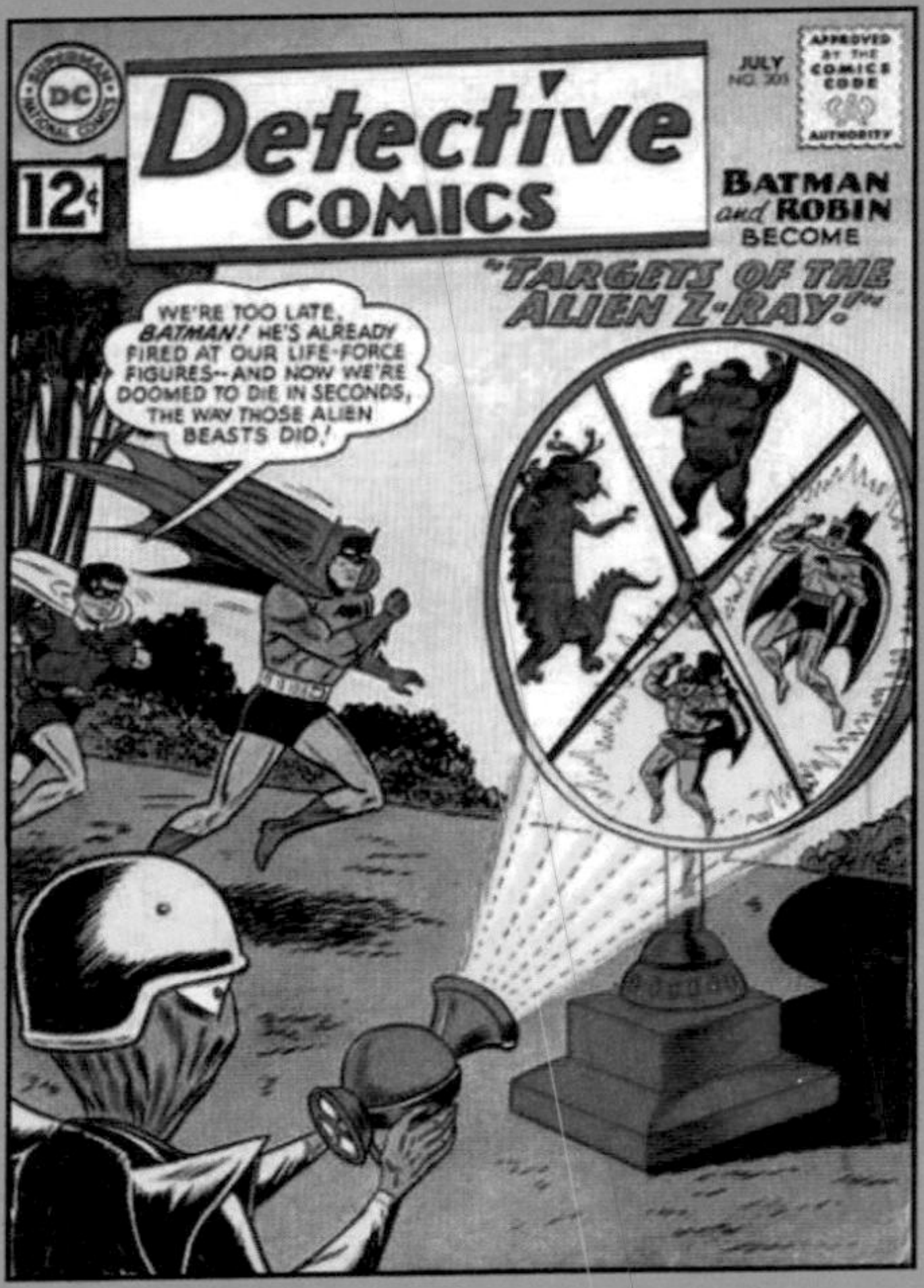
DC
Detective COMICS
12¢
JULY
APPROVED BY THE COMICS CODE AUTHORITY
BATMAN and ROBIN BECOME
"TARGETS OF THE ALIEN Z-RAY!"
WE'RE TOO LATE, BATMAN! HE'S ALREADY FIRED AT OUR LIFE-FORCE FIGURES--AND NOW WE'RE DOOMED TO DIE IN SECONDS, THE WAY THOSE ALIEN BEASTS DID!

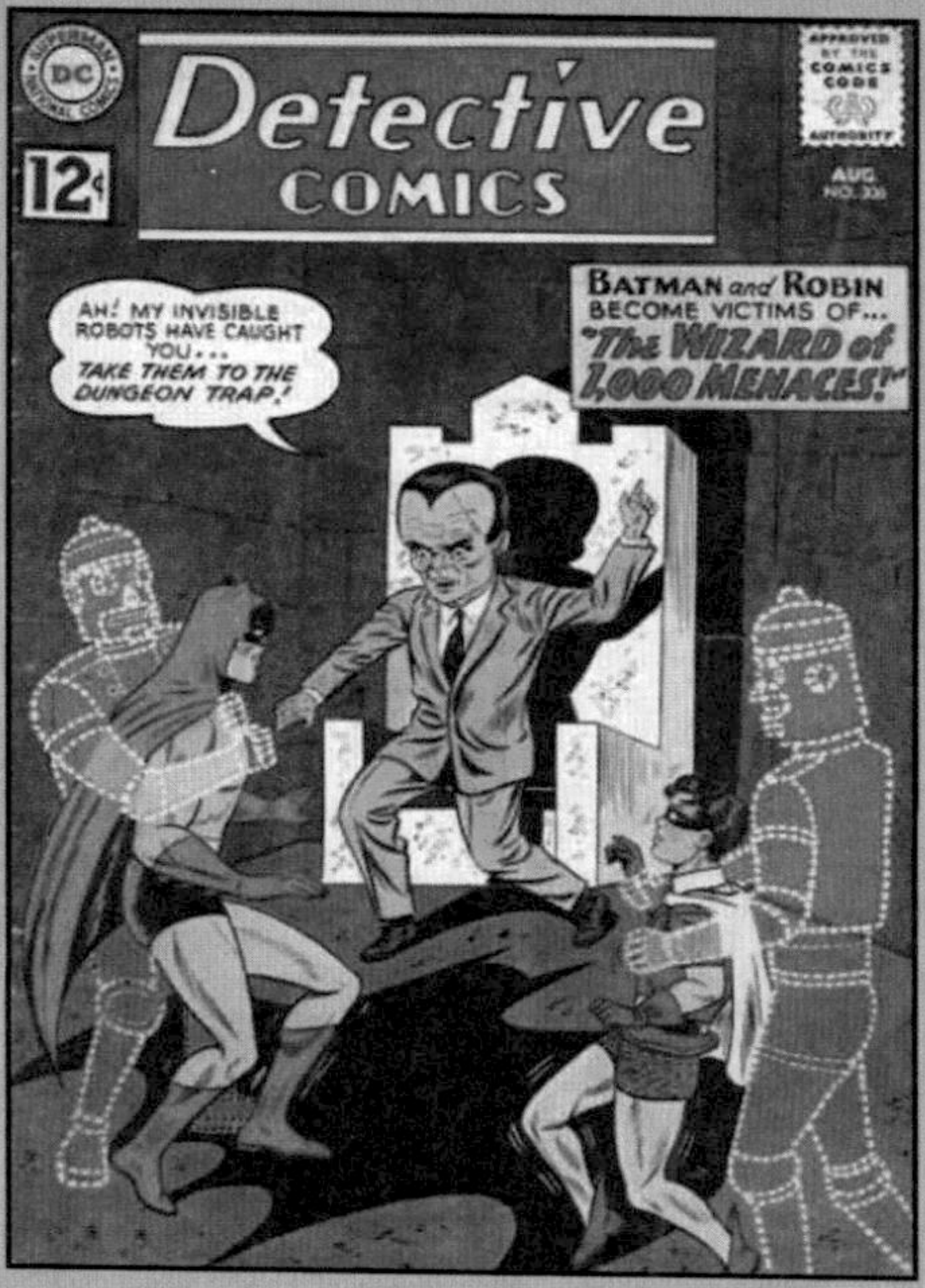
DC
Detective
COMICS
12¢
APPROVED BY THE COMICS CODE AUTHORITY
AUG.
BATMAN and ROBIN BECOME VICTIMS OF...
"The WIZARD of 1,000 MENACES!"
AH! MY INVISIBLE ROBOTS HAVE CAUGHT YOU... TAKE THEM TO THE DUNGEON TRAP!

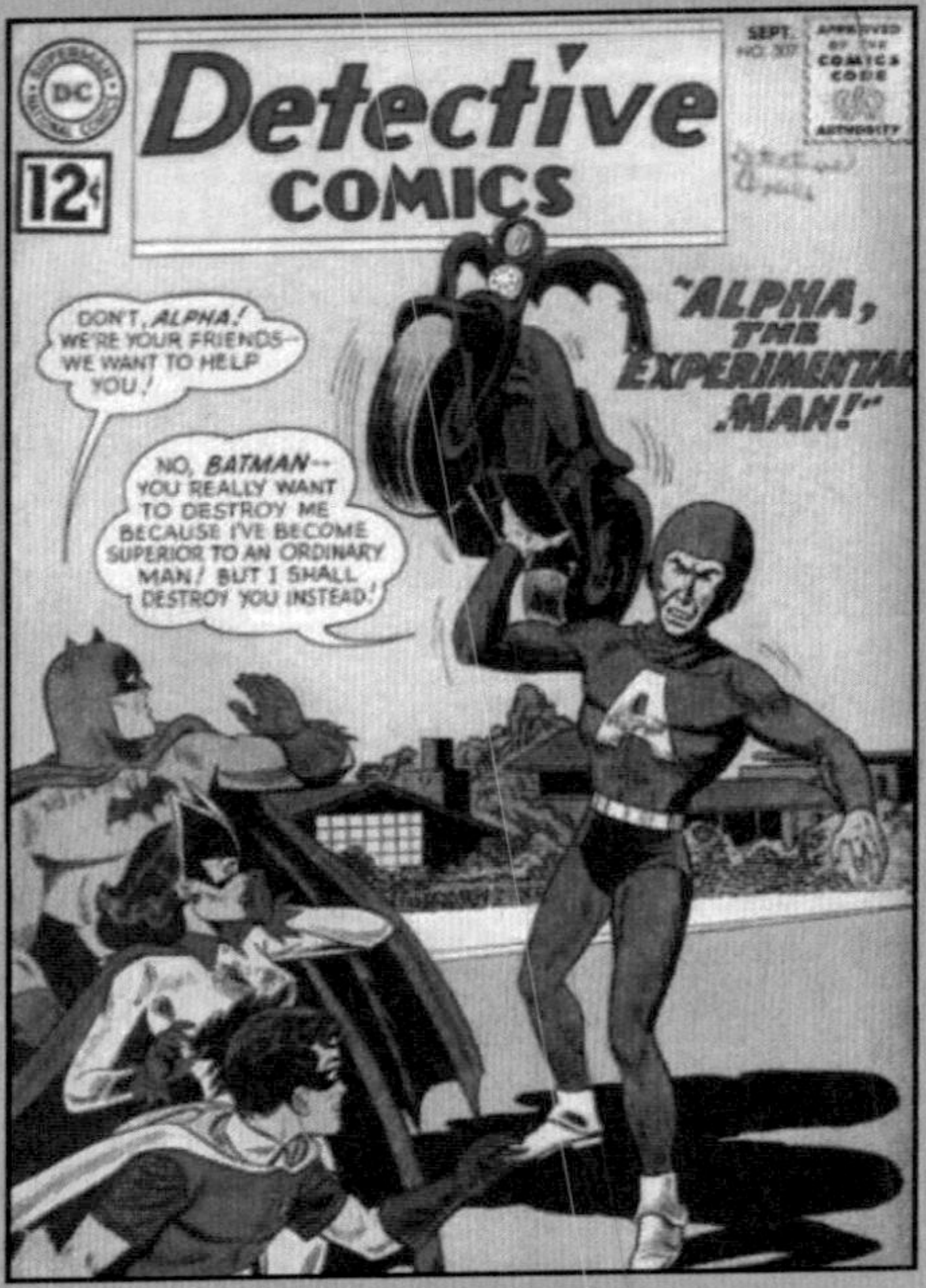
DC
12¢
Detective
COMICS
SEPT.
NO. 307
APPROVED BY THE COMICS CODE AUTHORITY
"ALPHA, THE EXPERIMENTAL MAN!"
DON'T, ALPHA! WE'RE YOUR FRIENDS—WE WANT TO HELP YOU!
NO, BATMAN—YOU REALLY WANT TO DESTROY ME BECAUSE I'VE BECOME SUPERIOR TO AN ORDINARY MAN! BUT I SHALL DESTROY YOU INSTEAD!

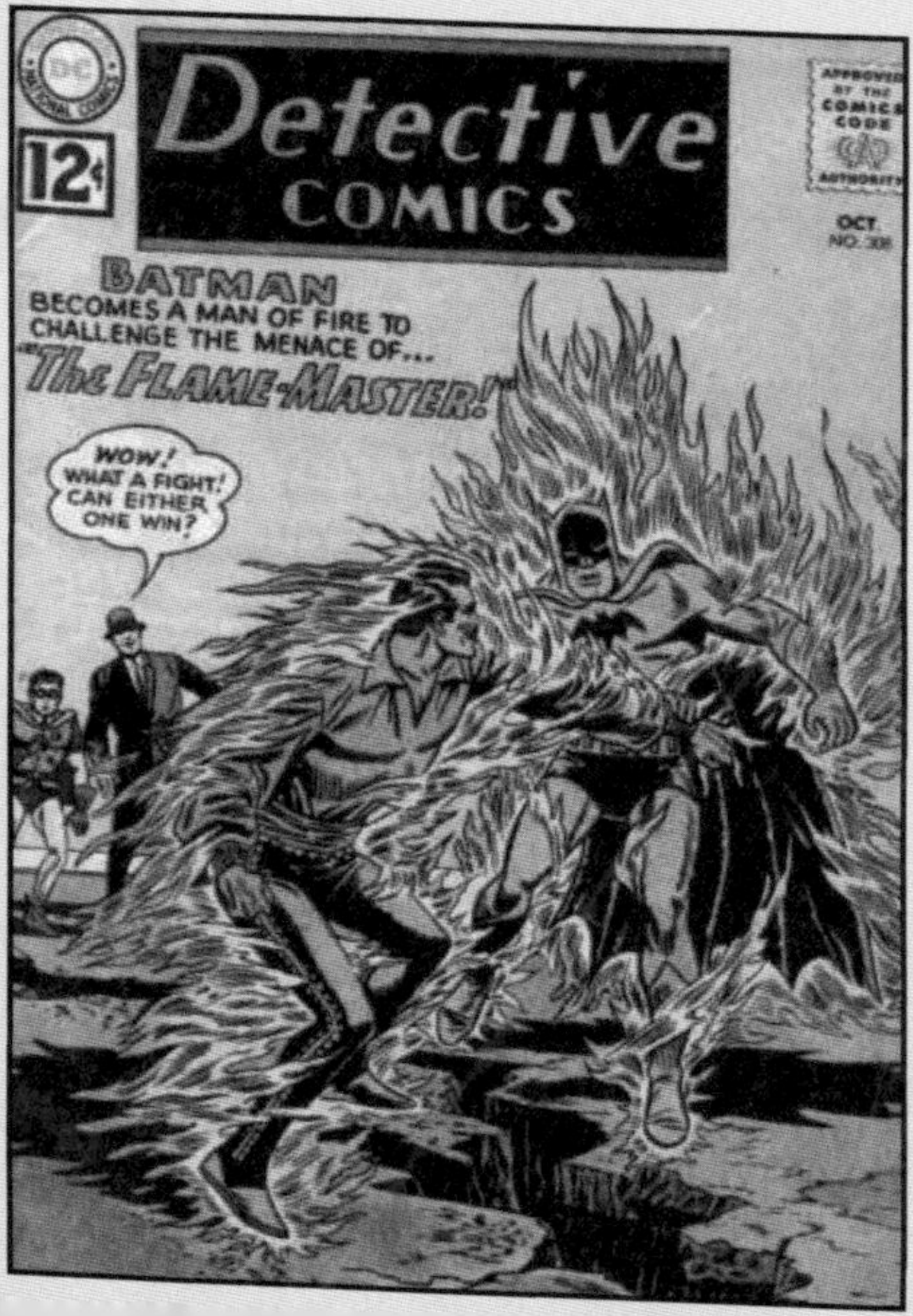
DC
NATIONAL COMICS
12¢
Detective
COMICS
APPROVED BY THE COMICS CODE AUTHORITY
OCT.
NO. 308
BATMAN
BECOMES A MAN OF FIRE TO CHALLENGE THE MENACE OF...
"The FLAME-MASTER!"
WOW! WHAT A FIGHT! CAN EITHER ONE WIN?

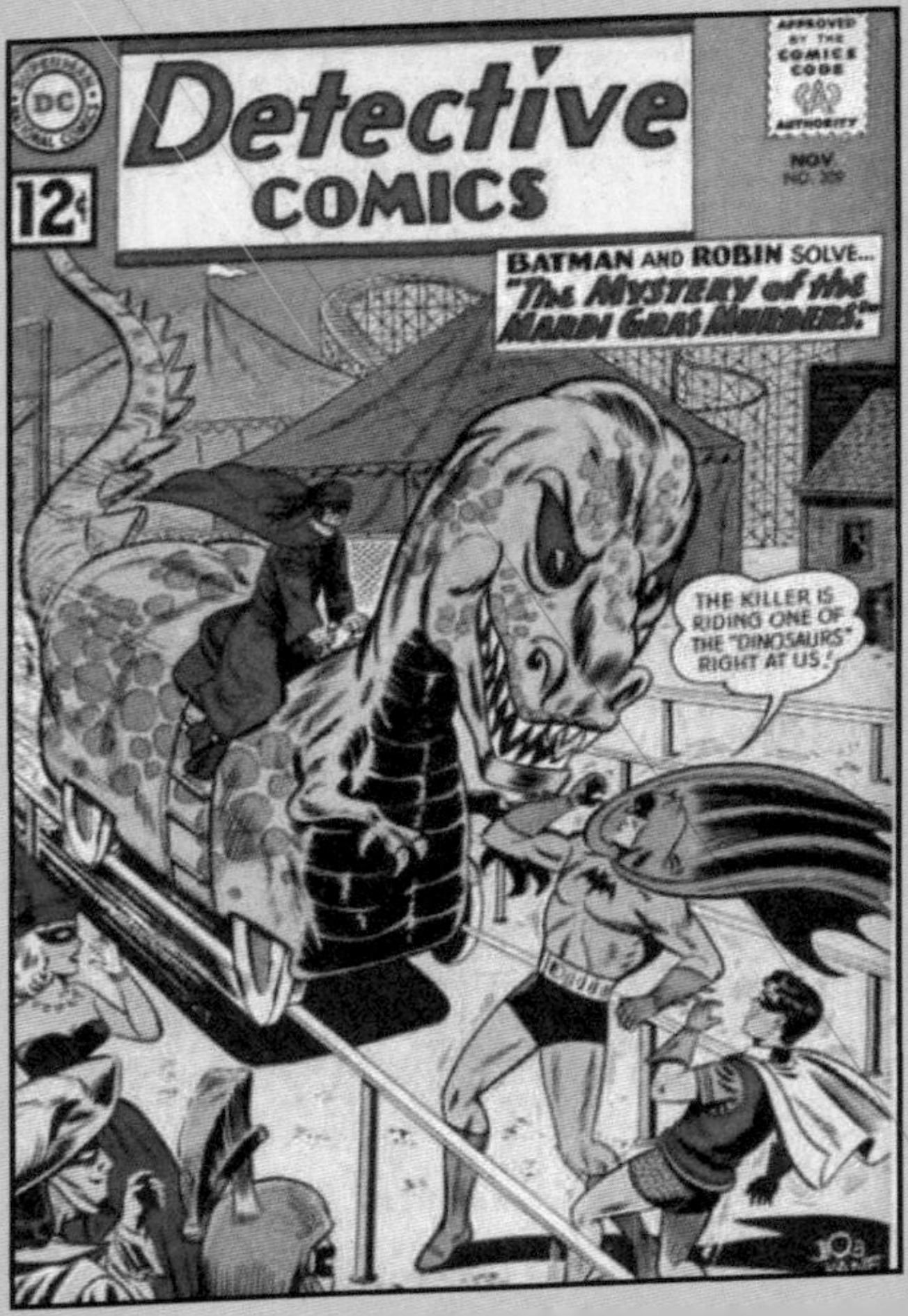
DC
Detective
COMICS
12¢
APPROVED BY THE COMICS CODE AUTHORITY
NOV.
BATMAN AND ROBIN SOLVE...
"The Mystery of the Mardi Gras Murders!"
THE KILLER IS RIDING ONE OF THE "DINOSAURS" RIGHT AT US!

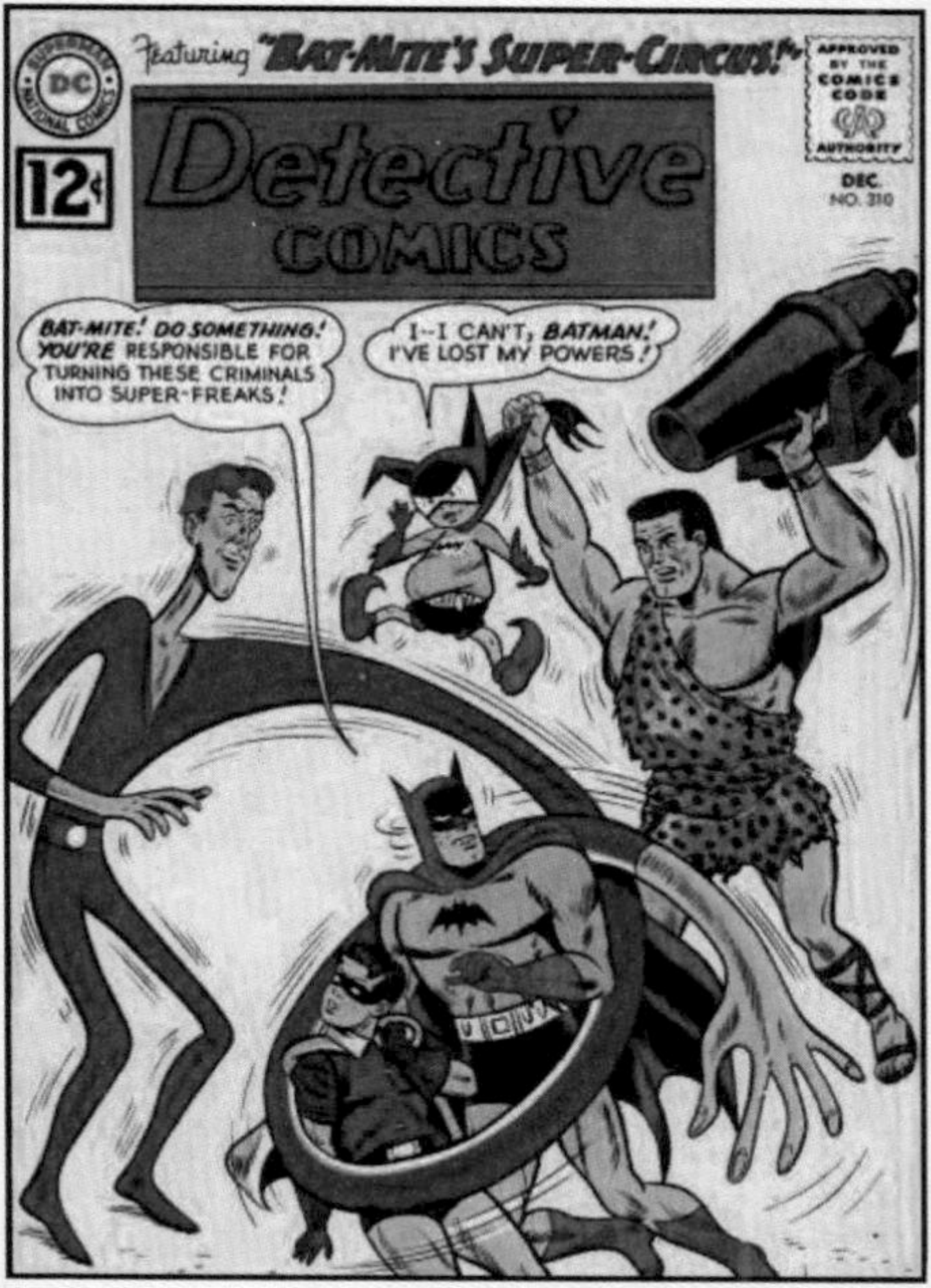
Featuring "BAT-MITE'S SUPER-CIRCUS!"
DC
12¢
Detective COMICS
APPROVED BY THE COMICS CODE AUTHORITY
DEC.
NO. 310
BAT-MITE! DO SOMETHING! YOU'RE RESPONSIBLE FOR TURNING THESE CRIMINALS INTO SUPER-FREAKS!
I--I CAN'T, BATMAN! I'VE LOST MY POWERS!

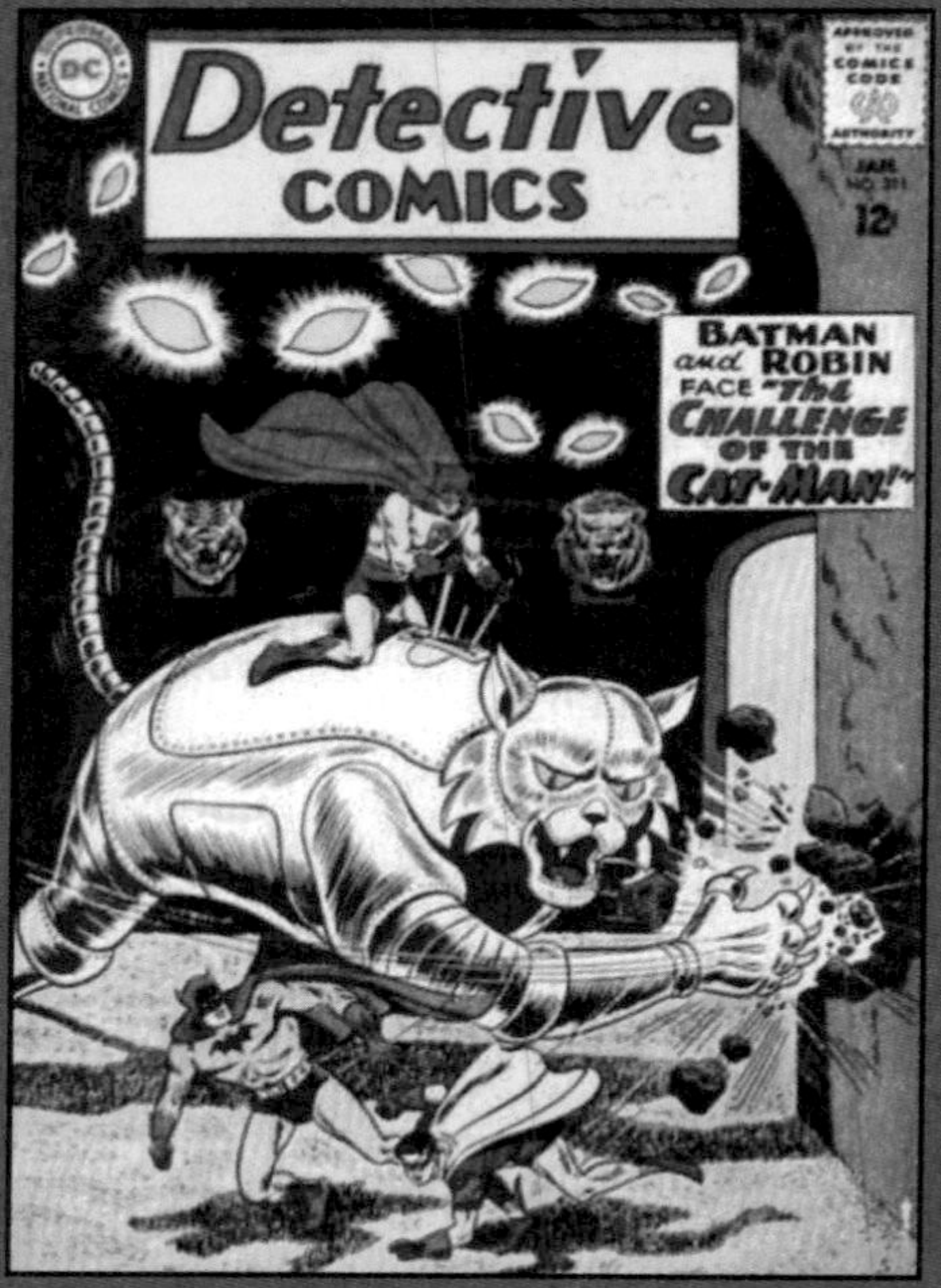
DC
Detective
COMICS
APPROVED BY THE COMICS CODE AUTHORITY
JAN.
NO. 311
12¢
BATMAN and ROBIN FACE "The CHALLENGE OF THE CAT-MAN!"

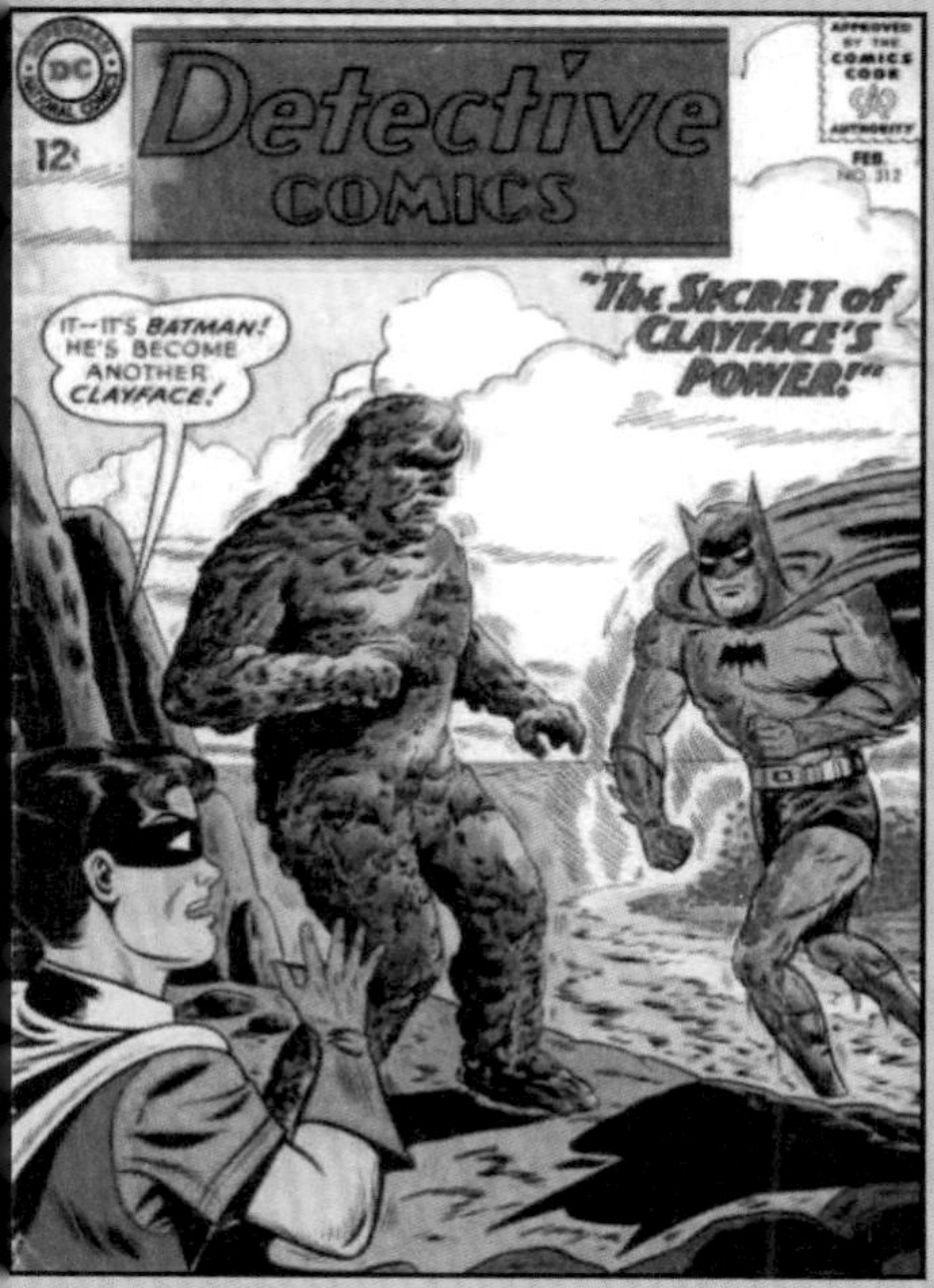
DC
12¢
Detective
COMICS
APPROVED BY THE COMICS CODE AUTHORITY
FEB.
NO. 312
"The SECRET of CLAYFACE'S POWER!"
IT—IT'S BATMAN! HE'S BECOME ANOTHER CLAYFACE!

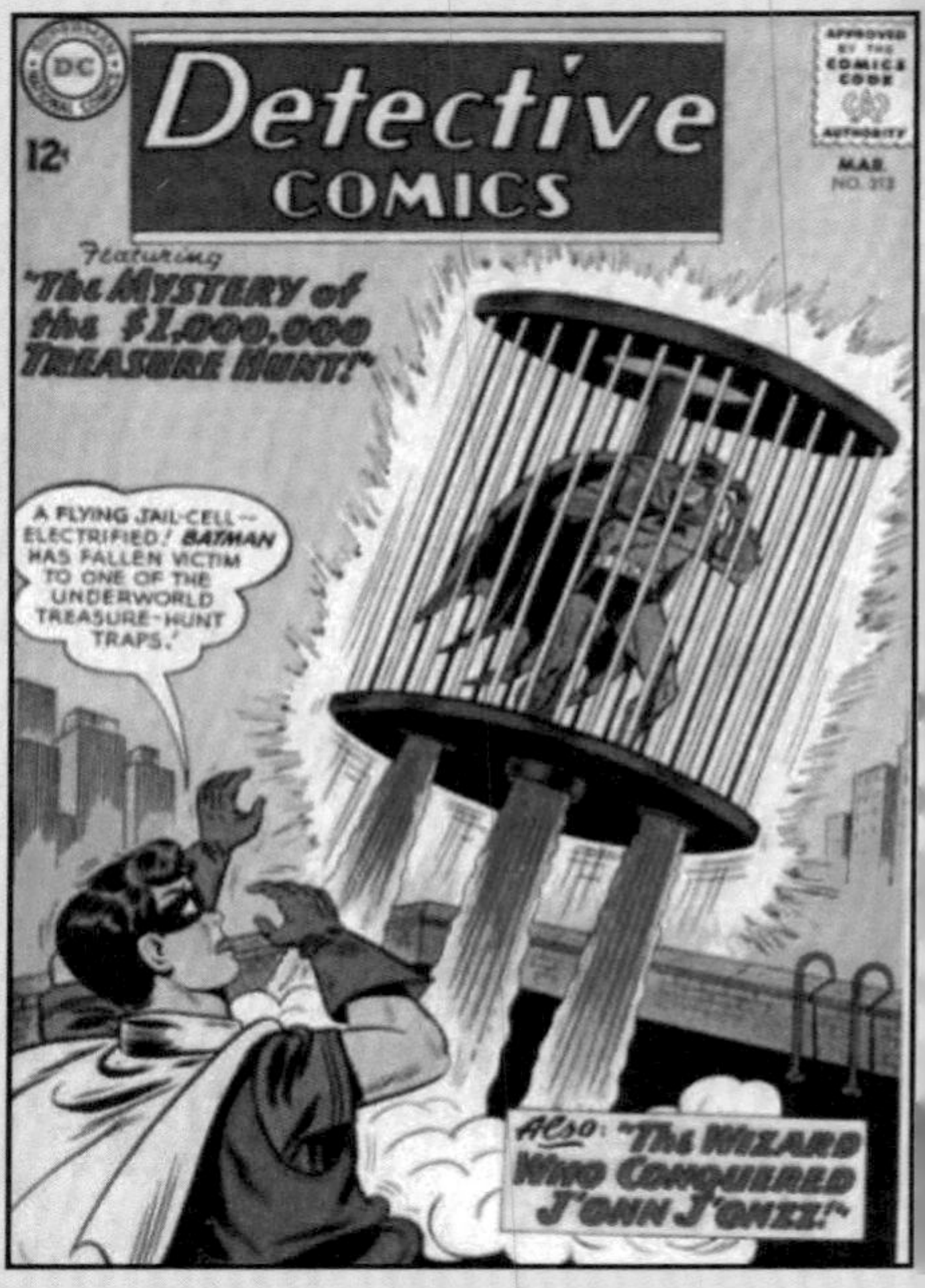
DC
12¢
Detective
COMICS
APPROVED BY THE COMICS CODE AUTHORITY
MAR.
NO. 313
Featuring
"The Mystery of the $1,000,000 Treasure Hunt!"
A FLYING JAIL-CELL—ELECTRIFIED! BATMAN HAS FALLEN VICTIM TO ONE OF THE UNDERWORLD TREASURE-HUNT TRAPS.
Also: "The Wizard Who Conquered J'onn J'onzz!"

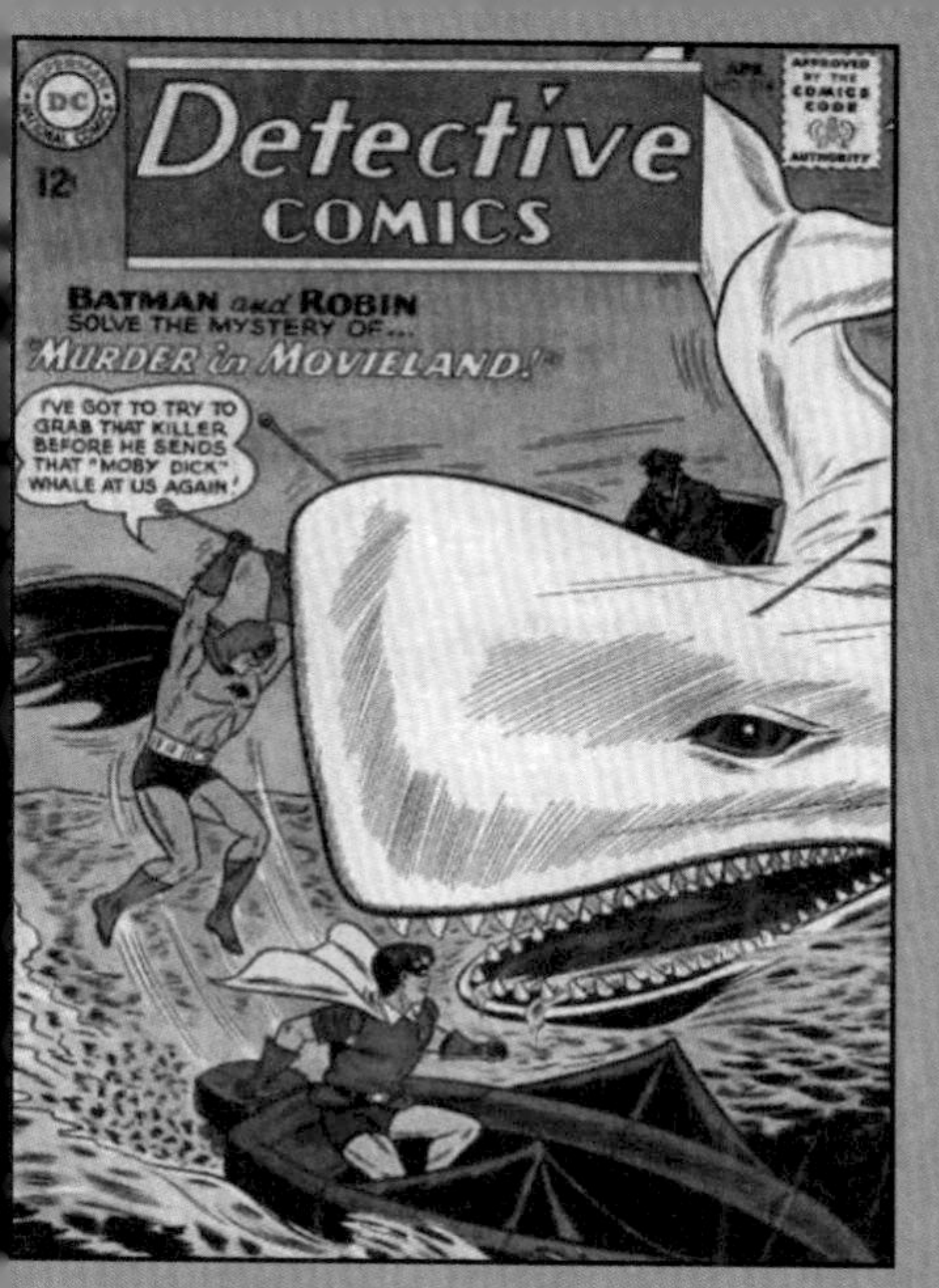
DC
12¢
Detective
COMICS
APPROVED BY THE COMICS CODE AUTHORITY
BATMAN and ROBIN
SOLVE THE MYSTERY OF...
"MURDER in MOVIELAND!"
I'VE GOT TO TRY TO GRAB THAT KILLER BEFORE HE SENDS THAT "MOBY DICK" WHALE AT US AGAIN!

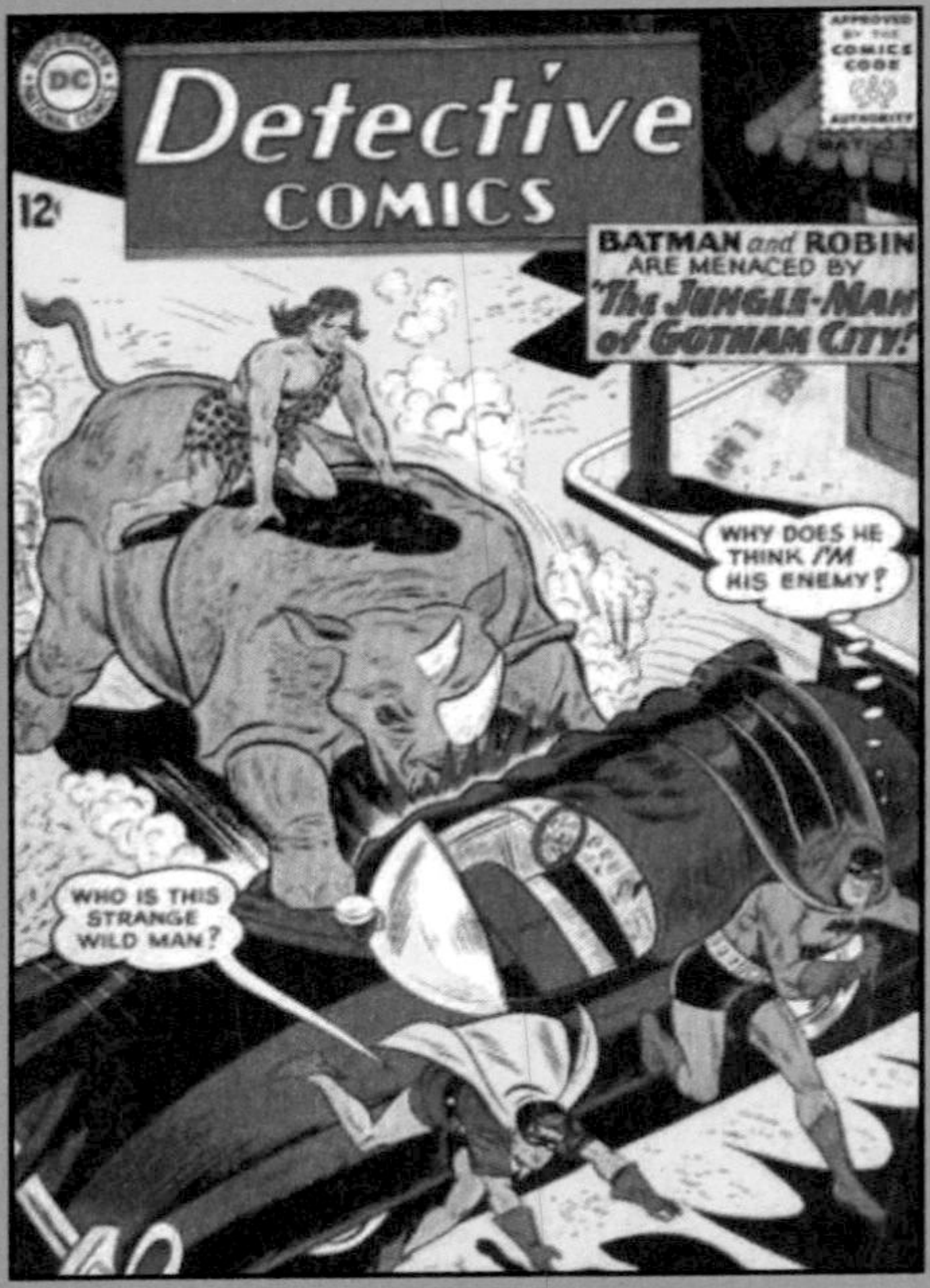
DC
Detective
COMICS
12¢
APPROVED BY THE COMICS CODE AUTHORITY
BATMAN and ROBIN ARE MENACED BY "The JUNGLE-MAN of GOTHAM CITY!"
WHY DOES HE THINK I'M HIS ENEMY?
WHO IS THIS STRANGE WILD MAN?

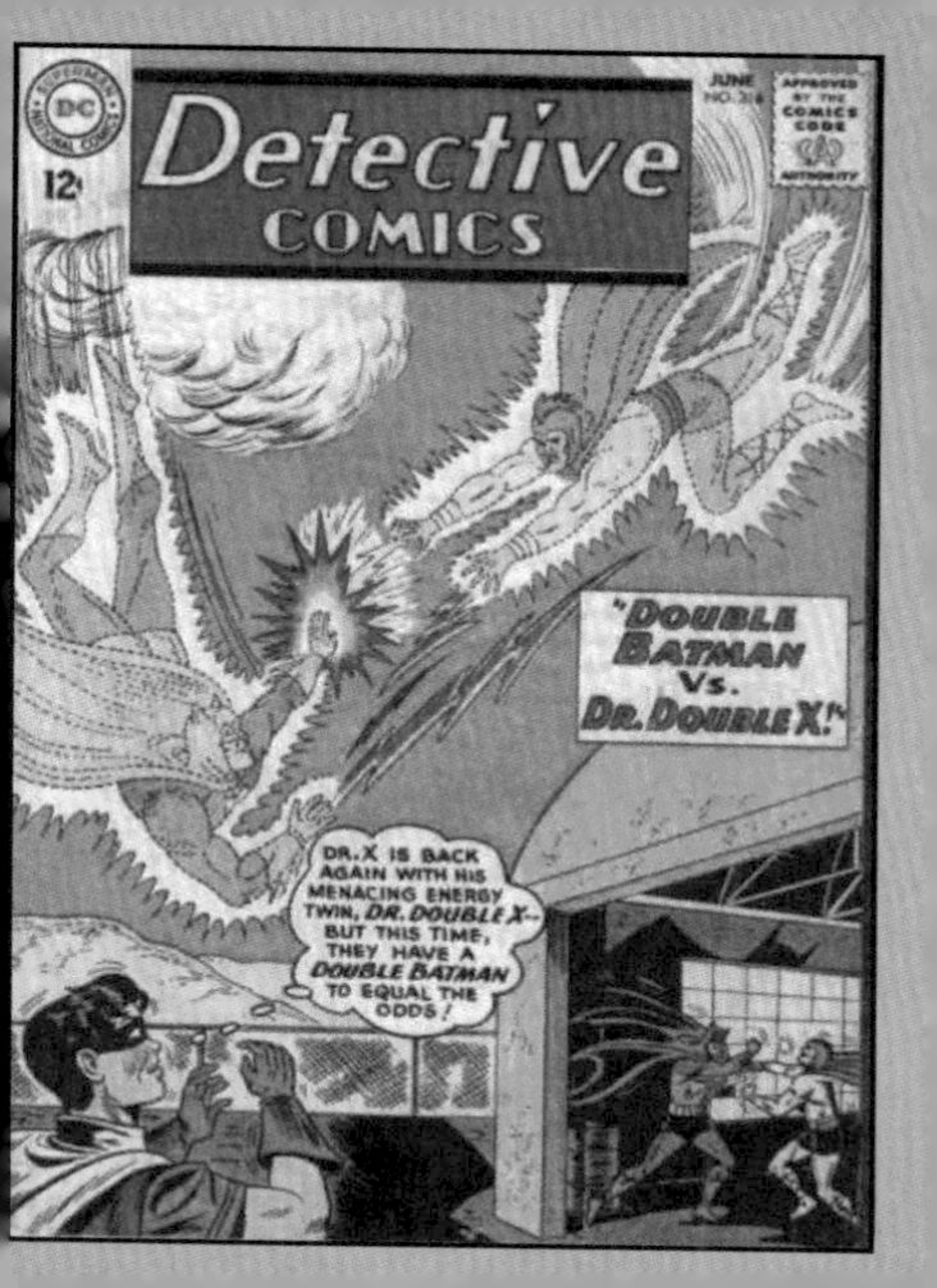
DC
12¢
Detective
COMICS
JUNE
APPROVED BY THE COMICS CODE AUTHORITY
"DOUBLE BATMAN Vs. DR. DOUBLE X!"
DR. X IS BACK AGAIN WITH HIS MENACING ENERGY TWIN, DR. DOUBLE X-- BUT THIS TIME, THEY HAVE A DOUBLE BATMAN TO EQUAL THE ODDS!

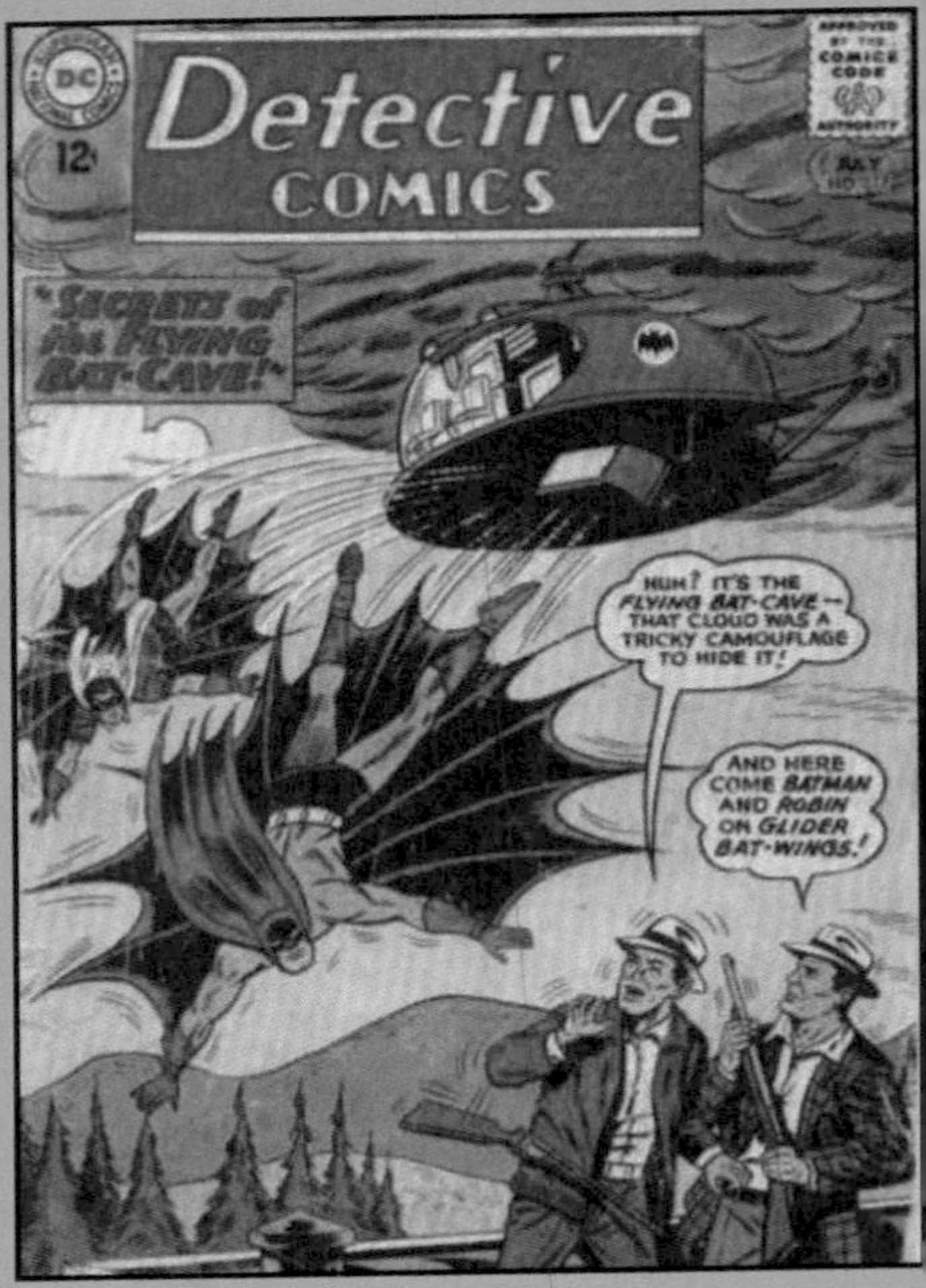
DC
12¢
Detective
COMICS
APPROVED BY THE COMICS CODE AUTHORITY
JULY
"SECRETS of the FLYING BAT-CAVE!"
HUH! IT'S THE FLYING BAT-CAVE — THAT CLOUD WAS A TRICKY CAMOUFLAGE TO HIDE IT!
AND HERE COME BATMAN AND ROBIN ON GLIDER BAT-WINGS!

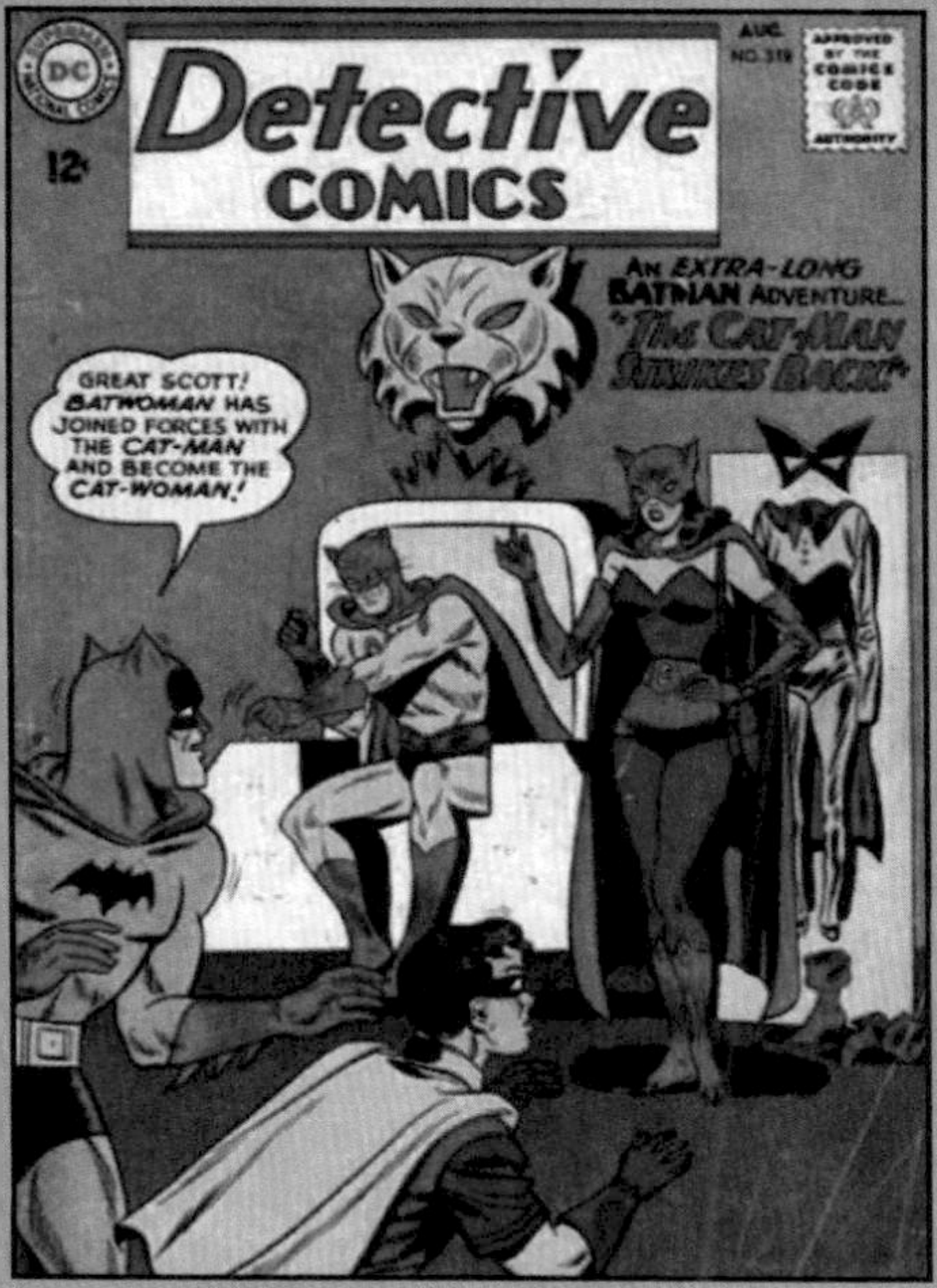
DC
Detective COMICS
12¢
AUG.
NO. 319
APPROVED BY THE COMICS CODE AUTHORITY
AN EXTRA-LONG BATMAN ADVENTURE...
"THE CAT-MAN STRIKES BACK!"
GREAT SCOTT! BATWOMAN HAS JOINED FORCES WITH THE CAT-MAN AND BECOME THE CAT-WOMAN!

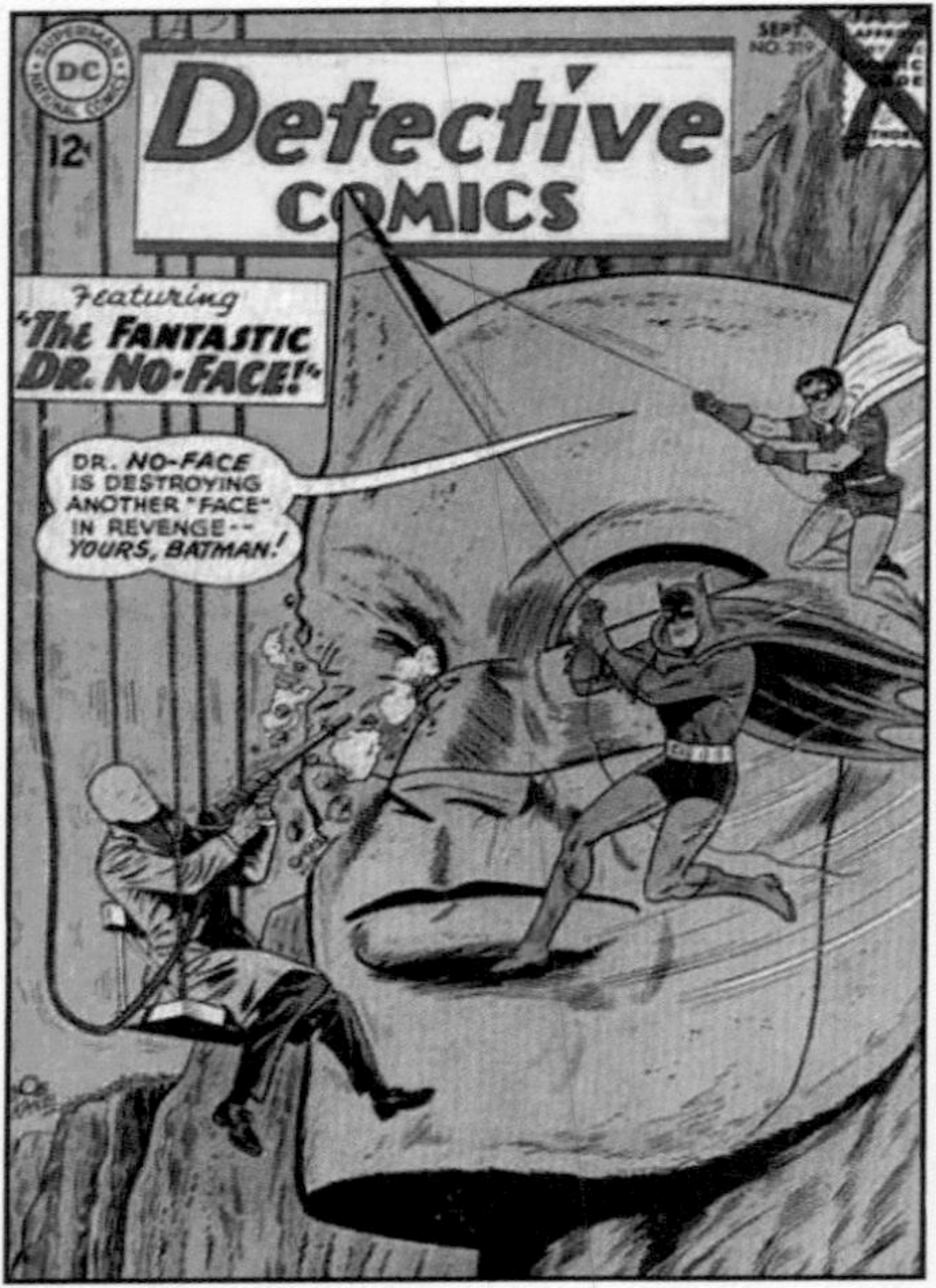
DC
12¢
Detective
COMICS
SEPT.
NO. 319
Featuring
"The Fantastic Dr. No-Face!"
DR. NO-FACE IS DESTROYING ANOTHER "FACE" IN REVENGE -- YOURS, BATMAN!

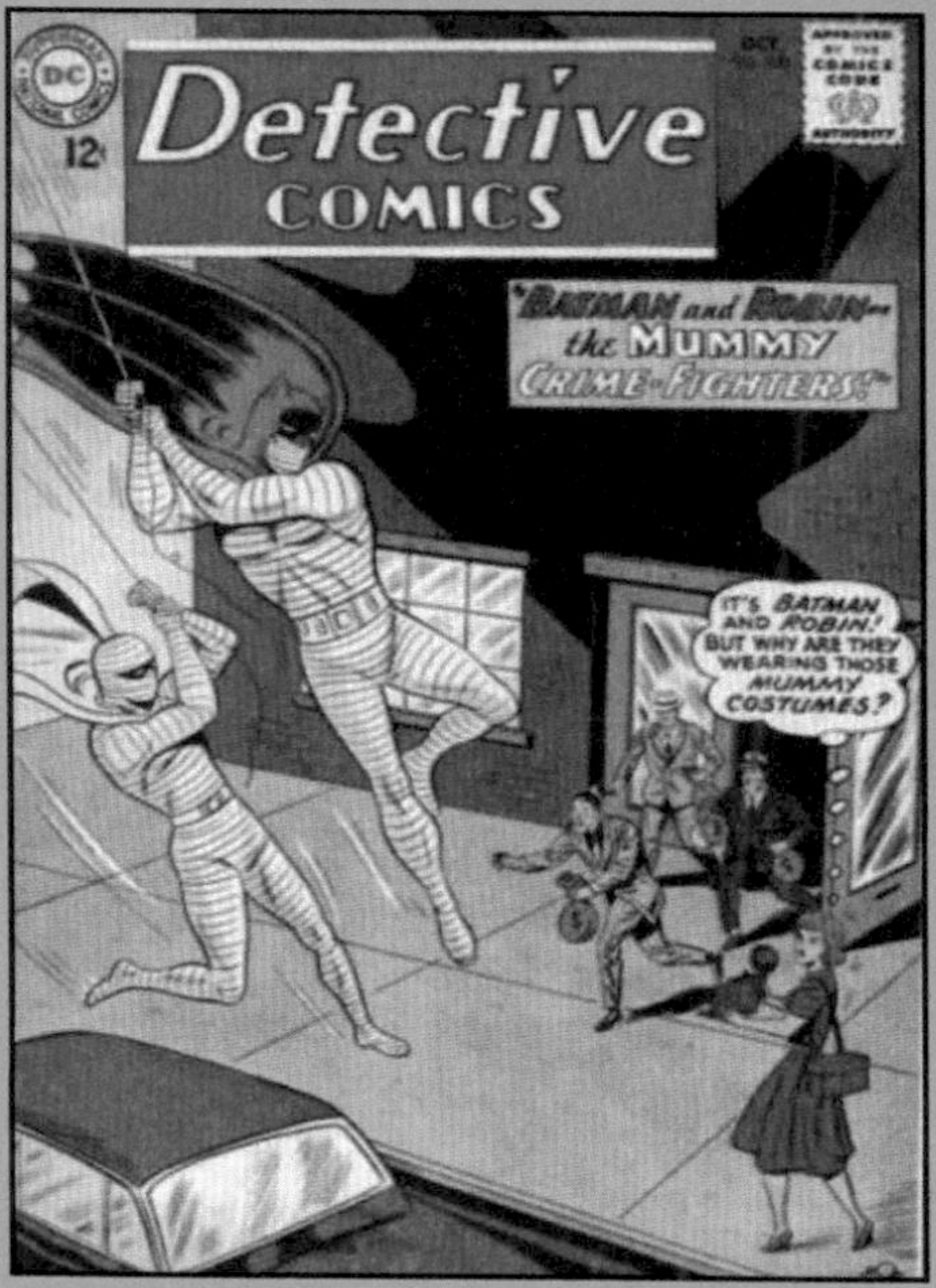
DC
12¢
Detective
COMICS
OCT.
APPROVED BY THE COMICS CODE AUTHORITY
"BATMAN and ROBIN— the MUMMY CRIME-FIGHTERS!"
IT'S BATMAN AND ROBIN! BUT WHY ARE THEY WEARING THOSE MUMMY COSTUMES?

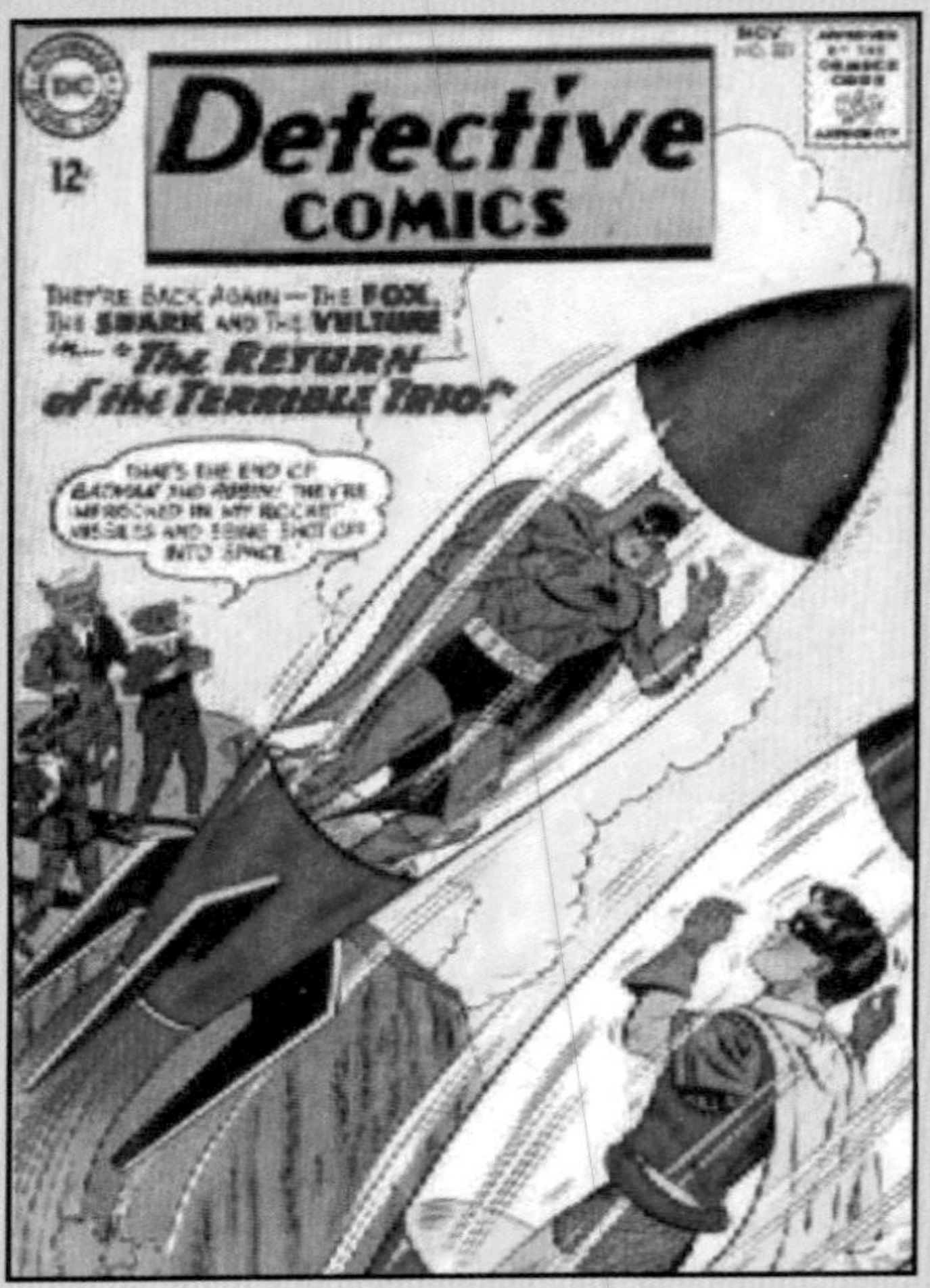
DC
12¢
Detective
COMICS
NOV.
THEY'RE BACK AGAIN — THE FOX, THE SHARK AND THE VULTURE in... "The RETURN of the TERRIBLE TRIO!"
THAT'S THE END OF BATMAN AND ROBIN! THEY'RE WRECKED IN MY ROCKET VEHICLES AND SOME SHOT OFF INTO SPACE!

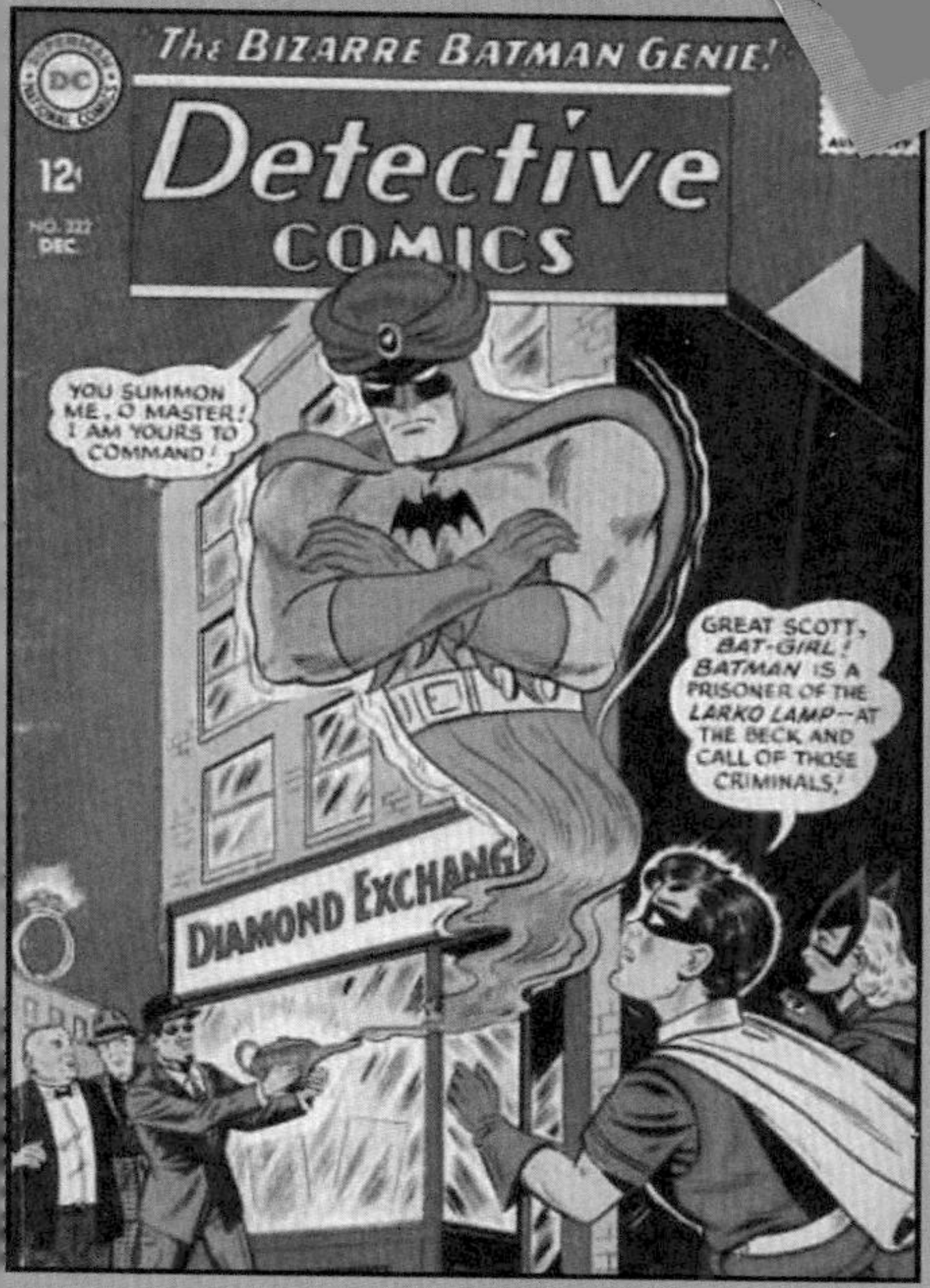
The BIZARRE BATMAN GENIE!
DC
12¢
NO. 227
DEC.
Detective
COMICS
YOU SUMMON ME, O MASTER! I AM YOURS TO COMMAND!
GREAT SCOTT, BAT-GIRL! BATMAN IS A PRISONER OF THE LARKO LAMP—AT THE BECK AND CALL OF THOSE CRIMINALS!
DIAMOND EXCHANGE

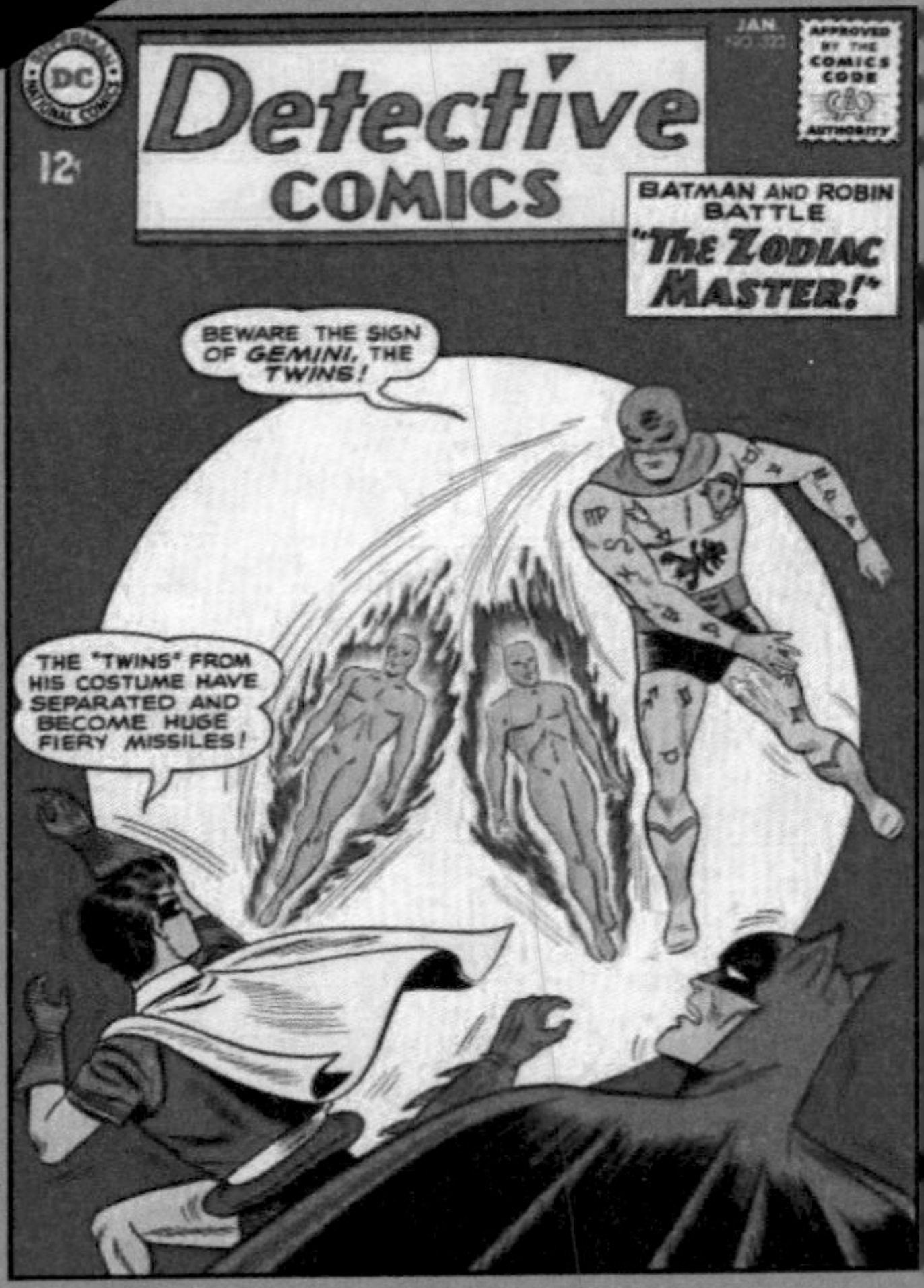
DC
12¢
Detective COMICS
JAN.
APPROVED BY THE COMICS CODE AUTHORITY
BATMAN AND ROBIN BATTLE "THE ZODIAC MASTER!"
BEWARE THE SIGN OF GEMINI, THE TWINS!
THE "TWINS" FROM HIS COSTUME HAVE SEPARATED AND BECOME HUGE FIERY MISSILES!

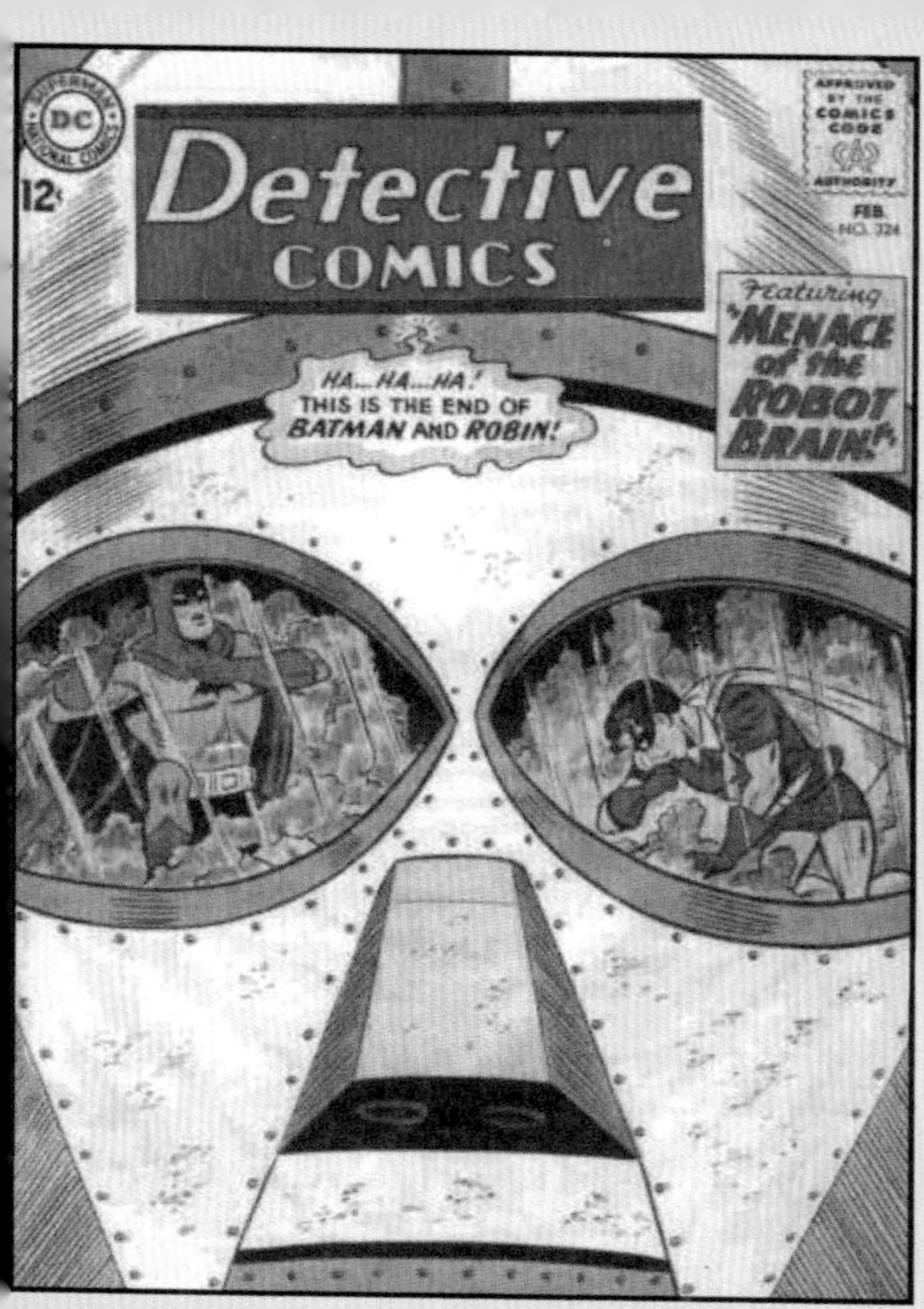
DC
SUPERMAN-BATMAN-NATIONAL COMICS
12¢
Detective
COMICS
APPROVED BY THE COMICS CODE AUTHORITY
FEB.
NO. 324
Featuring
"MENACE of the ROBOT BRAIN!"
HA...HA...HA!
THIS IS THE END OF
BATMAN AND ROBIN!

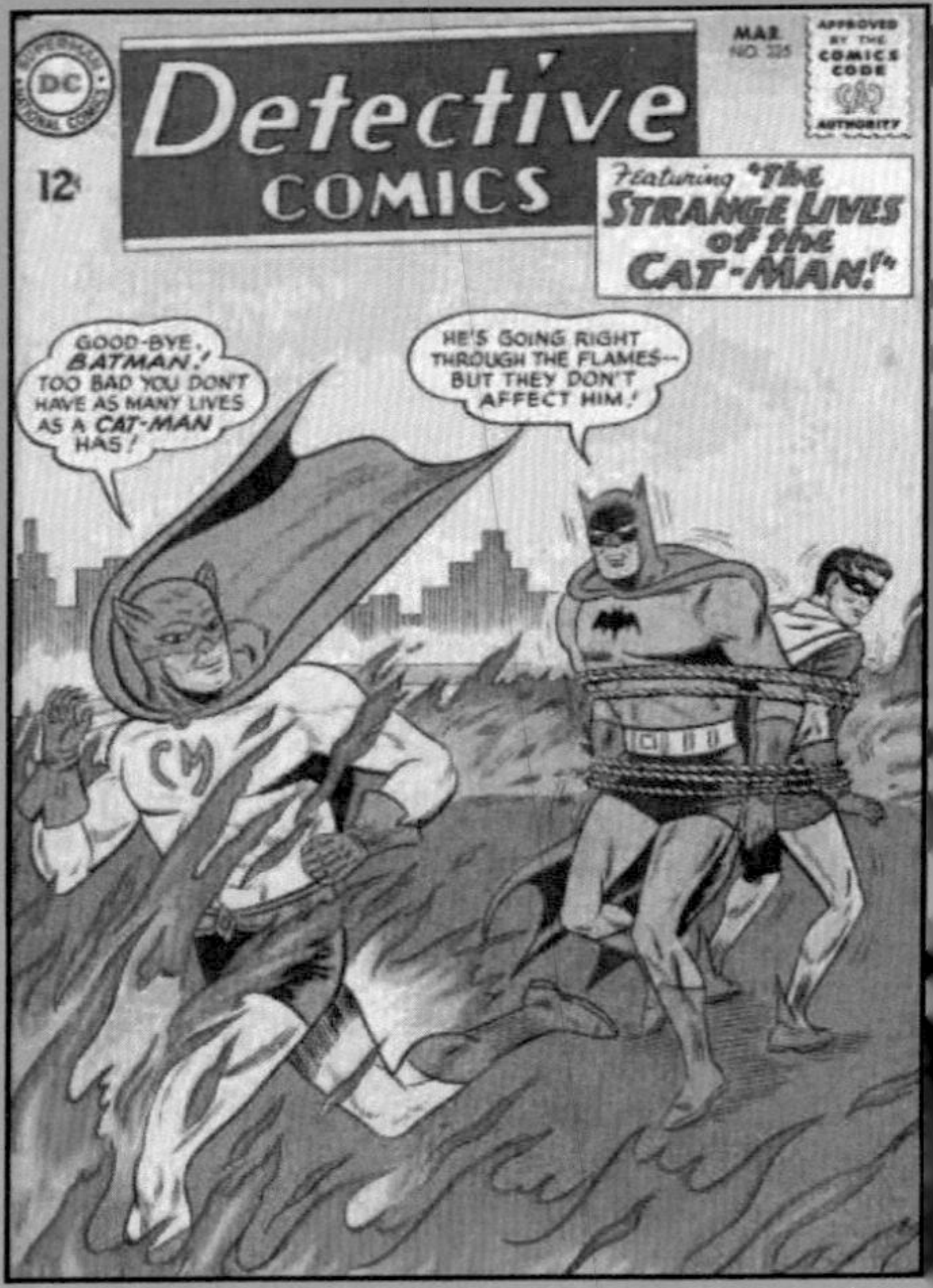
DC
Detective COMICS
12¢
MAR.
NO. 225
APPROVED BY THE COMICS CODE AUTHORITY
Featuring "The STRANGE LIVES of the CAT-MAN!"
GOOD-BYE, BATMAN! TOO BAD YOU DON'T HAVE AS MANY LIVES AS A CAT-MAN HAS!
HE'S GOING RIGHT THROUGH THE FLAMES-- BUT THEY DON'T AFFECT HIM!

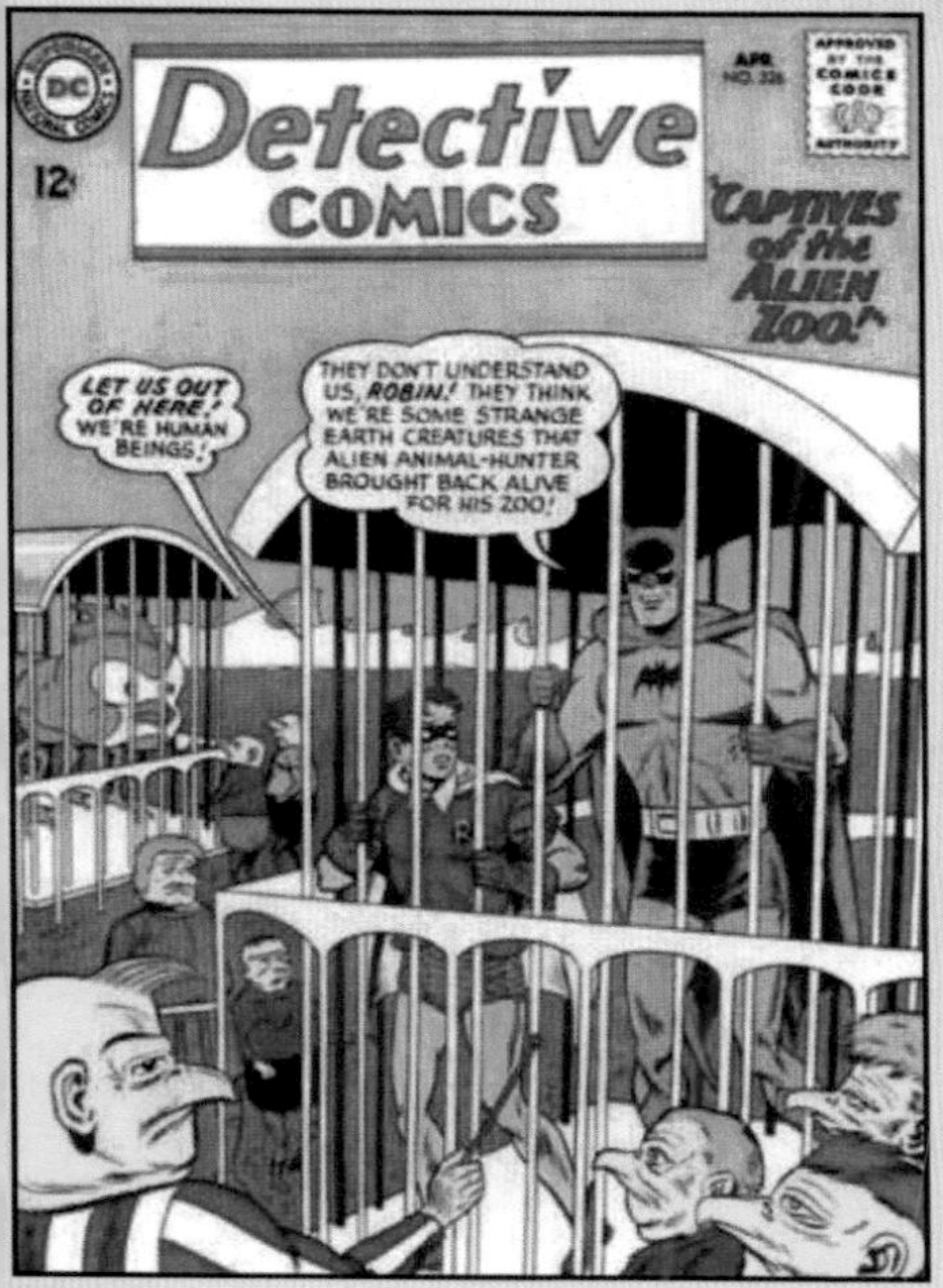
DC
Detective COMICS
12¢
APR. NO. 326
APPROVED BY THE COMICS CODE AUTHORITY
"CAPTIVES of the ALIEN ZOO!"
LET US OUT OF HERE! WE'RE HUMAN BEINGS!
THEY DON'T UNDERSTAND US, ROBIN! THEY THINK WE'RE SOME STRANGE EARTH CREATURES THAT ALIEN ANIMAL-HUNTER BROUGHT BACK ALIVE FOR HIS ZOO!

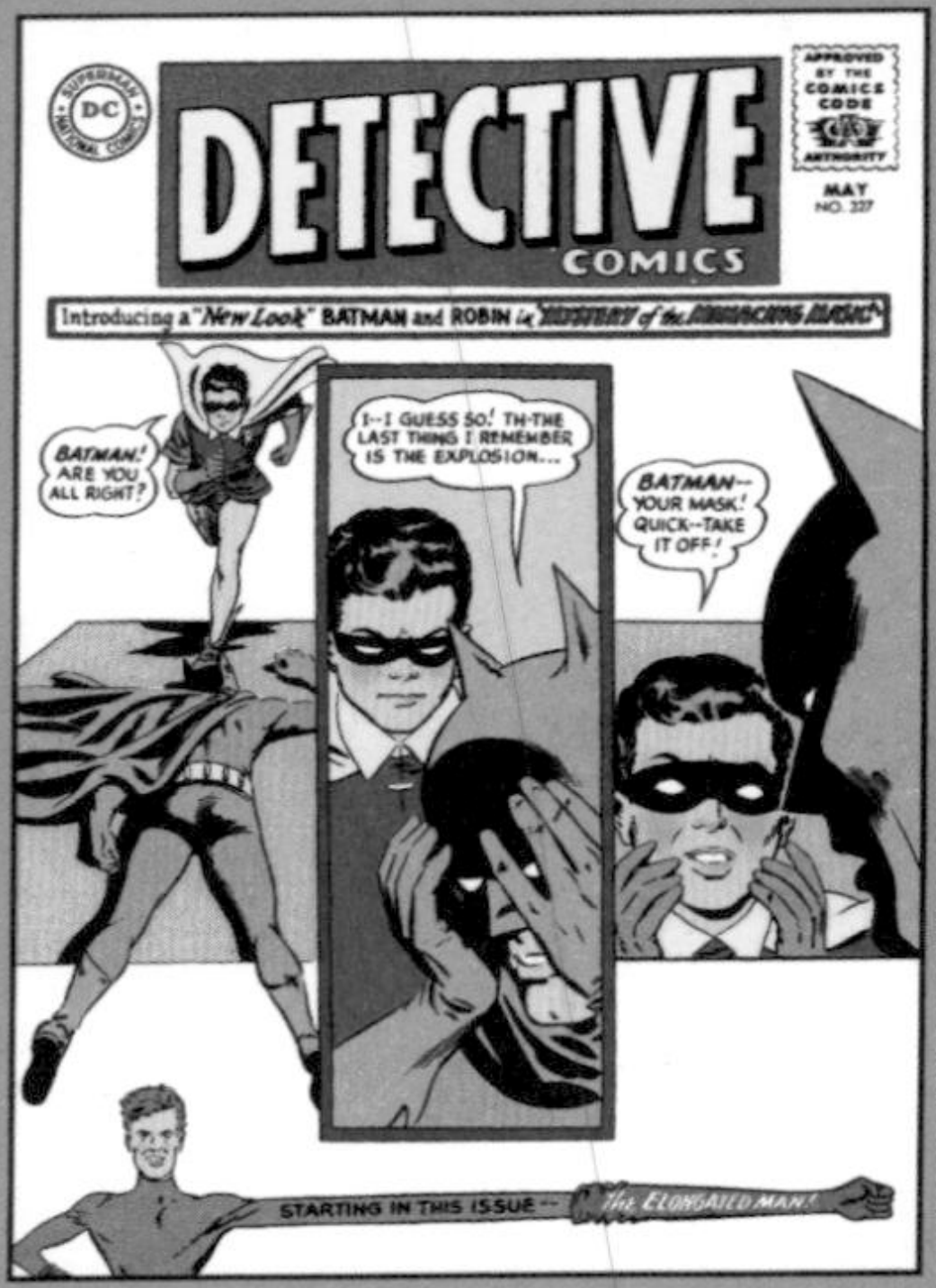

Detective Comics #327
This issue features a redesign for Batman and Robin and introduced the bat-symbol within the yellow oval.

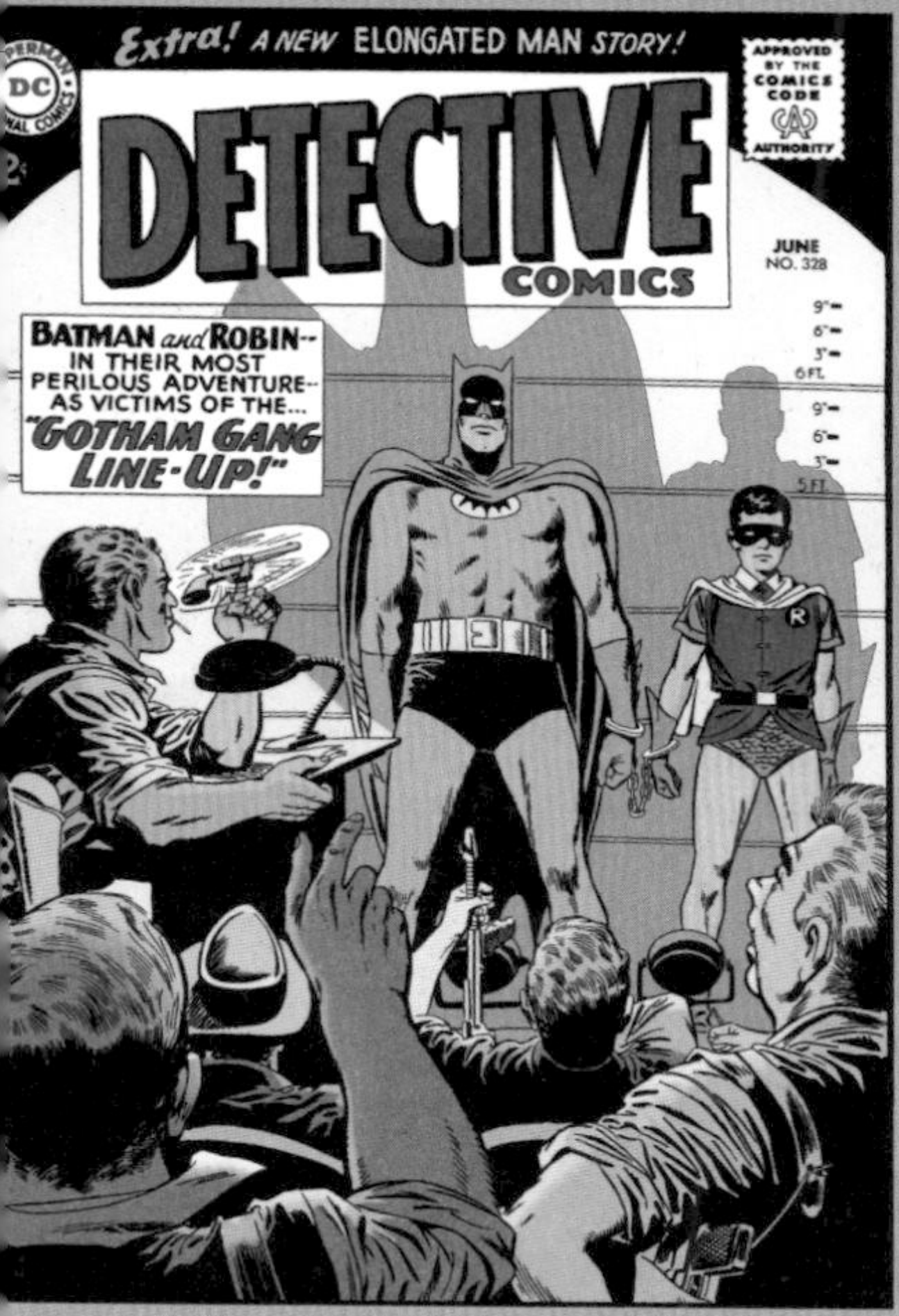
Extra! A NEW ELONGATED MAN STORY!
DC
APPROVED BY THE COMICS CODE AUTHORITY
DETECTIVE COMICS
JUNE
NO. 328
BATMAN and ROBIN-- IN THEIR MOST PERILOUS ADVENTURE-- AS VICTIMS OF THE... "GOTHAM GANG LINE-UP!"
9"
6"
3"
6 FT.
9"
6"
3"
5 FT.

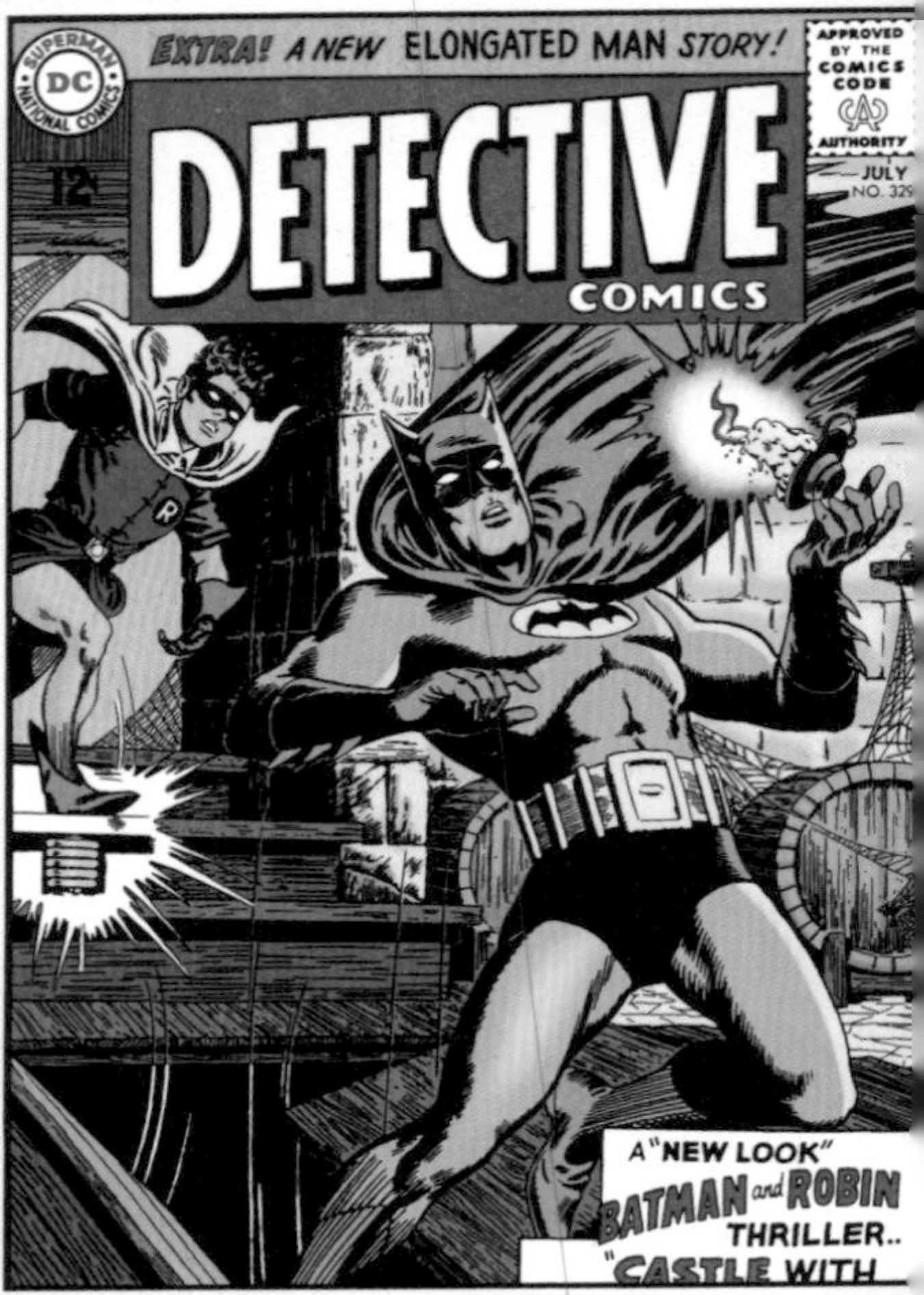
SUPERMAN
DC
NATIONAL COMICS
EXTRA! A NEW ELONGATED MAN STORY!
APPROVED BY THE COMICS CODE AUTHORITY
12¢
DETECTIVE COMICS
JULY
NO. 329
A "NEW LOOK" BATMAN and ROBIN THRILLER..
"CASTLE WITH

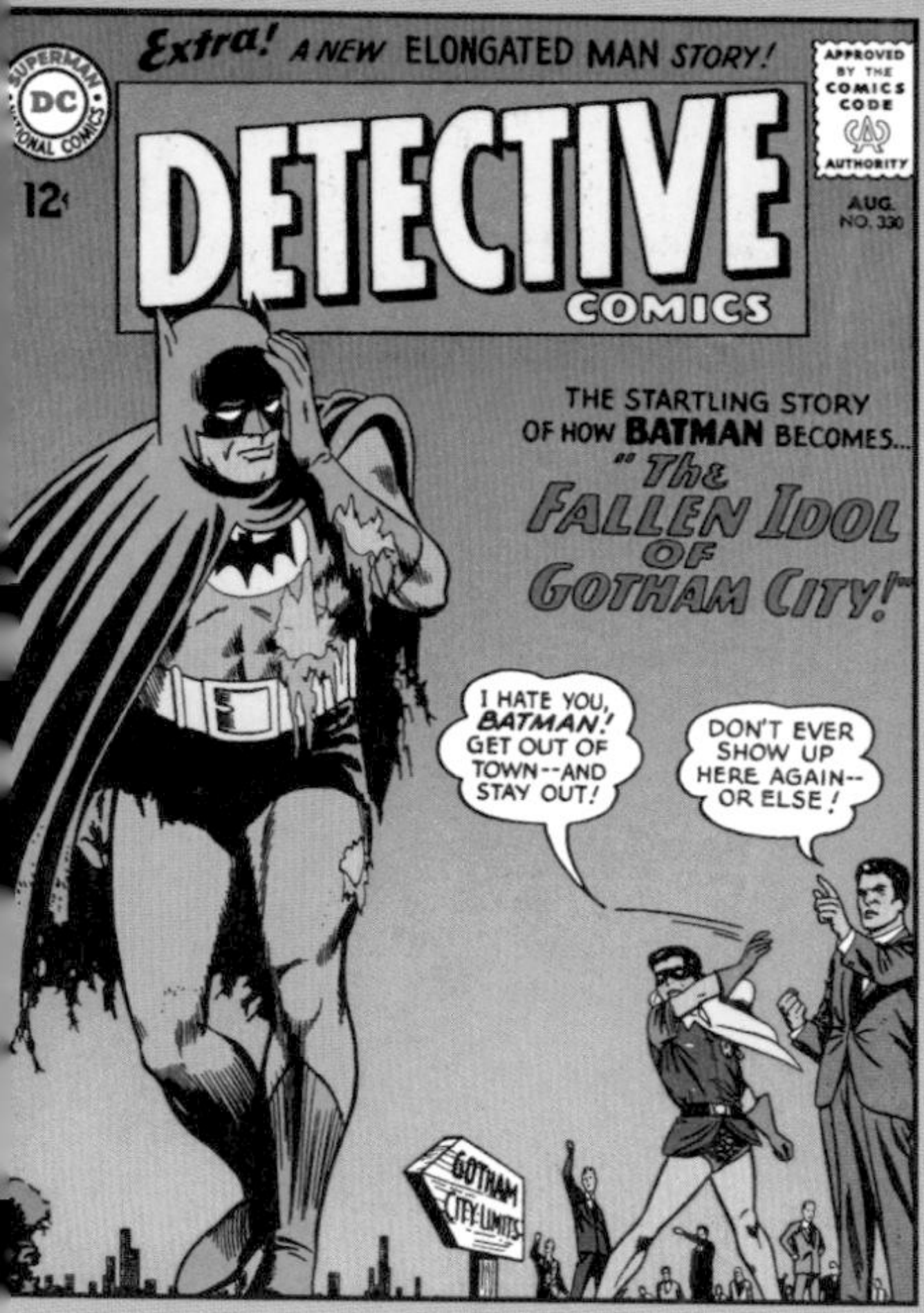
Extra! A NEW ELONGATED MAN STORY!
DC
SUPERMAN NATIONAL COMICS
12¢
DETECTIVE COMICS
APPROVED BY THE COMICS CODE AUTHORITY
AUG. NO. 330
THE STARTLING STORY OF HOW BATMAN BECOMES...
"The FALLEN IDOL OF GOTHAM CITY!"
I HATE YOU, BATMAN! GET OUT OF TOWN--AND STAY OUT!
DON'T EVER SHOW UP HERE AGAIN--OR ELSE!
GOTHAM CITY LIMITS

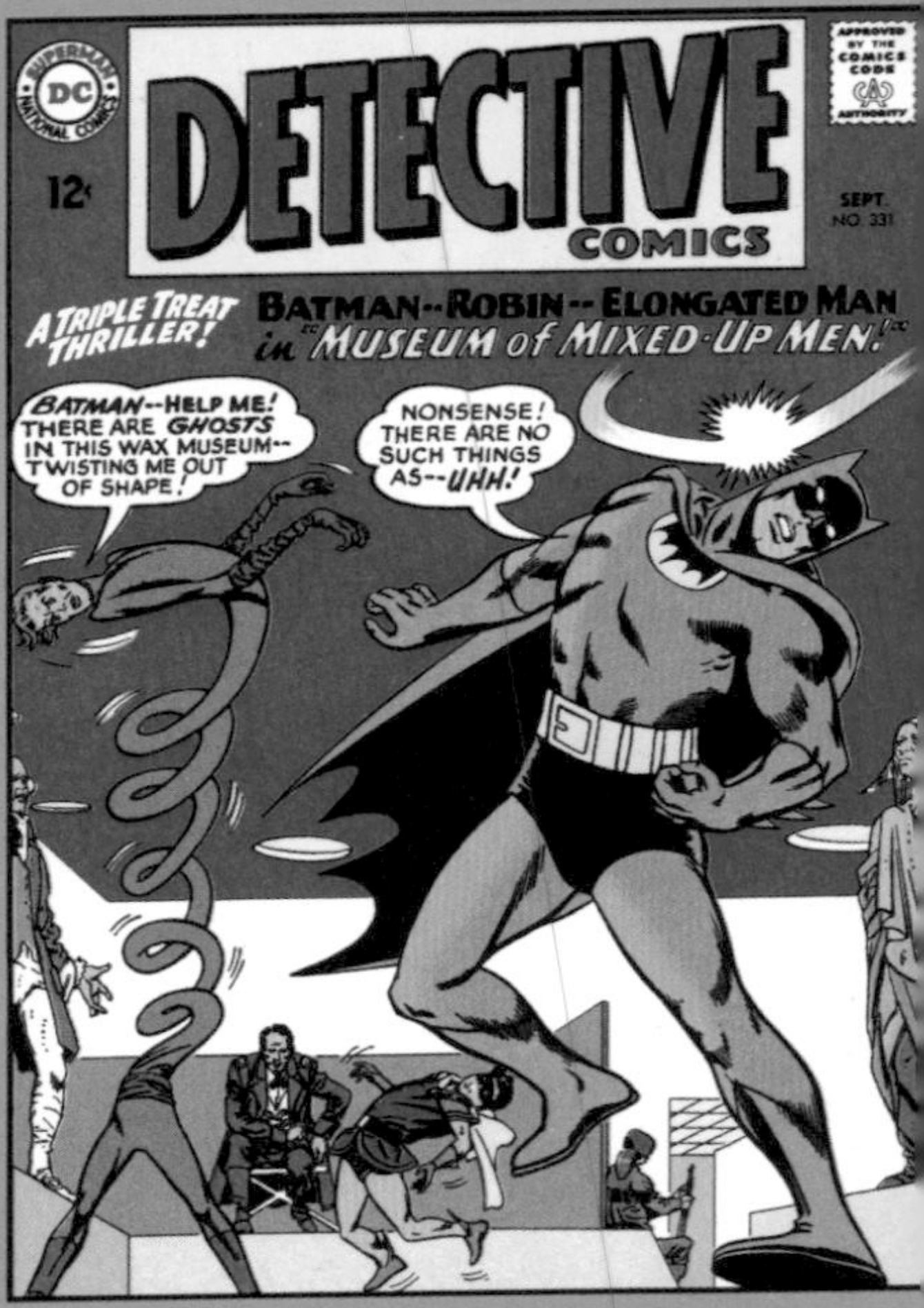
DC
SUPERMAN-BATMAN NATIONAL COMICS
DETECTIVE COMICS
12¢
SEPT. NO. 331
APPROVED BY THE COMICS CODE AUTHORITY
A TRIPLE TREAT THRILLER!
BATMAN--ROBIN--ELONGATED MAN in "MUSEUM of MIXED-UP MEN!"
BATMAN--HELP ME! THERE ARE GHOSTS IN THIS WAX MUSEUM--TWISTING ME OUT OF SHAPE!
NONSENSE! THERE ARE NO SUCH THINGS AS--UHH!

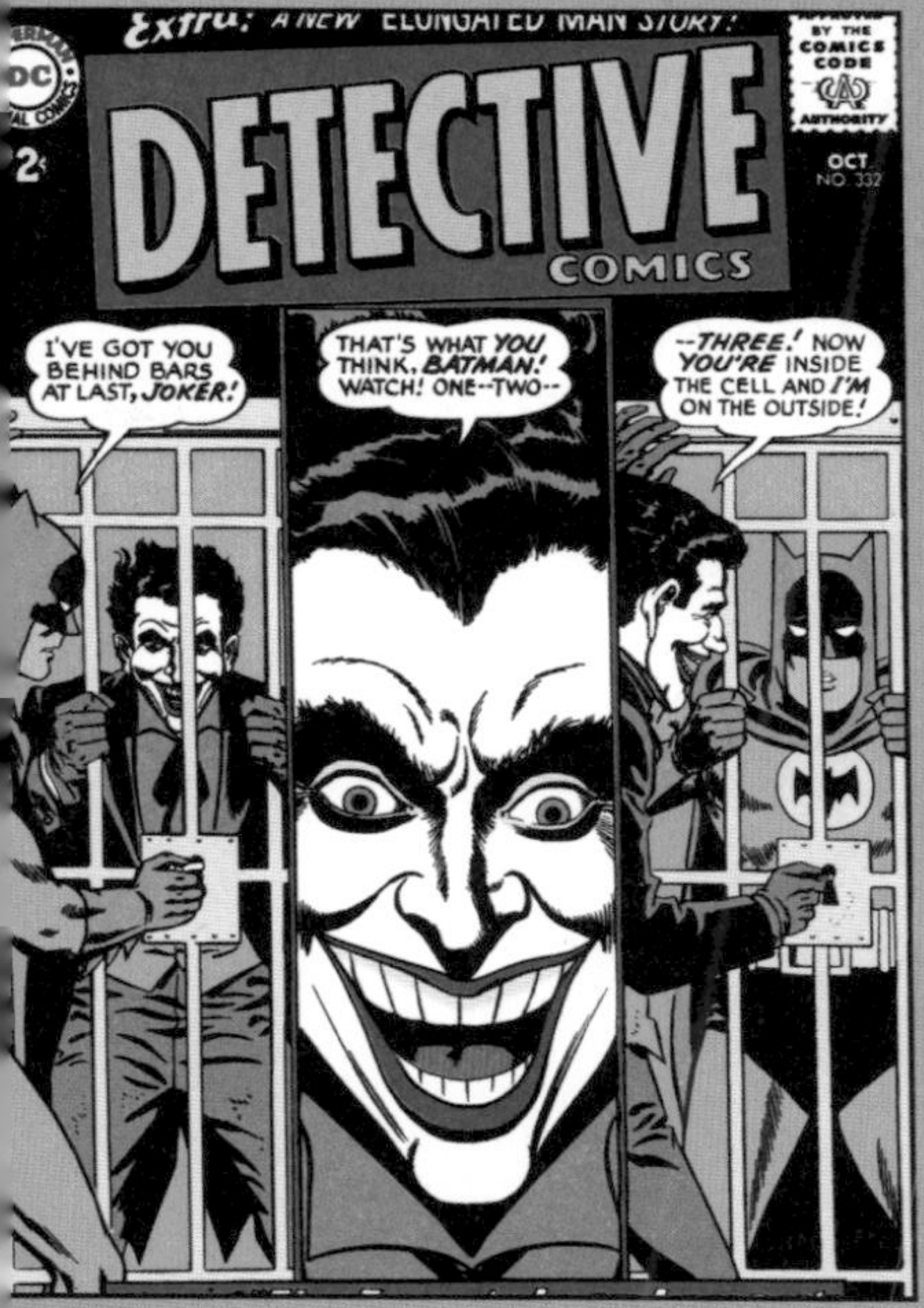
Extra! A NEW ELONGATED MAN STORY!
DC
2¢
DETECTIVE
COMICS
BY THE COMICS CODE AUTHORITY
OCT.
NO. 332
I'VE GOT YOU BEHIND BARS AT LAST, JOKER!
THAT'S WHAT YOU THINK, BATMAN! WATCH! ONE--TWO--
--THREE! NOW YOU'RE INSIDE THE CELL AND I'M ON THE OUTSIDE!

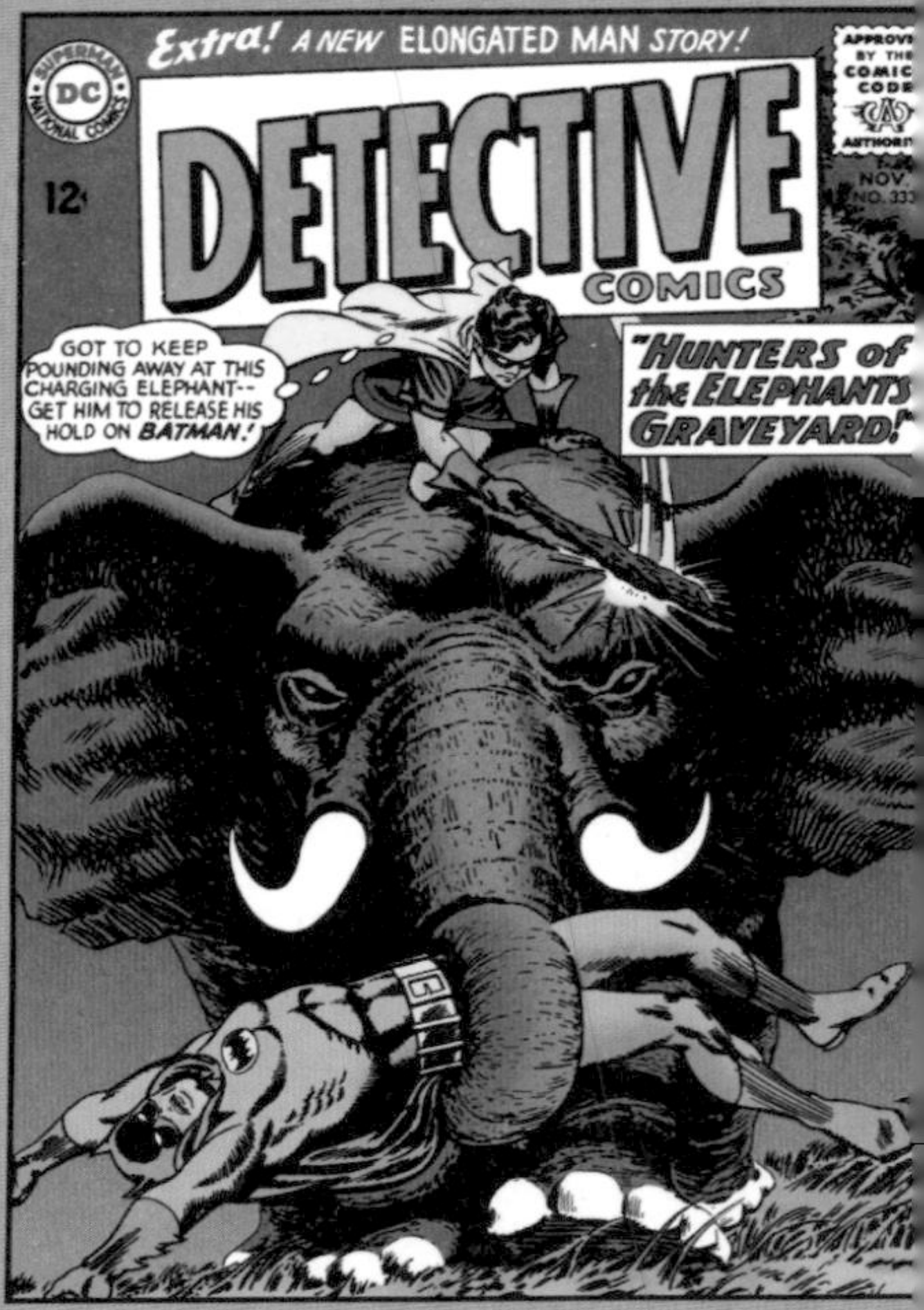
Extra! A NEW ELONGATED MAN STORY!
DC
SUPERMAN NATIONAL COMICS
12¢
DETECTIVE COMICS
APPROVED BY THE COMIC CODE AUTHORITY
NOV.
NO. 333
GOT TO KEEP POUNDING AWAY AT THIS CHARGING ELEPHANT-- GET HIM TO RELEASE HIS HOLD ON BATMAN!
"HUNTERS of the ELEPHANT'S GRAVEYARD!"

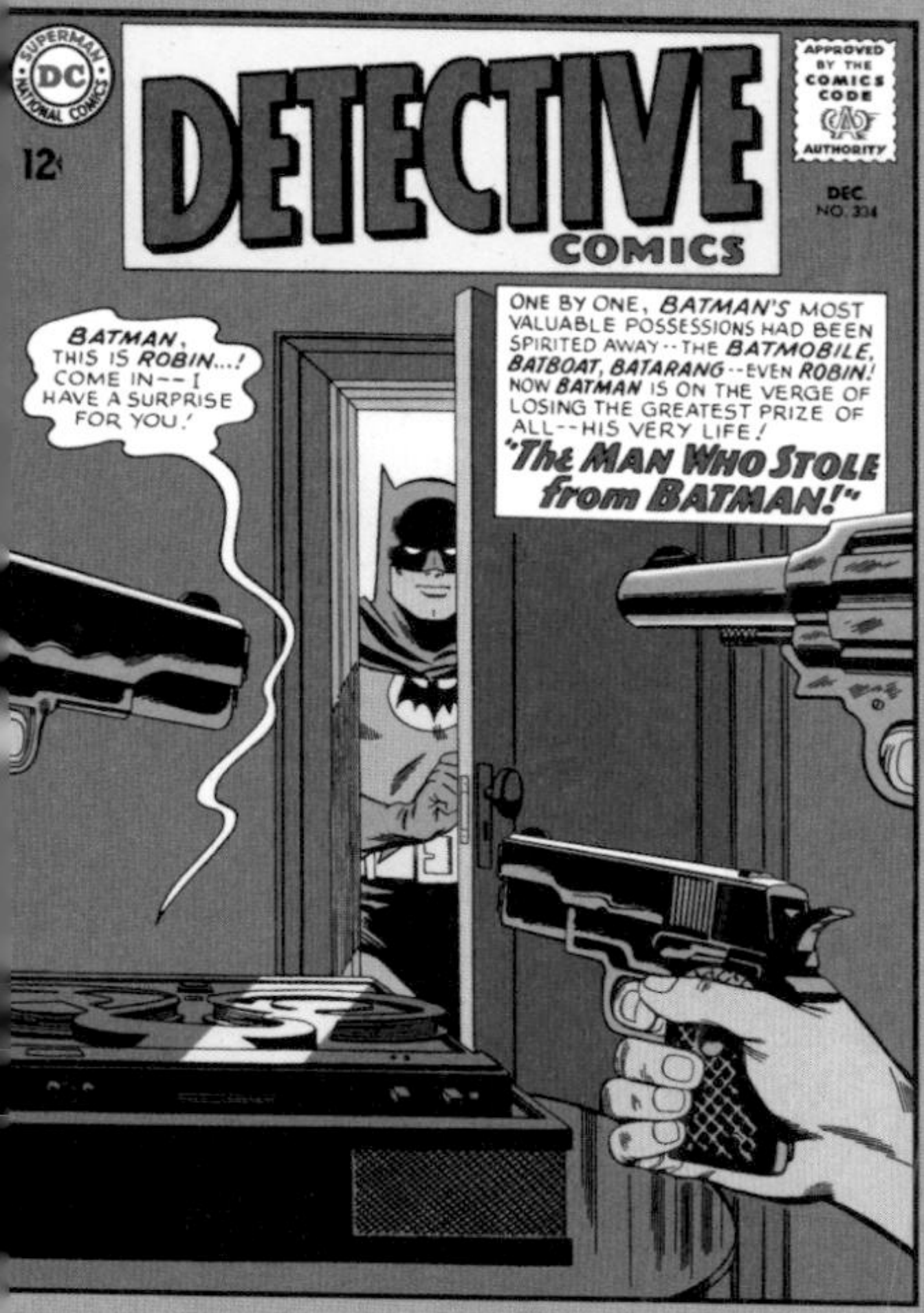
SUPERMAN
DC
NATIONAL COMICS
12¢
DETECTIVE
COMICS
APPROVED BY THE COMICS CODE AUTHORITY
DEC
NO. 334
BATMAN, THIS IS ROBIN...! COME IN-- I HAVE A SURPRISE FOR YOU!
ONE BY ONE, BATMAN'S MOST VALUABLE POSSESSIONS HAD BEEN SPIRITED AWAY-- THE BATMOBILE, BATBOAT, BATARANG-- EVEN ROBIN! NOW BATMAN IS ON THE VERGE OF LOSING THE GREATEST PRIZE OF ALL-- HIS VERY LIFE!
"The Man Who Stole from Batman!"

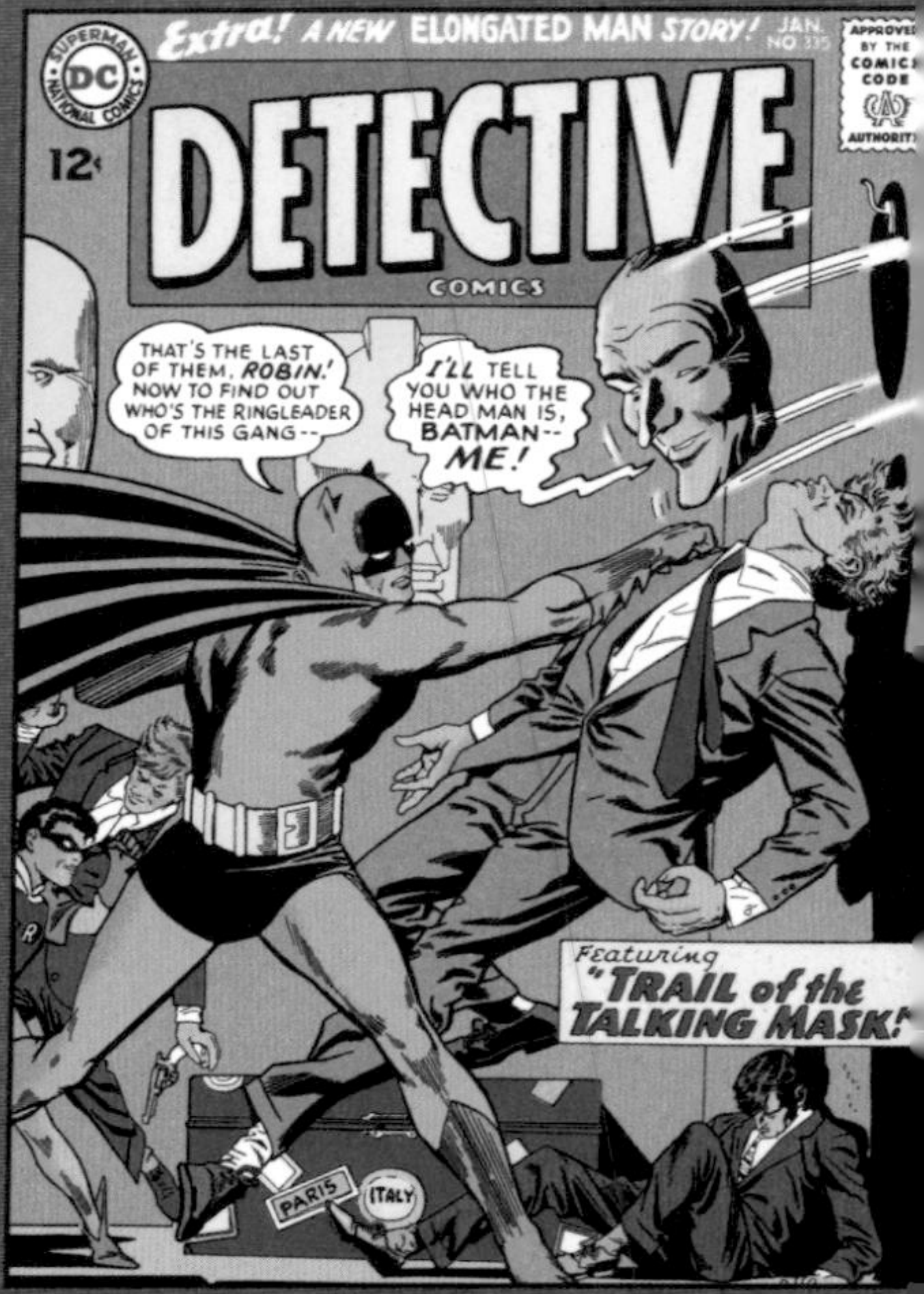
Extra! A NEW ELONGATED MAN STORY!
JAN. NO 335
SUPERMAN • NATIONAL COMICS • DC
12¢
DETECTIVE
COMICS
APPROVED BY THE COMICS CODE AUTHORITY
THAT'S THE LAST OF THEM, ROBIN! NOW TO FIND OUT WHO'S THE RINGLEADER OF THIS GANG--
I'LL TELL YOU WHO THE HEAD MAN IS, BATMAN-- ME!
Featuring "TRAIL of the TALKING MASK!"
PARIS
ITALY

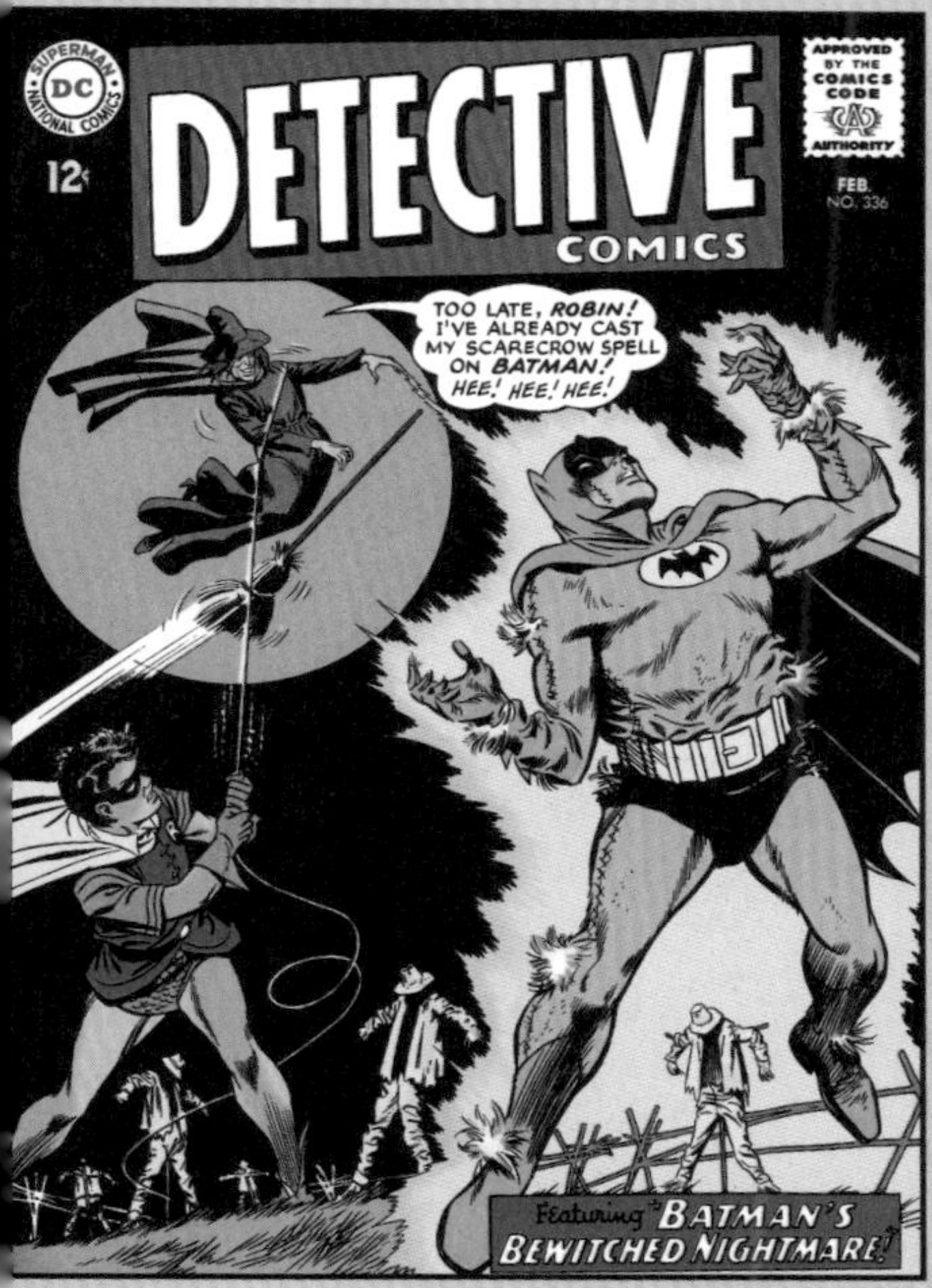
SUPERMAN
DC
NATIONAL COMICS
12¢
DETECTIVE
COMICS
APPROVED BY THE COMICS CODE AUTHORITY
FEB.
NO. 336
TOO LATE, ROBIN! I'VE ALREADY CAST MY SCARECROW SPELL ON BATMAN! HEE! HEE! HEE!
Featuring "BATMAN'S BEWITCHED NIGHTMARE!"

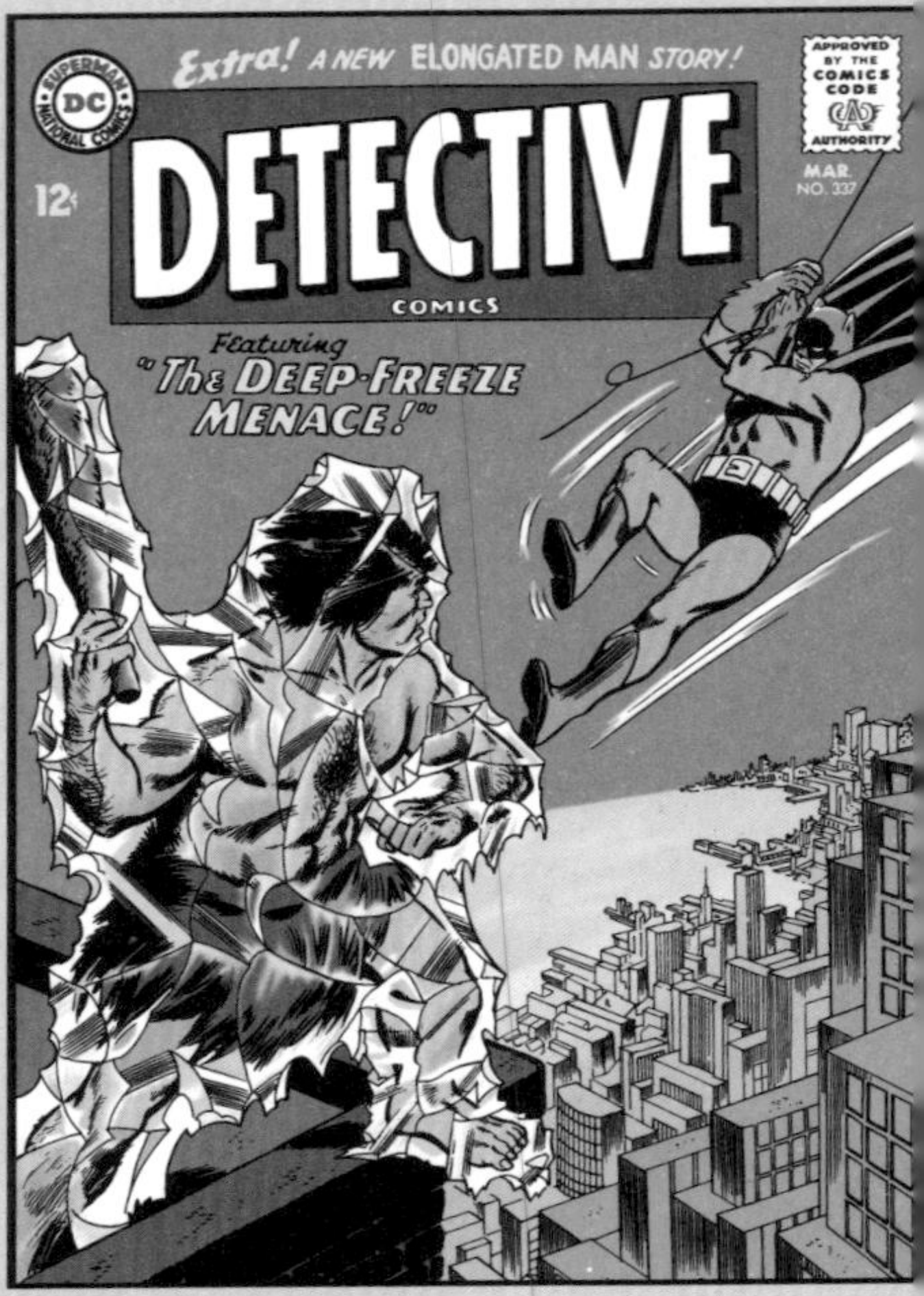
Extra! A NEW ELONGATED MAN STORY!
DC
SUPERMAN-BATMAN-ROBIN COMICS
APPROVED BY THE COMICS CODE AUTHORITY
12¢
MAR. NO. 337
DETECTIVE
COMICS
Featuring "The DEEP-FREEZE MENACE!"

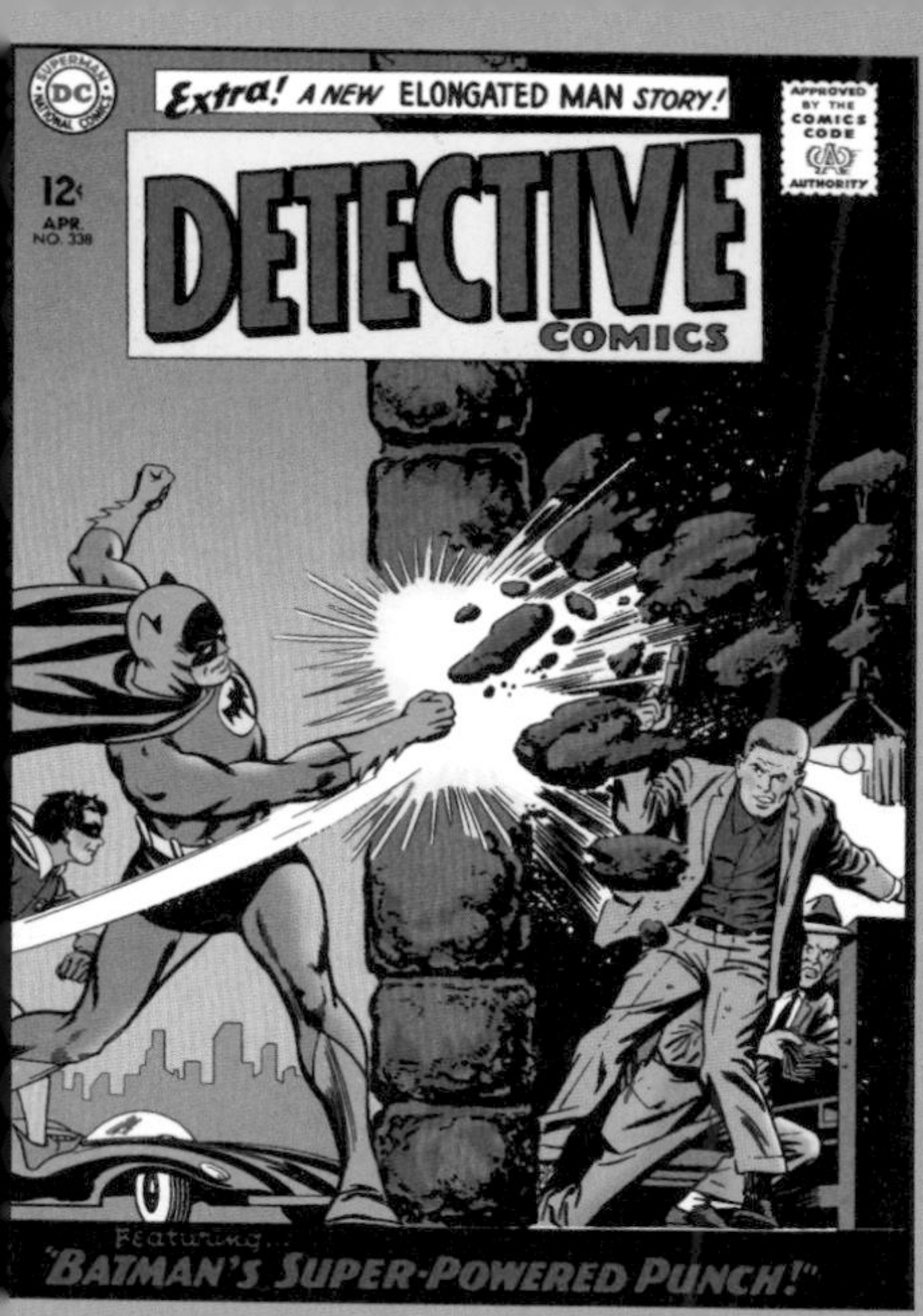
DC
SUPERMAN NATIONAL COMICS
Extra! A NEW ELONGATED MAN STORY!
APPROVED BY THE COMICS CODE AUTHORITY
12¢
APR.
NO. 338
DETECTIVE
COMICS
Featuring...
"BATMAN'S SUPER-POWERED PUNCH!"

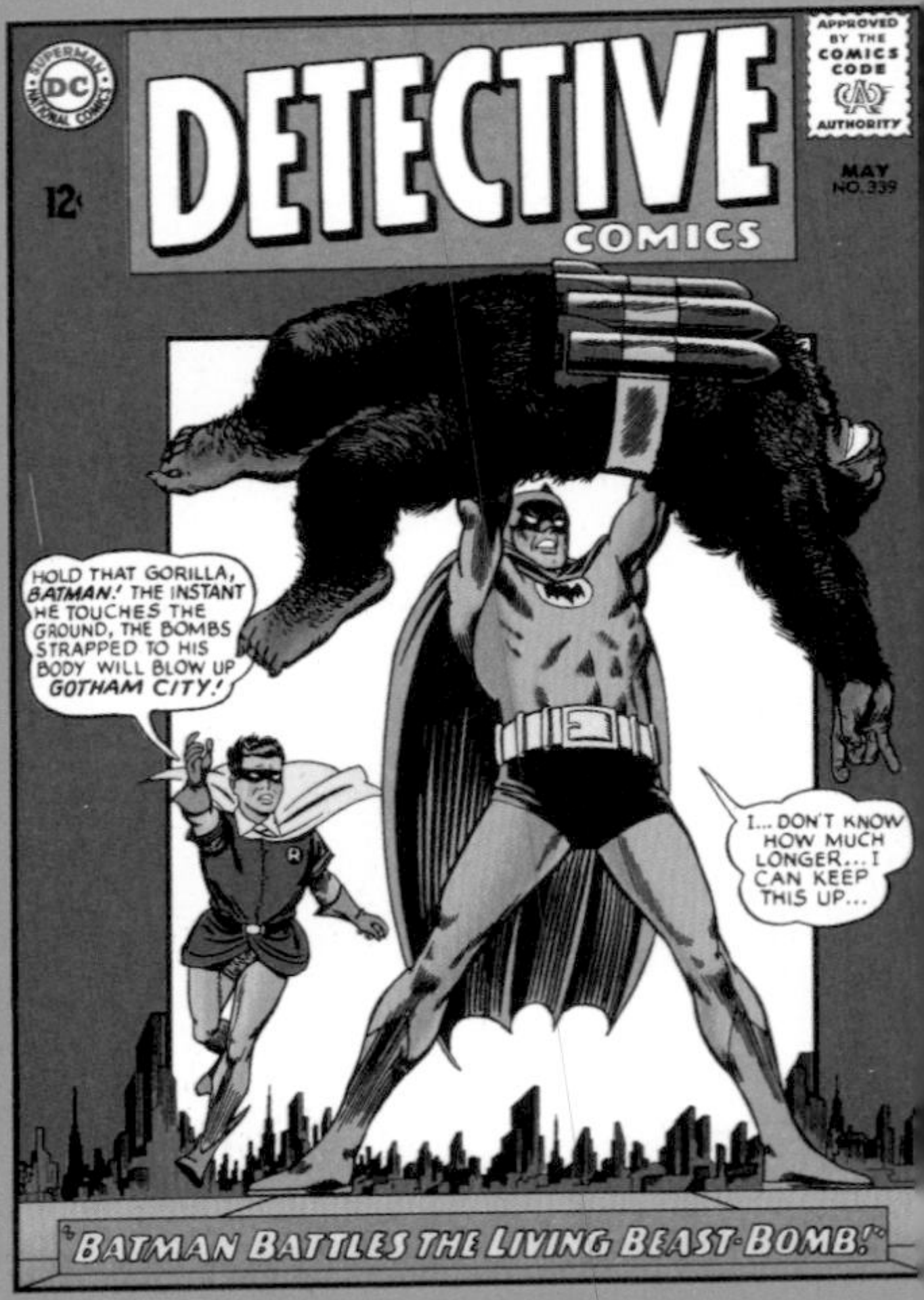
DC
SUPERMAN-BATMAN PRESENTS COMICS
DETECTIVE COMICS
12¢
APPROVED BY THE COMICS CODE AUTHORITY
MAY
NO. 339
HOLD THAT GORILLA, BATMAN! THE INSTANT HE TOUCHES THE GROUND, THE BOMBS STRAPPED TO HIS BODY WILL BLOW UP GOTHAM CITY!
I... DON'T KNOW HOW MUCH LONGER... I CAN KEEP THIS UP...
"BATMAN BATTLES THE LIVING BEAST-BOMB!"

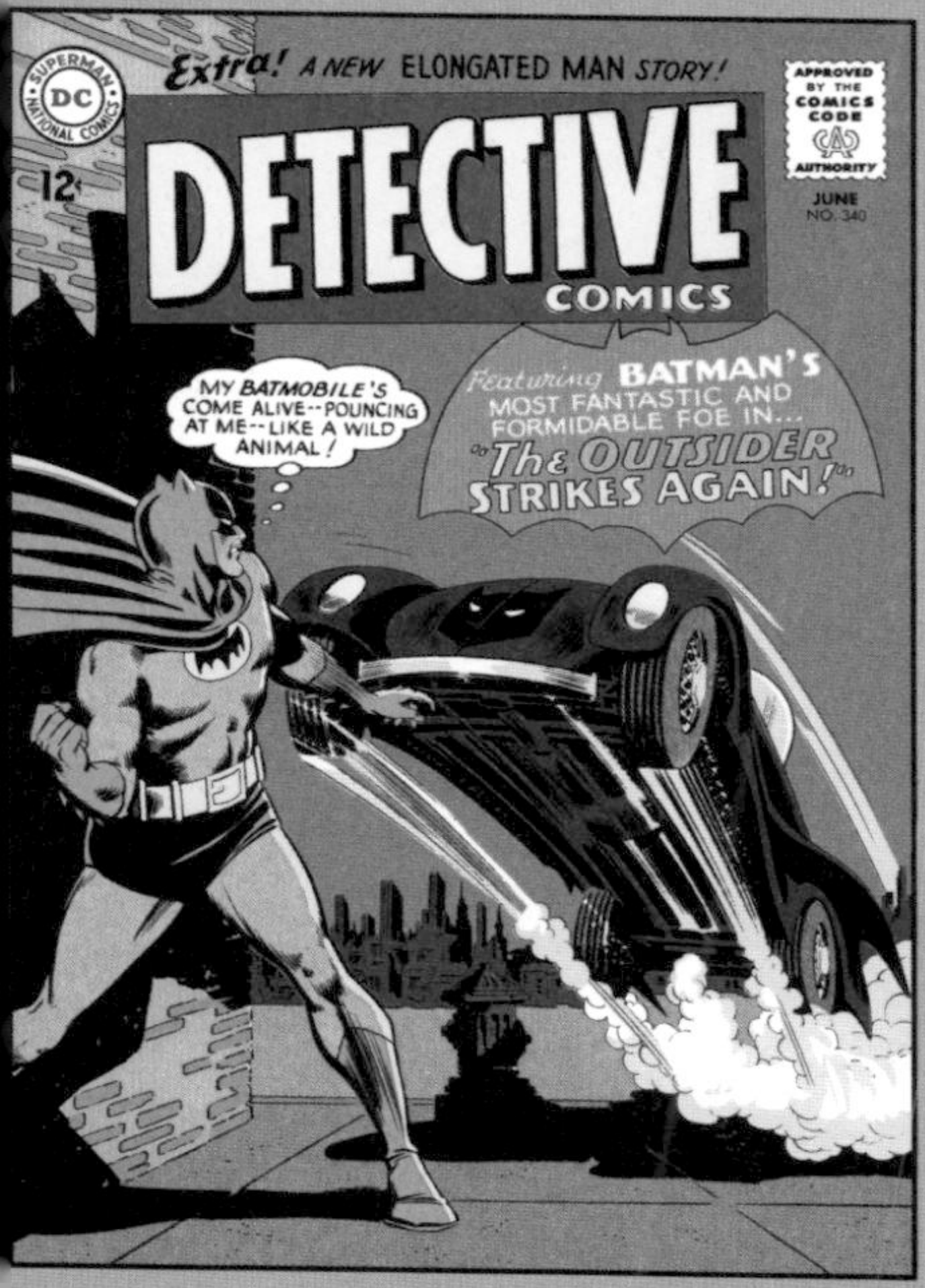
Extra! A NEW ELONGATED MAN STORY!
SUPERMAN DC NATIONAL COMICS
12¢
DETECTIVE COMICS
APPROVED BY THE COMICS CODE AUTHORITY
JUNE
NO. 340
MY BATMOBILE'S COME ALIVE--POUNCING AT ME--LIKE A WILD ANIMAL!
Featuring BATMAN'S MOST FANTASTIC AND FORMIDABLE FOE IN... "The OUTSIDER STRIKES AGAIN!"

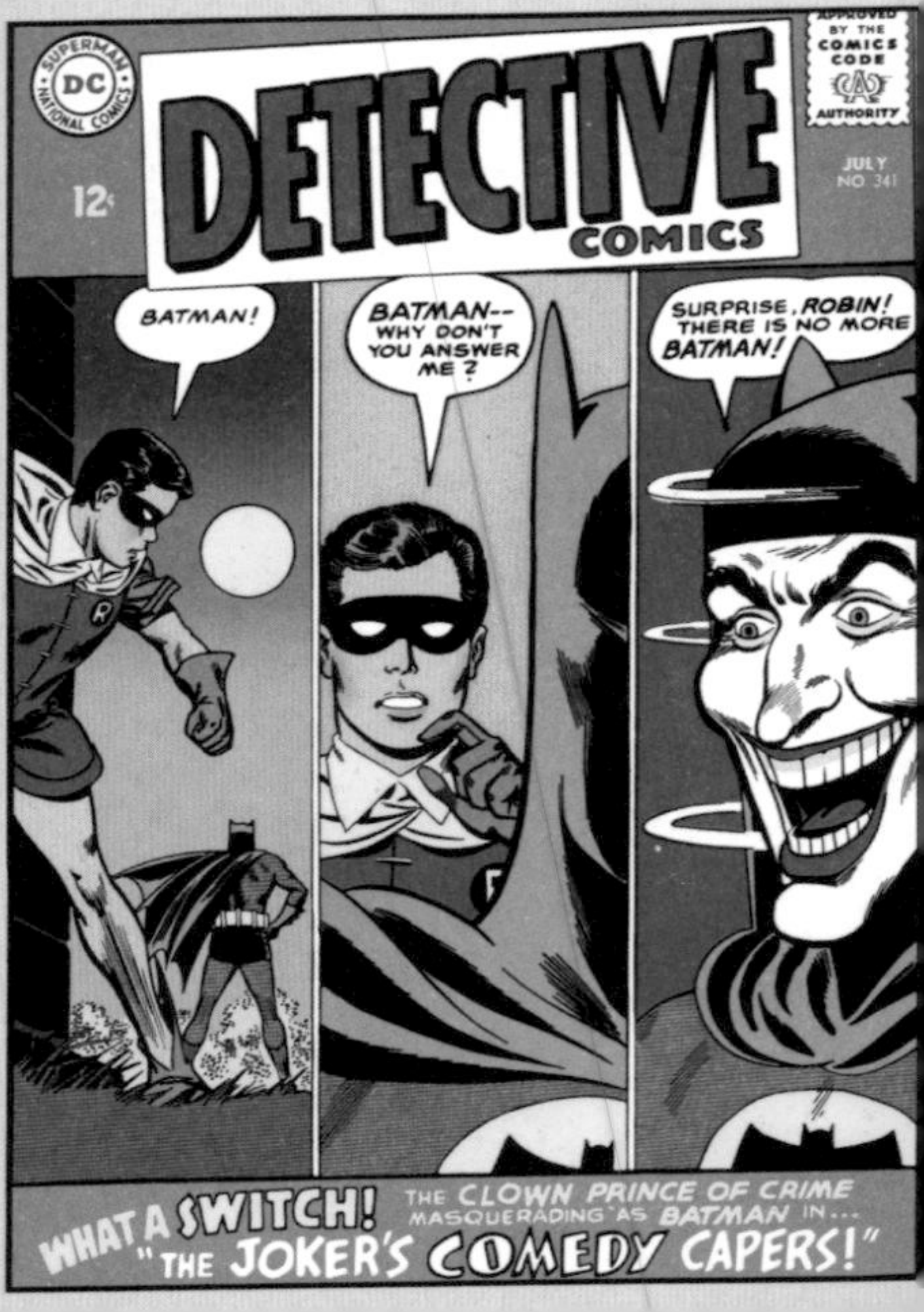
SUPERMAN
DC
NATIONAL COMICS
12¢
DETECTIVE COMICS
APPROVED BY THE COMICS CODE AUTHORITY
JULY
NO 341
BATMAN!
BATMAN-- WHY DON'T YOU ANSWER ME ?
SURPRISE, ROBIN! THERE IS NO MORE BATMAN!
WHAT A SWITCH! THE CLOWN PRINCE OF CRIME MASQUERADING AS BATMAN IN...
"THE JOKER'S COMEDY CAPERS!"

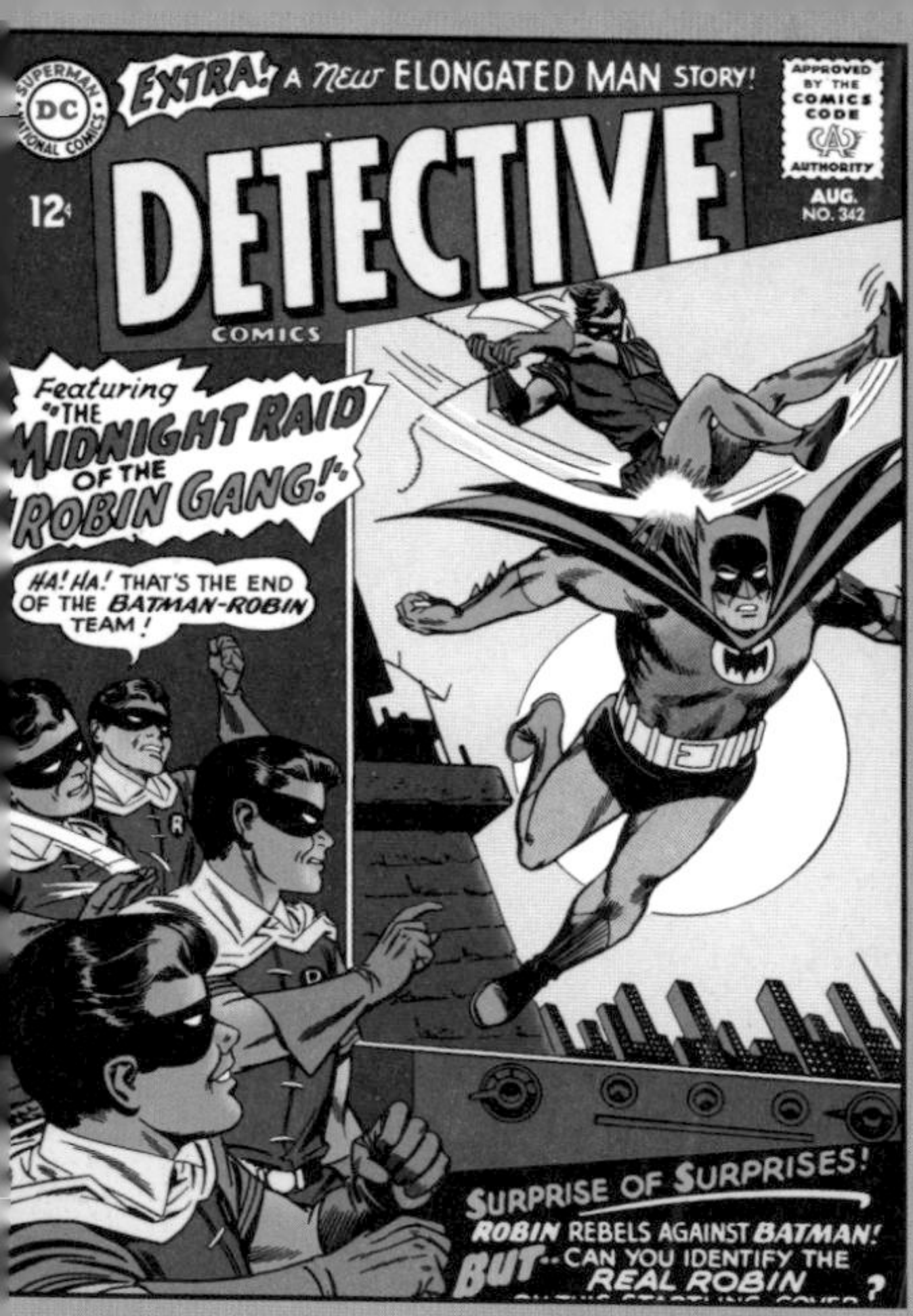
SUPERMAN-BATMAN NATIONAL COMICS
DC
EXTRA! A NEW ELONGATED MAN STORY!
APPROVED BY THE COMICS CODE AUTHORITY
12¢
DETECTIVE
COMICS
AUG.
NO. 342
Featuring "THE MIDNIGHT RAID OF THE ROBIN GANG!"
HA! HA! THAT'S THE END OF THE BATMAN-ROBIN TEAM!
SURPRISE OF SURPRISES!
ROBIN REBELS AGAINST BATMAN!
BUT-- CAN YOU IDENTIFY THE REAL ROBIN ?

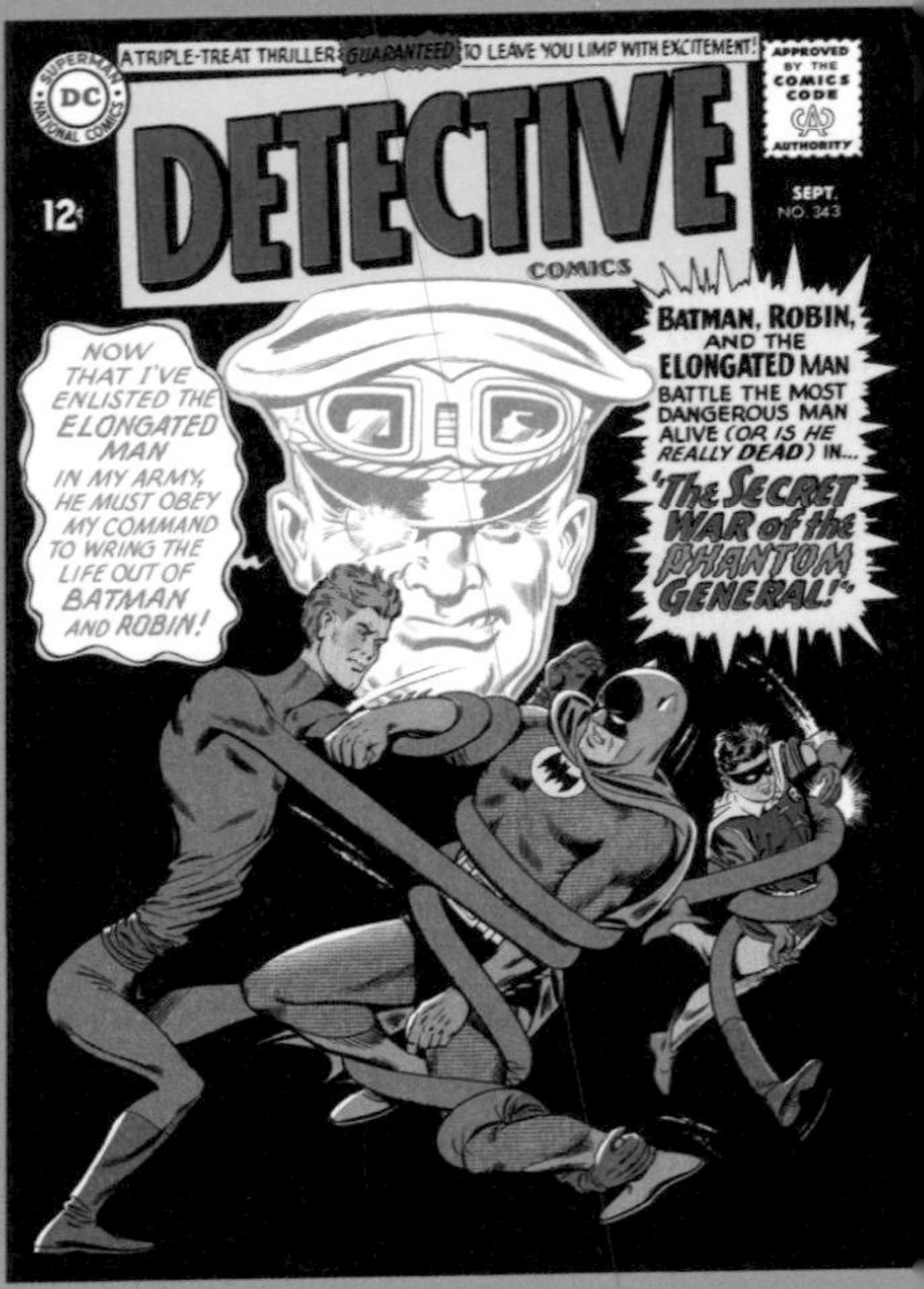
A TRIPLE-TREAT THRILLER GUARANTEED TO LEAVE YOU LIMP WITH EXCITEMENT!
DC
SUPERMAN NATIONAL COMICS
DETECTIVE
COMICS
12¢
APPROVED BY THE COMICS CODE AUTHORITY
SEPT.
NO. 343
NOW THAT I'VE ENLISTED THE ELONGATED MAN IN MY ARMY, HE MUST OBEY MY COMMAND TO WRING THE LIFE OUT OF BATMAN AND ROBIN!
BATMAN, ROBIN, AND THE ELONGATED MAN BATTLE THE MOST DANGEROUS MAN ALIVE (OR IS HE REALLY DEAD) IN...
"The SECRET WAR of the PHANTOM GENERAL!"

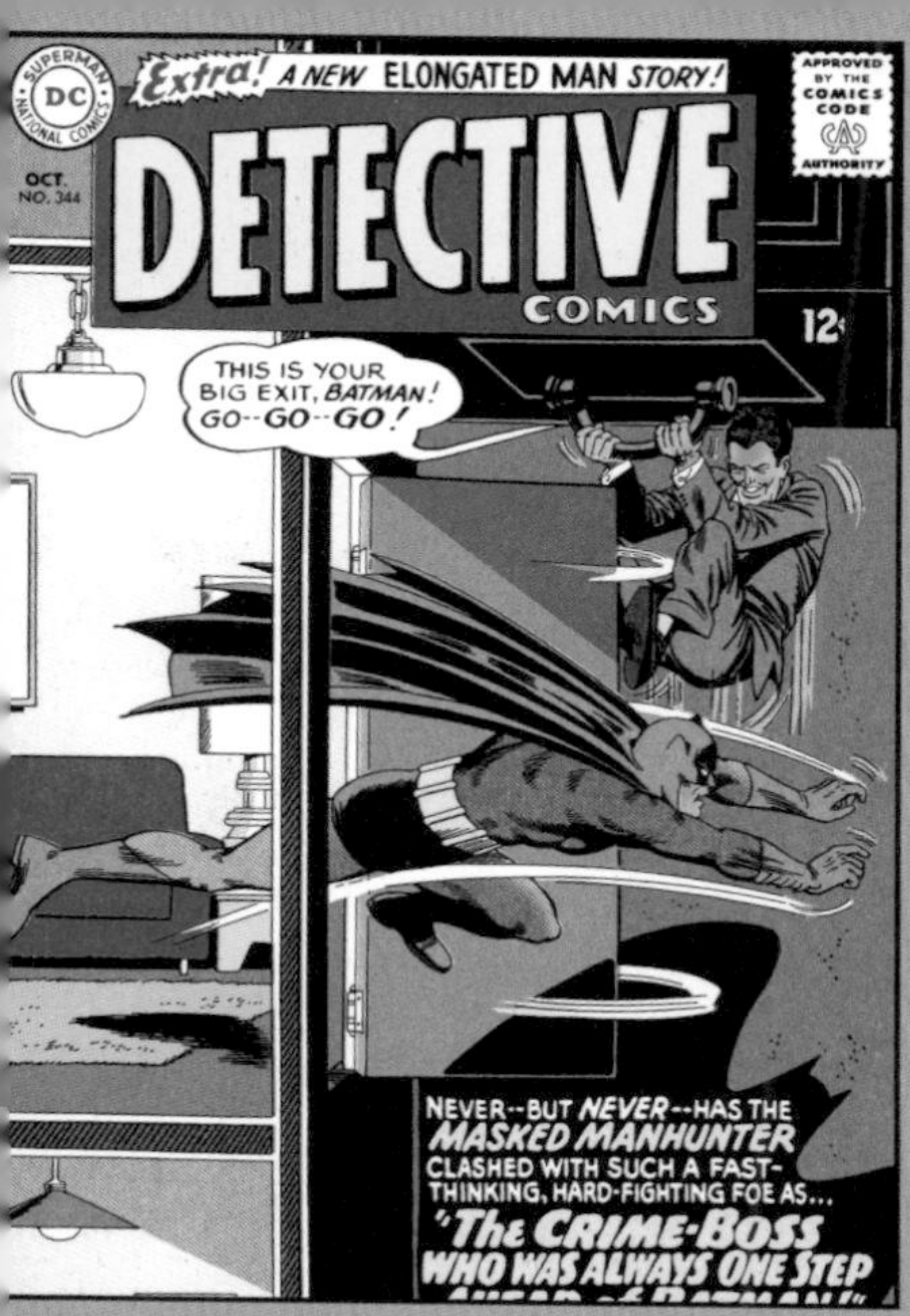
SUPERMAN DC NATIONAL COMICS
Extra! A NEW ELONGATED MAN STORY!
APPROVED BY THE COMICS CODE AUTHORITY
OCT. NO. 344
DETECTIVE COMICS
12¢
THIS IS YOUR BIG EXIT, BATMAN! GO--GO--GO!
NEVER--BUT NEVER--HAS THE MASKED MANHUNTER CLASHED WITH SUCH A FAST-THINKING, HARD-FIGHTING FOE AS...
"The CRIME-BOSS WHO WAS ALWAYS ONE STEP

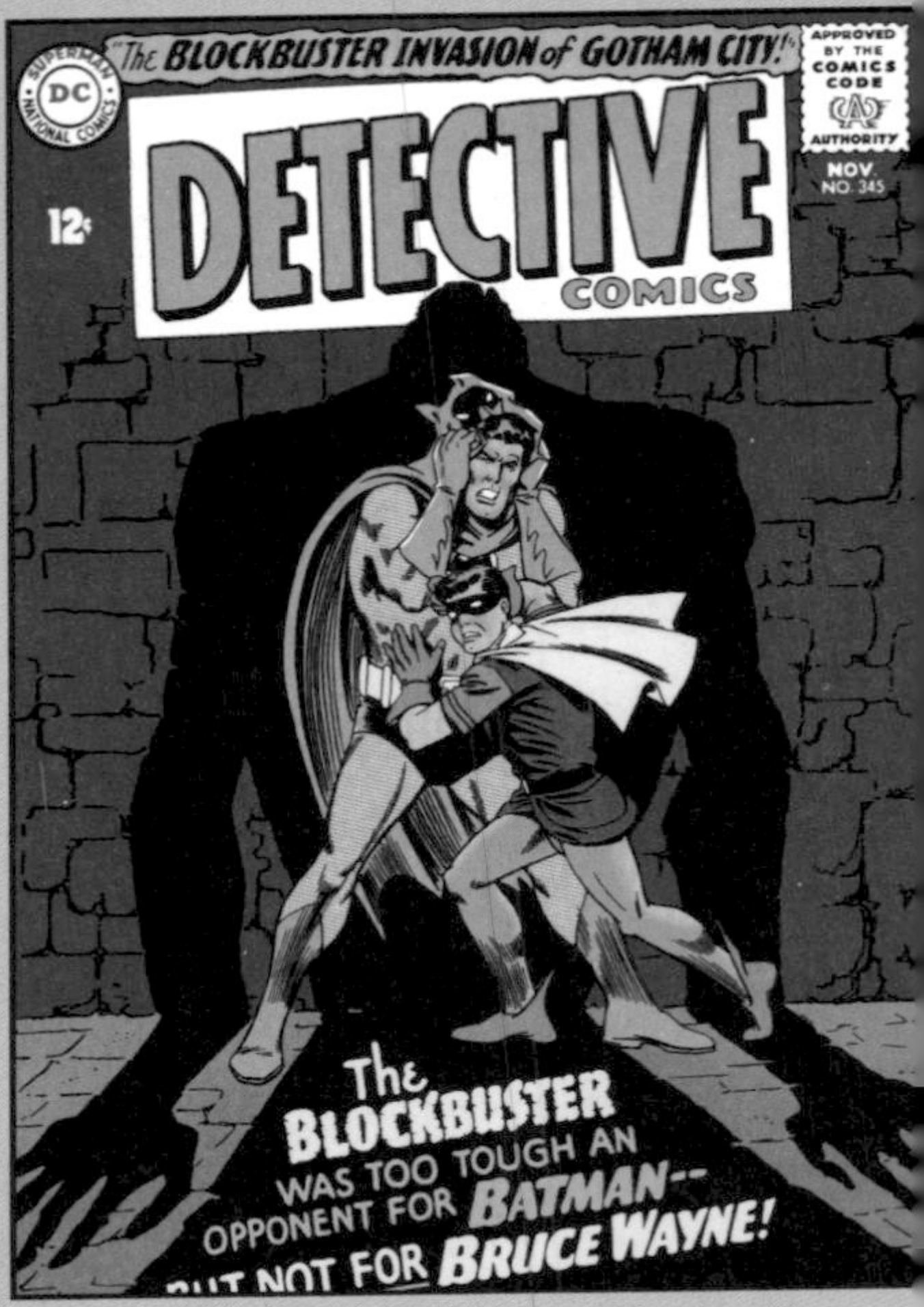
"The BLOCKBUSTER INVASION of GOTHAM CITY!"
DC
SUPERMAN • NATIONAL COMICS •
APPROVED BY THE COMICS CODE AUTHORITY
NOV. NO. 345
12¢
DETECTIVE COMICS
The BLOCKBUSTER WAS TOO TOUGH AN OPPONENT FOR BATMAN--
BUT NOT FOR BRUCE WAYNE!

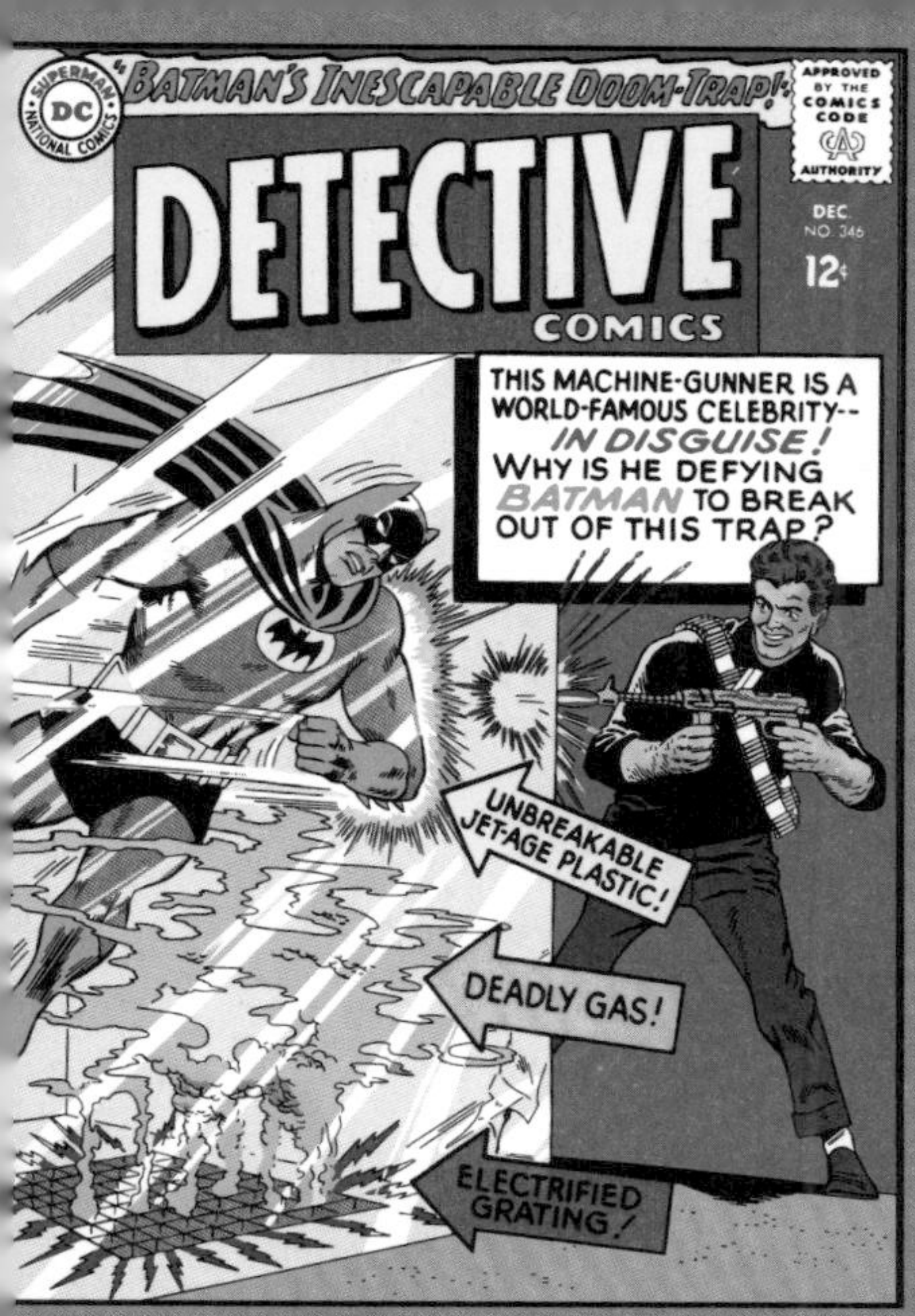
SUPERMAN • NATIONAL COMICS • DC
"BATMAN'S INESCAPABLE DOOM-TRAP!"
APPROVED BY THE COMICS CODE AUTHORITY
DETECTIVE COMICS
DEC. NO. 346
12¢
THIS MACHINE-GUNNER IS A WORLD-FAMOUS CELEBRITY-- IN DISGUISE! WHY IS HE DEFYING BATMAN TO BREAK OUT OF THIS TRAP?
UNBREAKABLE JET-AGE PLASTIC!
DEADLY GAS!
ELECTRIFIED GRATING!

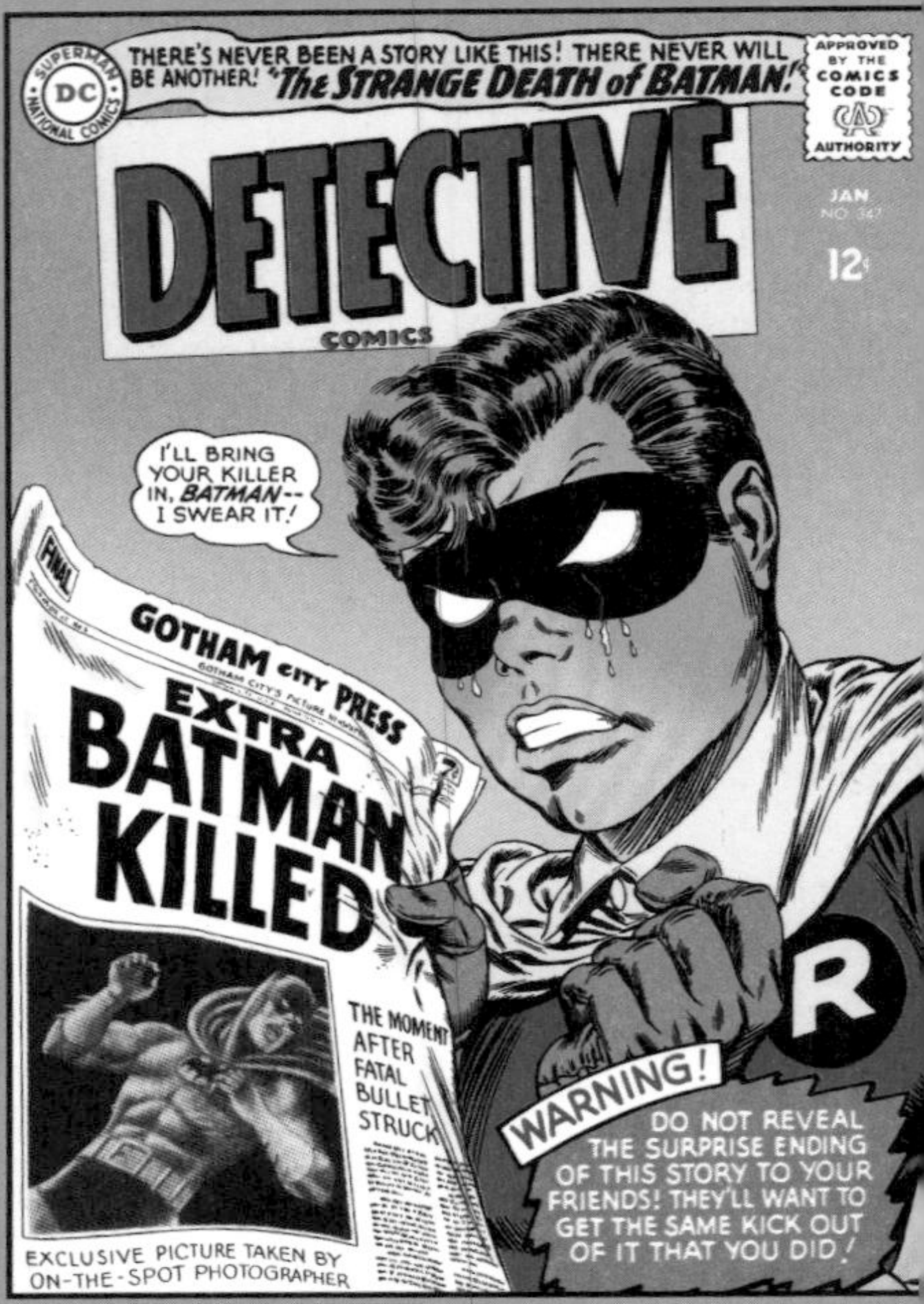
SUPERMAN DC NATIONAL COMICS
THERE'S NEVER BEEN A STORY LIKE THIS! THERE NEVER WILL BE ANOTHER! "The STRANGE DEATH of BATMAN!"
APPROVED BY THE COMICS CODE AUTHORITY
DETECTIVE COMICS
JAN
NO. 347
12¢
I'LL BRING YOUR KILLER IN, BATMAN-- I SWEAR IT!
FINAL
GOTHAM CITY PRESS
EXTRA
BATMAN KILLED
THE MOMENT AFTER FATAL BULLET STRUCK
EXCLUSIVE PICTURE TAKEN BY ON-THE-SPOT PHOTOGRAPHER
R
WARNING!
DO NOT REVEAL THE SURPRISE ENDING OF THIS STORY TO YOUR FRIENDS! THEY'LL WANT TO GET THE SAME KICK OUT OF IT THAT YOU DID!

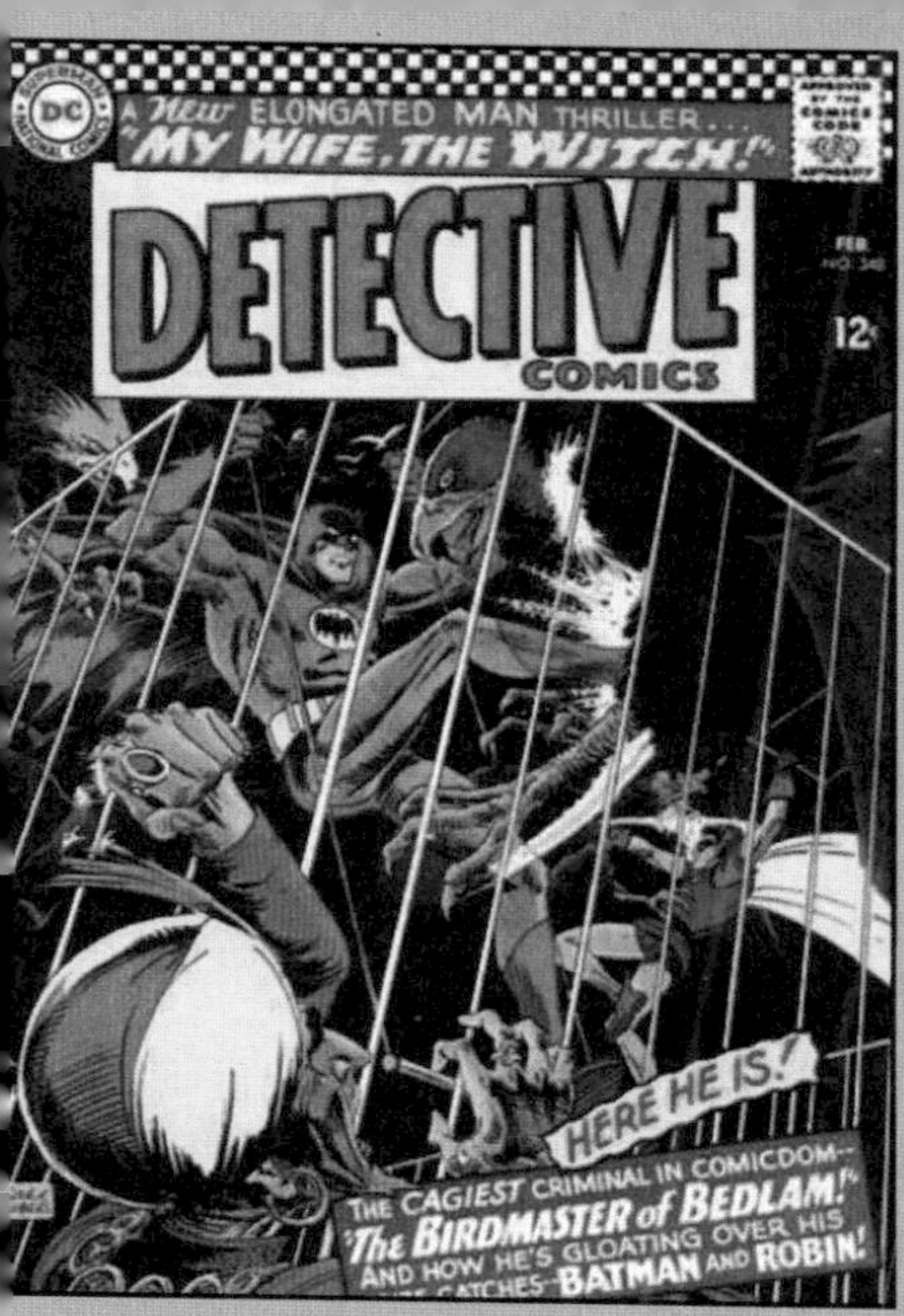
DC
A New ELONGATED MAN THRILLER...
"MY WIFE, THE WITCH!"
DETECTIVE
COMICS
FEB.
12¢
HERE HE IS!
THE CAGIEST CRIMINAL IN COMICDOM--
"The BIRDMASTER of BEDLAM!"
AND HOW HE'S GLOATING OVER HIS
CATCHES--BATMAN AND ROBIN!

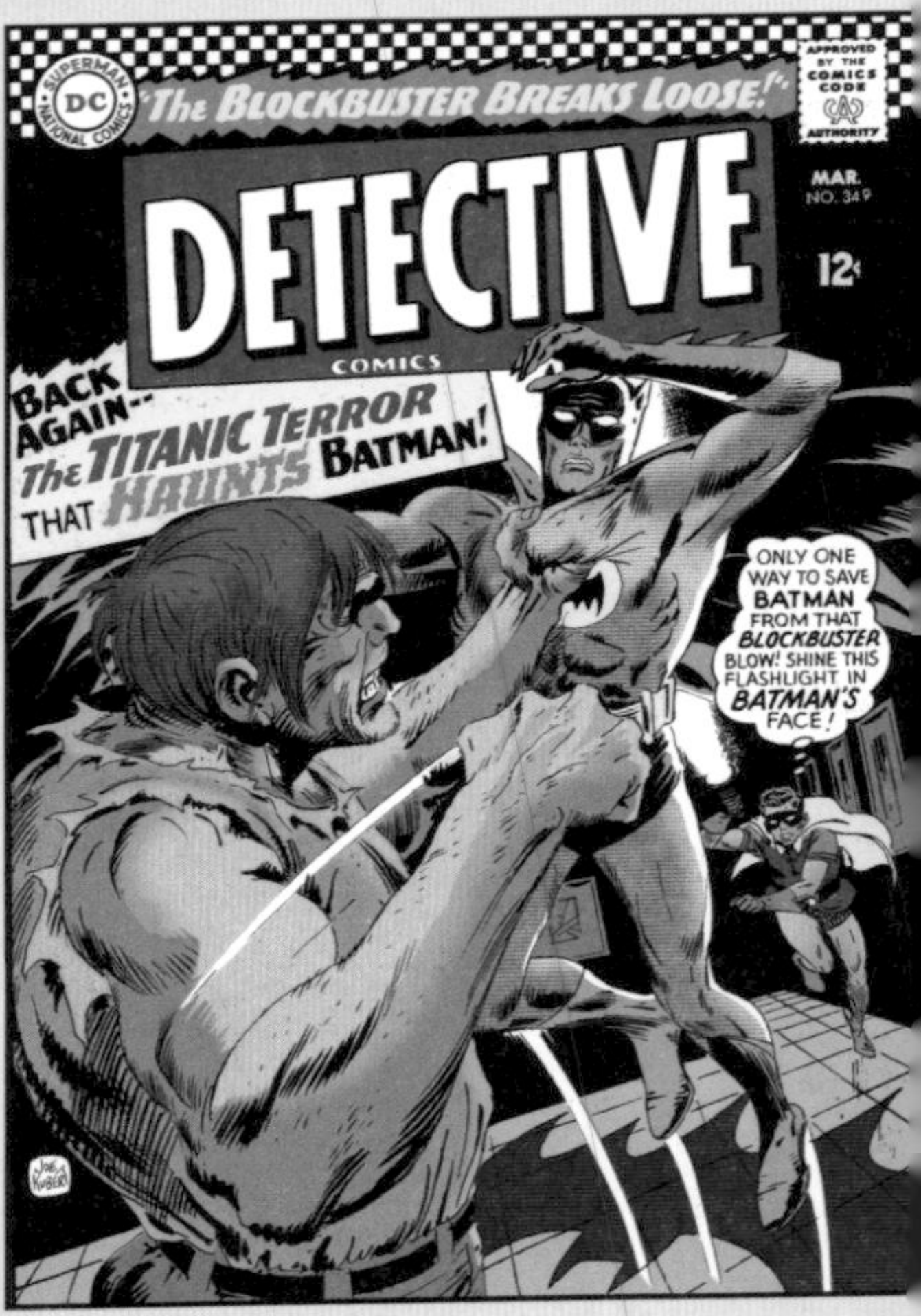
SUPERMAN
DC
NATIONAL COMICS
"The BLOCKBUSTER BREAKS LOOSE!"
APPROVED BY THE COMICS CODE AUTHORITY
DETECTIVE
COMICS
MAR.
NO. 349
12¢
BACK AGAIN--
The TITANIC TERROR
THAT HAUNTS BATMAN!
ONLY ONE WAY TO SAVE BATMAN FROM THAT BLOCKBUSTER BLOW! SHINE THIS FLASHLIGHT IN BATMAN'S FACE!

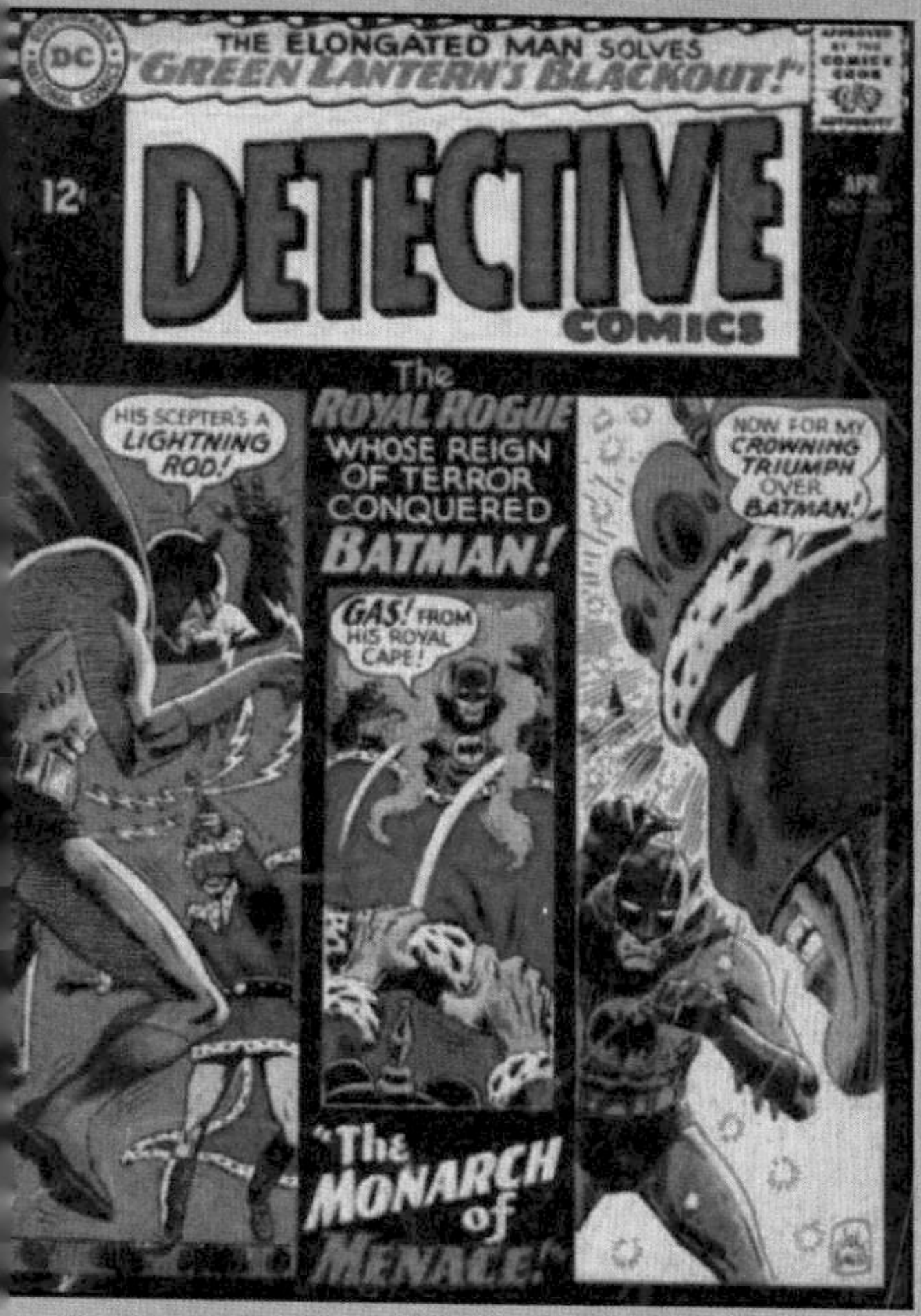
DC
THE ELONGATED MAN SOLVES
"GREEN LANTERN'S BLACKOUT!"
12¢
DETECTIVE
COMICS
APR
The
ROYAL ROGUE
WHOSE REIGN OF TERROR CONQUERED
BATMAN!
HIS SCEPTER'S A LIGHTNING ROD!
GAS! FROM HIS ROYAL CAPE!
NOW FOR MY CROWNING TRIUMPH OVER BATMAN!
"The MONARCH of MENACE!"

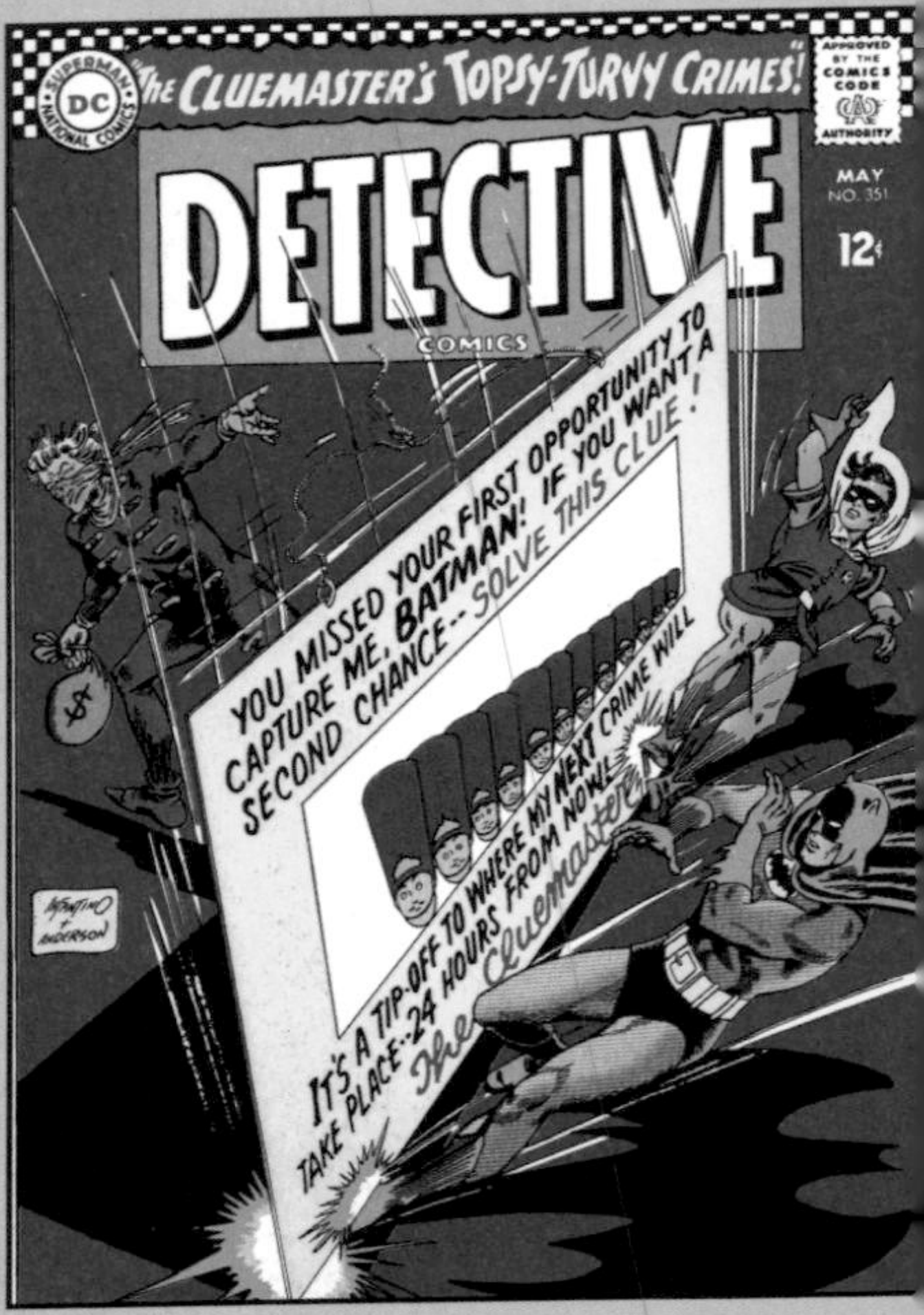
SUPERMAN-BATMAN NATIONAL COMICS
DC
"The CLUEMASTER'S TOPSY-TURVY CRIMES!"
APPROVED BY THE COMICS CODE AUTHORITY
DETECTIVE
COMICS
MAY
NO. 351
12¢
YOU MISSED YOUR FIRST OPPORTUNITY TO CAPTURE ME, BATMAN! IF YOU WANT A SECOND CHANCE-- SOLVE THIS CLUE!
IT'S A TIP-OFF TO WHERE MY NEXT CRIME WILL TAKE PLACE--24 HOURS FROM NOW!
The Cluemaster
MARTINEZ + ANDERSON

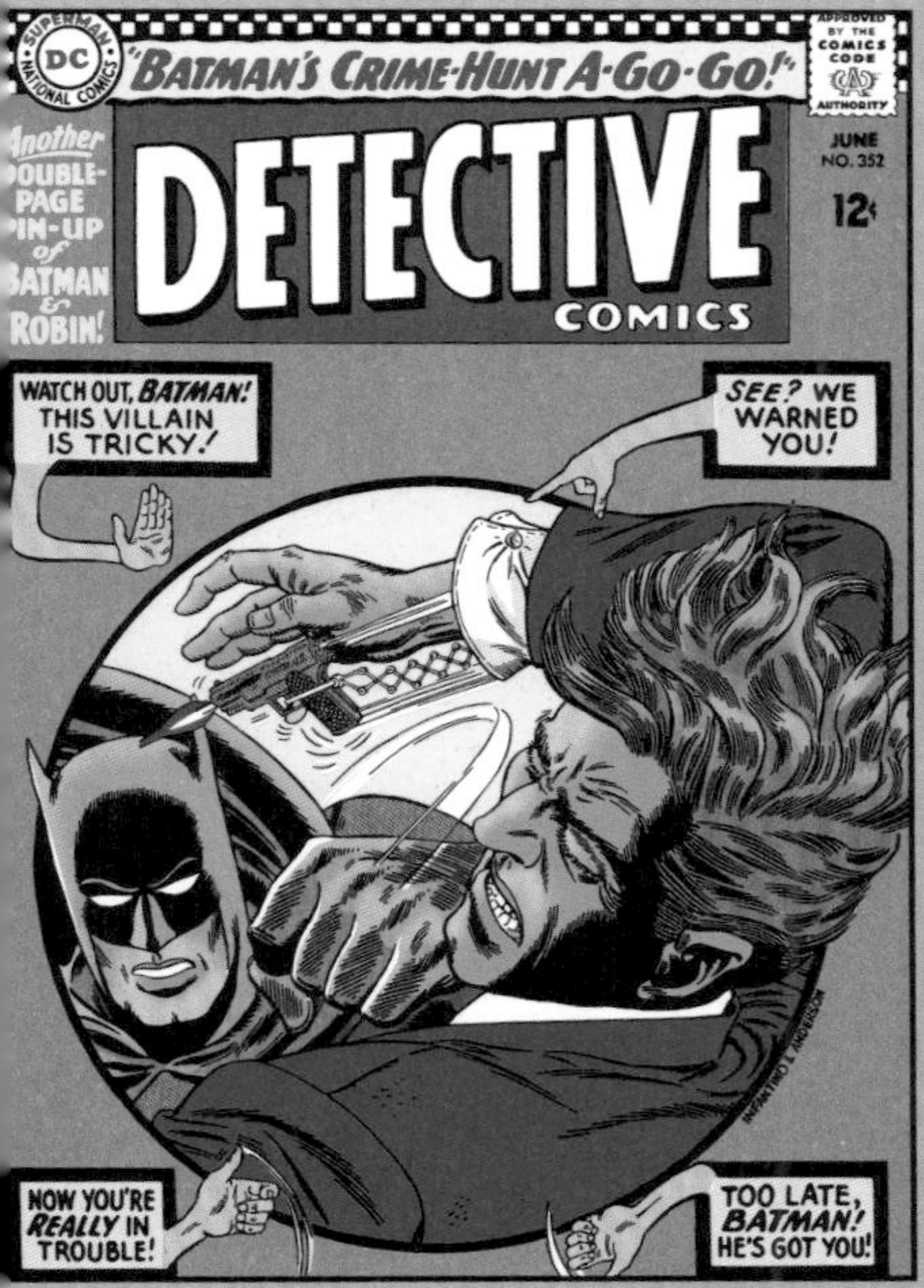
SUPERMAN NATIONAL COMICS
DC
"BATMAN'S CRIME-HUNT A-GO-GO!"
APPROVED BY THE COMICS CODE AUTHORITY
Another DOUBLE-PAGE PIN-UP of BATMAN & ROBIN!
DETECTIVE COMICS
JUNE
NO. 352
12¢
WATCH OUT, BATMAN! THIS VILLAIN IS TRICKY!
SEE? WE WARNED YOU!
NOW YOU'RE REALLY IN TROUBLE!
TOO LATE, BATMAN! HE'S GOT YOU!

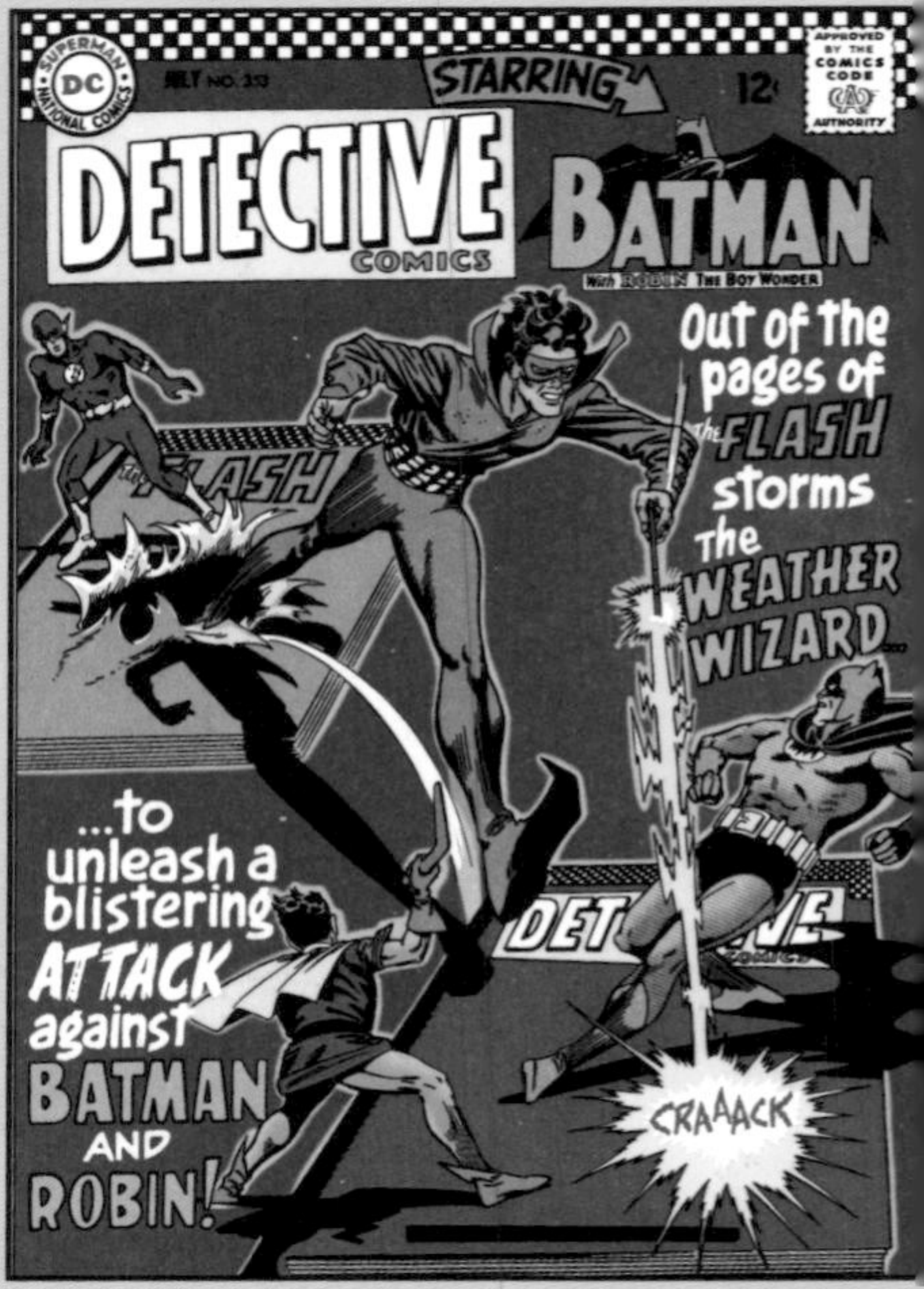
SUPERMAN NATIONAL COMICS
DC
NO. 33
STARRING
12¢
APPROVED BY THE COMICS CODE AUTHORITY
DETECTIVE COMICS
BATMAN
WITH ROBIN THE BOY WONDER
Out of the pages of The FLASH storms the WEATHER WIZARD...
...to unleash a blistering ATTACK against BATMAN AND ROBIN!
CRAAACK

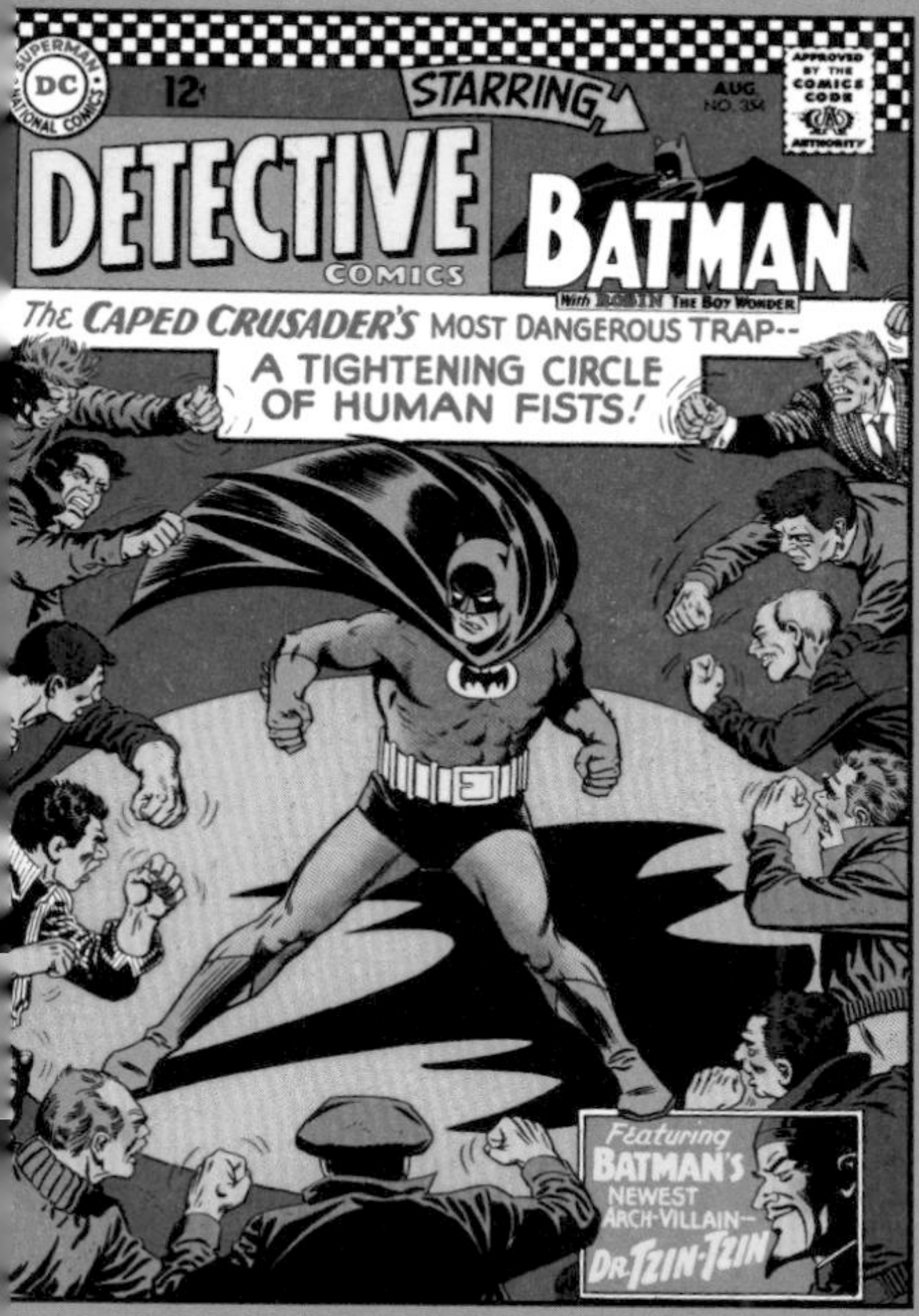
SUPERMAN • NATIONAL COMICS
DC
12¢
STARRING
AUG
NO. 354
APPROVED BY THE COMICS CODE AUTHORITY
DETECTIVE COMICS
BATMAN
With ROBIN THE BOY WONDER
The CAPED CRUSADER'S MOST DANGEROUS TRAP--
A TIGHTENING CIRCLE OF HUMAN FISTS!
Featuring BATMAN'S NEWEST ARCH-VILLAIN-- DR. TZIN-TZIN

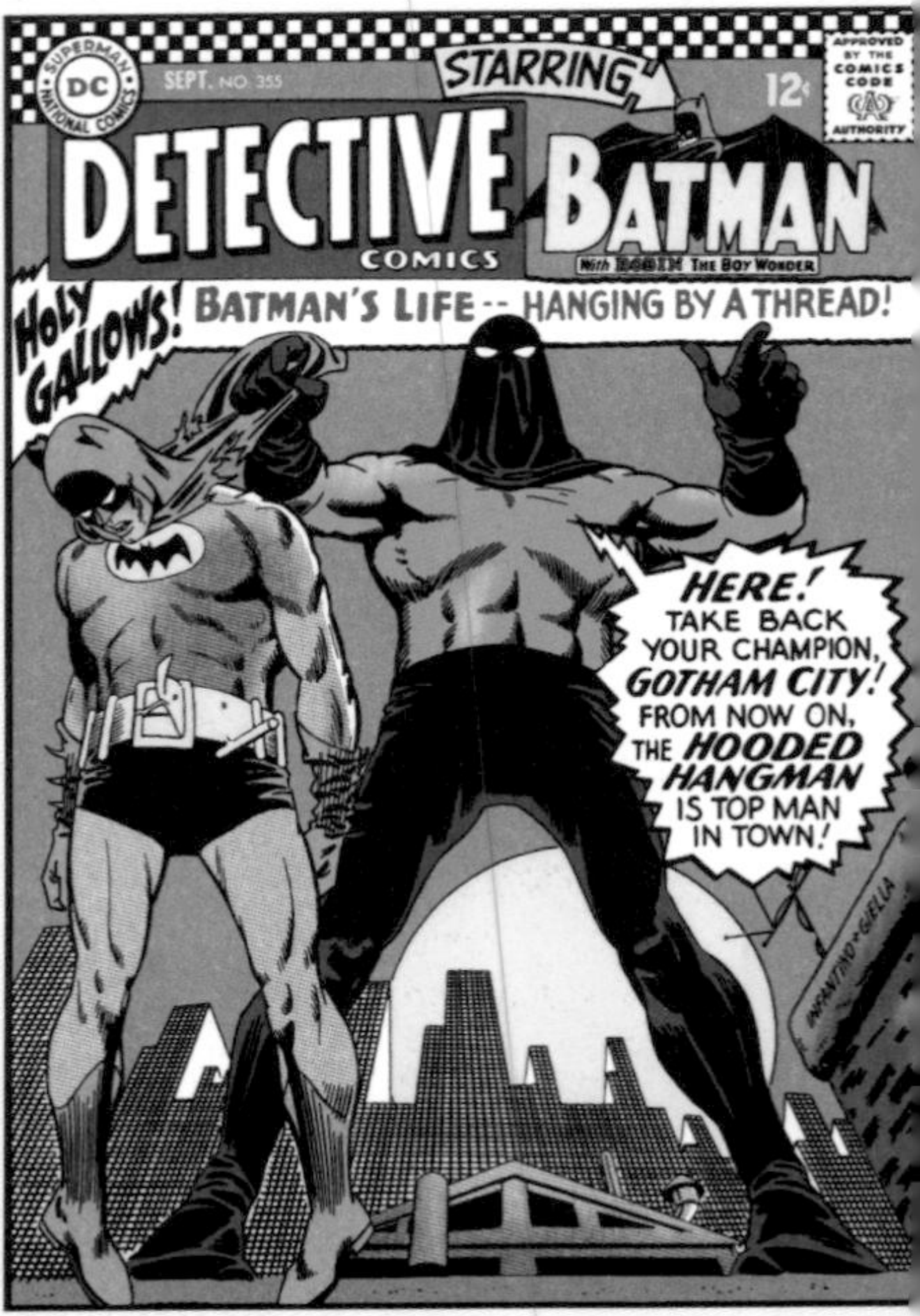
SUPERMAN NATIONAL COMICS
DC
SEPT. NO. 355
STARRING
12¢
APPROVED BY THE COMICS CODE AUTHORITY
DETECTIVE COMICS
BATMAN
With ROBIN THE BOY WONDER
HOLY GALLOWS!
BATMAN'S LIFE -- HANGING BY A THREAD!
HERE! TAKE BACK YOUR CHAMPION, GOTHAM CITY! FROM NOW ON, THE HOODED HANGMAN IS TOP MAN IN TOWN!

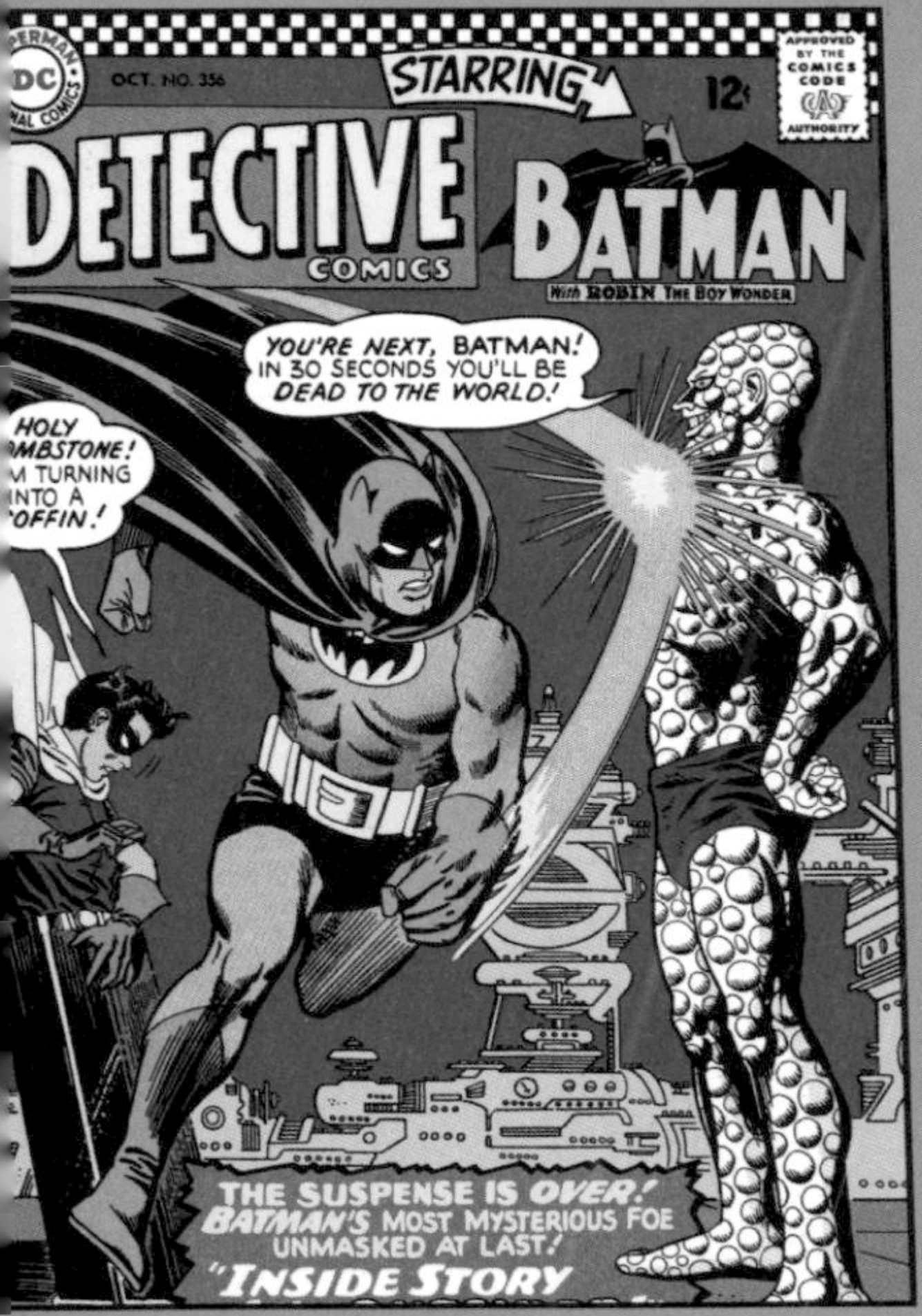
DC
OCT. NO. 356
STARRING
12¢
APPROVED BY THE COMICS CODE AUTHORITY
DETECTIVE COMICS
BATMAN
With ROBIN THE BOY WONDER
YOU'RE NEXT, BATMAN! IN 30 SECONDS YOU'LL BE DEAD TO THE WORLD!
HOLY OMBSTONE! M TURNING INTO A OFFIN!
THE SUSPENSE IS OVER! BATMAN'S MOST MYSTERIOUS FOE UNMASKED AT LAST!
"INSIDE STORY

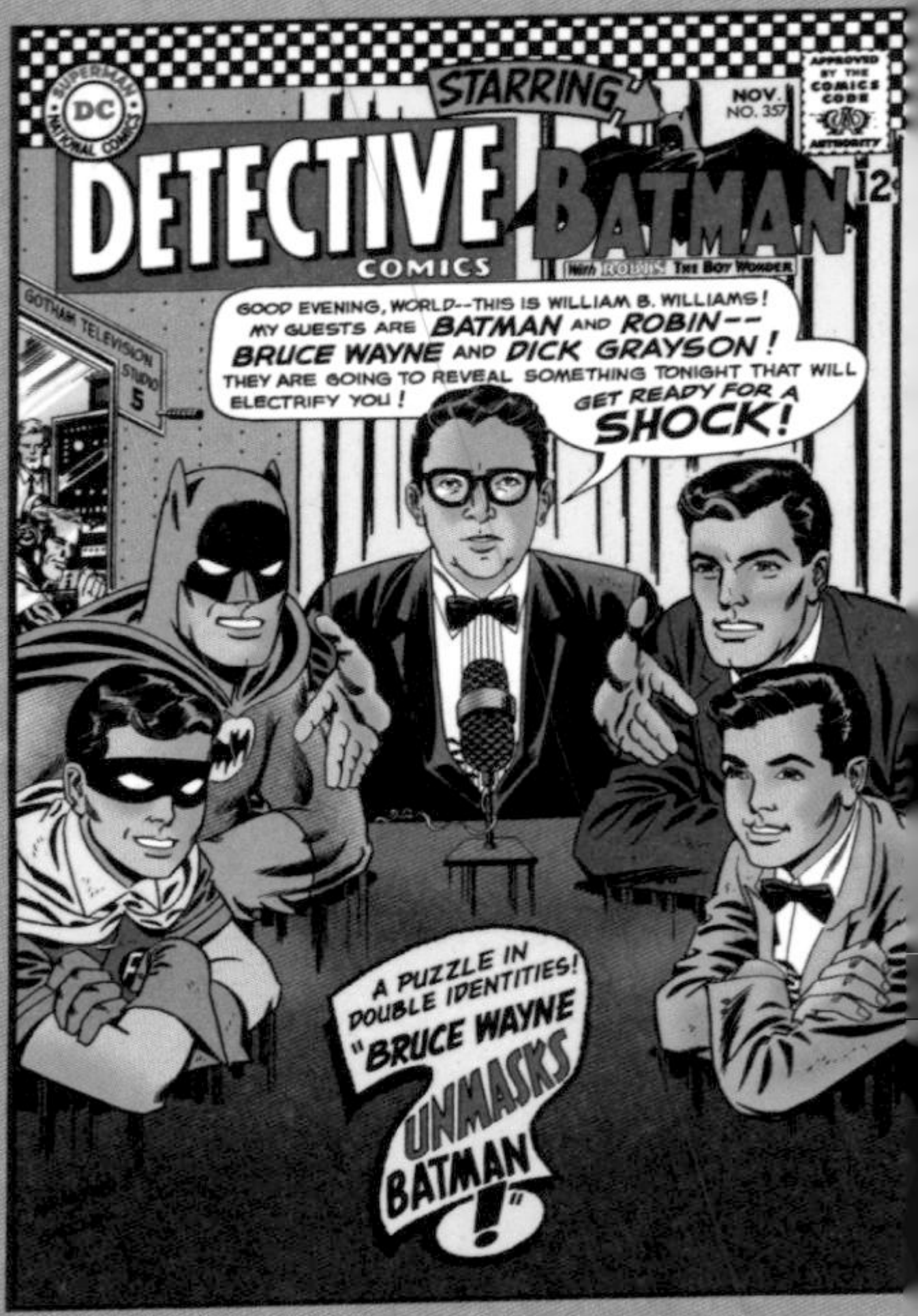
DC
SUPERMAN-BATMAN NATIONAL COMICS
STARRING
NOV. NO. 357
APPROVED BY THE COMICS CODE AUTHORITY
DETECTIVE COMICS
BATMAN
12¢
WITH ROBIN THE BOY WONDER
GOTHAM TELEVISION STUDIO 5
GOOD EVENING, WORLD--THIS IS WILLIAM B. WILLIAMS! MY GUESTS ARE BATMAN AND ROBIN-- BRUCE WAYNE AND DICK GRAYSON! THEY ARE GOING TO REVEAL SOMETHING TONIGHT THAT WILL ELECTRIFY YOU!
GET READY FOR A SHOCK!
A PUZZLE IN DOUBLE IDENTITIES!
"BRUCE WAYNE UNMASKS BATMAN!"

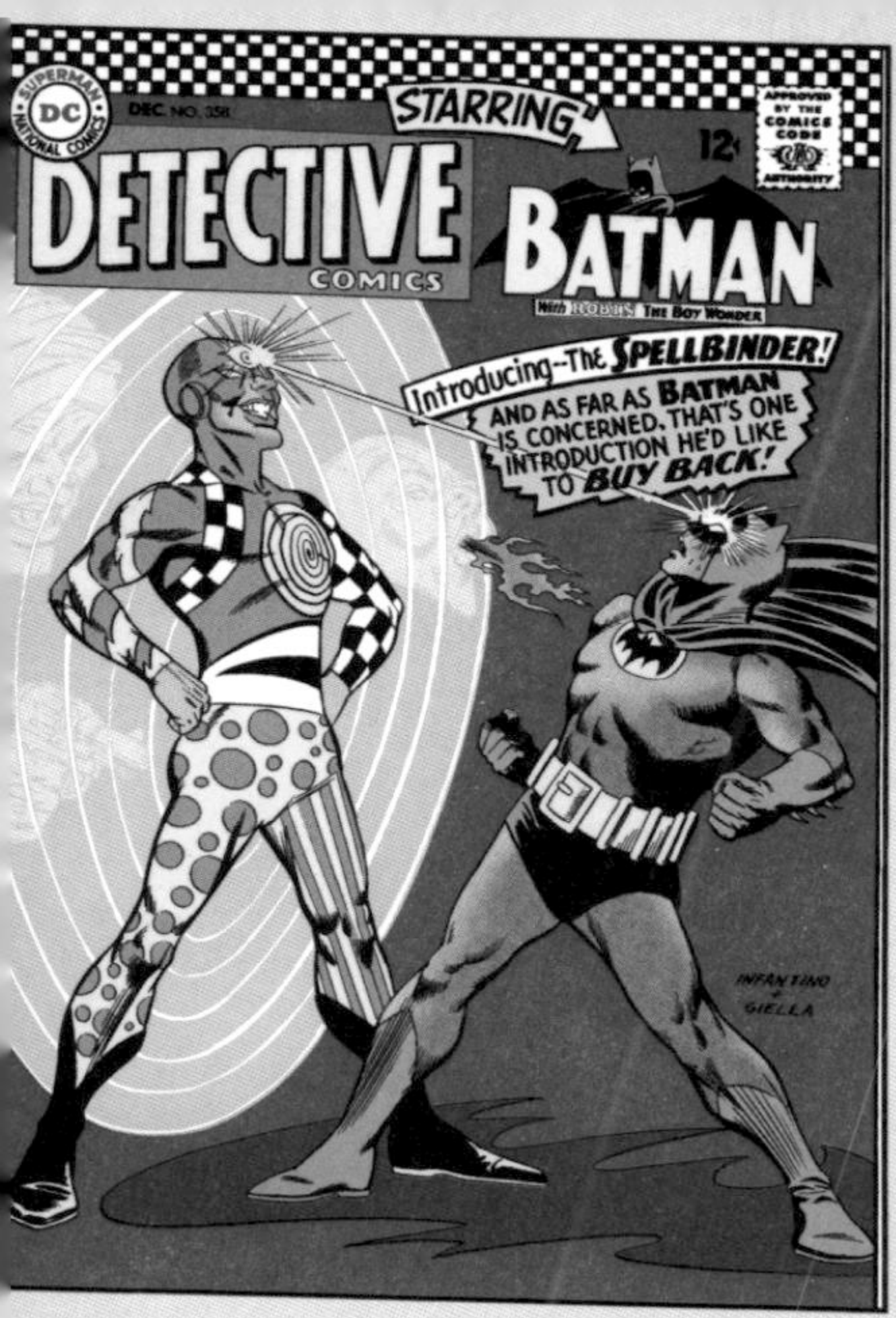
SUPERMAN NATIONAL COMICS
DC
DEC. NO. 358
STARRING
12¢
APPROVED BY THE COMICS CODE AUTHORITY
DETECTIVE COMICS
BATMAN
WITH ROBIN THE BOY WONDER
Introducing--The SPELLBINDER!
AND AS FAR AS BATMAN IS CONCERNED, THAT'S ONE INTRODUCTION HE'D LIKE TO BUY BACK!
INFANTINO & GIELLA

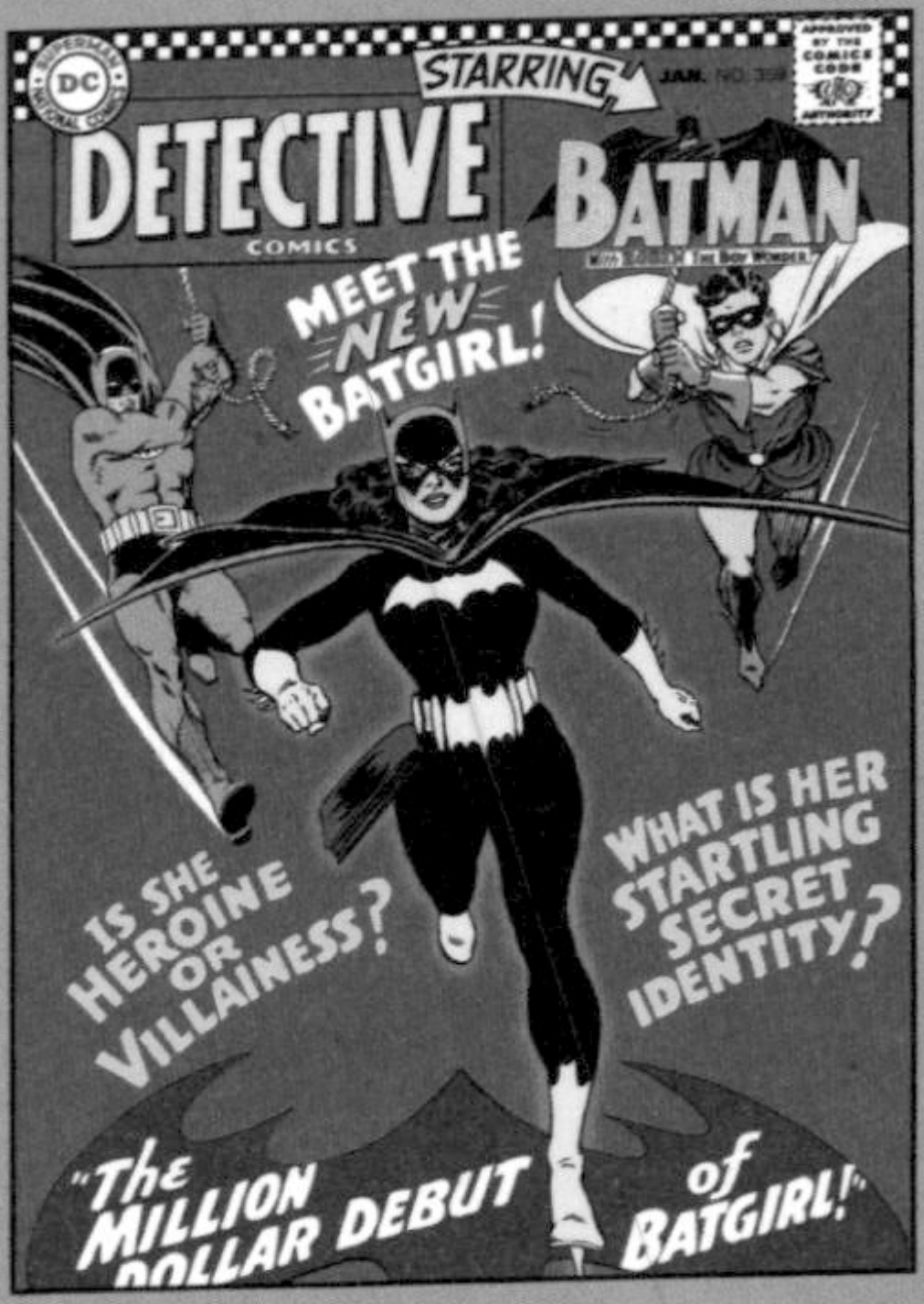

Detective Comics #359
This issue introduces Batgirl. Batgirl's secret identity is Barbara Gordon, daughter of Gotham City police commissioner James Gordon.

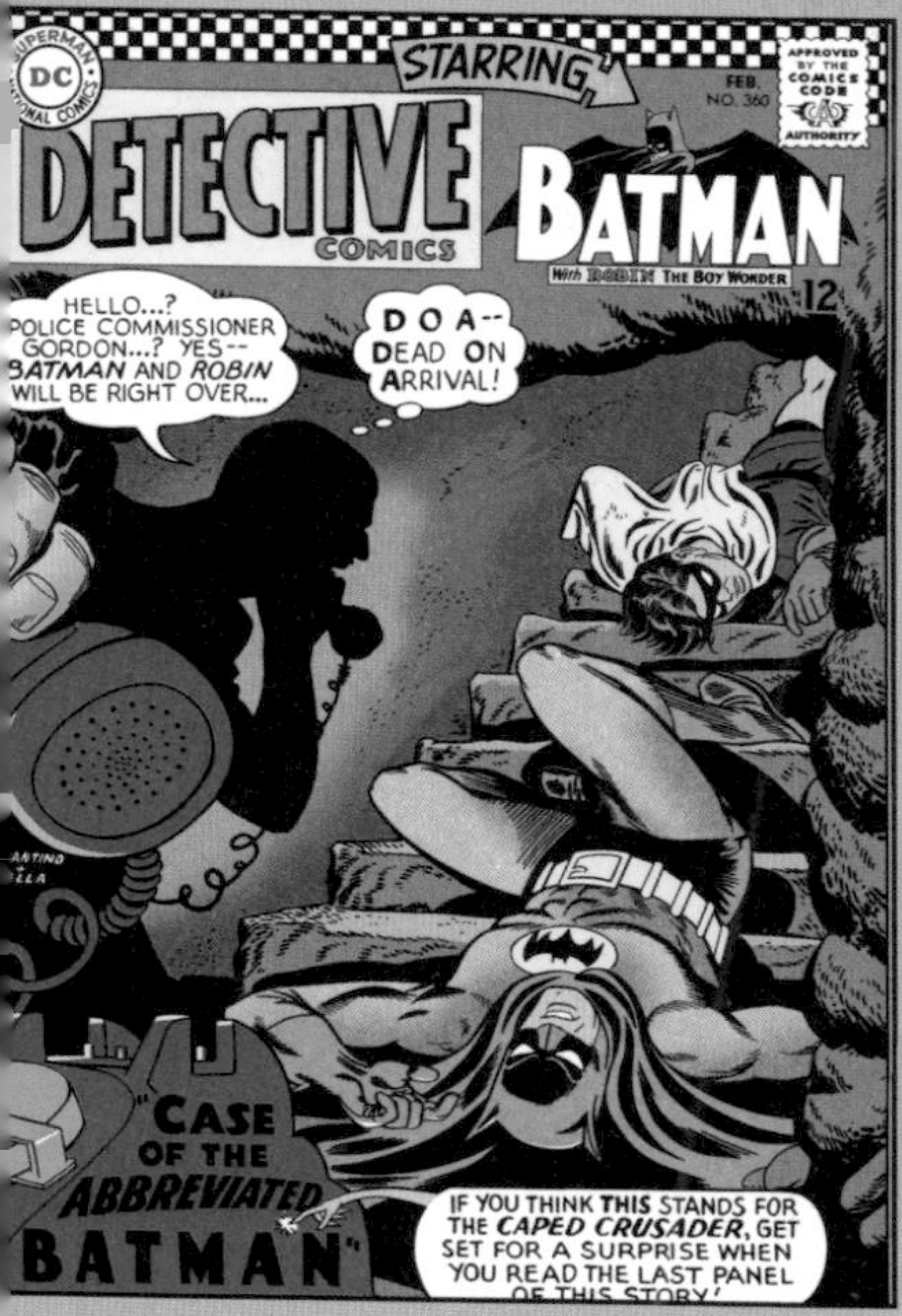
SUPERMAN
DC
NATIONAL COMICS
STARRING
FEB.
NO. 360
APPROVED BY THE COMICS CODE AUTHORITY
DETECTIVE COMICS
BATMAN
With ROBIN THE BOY WONDER
12
HELLO...? POLICE COMMISSIONER GORDON...? YES-- BATMAN AND ROBIN WILL BE RIGHT OVER...
D O A-- DEAD ON ARRIVAL!
"CASE OF THE ABBREVIATED BATMAN"
IF YOU THINK THIS STANDS FOR THE CAPED CRUSADER, GET SET FOR A SURPRISE WHEN YOU READ THE LAST PANEL OF THIS STORY!

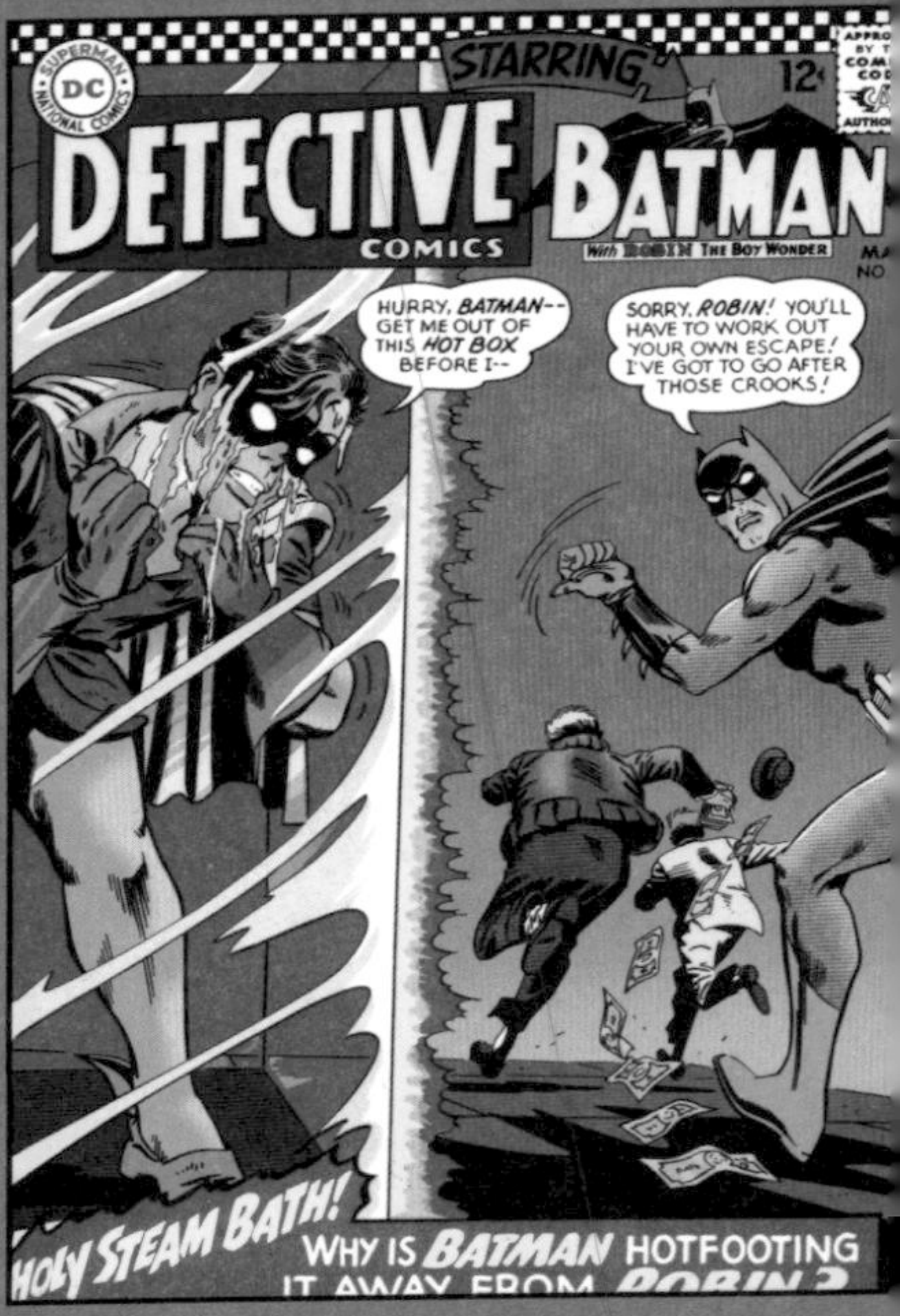
SUPERMAN
DC
NATIONAL COMICS
STARRING
12¢
DETECTIVE COMICS
BATMAN
With ROBIN The Boy Wonder
HURRY, BATMAN-- GET ME OUT OF THIS HOT BOX BEFORE I--
SORRY, ROBIN! YOU'LL HAVE TO WORK OUT YOUR OWN ESCAPE! I'VE GOT TO GO AFTER THOSE CROOKS!
HOLY STEAM BATH!
WHY IS BATMAN HOTFOOTING

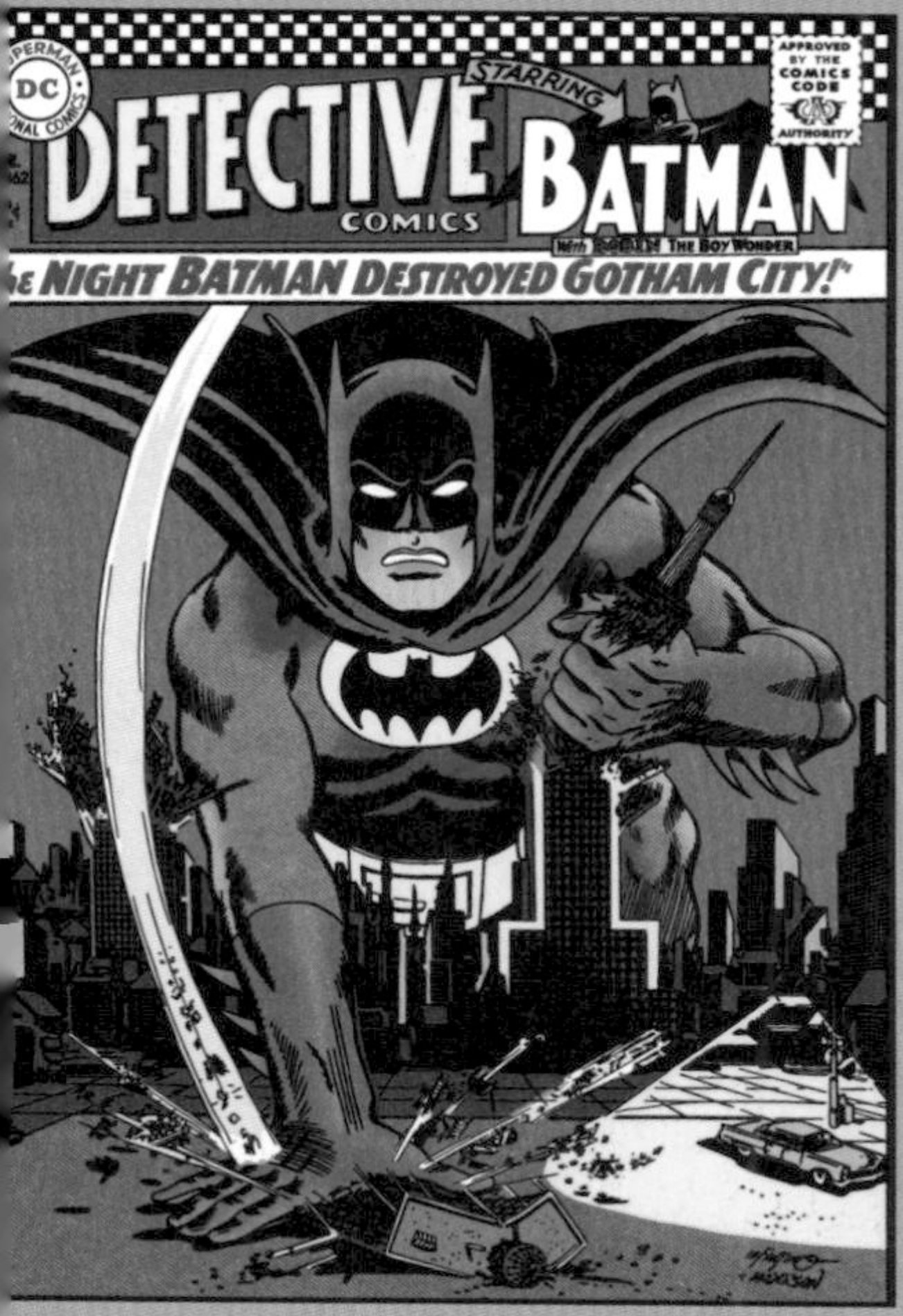
DC
DETECTIVE COMICS
STARRING BATMAN
APPROVED BY THE COMICS CODE AUTHORITY
NIGHT BATMAN DESTROYED GOTHAM CITY!

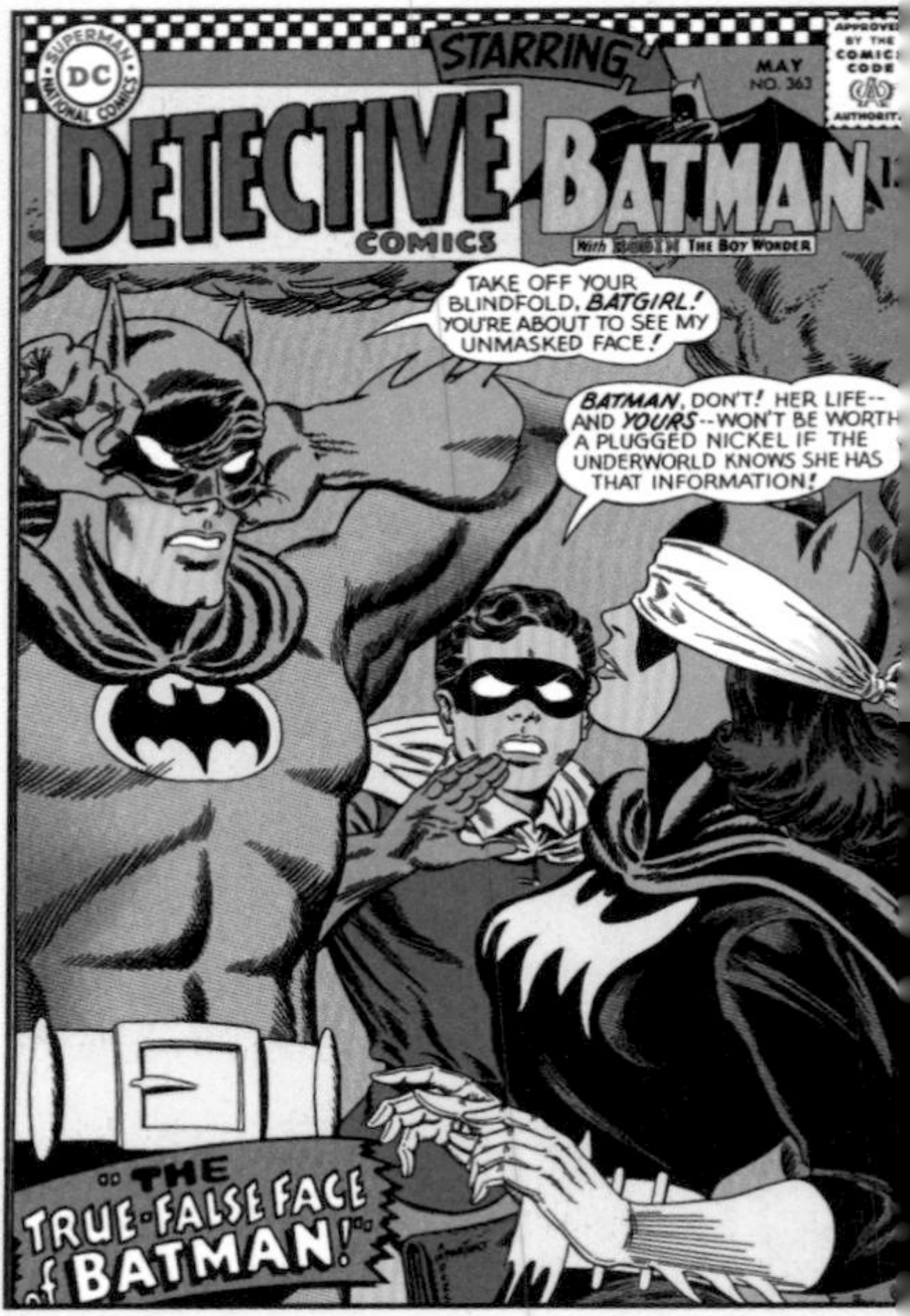
SUPERMAN
DC
NATIONAL COMICS
STARRING
MAY
NO. 363
APPROVED BY THE COMICS CODE AUTHORITY
DETECTIVE COMICS
BATMAN
With ROBIN THE BOY WONDER
TAKE OFF YOUR BLINDFOLD, BATGIRL! YOU'RE ABOUT TO SEE MY UNMASKED FACE!
BATMAN, DON'T! HER LIFE-- AND YOURS--WON'T BE WORTH A PLUGGED NICKEL IF THE UNDERWORLD KNOWS SHE HAS THAT INFORMATION!
"THE TRUE-FALSE FACE of BATMAN!"

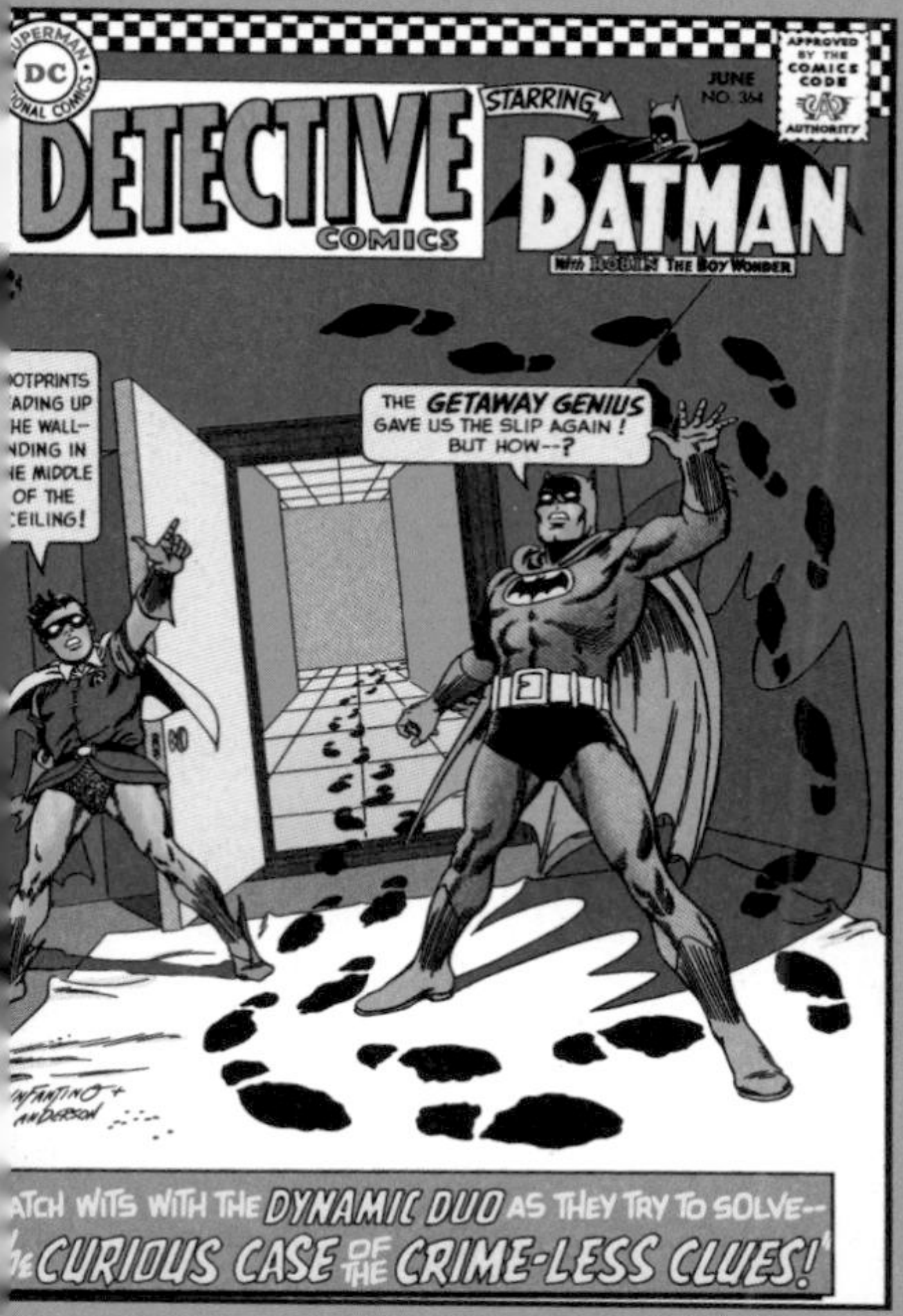
DC
SUPERMAN • NATIONAL COMICS
DETECTIVE COMICS
STARRING BATMAN
WITH ROBIN THE BOY WONDER
JUNE
NO. 364
APPROVED BY THE COMICS CODE AUTHORITY
OOTPRINTS ADING UP HE WALL- NDING IN HE MIDDLE OF THE CEILING!
THE GETAWAY GENIUS GAVE US THE SLIP AGAIN! BUT HOW--?
INFANTINO + ANDERSON
ATCH WITS WITH THE DYNAMIC DUO AS THEY TRY TO SOLVE--
HE CURIOUS CASE OF THE CRIME-LESS CLUES!

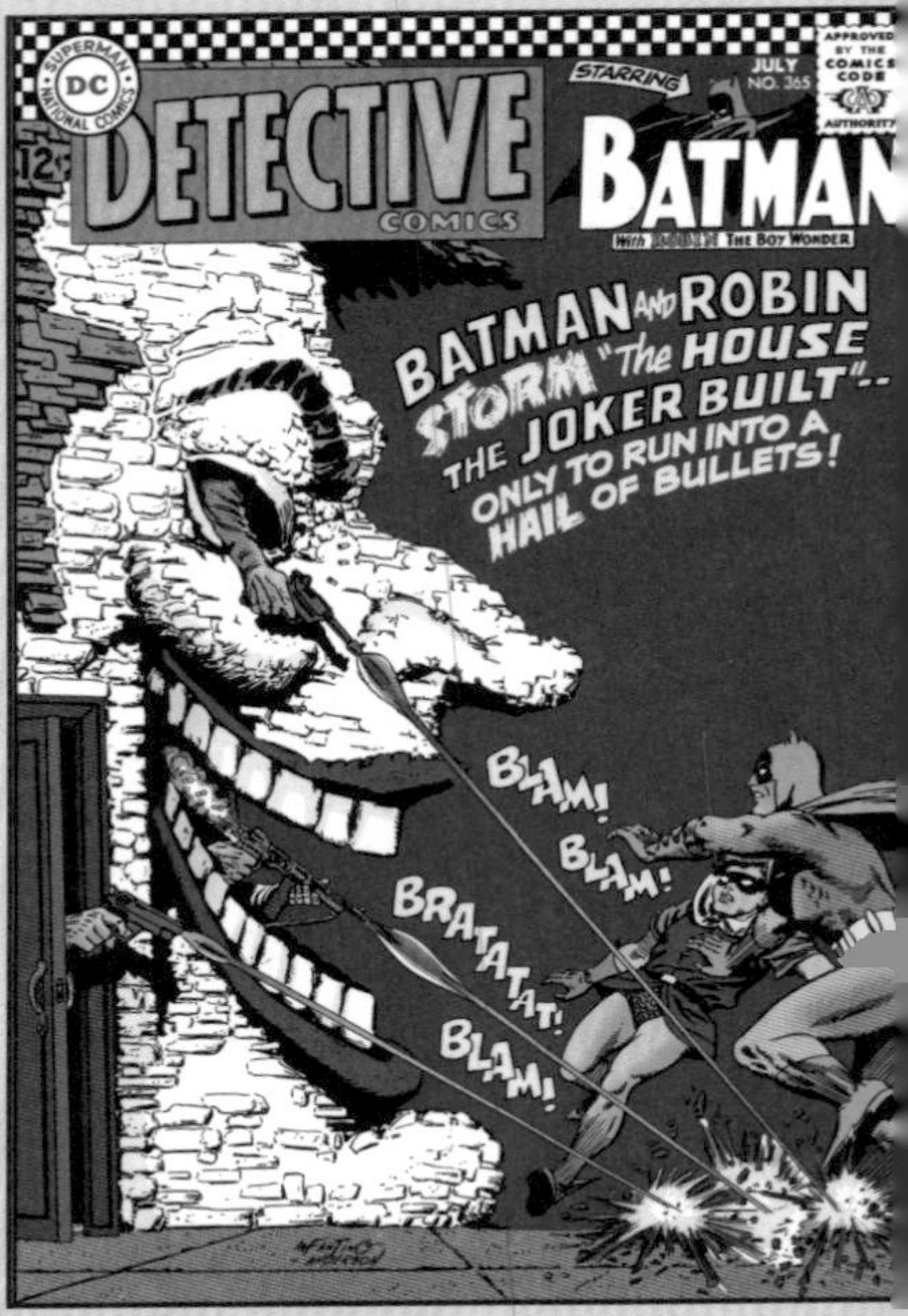
SUPERMAN
DC
NATIONAL COMICS
12¢
DETECTIVE
COMICS
STARRING
JULY
NO. 365
APPROVED BY THE COMICS CODE AUTHORITY
BATMAN
WITH ROBIN THE BOY WONDER
BATMAN AND ROBIN
STORM "The HOUSE
THE JOKER BUILT"--
ONLY TO RUN INTO A
HAIL OF BULLETS!
BLAM!
BLAM!
BRATATAT!
BLAM!

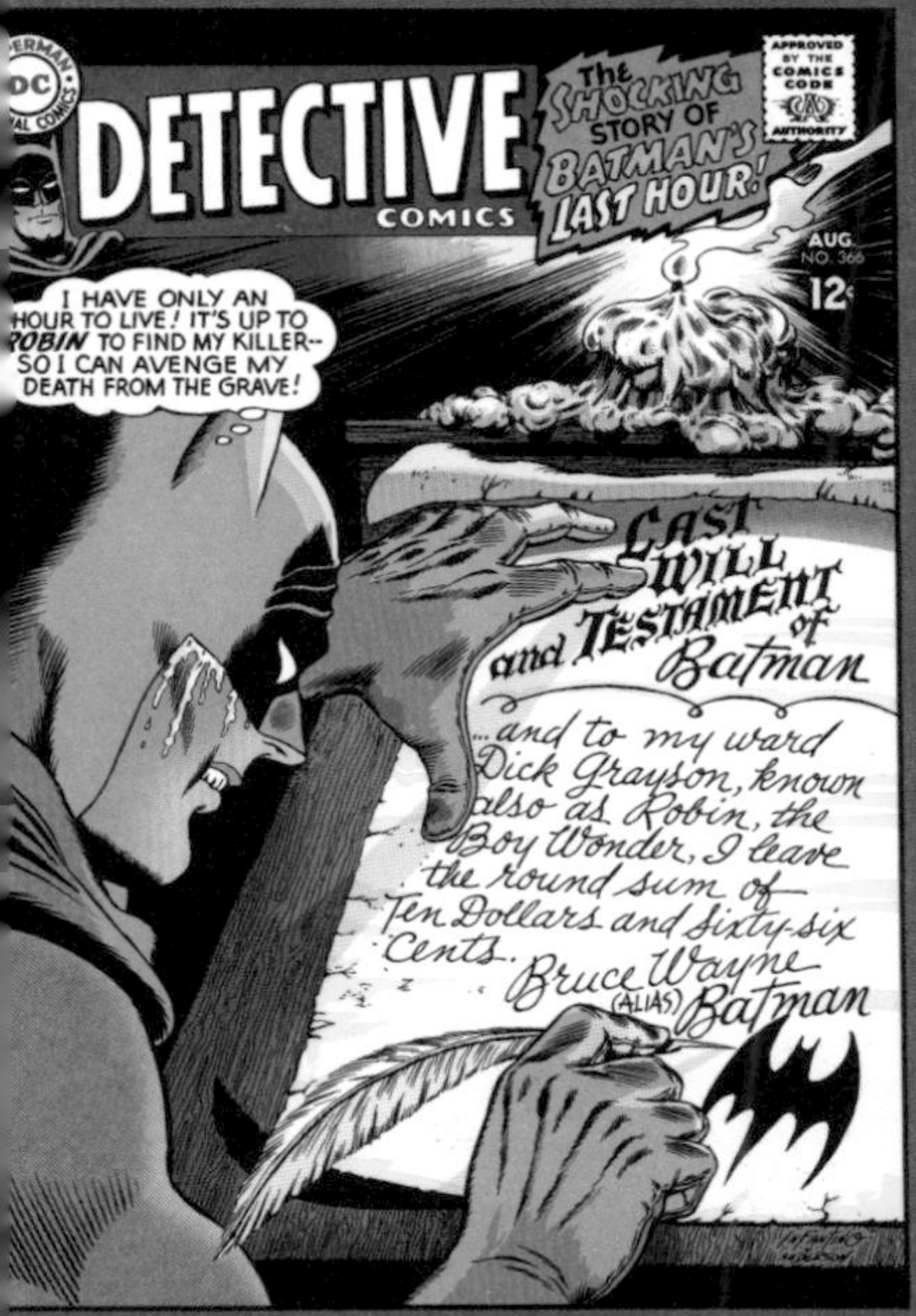
DC
DETECTIVE
COMICS
The SHOCKING STORY OF BATMAN'S LAST HOUR!
APPROVED BY THE COMICS CODE AUTHORITY
AUG.
NO. 366
12¢
I HAVE ONLY AN HOUR TO LIVE! IT'S UP TO ROBIN TO FIND MY KILLER-- SO I CAN AVENGE MY DEATH FROM THE GRAVE!
LAST WILL and TESTAMENT of Batman
...and to my ward Dick Grayson, known also as Robin, the Boy Wonder, I leave the round sum of Ten Dollars and Sixty-six Cents.
Bruce Wayne (ALIAS) Batman

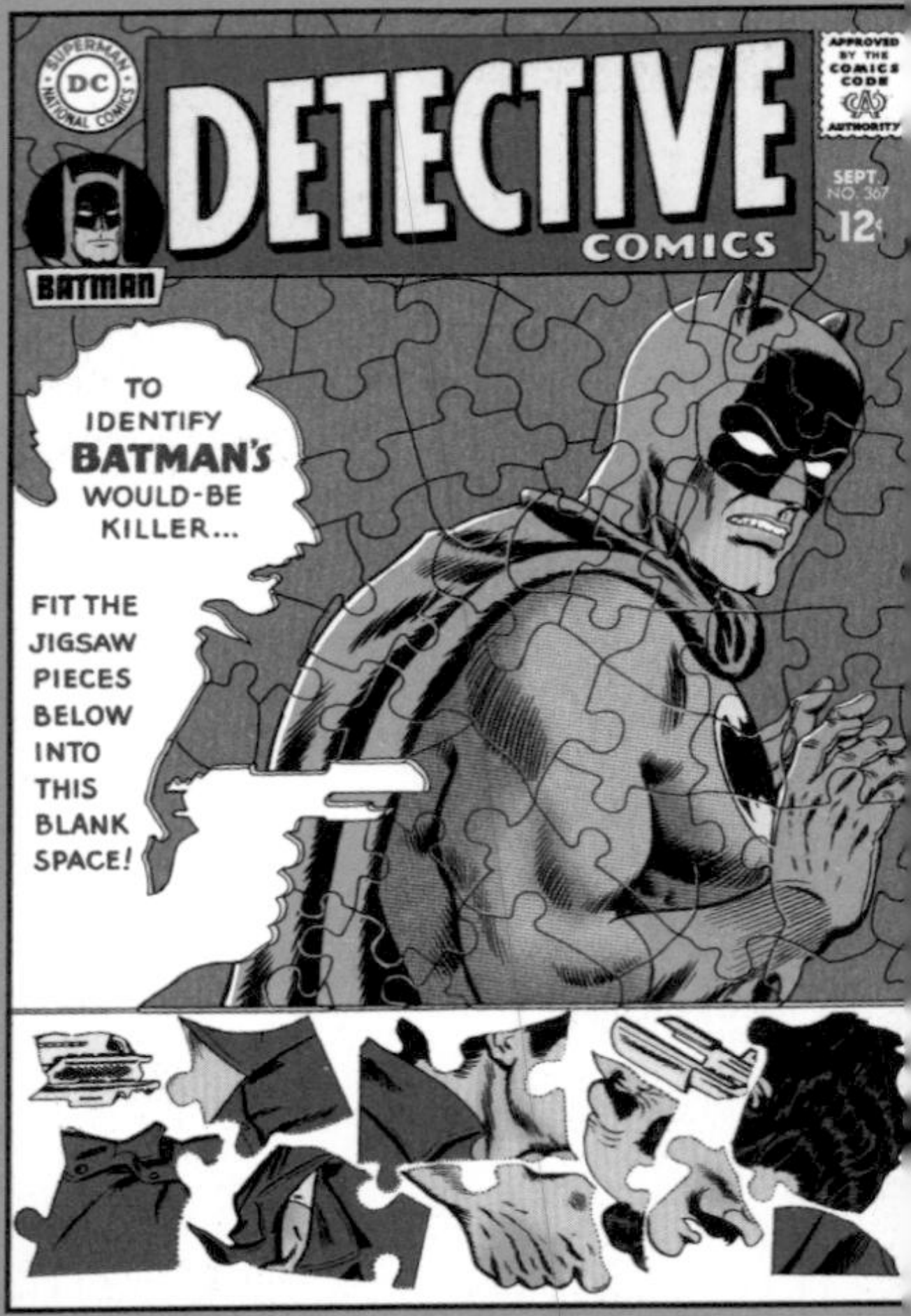
SUPERMAN
DC
NATIONAL COMICS
DETECTIVE
COMICS
APPROVED BY THE COMICS CODE AUTHORITY
SEPT.
NO. 367
12¢
BATMAN
TO IDENTIFY BATMAN'S WOULD-BE KILLER...
FIT THE JIGSAW PIECES BELOW INTO THIS BLANK SPACE!

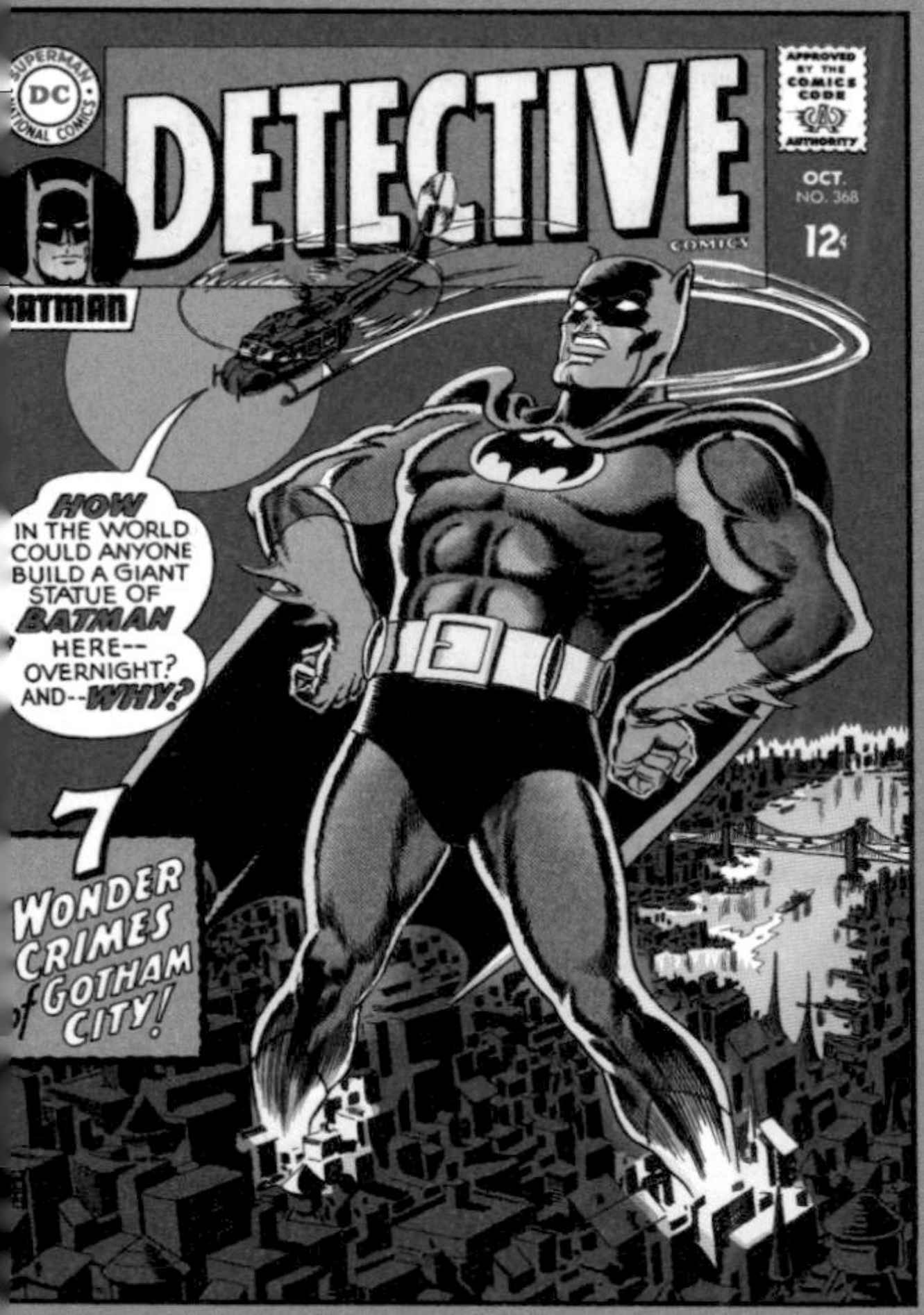
DC
SUPERMAN • NATIONAL COMICS
DETECTIVE
COMICS
APPROVED BY THE COMICS CODE AUTHORITY
OCT.
NO. 368
12¢
BATMAN
HOW IN THE WORLD COULD ANYONE BUILD A GIANT STATUE OF BATMAN HERE-- OVERNIGHT? AND--WHY?
7 WONDER CRIMES of GOTHAM CITY!

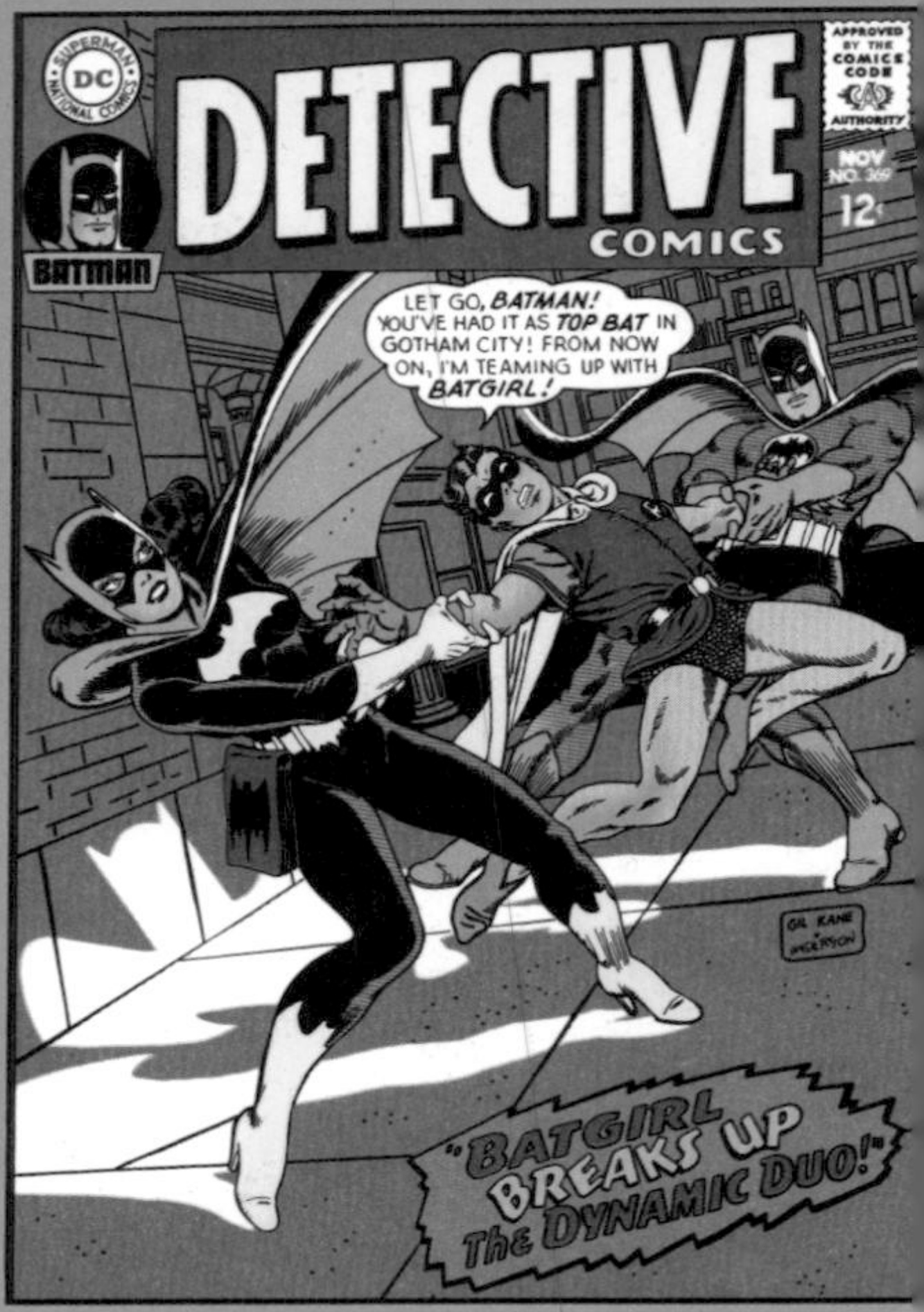
SUPERMAN
DC
NATIONAL COMICS
DETECTIVE
COMICS
APPROVED BY THE COMICS CODE AUTHORITY
NOV
NO. 369
12¢
BATMAN
LET GO, BATMAN! YOU'VE HAD IT AS TOP BAT IN GOTHAM CITY! FROM NOW ON, I'M TEAMING UP WITH BATGIRL!
GIL KANE
ANDERSON
"BATGIRL BREAKS UP THE DYNAMIC DUO!"

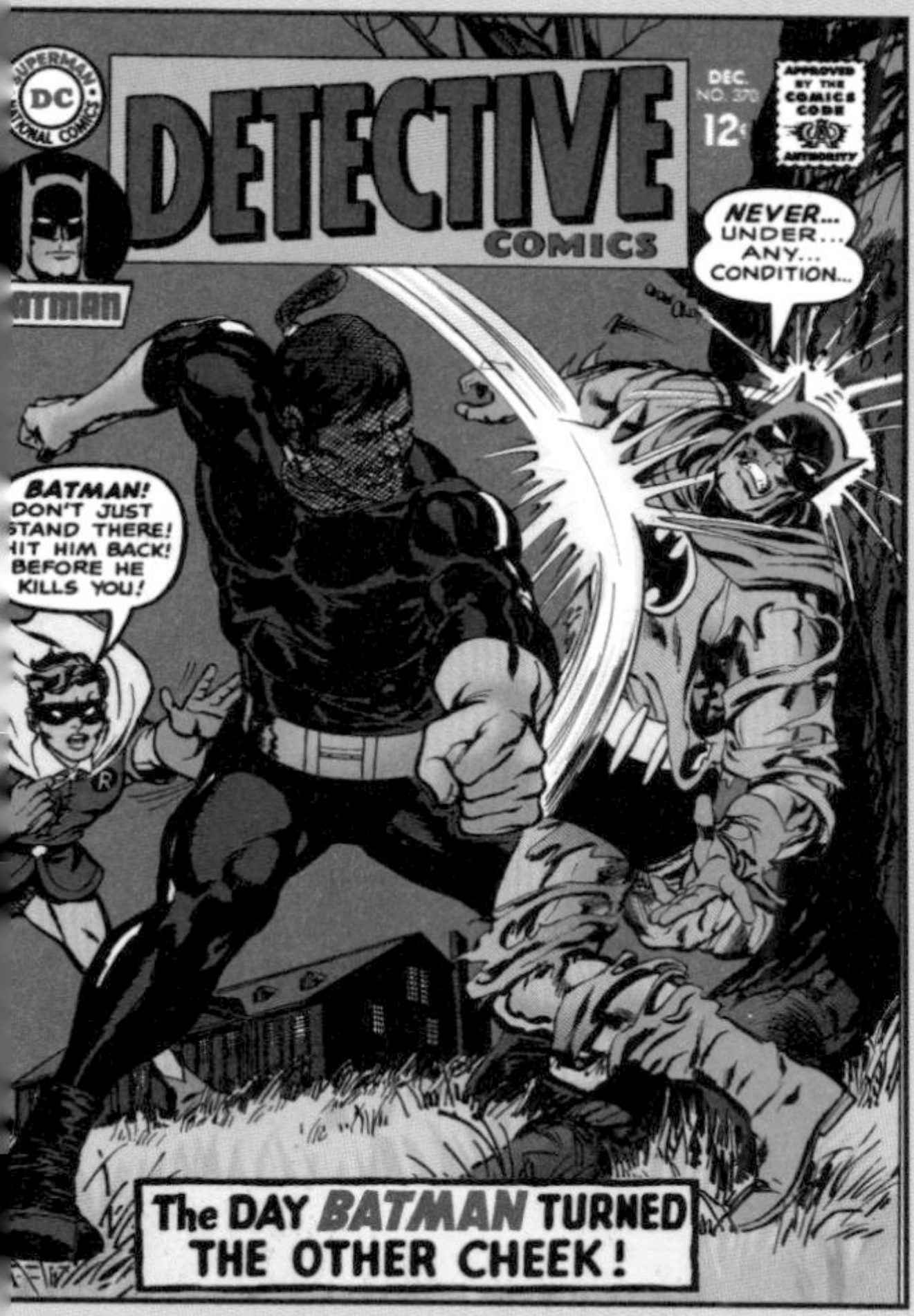
DC
SUPERMAN
NATIONAL COMICS
DETECTIVE
COMICS
DEC.
NO. 370
12¢
APPROVED BY THE COMICS CODE AUTHORITY
BATMAN
NEVER... UNDER... ANY... CONDITION...
BATMAN! DON'T JUST STAND THERE! HIT HIM BACK! BEFORE HE KILLS YOU!
The DAY BATMAN TURNED THE OTHER CHEEK!

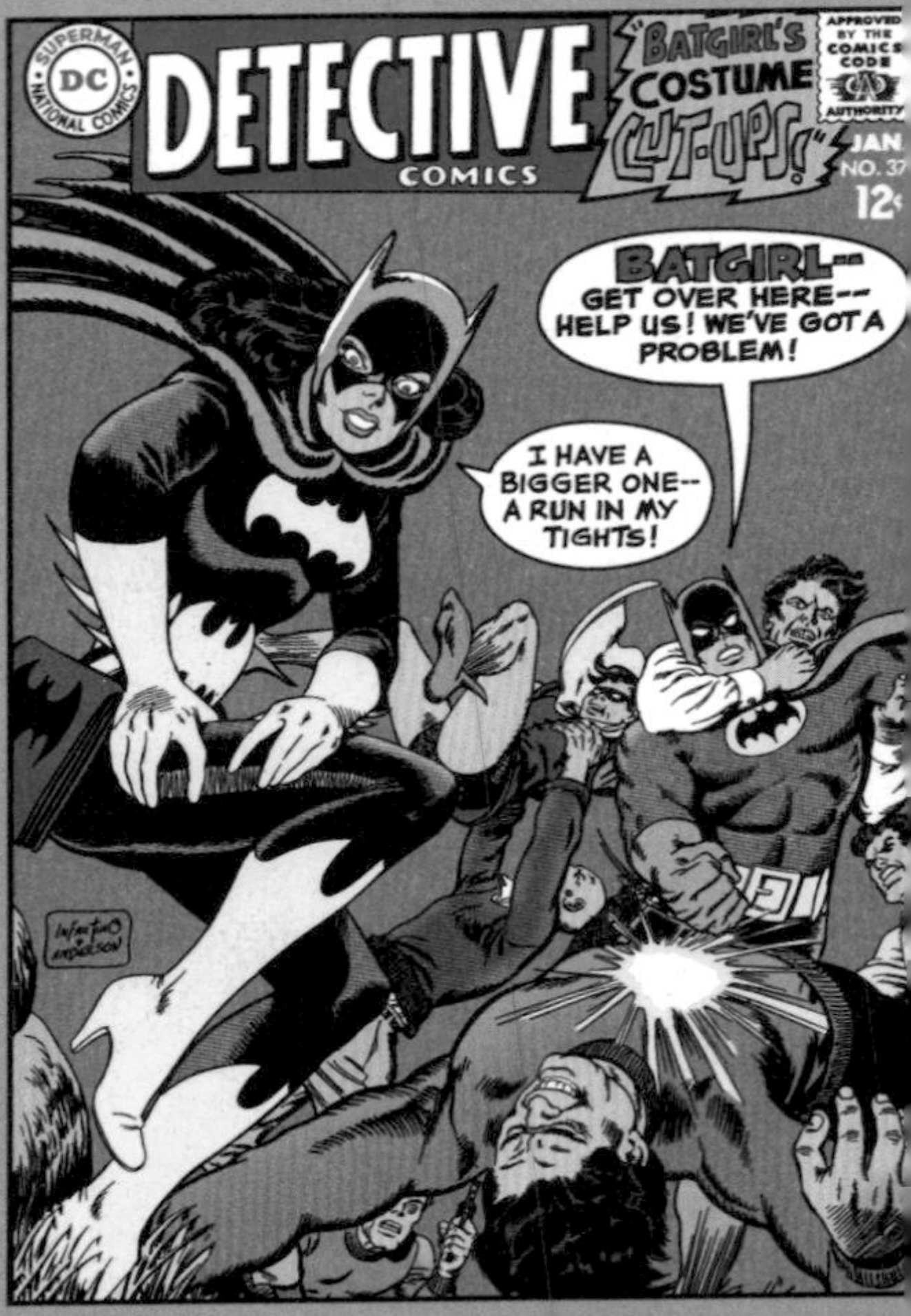
SUPERMAN
DC
NATIONAL COMICS
DETECTIVE
COMICS
"BATGIRL'S COSTUME CUT-UPS!"
APPROVED BY THE COMICS CODE AUTHORITY
JAN.
NO. 37
12¢
BATGIRL--
GET OVER HERE--
HELP US! WE'VE GOT A PROBLEM!
I HAVE A BIGGER ONE--
A RUN IN MY TIGHTS!

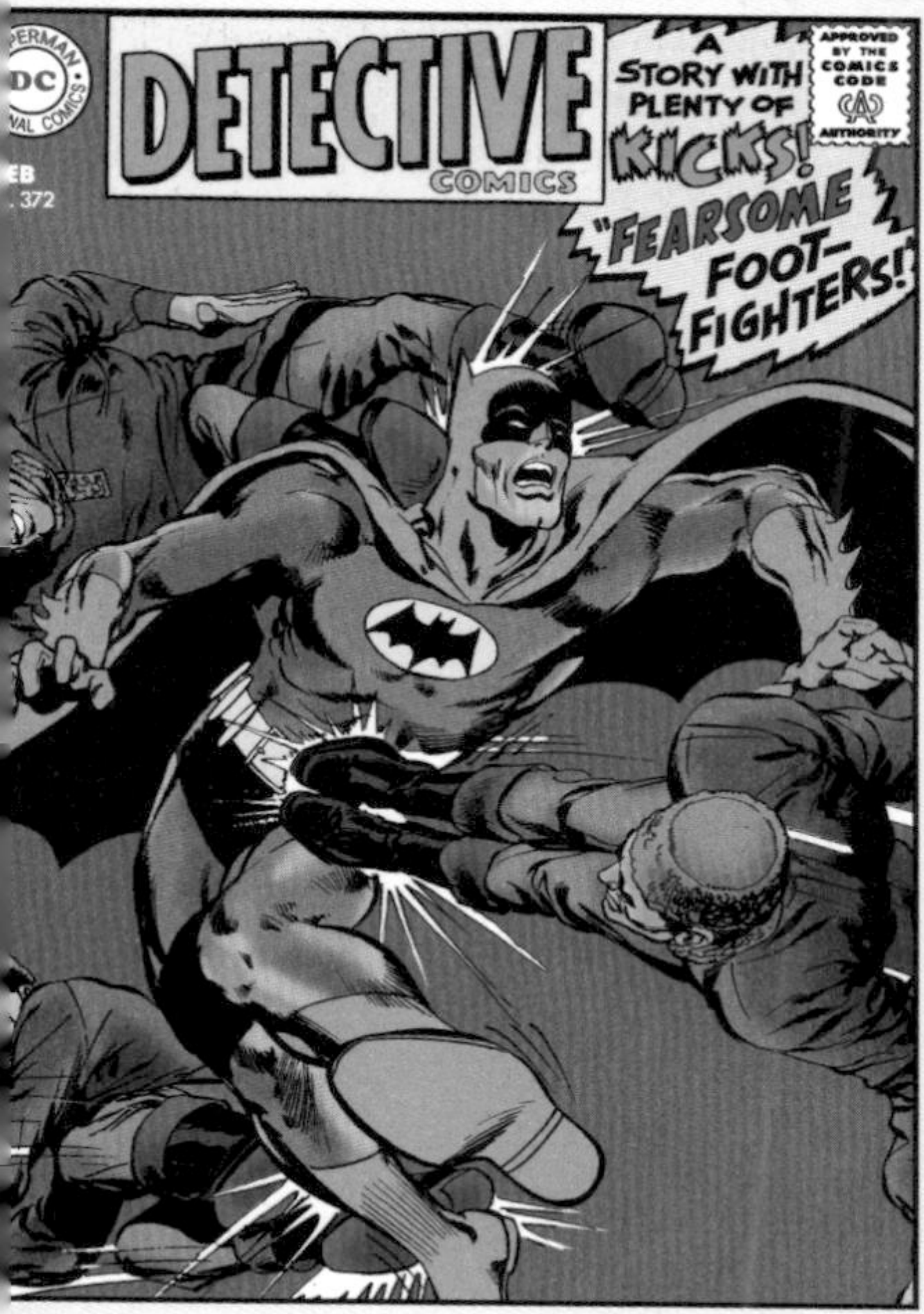
PERMAN
DC
NAL COMICS
EB
. 372
DETECTIVE
COMICS
A STORY WITH PLENTY OF KICKS!
APPROVED BY THE COMICS CODE AUTHORITY
"FEARSOME FOOT-FIGHTERS!"

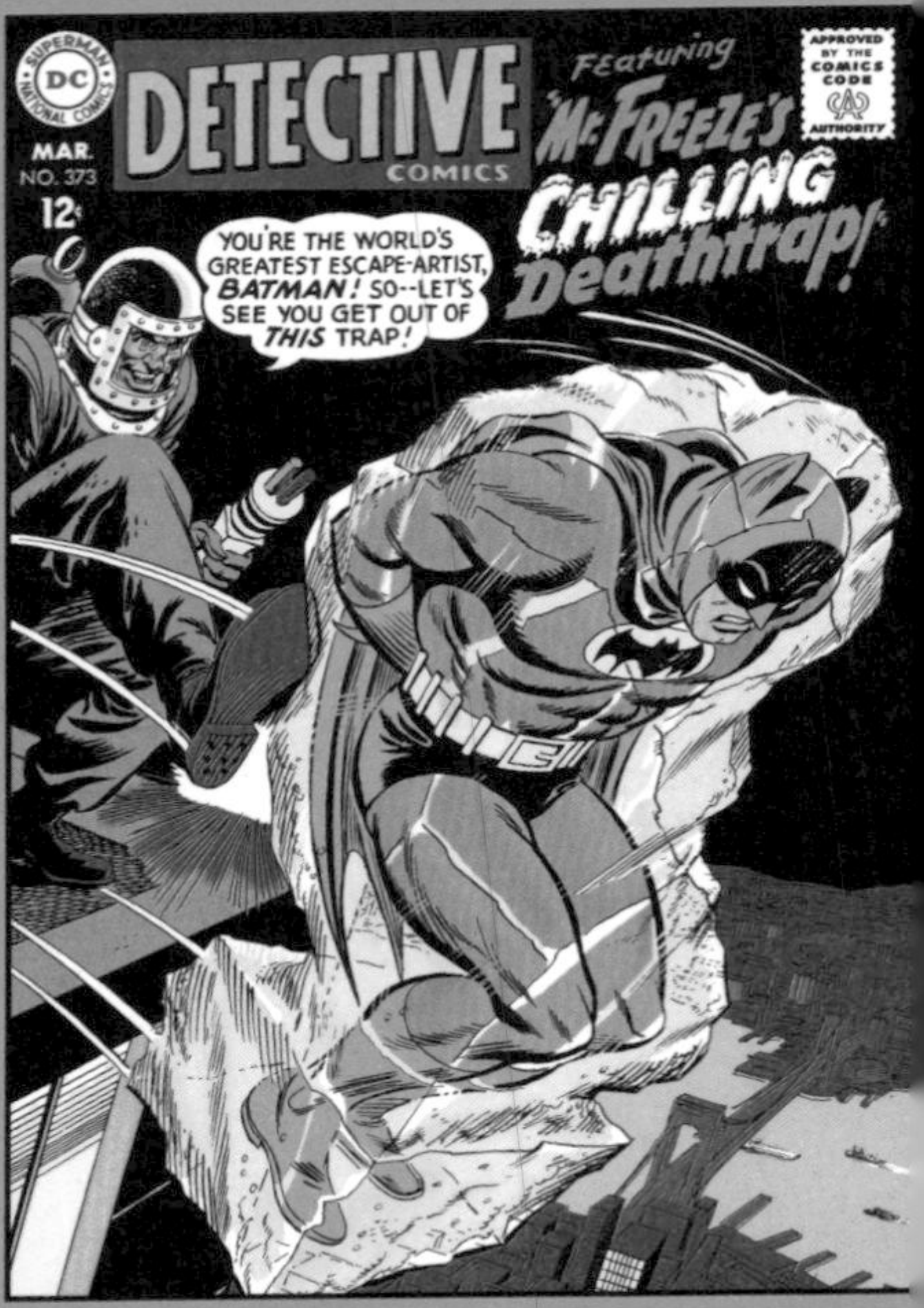
SUPERMAN
DC
NATIONAL COMICS
DETECTIVE
COMICS
MAR.
NO. 373
12¢
Featuring
"Mr. FREEZE'S CHILLING Deathtrap!"
APPROVED BY THE COMICS CODE AUTHORITY
YOU'RE THE WORLD'S GREATEST ESCAPE-ARTIST, BATMAN! SO--LET'S SEE YOU GET OUT OF THIS TRAP!

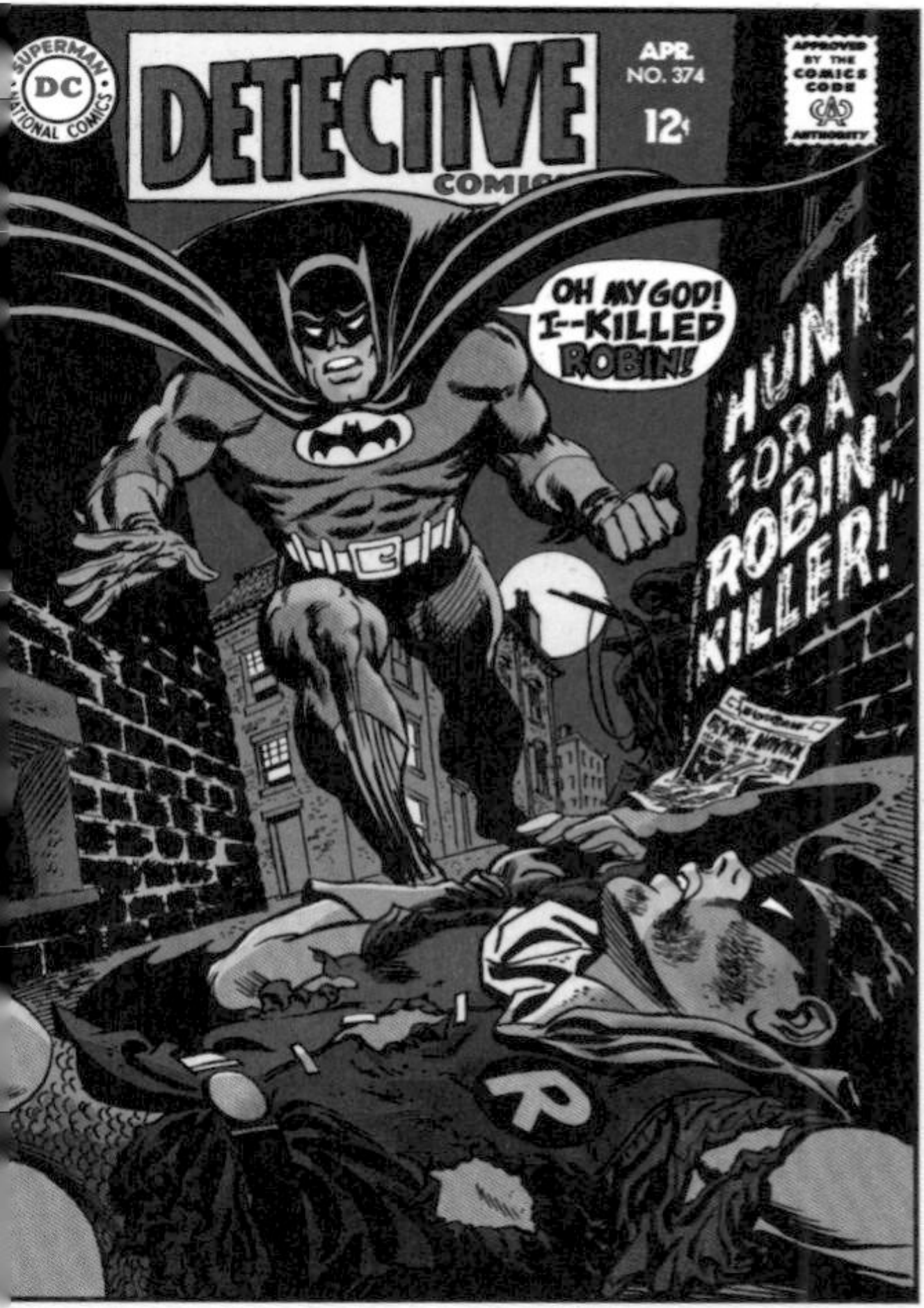
SUPERMAN
DC
NATIONAL COMICS
DETECTIVE
COMIC
APR.
NO. 374
12¢
APPROVED BY THE COMICS CODE AUTHORITY
OH MY GOD! I--KILLED ROBIN!
"HUNT FOR A ROBIN-KILLER!"

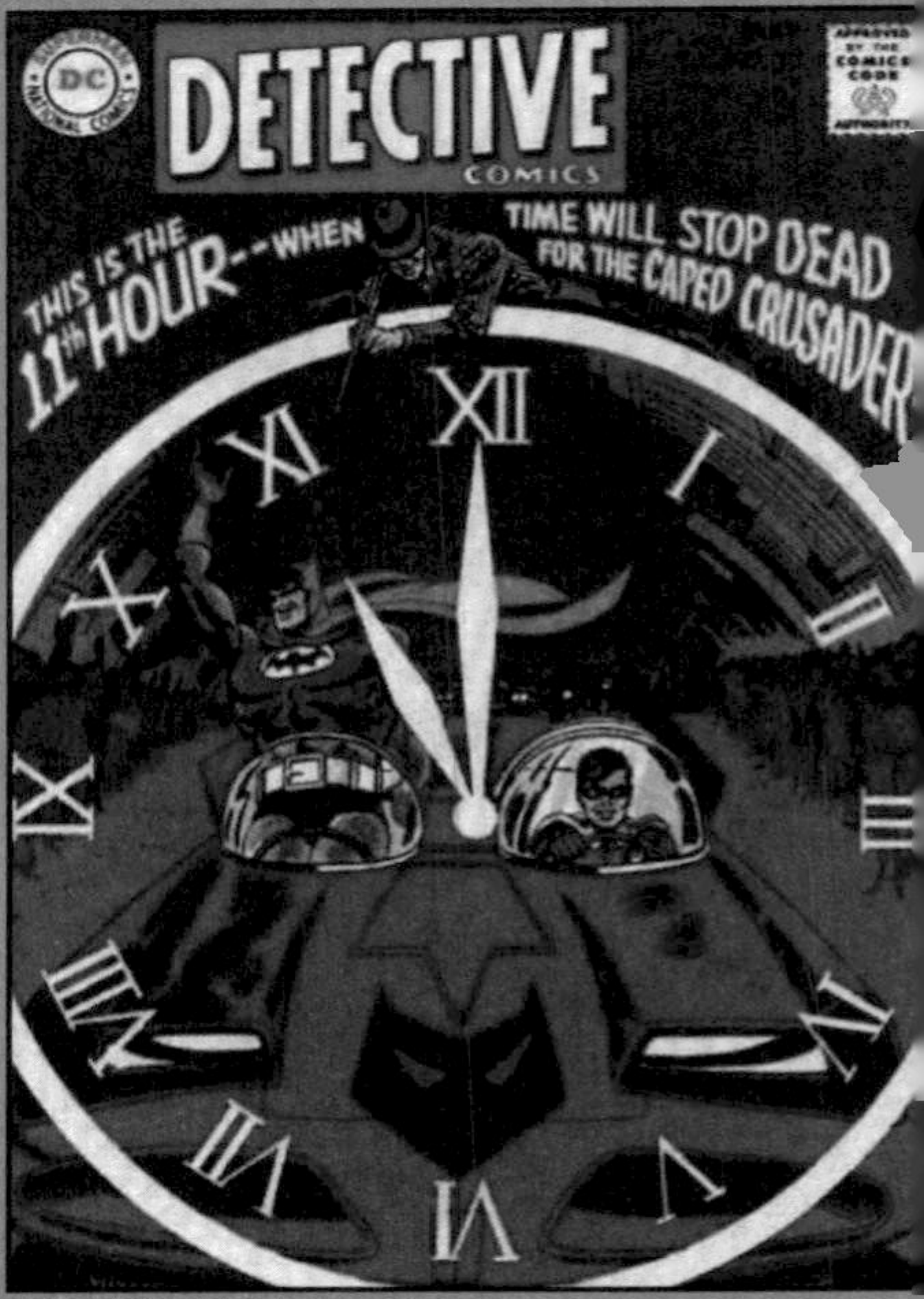
DC
DETECTIVE
COMICS
APPROVED BY THE COMICS CODE AUTHORITY
THIS IS THE 11TH HOUR--WHEN
TIME WILL STOP DEAD FOR THE CAPED CRUSADER

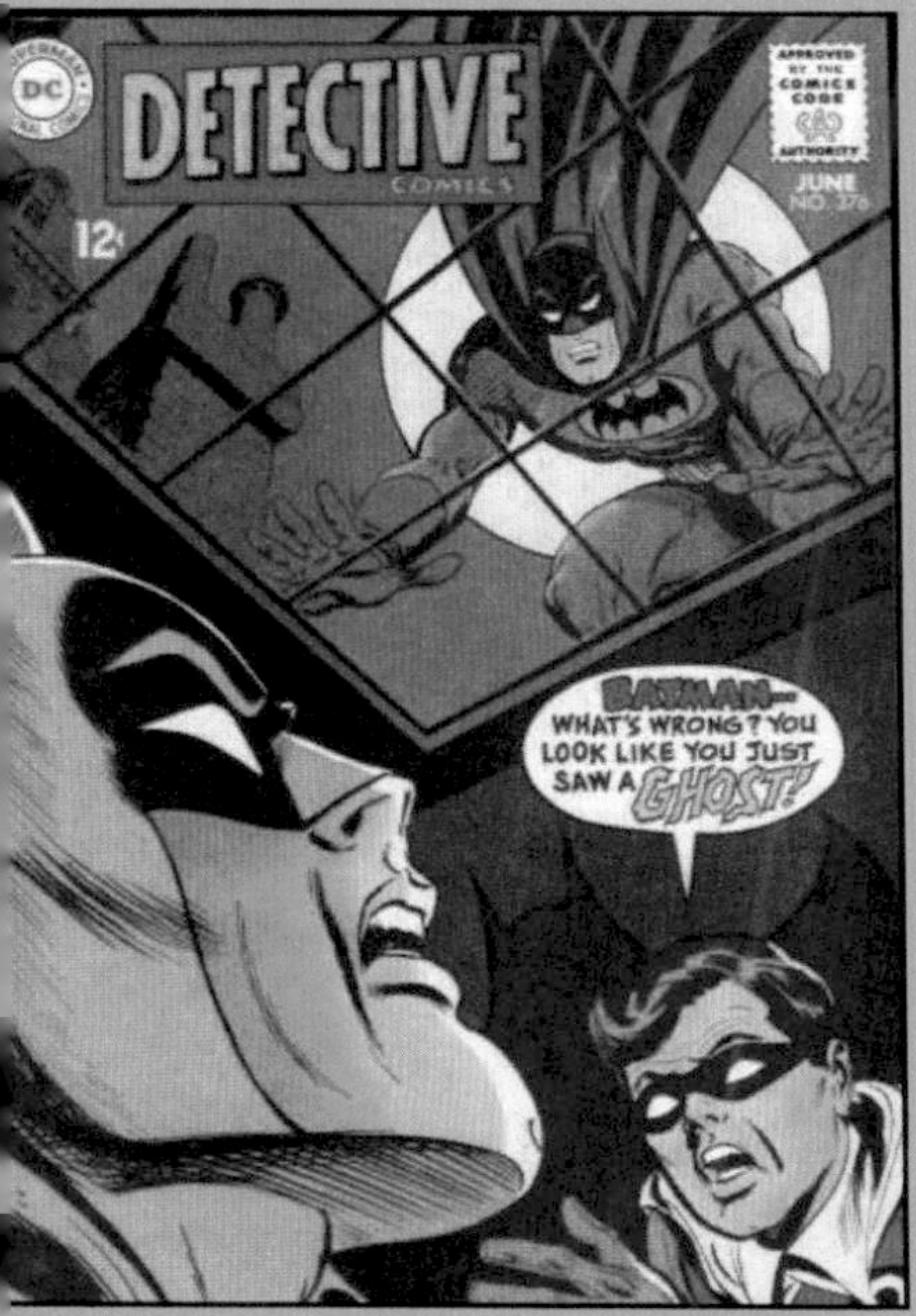
DC
DETECTIVE
COMICS
12¢
APPROVED BY THE COMICS CODE AUTHORITY
JUNE
NO. 276
BATMAN—
WHAT'S WRONG? YOU LOOK LIKE YOU JUST SAW A GHOST!

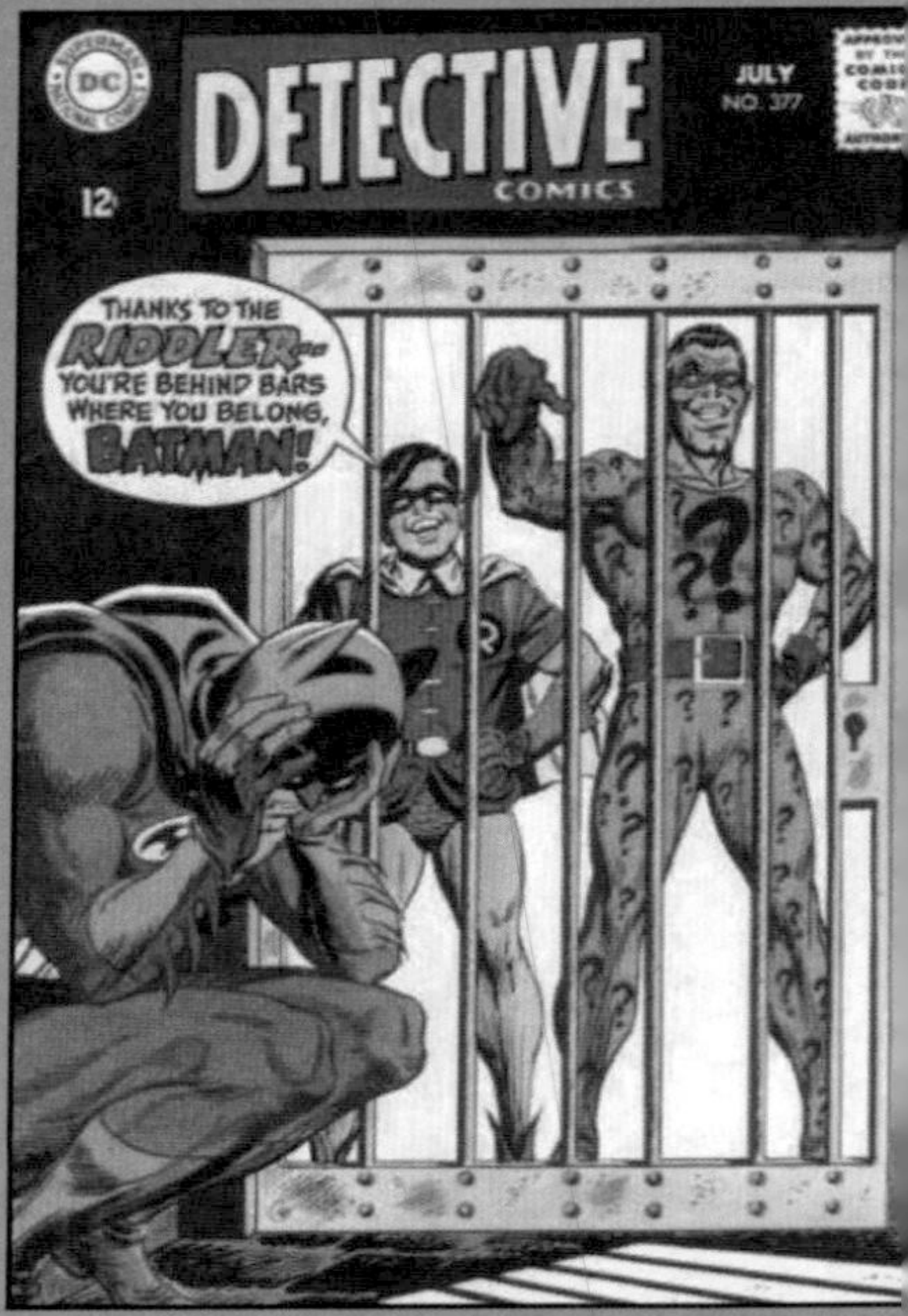
DC
DETECTIVE
COMICS
JULY
NO. 377
12¢
THANKS TO THE RIDDLER, YOU'RE BEHIND BARS WHERE YOU BELONG, BATMAN!

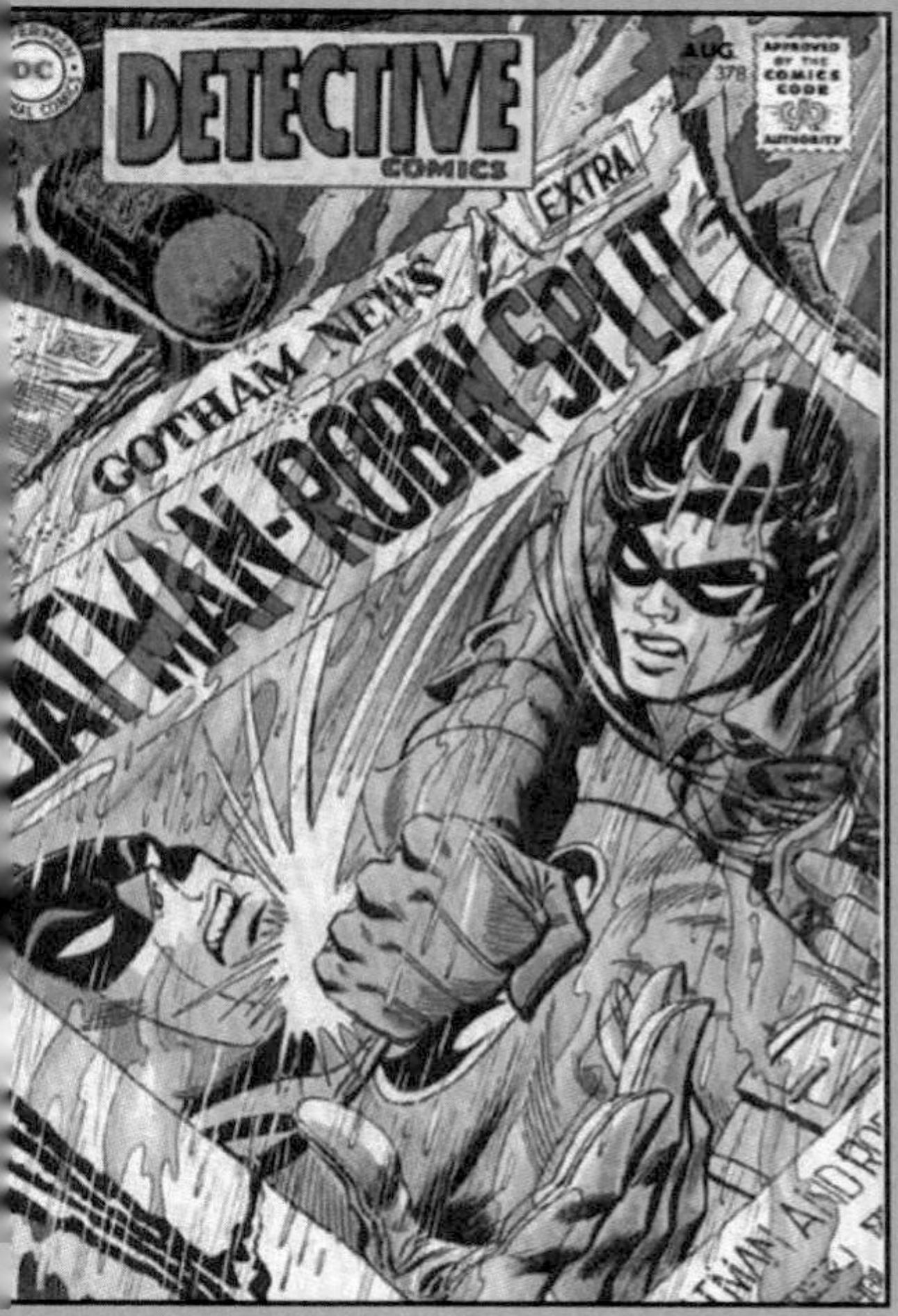
DC
DETECTIVE
COMICS
AUG.
No. 378
APPROVED BY THE COMICS CODE AUTHORITY
EXTRA
GOTHAM NEWS
BATMAN-ROBIN SPLIT

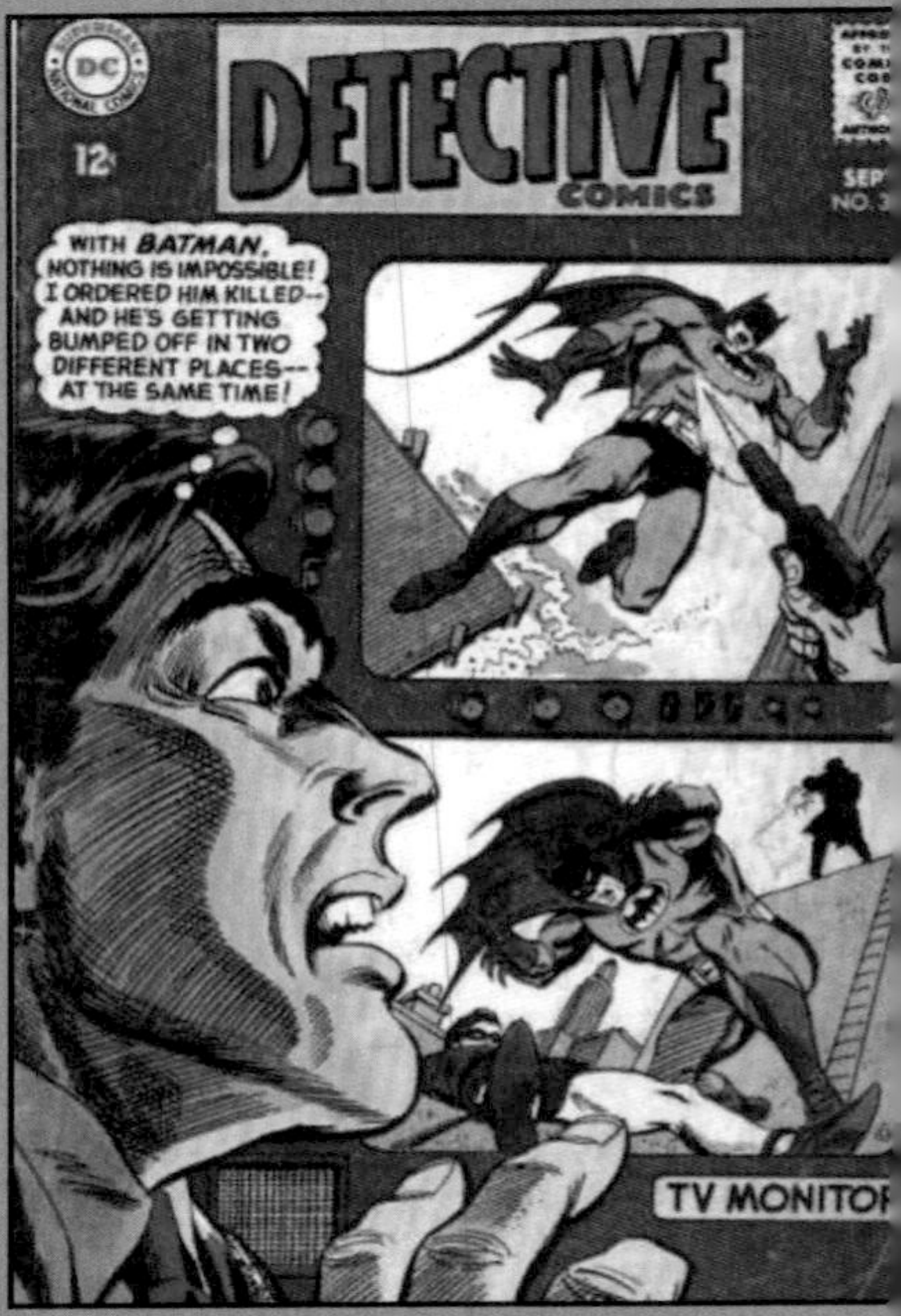
DC
12¢
DETECTIVE
COMICS
SEP
NO. 3
WITH BATMAN, NOTHING IS IMPOSSIBLE! I ORDERED HIM KILLED-- AND HE'S GETTING BUMPED OFF IN TWO DIFFERENT PLACES--- AT THE SAME TIME!
TV MONITOR

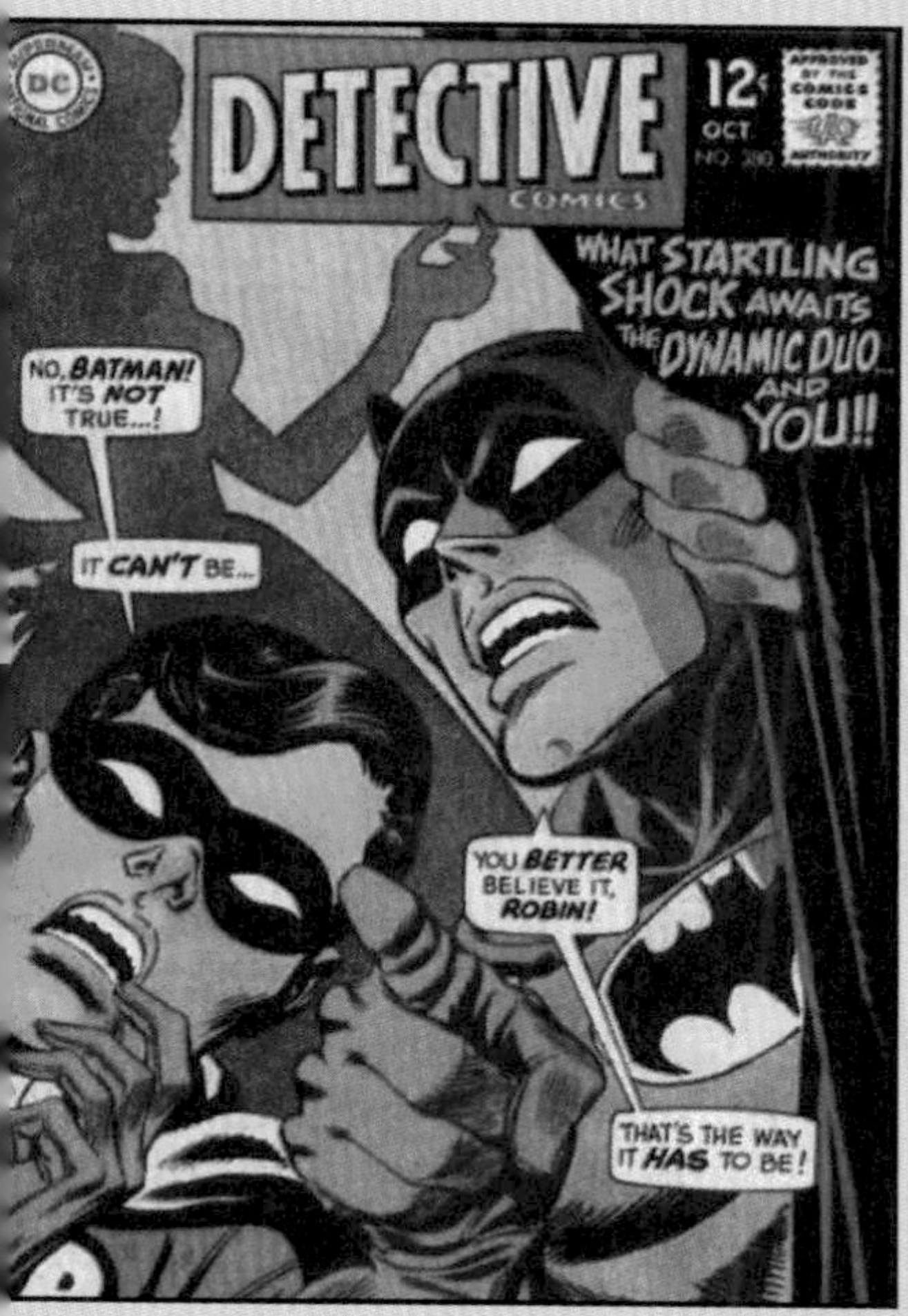
DC
DETECTIVE
COMICS
12¢
OCT.
NO. 300
APPROVED BY THE COMICS CODE AUTHORITY
WHAT STARTLING SHOCK AWAITS THE DYNAMIC DUO... AND YOU!!
NO, BATMAN! IT'S NOT TRUE...!
IT CAN'T BE...
YOU BETTER BELIEVE IT, ROBIN!
THAT'S THE WAY IT HAS TO BE!

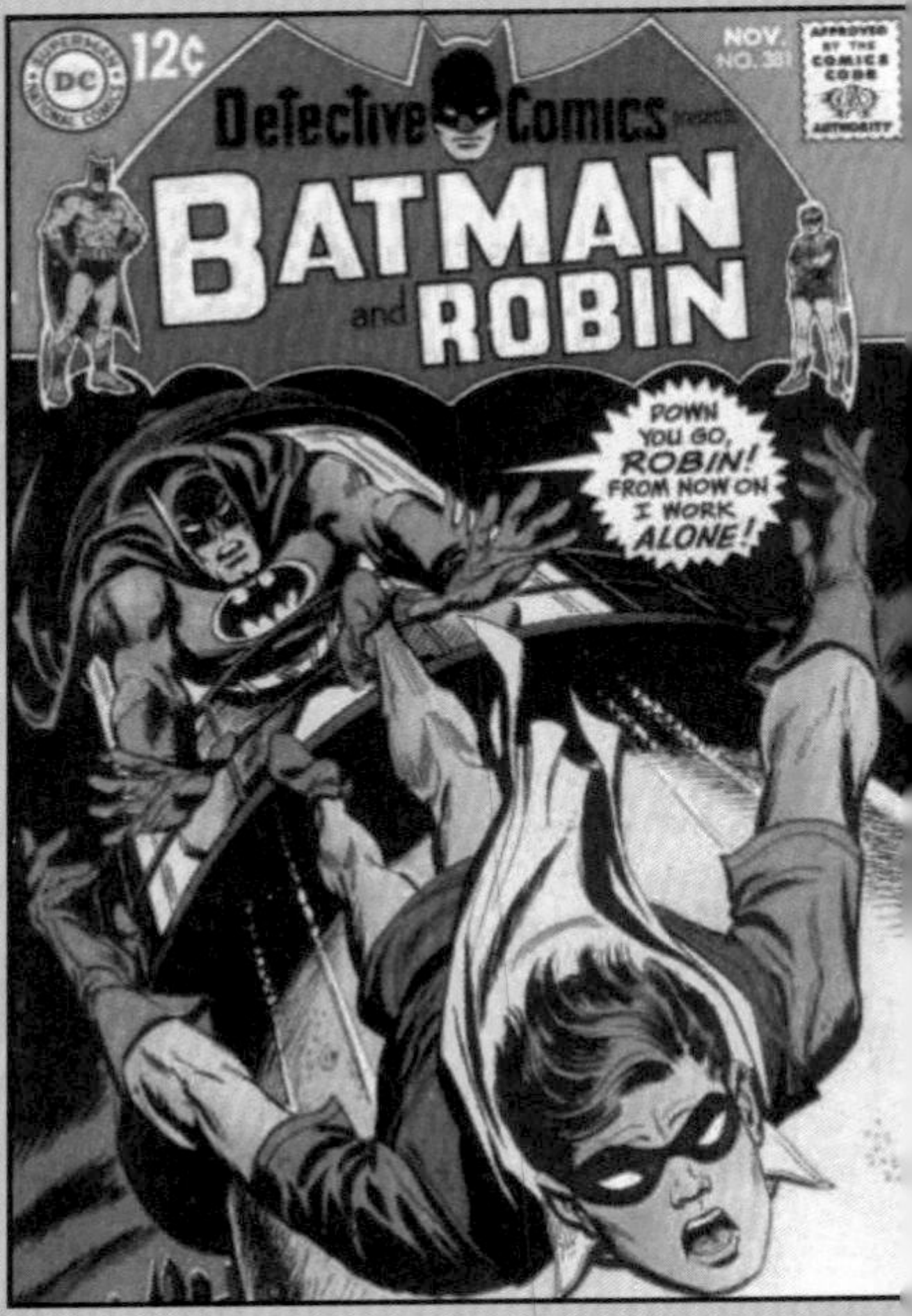
DC
12¢
NOV.
NO. 381
APPROVED BY THE COMICS CODE AUTHORITY
Detective Comics
BATMAN
and ROBIN
DOWN YOU GO, ROBIN! FROM NOW ON I WORK ALONE!

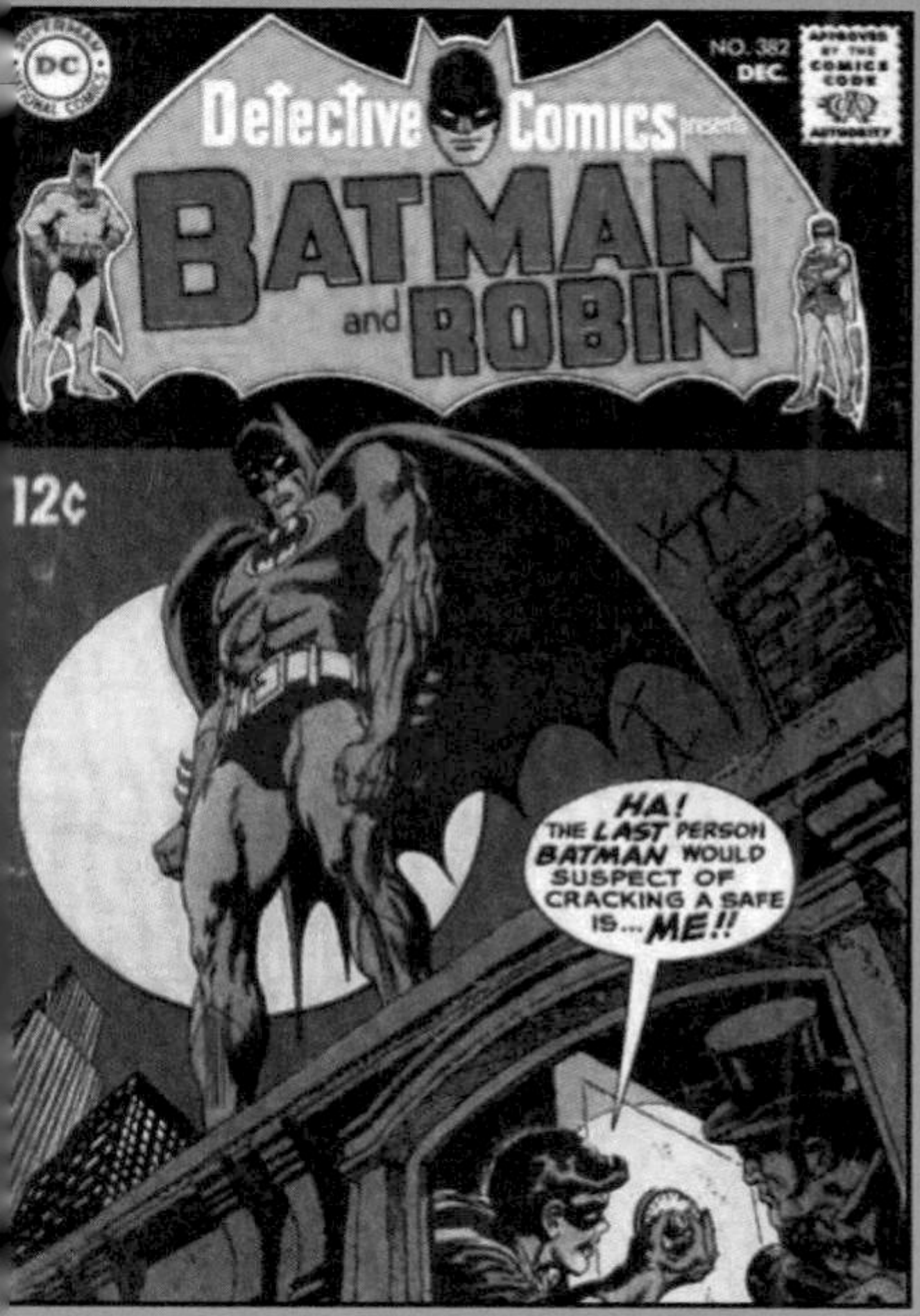
DC
NO. 382
DEC.
APPROVED BY THE COMICS CODE AUTHORITY
Detective Comics presents
BATMAN and ROBIN
12¢
HA! THE LAST PERSON BATMAN WOULD SUSPECT OF CRACKING A SAFE IS... ME!!

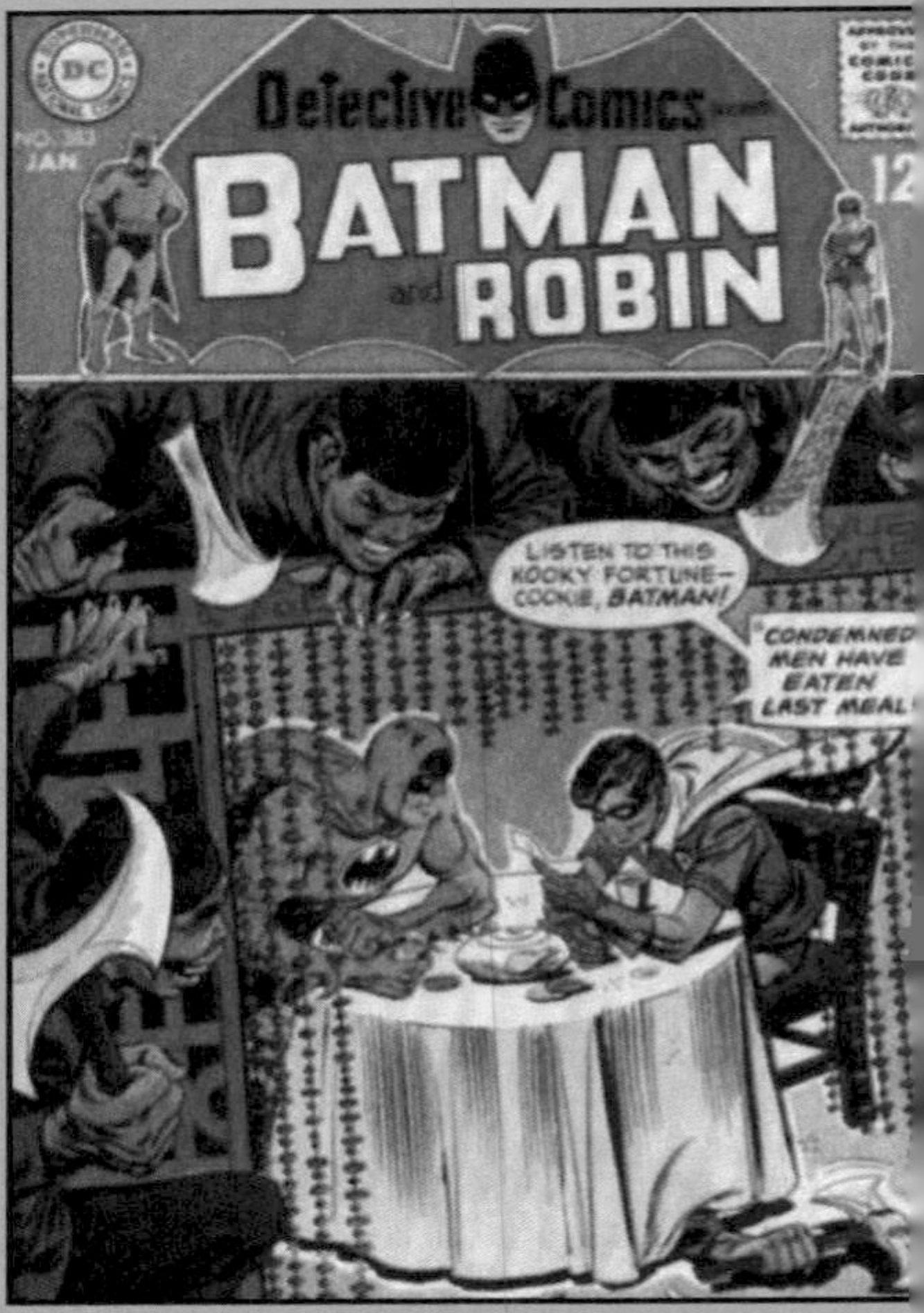
DC
Detective Comics
NO. 383
JAN.
BATMAN
and ROBIN
12
LISTEN TO THIS KOOKY FORTUNE-COOKIE, BATMAN!
"CONDEMNED MEN HAVE EATEN LAST MEAL!"

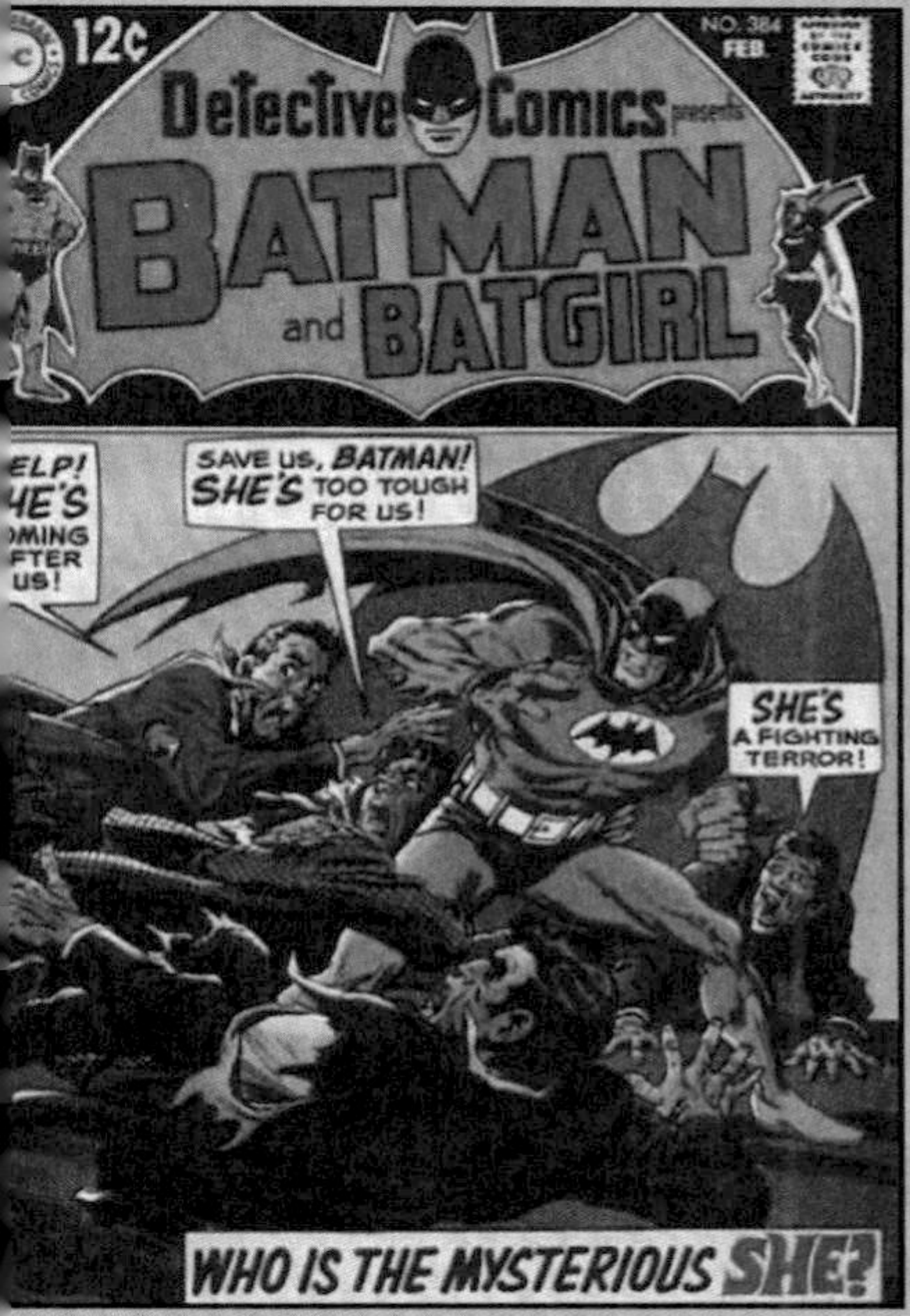
12¢
NO. 384
FEB.
Detective Comics presents
BATMAN
and BATGIRL
ELP! HE'S OMING FTER US!
SAVE US, BATMAN! SHE'S TOO TOUGH FOR US!
SHE'S A FIGHTING TERROR!
WHO IS THE MYSTERIOUS SHE?

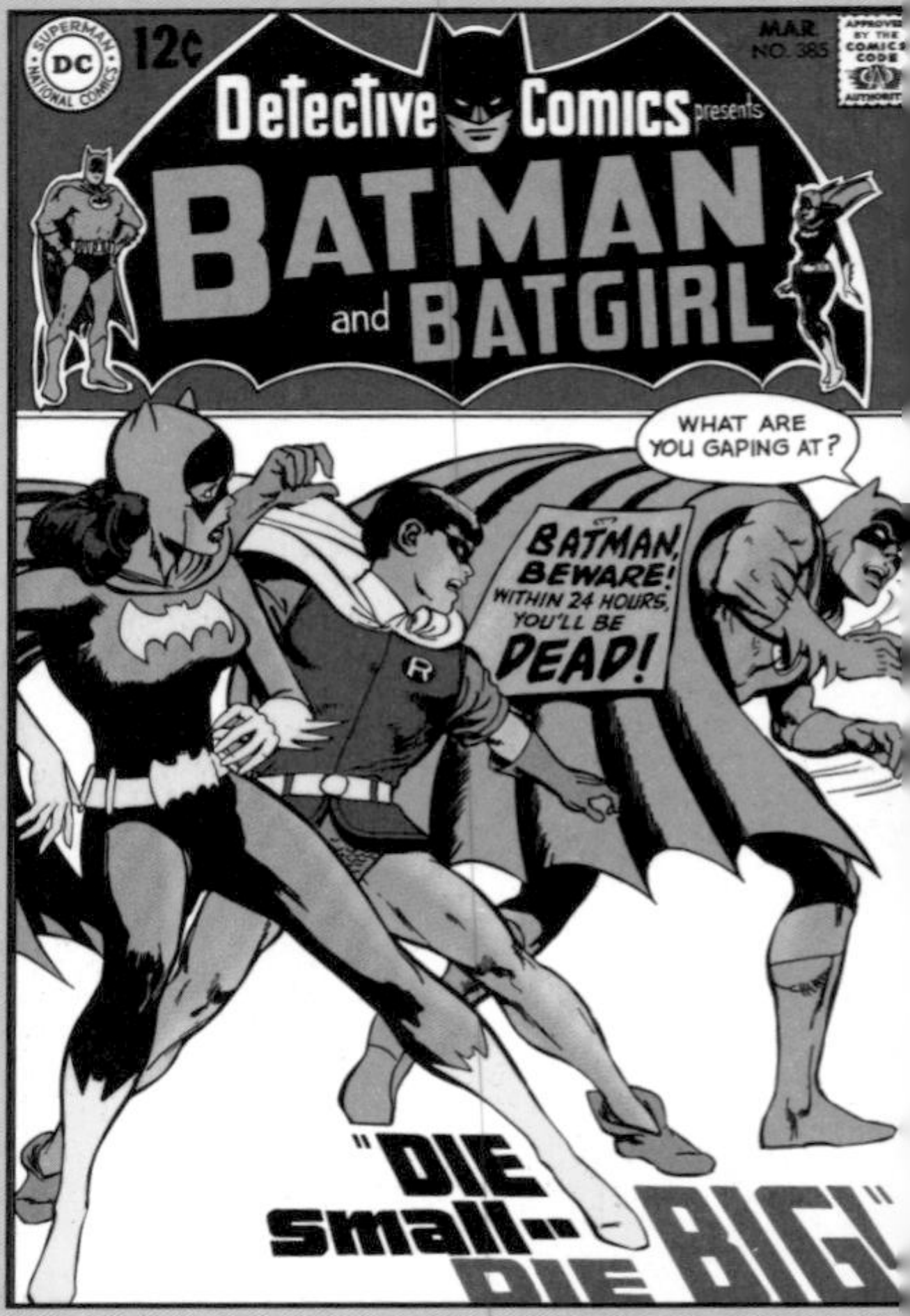
SUPERMAN NATIONAL COMICS
DC
12¢
MAR
NO. 385
APPROVED BY THE COMICS CODE AUTHORITY
Detective Comics presents
BATMAN and BATGIRL
WHAT ARE YOU GAPING AT?
BATMAN, BEWARE! WITHIN 24 HOURS, YOU'LL BE DEAD!
"DIE small.. DIE BIG!"

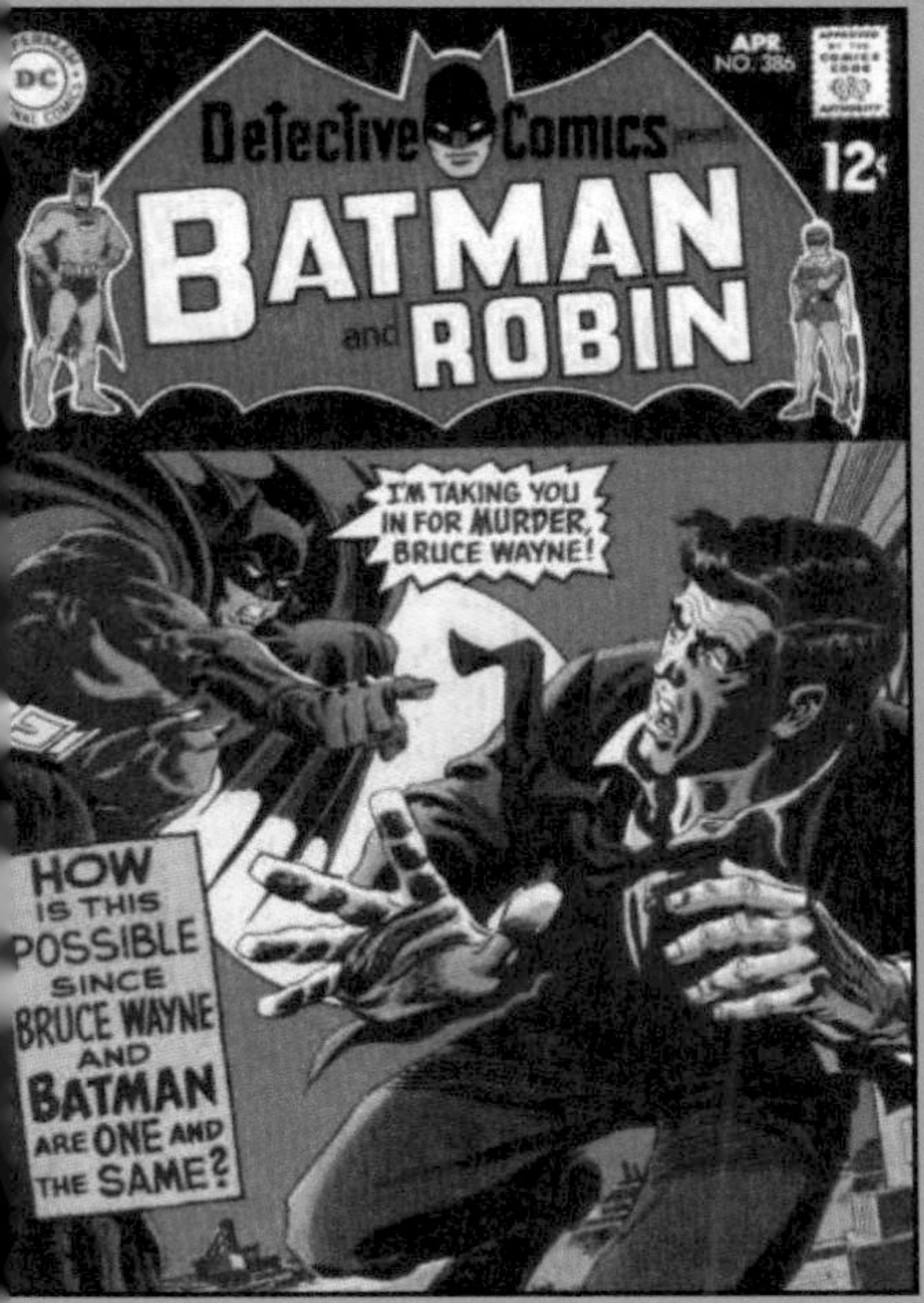
DC
APR.
NO. 386
Detective Comics
12¢
BATMAN
and ROBIN
I'M TAKING YOU IN FOR MURDER, BRUCE WAYNE!
HOW IS THIS POSSIBLE SINCE BRUCE WAYNE AND BATMAN ARE ONE AND THE SAME?

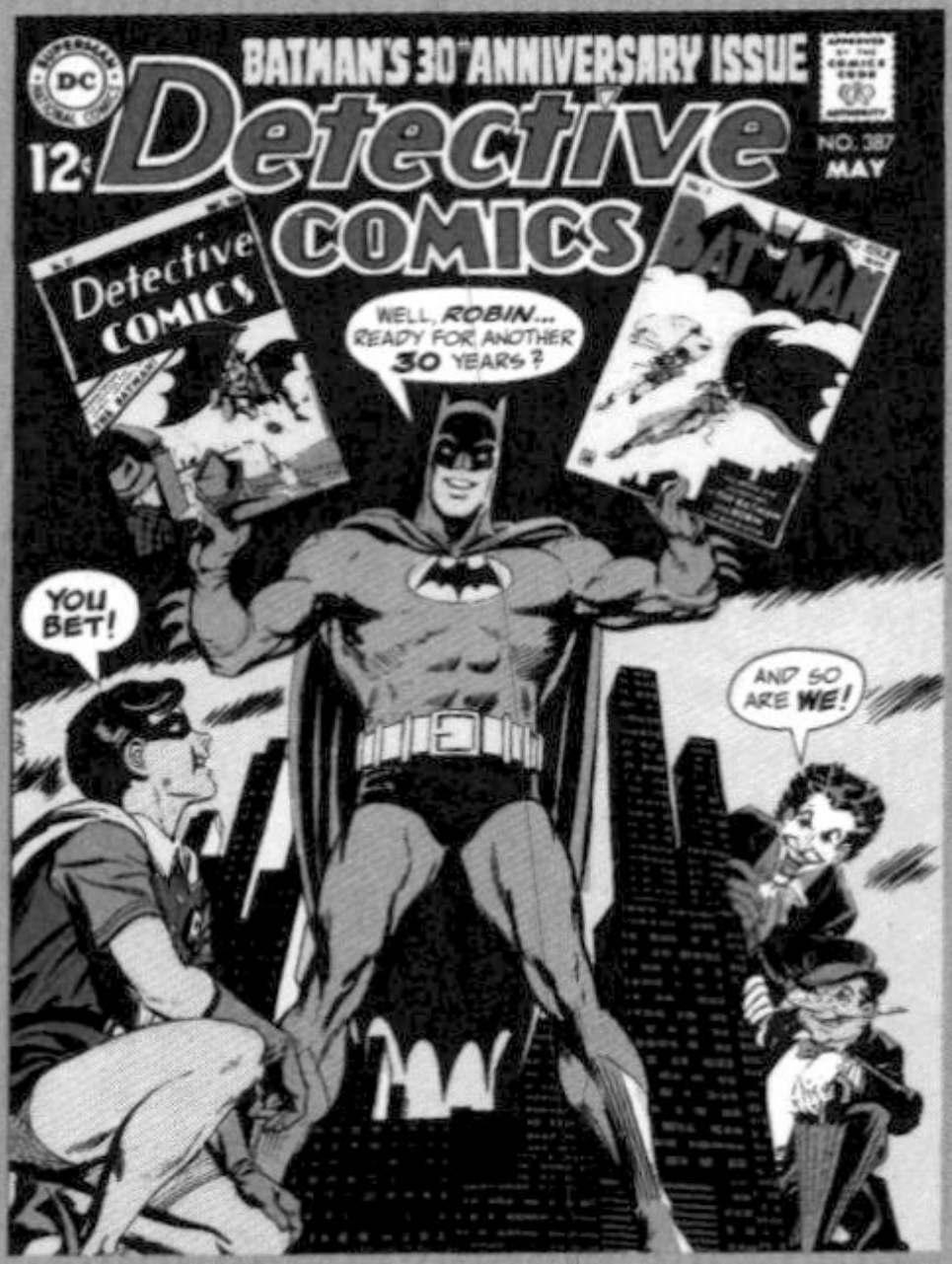

Detective Comics #387
This issue celebrates the thirty-year anniversary of Batman's first appearance. Irv Novick and Gaspar Saladino worked on the cover alongside Bob Kane.

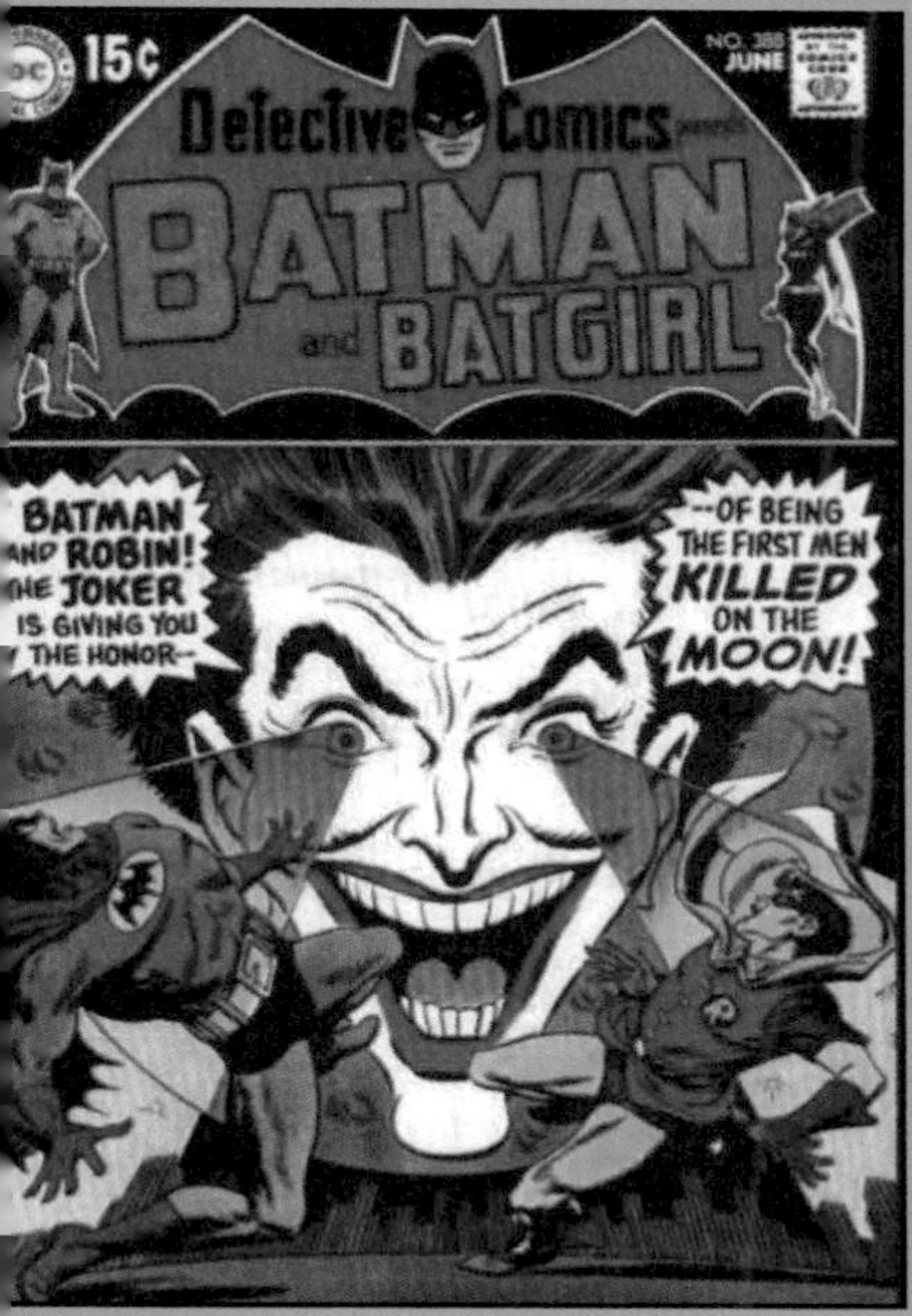
15¢
NO. 388
JUNE
Detective Comics
BATMAN
and BATGIRL
BATMAN
AND ROBIN!
THE JOKER
IS GIVING YOU
THE HONOR--
--OF BEING
THE FIRST MEN
KILLED
ON THE
MOON!

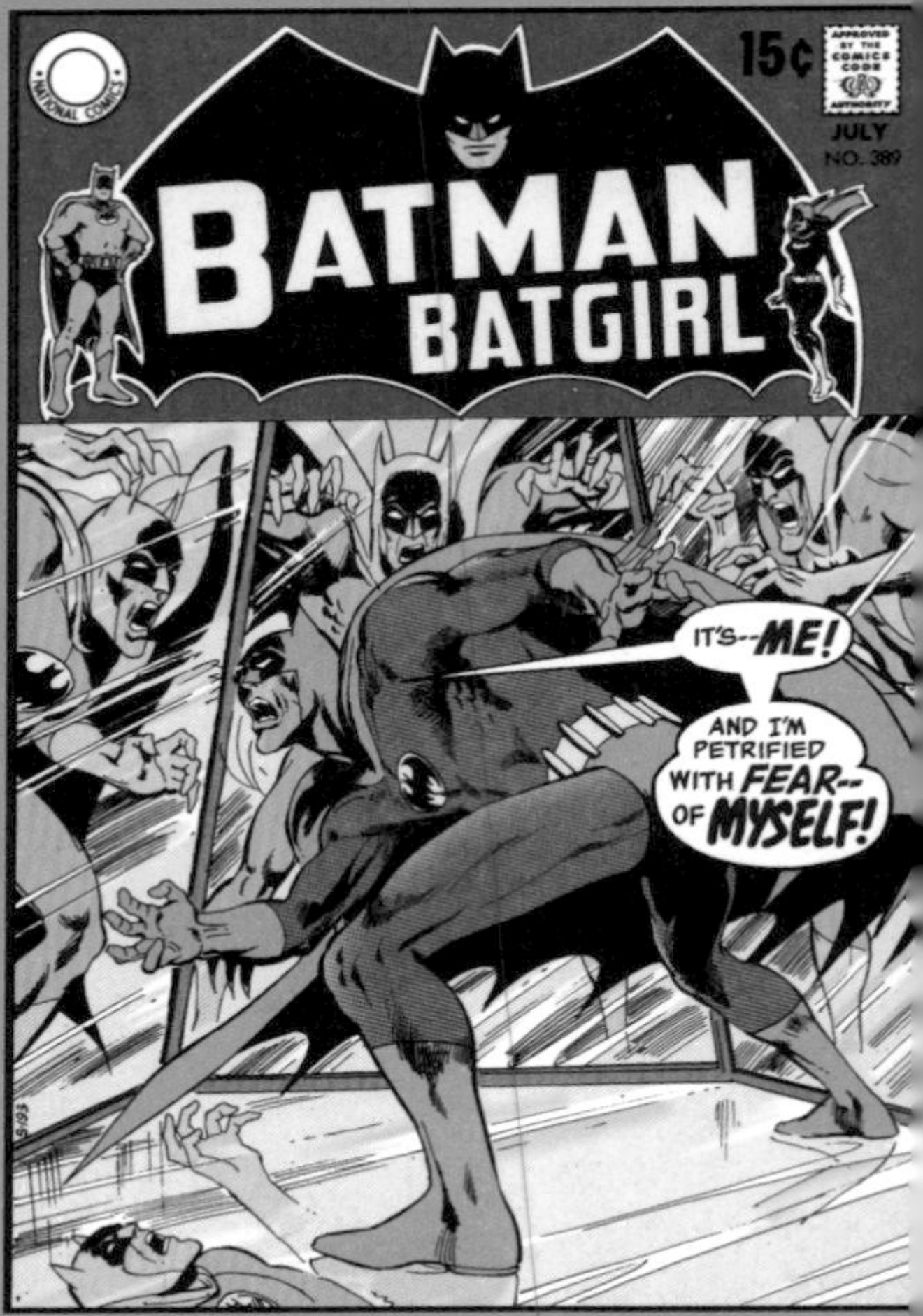
NATIONAL COMICS
15¢
APPROVED BY THE COMICS CODE AUTHORITY
JULY
NO. 389
BATMAN
BATGIRL
IT'S--ME!
AND I'M PETRIFIED WITH FEAR--OF MYSELF!

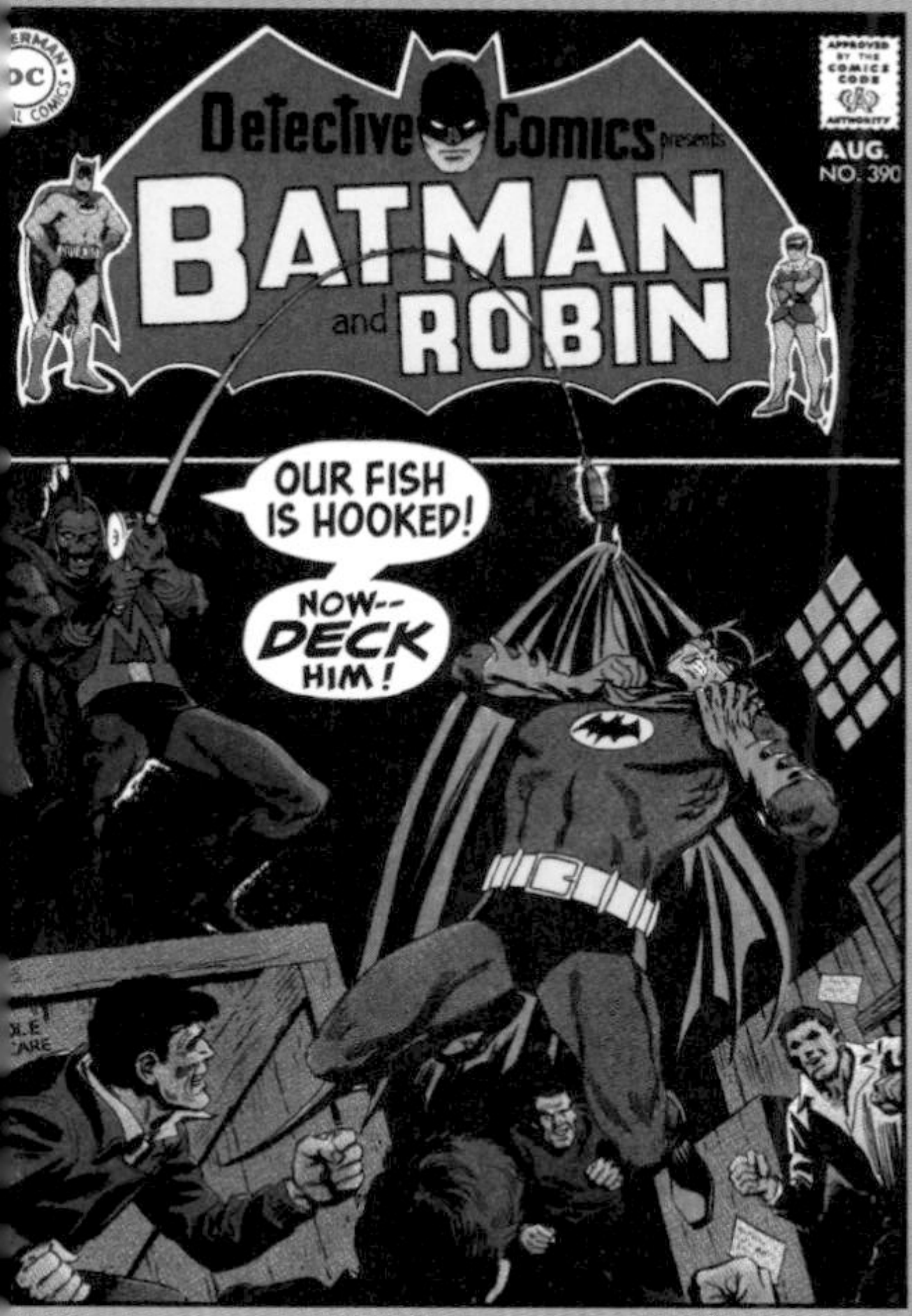
DC
Detective Comics presents
BATMAN and ROBIN
APPROVED BY THE COMICS CODE AUTHORITY
AUG.
NO. 390
OUR FISH IS HOOKED!
NOW-- DECK HIM!

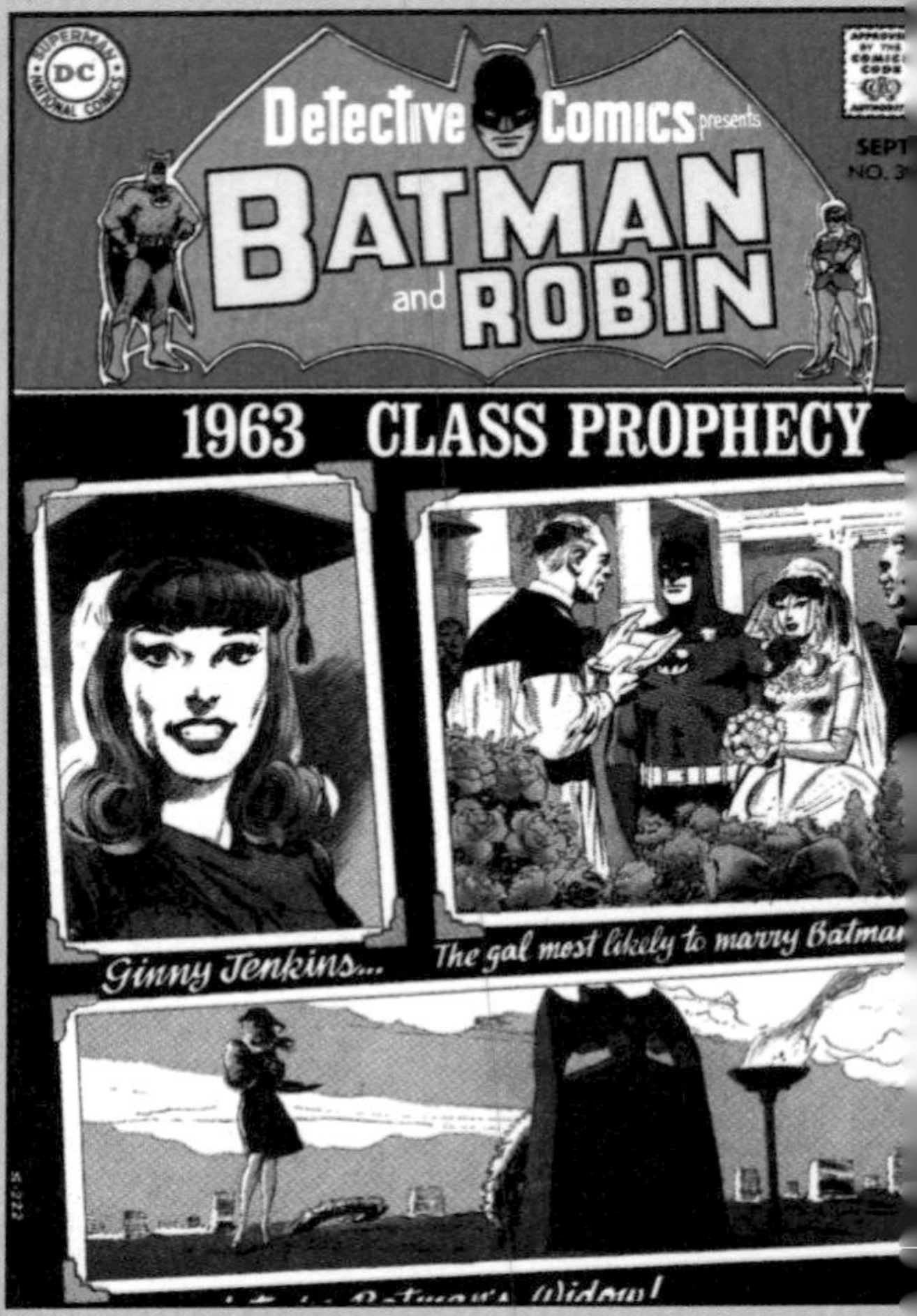
DC
SUPERMAN NATIONAL COMICS
Detective Comics presents
BATMAN and ROBIN
SEPT
NO. 3
1963 CLASS PROPHECY
Ginny Jenkins...
The gal most likely to marry Batman
Widow!

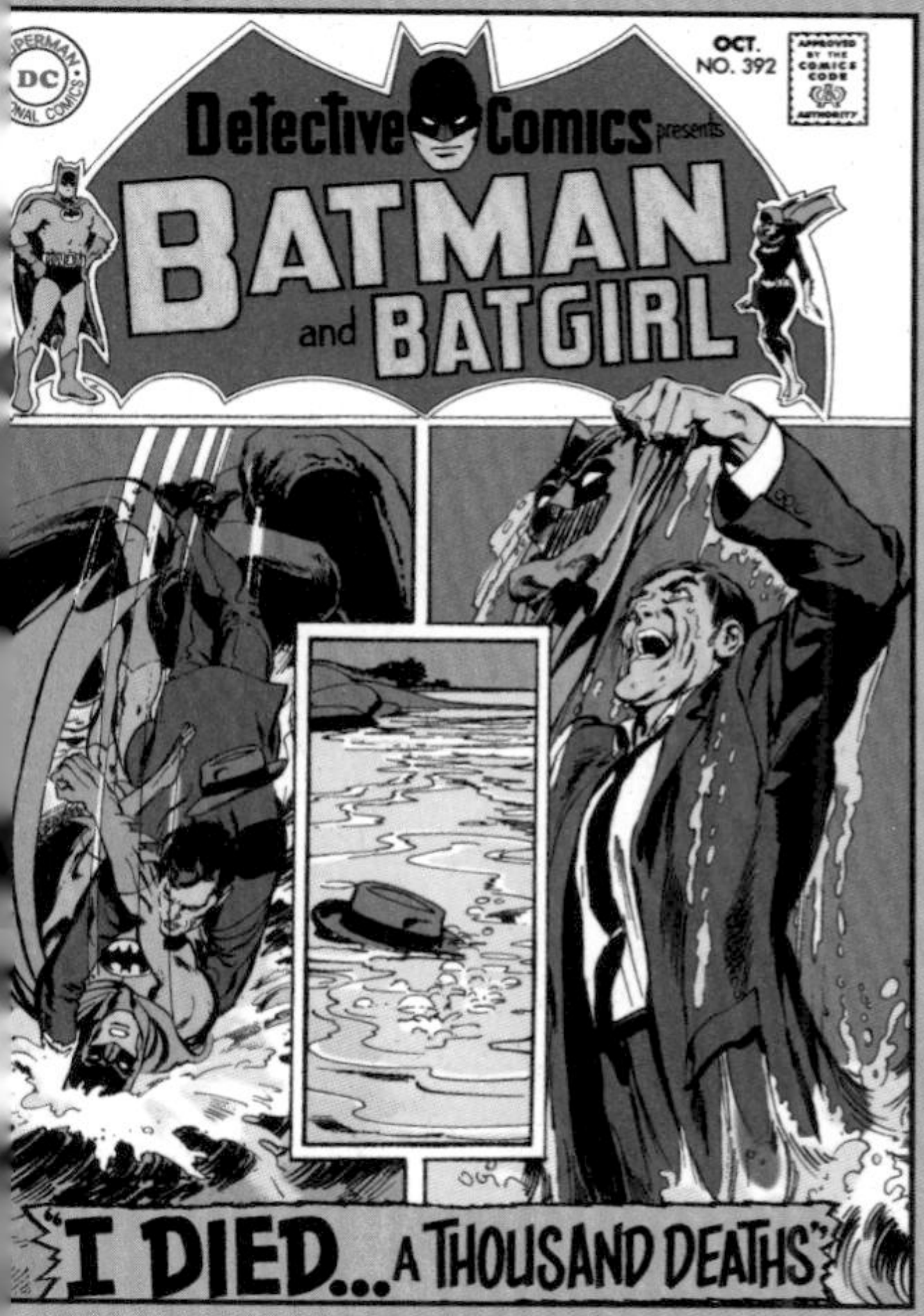
DC
OCT.
NO. 392
APPROVED BY THE COMICS CODE AUTHORITY
Detective Comics presents
BATMAN
and BATGIRL
"I DIED... A THOUSAND DEATHS"

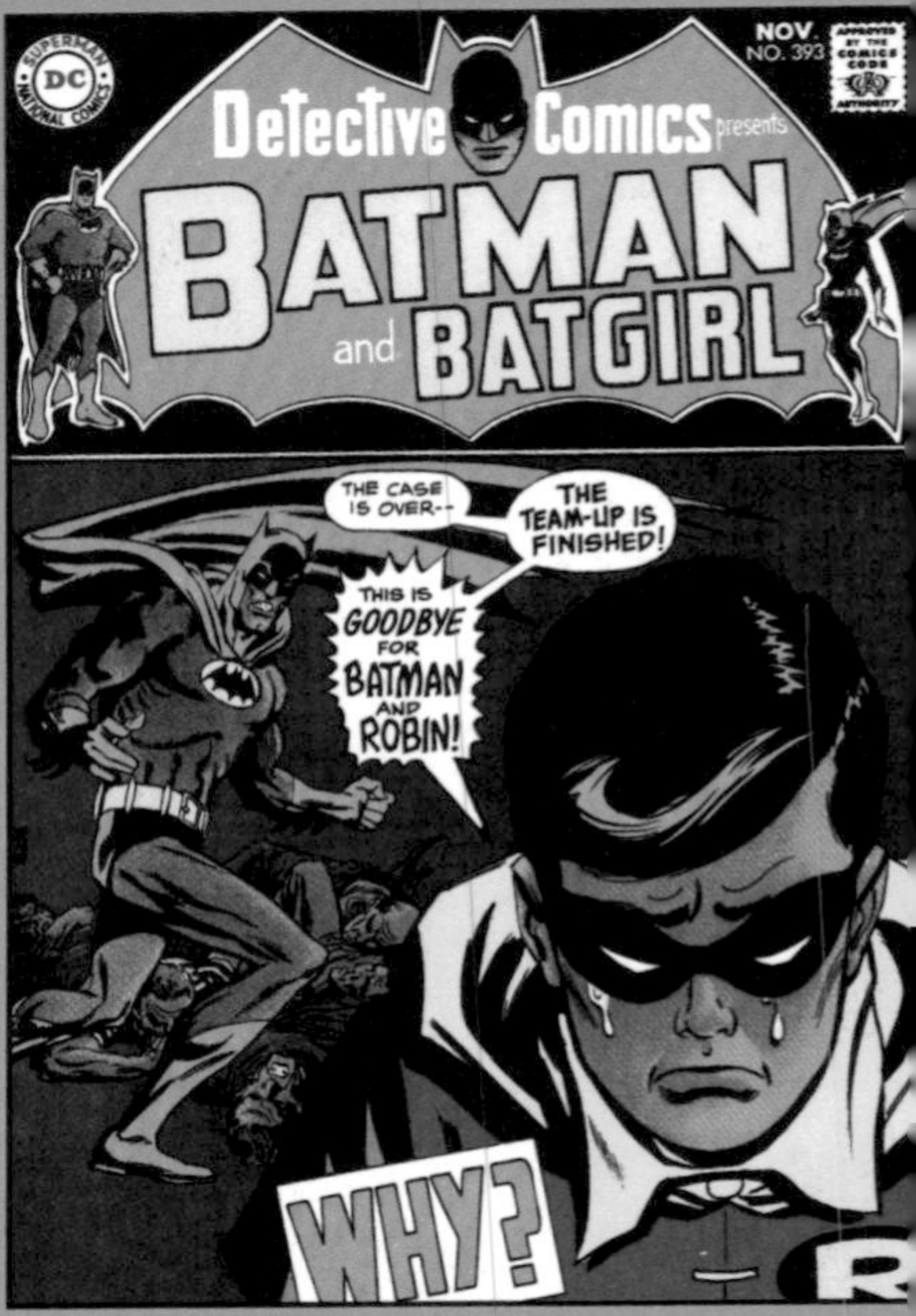
SUPERMAN NATIONAL COMICS
DC
NOV.
NO. 393
APPROVED BY THE COMICS CODE AUTHORITY
Detective Comics presents
BATMAN and BATGIRL
THE CASE IS OVER--
THE TEAM-UP IS FINISHED!
THIS IS GOODBYE FOR BATMAN AND ROBIN!
WHY?

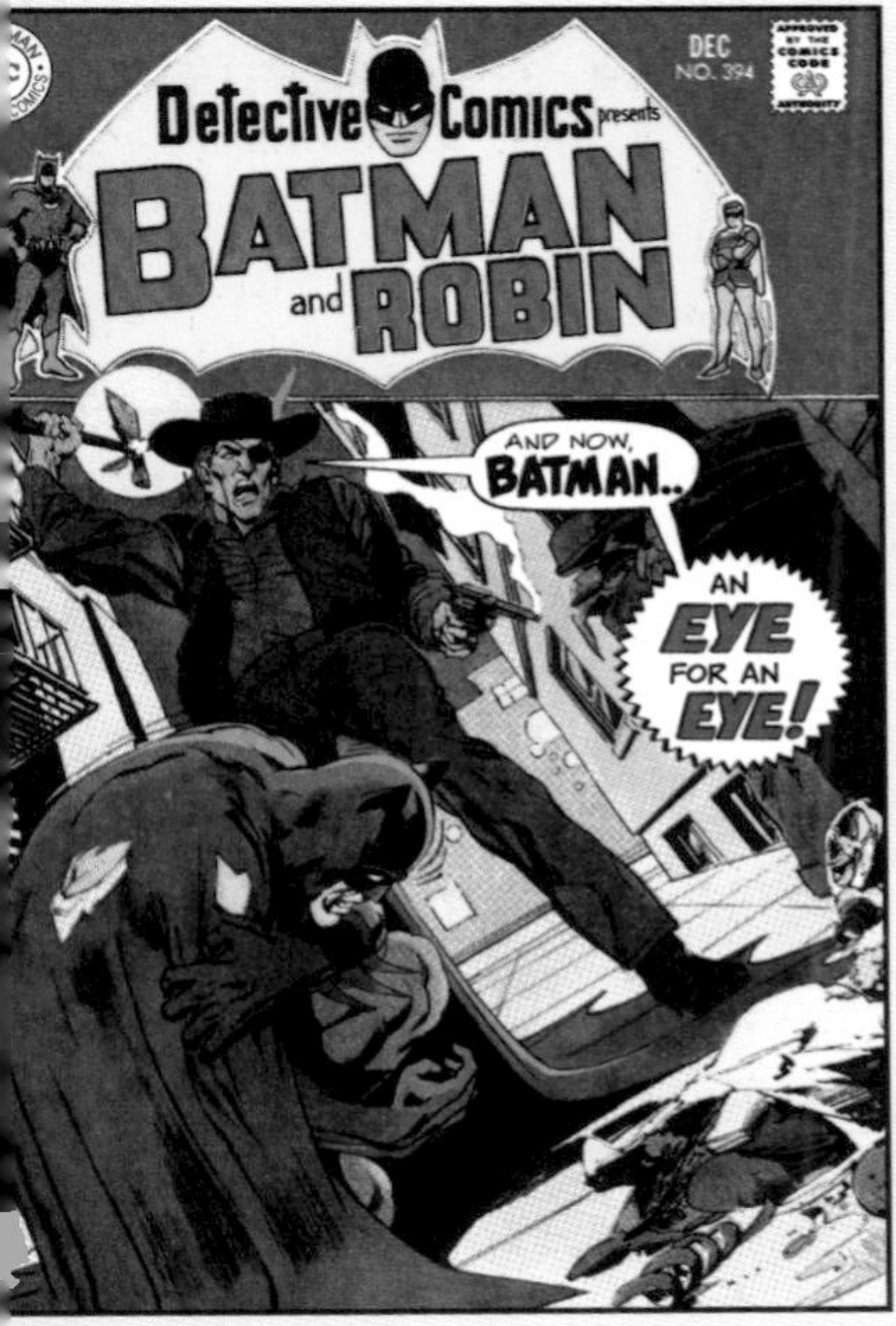
Detective Comics presents
BATMAN and ROBIN
DEC
NO. 394
APPROVED BY THE COMICS CODE AUTHORITY
AND NOW, BATMAN..
AN EYE FOR AN EYE!

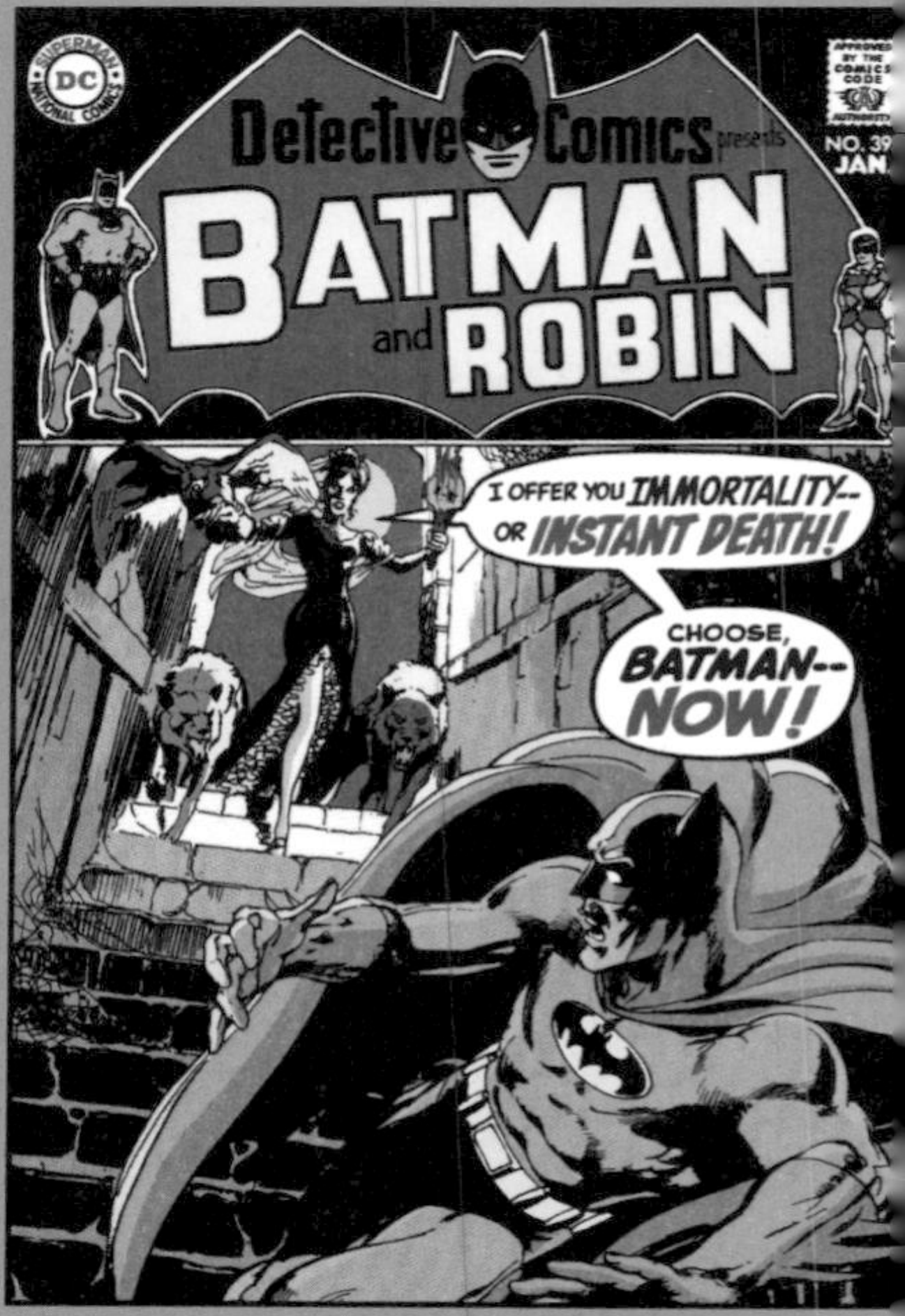
DC
SUPERMAN NATIONAL COMICS
Detective Comics presents
BATMAN and ROBIN
APPROVED BY THE COMICS CODE AUTHORITY
NO. 39
JAN.
I OFFER YOU IMMORTALITY-- OR INSTANT DEATH!
CHOOSE, BATMAN-- NOW!

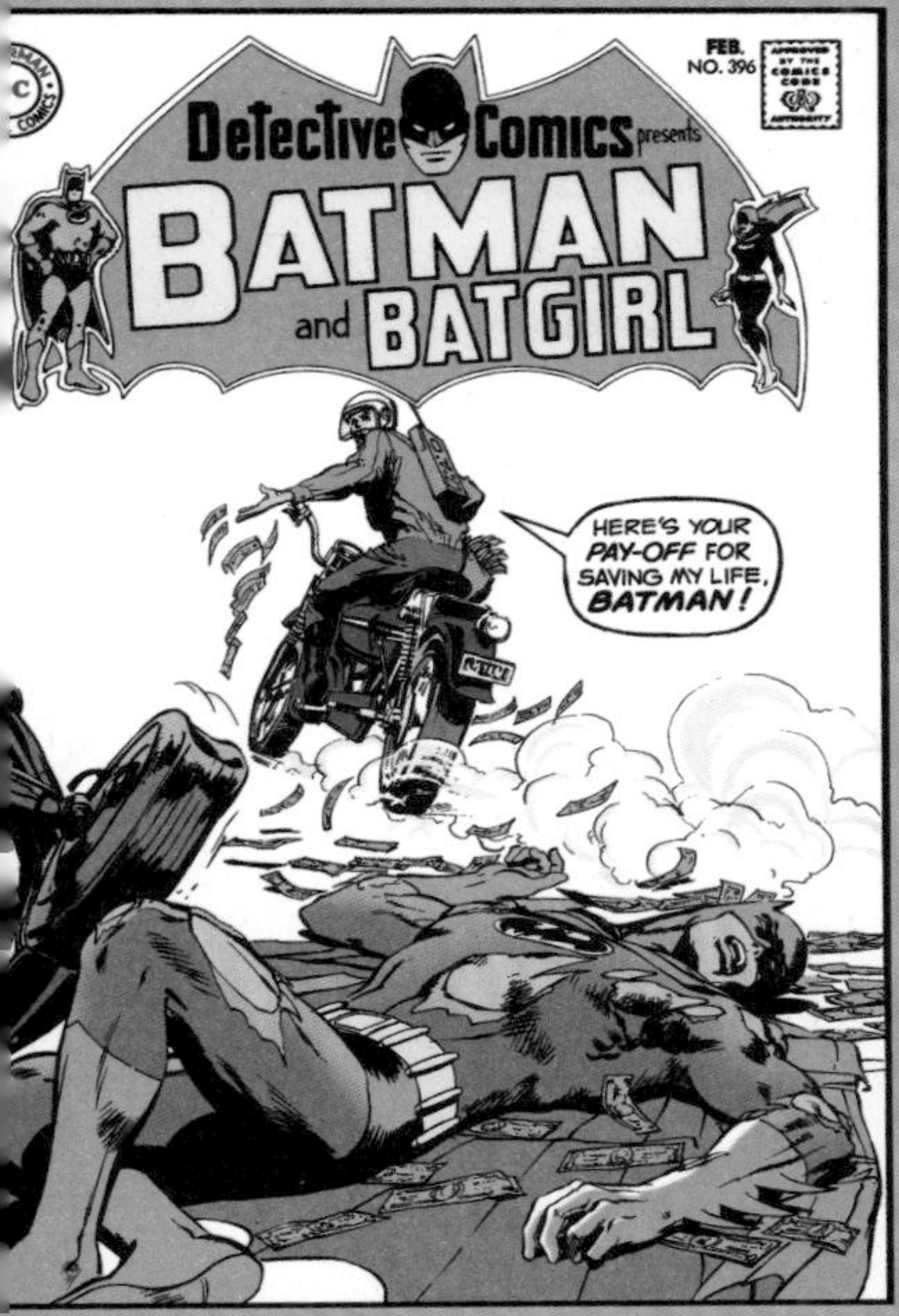
FEB.
NO. 396
APPROVED BY THE COMICS CODE AUTHORITY
Detective Comics presents
BATMAN
and BATGIRL
HERE'S YOUR PAY-OFF FOR SAVING MY LIFE, BATMAN!

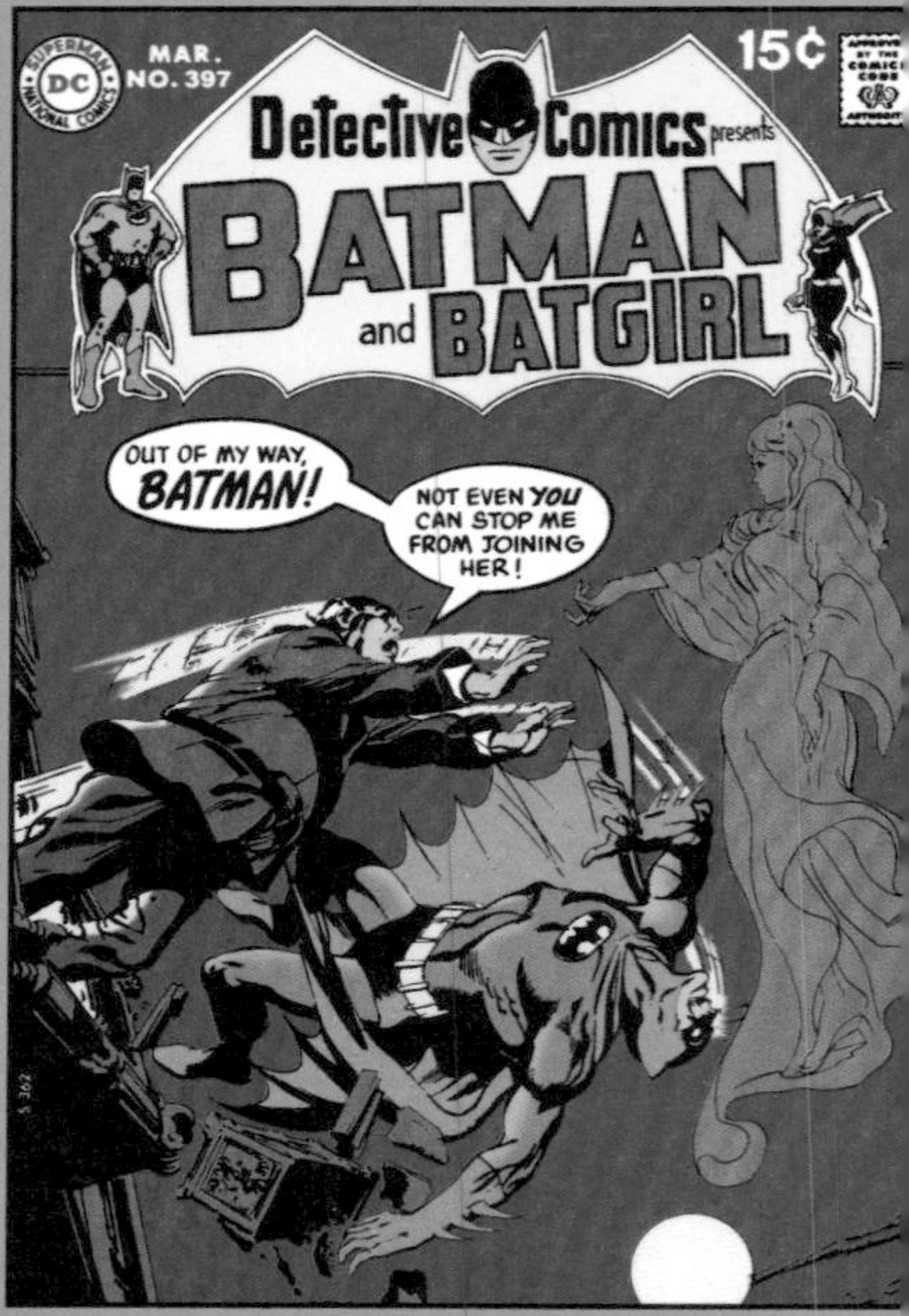
SUPERMAN NATIONAL COMICS
DC
MAR.
NO. 397
15¢
Detective Comics presents
BATMAN
and BATGIRL
OUT OF MY WAY, BATMAN!
NOT EVEN YOU CAN STOP ME FROM JOINING HER!

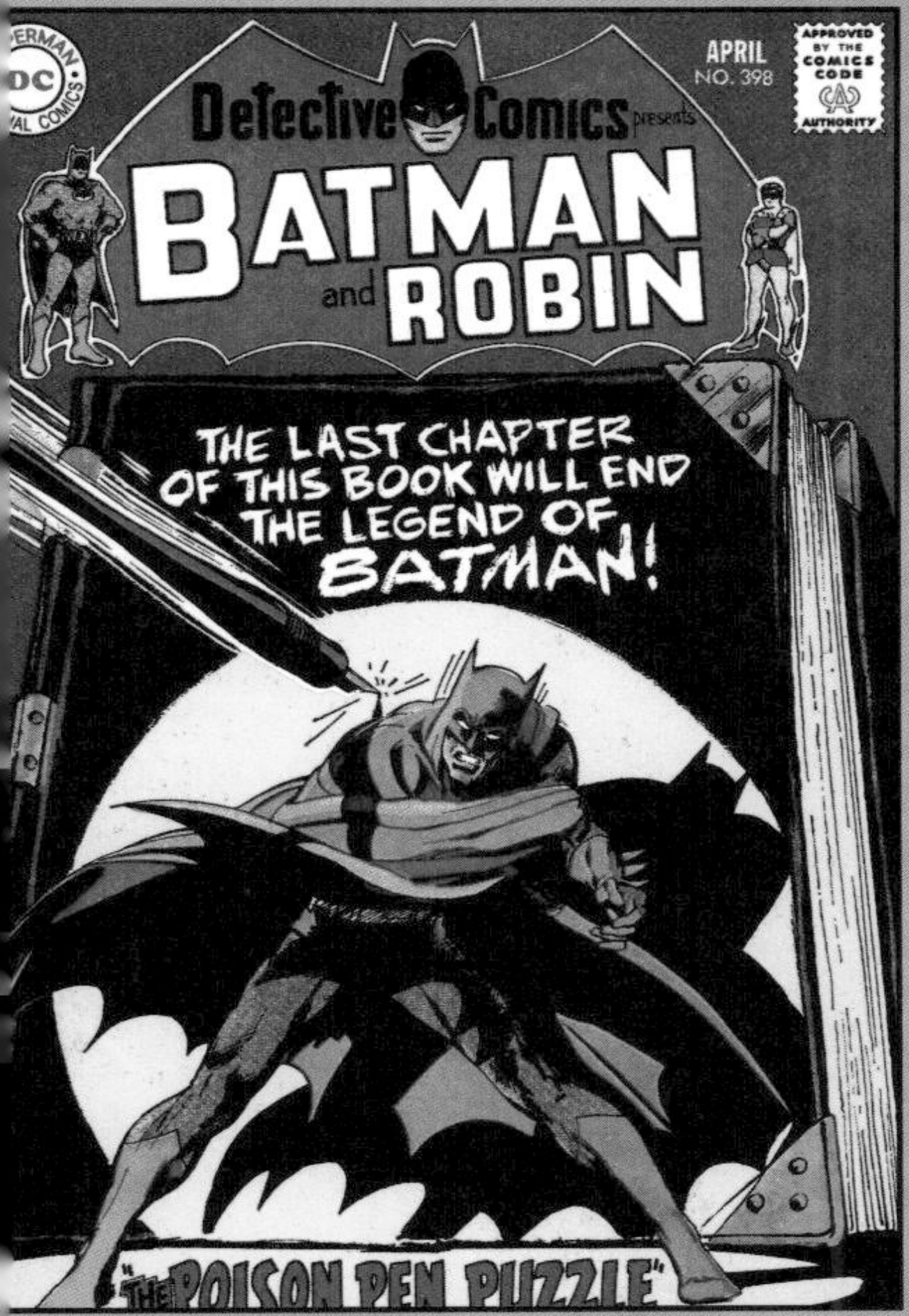
DC
Detective Comics presents
BATMAN and ROBIN
APRIL
NO. 398
APPROVED BY THE COMICS CODE AUTHORITY
THE LAST CHAPTER OF THIS BOOK WILL END THE LEGEND OF BATMAN!
"THE POISON PEN PUZZLE"

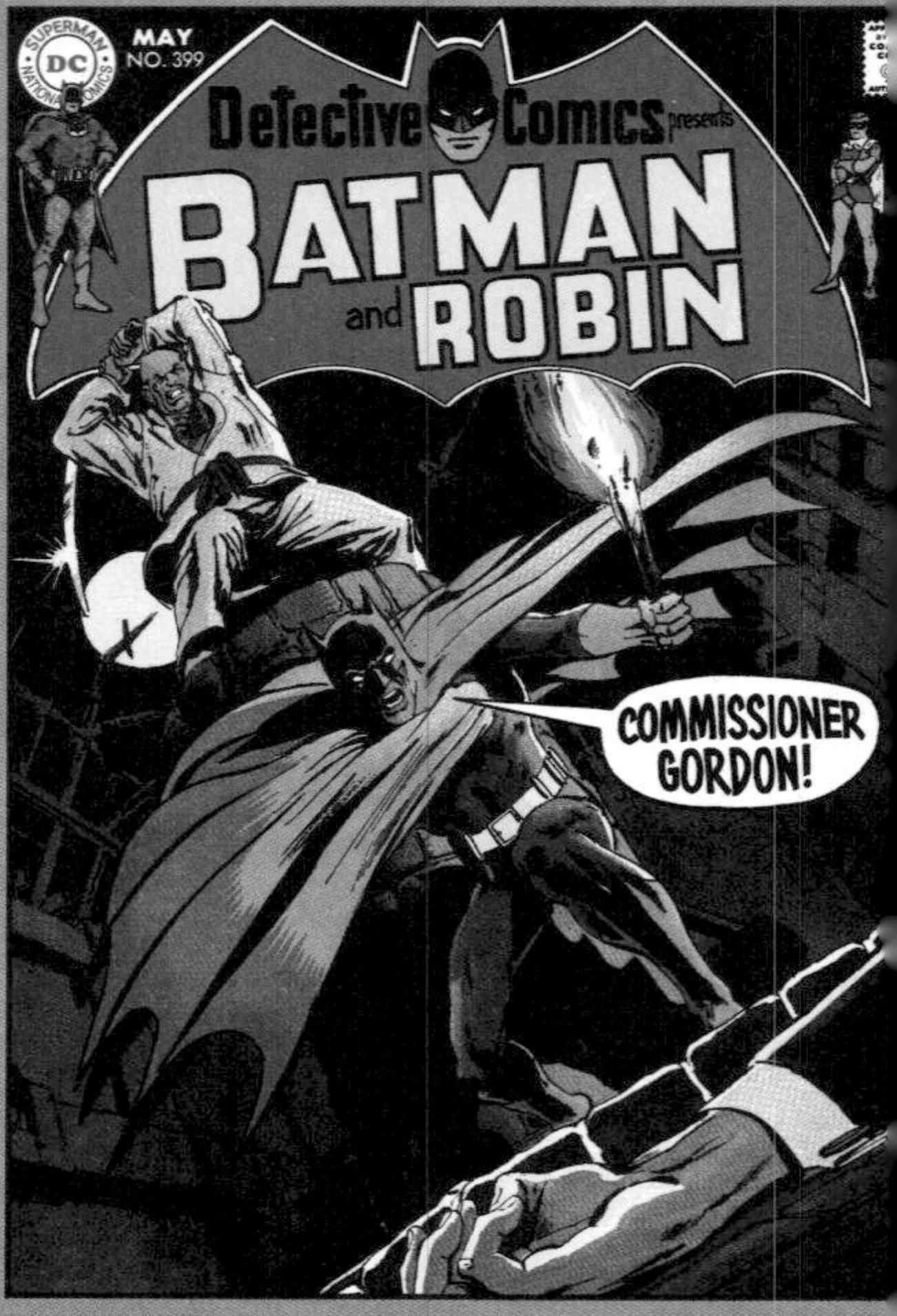
SUPERMAN
DC
NATIONAL COMICS
MAY
NO. 399
Detective Comics presents
BATMAN
and ROBIN
COMMISSIONER GORDON!

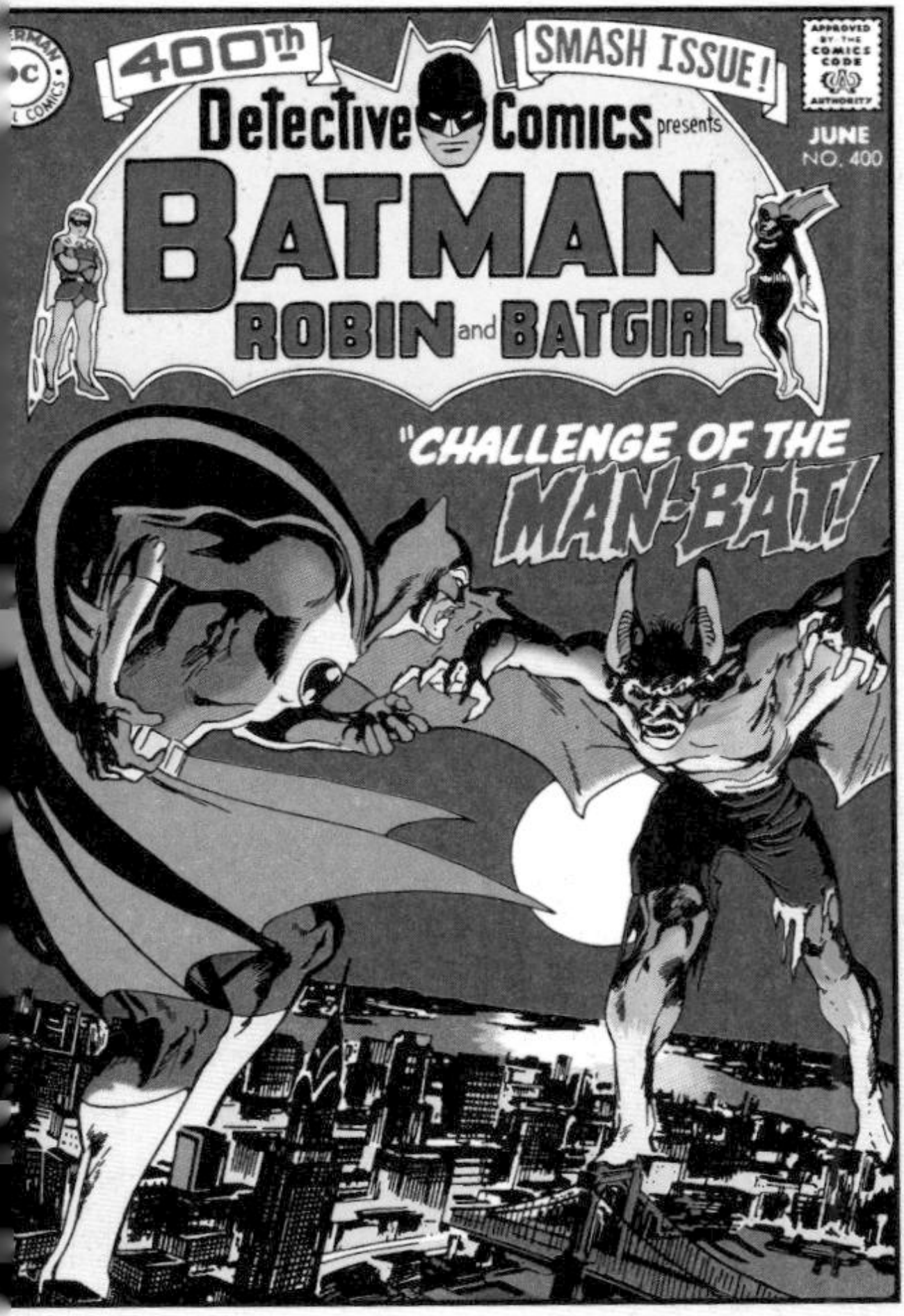
400th
SMASH ISSUE!
APPROVED BY THE COMICS CODE AUTHORITY
Detective Comics presents
JUNE
NO. 400
BATMAN
ROBIN and BATGIRL
"CHALLENGE OF THE MAN-BAT!"

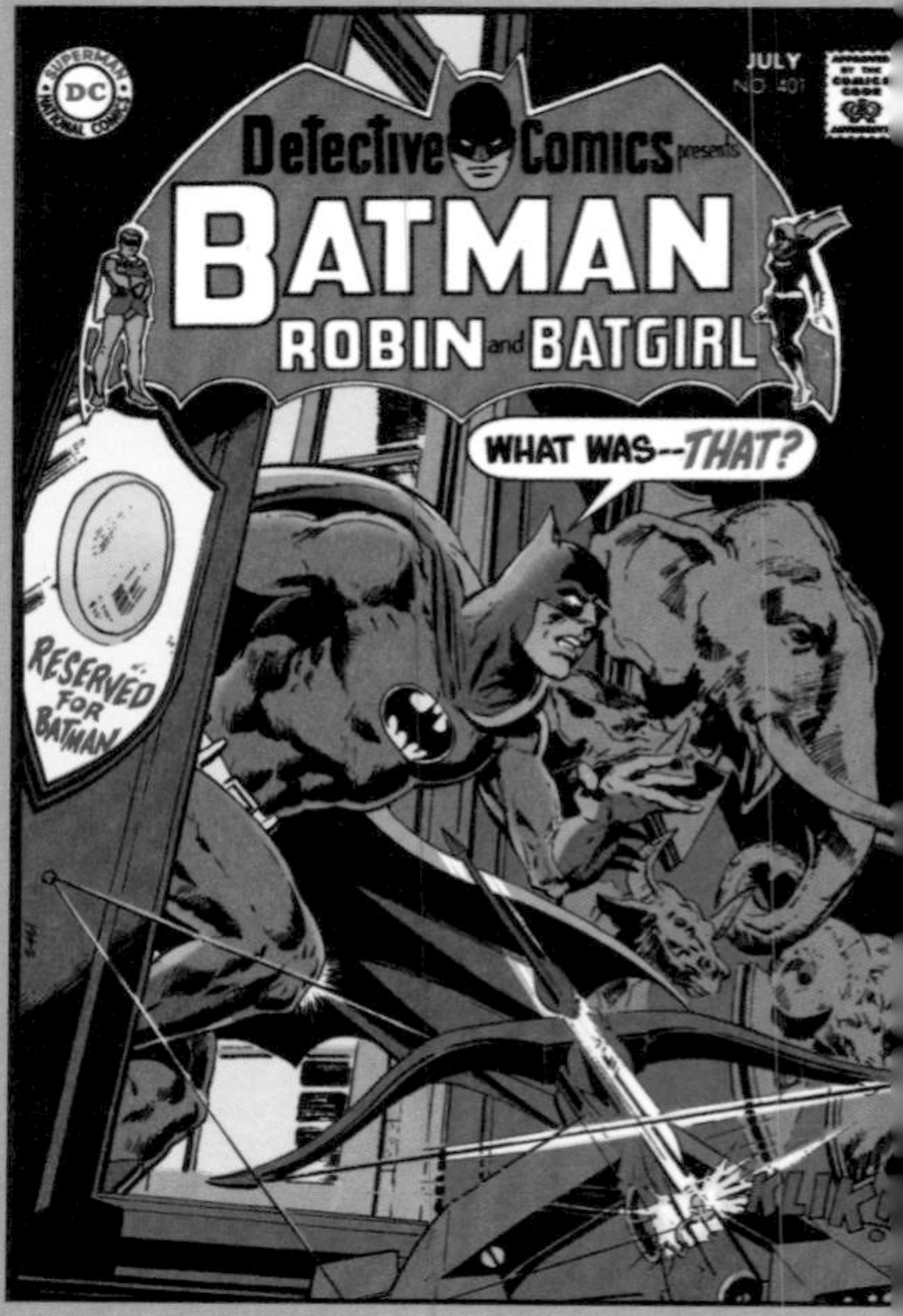
SUPERMAN
DC
NATIONAL COMICS
JULY
NO. 401
Detective Comics presents
BATMAN
ROBIN and BATGIRL
WHAT WAS--THAT?
RESERVED FOR BATMAN
KLIK!

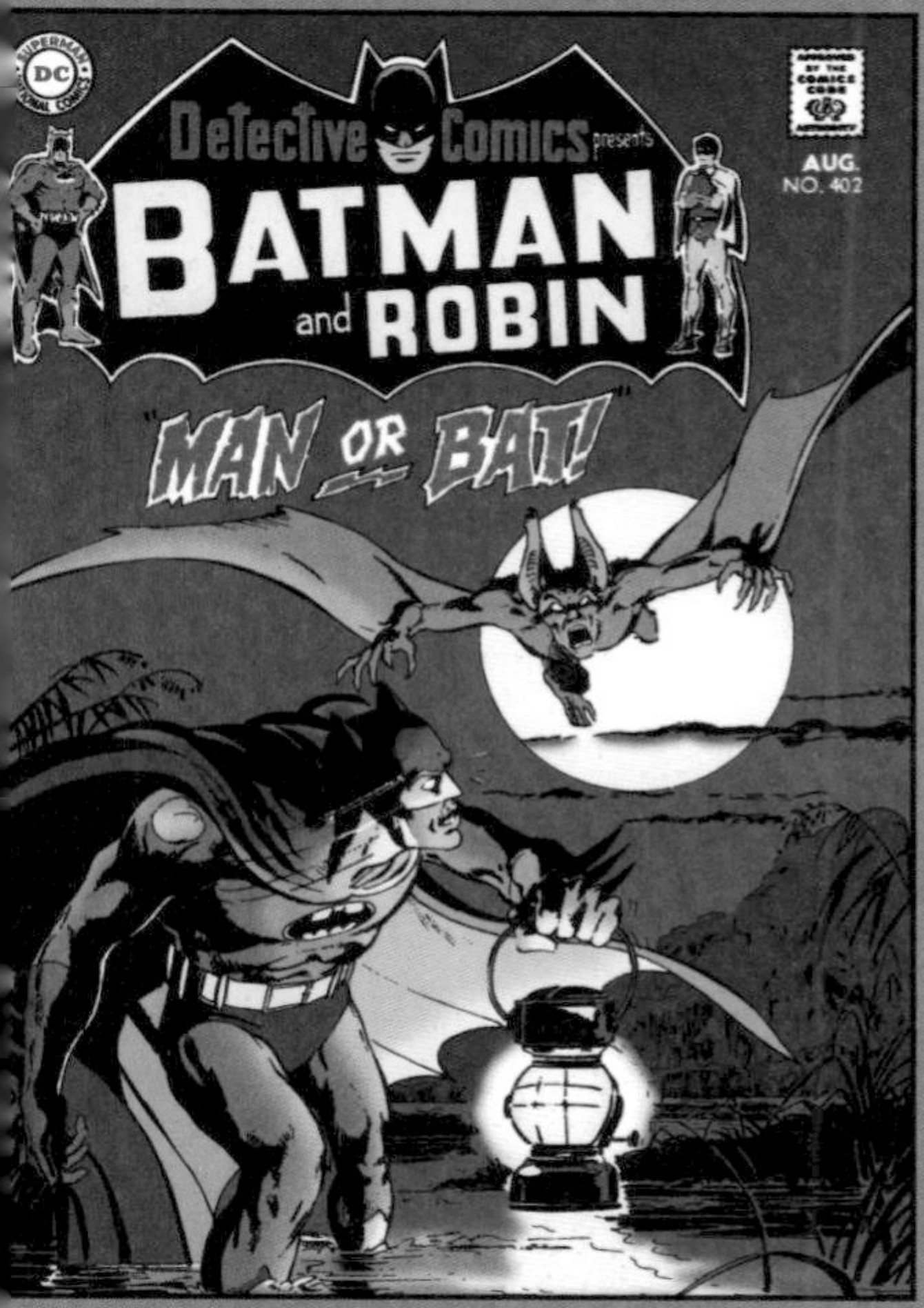
DC
SUPERMAN-BATMAN-WONDER WOMAN COMICS
Detective Comics presents
BATMAN and ROBIN
APPROVED BY THE COMICS CODE
AUG.
NO. 402
"MAN OR BAT!"

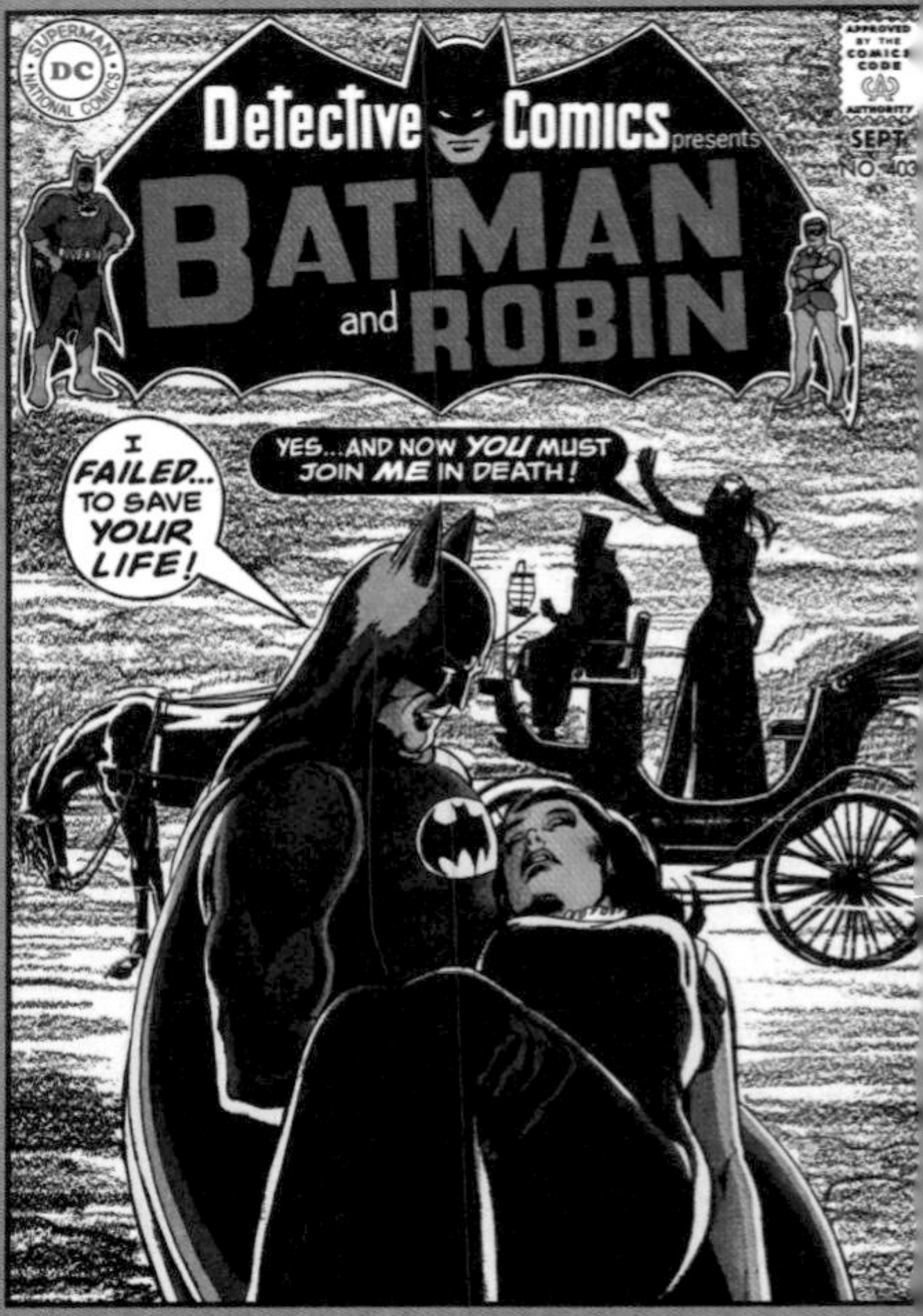
SUPERMAN • NATIONAL COMICS •
DC
Detective Comics presents
BATMAN and ROBIN
APPROVED BY THE COMICS CODE AUTHORITY
SEPT.
NO. 403
I FAILED... TO SAVE YOUR LIFE!
YES...AND NOW YOU MUST JOIN ME IN DEATH!

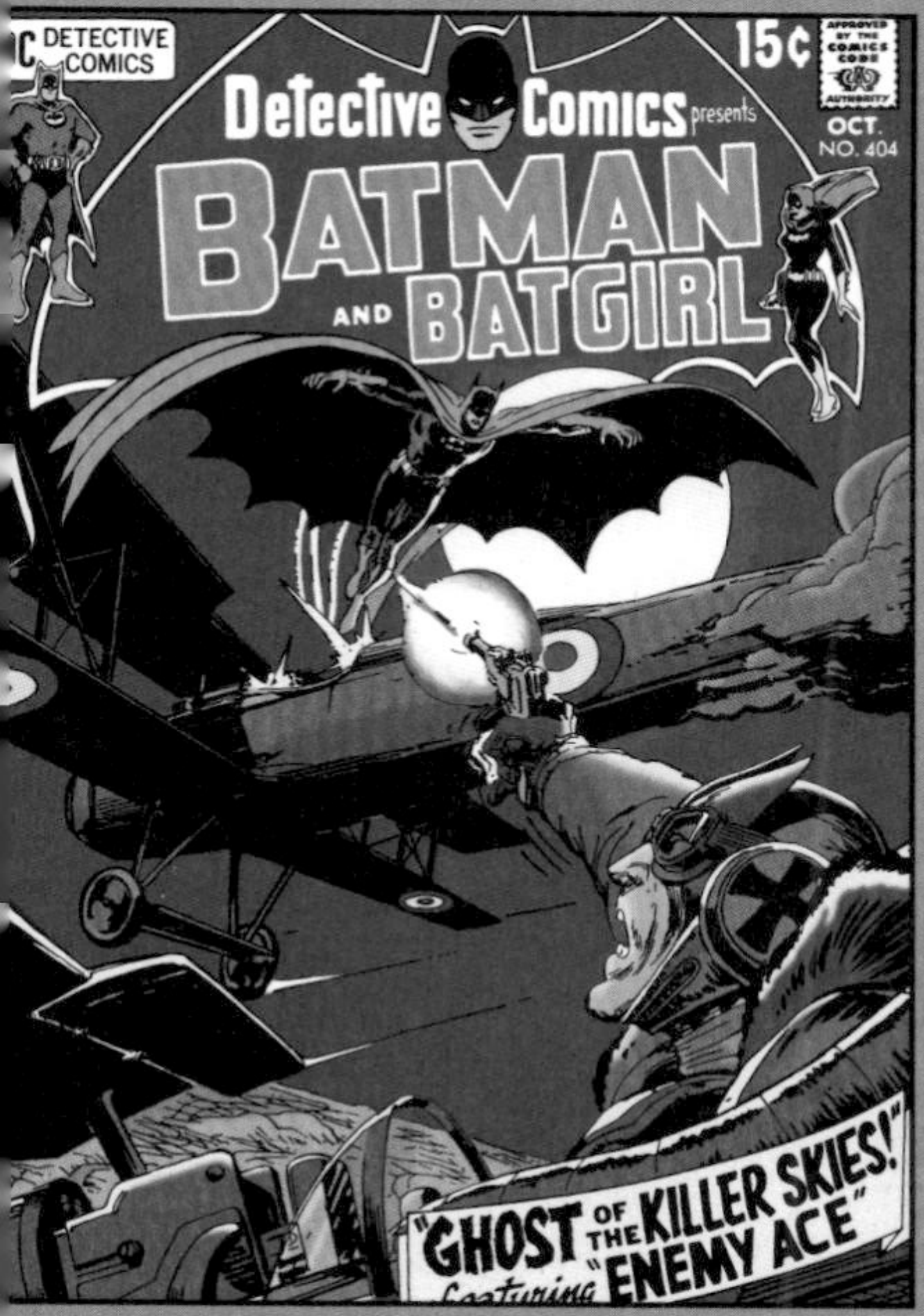
DC DETECTIVE COMICS
15¢
APPROVED BY THE COMICS CODE AUTHORITY
Detective Comics presents
OCT.
NO. 404
BATMAN AND BATGIRL
"GHOST OF THE KILLER SKIES!"
featuring "ENEMY ACE"

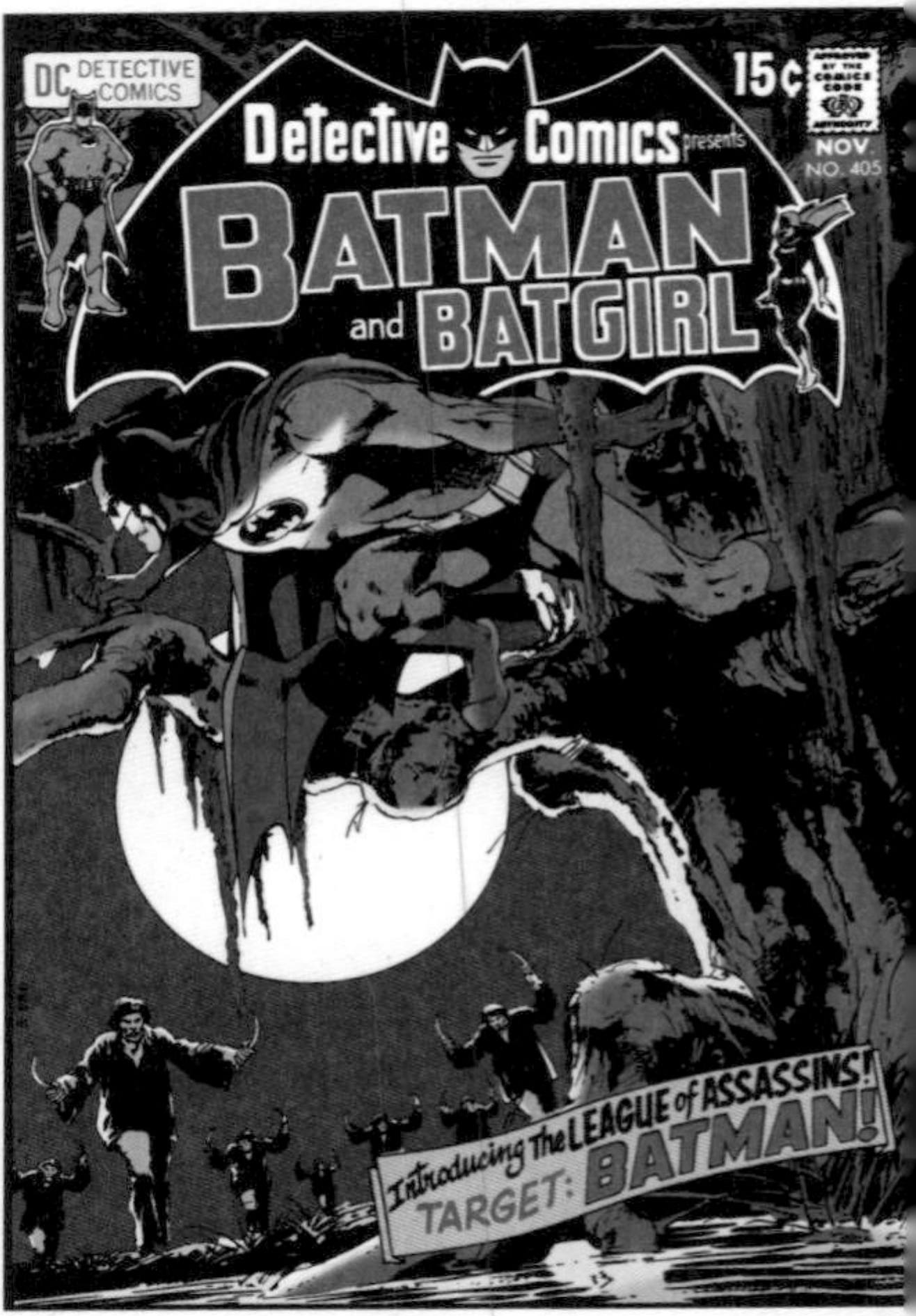
DC DETECTIVE COMICS
15¢
APPROVED BY THE COMICS CODE AUTHORITY
Detective Comics presents
NOV.
NO. 405
BATMAN
and BATGIRL
Introducing The LEAGUE of ASSASSINS!
TARGET: BATMAN!

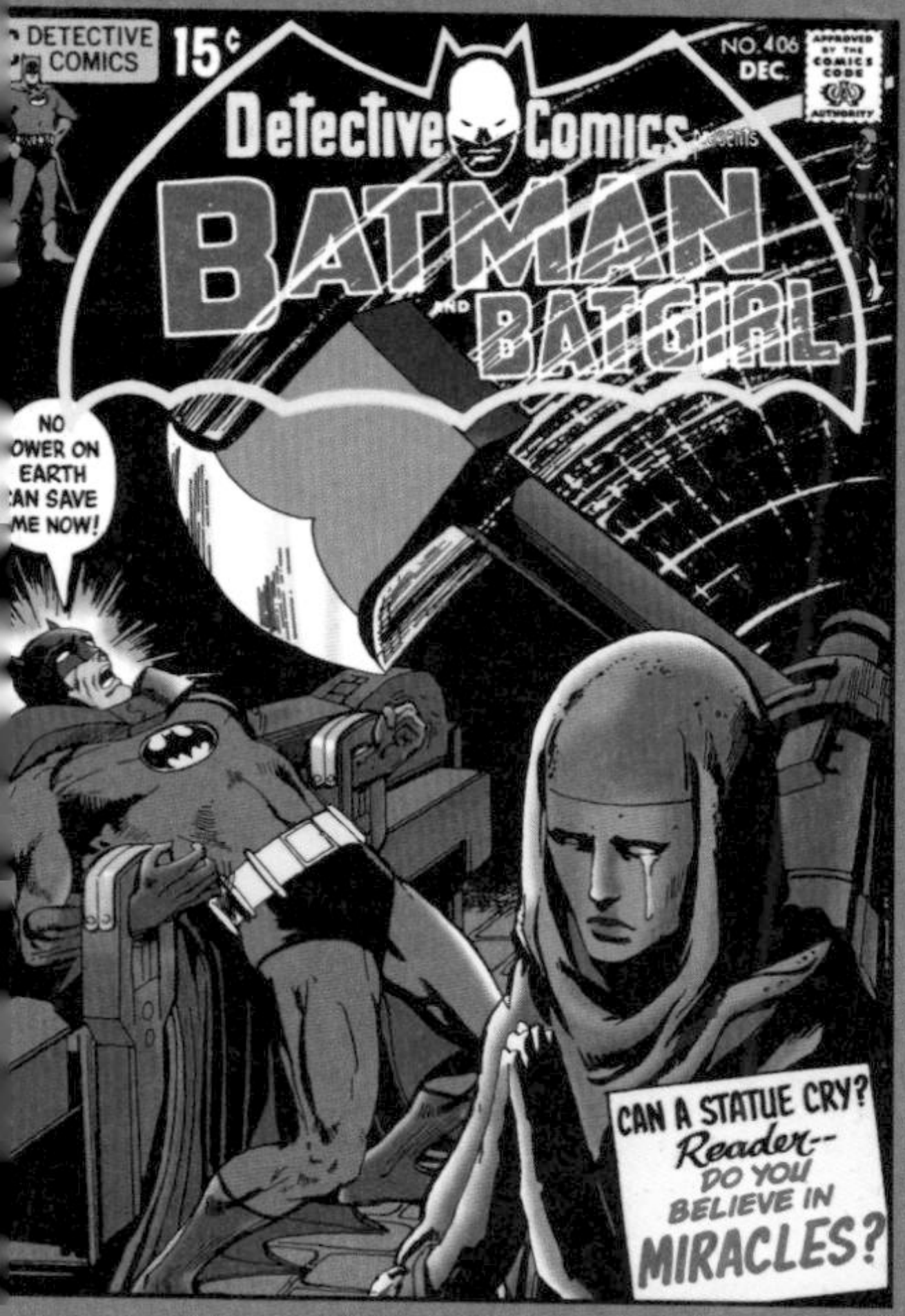
DETECTIVE COMICS
15¢
NO. 406
DEC.
APPROVED BY THE COMICS CODE AUTHORITY
Detective Comics presents
BATMAN AND BATGIRL
NO POWER ON EARTH CAN SAVE ME NOW!
CAN A STATUE CRY?
Reader-- DO YOU BELIEVE IN MIRACLES?

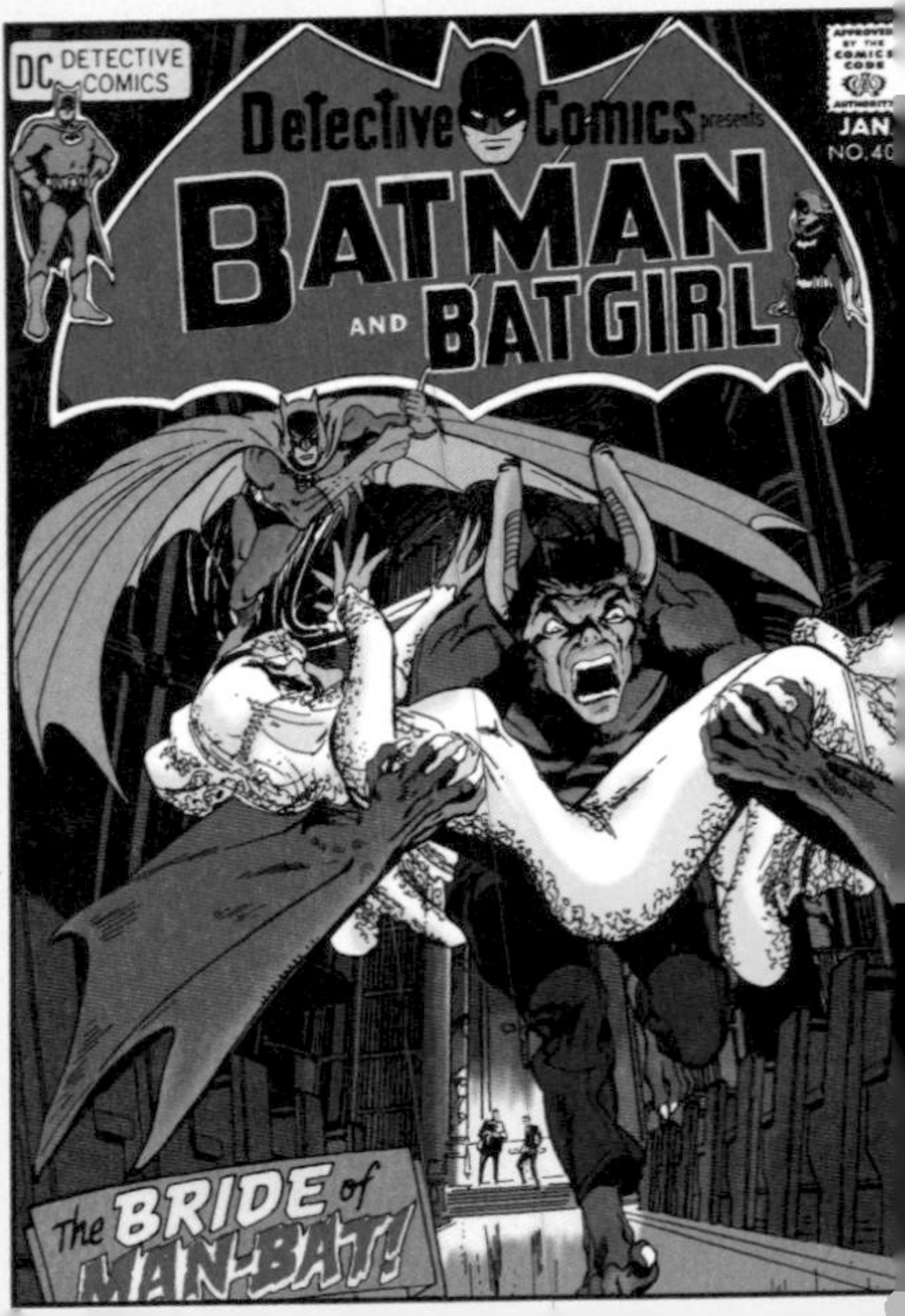
DC DETECTIVE COMICS
Detective Comics presents
BATMAN AND BATGIRL
APPROVED BY THE COMICS CODE AUTHORITY
JAN.
NO. 40
The BRIDE of MAN-BAT!

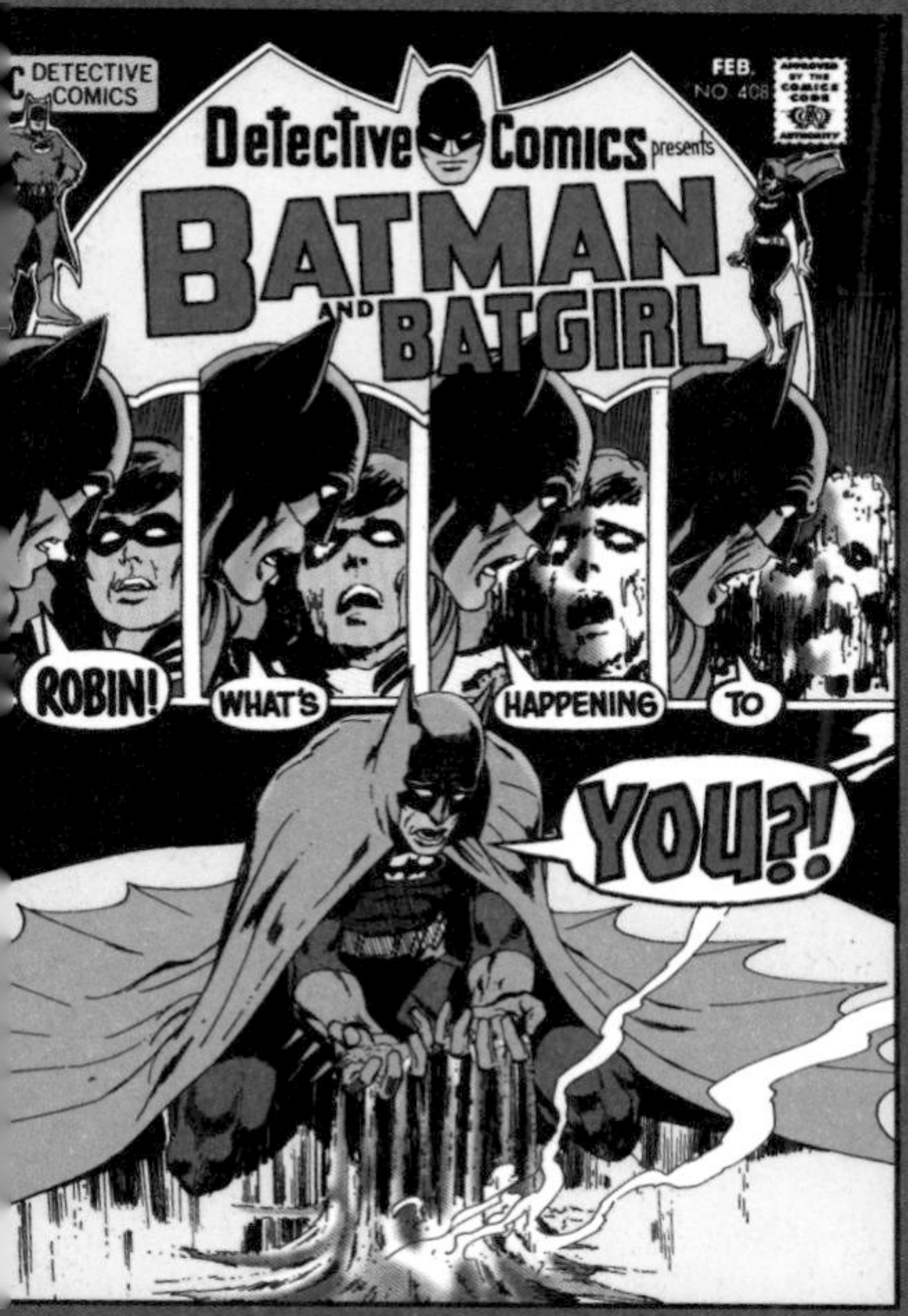
DETECTIVE COMICS
FEB.
NO. 408
APPROVED BY THE COMICS CODE AUTHORITY
Detective Comics presents
BATMAN AND BATGIRL
ROBIN!
WHAT'S
HAPPENING
TO
YOU?!

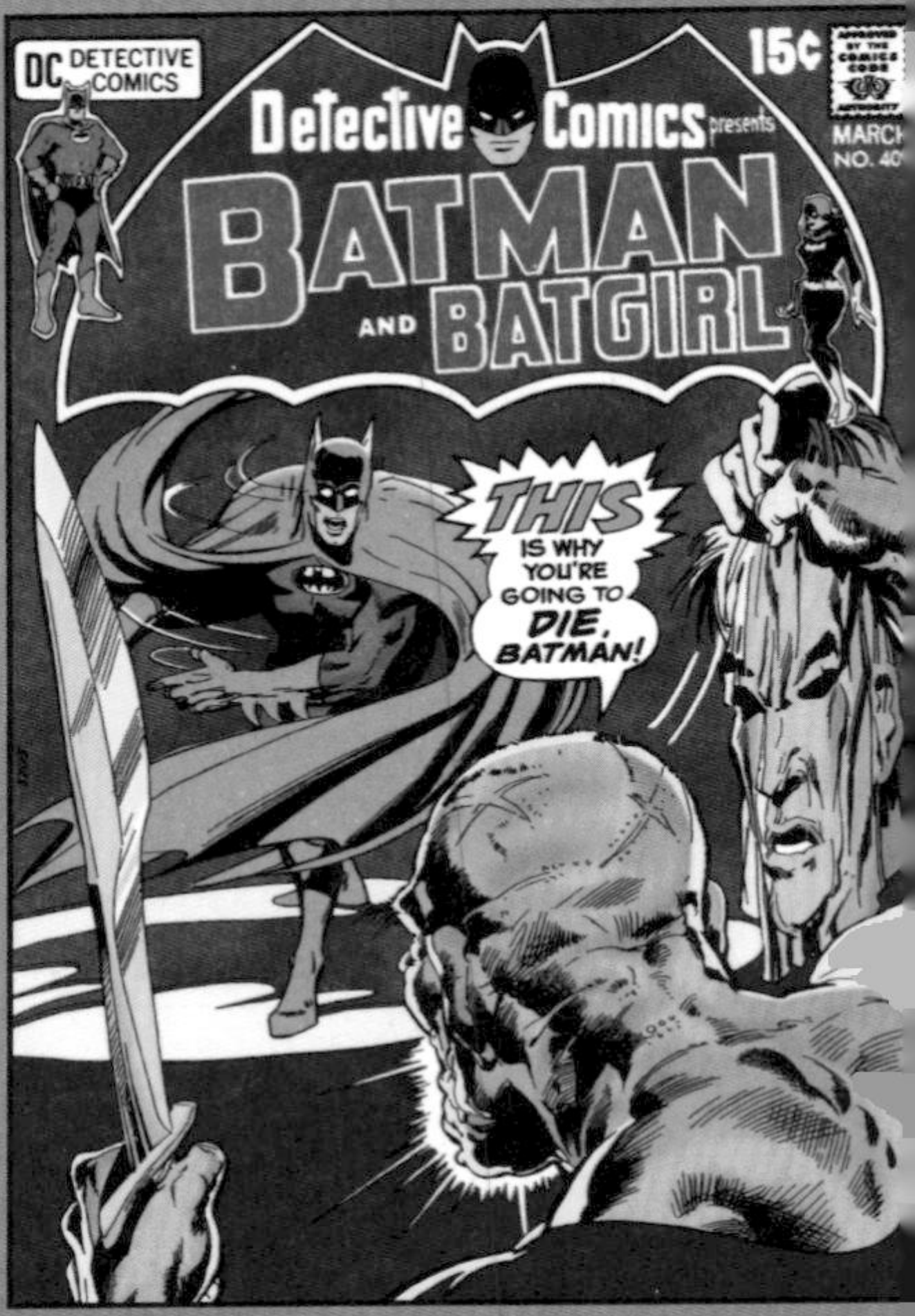
DC DETECTIVE COMICS
15¢
APPROVED BY THE COMICS CODE AUTHORITY
Detective Comics presents
MARCH
NO. 40
BATMAN AND BATGIRL
THIS IS WHY YOU'RE GOING TO DIE, BATMAN!

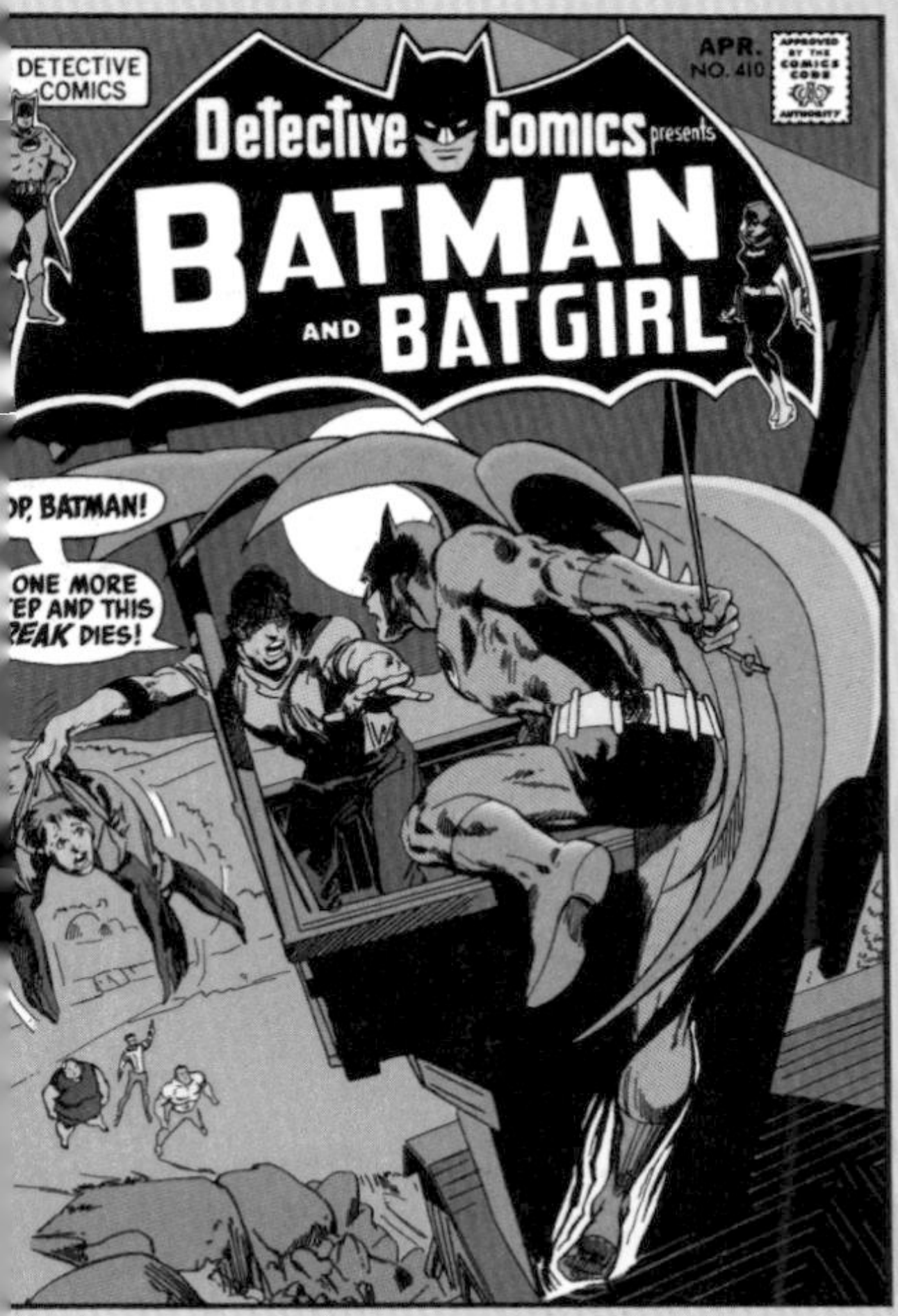
DETECTIVE COMICS
APR.
NO. 410
APPROVED BY THE COMICS CODE AUTHORITY
Detective Comics presents
BATMAN
AND BATGIRL
OP, BATMAN!
ONE MORE
EP AND THIS
EAK DIES!

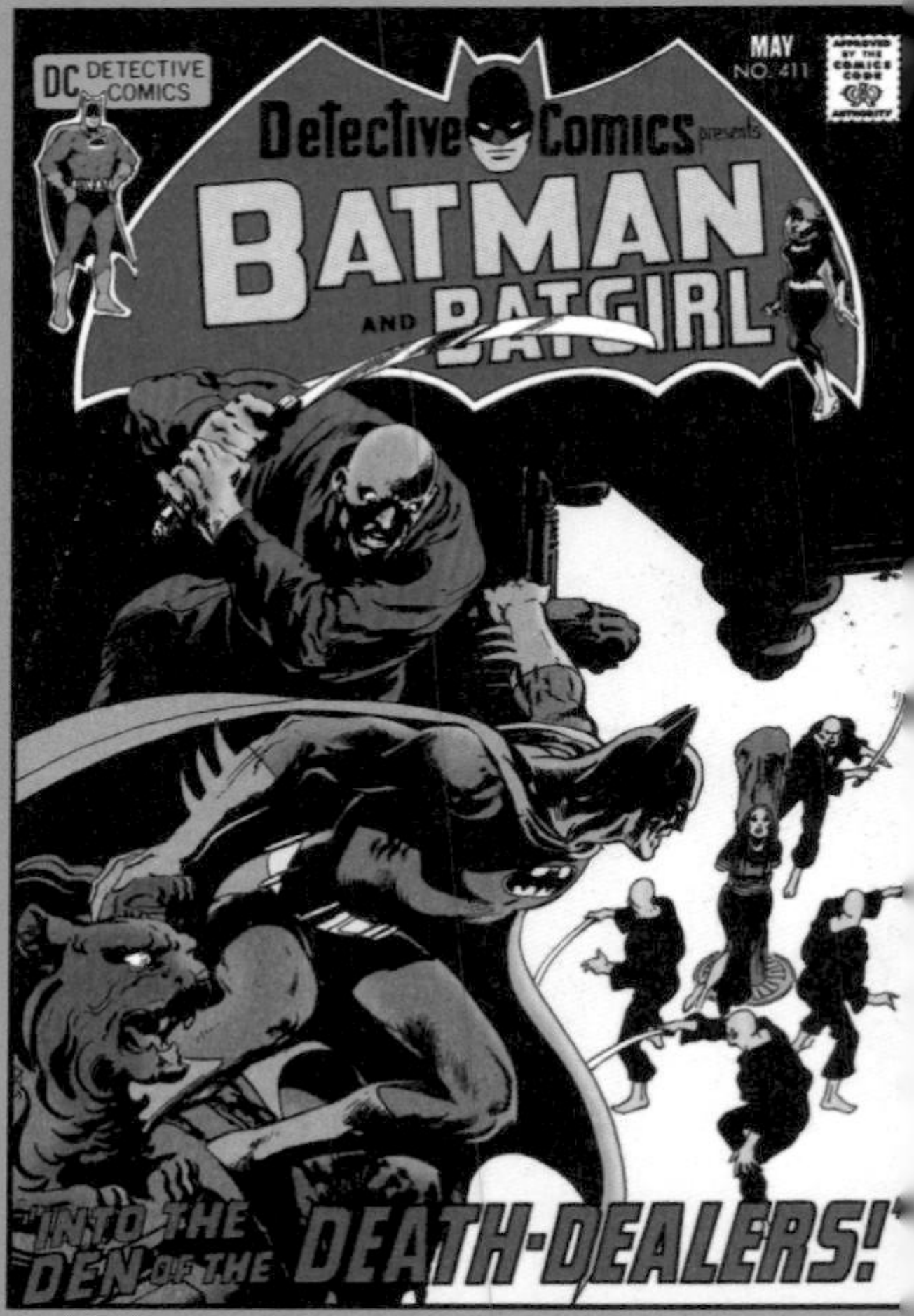
DC DETECTIVE COMICS
MAY
NO. 411
APPROVED BY THE COMICS CODE AUTHORITY
Detective Comics presents
BATMAN
AND BATGIRL
INTO THE DEN OF THE DEATH-DEALERS!

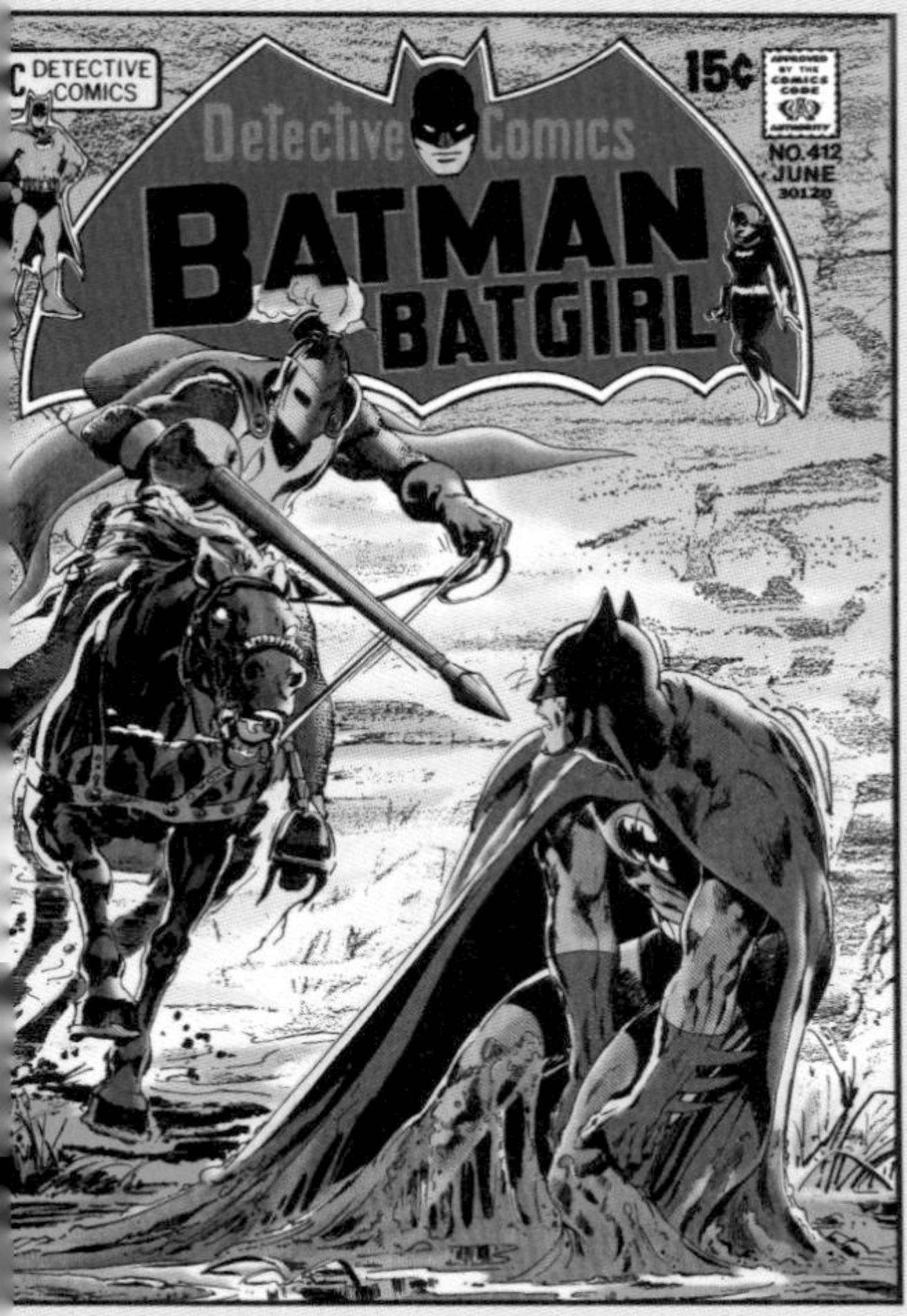
DETECTIVE COMICS
15¢
APPROVED BY THE COMICS CODE AUTHORITY
Detective Comics
NO. 412
JUNE
30120
BATMAN
BATGIRL

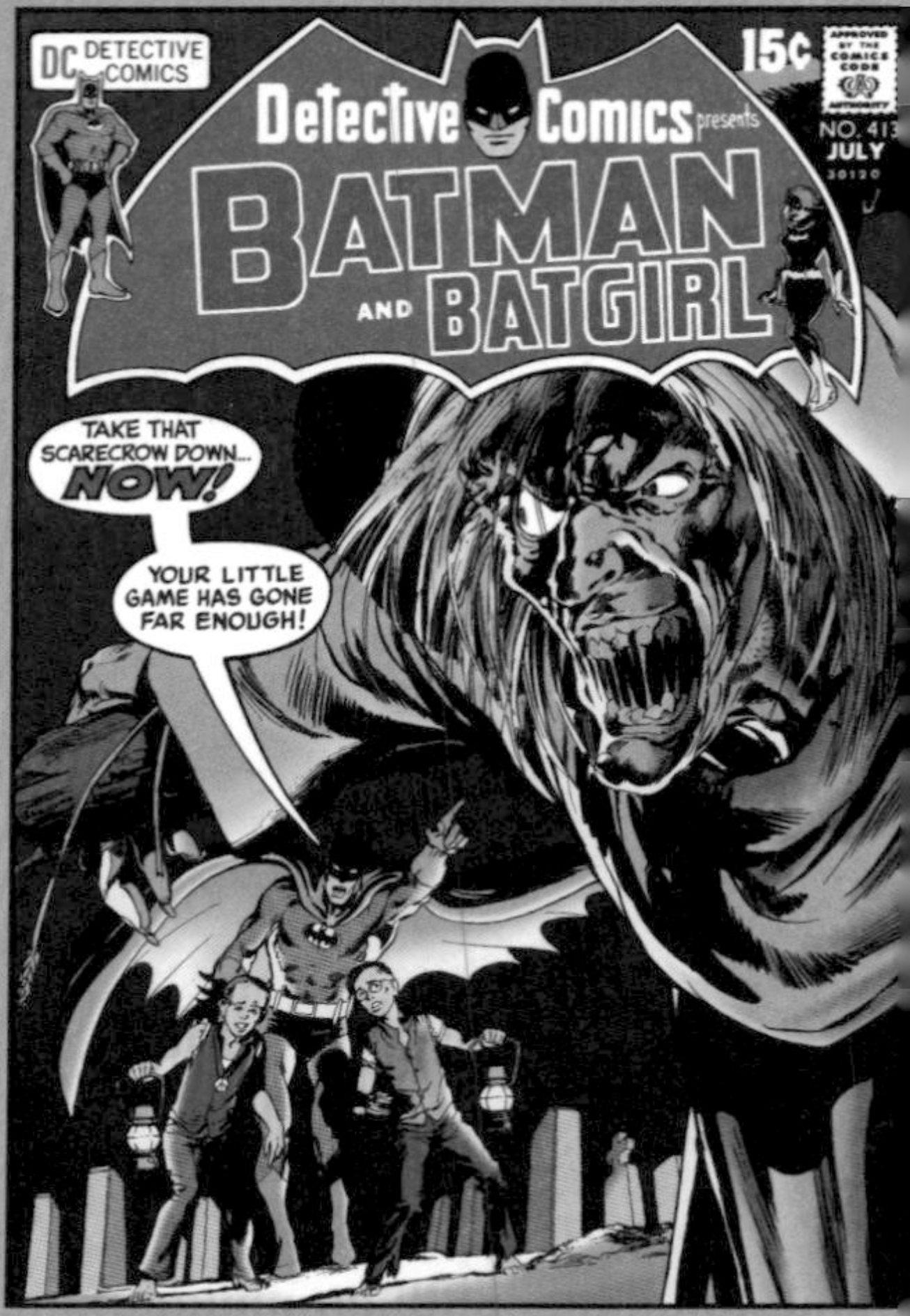
DC DETECTIVE COMICS
15¢
APPROVED BY THE COMICS CODE AUTHORITY
Detective Comics presents
NO. 413
JULY
BATMAN AND BATGIRL
TAKE THAT SCARECROW DOWN... NOW!
YOUR LITTLE GAME HAS GONE FAR ENOUGH!

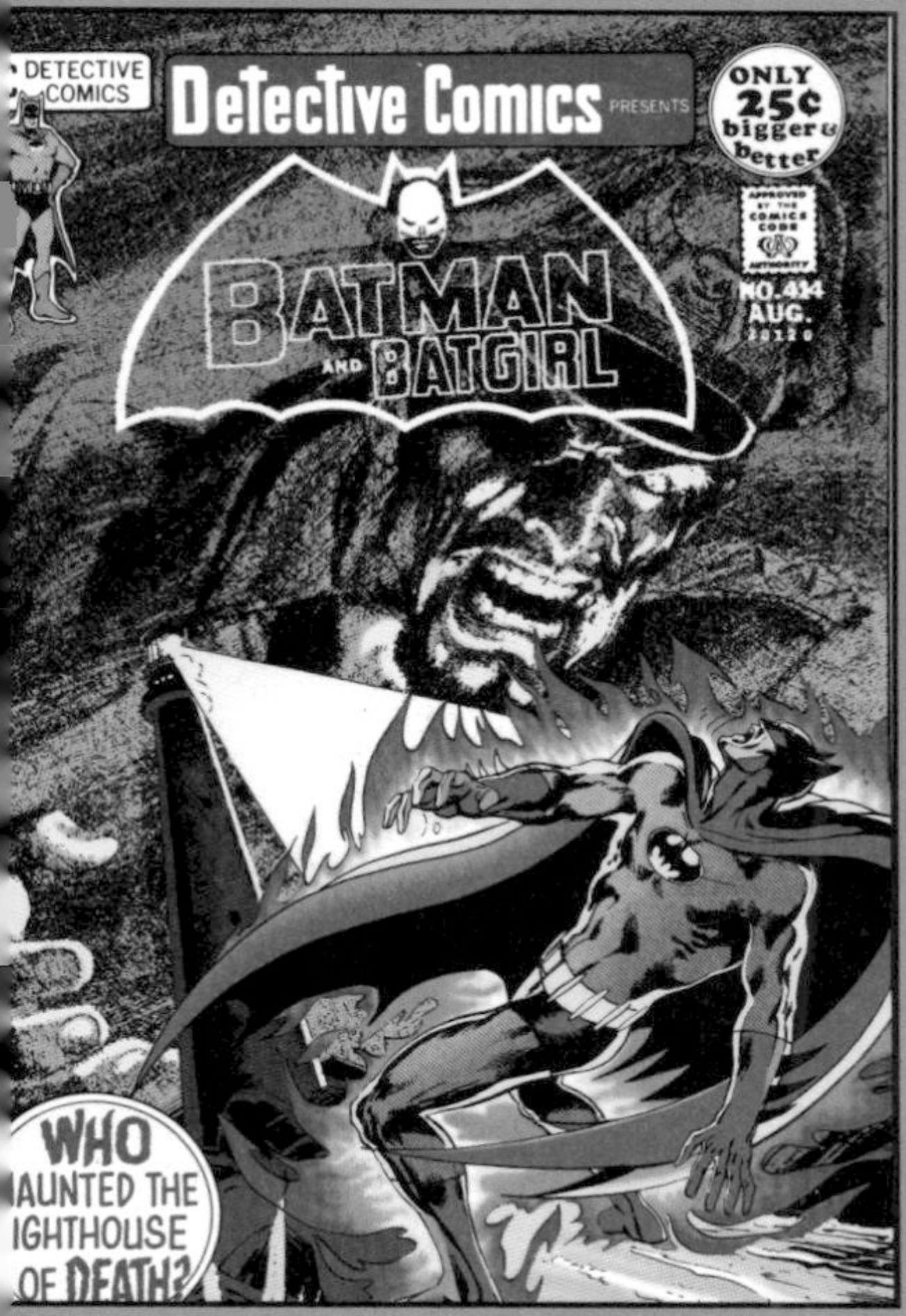
DETECTIVE COMICS
Detective Comics PRESENTS
ONLY 25¢ bigger & better
APPROVED BY THE COMICS CODE AUTHORITY
NO. 414
AUG.
BATMAN AND BATGIRL
WHO HAUNTED THE LIGHTHOUSE OF DEATH?

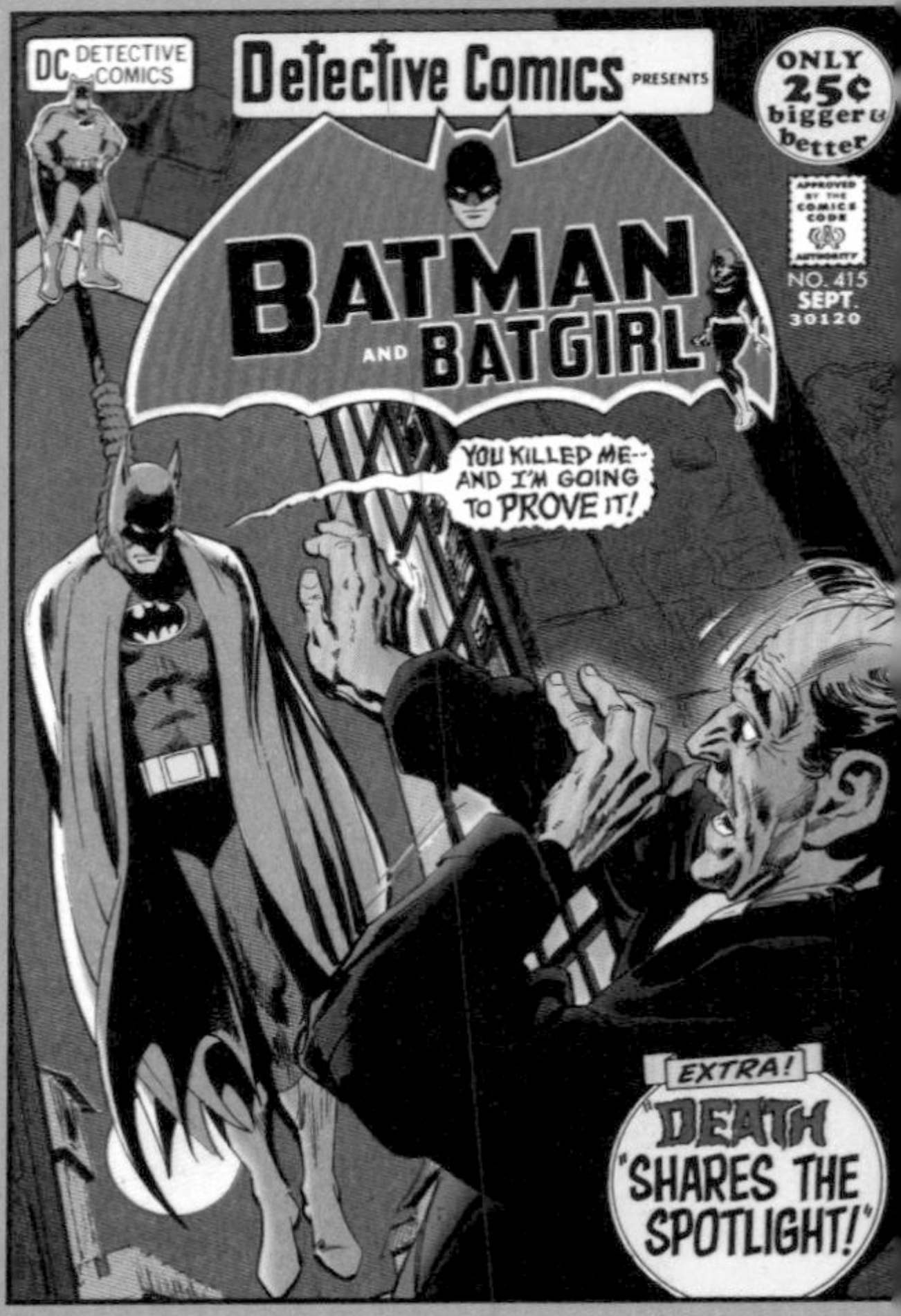
DC DETECTIVE COMICS
Detective Comics PRESENTS
ONLY 25¢ bigger & better
APPROVED BY THE COMICS CODE AUTHORITY
NO. 415
SEPT.
30120
BATMAN AND BATGIRL
YOU KILLED ME-- AND I'M GOING TO PROVE IT!
EXTRA!
"DEATH "SHARES THE SPOTLIGHT!"

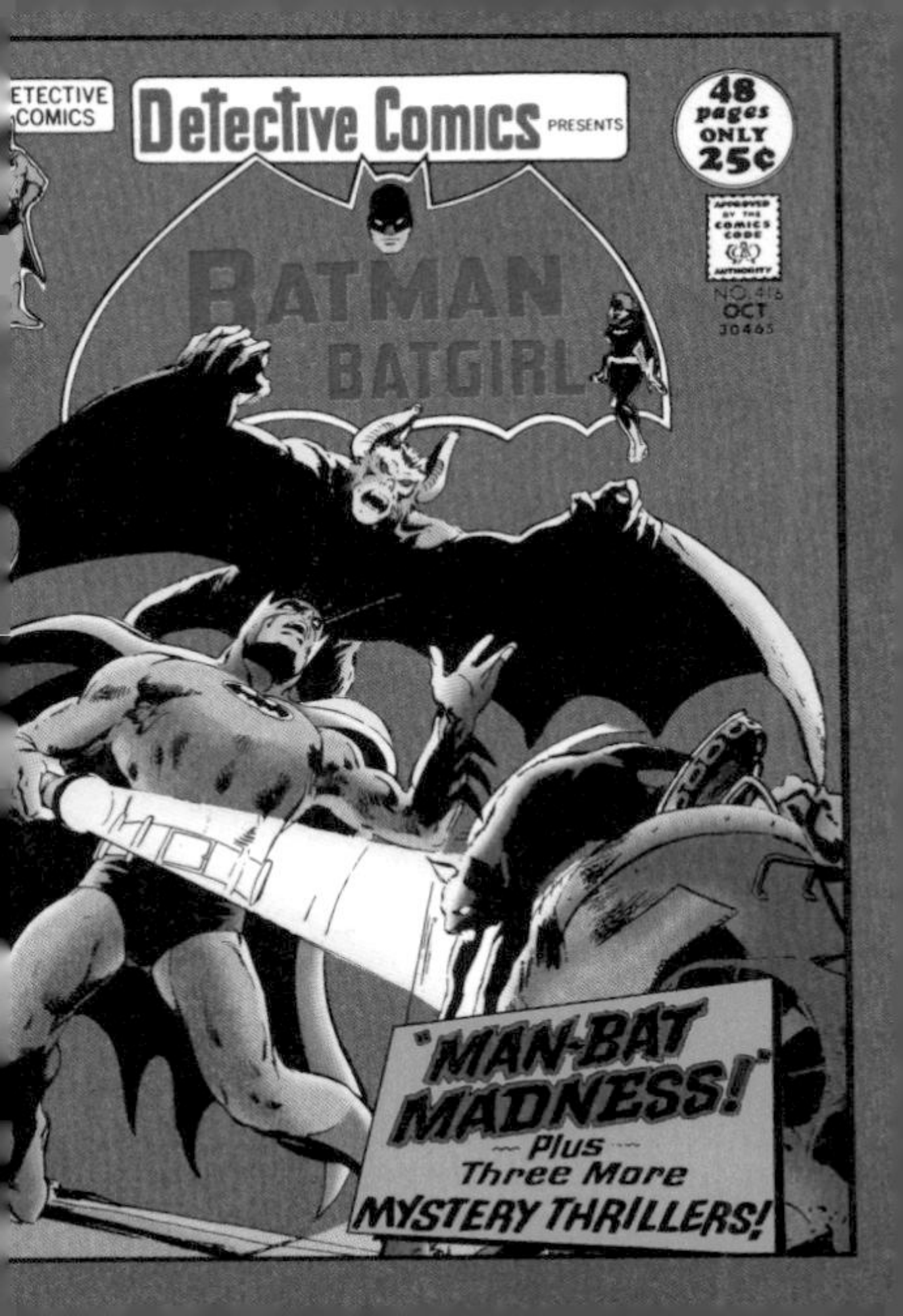
ETECTIVE COMICS
Detective Comics PRESENTS
48 pages ONLY 25¢
APPROVED BY THE COMICS CODE AUTHORITY
NO. 416
OCT
30465
BATMAN
BATGIRL
"MAN-BAT MADNESS!"
Plus
Three More
MYSTERY THRILLERS!

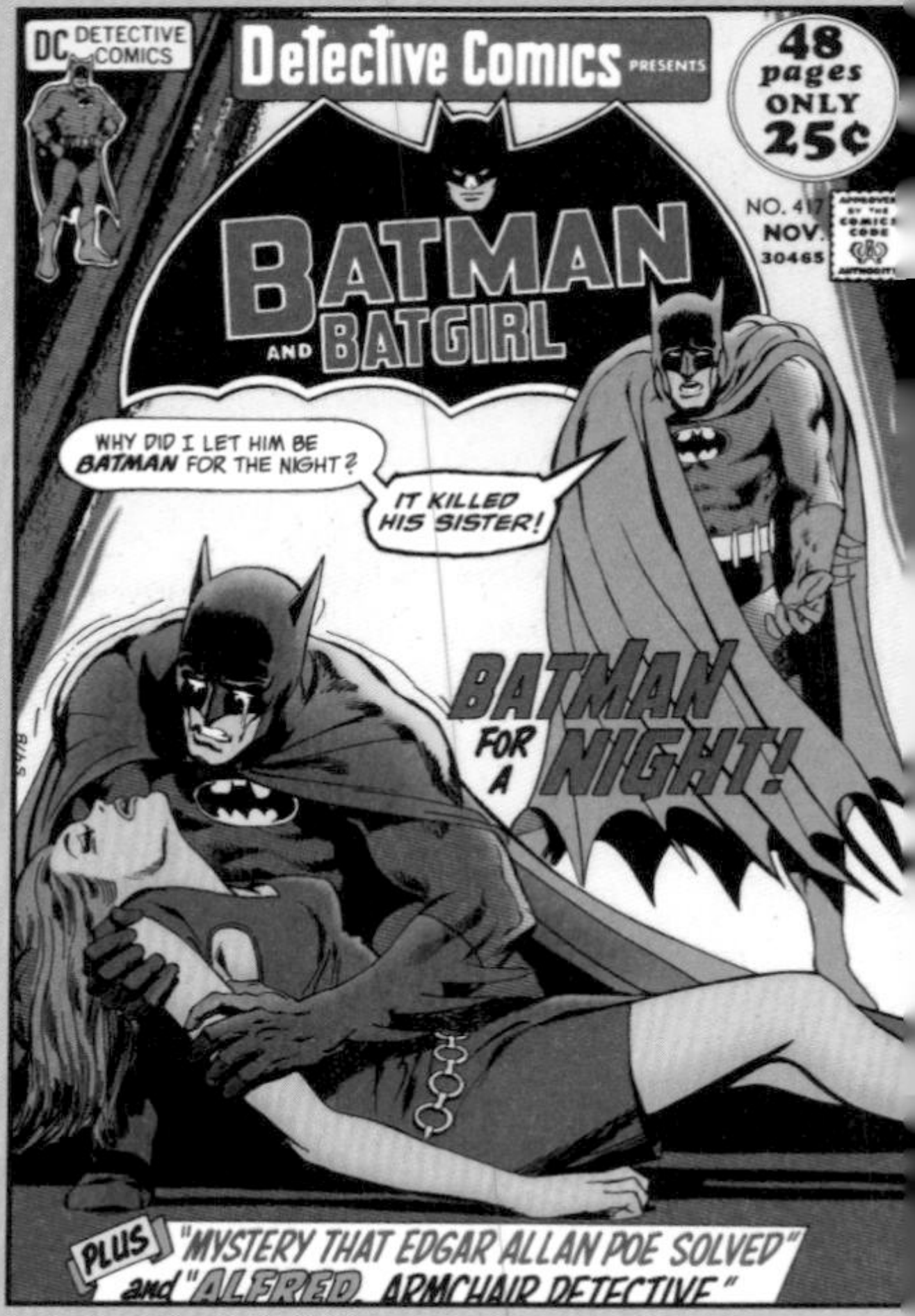
DC DETECTIVE COMICS
Detective Comics PRESENTS
48 pages ONLY 25¢
NO. 417
NOV.
30465
BATMAN AND BATGIRL
WHY DID I LET HIM BE BATMAN FOR THE NIGHT?
IT KILLED HIS SISTER!
BATMAN FOR A NIGHT!
PLUS "MYSTERY THAT EDGAR ALLAN POE SOLVED" and "ALFRED, ARMCHAIR DETECTIVE"

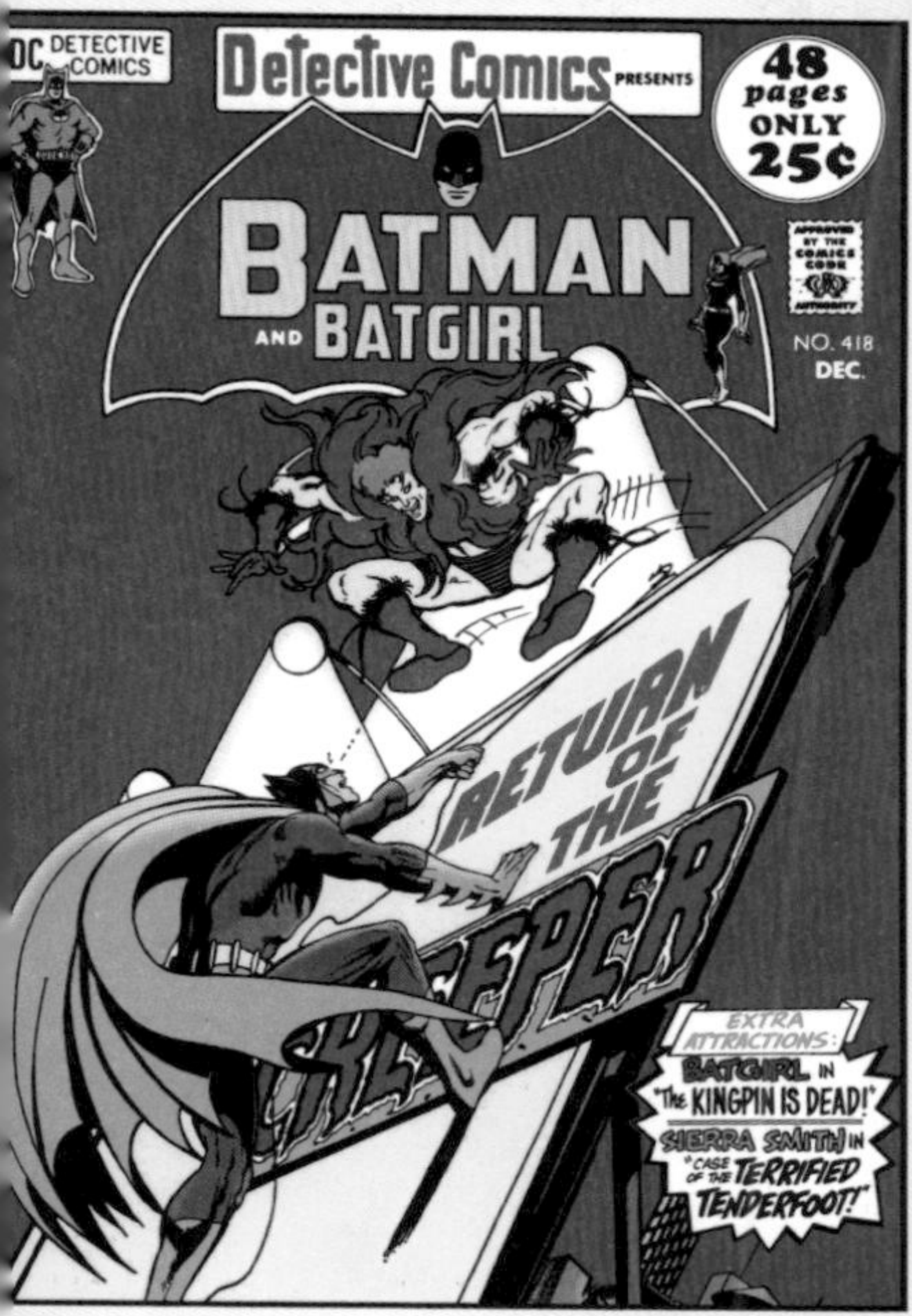
DC DETECTIVE COMICS
Detective Comics PRESENTS
48 pages ONLY 25¢
BATMAN AND BATGIRL
APPROVED BY THE COMICS CODE AUTHORITY
NO. 418
DEC.
RETURN OF THE
SKEEPER
EXTRA ATTRACTIONS:
BATGIRL IN "The KINGPIN IS DEAD!"
SIERRA SMITH IN "CASE OF THE TERRIFIED TENDERFOOT!"

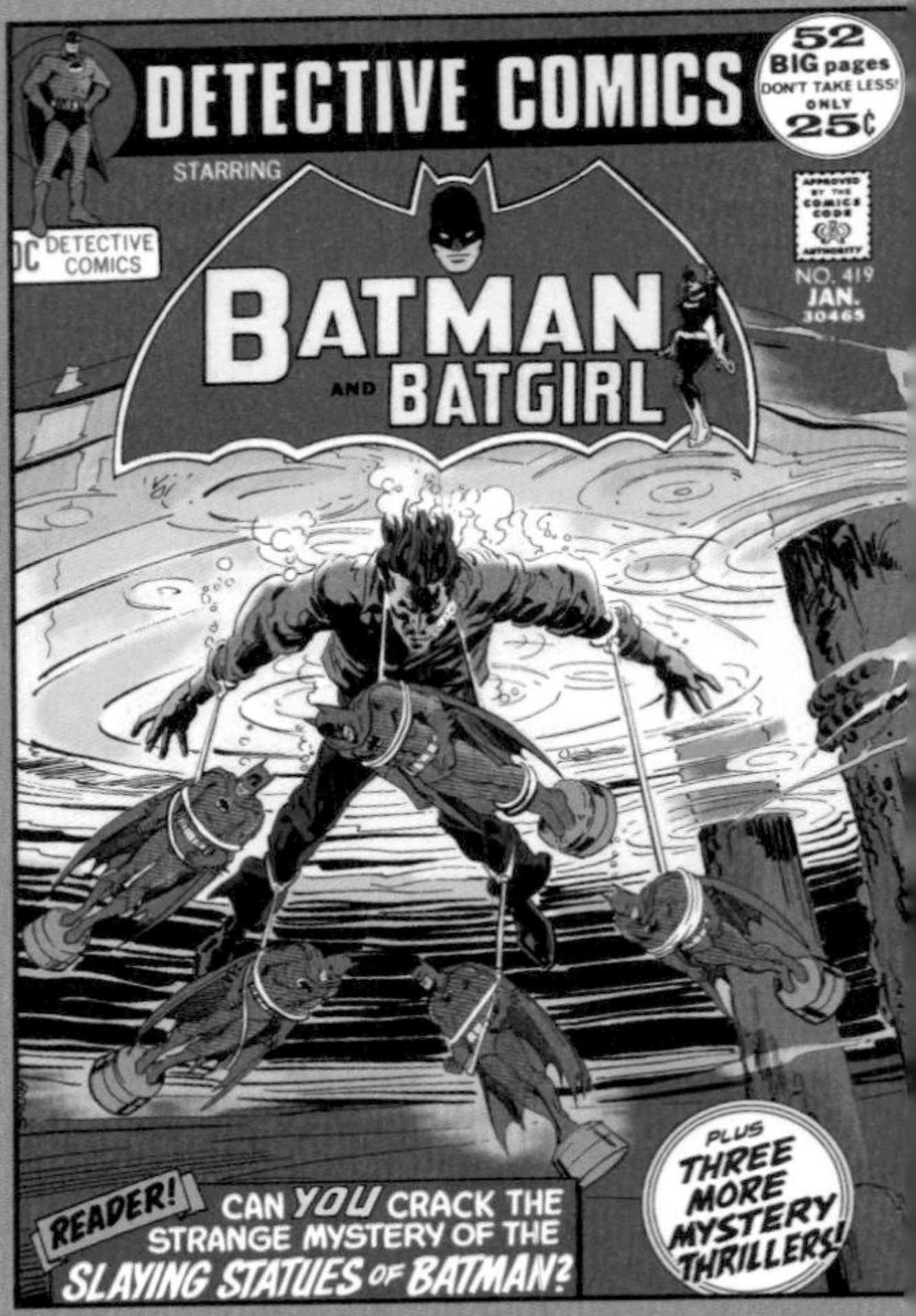
DETECTIVE COMICS
52 BIG pages DON'T TAKE LESS! ONLY 25¢
STARRING
DC DETECTIVE COMICS
APPROVED BY THE COMICS CODE AUTHORITY
NO. 419
JAN.
30465
BATMAN AND BATGIRL
PLUS THREE MORE MYSTERY THRILLERS!
READER! CAN YOU CRACK THE STRANGE MYSTERY OF THE SLAYING STATUES OF BATMAN?

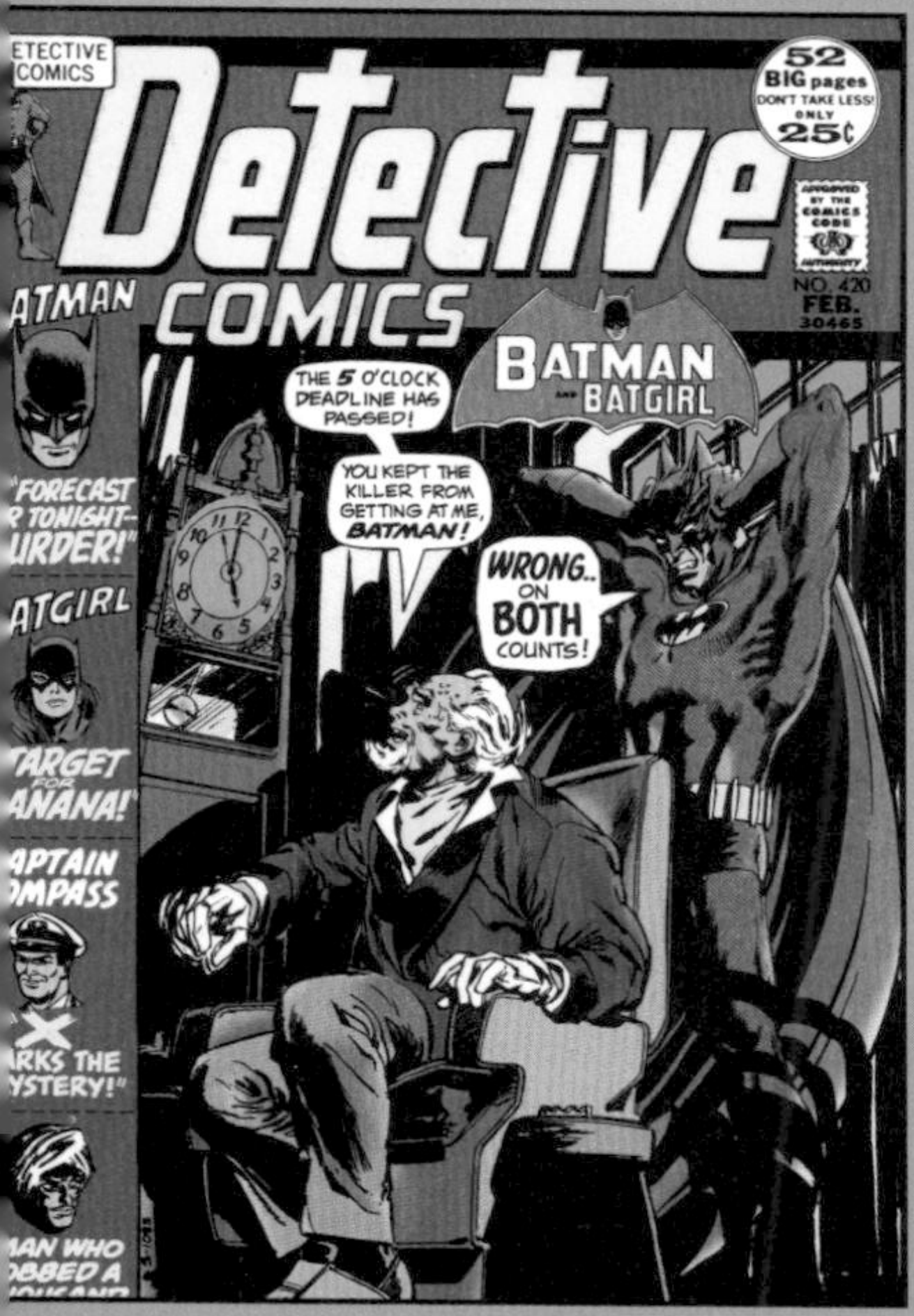
ETECTIVE COMICS
Detective COMICS
52 BIG pages DON'T TAKE LESS! ONLY 25¢
APPROVED BY THE COMICS CODE AUTHORITY
NO. 420 FEB. 30465
BATMAN AND BATGIRL
THE 5 O'CLOCK DEADLINE HAS PASSED!
YOU KEPT THE KILLER FROM GETTING AT ME, BATMAN!
WRONG.. ON BOTH COUNTS!
ATMAN
"FORECAST R TONIGHT— URDER!"
ATGIRL
TARGET FOR ANANA!"
APTAIN OMPASS
X ARKS THE YSTERY!"
AN WHO OBBED A

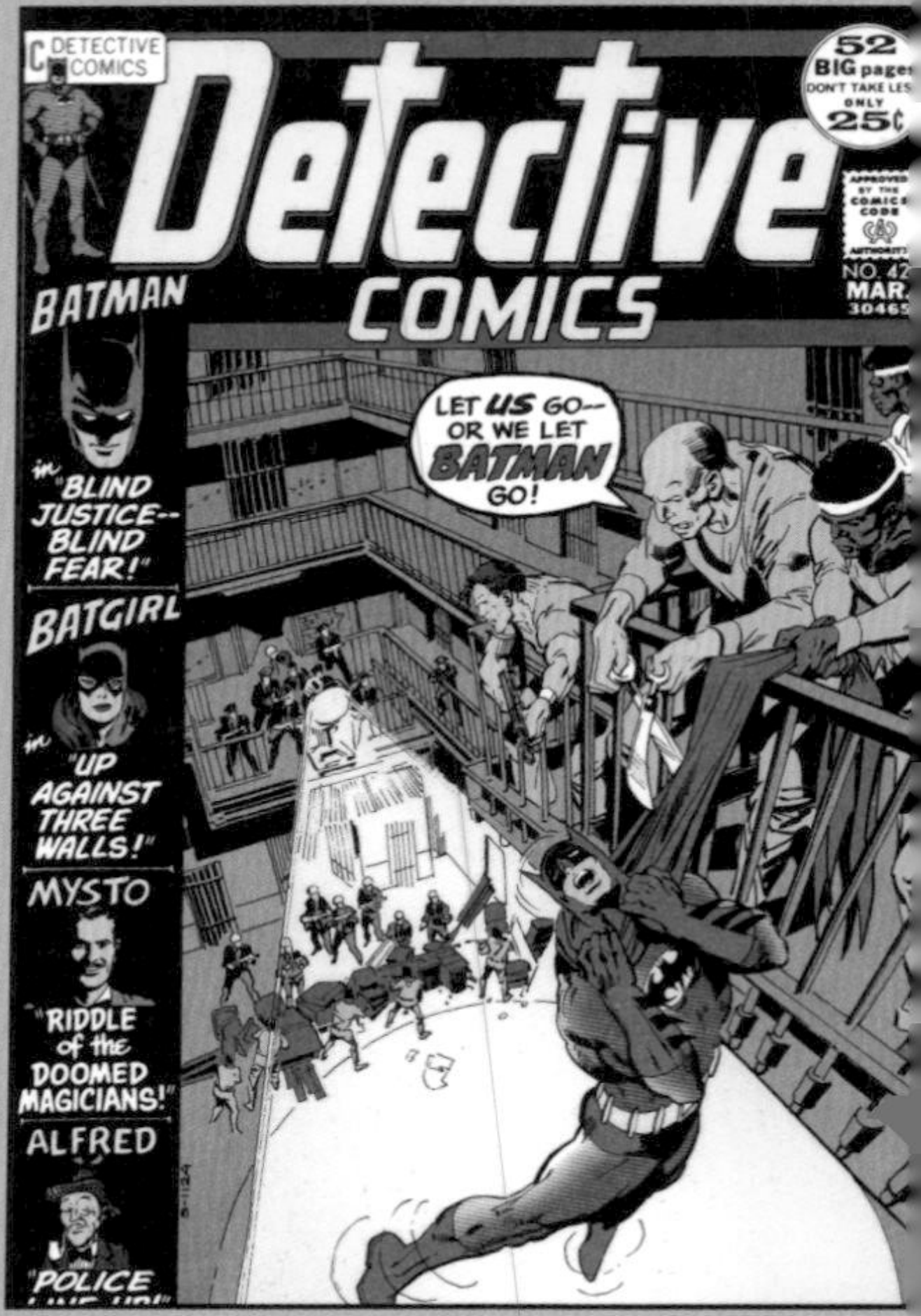
DETECTIVE COMICS
Detective
COMICS
52 BIG pages DON'T TAKE LES ONLY 25¢
APPROVED BY THE COMICS CODE AUTHORITY
NO. 42
MAR.
BATMAN
in "BLIND JUSTICE-- BLIND FEAR!"
BATGIRL
in "UP AGAINST THREE WALLS!"
MYSTO
"RIDDLE of the DOOMED MAGICIANS!"
ALFRED
"POLICE
LET US GO-- OR WE LET BATMAN GO!

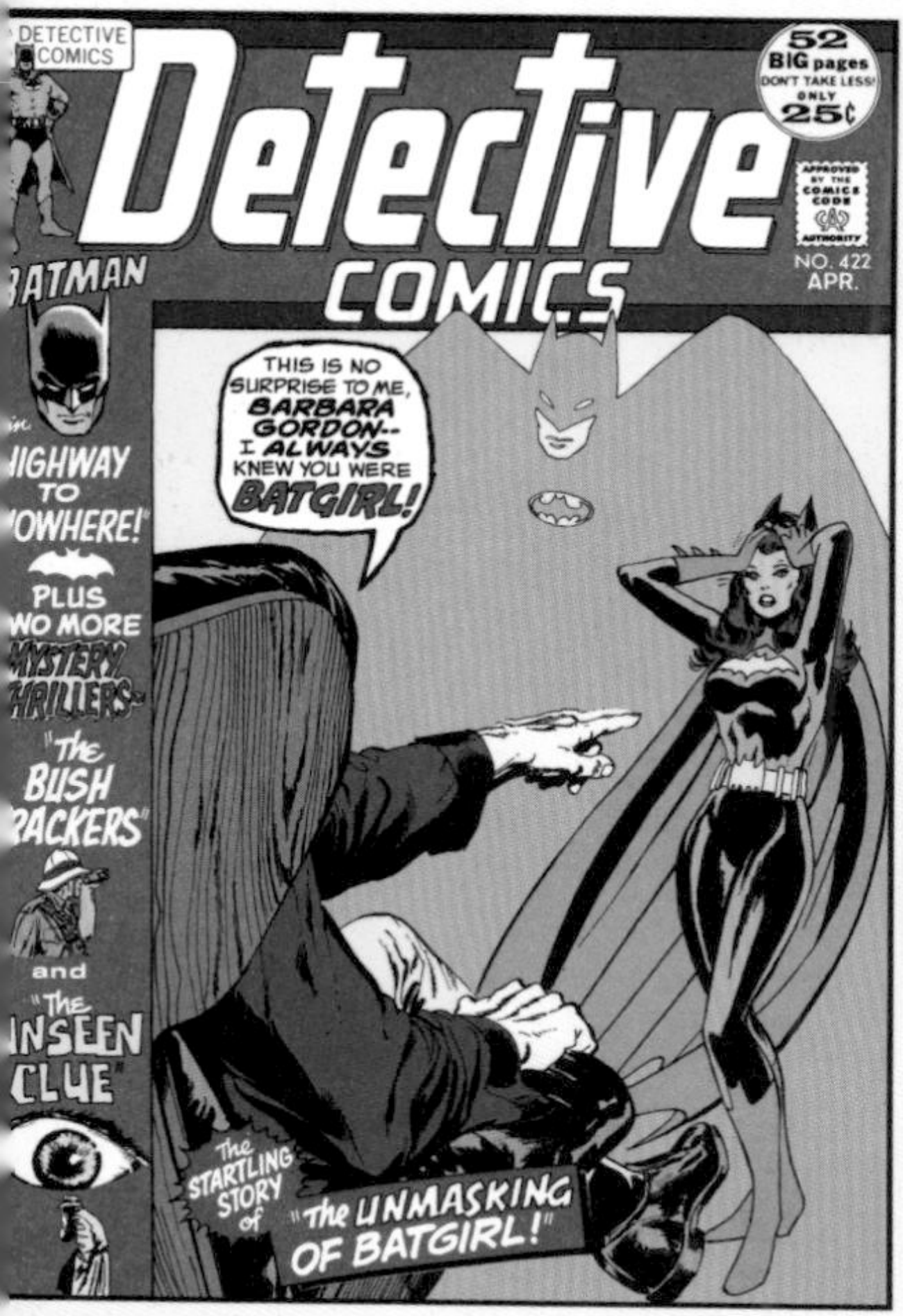
DETECTIVE COMICS
Detective COMICS
52 BIG pages DON'T TAKE LESS! ONLY 25¢
APPROVED BY THE COMICS CODE AUTHORITY
NO. 422 APR.
BATMAN in HIGHWAY TO NOWHERE!
PLUS TWO MORE MYSTERY THRILLERS-
"The BUSH WACKERS"
and "The UNSEEN CLUE"
THIS IS NO SURPRISE TO ME, BARBARA GORDON-- I ALWAYS KNEW YOU WERE BATGIRL!
The STARTLING STORY of "The UNMASKING OF BATGIRL!"

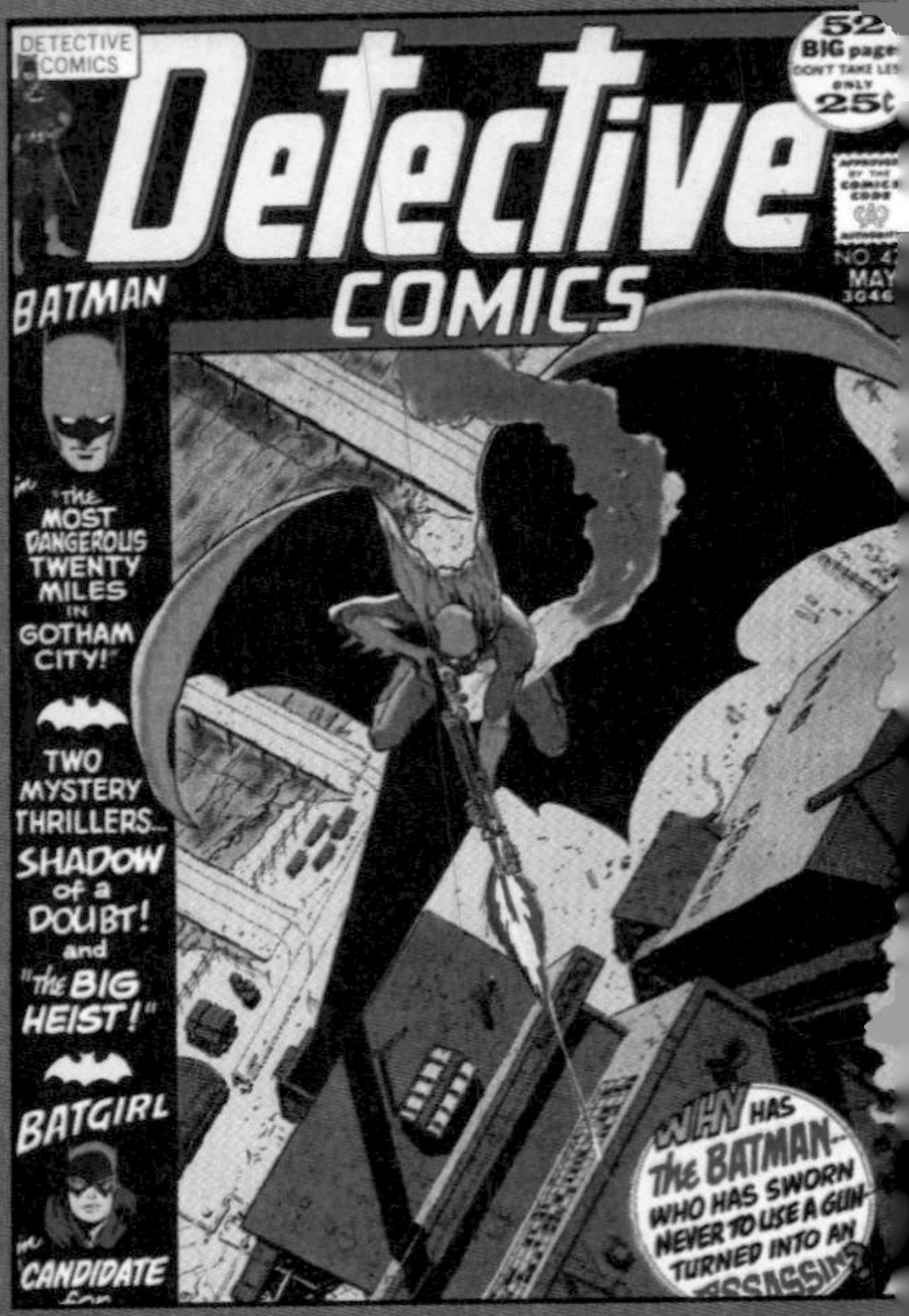
DETECTIVE COMICS
Detective
COMICS
52 BIG page DON'T TAKE LESS ONLY 25¢
APPROVED BY THE COMICS CODE
NO. 4
MAY
1946
BATMAN
in "The MOST DANGEROUS TWENTY MILES IN GOTHAM CITY!"
TWO MYSTERY THRILLERS... SHADOW of a DOUBT! and "The BIG HEIST!"
BATGIRL
in CANDIDATE
JOHN HAS The BATMAN- WHO HAS SWORN NEVER TO USE A GUN TURNED INTO AN ASSASSIN?

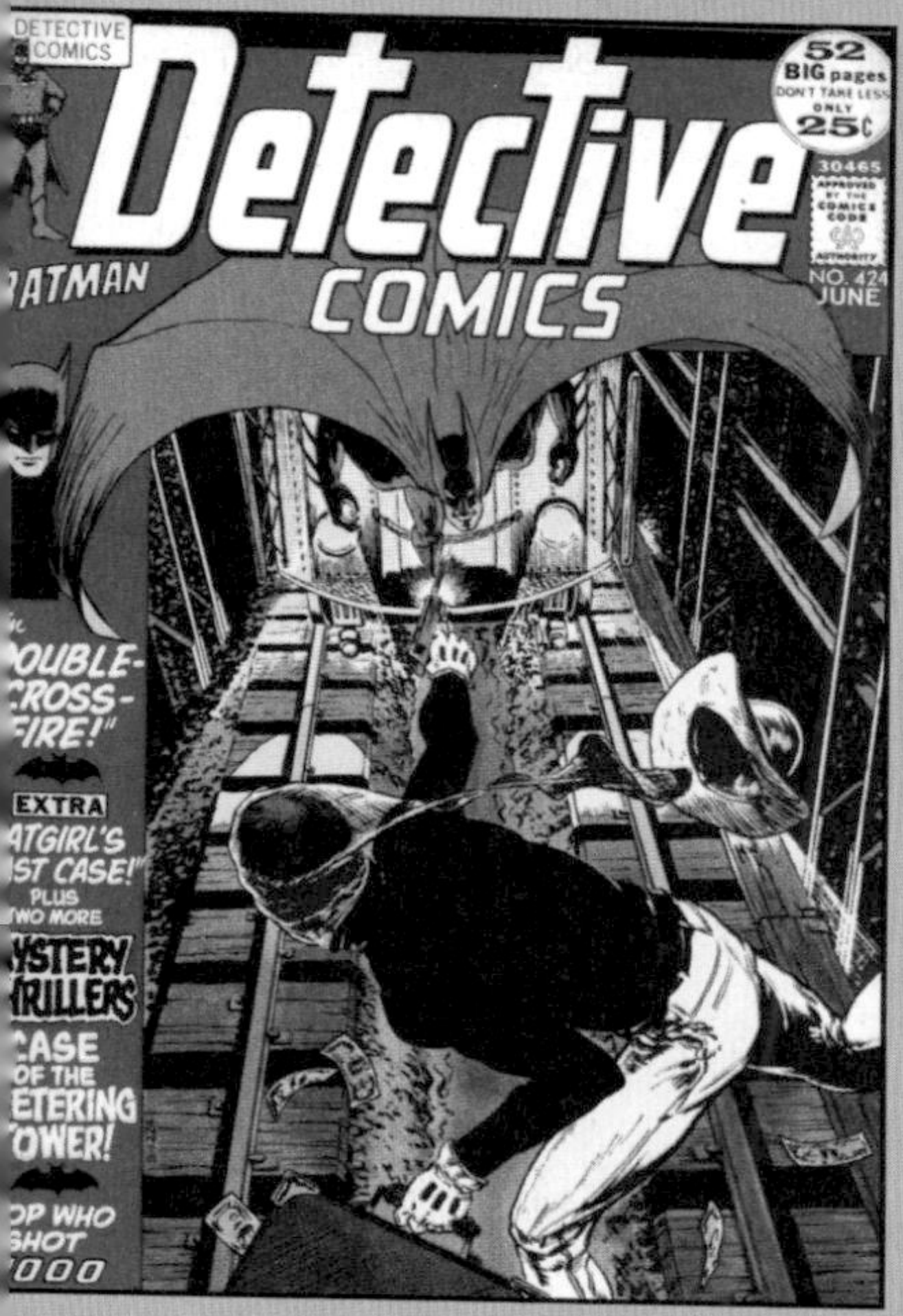
DETECTIVE COMICS
Detective
COMICS
52 BIG pages DON'T TAKE LESS ONLY 25¢
30465
APPROVED BY THE COMICS CODE AUTHORITY
NO. 424 JUNE
BATMAN
"DOUBLE-CROSS-FIRE!"
EXTRA
BATGIRL'S LAST CASE!"
PLUS TWO MORE
MYSTERY THRILLERS
CASE OF THE VETERING TOWER!
TOP WHO SHOT

DETECTIVE DC COMICS

ALL NEW STORIES
BEST IN COMICS

NOW ONLY 20¢

NO. 425
JULY
30465

Detective COMICS

DEATH LURKS IN THE WINGS, AS BATMAN

PLAYS THE STARRING ROLE IN...

"the STAGE IS SET FOR MURDER!"

INTRODUCING A NEW SERIES...

the MASTER CRIME-FILE OF Jason Bard

"the OPEN-AND-SHUT CASE!"

DC COMICS

ALL NEW STORIES
BEST IN COMICS

NOW ONLY 20¢

Detective COMICS

APPROVED BY THE COMICS CODE AUTHORITY

NO. 426
AUG.
30465

TMAN

AYS A
ADLY
ME OF
LER'S
LETTE!

NGATED
MAN
LVES A
FFLING
EW
STERY...
AIL of the
EAWAY
TDOINTS!

To Robin, Batgirl, Superman...
and all those near and dear to me...
Shortly I will take gun in
hand and put an end to what
has become a meaningless life...
a life without honor...
Signed
The Batman

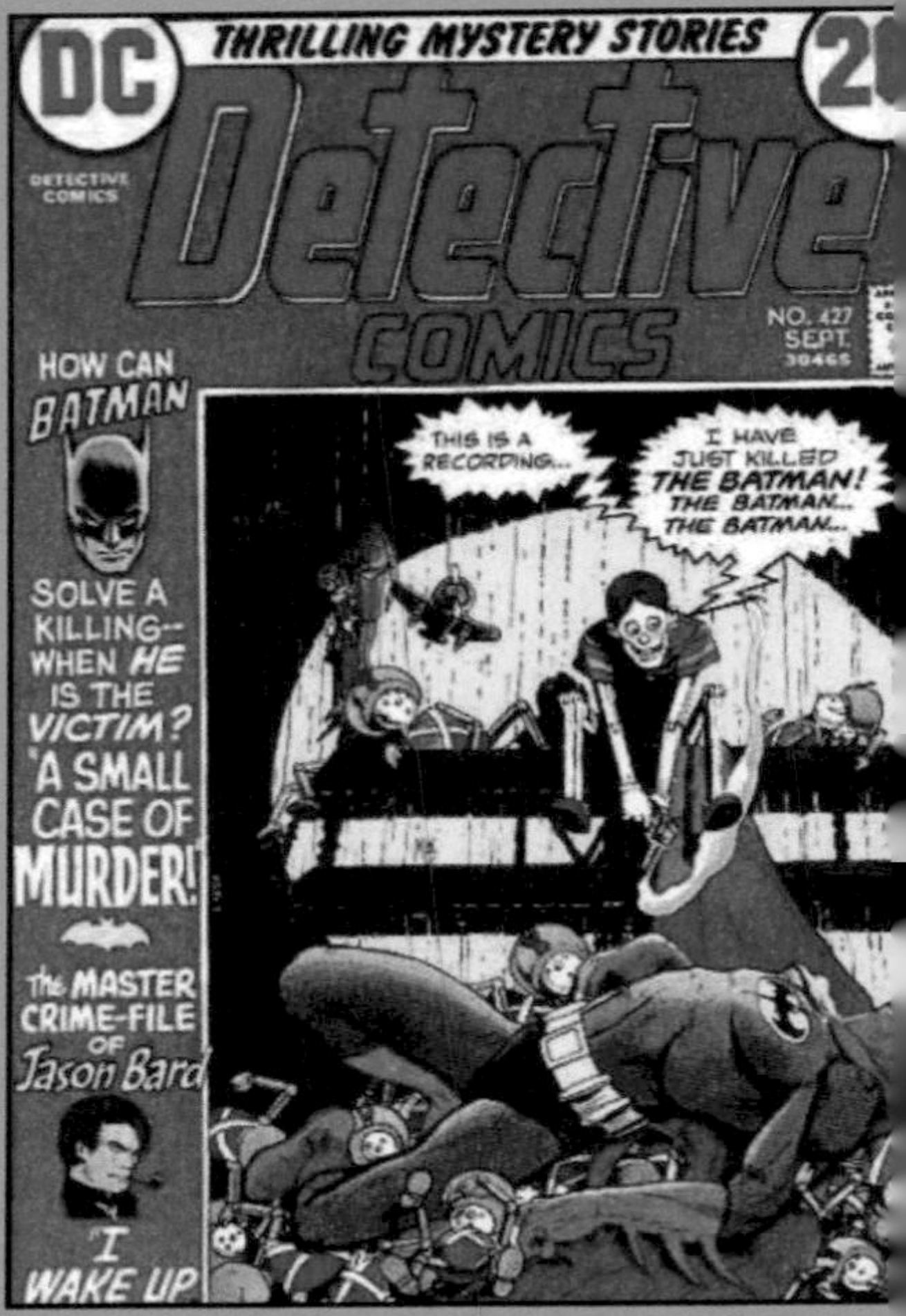
DC
THRILLING MYSTERY STORIES
20
DETECTIVE COMICS
Detective
COMICS
NO. 427
SEPT.
30465
HOW CAN BATMAN
SOLVE A KILLING-- WHEN HE IS THE VICTIM?
"A SMALL CASE OF MURDER!"
The MASTER CRIME-FILE OF Jason Bard
"I WAKE UP
THIS IS A RECORDING...
I HAVE JUST KILLED THE BATMAN! THE BATMAN... THE BATMAN...

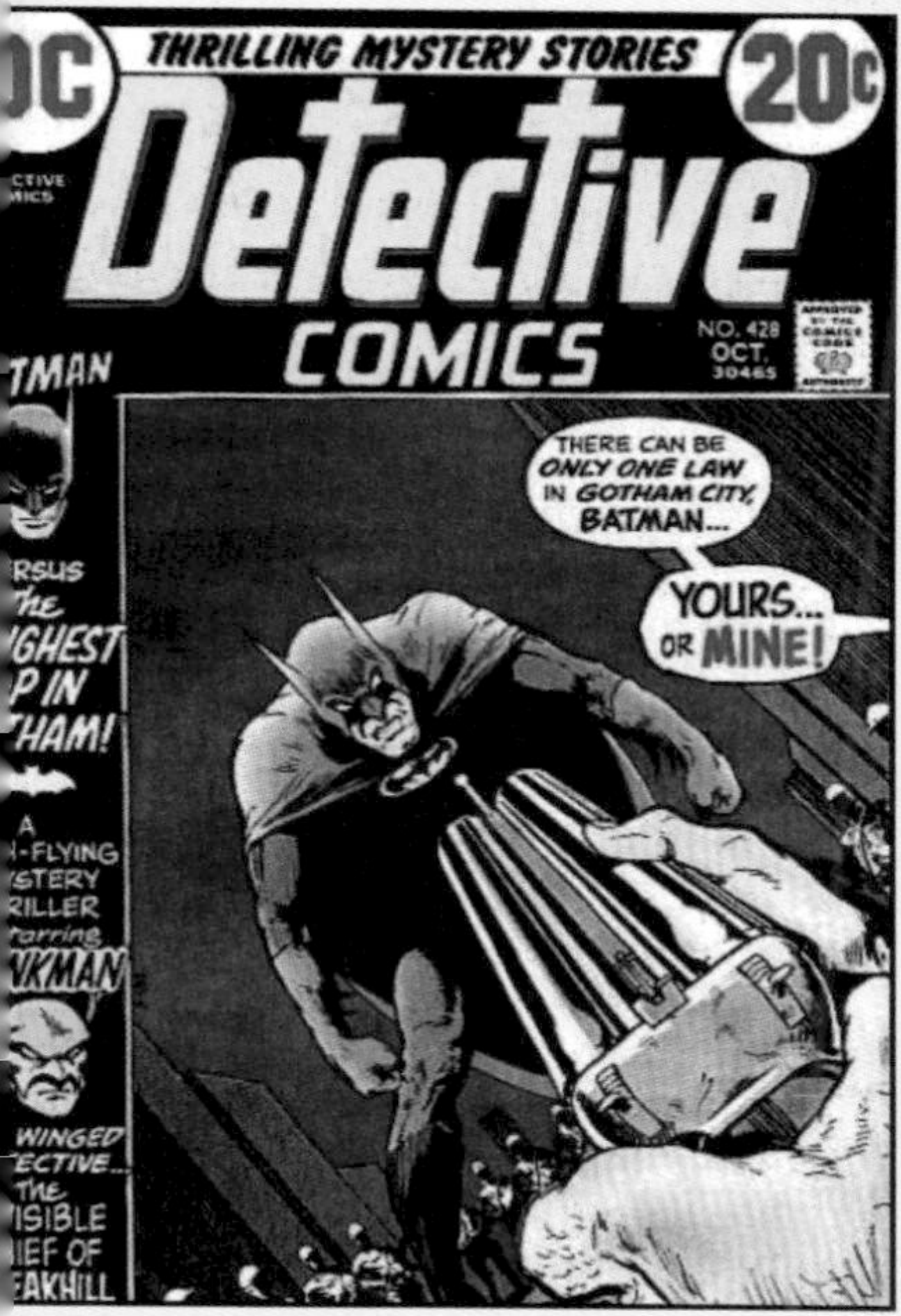
THRILLING MYSTERY STORIES
20c
Detective
COMICS
NO. 428
OCT.
30465
THERE CAN BE ONLY ONE LAW IN GOTHAM CITY, BATMAN...
YOURS... OR MINE!

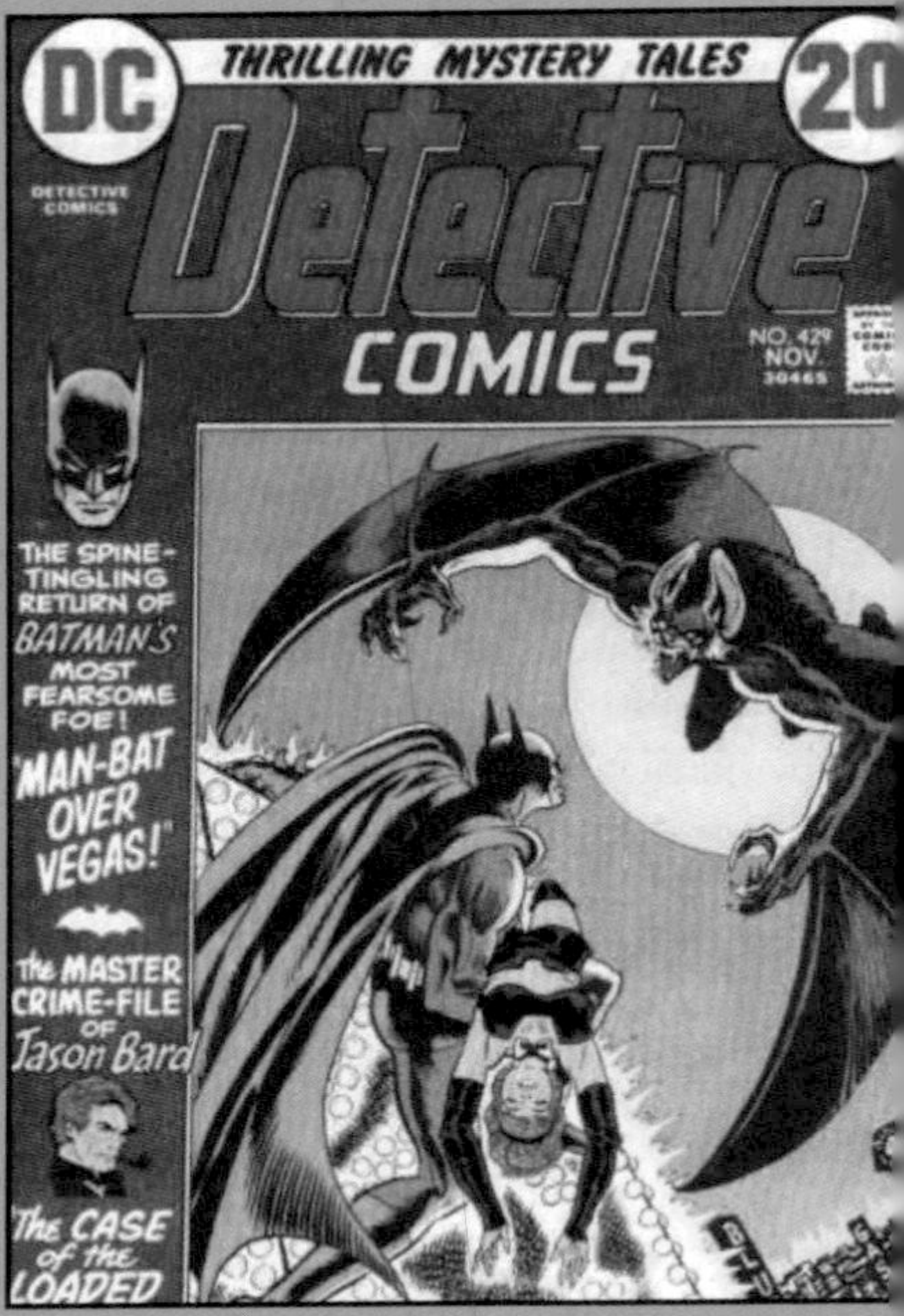
DC
THRILLING MYSTERY TALES
20
DETECTIVE COMICS
Detective
COMICS
NO. 429
NOV.
30465
THE SPINE-TINGLING RETURN OF BATMAN'S MOST FEARSOME FOE!
"MAN-BAT OVER VEGAS!"
The MASTER CRIME-FILE OF Jason Bard
"The CASE of the LOADED

DC

THRILLING MYSTERY TALES

20c

ETECTIVE COMICS

Detective COMICS

NO. 430
DEC.
30465

APPROVED BY THE COMICS CODE AUTHORITY

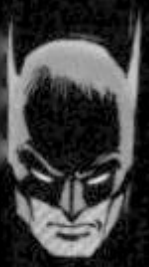

THE ARTLING STORY OF A ANGSTER WHO SCOVERED BATMAN'S ECRET DENTITY! CLUE OF THE ALSE ACES!"

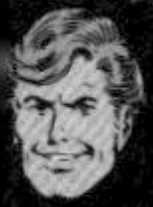

THE ONGATED MAN LVES THE AFFLING ASE OF "THE UNTED TUDIO YSTERY!"

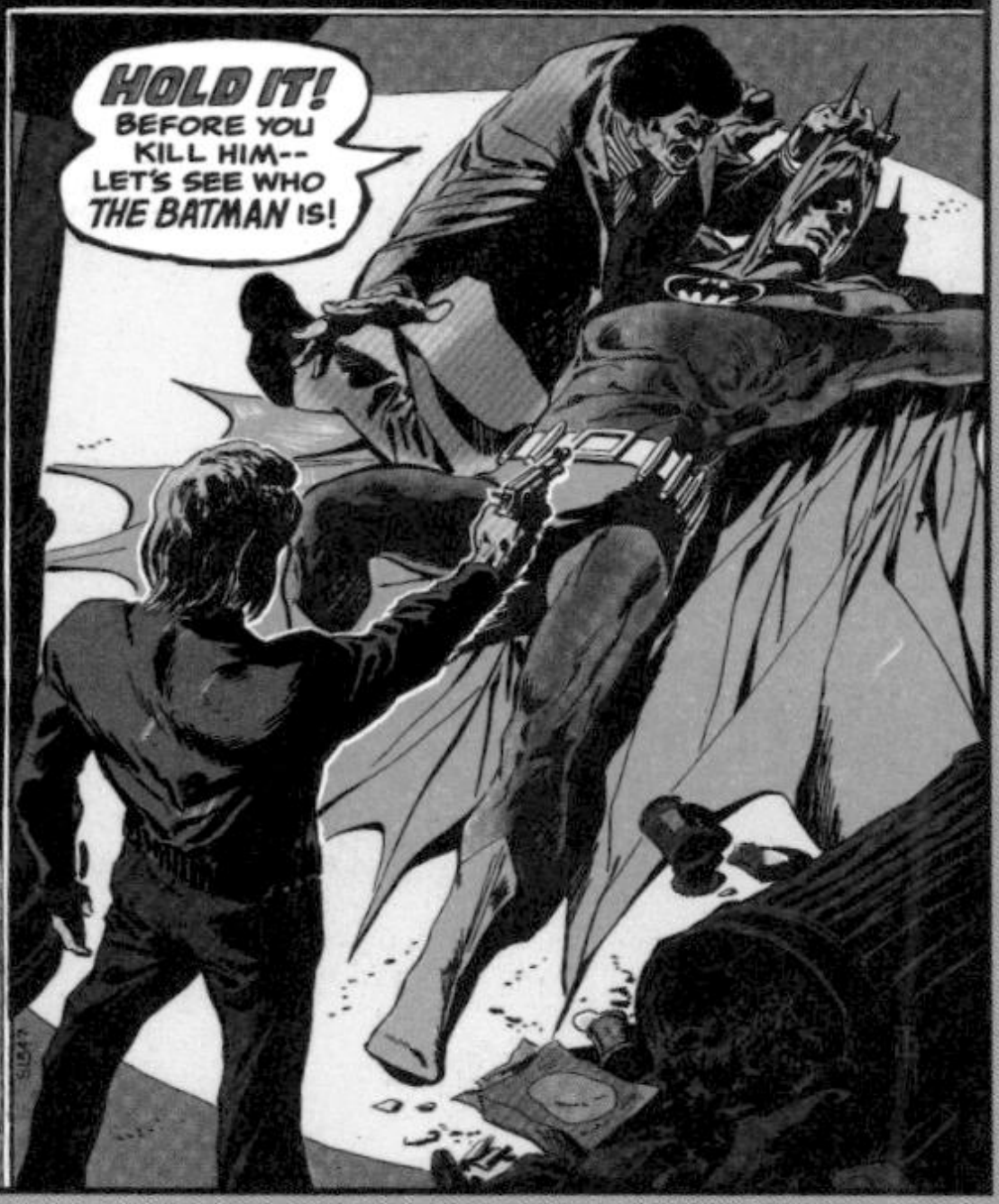

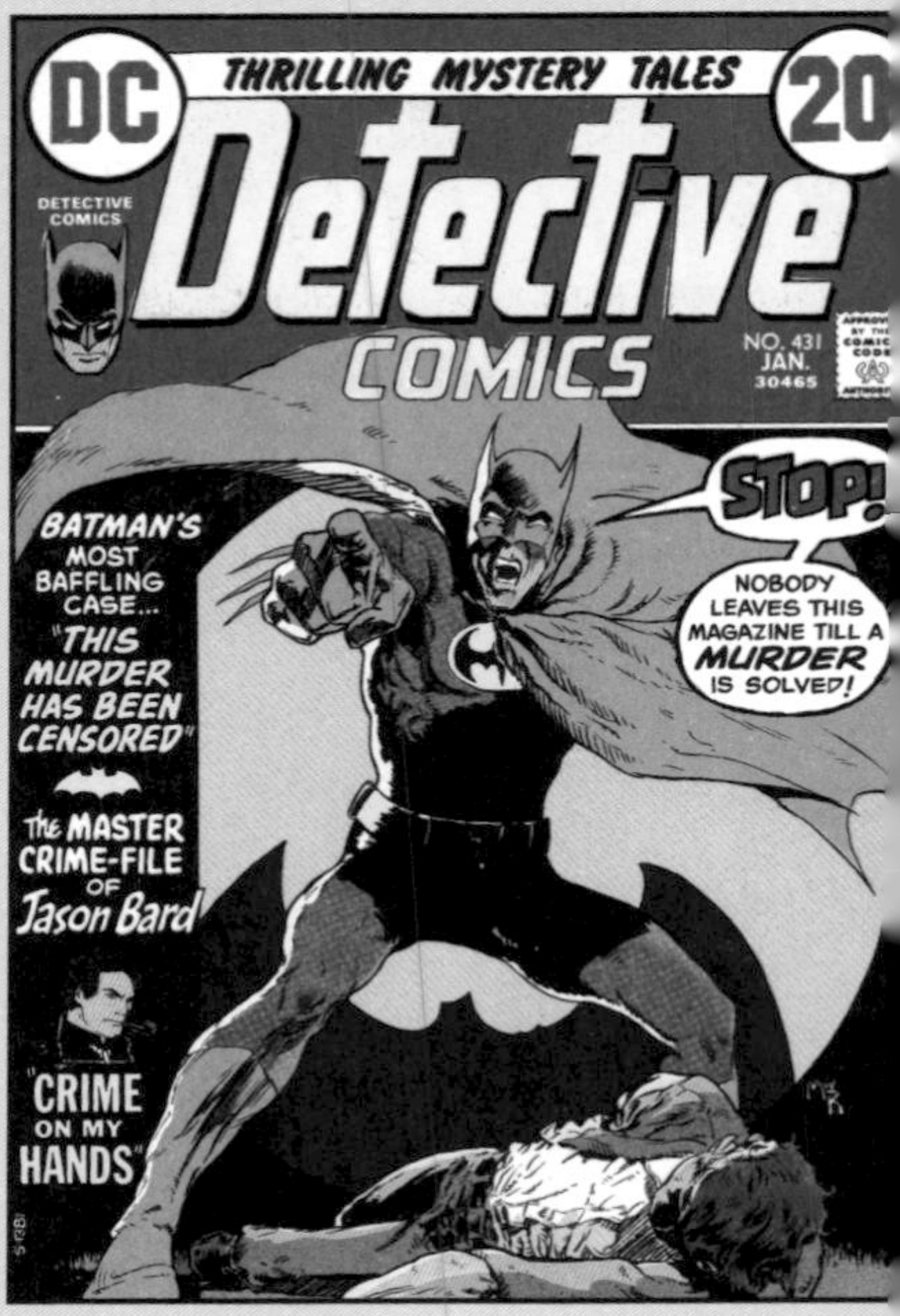
DC
THRILLING MYSTERY TALES
20
DETECTIVE COMICS
Detective
COMICS
NO. 431
JAN.
30465
STOP!
NOBODY LEAVES THIS MAGAZINE TILL A MURDER IS SOLVED!
BATMAN'S MOST BAFFLING CASE...
"THIS MURDER HAS BEEN CENSORED"
The MASTER CRIME-FILE OF Jason Bard
"CRIME ON MY HANDS"

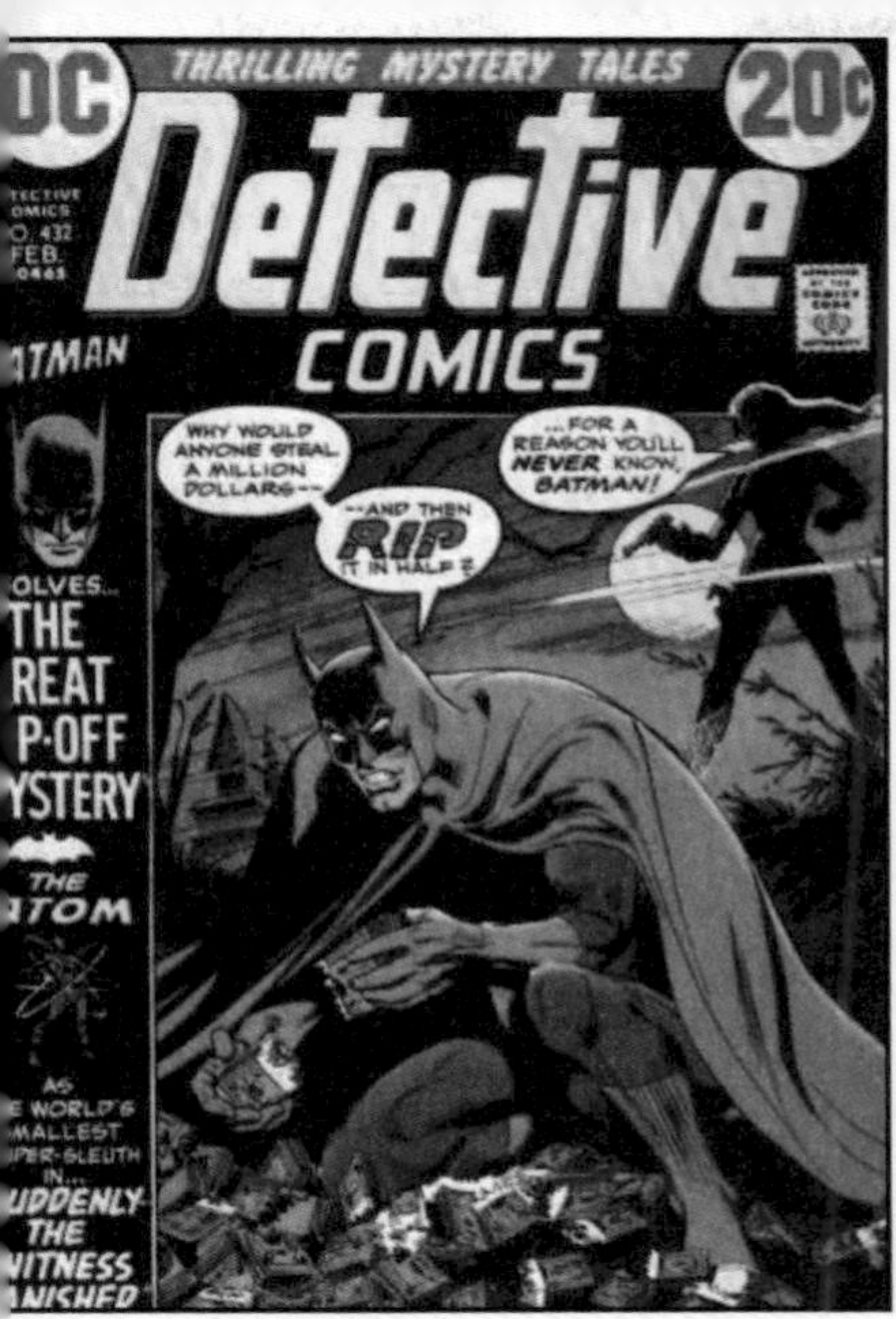
THRILLING MYSTERY TALES
DC
20c
Detective
COMICS
TECTIVE
OMICS
O. 432
FEB.
ATMAN
OLVES...
THE
REAT
P-OFF
YSTERY
THE
ITOM
AS
E WORLD'S
MALLEST
PER-SLEUTH
IN...
UDDENLY
THE
ITNESS
ANISHED
WHY WOULD ANYONE STEAL A MILLION DOLLARS--
--AND THEN RIP IT IN HALF?
...FOR A REASON YOU'LL NEVER KNOW, BATMAN!

DC

THRILLING MYSTERY TALES

20

DETECTIVE COMICS

Detective COMICS

NO. 433
MAR.

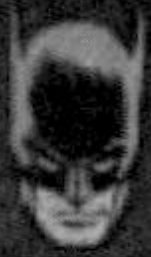

BATMAN CHALLENGES THE READER TO GUESS WHO IS... "The KILLER IN THE SMOG!"

The MASTER CRIME-FILE OF Jason Bard

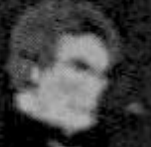

"CASE OF THE FORGED

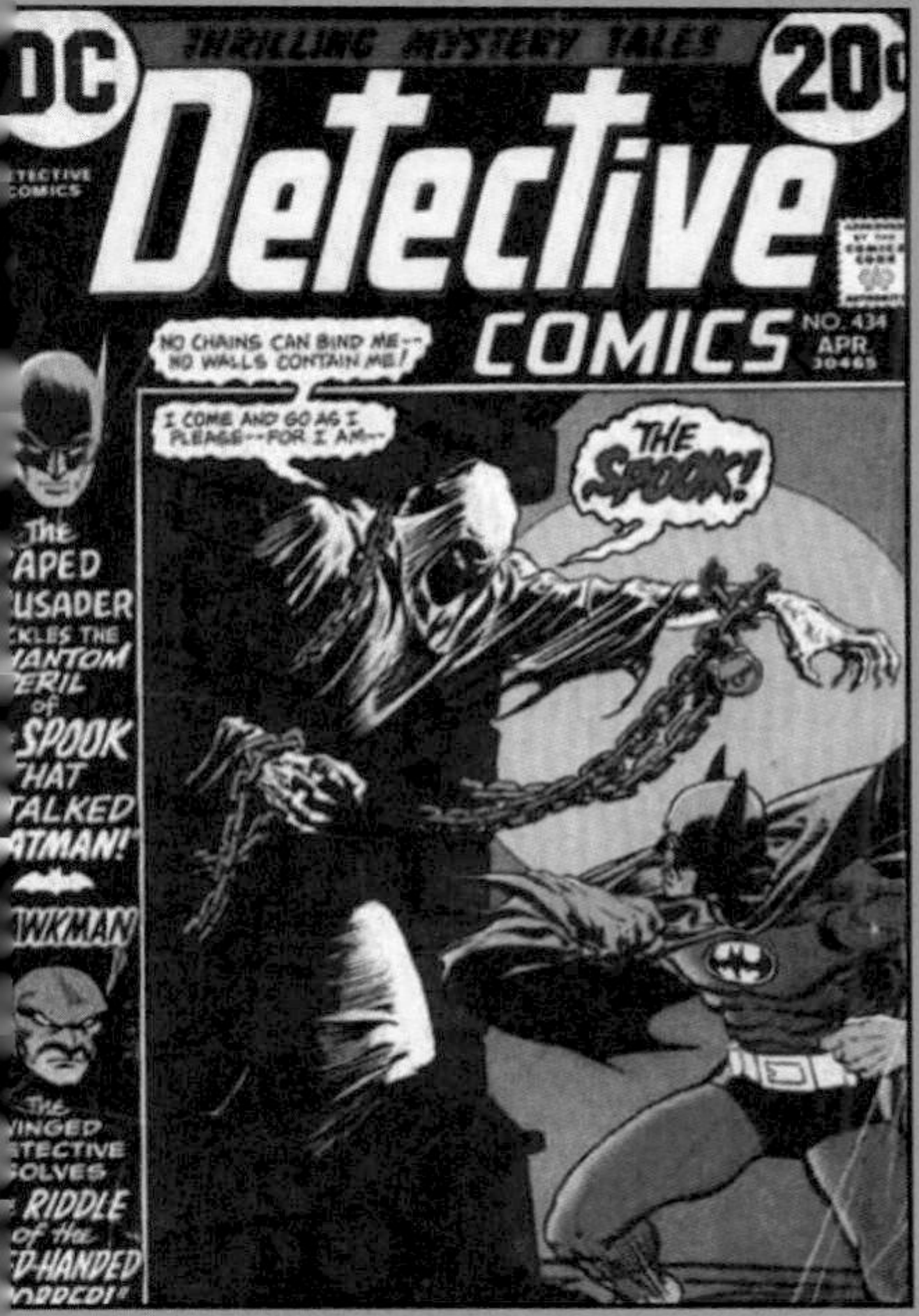
DC
THRILLING MYSTERY TALES
20¢
Detective
COMICS
NO. 434
APR.
NO CHAINS CAN BIND ME-- NO WALLS CONTAIN ME!
I COME AND GO AS I PLEASE--FOR I AM--
THE SPOOK!
The CAPED CRUSADER TACKLES THE PHANTOM PERIL of the SPOOK THAT STALKED BATMAN!
HAWKMAN
The WINGED DETECTIVE SOLVES THE RIDDLE of the RED-HANDED MURDER!

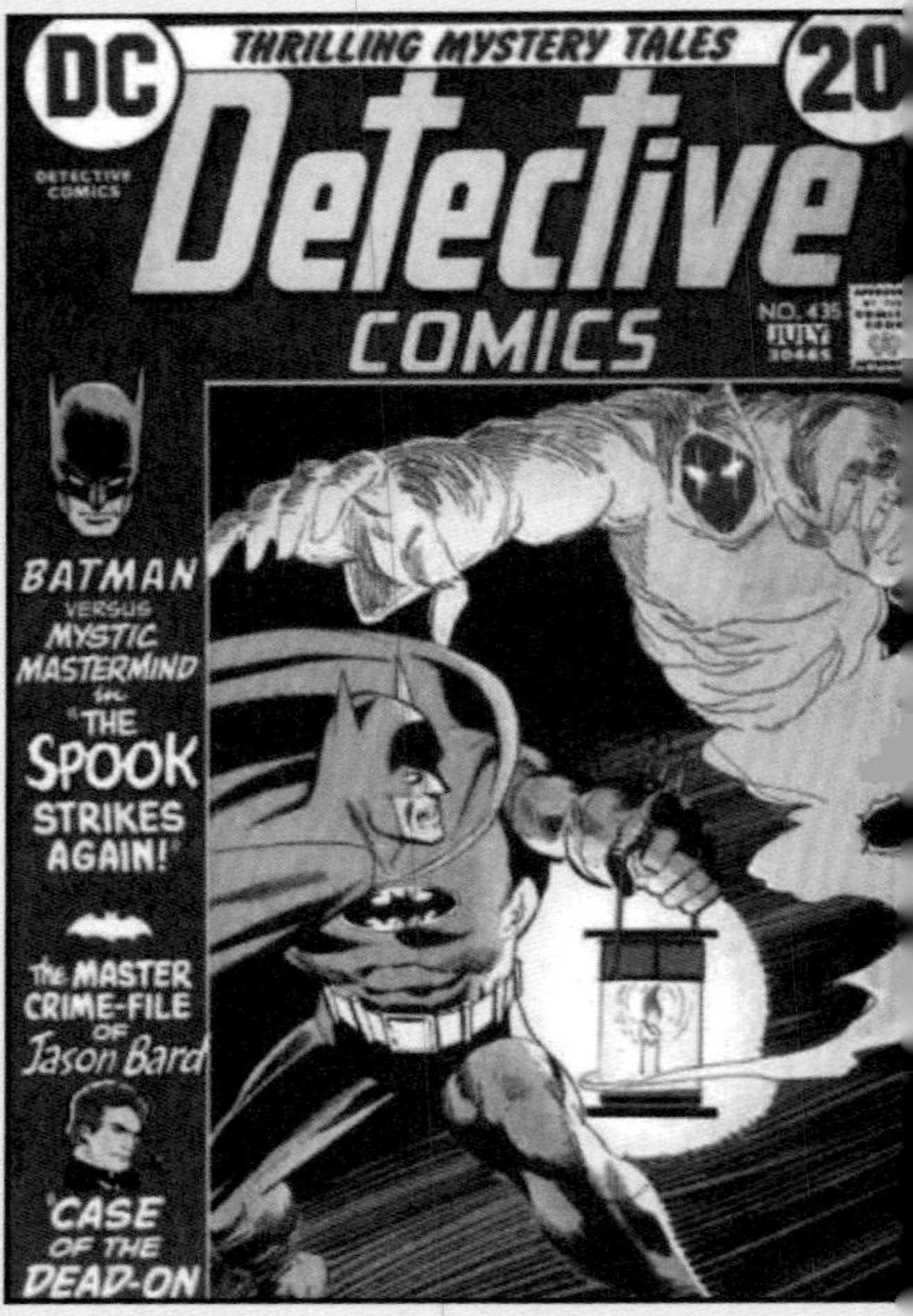
DC
THRILLING MYSTERY TALES
20
DETECTIVE COMICS
Detective
COMICS
NO. 435
JULY
BATMAN
VERSUS
MYSTIC MASTERMIND
in
"THE SPOOK STRIKES AGAIN!"
The MASTER CRIME-FILE OF Jason Bard
"CASE OF THE DEAD-ON

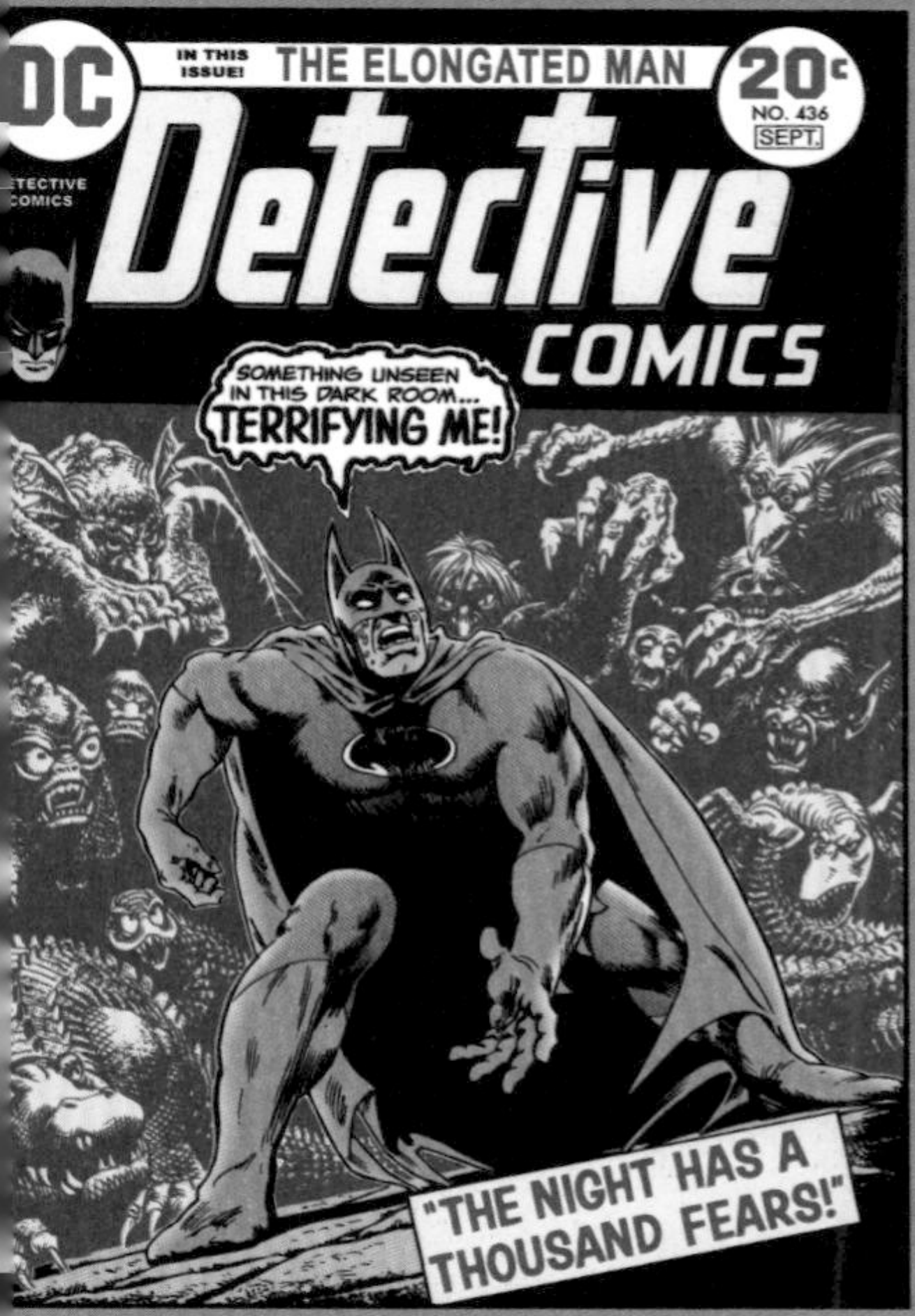
DC
IN THIS ISSUE!
THE ELONGATED MAN
20c
NO. 436
SEPT.
ETECTIVE COMICS
Detective
COMICS
SOMETHING UNSEEN IN THIS DARK ROOM... TERRIFYING ME!
"THE NIGHT HAS A THOUSAND FEARS!"

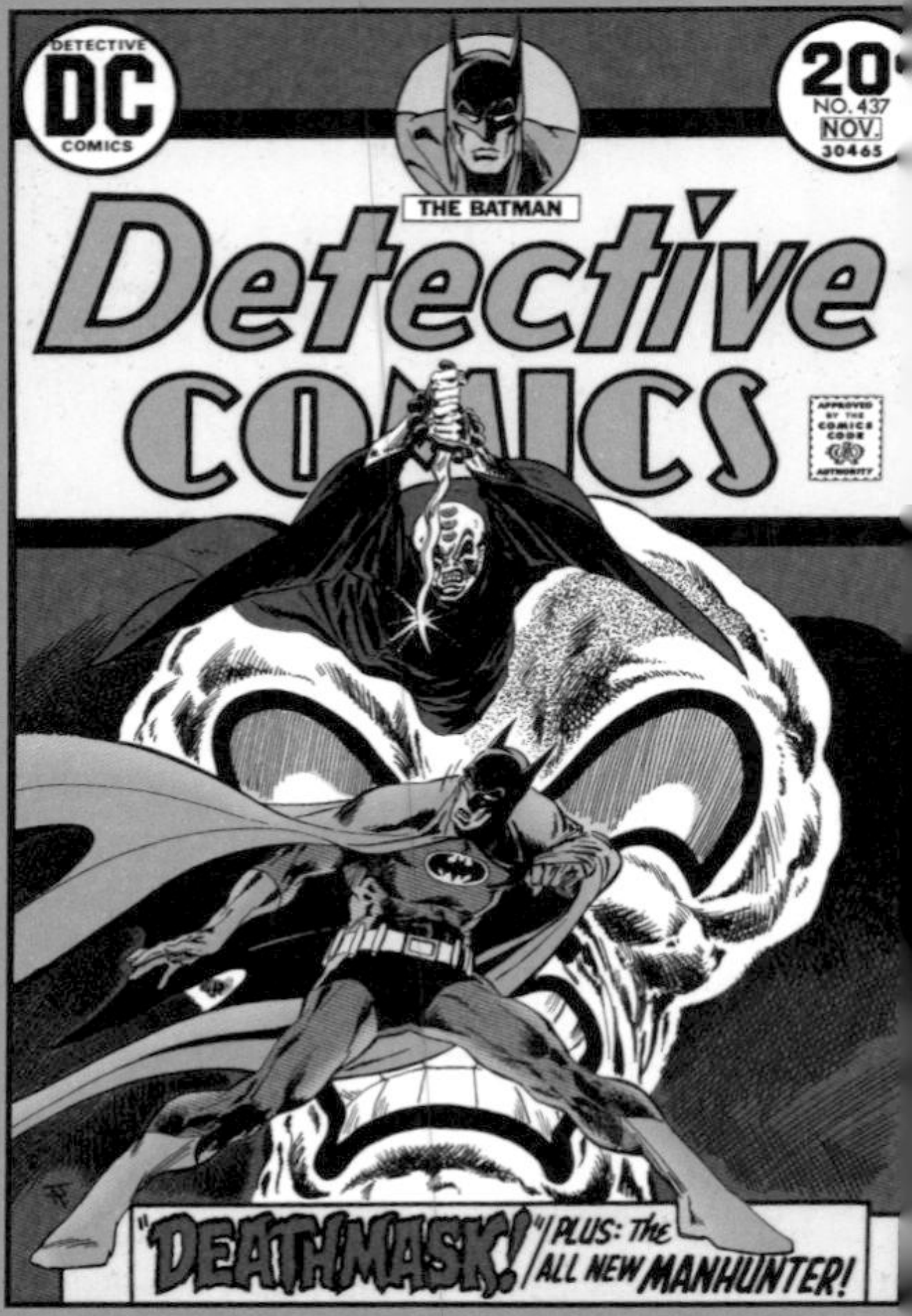
DETECTIVE
DC
COMICS
20¢
NO. 437
NOV.
30465
THE BATMAN
Detective
COMICS
APPROVED BY THE COMICS CODE AUTHORITY
"DEATHMASK!"
PLUS: THE ALL NEW MANHUNTER!

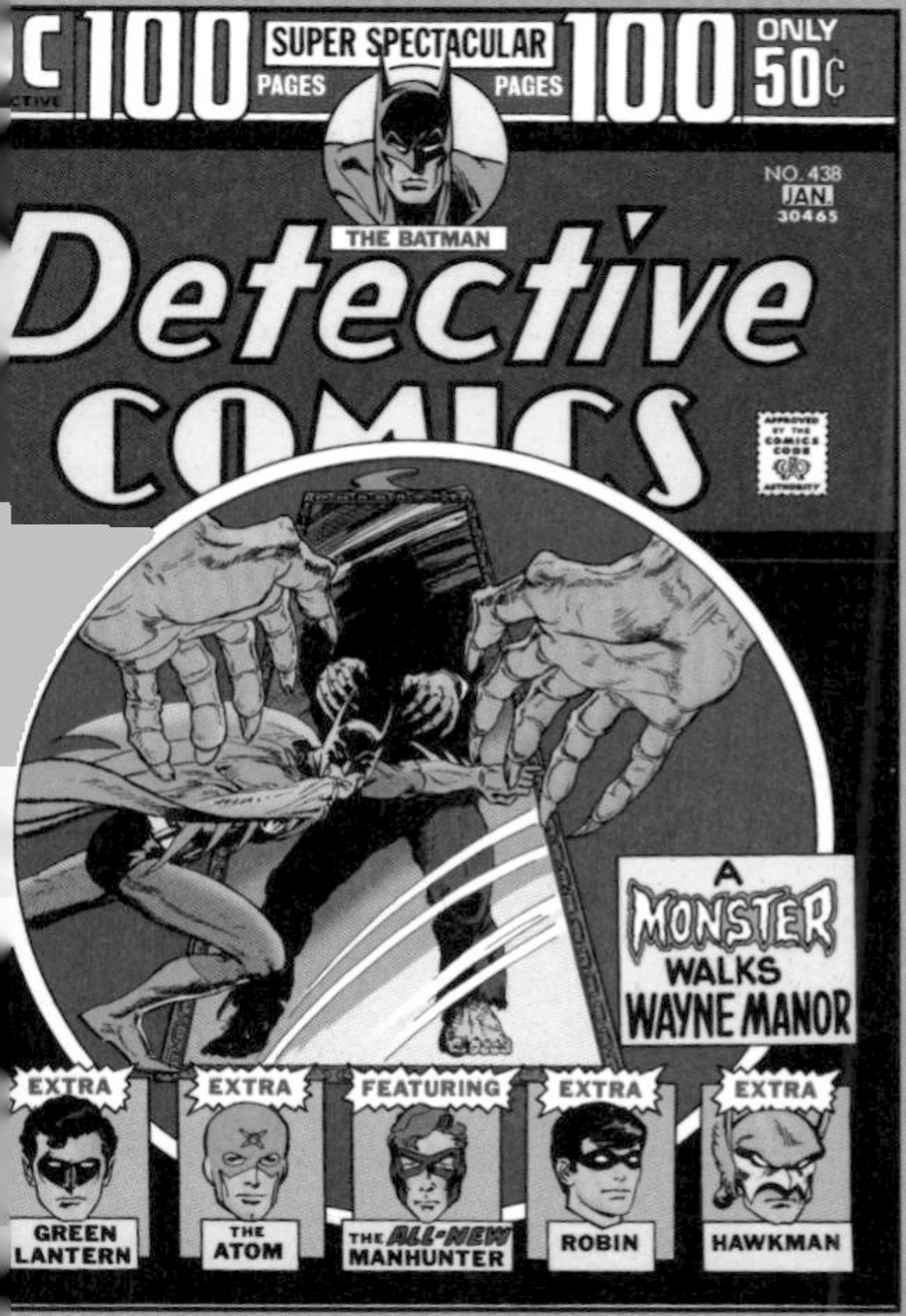
100 PAGES
SUPER SPECTACULAR
100 PAGES
ONLY 50¢
NO. 438
JAN.
30465
THE BATMAN
Detective COMICS
APPROVED BY THE COMICS CODE AUTHORITY
A MONSTER WALKS WAYNE MANOR
EXTRA
GREEN LANTERN
EXTRA
THE ATOM
FEATURING
THE ALL-NEW MANHUNTER
EXTRA
ROBIN
EXTRA
HAWKMAN

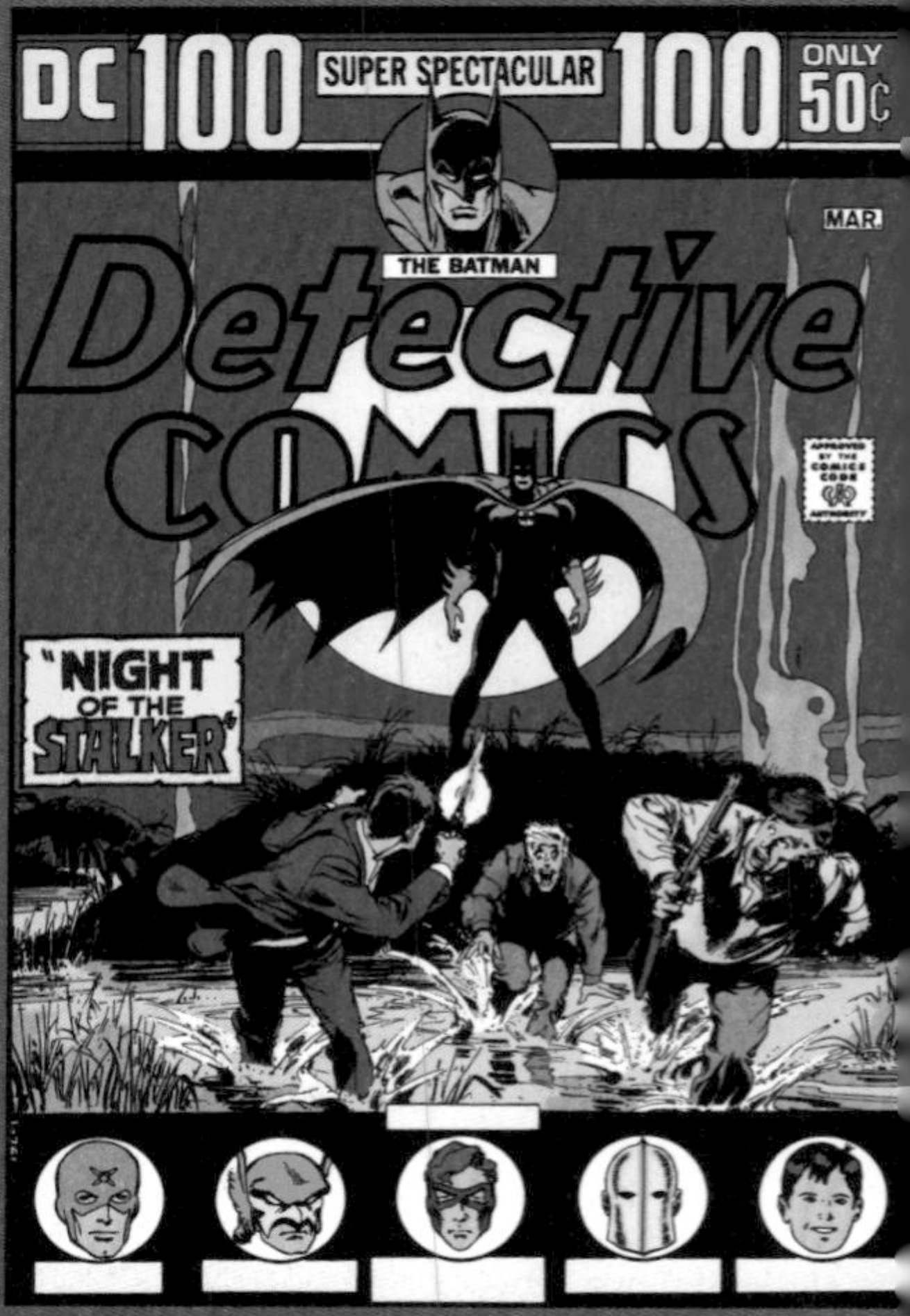
DC 100 SUPER SPECTACULAR 100
ONLY 50¢
MAR.
THE BATMAN
Detective COMICS
APPROVED BY THE COMICS CODE AUTHORITY
"NIGHT OF THE STALKER"

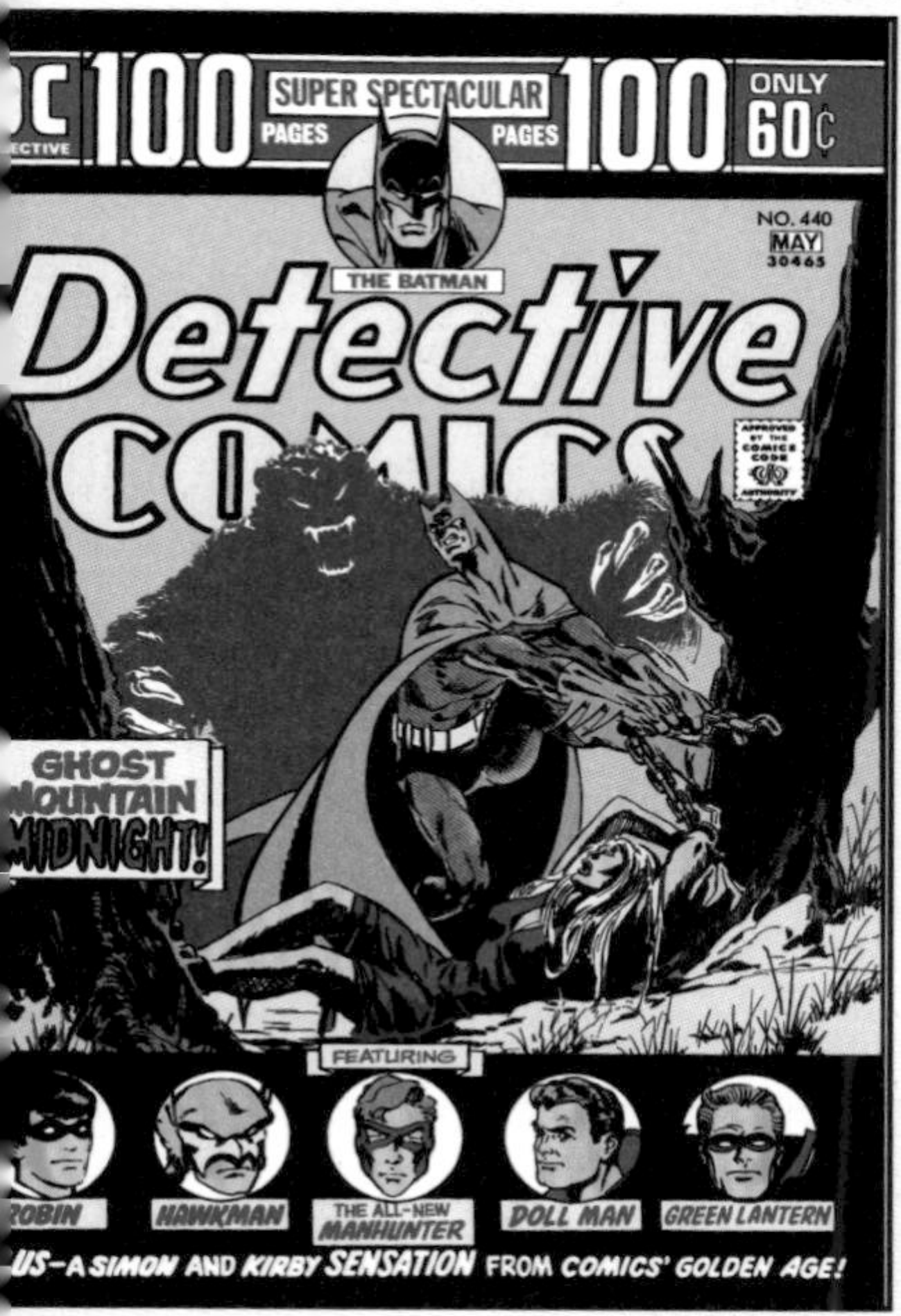
DC
ECTIVE
100
PAGES
SUPER SPECTACULAR
100
PAGES
ONLY
60¢
NO. 440
MAY
30465
THE BATMAN
Detective
COMICS
APPROVED BY THE COMICS CODE AUTHORITY
GHOST MOUNTAIN MIDNIGHT!
FEATURING
ROBIN
HAWKMAN
THE ALL-NEW MANHUNTER
DOLL MAN
GREEN LANTERN
US—A SIMON AND KIRBY SENSATION FROM COMICS' GOLDEN AGE!

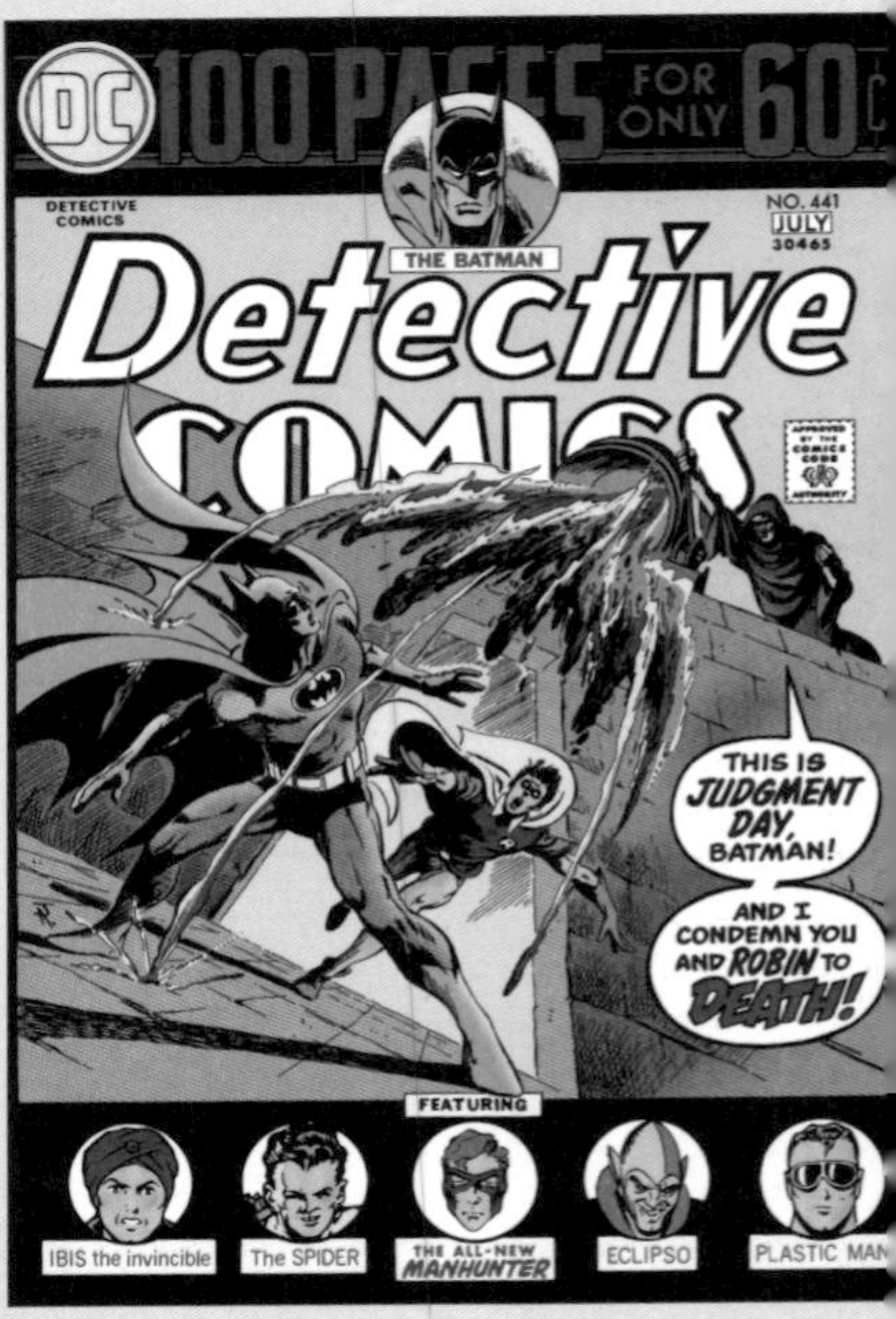
DC
100 PAGES FOR ONLY 60¢
DETECTIVE COMICS
NO. 441
JULY
30465
THE BATMAN
Detective COMICS
APPROVED BY THE COMICS CODE AUTHORITY
THIS IS JUDGMENT DAY, BATMAN!
AND I CONDEMN YOU AND ROBIN TO DEATH!
FEATURING
IBIS the invincible
The SPIDER
THE ALL-NEW MANHUNTER
ECLIPSO
PLASTIC MAN

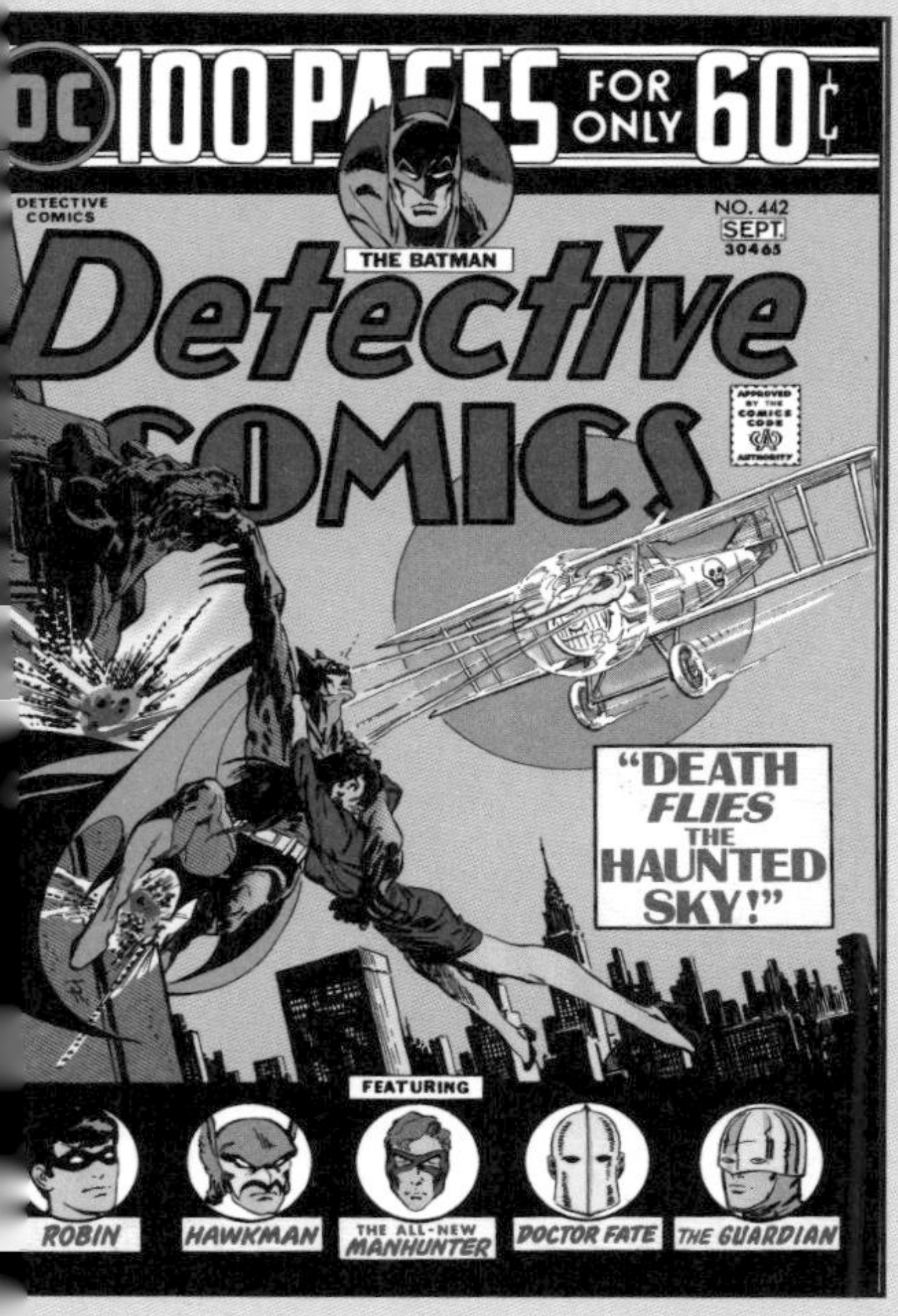
DC 100 PAGES FOR ONLY 60¢
DETECTIVE COMICS
NO. 442
SEPT.
30465
THE BATMAN
Detective COMICS
APPROVED BY THE COMICS CODE AUTHORITY
"DEATH FLIES THE HAUNTED SKY!"
FEATURING
ROBIN
HAWKMAN
THE ALL-NEW MANHUNTER
DOCTOR FATE
THE GUARDIAN

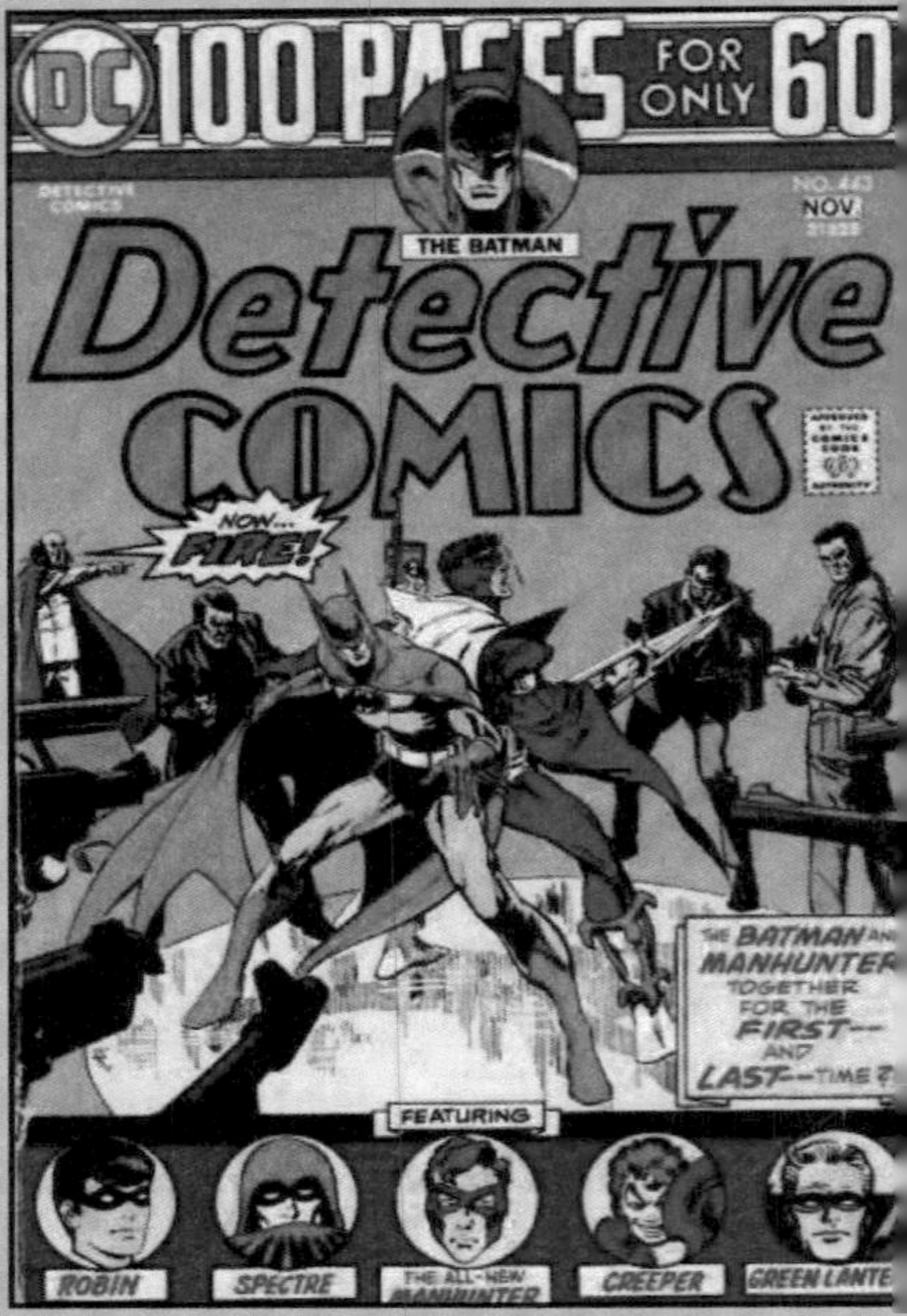
DC
100 PAGES FOR ONLY 60
DETECTIVE COMICS
NO. 463
NOV.
THE BATMAN
Detective COMICS
NOW... FIRE!
THE BATMAN AND MANHUNTER TOGETHER FOR THE FIRST-- AND LAST--TIME?
FEATURING
ROBIN
SPECTRE
THE ALL-NEW MANHUNTER
CREEPER
GREEN LANTE

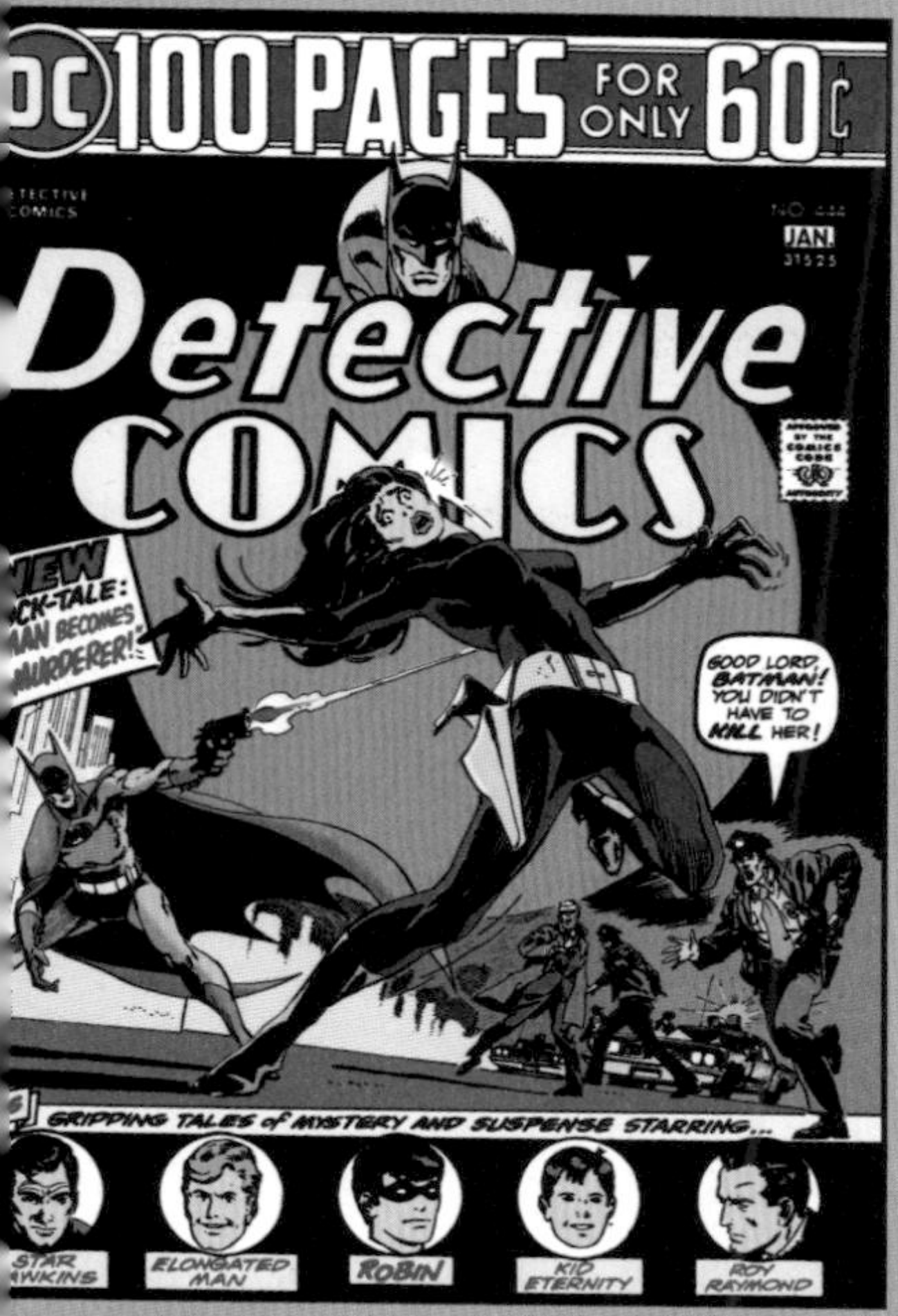
DC 100 PAGES FOR ONLY 60¢
DETECTIVE COMICS
JAN.
Detective COMICS
APPROVED BY THE COMICS CODE AUTHORITY
NEW ROCK-TALE: MAN BECOMES MURDERER!
GOOD LORD, BATMAN! YOU DIDN'T HAVE TO KILL HER!
GRIPPING TALES of MYSTERY AND SUSPENSE STARRING...
STAR HAWKINS
ELONGATED MAN
ROBIN
KID ETERNITY
ROY RAYMOND

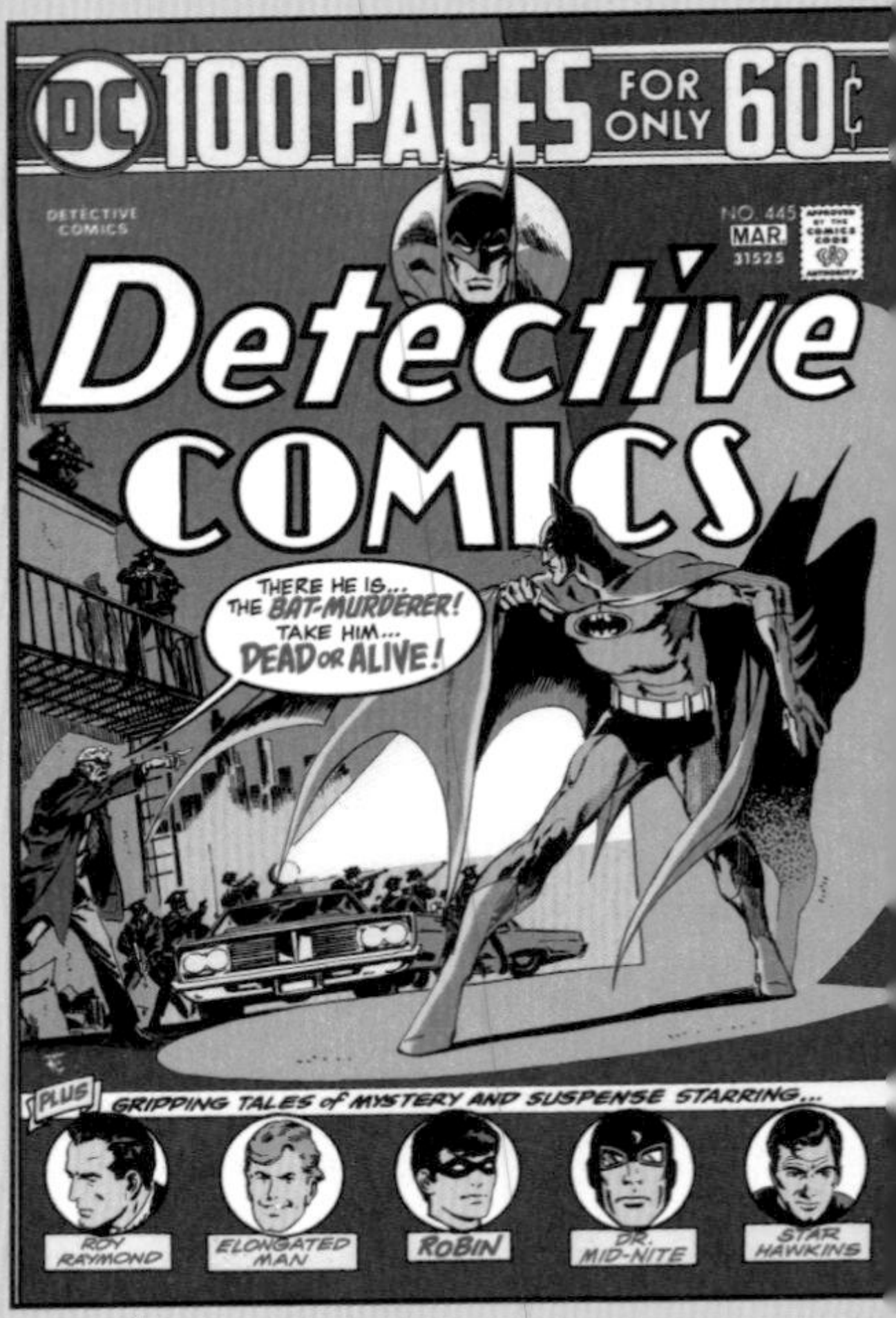
DC
100 PAGES FOR ONLY 60¢
DETECTIVE COMICS
NO. 445
MAR.
31525
Detective COMICS
THERE HE IS... THE BAT-MURDERER! TAKE HIM... DEAD OR ALIVE!
PLUS
GRIPPING TALES of MYSTERY AND SUSPENSE STARRING...
ROY RAYMOND
ELONGATED MAN
ROBIN
DR. MID-NITE
STAR HAWKINS

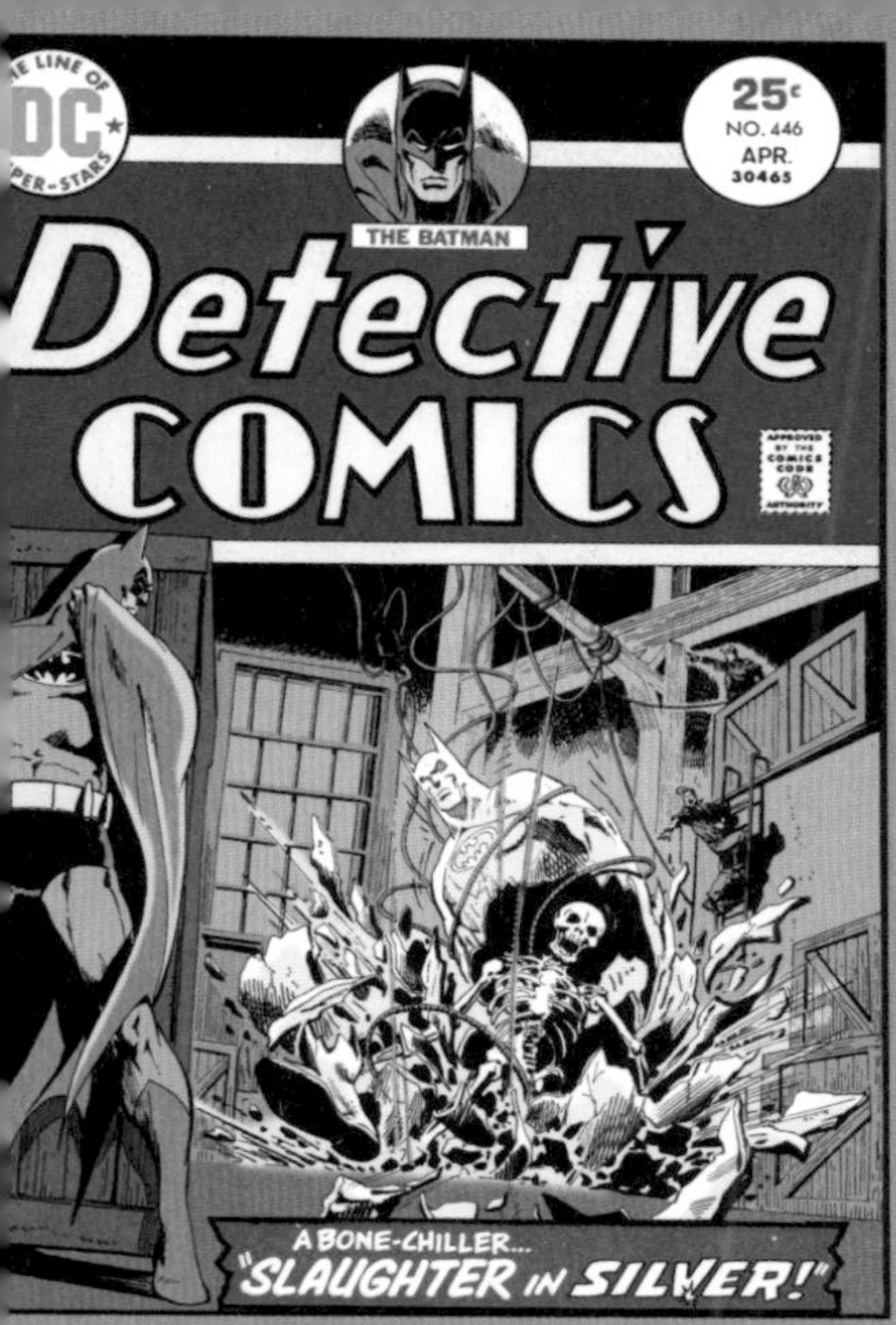
THE LINE OF DC SUPER-STARS
25¢
NO. 446
APR.
30465
THE BATMAN
Detective COMICS
APPROVED BY THE COMICS CODE AUTHORITY
A BONE-CHILLER...
"SLAUGHTER IN SILVER!"

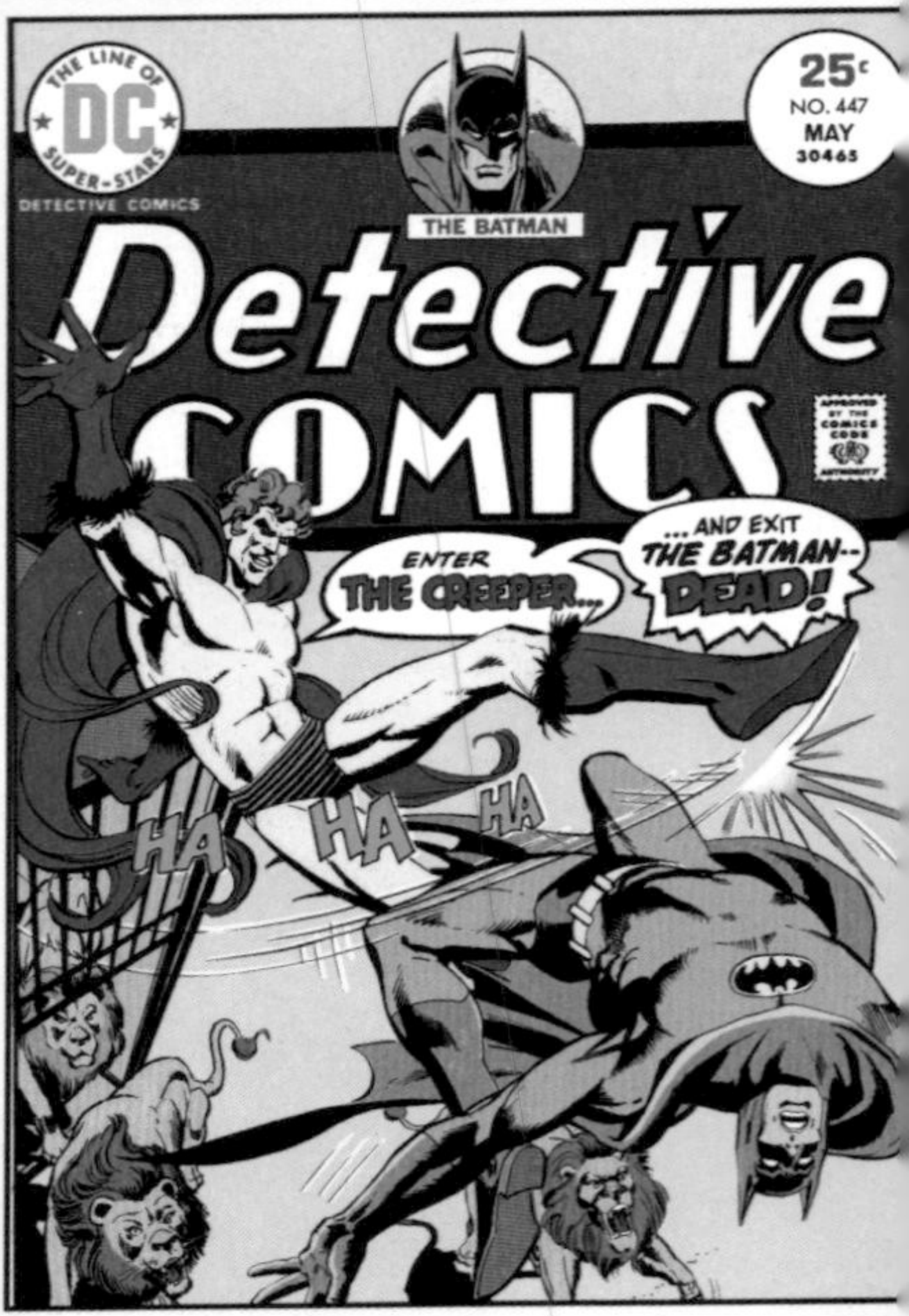
THE LINE OF DC SUPER-STARS
DETECTIVE COMICS
THE BATMAN
Detective COMICS
25¢
NO. 447
MAY
30465
APPROVED BY THE COMICS CODE AUTHORITY
ENTER THE CREEPER...
...AND EXIT THE BATMAN-- DEAD!
HA
HA
HA

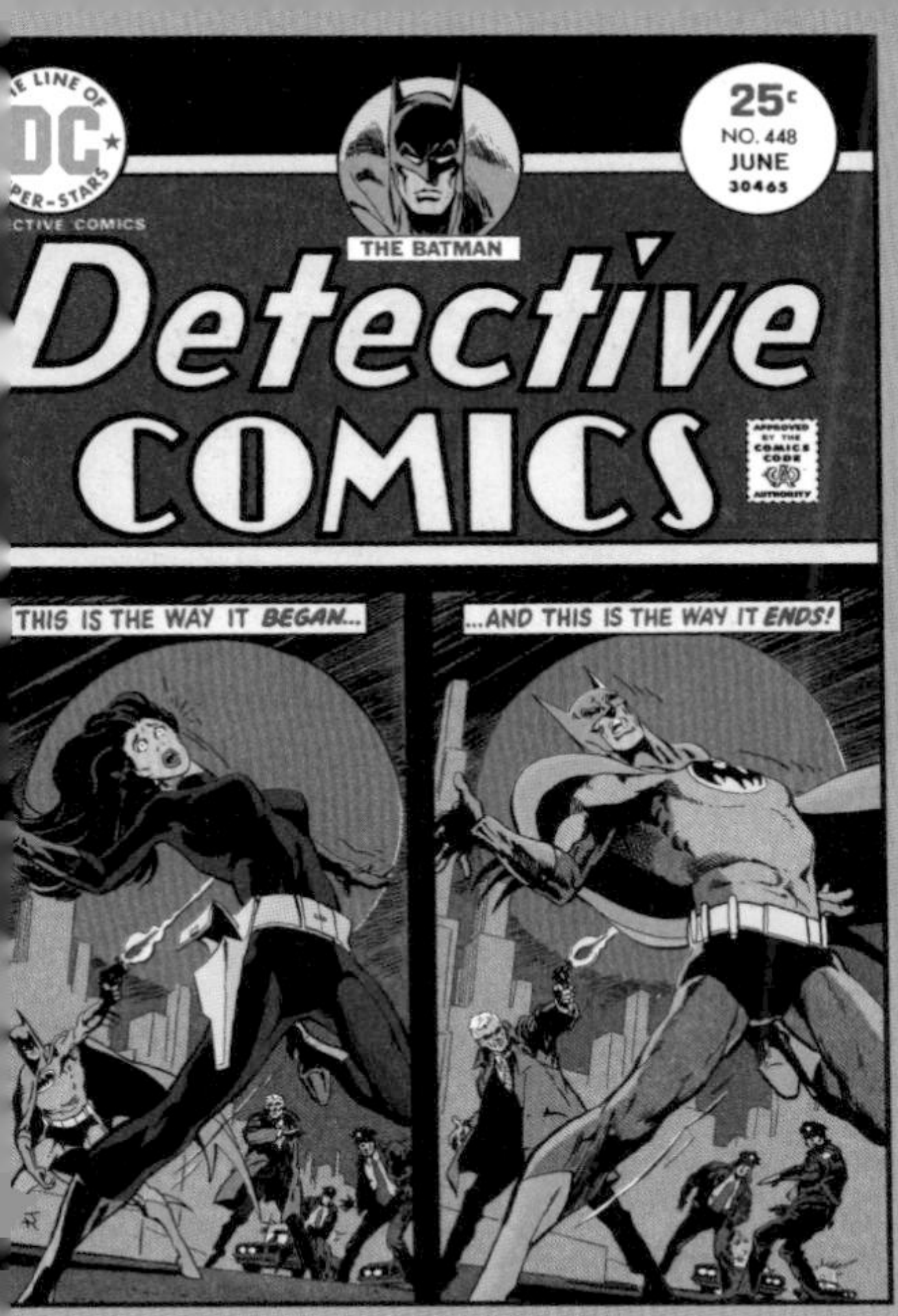
THE LINE OF
DC
PER-STARS
CTIVE COMICS
25c
NO. 448
JUNE
30465
THE BATMAN
Detective
COMICS
APPROVED BY THE COMICS CODE AUTHORITY
THIS IS THE WAY IT BEGAN...
...AND THIS IS THE WAY IT ENDS!

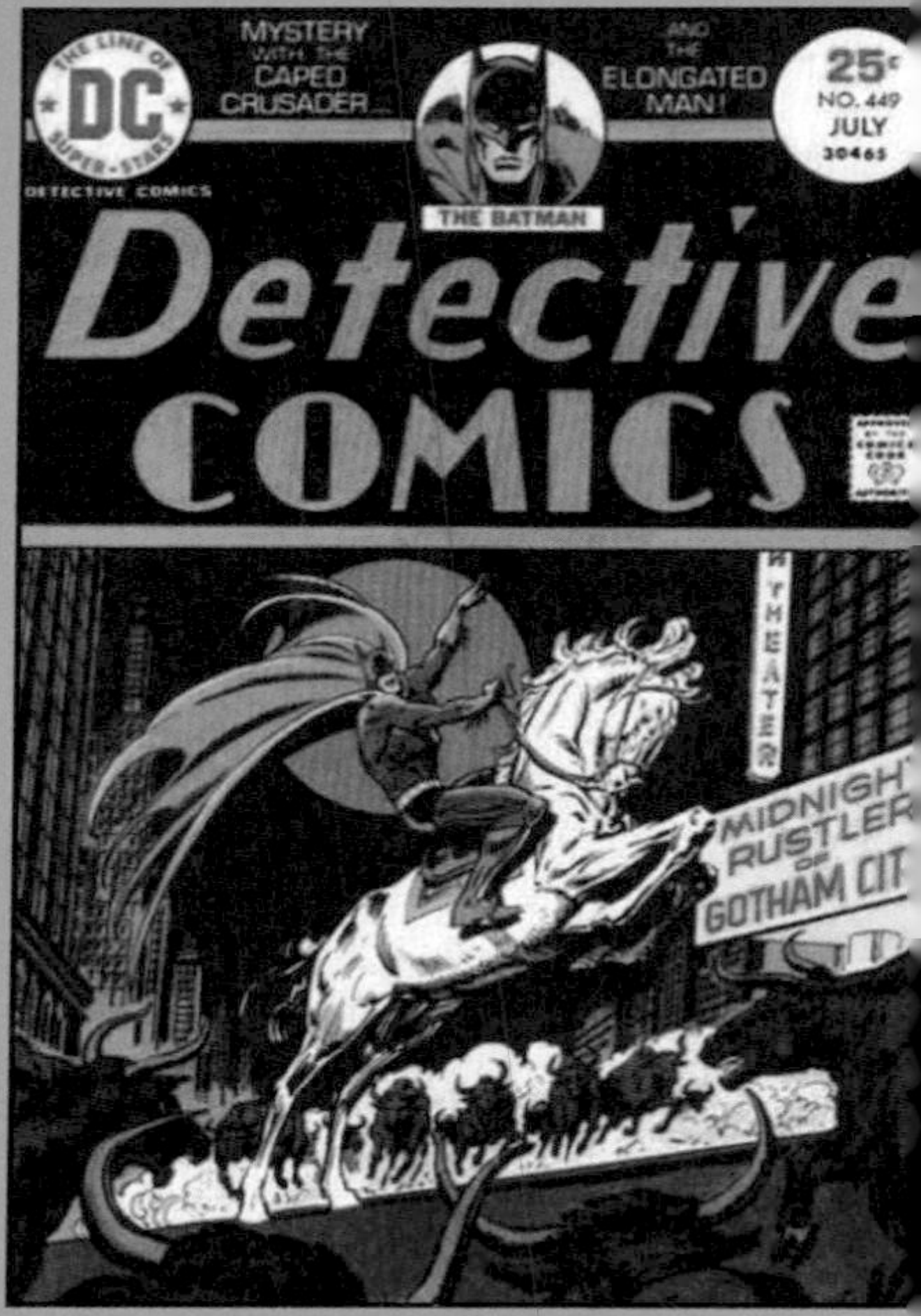
THE LINE OF DC SUPER-STARS
MYSTERY WITH THE CAPED CRUSADER
AND THE ELONGATED MAN!
25¢
NO. 449
JULY
30465
DETECTIVE COMICS
THE BATMAN
Detective COMICS
THEATER
MIDNIGHT RUSTLER OF GOTHAM CIT

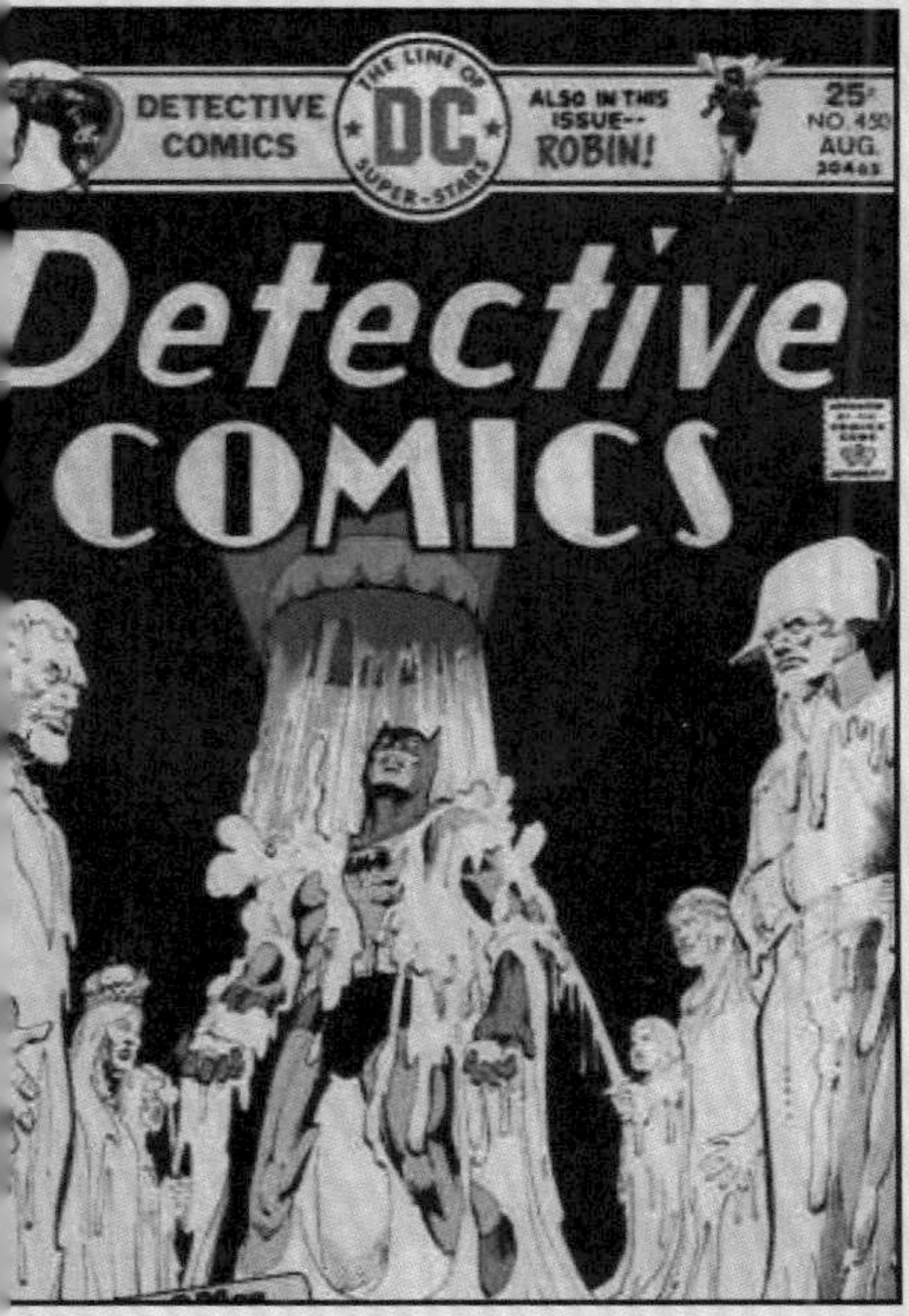
DETECTIVE COMICS
THE LINE OF DC SUPER-STARS
ALSO IN THIS ISSUE-- ROBIN!
25¢
NO. 450
AUG.
Detective COMICS

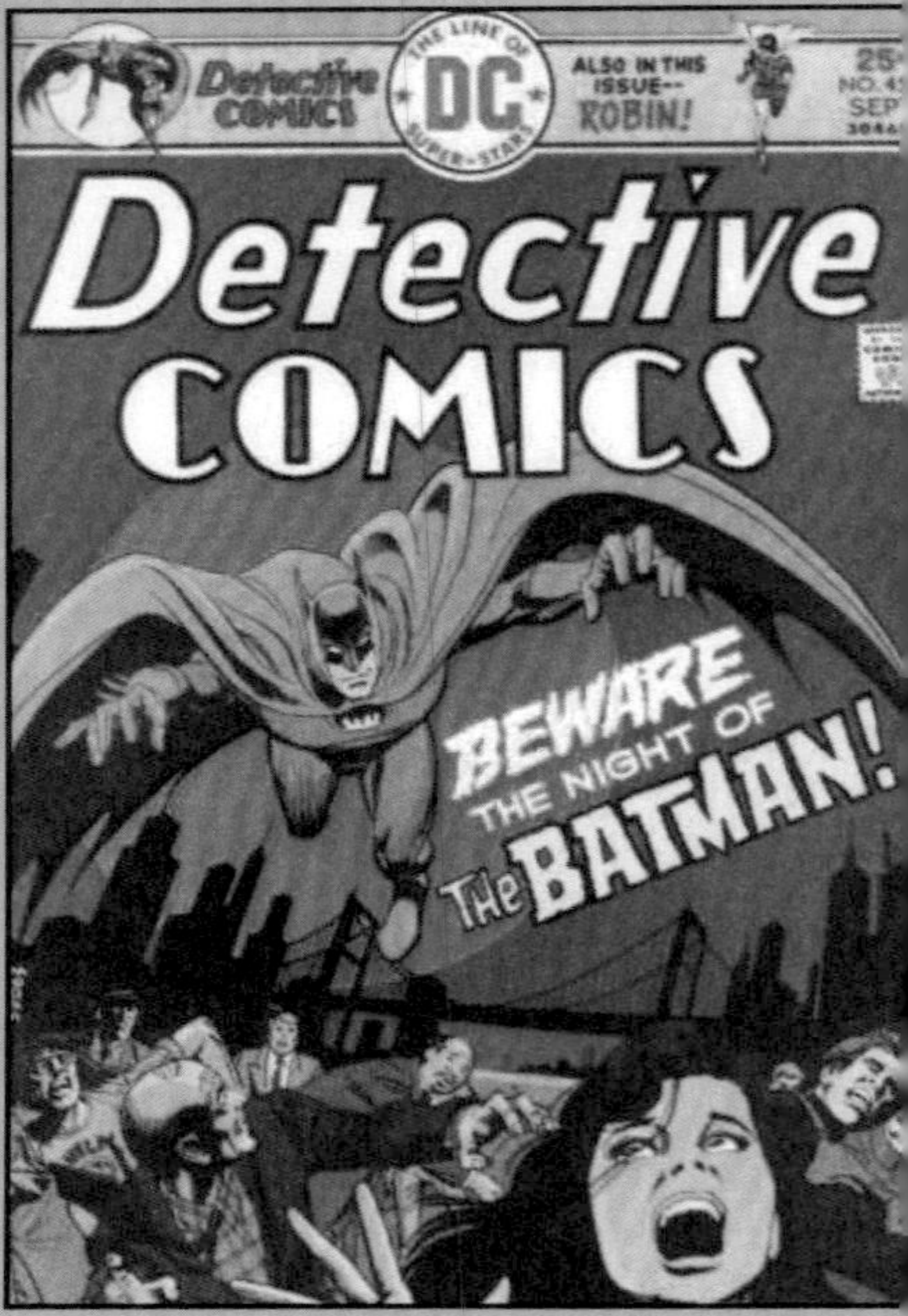
Detective COMICS
THE LINE OF DC SUPER-STARS
ALSO IN THIS ISSUE-- ROBIN!
25¢
NO. 4
SEP
Detective COMICS
BEWARE THE NIGHT OF The BATMAN!

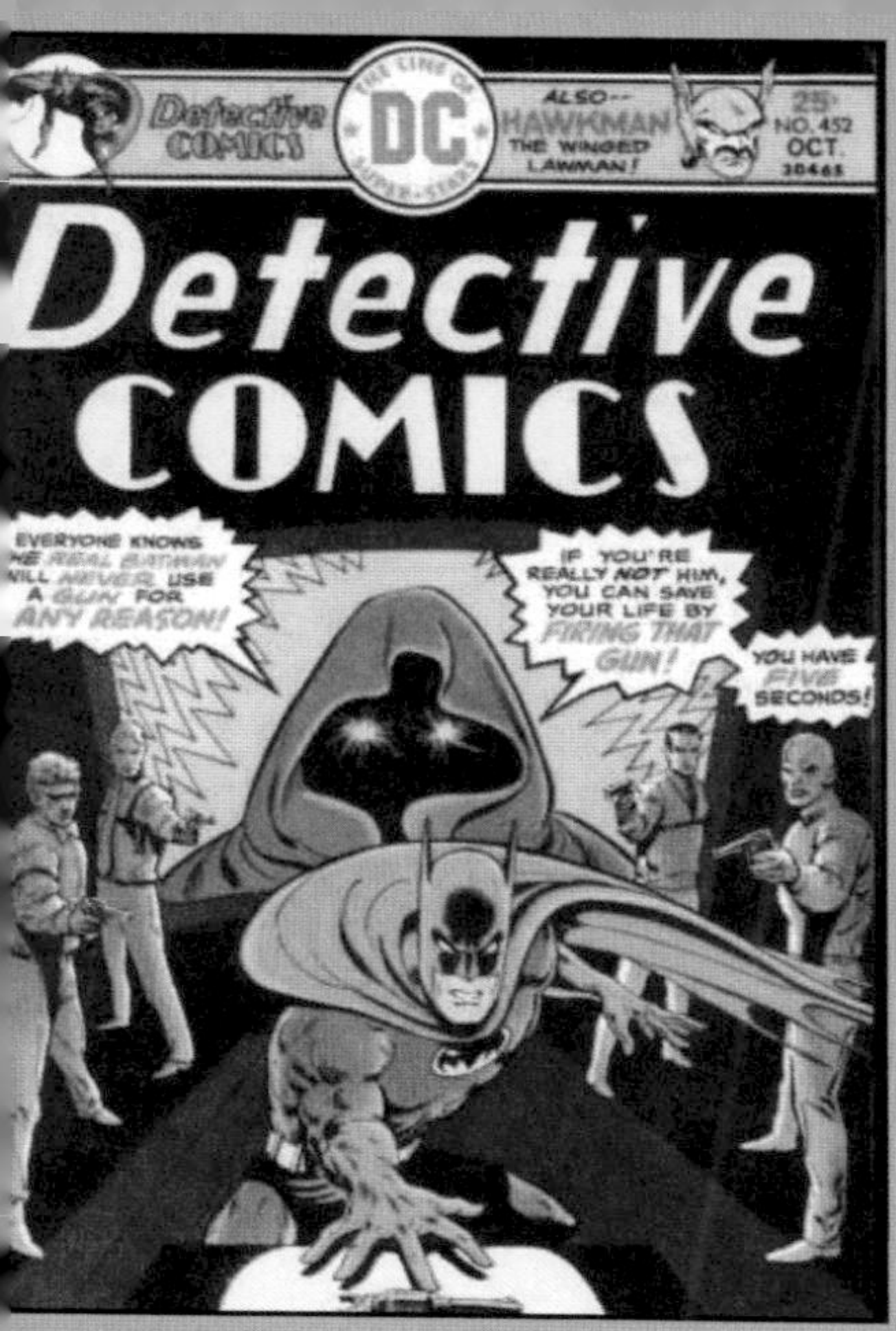
Detective COMICS
DC
ALSO--
HAWKMAN
THE WINGED LAWMAN!
25¢
NO. 452
OCT.
Detective
COMICS
EVERYONE KNOWS THE REAL BATMAN WILL NEVER USE A GUN FOR ANY REASON!
IF YOU'RE REALLY NOT HIM, YOU CAN SAVE YOUR LIFE BY FIRING THAT GUN!
YOU HAVE FIVE SECONDS!

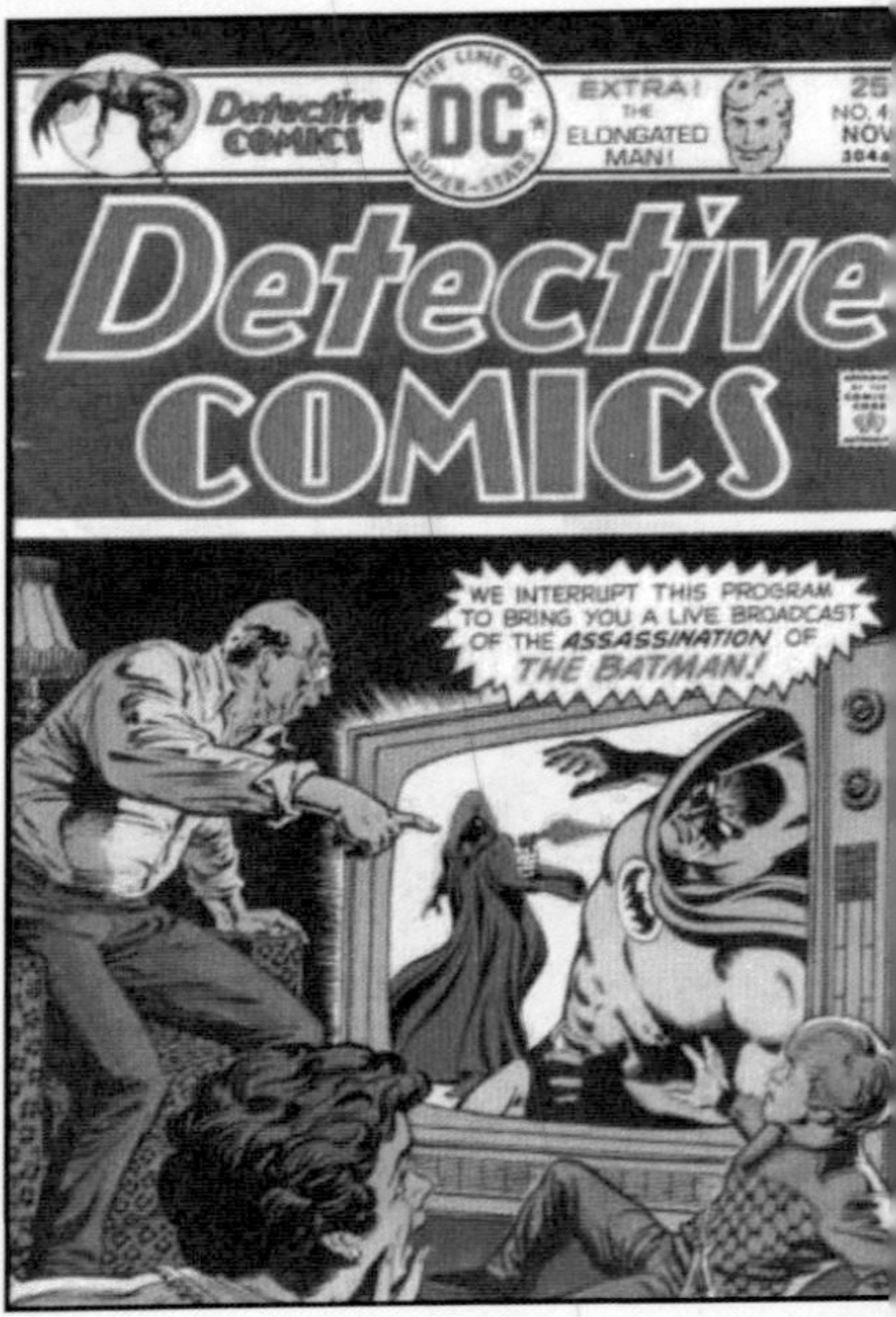
Detective COMICS
THE LINE OF DC SUPER-STARS
EXTRA! THE ELONGATED MAN!
25
NO. 4
NOV
Detective COMICS
WE INTERRUPT THIS PROGRAM TO BRING YOU A LIVE BROADCAST OF THE ASSASSINATION OF THE BATMAN!

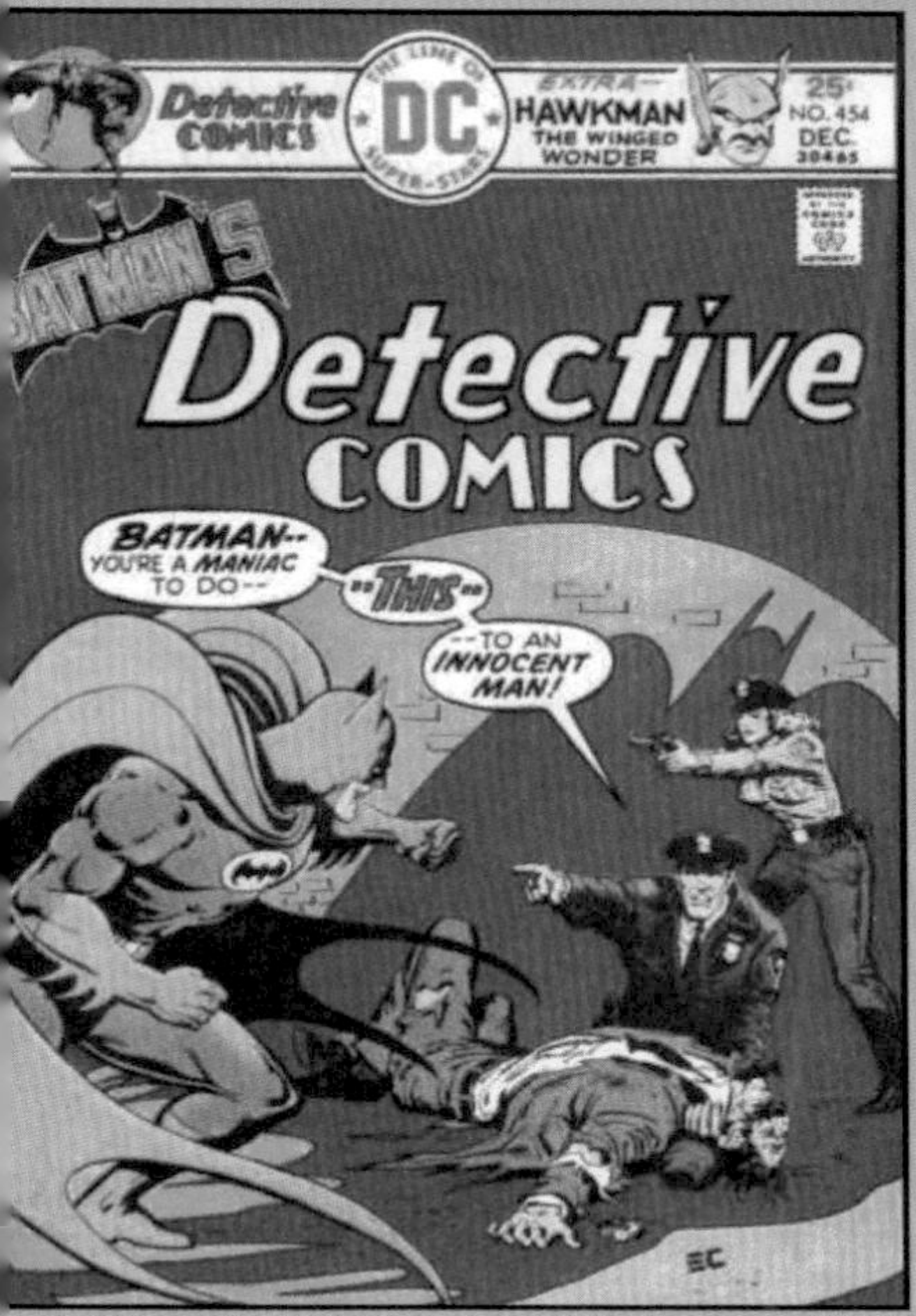
Detective COMICS
THE LINE OF SUPER-STARS
DC
EXTRA— HAWKMAN THE WINGED WONDER
25¢
NO. 454
DEC.
BATMAN'S
Detective COMICS
BATMAN-- YOU'RE A MANIAC TO DO--
--THIS--
--TO AN INNOCENT MAN!
EC

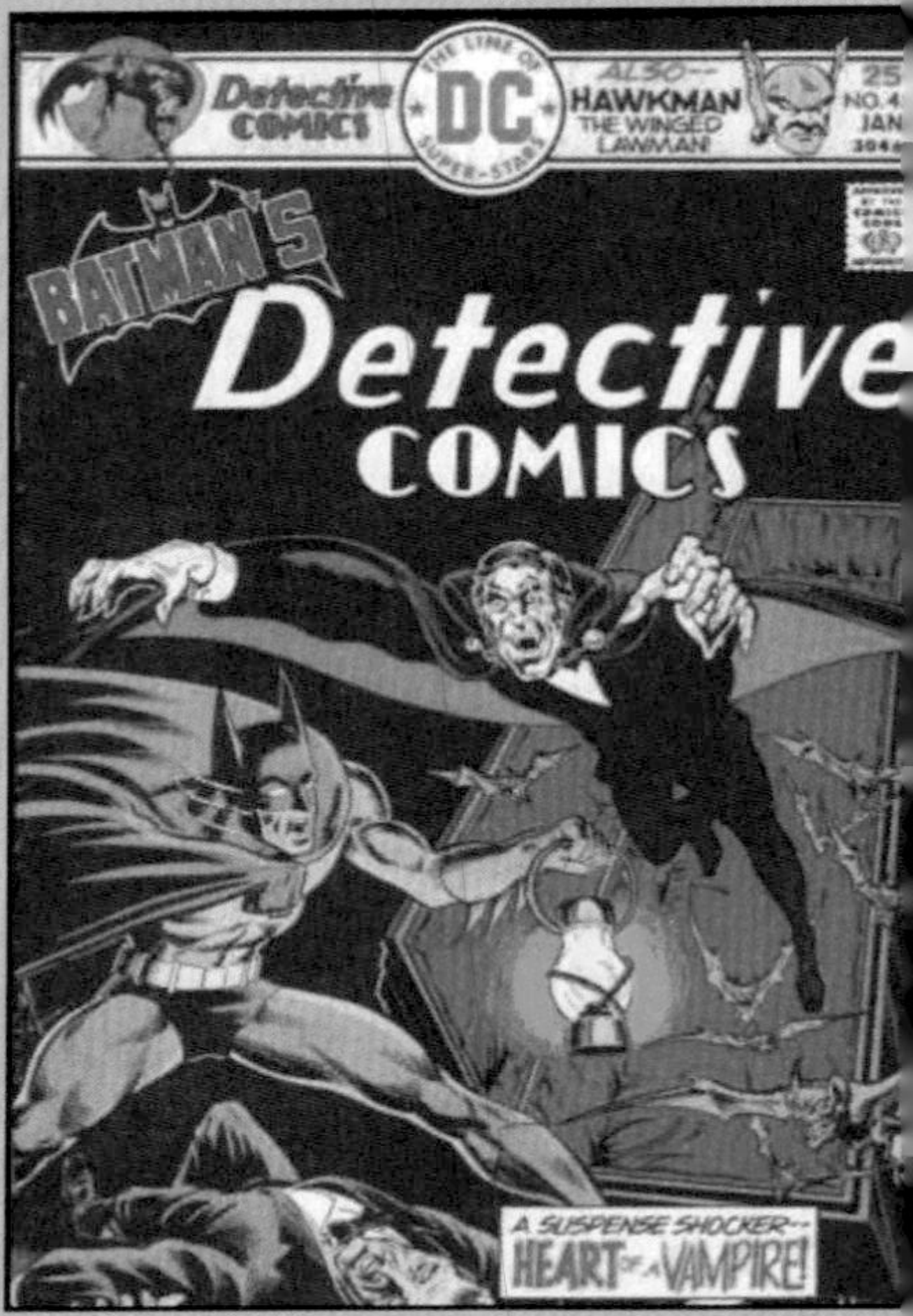
Detective COMICS
THE LINE OF SUPER-STARS
DC
ALSO--
HAWKMAN
THE WINGED LAWMAN
25
NO. 4
JAN
BATMAN'S
Detective
COMICS
A SUSPENSE SHOCKER--
HEART OF A VAMPIRE!

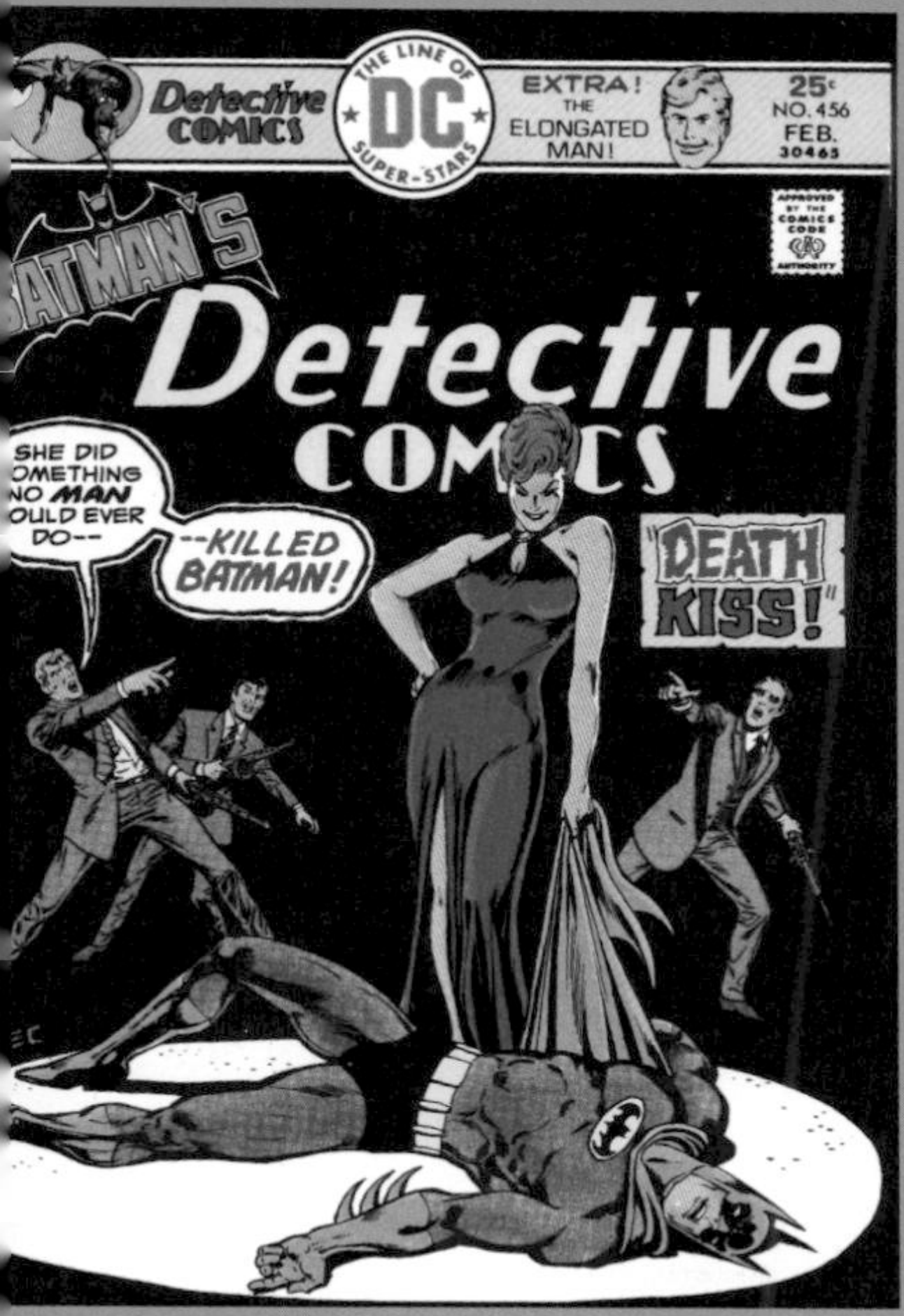
Detective COMICS
THE LINE OF DC SUPER-STARS
EXTRA! THE ELONGATED MAN!
25¢
NO. 456
FEB.
30465
APPROVED BY THE COMICS CODE AUTHORITY
BATMAN'S
Detective COMICS
SHE DID SOMETHING NO MAN COULD EVER DO--
--KILLED BATMAN!
"DEATH KISS!"

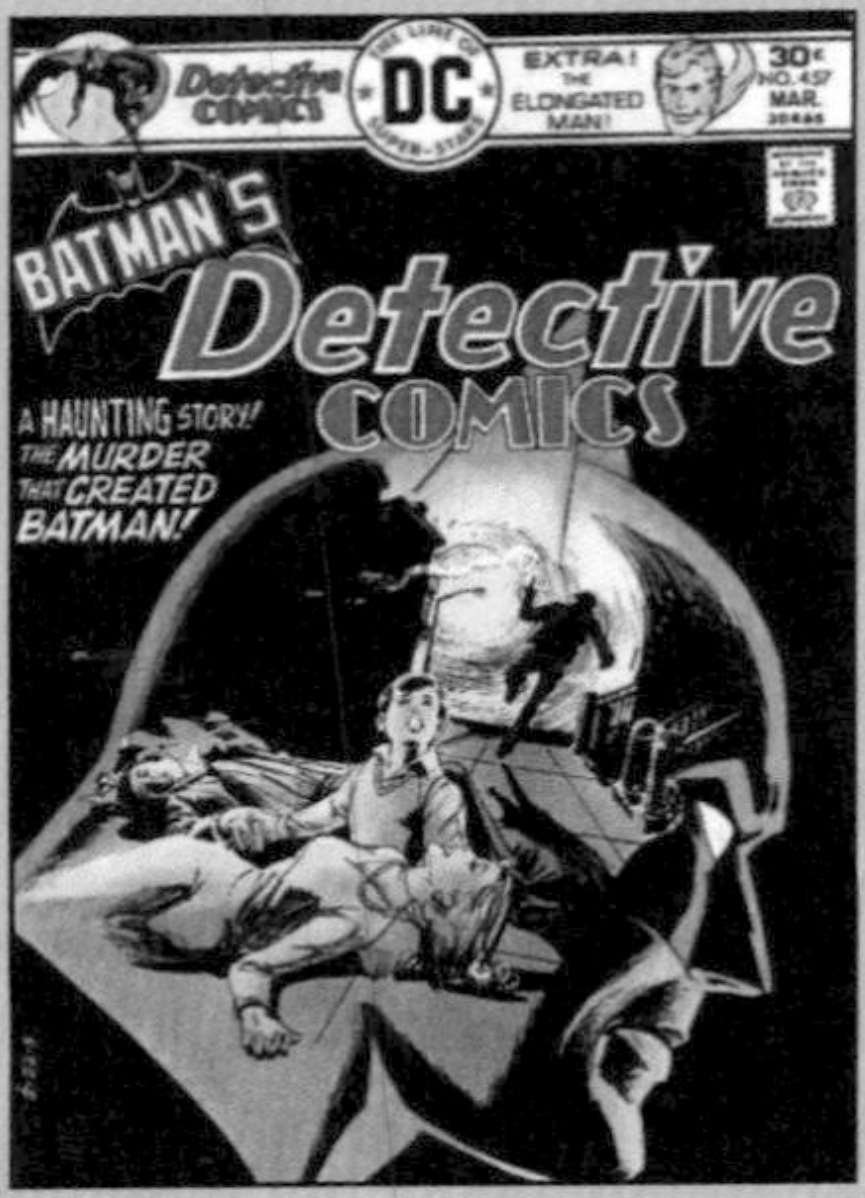

Detective Comics #457

A retelling of Batman's tragic backstory, issue #457 added more detail to Thomas and Martha Waynes' fateful night in Crime Alley. This issue also introduces readers to Dr. Leslie Thompkins, a close colleague of the Waynes who eventually becomes an ally of Batman.

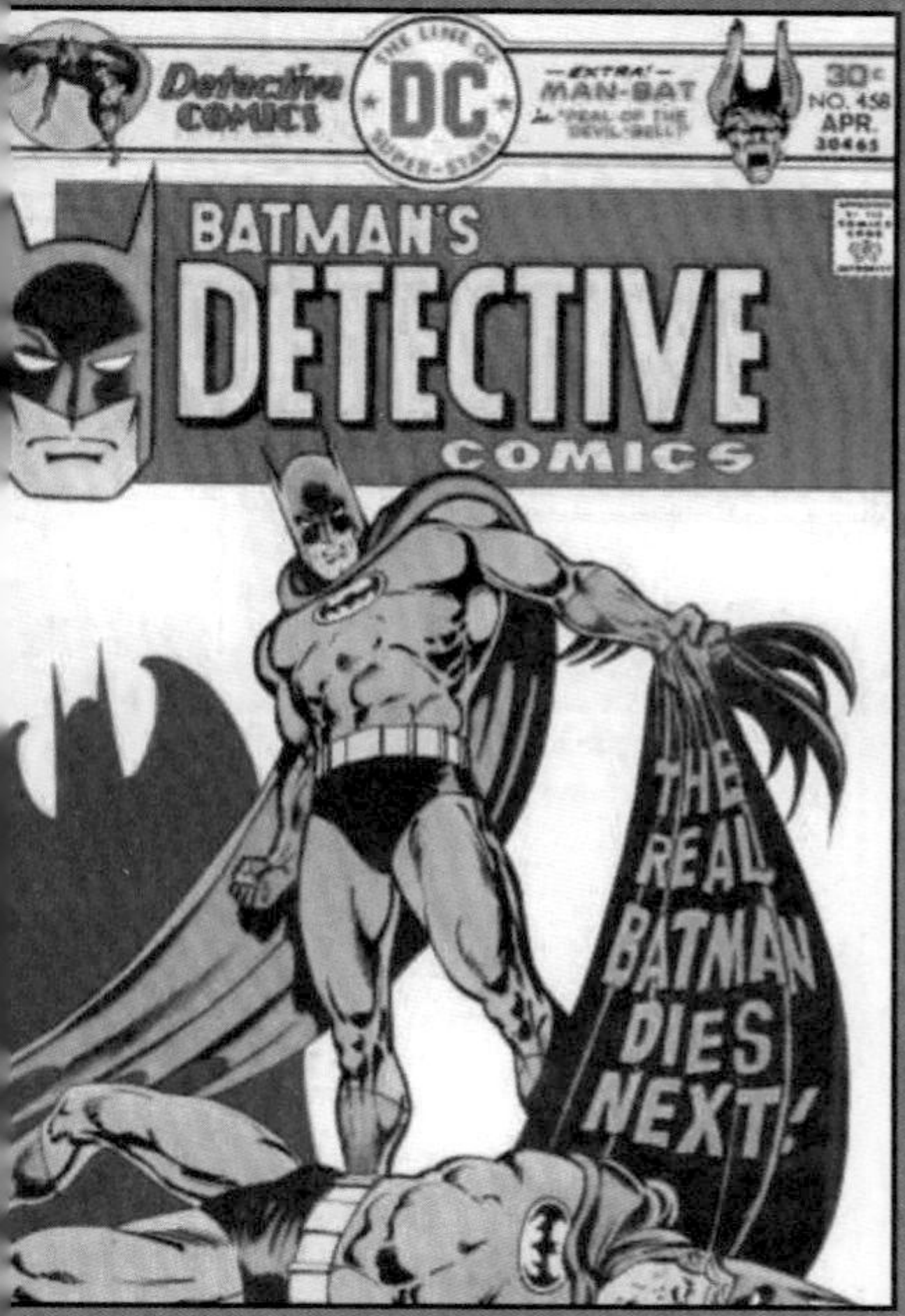
Detective COMICS
THE LINE OF SUPER-STARS
DC
—EXTRA!—
MAN-BAT
30¢
NO. 458
APR.
BATMAN'S
DETECTIVE
COMICS
THE REAL BATMAN DIES NEXT!

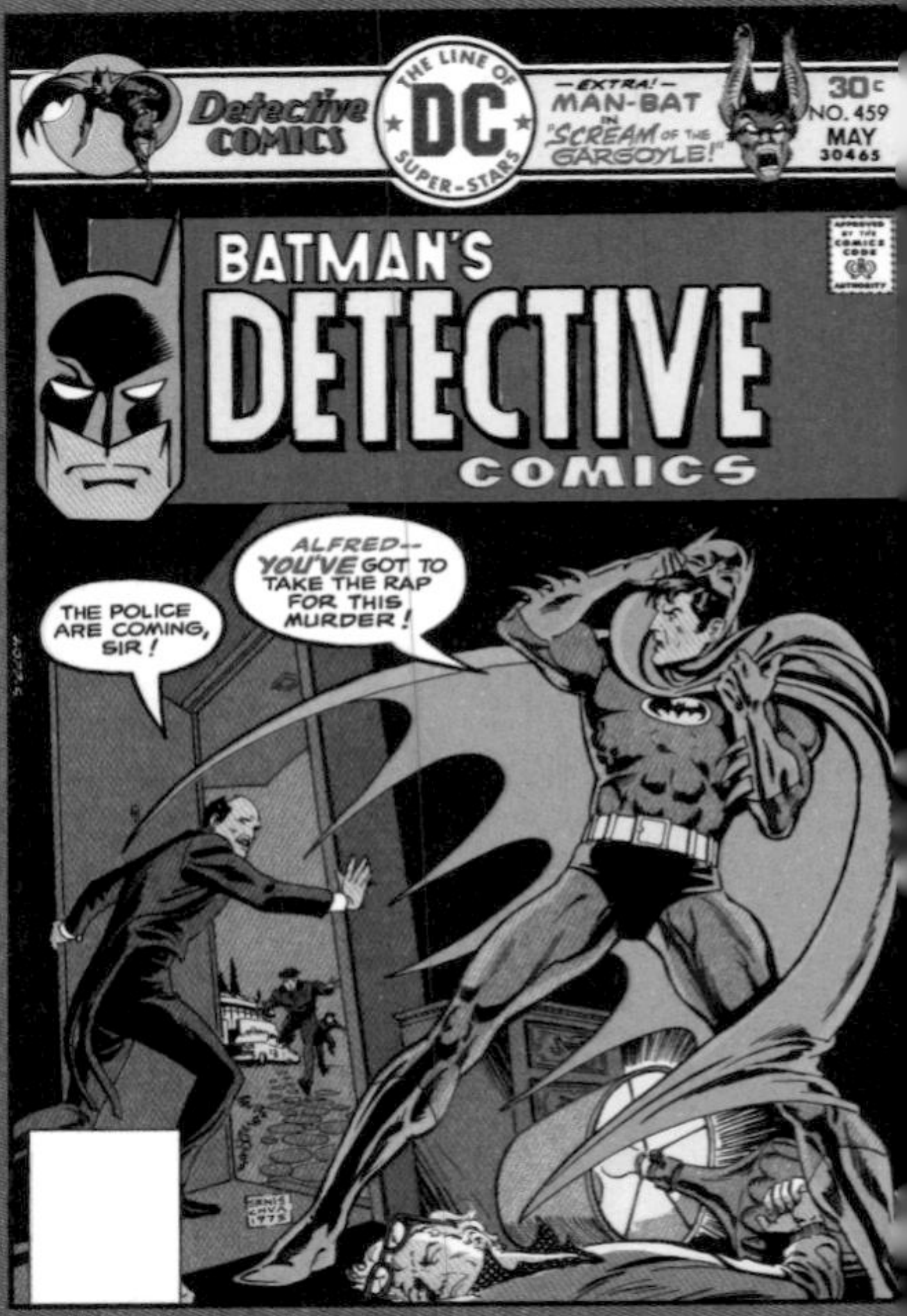
Detective COMICS
THE LINE OF DC SUPER-STARS
—EXTRA!—
MAN-BAT
IN "SCREAM OF THE GARGOYLE!"
30¢
NO. 459
MAY
30465
BATMAN'S
DETECTIVE
COMICS
ALFRED-- YOU'VE GOT TO TAKE THE RAP FOR THIS MURDER!
THE POLICE ARE COMING, SIR!

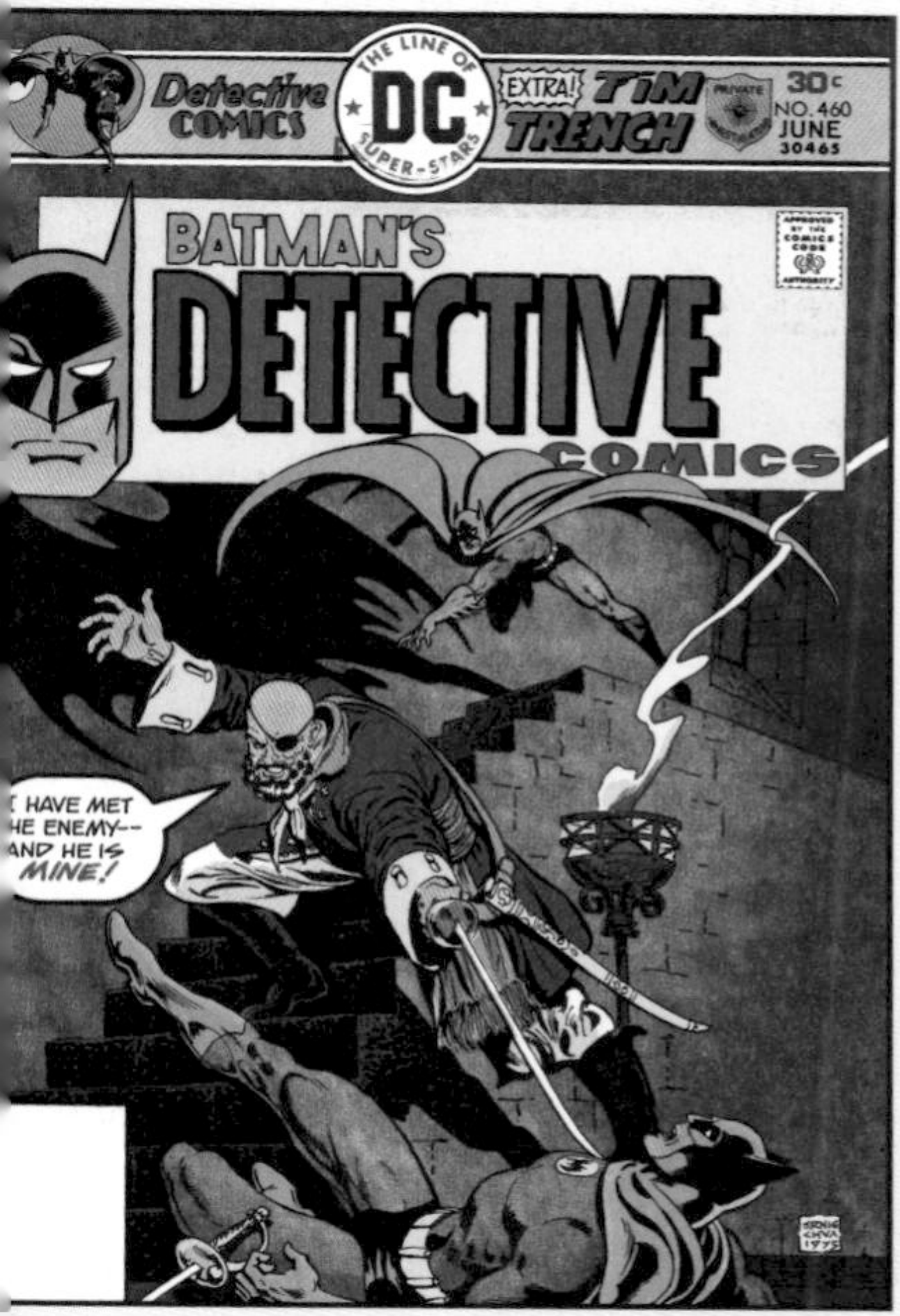
Detective COMICS
THE LINE OF DC SUPER-STARS
EXTRA! TIM TRENCH
30¢
NO. 460
JUNE
30465
BATMAN'S
DETECTIVE
COMICS
I HAVE MET THE ENEMY-- AND HE IS MINE!

DC COMICS SALUTES THE BICENTENNIAL 29

Detective COMICS

THE LINE OF DC SUPER-STARS

EXTRA! TIM TRENCH

PRIVATE INVESTIGATOR

30¢ NO. 46 JULY 30465

APPROVED BY THE COMICS CODE AUTHORITY

BATMAN'S DETECTIVE COMICS

"BAIT IN A BAT-TRAP!"

ERNIE CHUA 1976

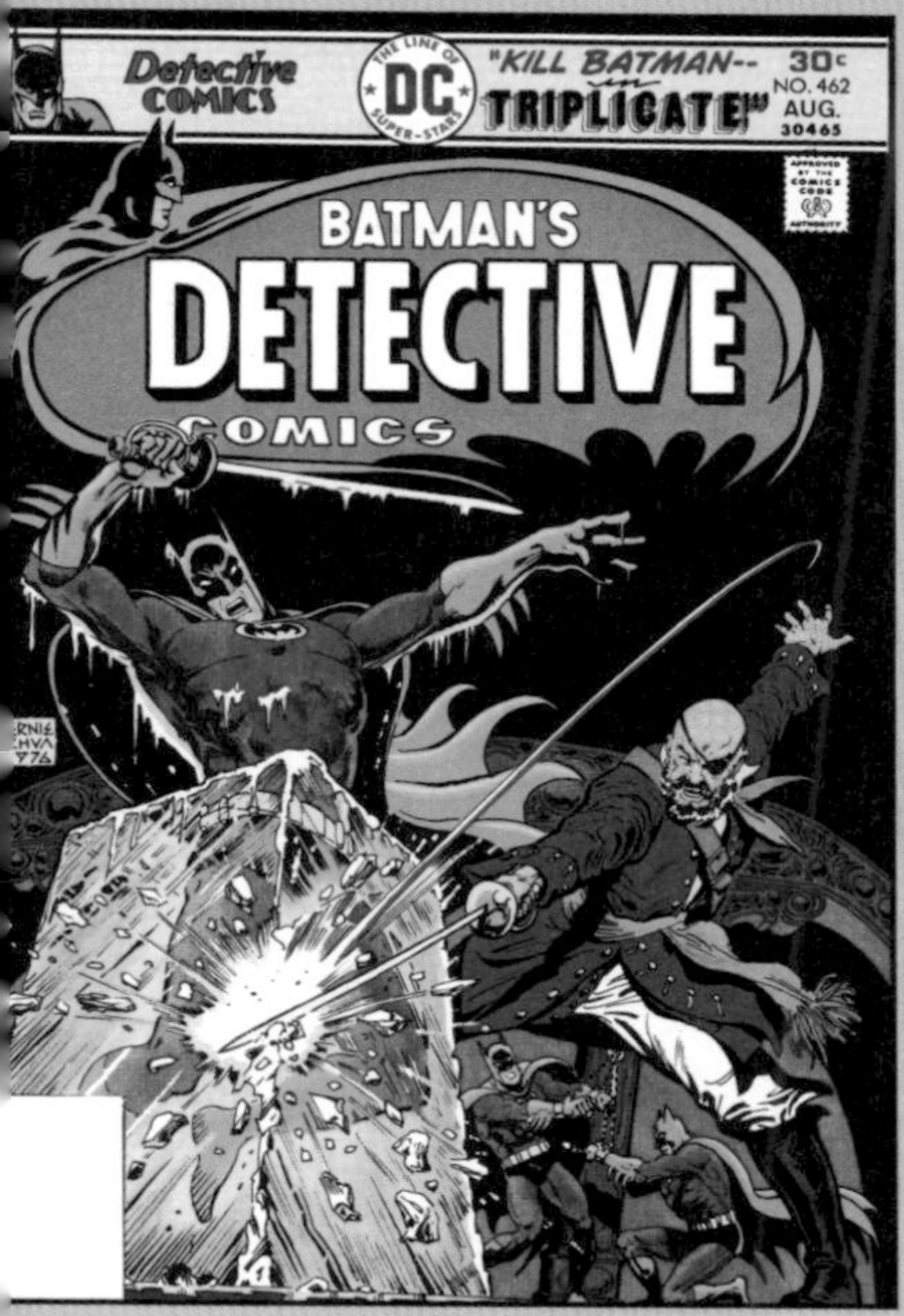
Detective COMICS
THE LINE OF DC SUPER-STARS
"KILL BATMAN-- in TRIPLICATE!"
30c
NO. 462
AUG.
30465
APPROVED BY THE COMICS CODE AUTHORITY
BATMAN'S
DETECTIVE
COMICS

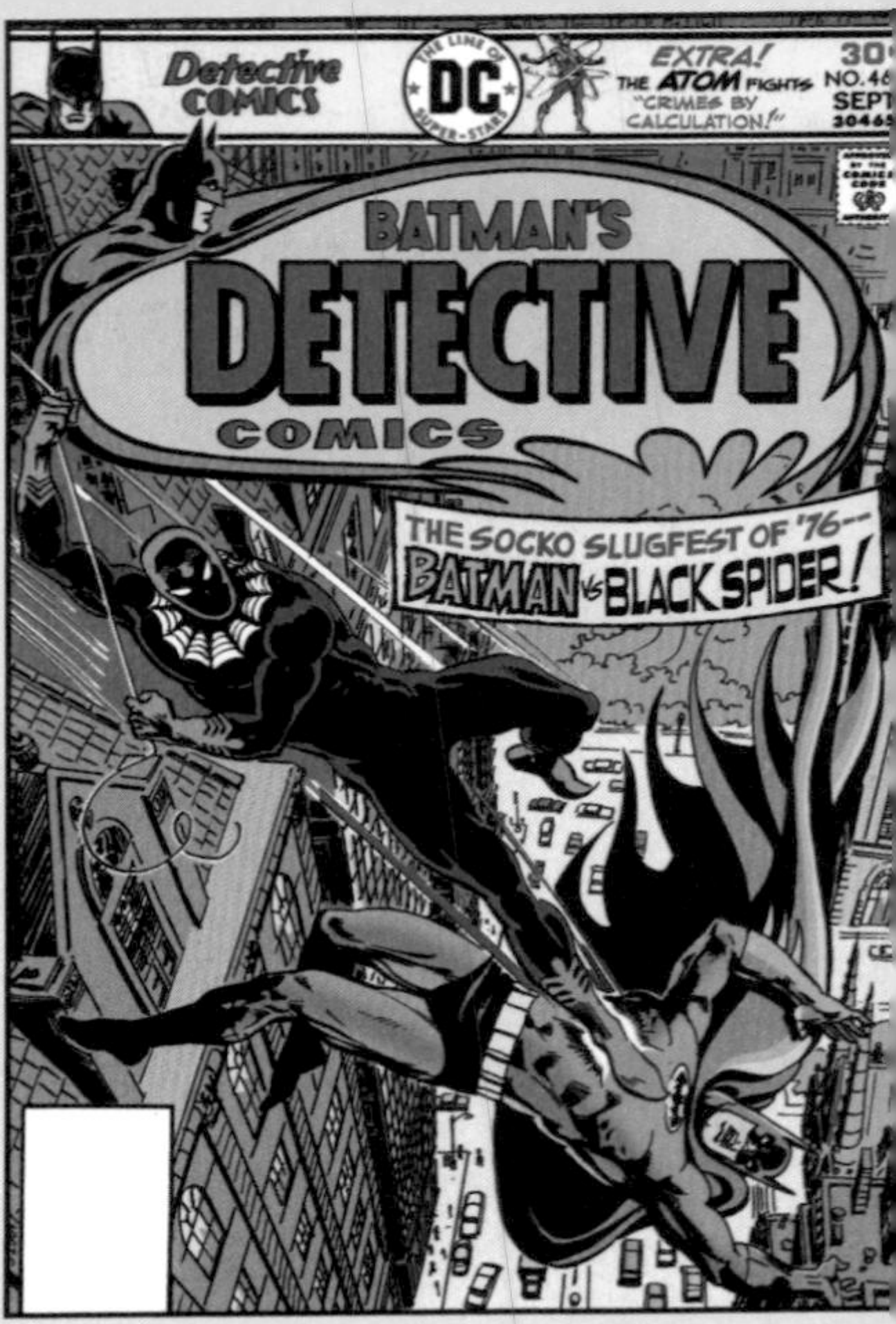
Detective COMICS
THE LINE OF SUPER-STARS
DC
EXTRA! THE ATOM FIGHTS "CRIMES BY CALCULATION!"
30¢
NO. 46
SEPT
BATMAN'S
DETECTIVE
COMICS
THE SOCKO SLUGFEST OF '76--
BATMAN vs BLACK SPIDER!

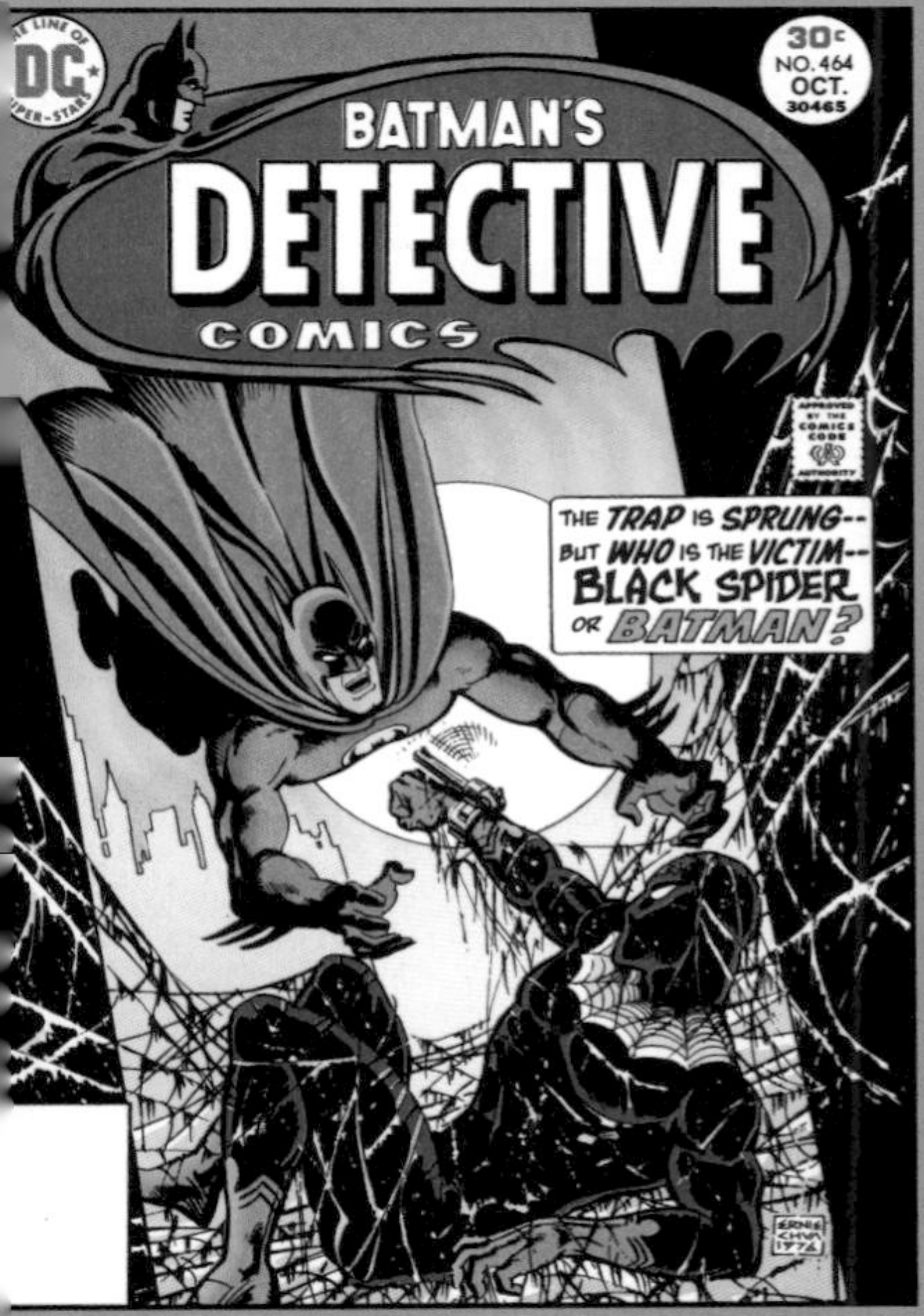
THE LINE OF DC SUPER-STARS
30c
NO. 464
OCT.
30465
BATMAN'S
DETECTIVE
COMICS
APPROVED BY THE COMICS CODE AUTHORITY
THE TRAP IS SPRUNG--
BUT WHO IS THE VICTIM--
BLACK SPIDER
OR BATMAN?

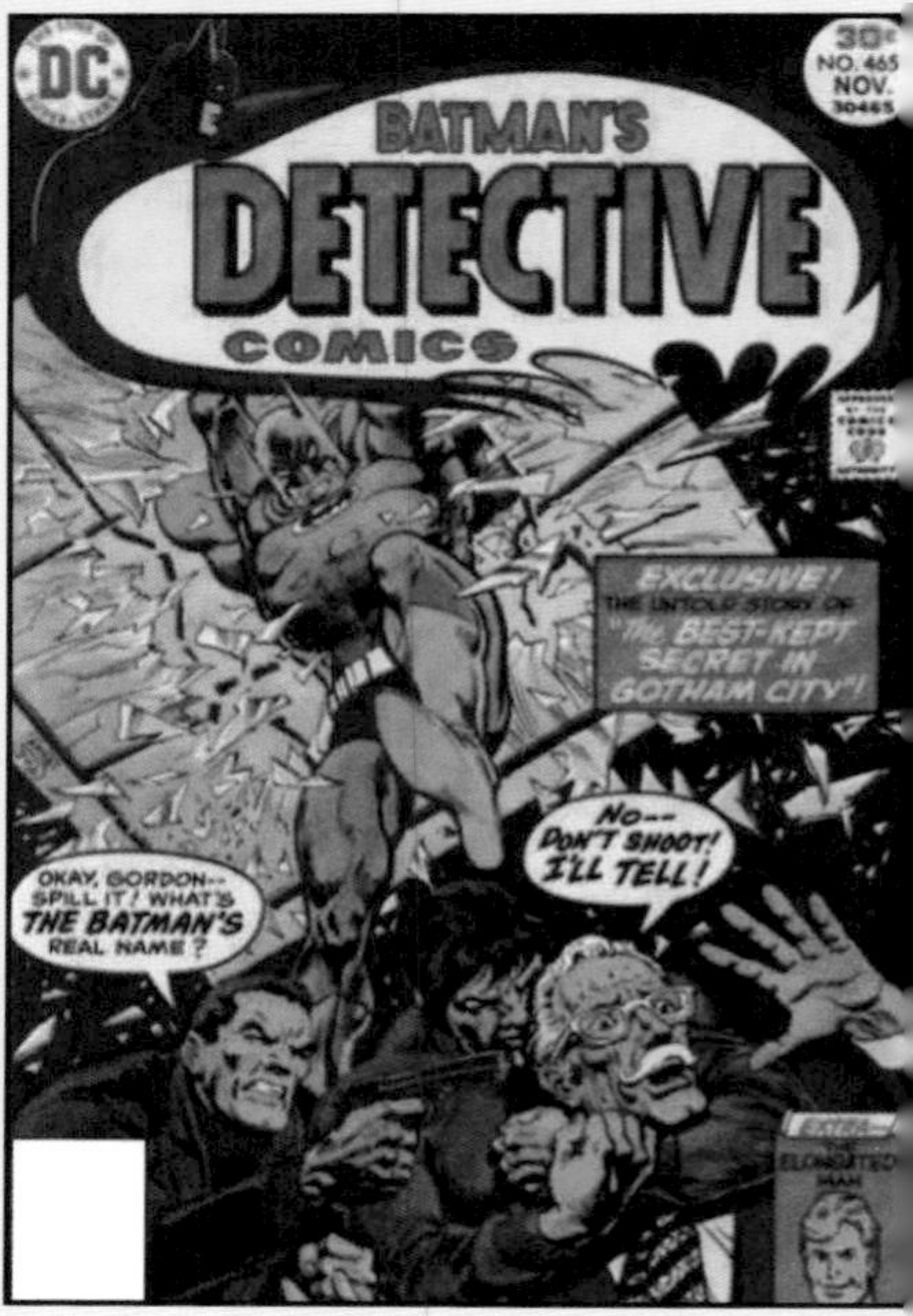
DC
30¢
NO. 465
NOV.
30465
BATMAN'S
DETECTIVE
COMICS
EXCLUSIVE!
THE UNTOLD STORY OF
"The BEST-KEPT SECRET IN GOTHAM CITY"!
No-- DON'T SHOOT! I'LL TELL!
OKAY, GORDON-- SPILL IT! WHAT'S THE BATMAN'S REAL NAME?
EXTRA!
ELONGATED MAN

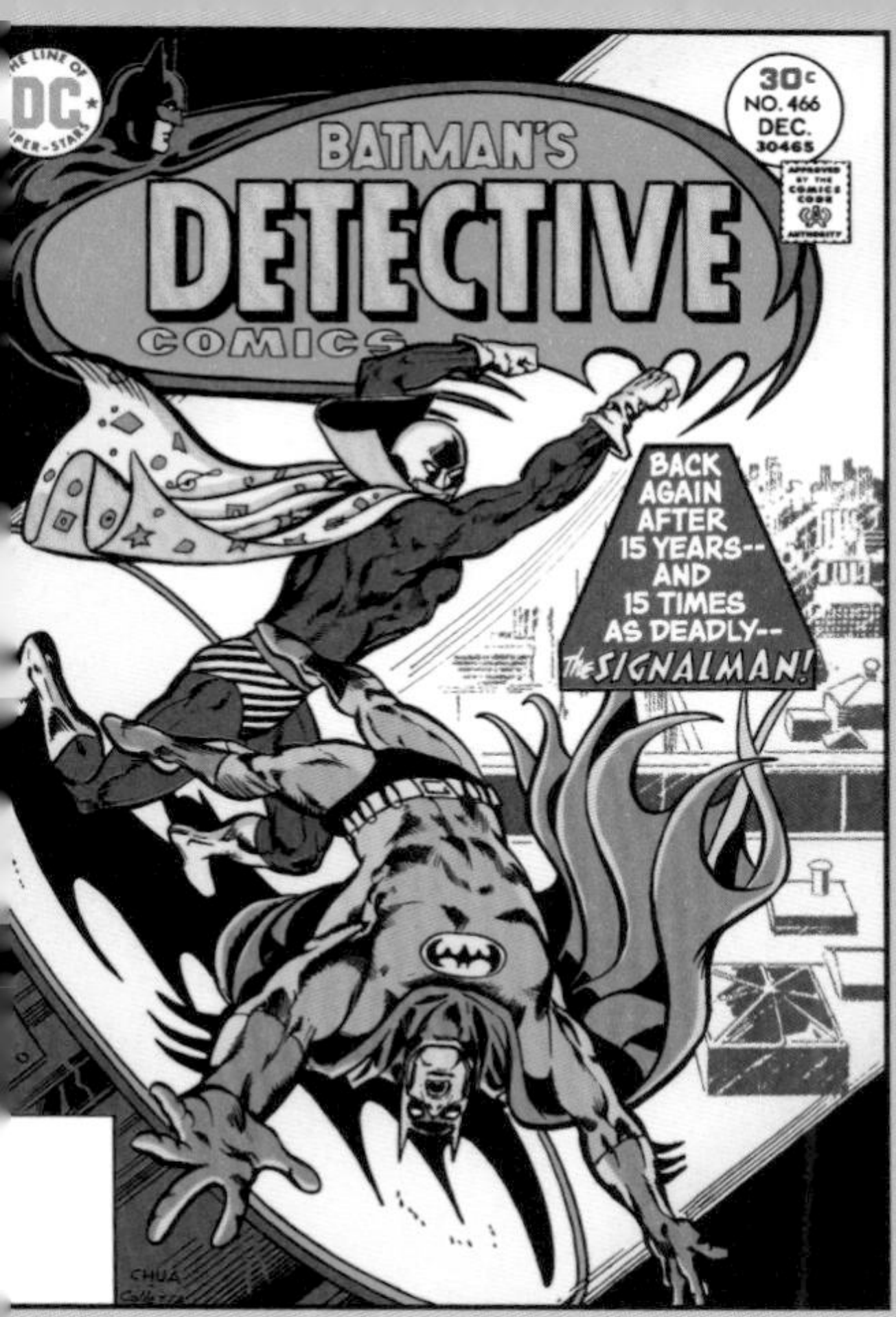
THE LINE OF
DC
SUPER-STARS
30¢
NO. 466
DEC.
30465
APPROVED BY THE COMICS CODE AUTHORITY
BATMAN'S
DETECTIVE
COMICS
BACK AGAIN AFTER 15 YEARS-- AND 15 TIMES AS DEADLY--
THE SIGNALMAN!
CHUA

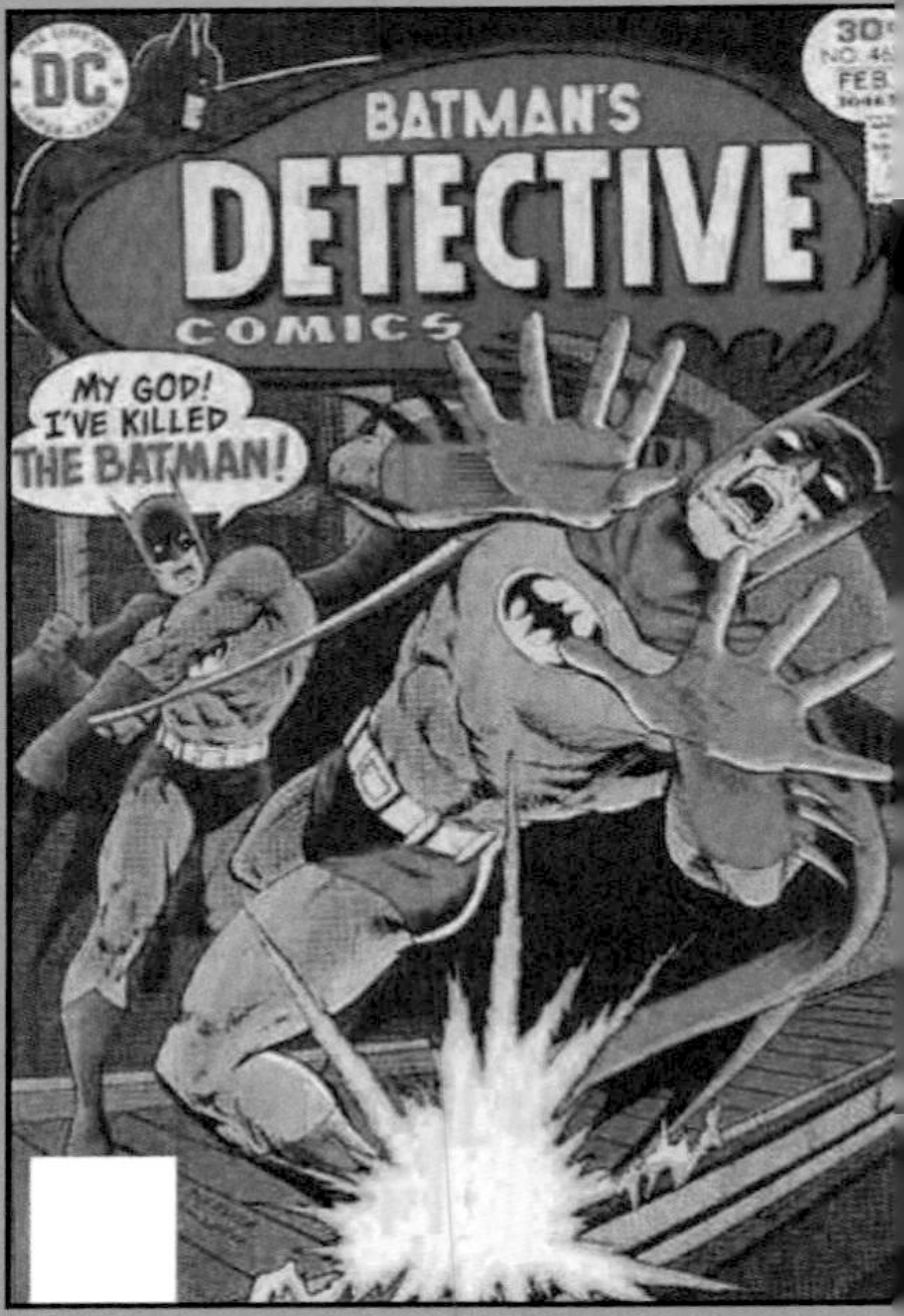
DC
30¢
NO. 46
FEB.
BATMAN'S
DETECTIVE
COMICS
MY GOD! I'VE KILLED THE BATMAN!

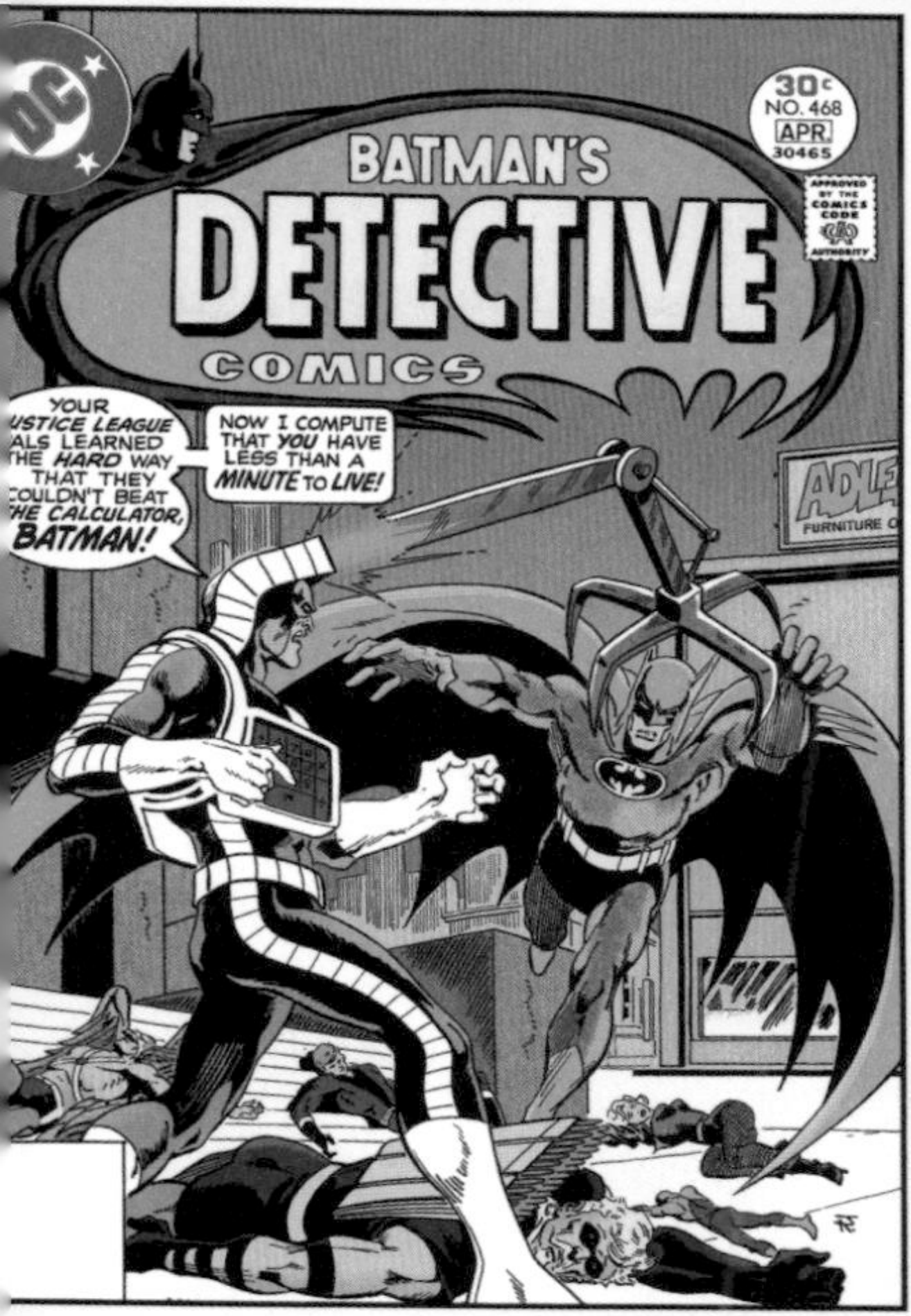
30c
NO. 468
APR.
30465
APPROVED BY THE COMICS CODE AUTHORITY
BATMAN'S
DETECTIVE
COMICS
YOUR JUSTICE LEAGUE PALS LEARNED THE HARD WAY THAT THEY COULDN'T BEAT THE CALCULATOR, BATMAN!
NOW I COMPUTE THAT YOU HAVE LESS THAN A MINUTE TO LIVE!
FURNITURE

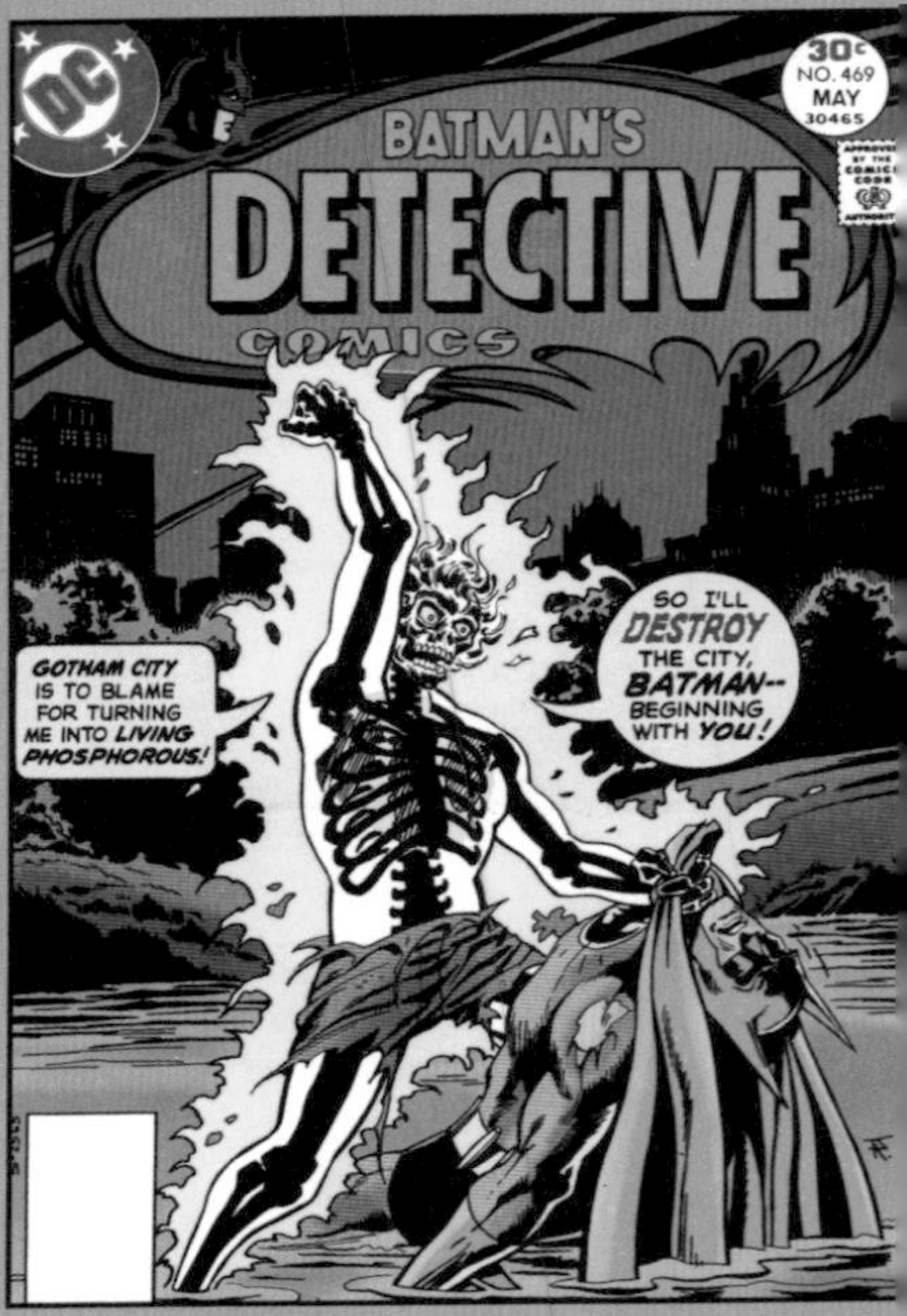
DC
30¢
NO. 469
MAY
30465
BATMAN'S
DETECTIVE
COMICS
GOTHAM CITY IS TO BLAME FOR TURNING ME INTO LIVING PHOSPHOROUS!
SO I'LL DESTROY THE CITY, BATMAN-- BEGINNING WITH YOU!

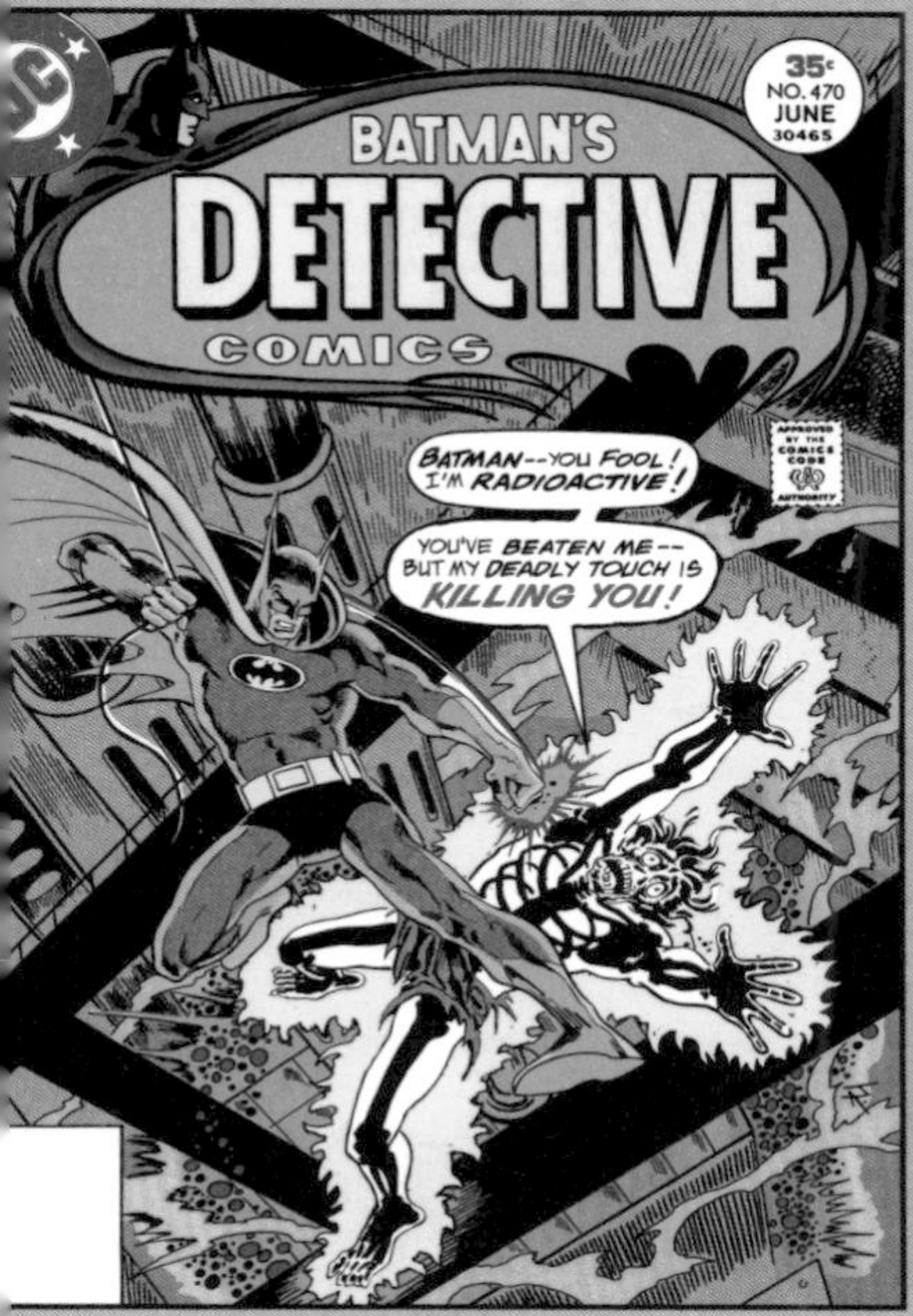
35¢
NO. 470
JUNE
30465
BATMAN'S
DETECTIVE
COMICS
APPROVED BY THE COMICS CODE AUTHORITY
BATMAN--YOU FOOL! I'M RADIOACTIVE!
YOU'VE BEATEN ME-- BUT MY DEADLY TOUCH IS KILLING YOU!

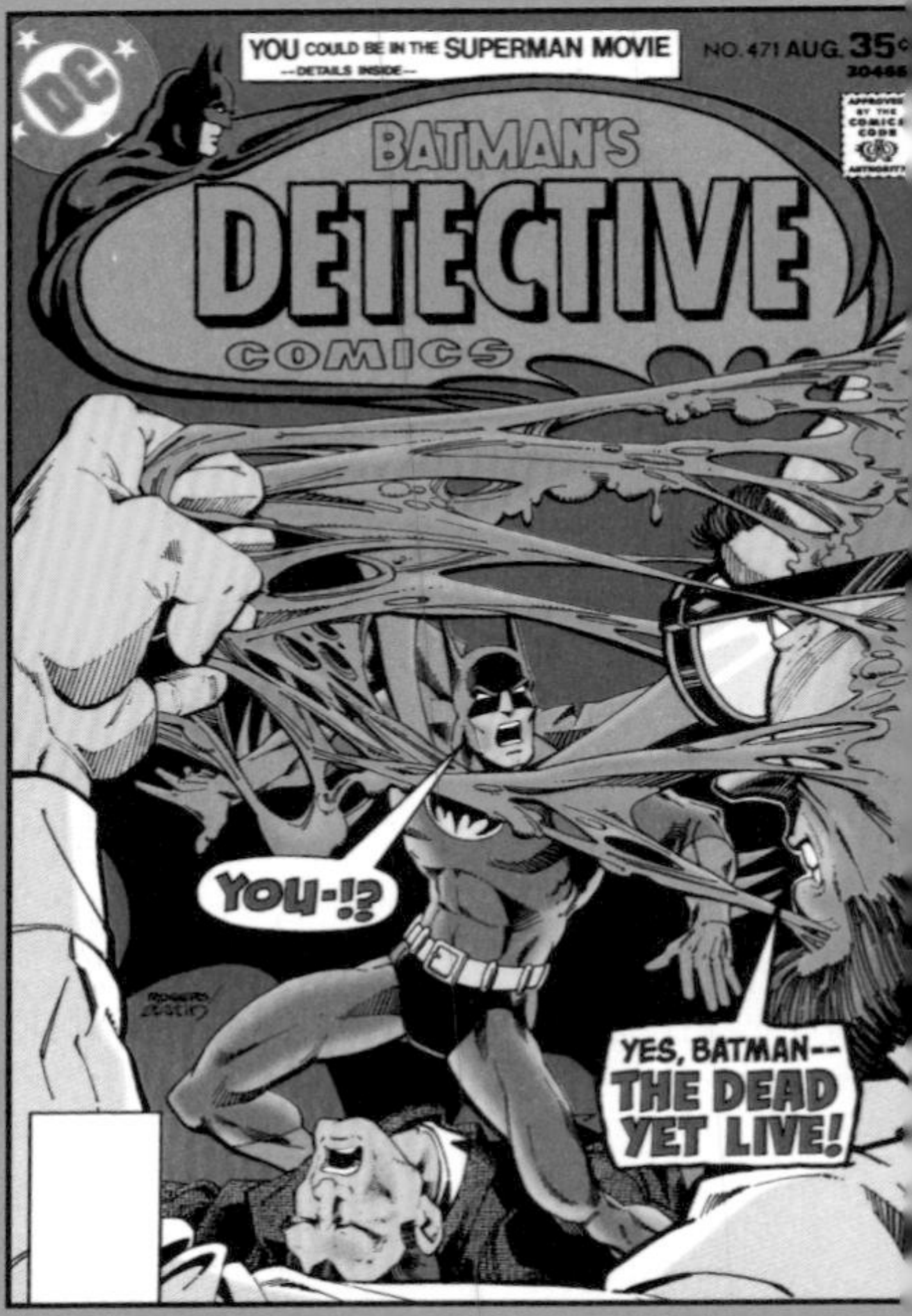
YOU COULD BE IN THE SUPERMAN MOVIE
--DETAILS INSIDE--
NO. 471 AUG. 35¢
20466
APPROVED BY THE COMICS CODE AUTHORITY
BATMAN'S
DETECTIVE
COMICS
YOU-!?
YES, BATMAN--
THE DEAD
YET LIVE!

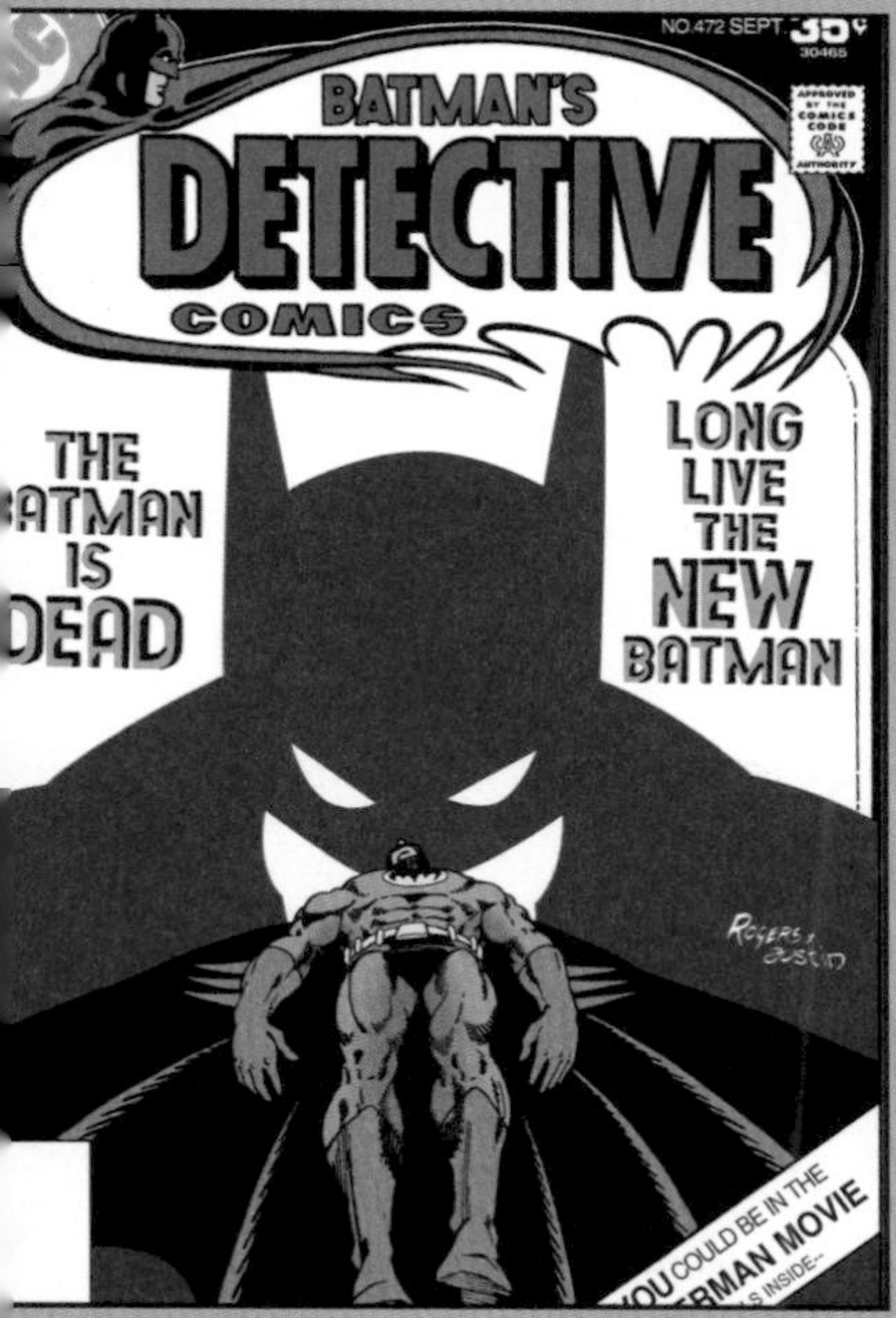
NO.472 SEPT. 35¢
30465
APPROVED BY THE COMICS CODE AUTHORITY
BATMAN'S
DETECTIVE
COMICS
THE BATMAN IS DEAD
LONG LIVE THE NEW BATMAN
ROGERS & AUSTIN
YOU COULD BE IN THE BATMAN MOVIE
INSIDE--

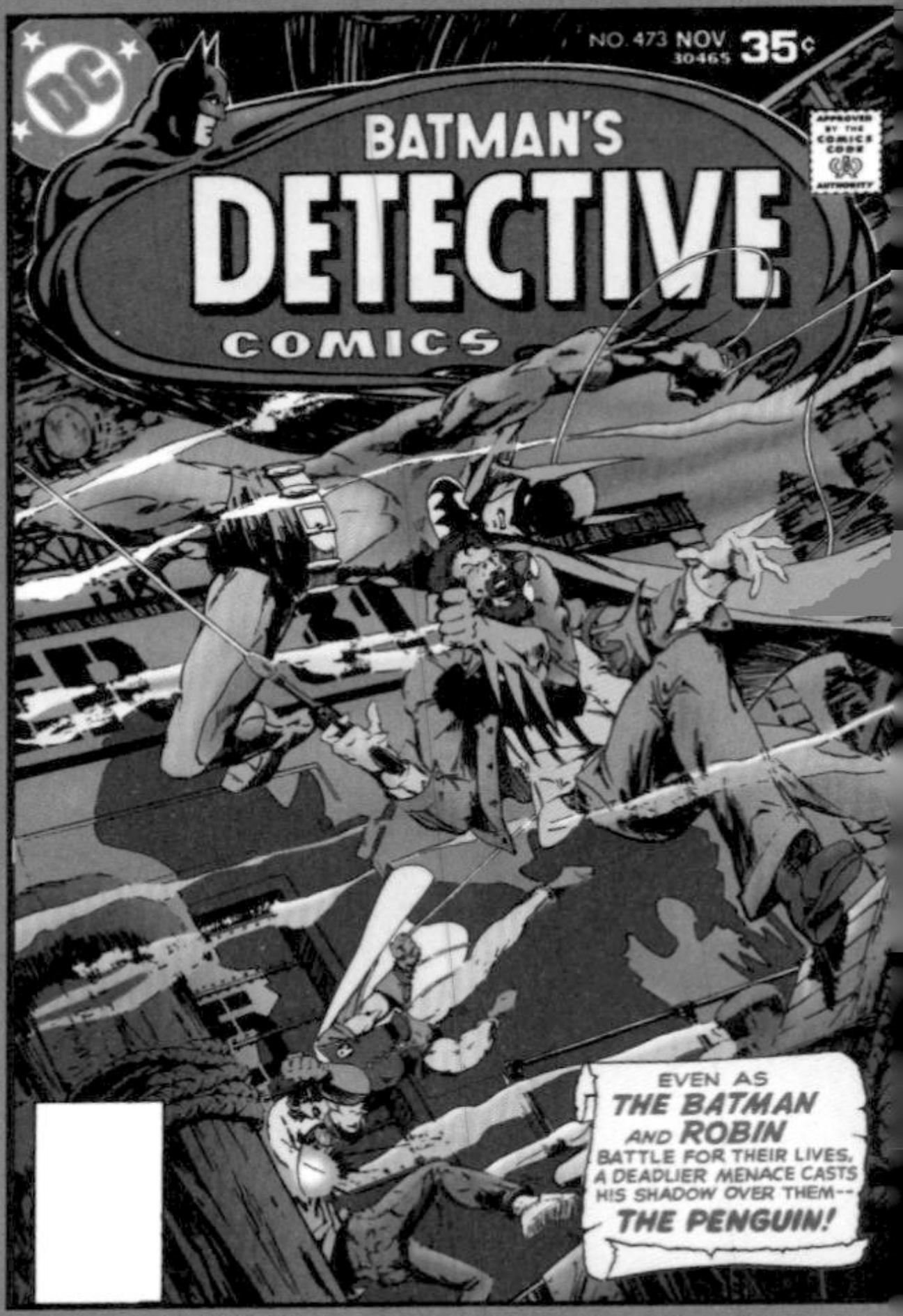
DC
NO. 473 NOV. 30465 35¢
BATMAN'S
DETECTIVE
COMICS
APPROVED BY THE COMICS CODE AUTHORITY
EVEN AS THE BATMAN AND ROBIN BATTLE FOR THEIR LIVES, A DEADLIER MENACE CASTS HIS SHADOW OVER THEM-- THE PENGUIN!

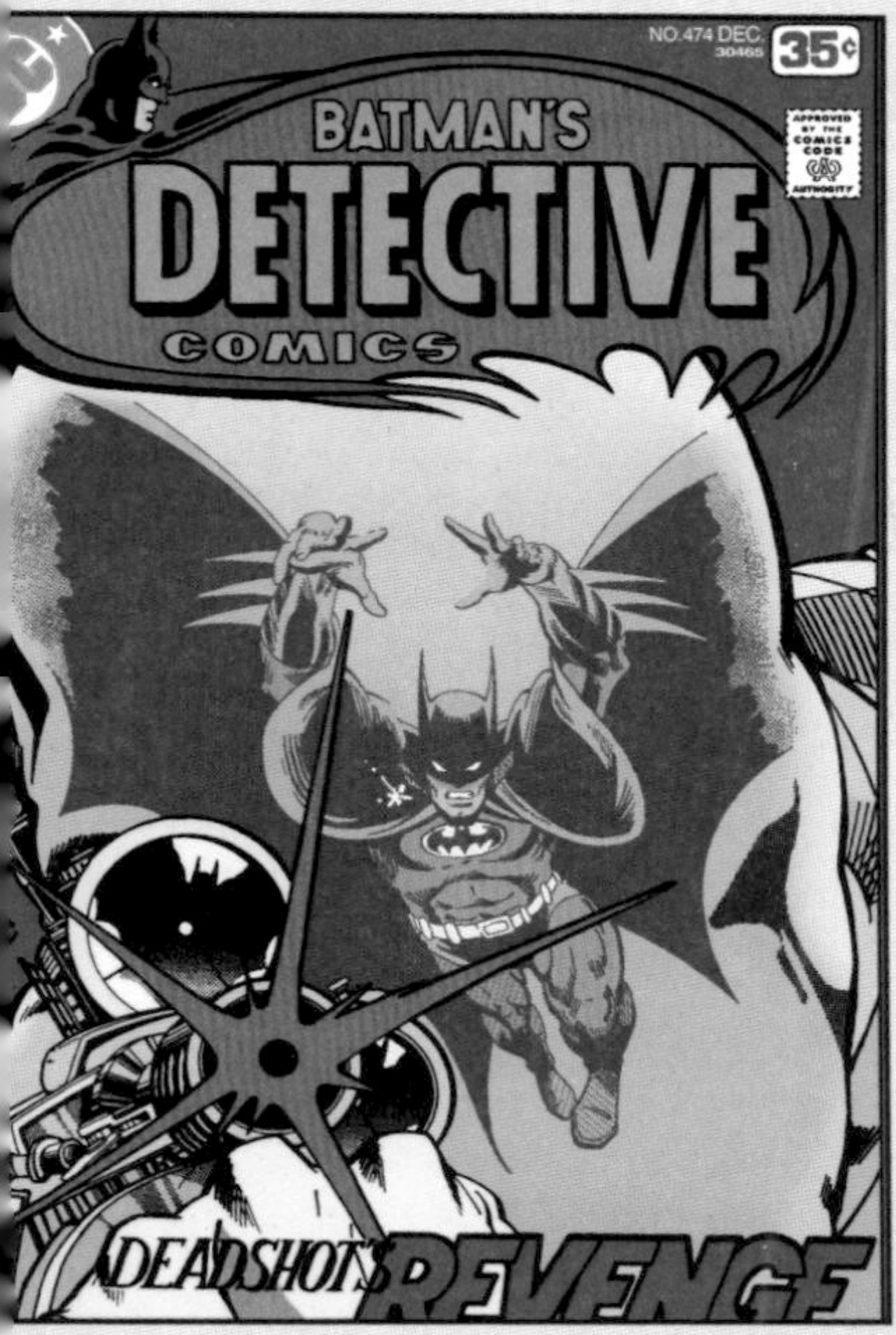
NO.474 DEC.
30465
35¢
APPROVED BY THE COMICS CODE AUTHORITY
BATMAN'S
DETECTIVE
COMICS
DEADSHOT'S REVENGE

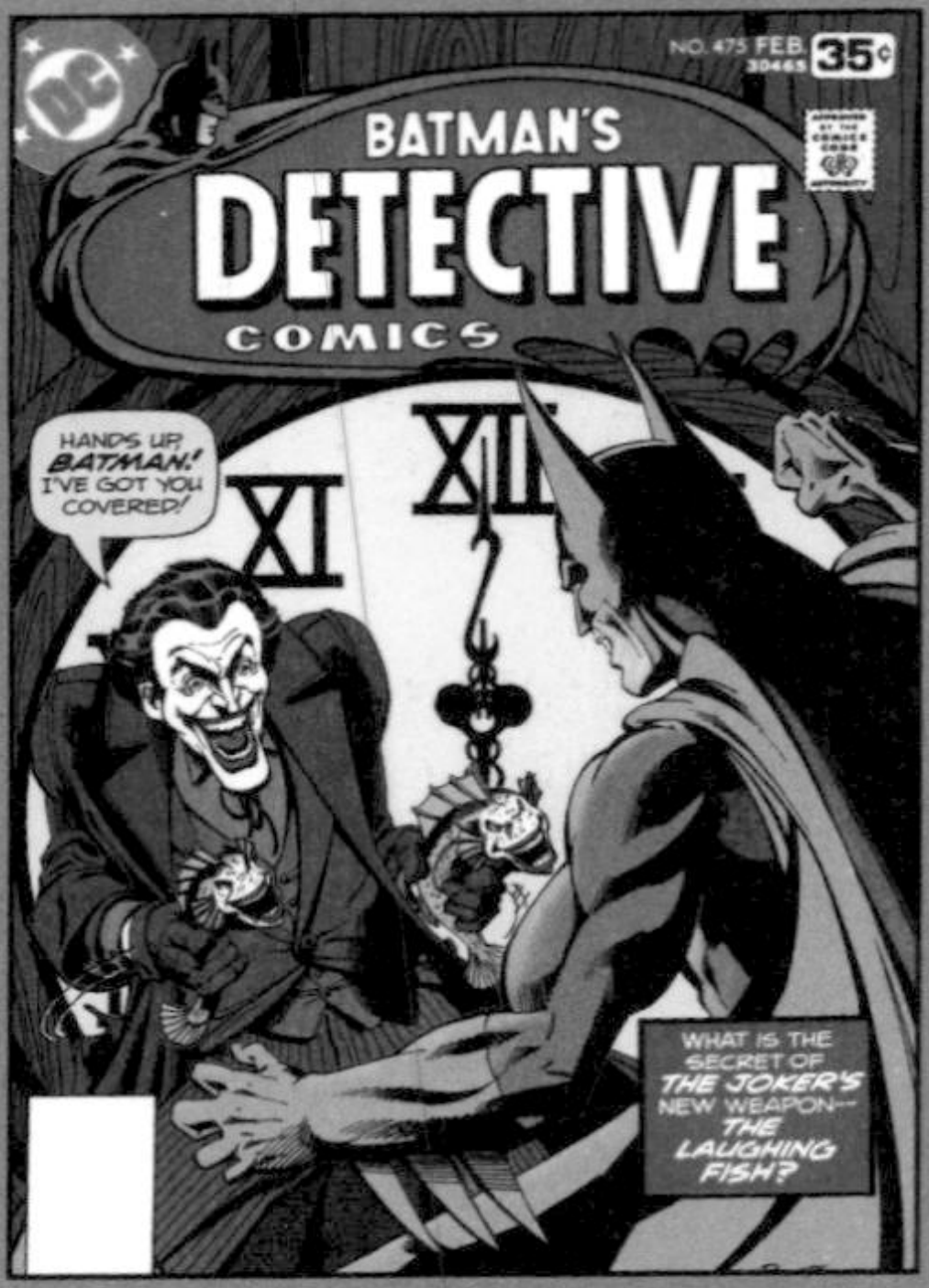

Detective Comics #475
In the popular "Laughing Fish" story arc, the Joker tries to trademark his sinister grin after it appears on the fish of Gotham City.

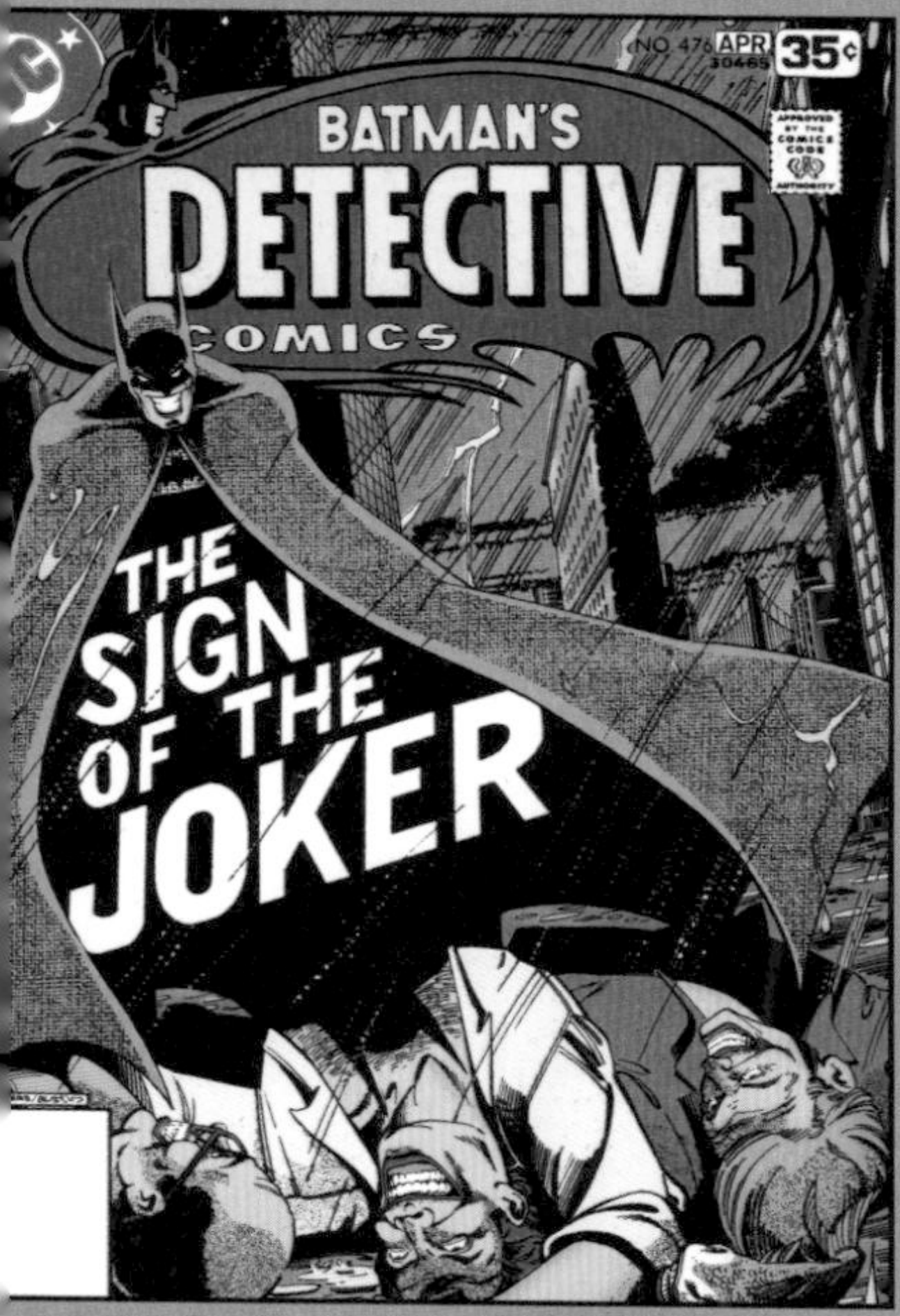
NO. 476 APR. 30465
35¢
APPROVED BY THE COMICS CODE AUTHORITY
BATMAN'S
DETECTIVE
COMICS
THE SIGN OF THE JOKER

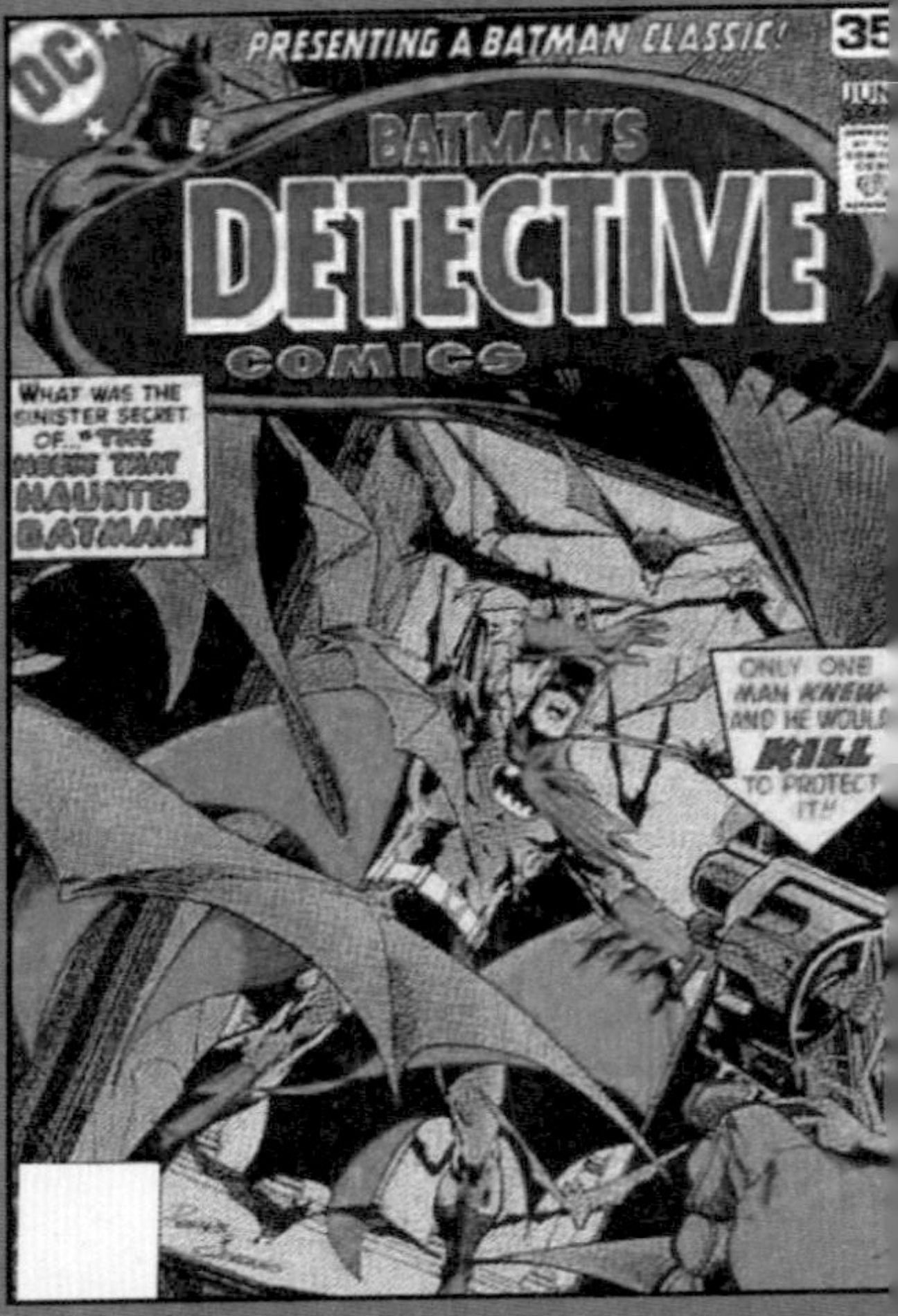
PRESENTING A BATMAN CLASSIC!
35
BATMAN'S
DETECTIVE
COMICS
WHAT WAS THE SINISTER SECRET OF... "THE MOON THAT HAUNTED BATMAN"
ONLY ONE MAN KNEW AND HE WOULD KILL TO PROTECT IT!

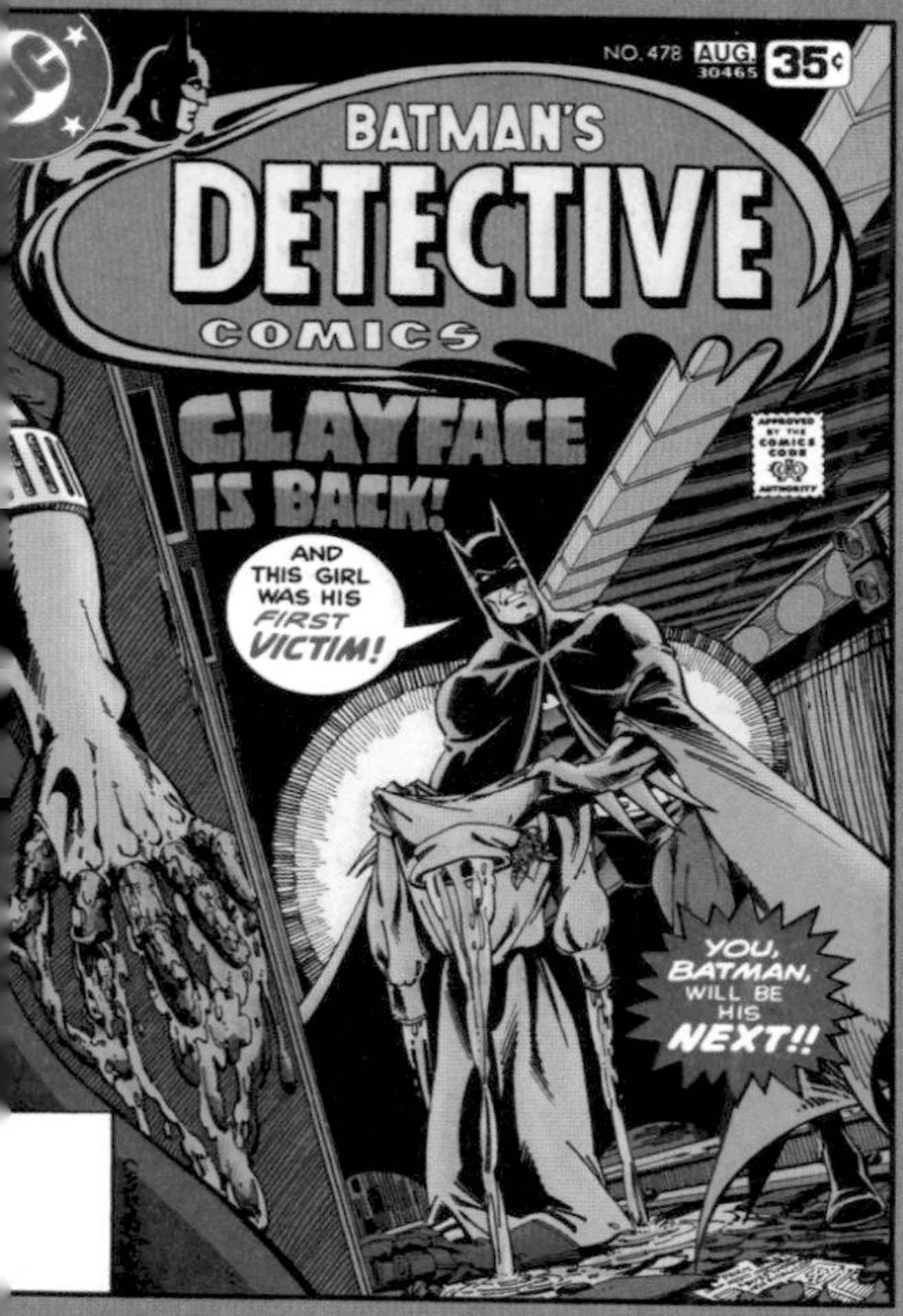
NO. 478 AUG. 30465 35¢
BATMAN'S
DETECTIVE
COMICS
CLAYFACE IS BACK!
APPROVED BY THE COMICS CODE AUTHORITY
AND THIS GIRL WAS HIS FIRST VICTIM!
YOU, BATMAN, WILL BE HIS NEXT!!

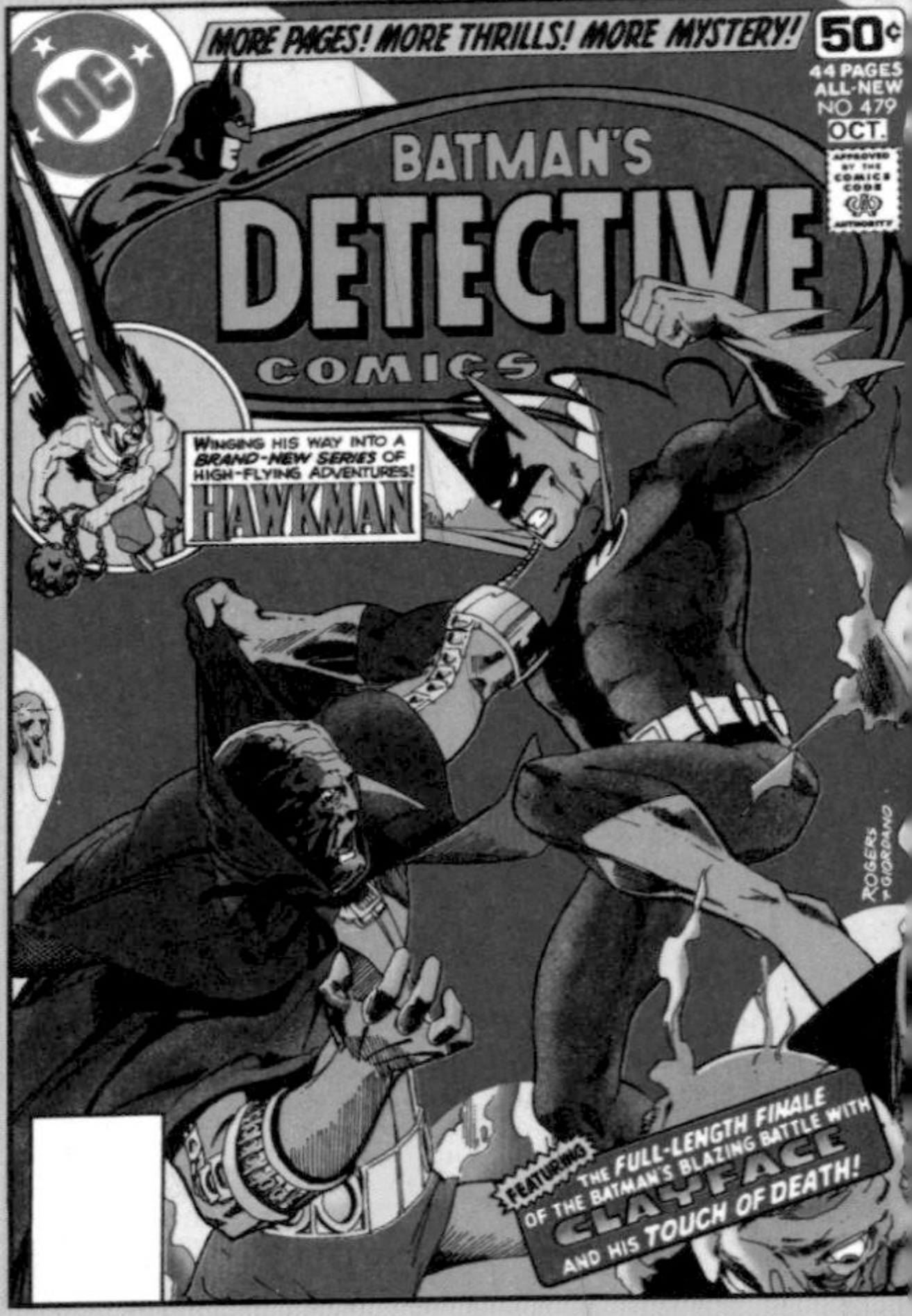
MORE PAGES! MORE THRILLS! MORE MYSTERY!
50¢
44 PAGES
ALL-NEW
NO 479
OCT.
APPROVED BY THE COMICS CODE AUTHORITY
DC
BATMAN'S
DETECTIVE
COMICS
WINGING HIS WAY INTO A BRAND-NEW SERIES OF HIGH-FLYING ADVENTURES!
HAWKMAN
ROGERS + GIORDANO
FEATURING THE FULL-LENGTH FINALE OF THE BATMAN'S BLAZING BATTLE WITH
CLAYFACE
AND HIS TOUCH OF DEATH!

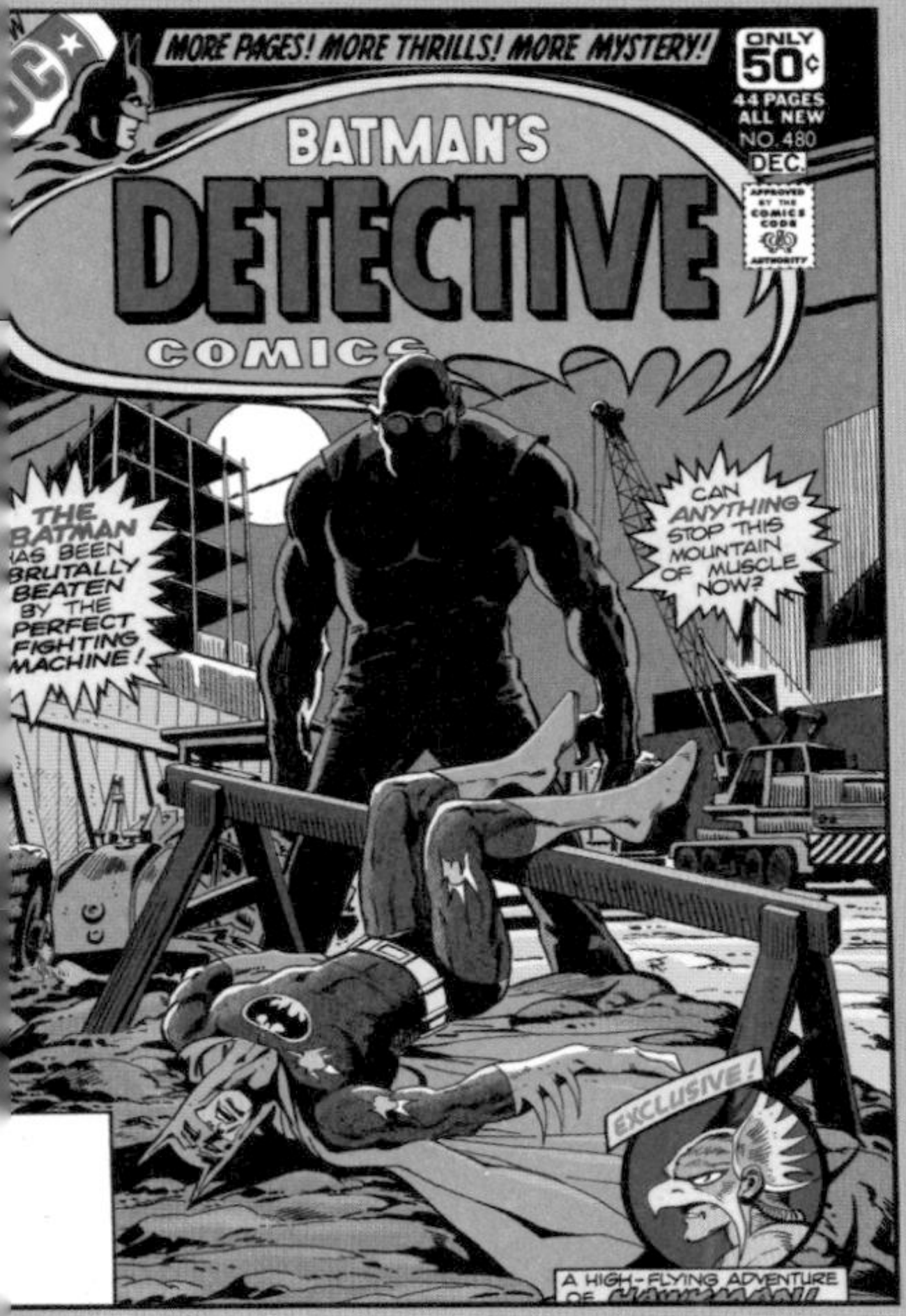
MORE PAGES! MORE THRILLS! MORE MYSTERY!
ONLY 50¢
44 PAGES ALL NEW
NO. 480
DEC.
APPROVED BY THE COMICS CODE AUTHORITY
BATMAN'S
DETECTIVE
COMICS
THE BATMAN HAS BEEN BRUTALLY BEATEN BY THE PERFECT FIGHTING MACHINE!
CAN ANYTHING STOP THIS MOUNTAIN OF MUSCLE NOW?
EXCLUSIVE!
A HIGH-FLYING ADVENTURE OF

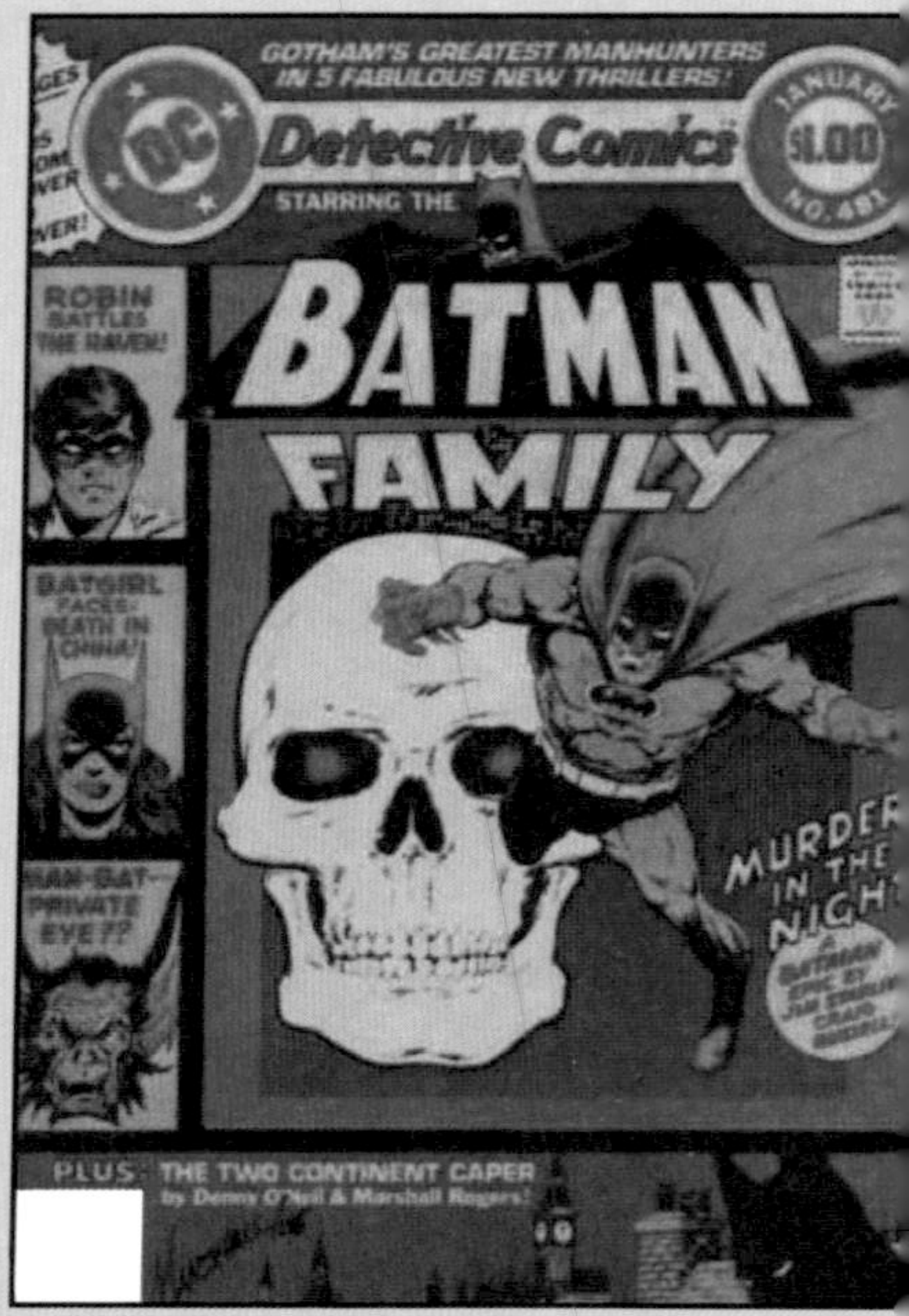
GOTHAM'S GREATEST MANHUNTERS
IN 5 FABULOUS NEW THRILLERS!
DC
Detective Comics
JANUARY
$1.00
NO. 481
STARRING THE
BATMAN
FAMILY
ROBIN
BATTLES
THE RAVEN!
BATGIRL
FACES:
DEATH IN
CHINA!
MAN-BAT
PRIVATE
EYE??
MURDER
IN THE
NIGHT
PLUS: THE TWO CONTINENT CAPER
by Denny O'Neil & Marshall Rogers!

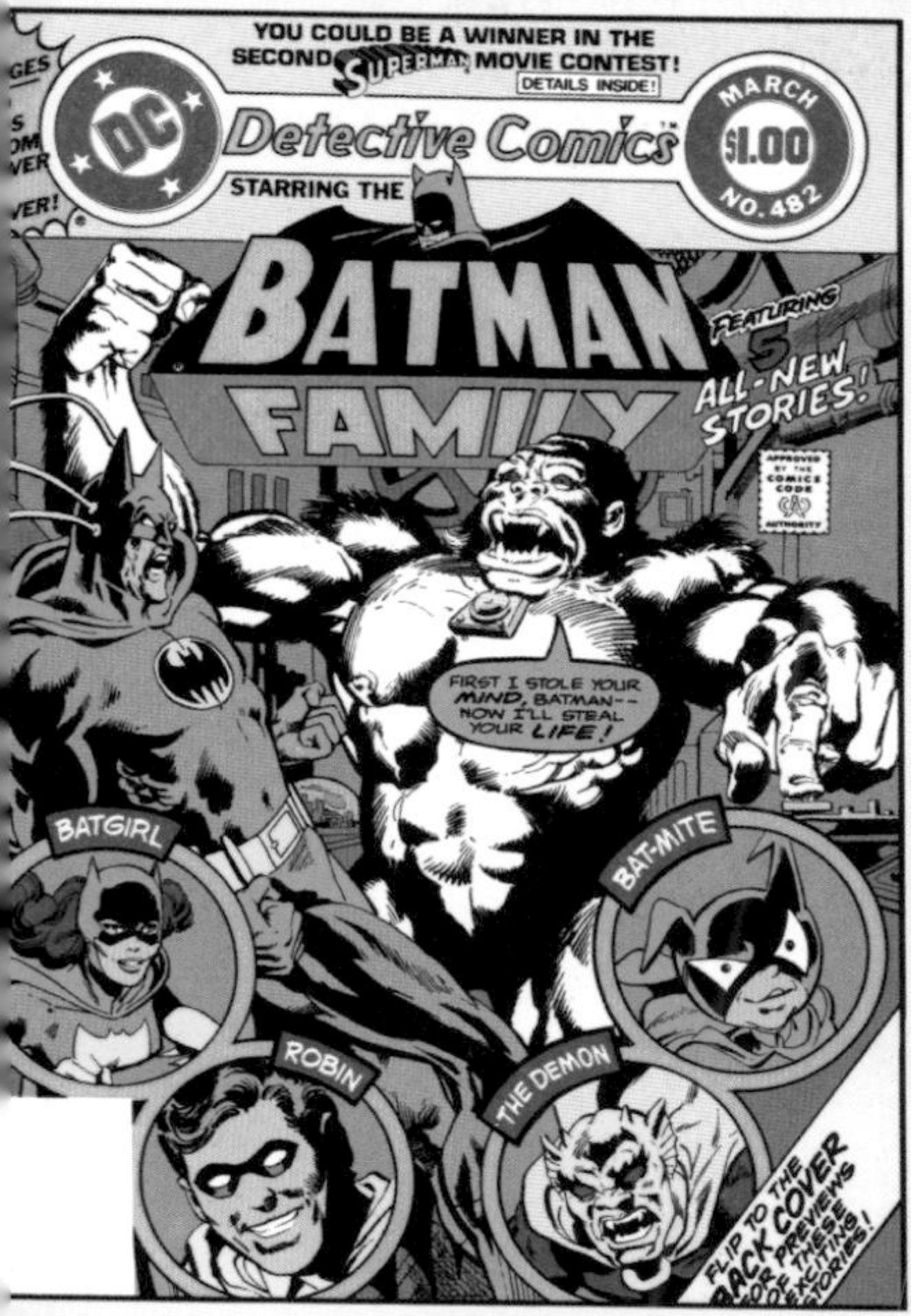
YOU COULD BE A WINNER IN THE SECOND SUPERMAN MOVIE CONTEST!
DETAILS INSIDE!
DC
Detective Comics
MARCH
$1.00
NO. 482
STARRING THE
BATMAN
FEATURING 5 ALL-NEW STORIES!
FAMILY
APPROVED BY THE COMICS CODE AUTHORITY
FIRST I STOLE YOUR MIND, BATMAN-- NOW I'LL STEAL YOUR LIFE!
BATGIRL
BAT-MITE
ROBIN
THE DEMON
FLIP TO THE BACK COVER FOR PREVIEWS OF THESE EXCITING STORIES!

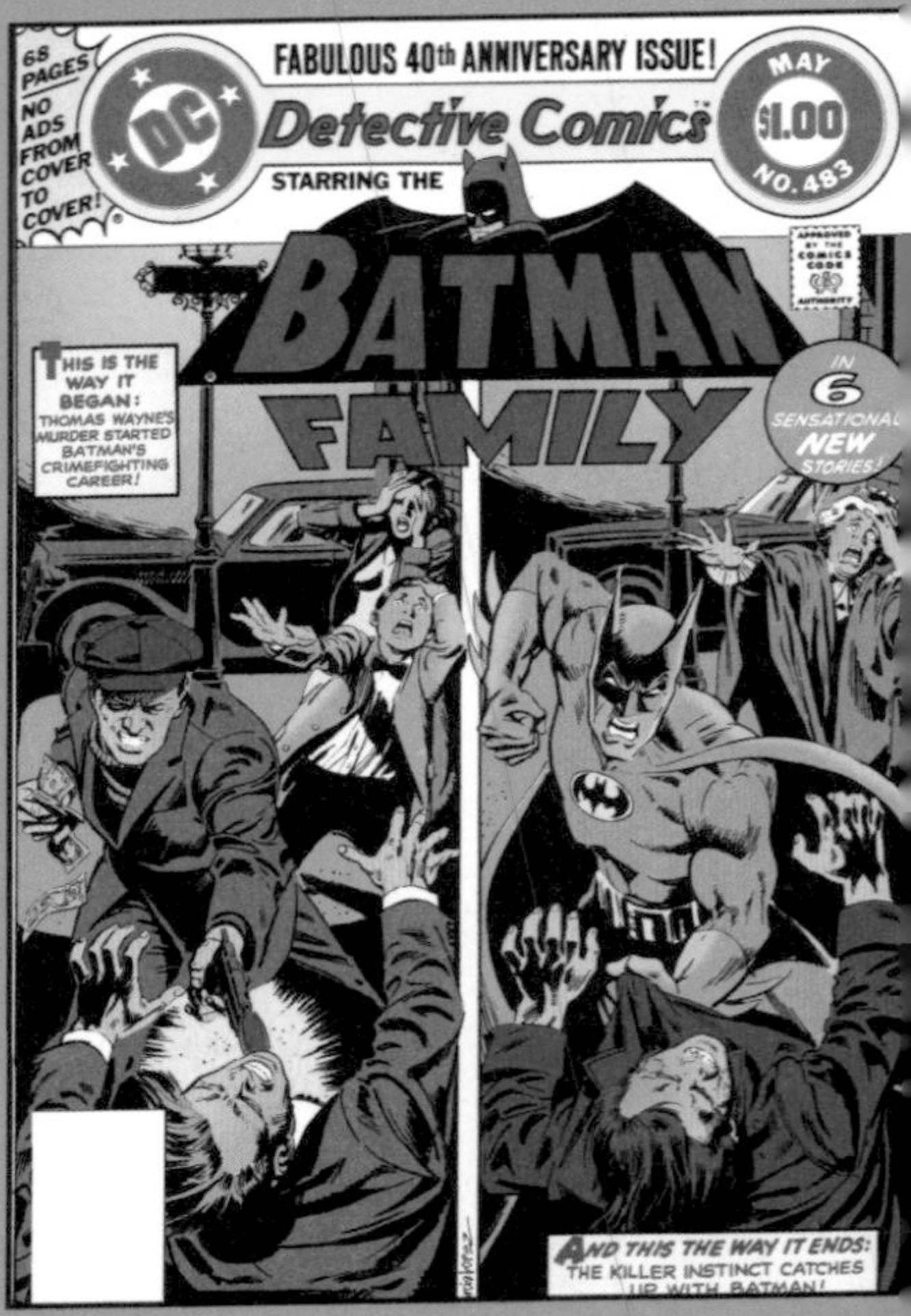
68 PAGES
NO ADS FROM COVER TO COVER!
FABULOUS 40th ANNIVERSARY ISSUE!
DC
Detective Comics
MAY
$1.00
NO. 483
STARRING THE
BATMAN
FAMILY
APPROVED BY THE COMICS CODE AUTHORITY
IN 6 SENSATIONAL NEW STORIES!
THIS IS THE WAY IT BEGAN: THOMAS WAYNE'S MURDER STARTED BATMAN'S CRIMEFIGHTING CAREER!
AND THIS THE WAY IT ENDS: THE KILLER INSTINCT CATCHES UP WITH BATMAN!

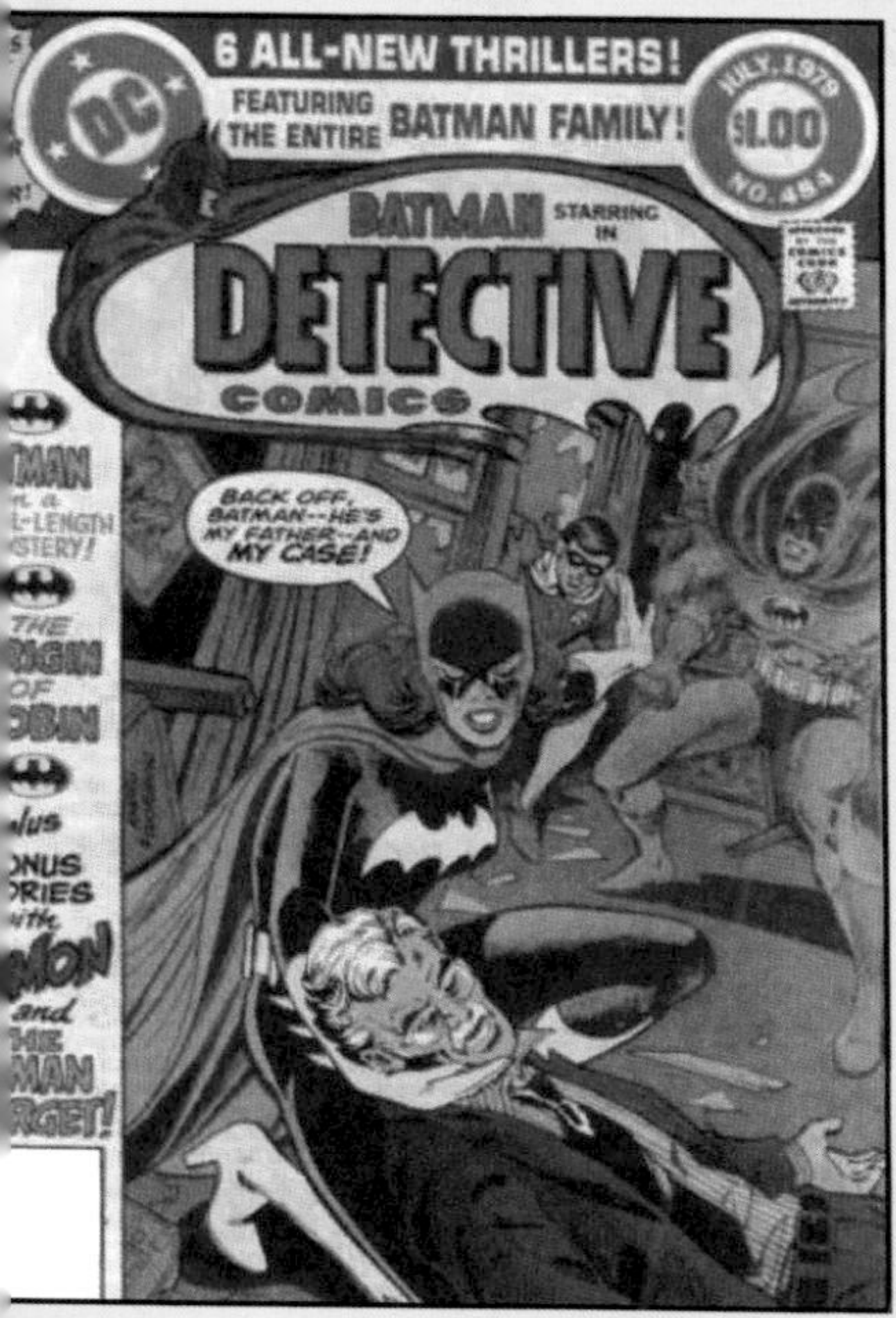
6 ALL-NEW THRILLERS!
FEATURING THE ENTIRE BATMAN FAMILY!
JULY, 1979
$1.00
NO. 481
BATMAN STARRING IN
DETECTIVE COMICS
BACK OFF, BATMAN--HE'S MY FATHER--AND MY CASE!

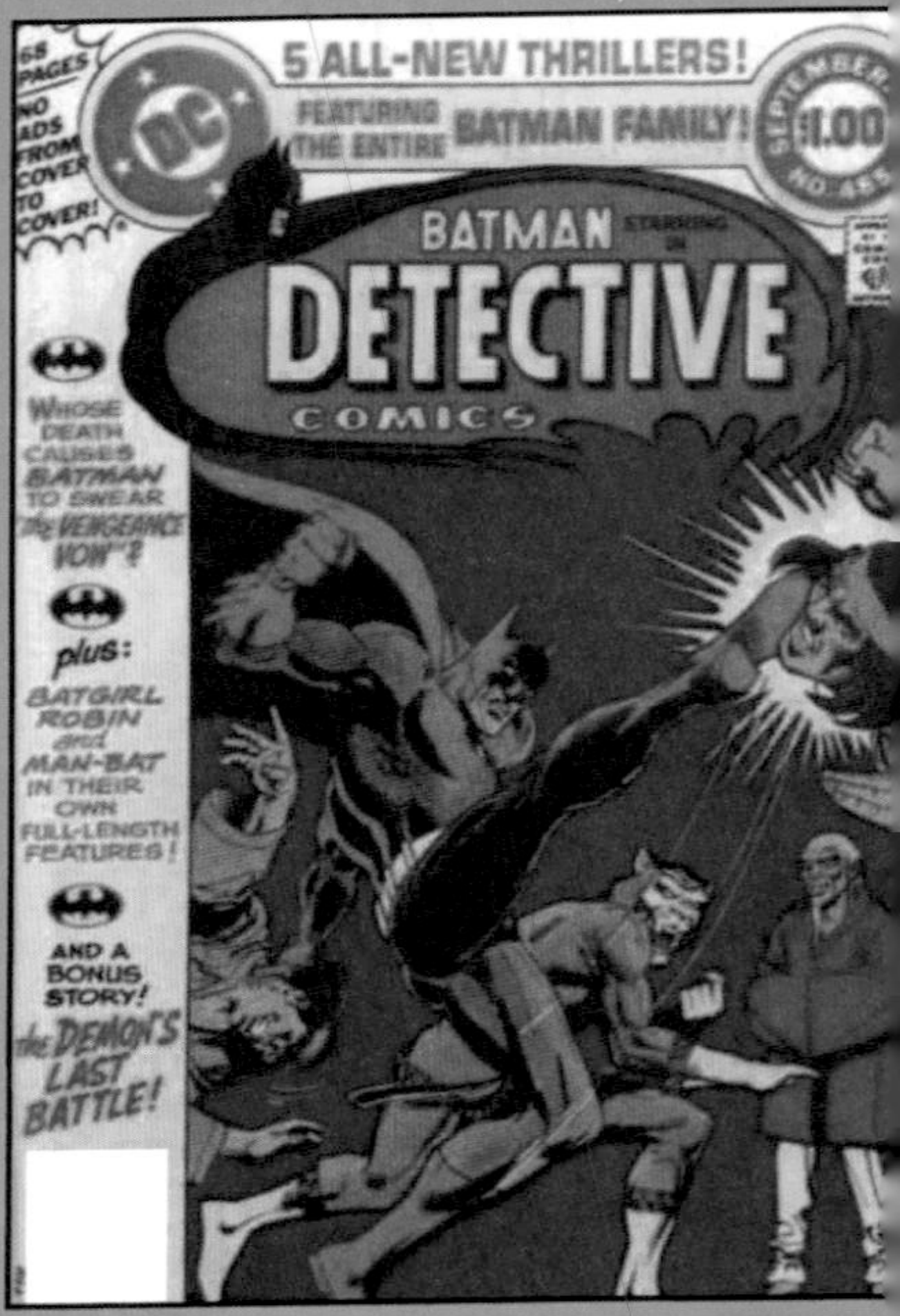
65 PAGES
NO ADS FROM COVER TO COVER!
DC
5 ALL-NEW THRILLERS!
FEATURING THE ENTIRE BATMAN FAMILY!
SEPTEMBER
$1.00
NO ADS
BATMAN STARRING IN
DETECTIVE
COMICS
WHOSE DEATH CAUSES BATMAN TO SWEAR the VENGEANCE VOW"?
plus:
BATGIRL ROBIN and MAN-BAT IN THEIR OWN FULL-LENGTH FEATURES!
AND A BONUS STORY!
the DEMON'S LAST BATTLE!

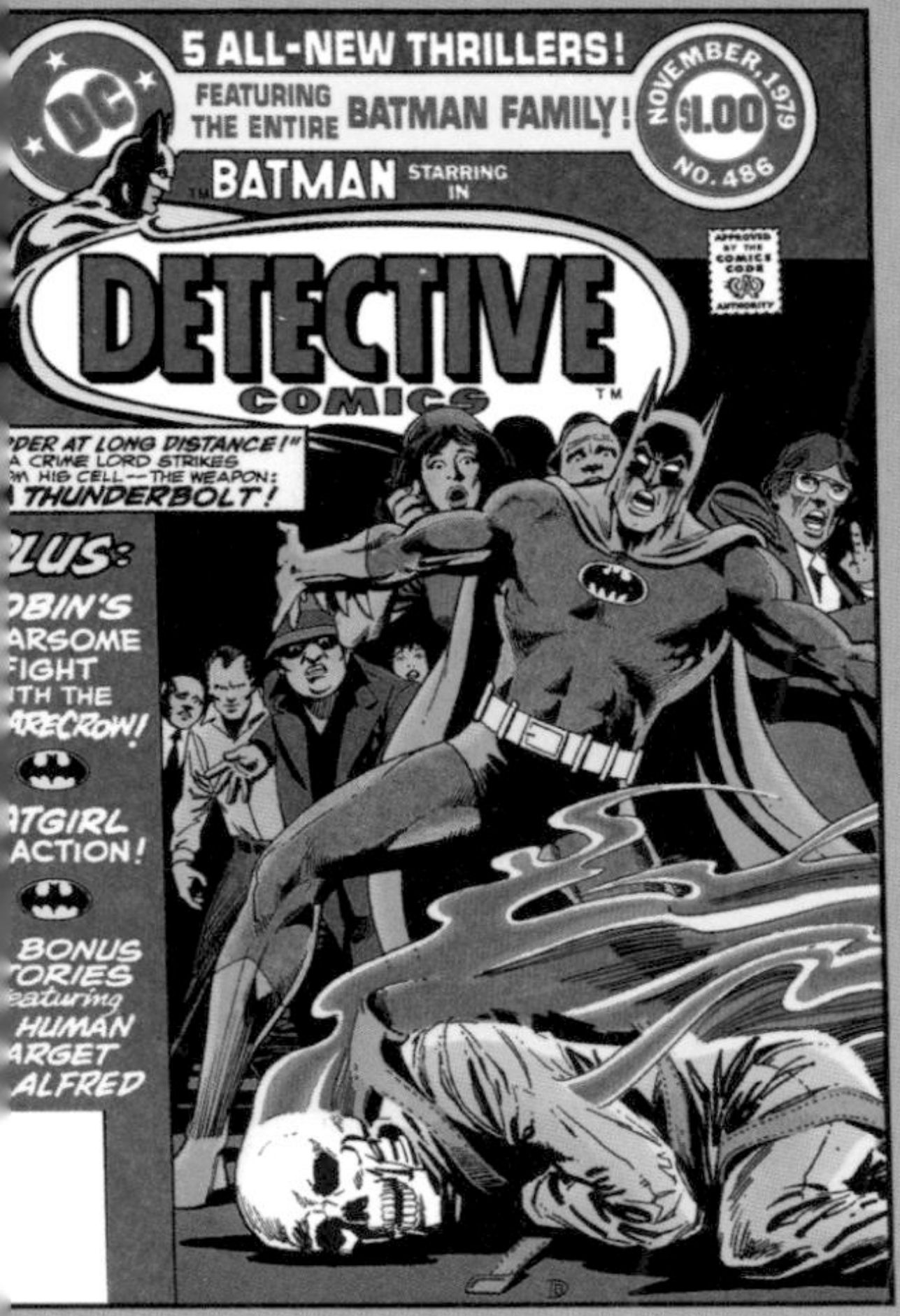
5 ALL-NEW THRILLERS!
FEATURING THE ENTIRE BATMAN FAMILY!
NOVEMBER, 1979
$1.00
NO. 486
BATMAN STARRING IN
DETECTIVE COMICS
APPROVED BY THE COMICS CODE AUTHORITY
DER AT LONG DISTANCE!"
A CRIME LORD STRIKES
M HIS CELL — THE WEAPON:
THUNDERBOLT!
LUS:
OBIN'S
ARSOME
IGHT
ITH THE
ARECROW!
ATGIRL
ACTION!
BONUS
TORIES
eaturing
HUMAN
ARGET
ALFRED

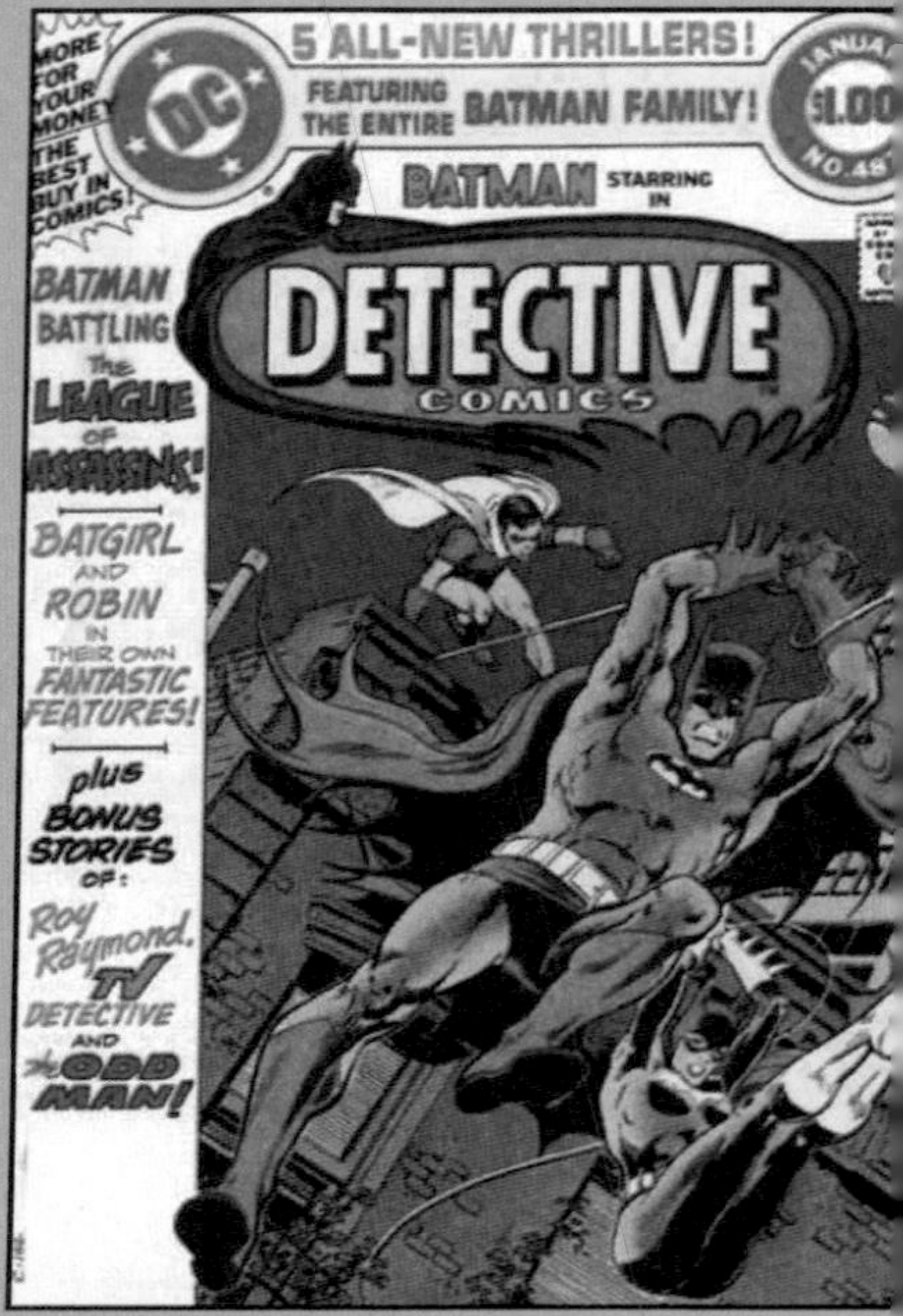
MORE FOR YOUR MONEY
THE BEST BUY IN COMICS!
DC
5 ALL-NEW THRILLERS!
FEATURING THE ENTIRE BATMAN FAMILY!
JANUARY
$1.00
NO. 48
BATMAN STARRING IN
DETECTIVE COMICS
BATMAN BATTLING The LEAGUE OF ASSASSINS!
BATGIRL AND ROBIN IN THEIR OWN FANTASTIC FEATURES!
plus BONUS STORIES OF: Roy Raymond, TV DETECTIVE AND the ODD MAN!

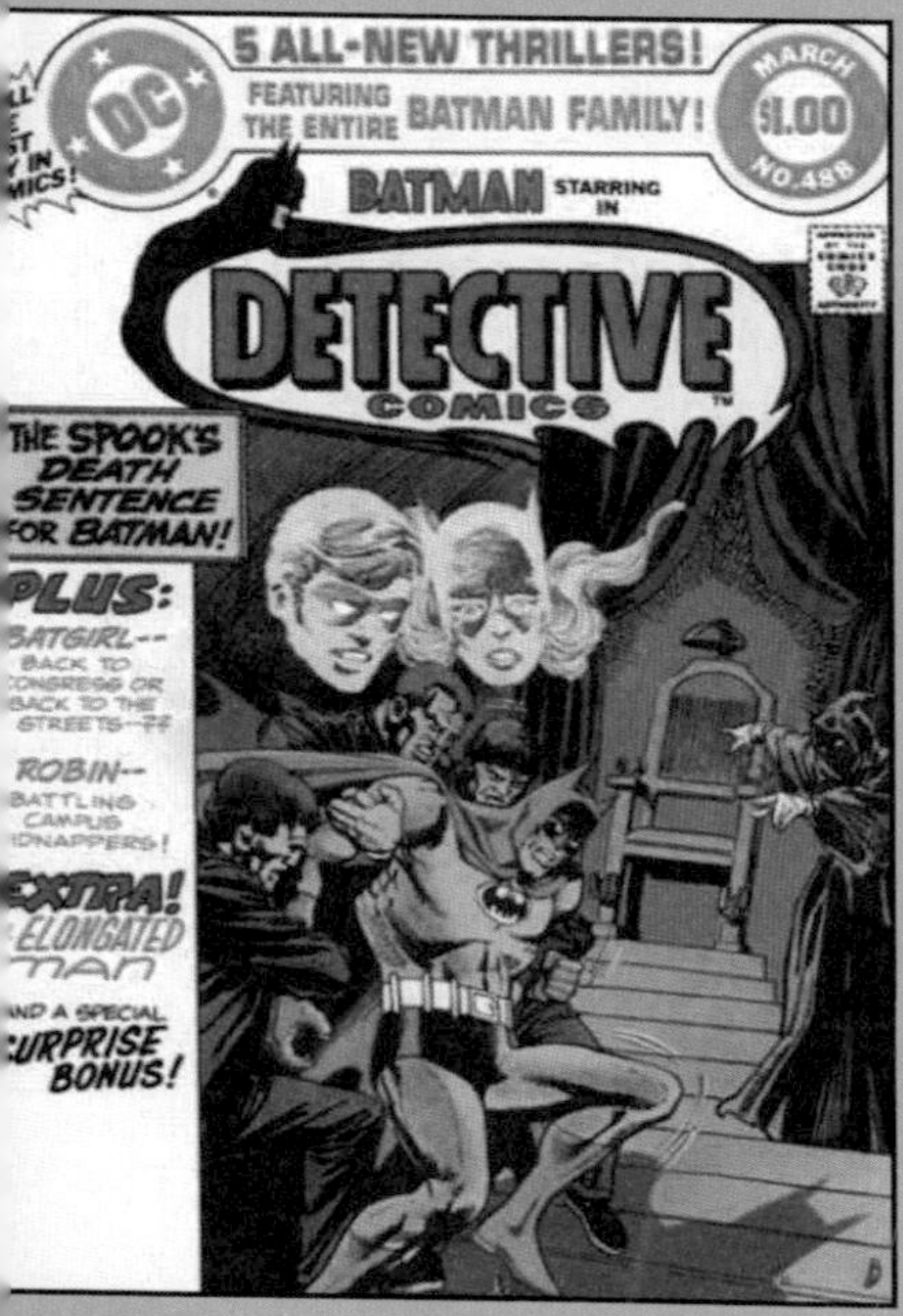
5 ALL-NEW THRILLERS!
FEATURING THE ENTIRE BATMAN FAMILY!
DC
MARCH
$1.00
NO. 488
BATMAN STARRING IN
DETECTIVE COMICS
THE SPOOK'S DEATH SENTENCE FOR BATMAN!
PLUS:
BATGIRL--
BACK TO CONGRESS OR BACK TO THE STREETS--??
ROBIN--
BATTLING CAMPUS KIDNAPPERS!
EXTRA!
ELONGATED MAN
AND A SPECIAL SURPRISE BONUS!

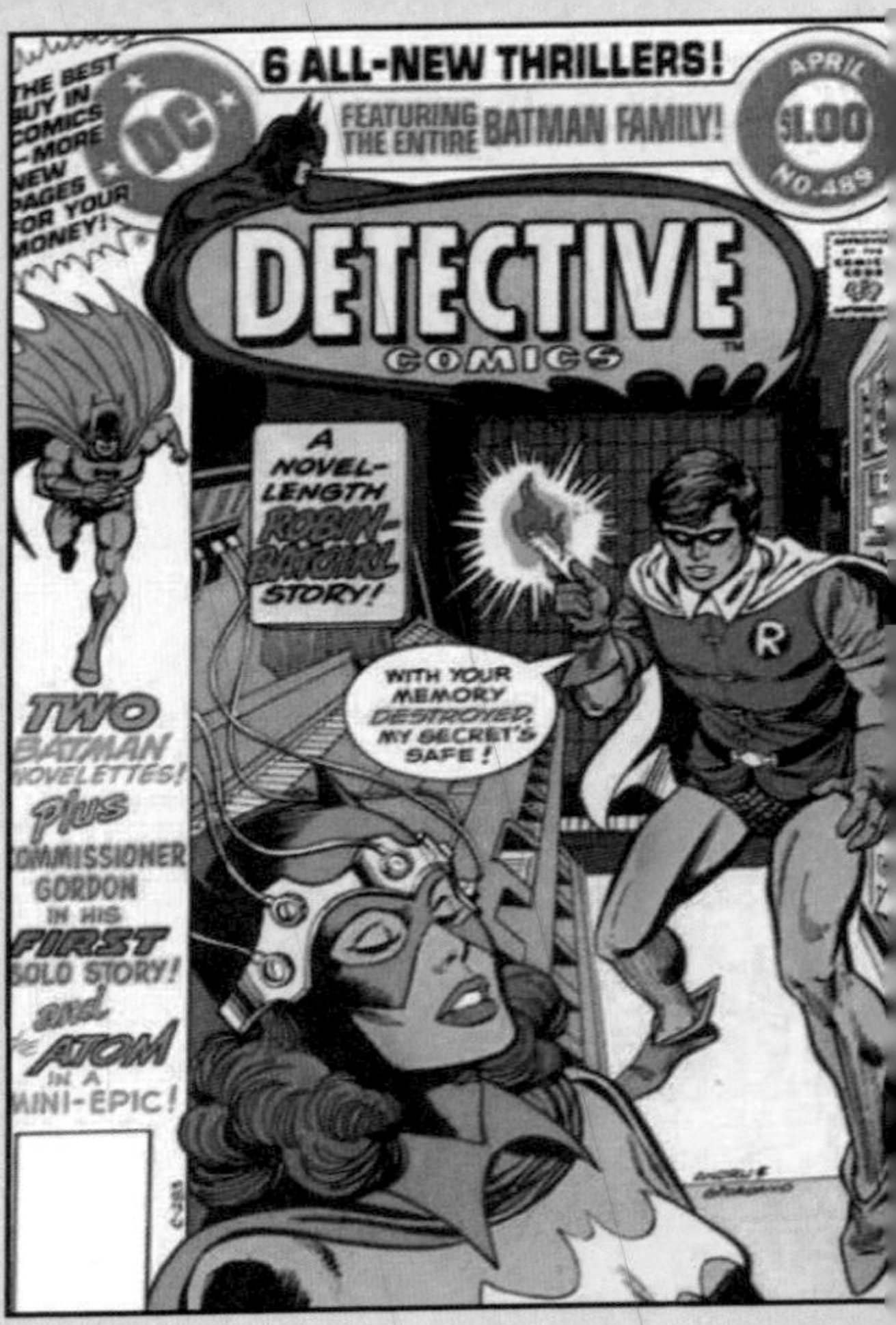
THE BEST BUY IN COMICS – MORE NEW PAGES FOR YOUR MONEY!
DC
6 ALL-NEW THRILLERS!
FEATURING THE ENTIRE BATMAN FAMILY!
APRIL
$1.00
NO. 489
DETECTIVE COMICS
A NOVEL-LENGTH ROBIN-BATGIRL STORY!
WITH YOUR MEMORY DESTROYED, MY SECRET'S SAFE!
R
TWO BATMAN NOVELETTES!
plus
COMMISSIONER GORDON IN HIS FIRST SOLO STORY!
and the ATOM IN A MINI-EPIC!

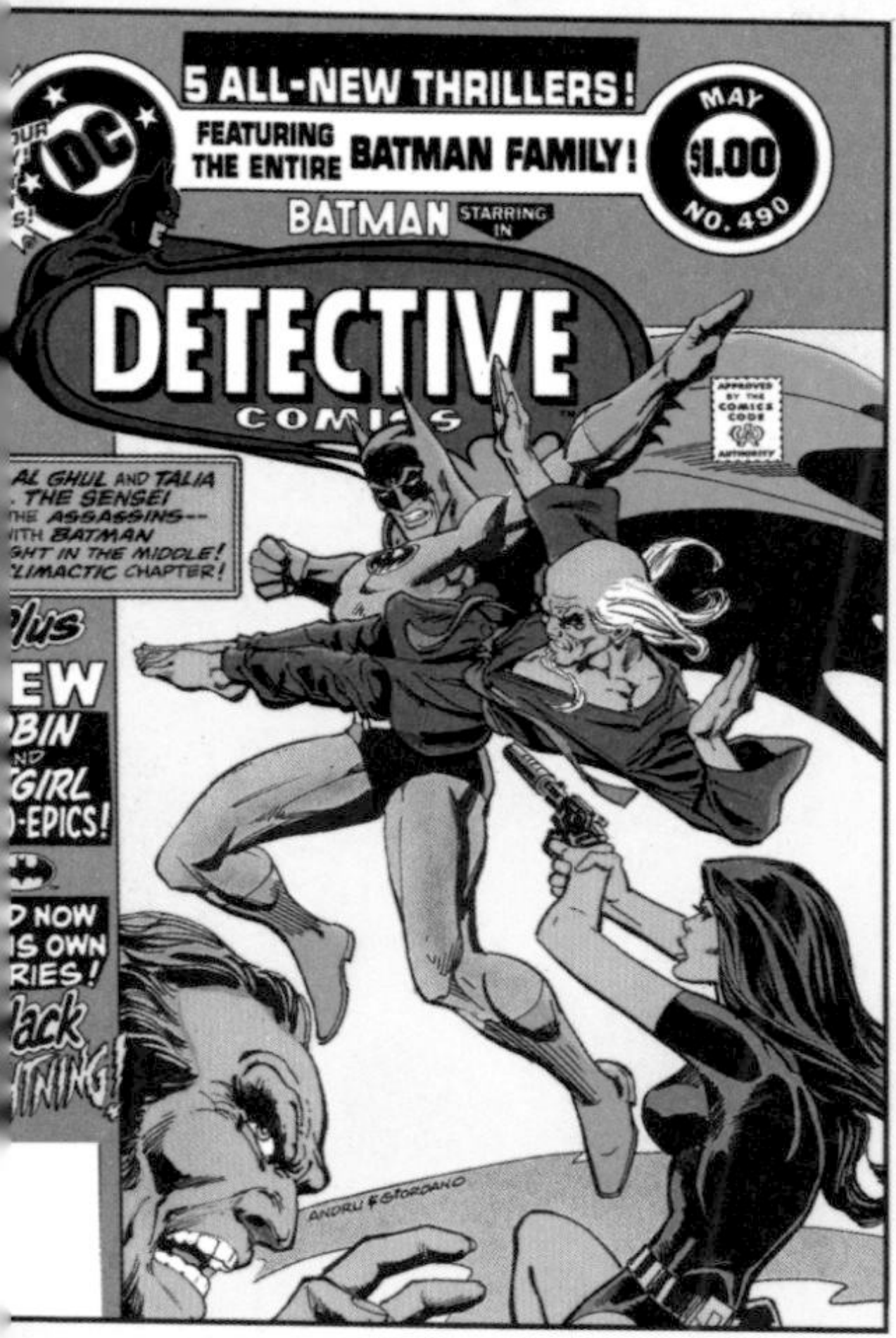
5 ALL-NEW THRILLERS!
FEATURING THE ENTIRE BATMAN FAMILY!
MAY
$1.00
NO. 490
BATMAN STARRING IN
DETECTIVE COMICS
APPROVED BY THE COMICS CODE AUTHORITY
AL GHUL AND TALIA
. THE SENSEI
THE ASSASSINS--
ITH BATMAN
GHT IN THE MIDDLE!
LIMACTIC CHAPTER!
lus
EW
BIN
ND
GIRL
-EPICS!
D NOW
IS OWN
RIES!
lack
ITNING!
ANDRU & GIORDANO

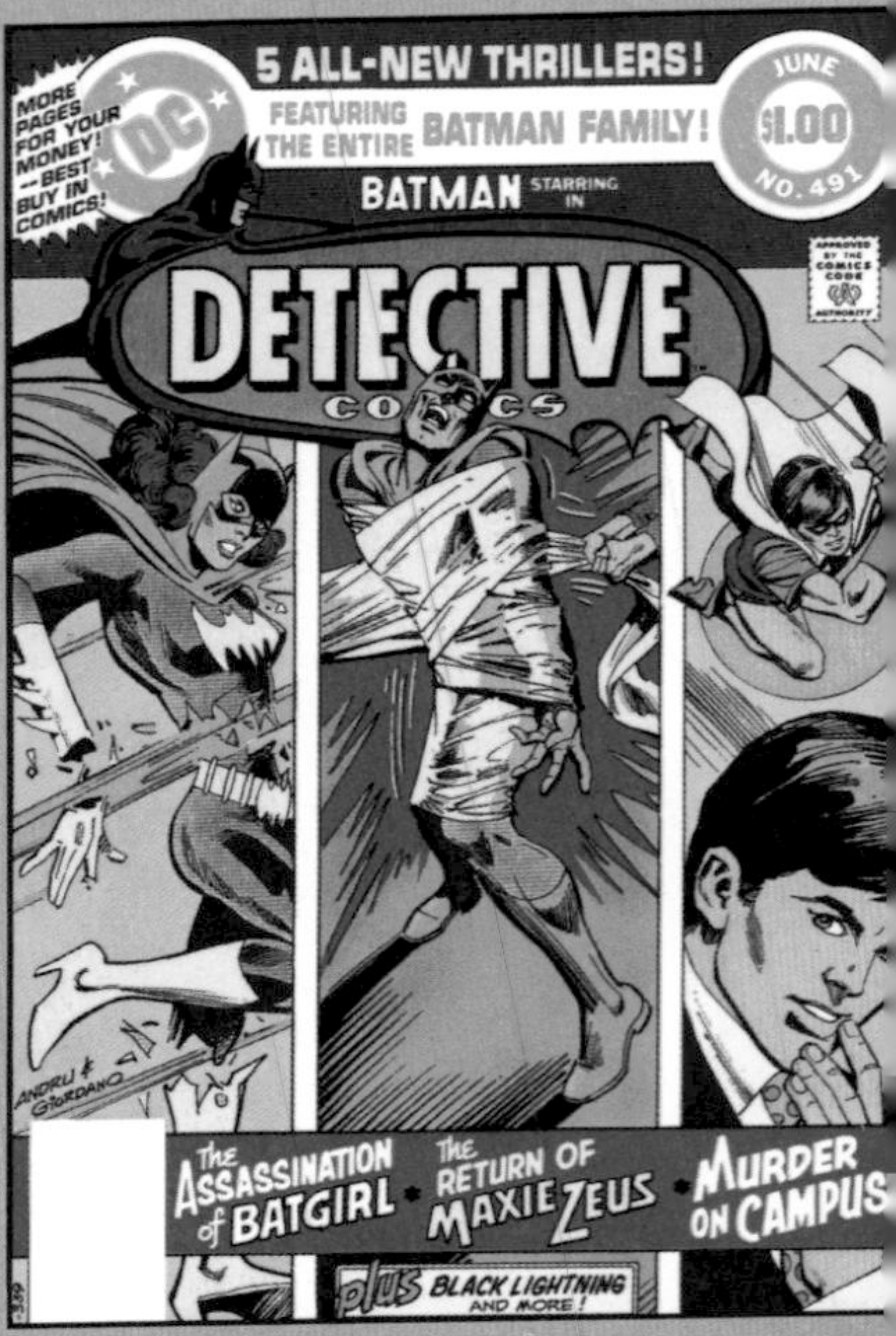
5 ALL-NEW THRILLERS!
MORE PAGES FOR YOUR MONEY! —BEST BUY IN COMICS!
DC
FEATURING THE ENTIRE BATMAN FAMILY!
JUNE
$1.00
NO. 491
BATMAN STARRING IN
DETECTIVE COMICS
APPROVED BY THE COMICS CODE AUTHORITY
ANDRU & GIORDANO
THE ASSASSINATION of BATGIRL
THE RETURN OF MAXIE ZEUS
MURDER ON CAMPUS
plus BLACK LIGHTNING AND MORE!

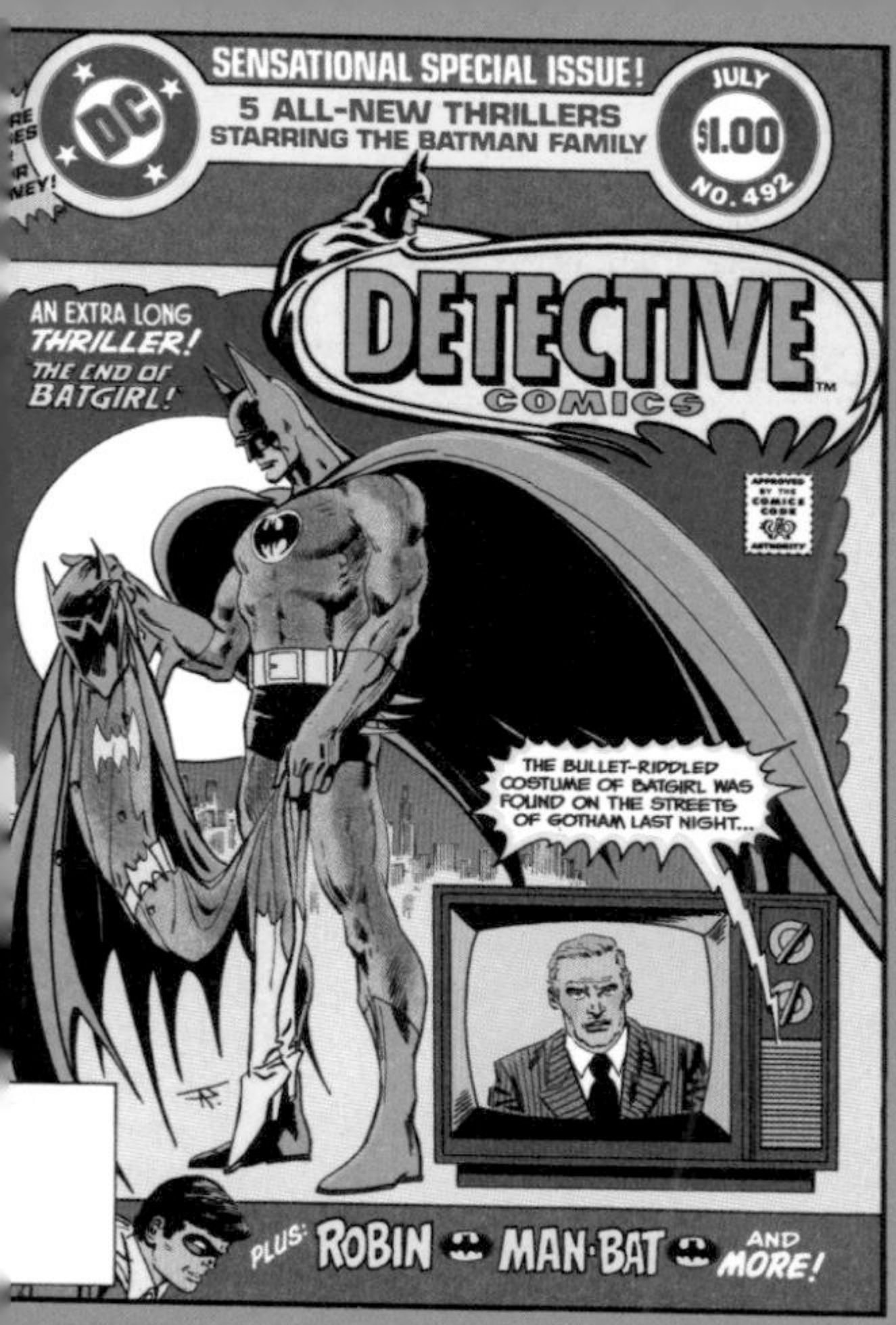
SENSATIONAL SPECIAL ISSUE!
5 ALL-NEW THRILLERS
STARRING THE BATMAN FAMILY
JULY
$1.00
NO. 492
DETECTIVE
COMICS
AN EXTRA LONG THRILLER!
THE END OF BATGIRL!
APPROVED BY THE COMICS CODE AUTHORITY
THE BULLET-RIDDLED COSTUME OF BATGIRL WAS FOUND ON THE STREETS OF GOTHAM LAST NIGHT...
PLUS: ROBIN MAN-BAT AND MORE!

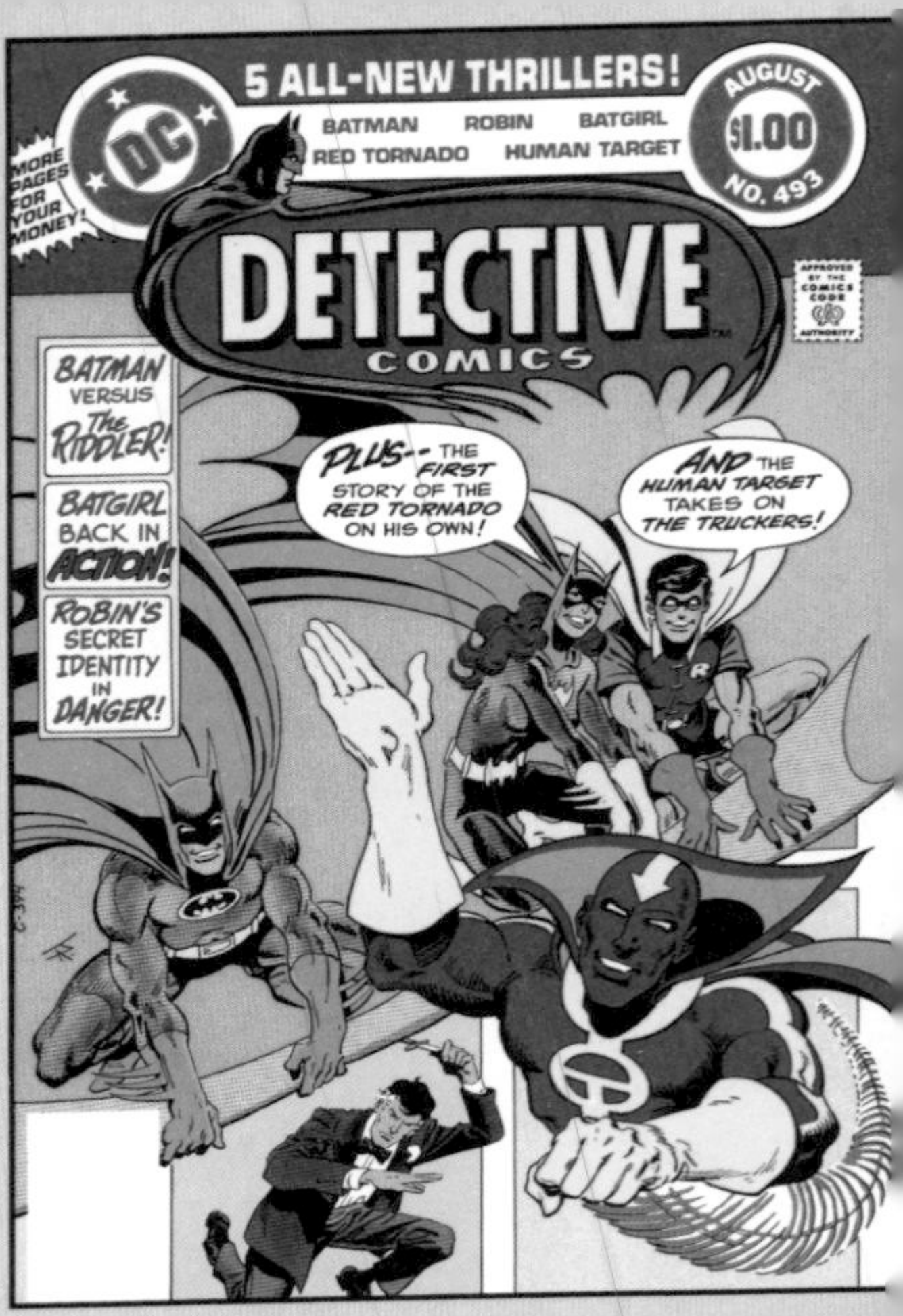
5 ALL-NEW THRILLERS!
BATMAN
ROBIN
BATGIRL
RED TORNADO
HUMAN TARGET
AUGUST
$1.00
NO. 493
DC
MORE PAGES FOR YOUR MONEY!
DETECTIVE
COMICS
APPROVED BY THE COMICS CODE AUTHORITY
BATMAN VERSUS The RIDDLER!
BATGIRL BACK IN ACTION!
ROBIN'S SECRET IDENTITY IN DANGER!
PLUS-- THE FIRST STORY OF THE RED TORNADO ON HIS OWN!
AND THE HUMAN TARGET TAKES ON THE TRUCKERS!

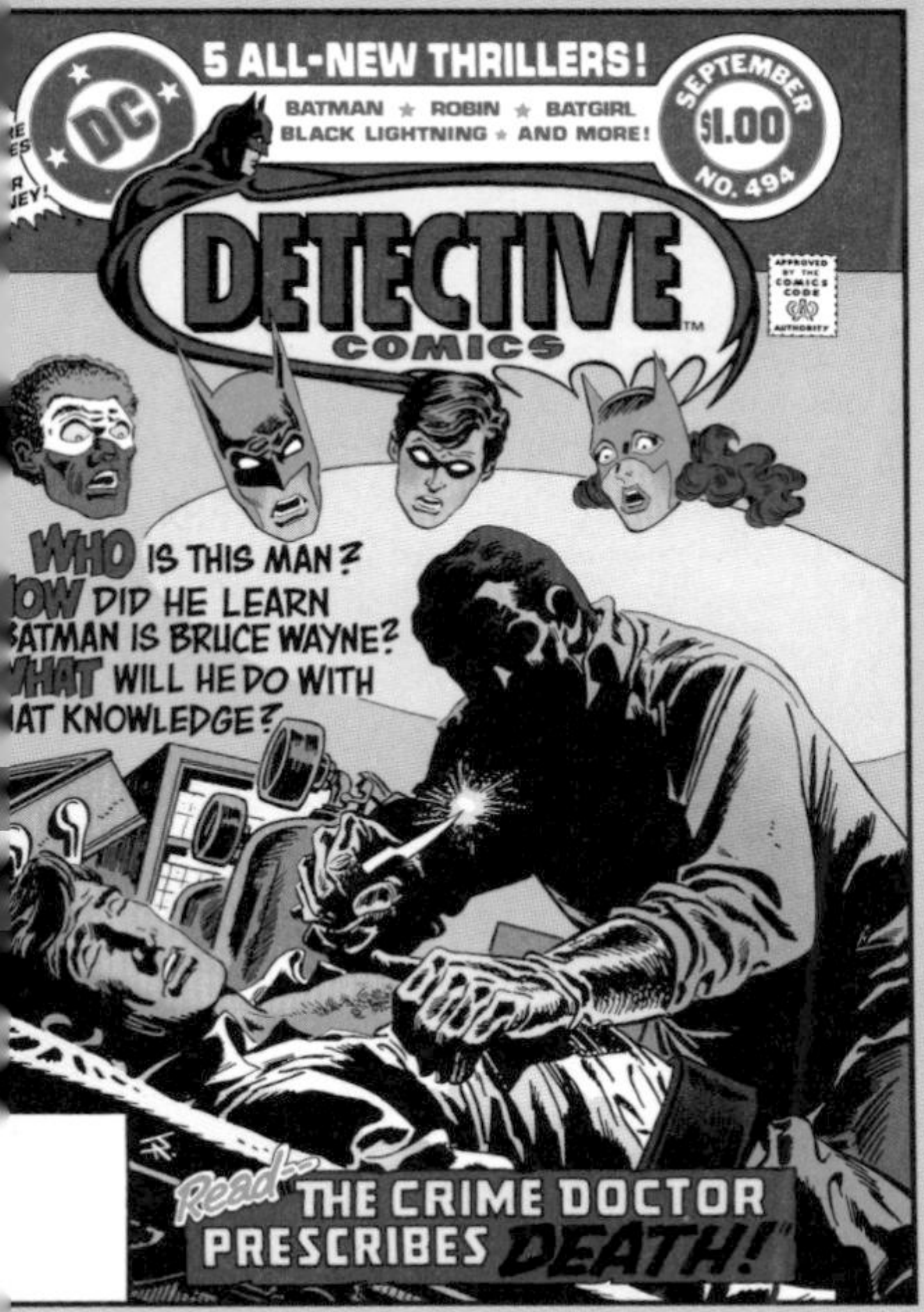
5 ALL-NEW THRILLERS!
DC
BATMAN ★ ROBIN ★ BATGIRL
BLACK LIGHTNING ★ AND MORE!
SEPTEMBER
$1.00
NO. 494
DETECTIVE
COMICS
APPROVED BY THE COMICS CODE AUTHORITY
WHO IS THIS MAN?
OW DID HE LEARN
ATMAN IS BRUCE WAYNE?
HAT WILL HE DO WITH
AT KNOWLEDGE?
Read: THE CRIME DOCTOR PRESCRIBES DEATH!

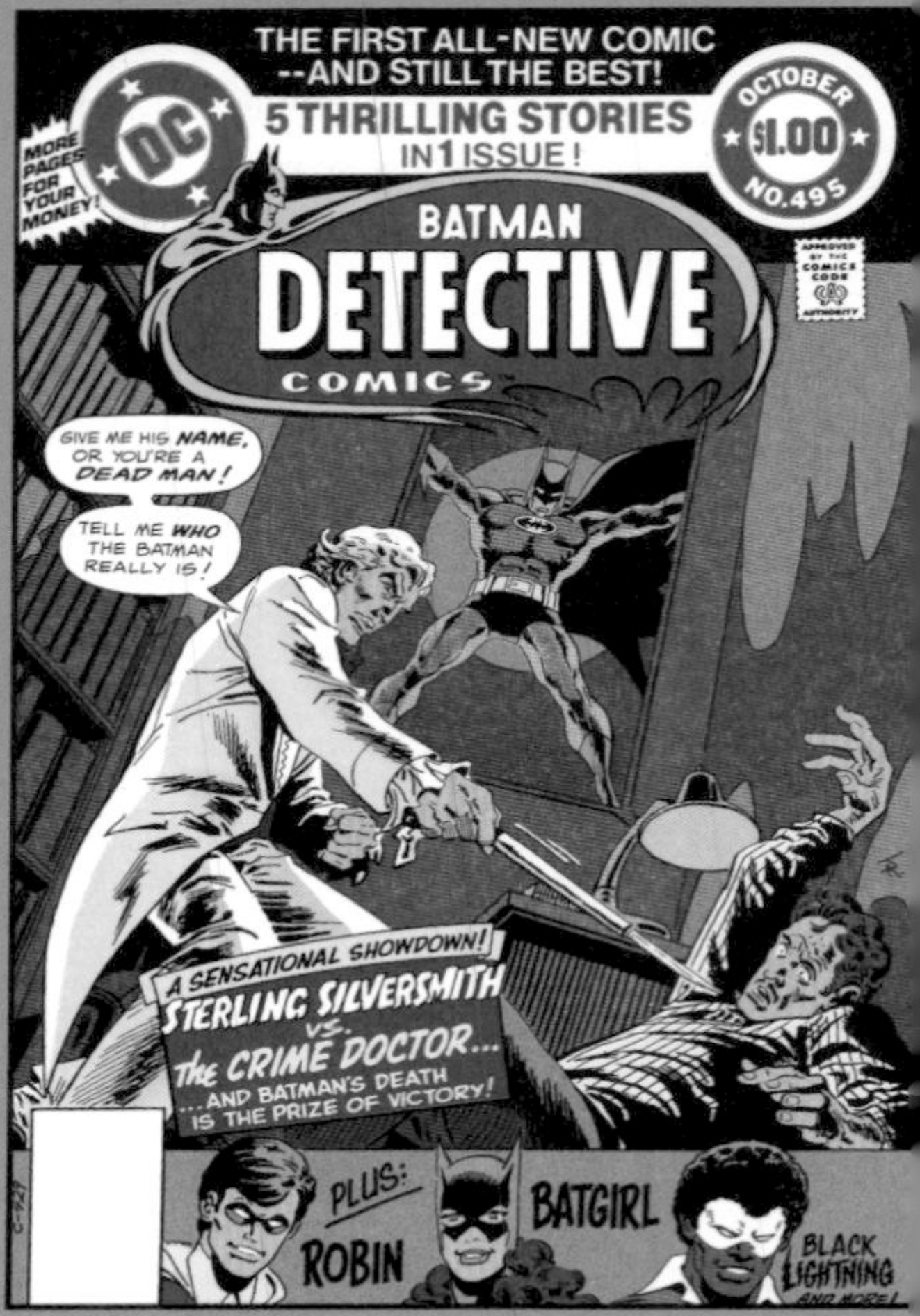
THE FIRST ALL-NEW COMIC
--AND STILL THE BEST!
DC
5 THRILLING STORIES
IN 1 ISSUE!
OCTOBER
$1.00
NO. 495
MORE PAGES FOR YOUR MONEY!
BATMAN
DETECTIVE
COMICS
APPROVED BY THE COMICS CODE AUTHORITY
GIVE ME HIS NAME, OR YOU'RE A DEAD MAN!
TELL ME WHO THE BATMAN REALLY IS!
A SENSATIONAL SHOWDOWN!
STERLING SILVERSMITH
VS.
THE CRIME DOCTOR...
...AND BATMAN'S DEATH IS THE PRIZE OF VICTORY!
PLUS:
ROBIN
BATGIRL
BLACK LIGHTNING
AND MORE!

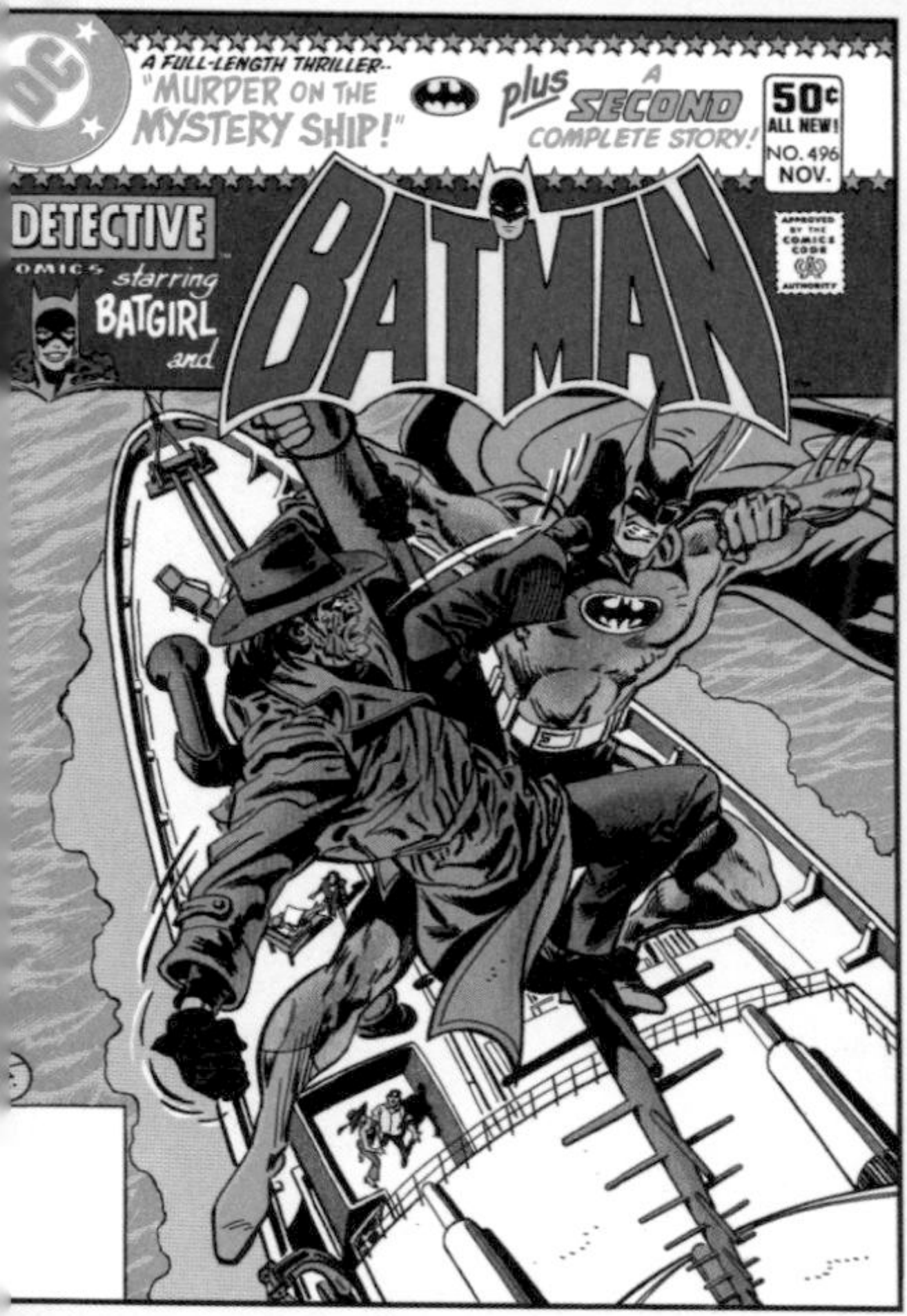
DC
A FULL-LENGTH THRILLER--
"MURDER ON THE MYSTERY SHIP!"
plus A SECOND COMPLETE STORY!
50¢
ALL NEW!
NO. 496
NOV.
DETECTIVE
OMICS starring BATGIRL and
BATMAN
APPROVED BY THE COMICS CODE AUTHORITY

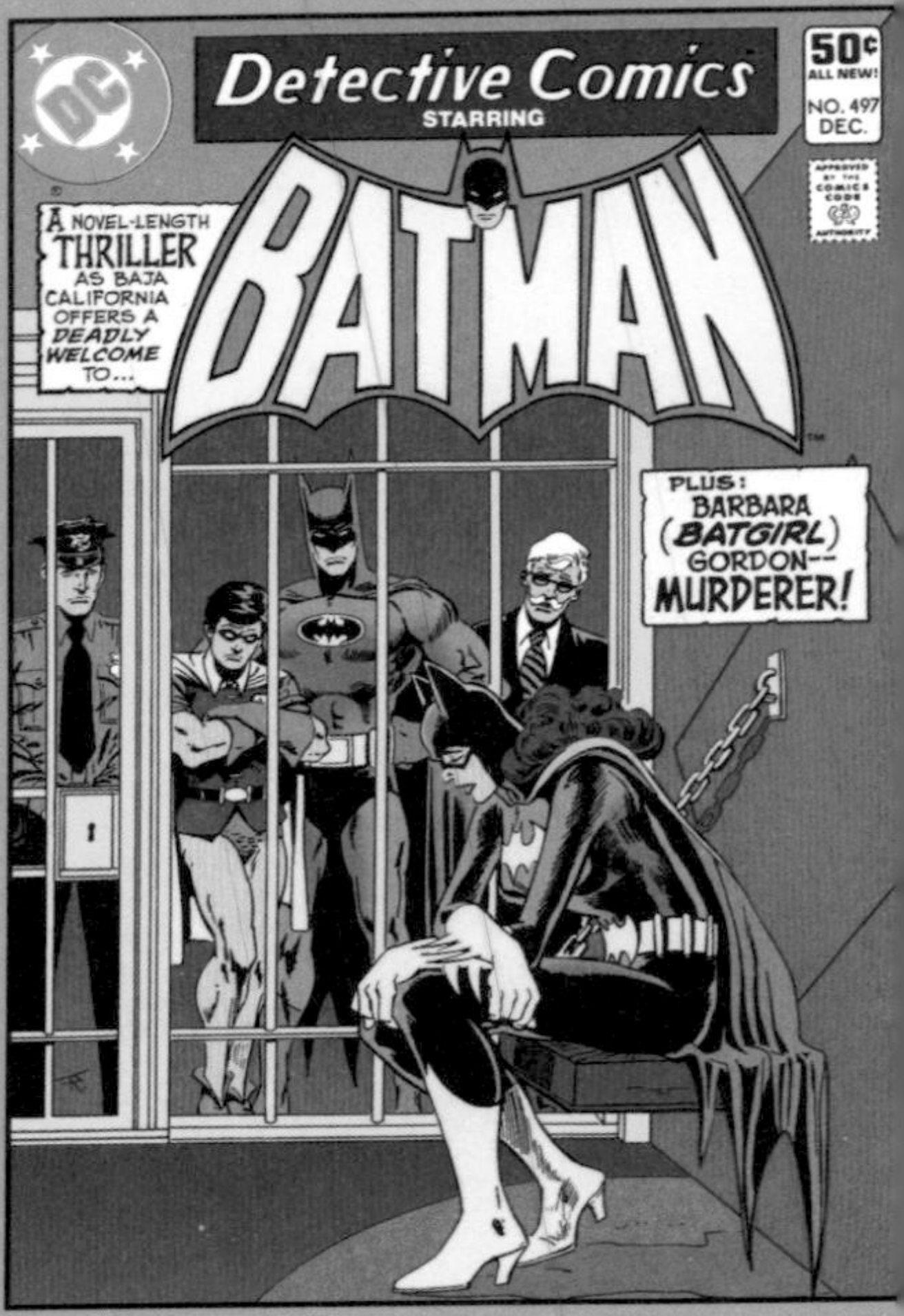
Detective Comics
STARRING
BATMAN
50¢
ALL NEW!
NO. 497
DEC.
A NOVEL-LENGTH THRILLER AS BAJA CALIFORNIA OFFERS A DEADLY WELCOME TO...
PLUS: BARBARA (BATGIRL) GORDON-- MURDERER!

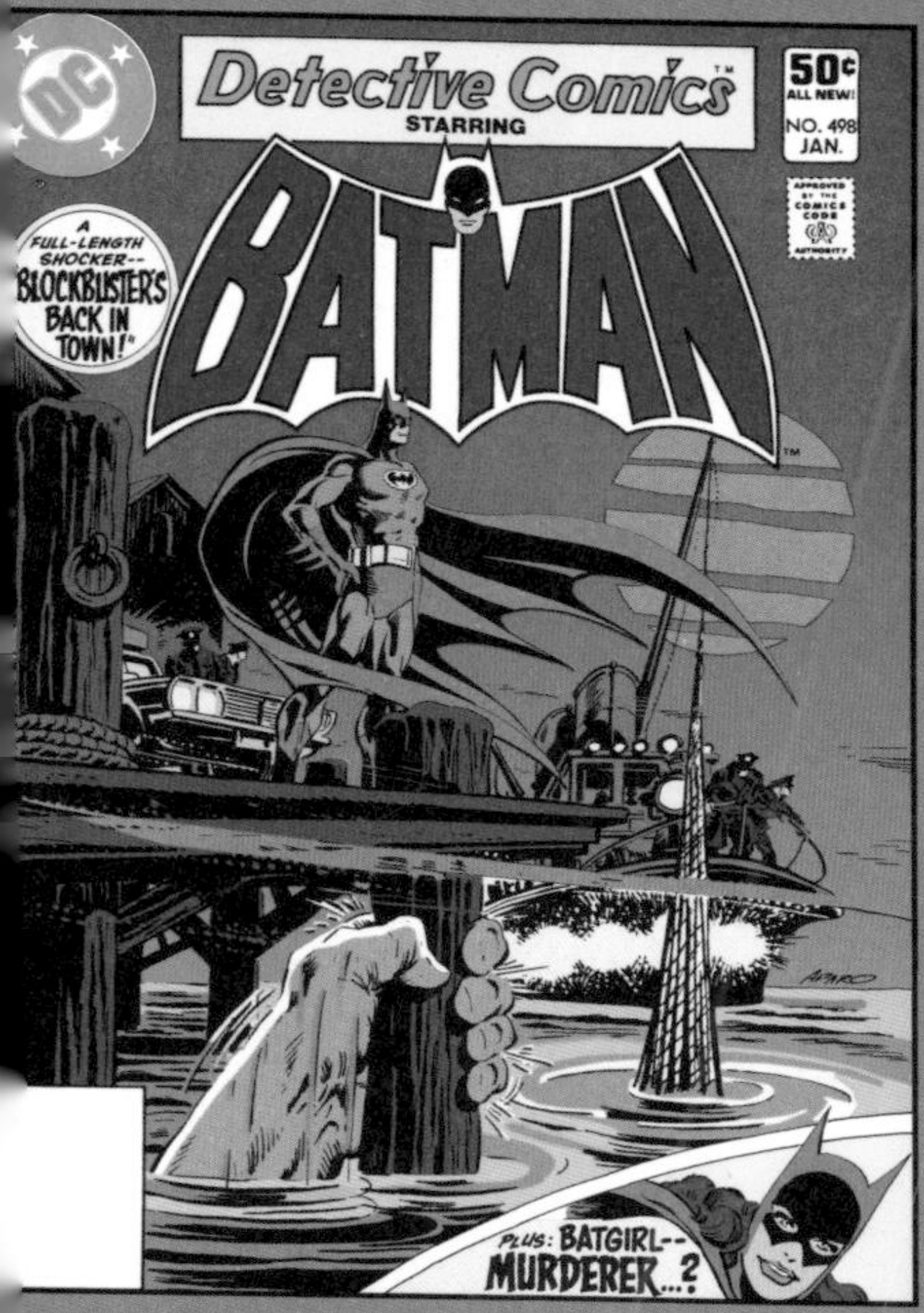
DC
Detective Comics™
STARRING
BATMAN™
50¢
ALL NEW!
NO. 498
JAN.
APPROVED BY THE COMICS CODE AUTHORITY
A FULL-LENGTH SHOCKER-- "BLOCKBUSTER'S BACK IN TOWN!"
PLUS: BATGIRL-- MURDERER...?

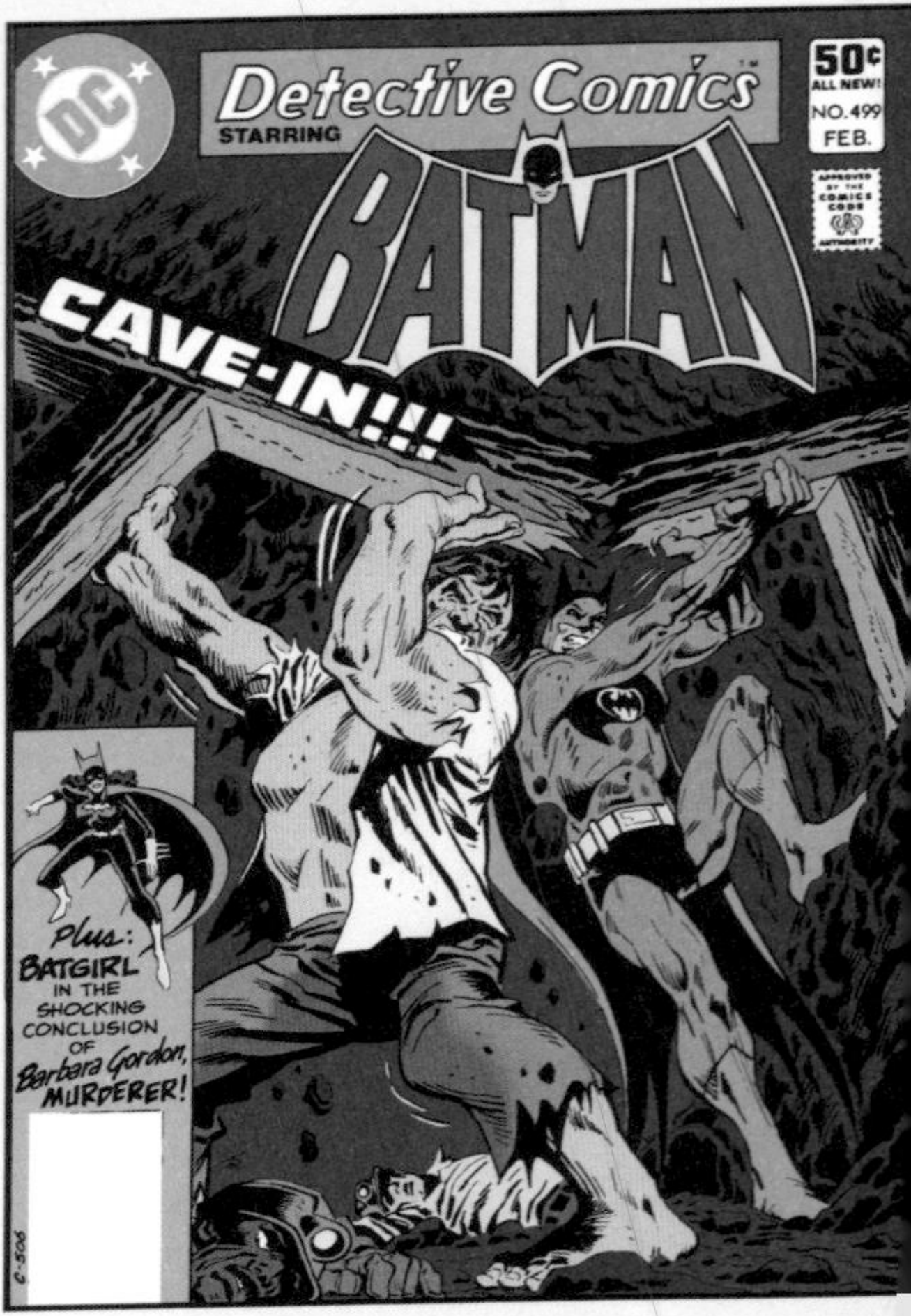
DC
Detective Comics
STARRING
BATMAN
50¢
ALL NEW!
NO. 499
FEB.
APPROVED BY THE COMICS CODE AUTHORITY
CAVE-IN!!!
Plus:
BATGIRL
IN THE
SHOCKING
CONCLUSION
OF
Barbara Gordon,
MURDERER!
C-506

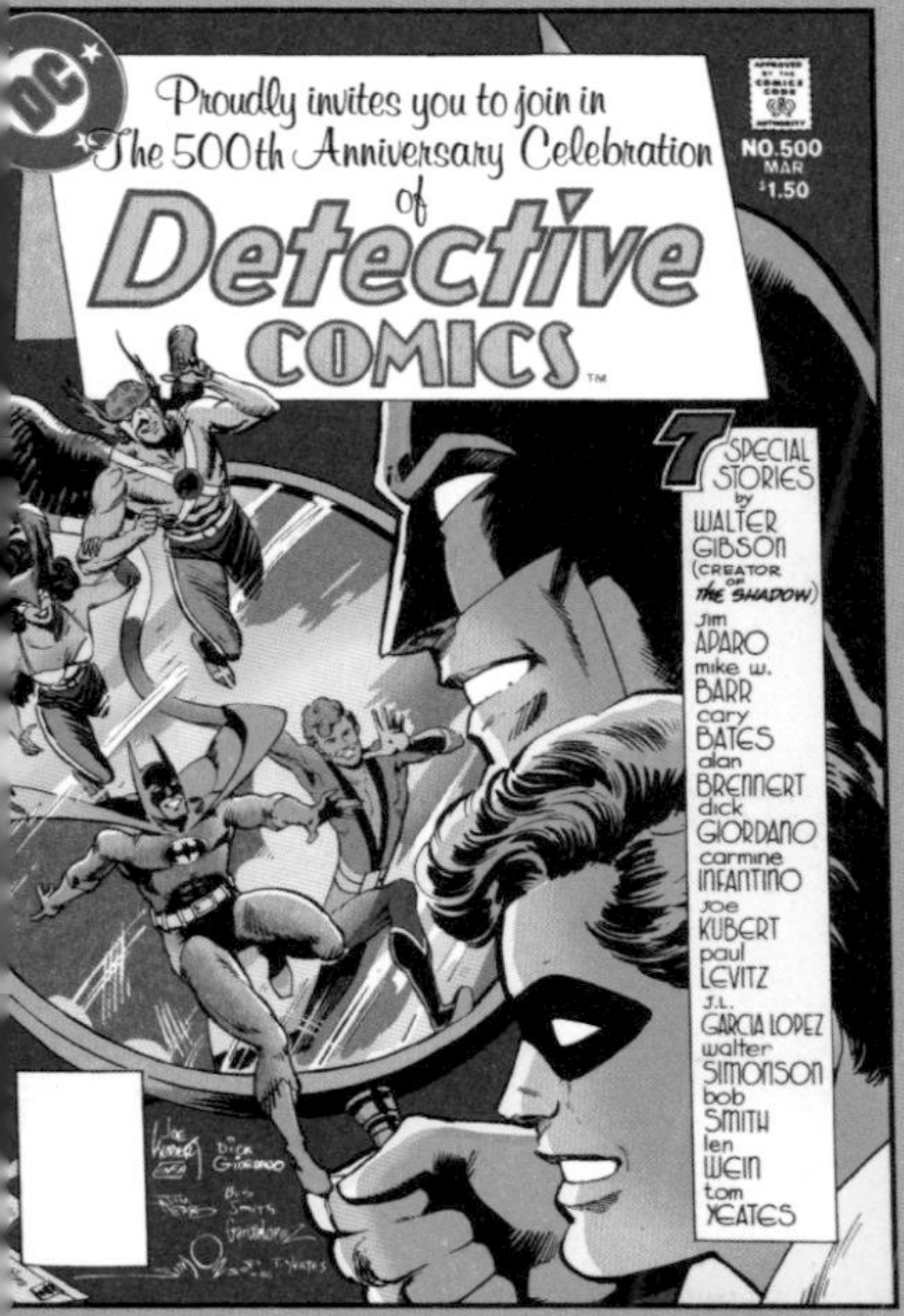
DC
Proudly invites you to join in
The 500th Anniversary Celebration
of
Detective
COMICS
NO.500
MAR
$1.50
7 SPECIAL STORIES
by
WALTER GIBSON
(CREATOR OF THE SHADOW)
Jim APARO
mike w. BARR
cary BATES
alan BRENNERT
dick GIORDANO
carmine INFANTINO
joe KUBERT
paul LEVITZ
J.L. GARCIA LOPEZ
walter SIMONSON
bob SMITH
len WEIN
tom YEATES

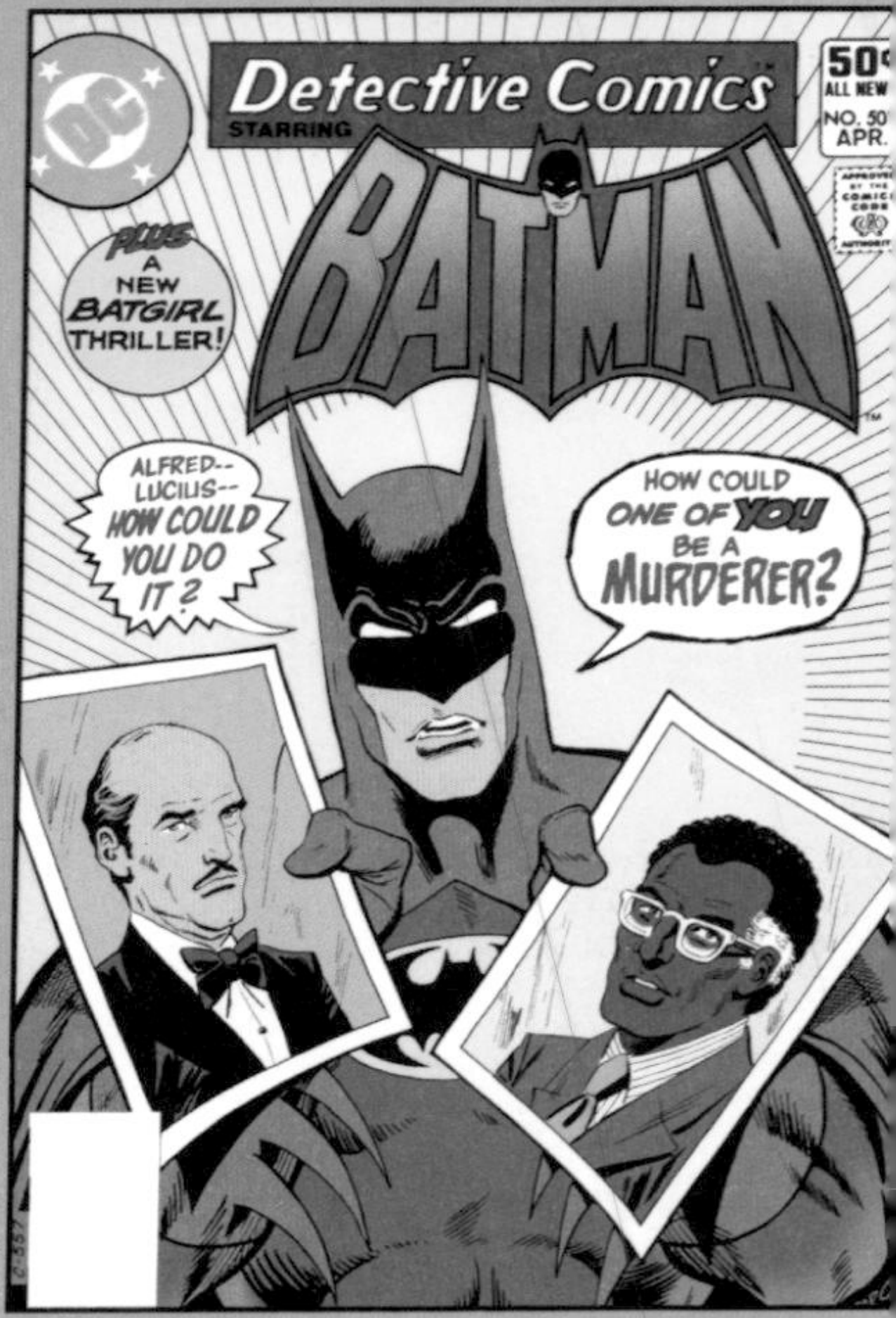
Detective Comics
STARRING
BATMAN
50¢
ALL NEW
NO. 50
APR.
PLUS A NEW BATGIRL THRILLER!
ALFRED-- LUCIUS-- HOW COULD YOU DO IT?
HOW COULD ONE OF YOU BE A MURDERER?

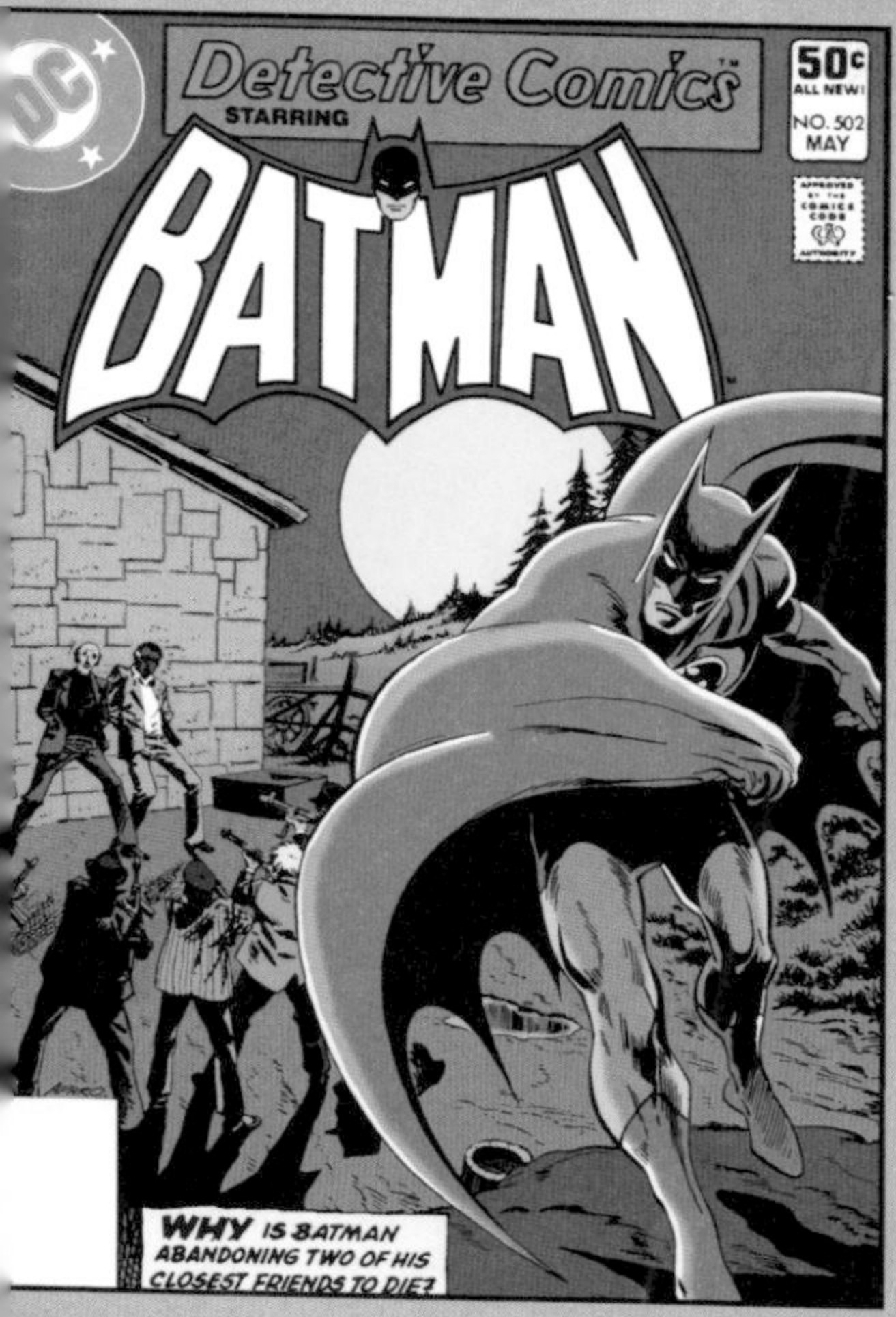
DC
Detective Comics
STARRING
BATMAN
50c
ALL NEW!
NO. 502
MAY
APPROVED BY THE COMICS CODE AUTHORITY
WHY IS BATMAN ABANDONING TWO OF HIS CLOSEST FRIENDS TO DIE?

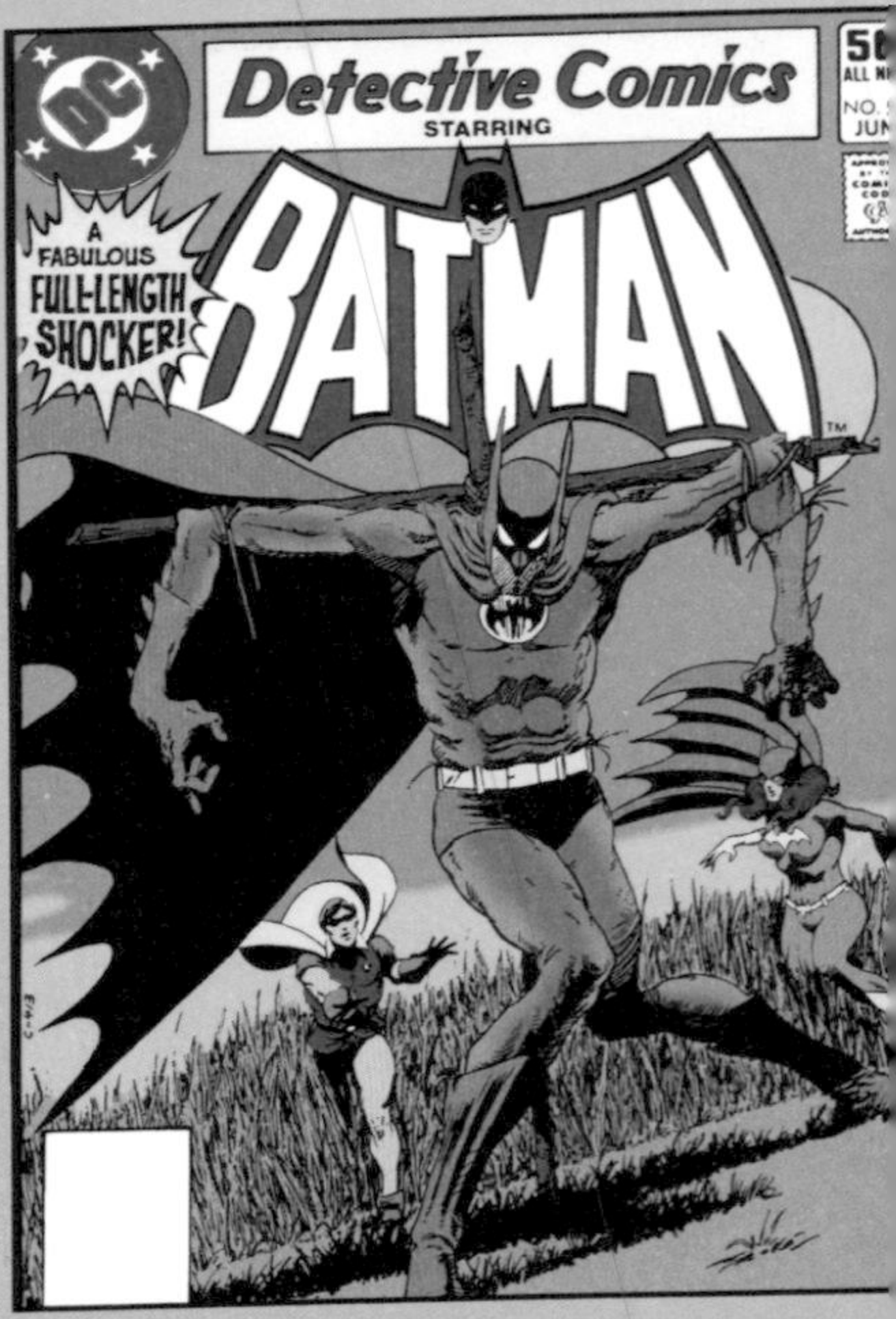
DC
Detective Comics
STARRING
BATMAN
A FABULOUS FULL-LENGTH SHOCKER!
50
ALL NE
NO.
JUN

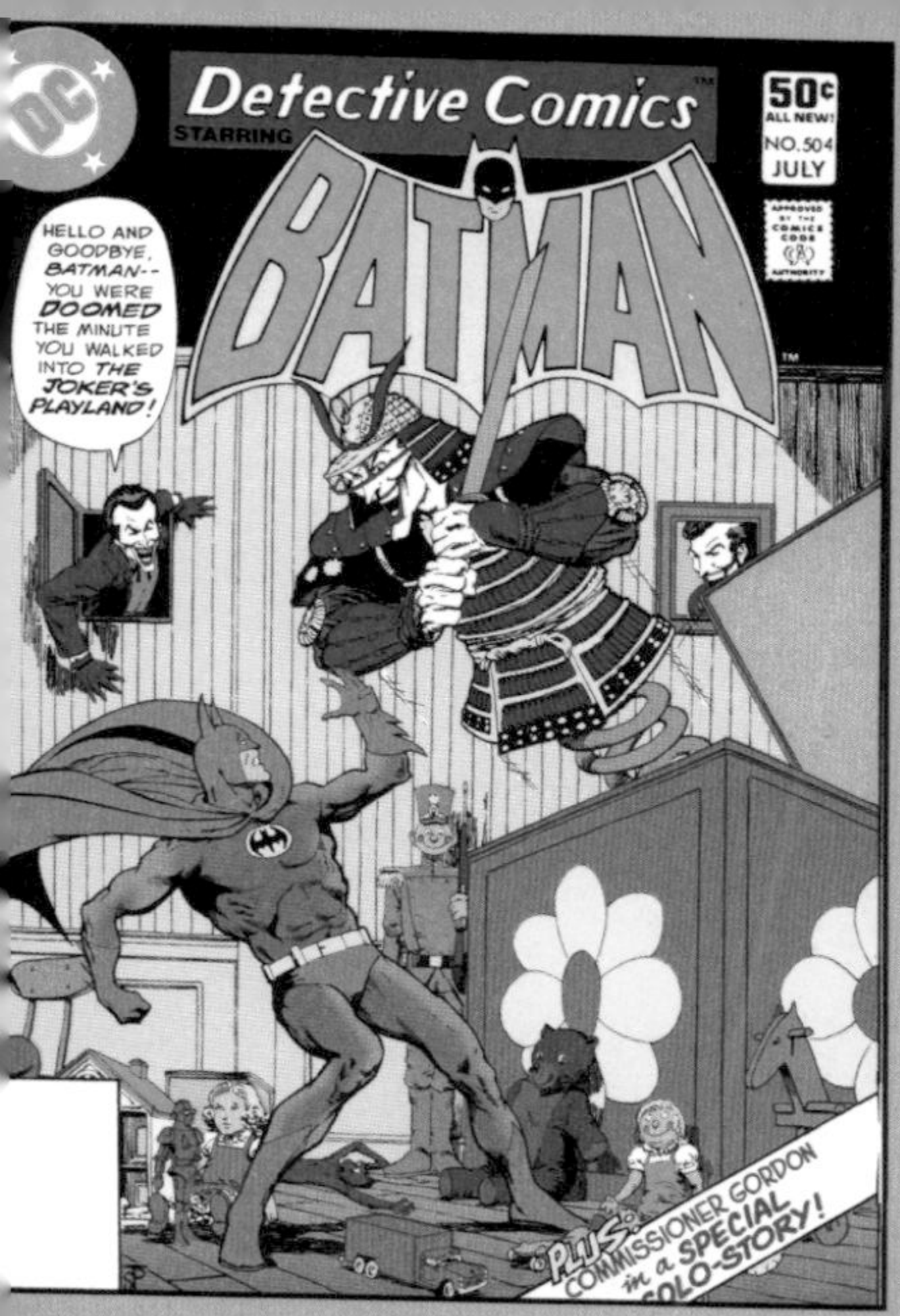
DC
Detective Comics
STARRING
BATMAN
50¢
ALL NEW!
NO. 504
JULY
APPROVED BY THE COMICS CODE AUTHORITY
HELLO AND GOODBYE, BATMAN-- YOU WERE DOOMED THE MINUTE YOU WALKED INTO THE JOKER'S PLAYLAND!
PLUS: COMMISSIONER GORDON in a SPECIAL SOLO-STORY!

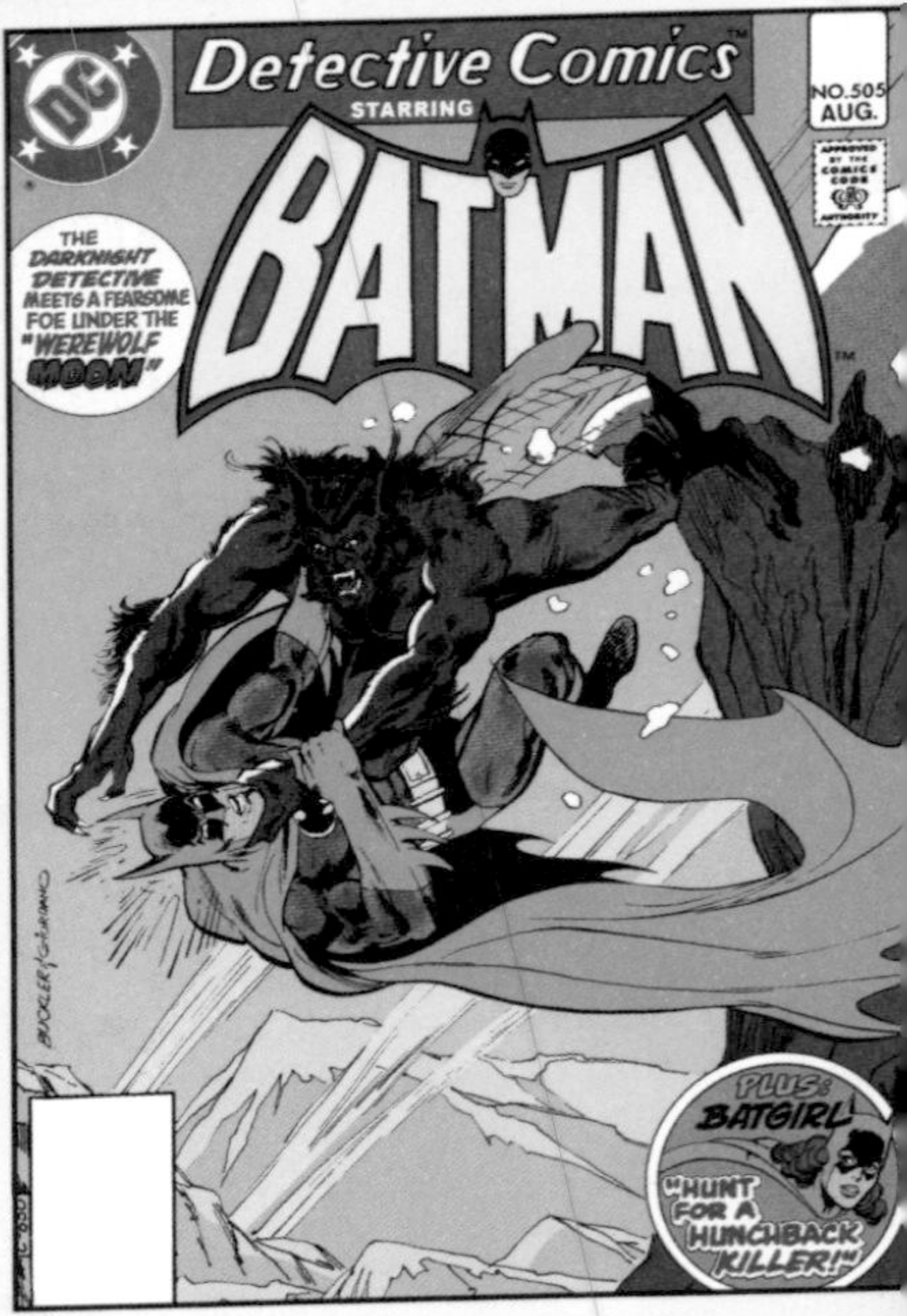
DC
Detective Comics
STARRING
BATMAN
NO. 505
AUG.
APPROVED BY THE COMICS CODE AUTHORITY
THE DARKNIGHT DETECTIVE MEETS A FEARSOME FOE UNDER THE "WEREWOLF MOON"
BUCKLER & GIORDANO
PLUS: BATGIRL
"HUNT FOR A HUNCHBACK KILLER!"

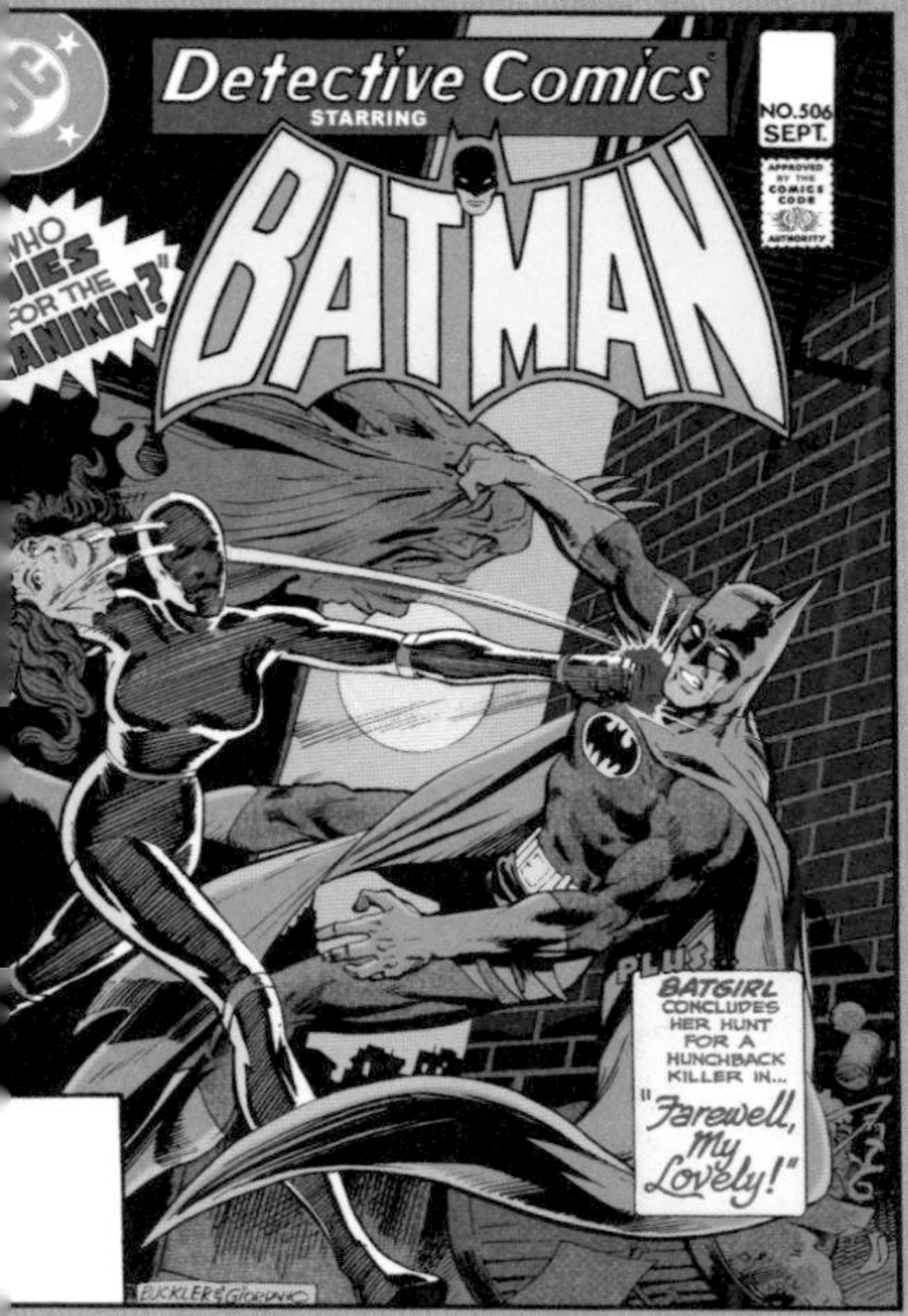
Detective Comics
STARRING
BATMAN
NO. 506
SEPT.
APPROVED BY THE COMICS CODE AUTHORITY
WHO DIES FOR THE ANIKIN?"
PLUS...
BATGIRL CONCLUDES HER HUNT FOR A HUNCHBACK KILLER IN...
"Farewell, My Lovely!"
BUCKLER & GIORDANO

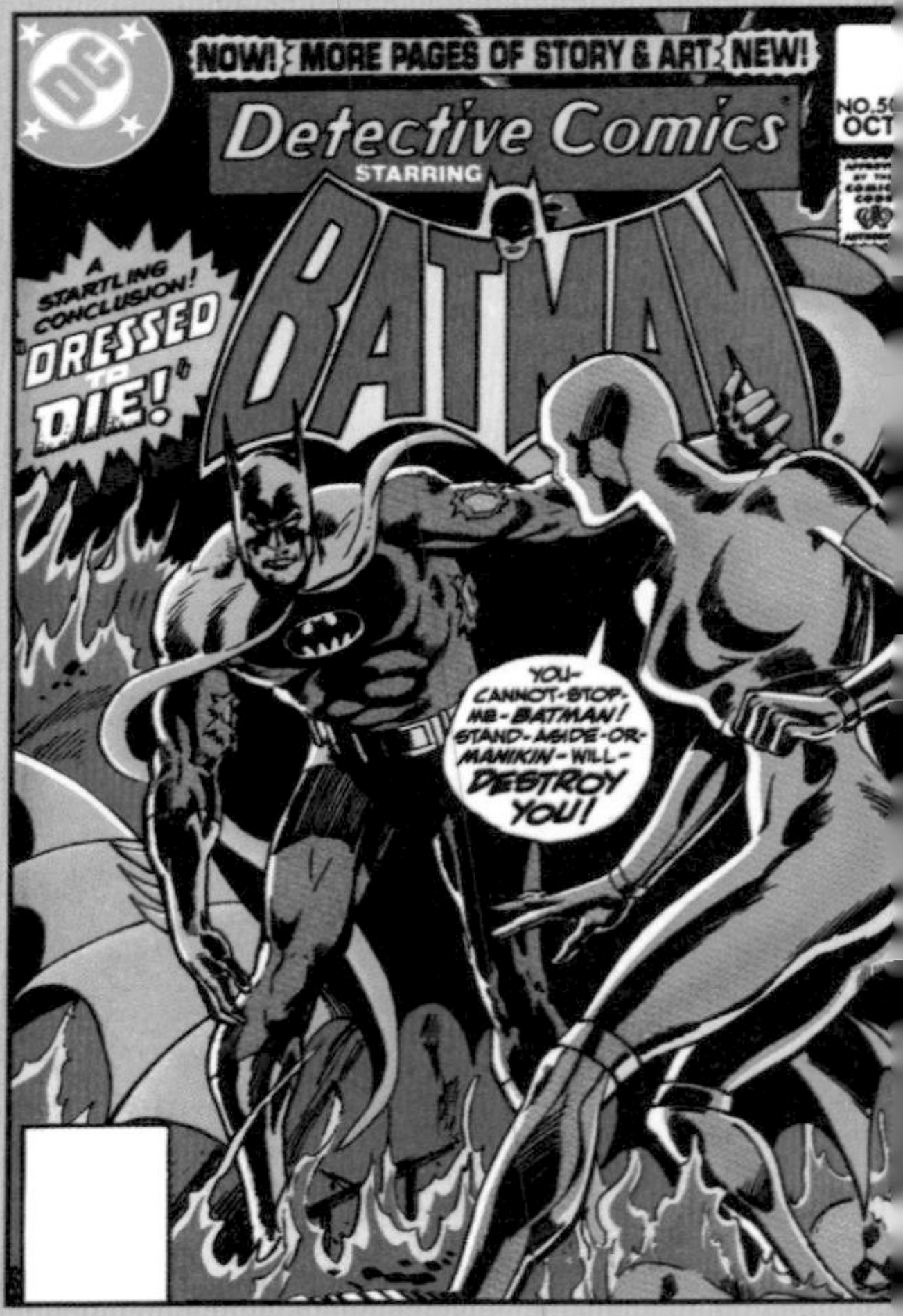
NOW! MORE PAGES OF STORY & ART NEW!
Detective Comics
STARRING
BATMAN
A STARTLING CONCLUSION!
DRESSED TO DIE!
YOU-CANNOT-STOP-ME-BATMAN! STAND-ASIDE-OR-MANIKIN-WILL-DESTROY YOU!

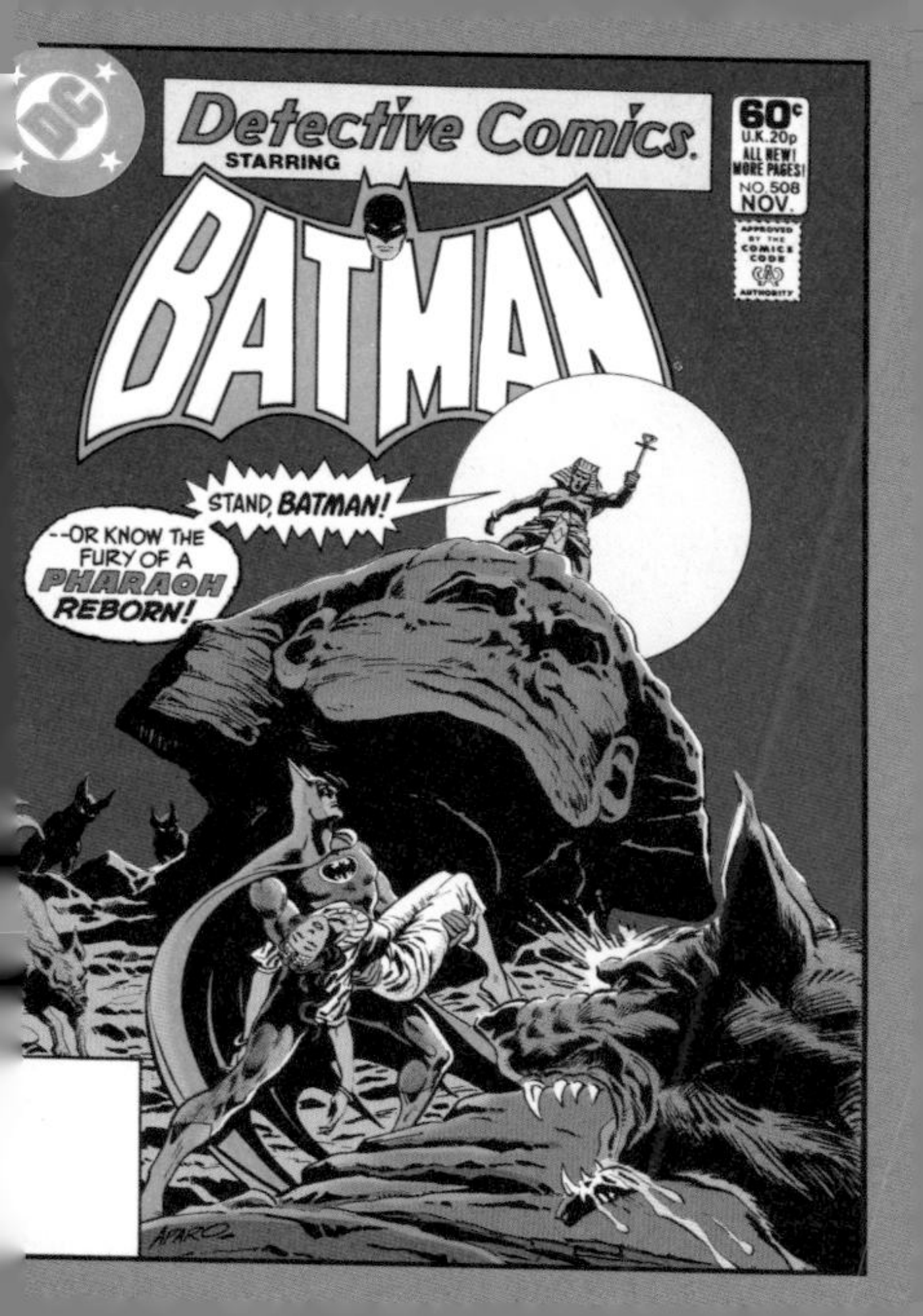
DC
Detective Comics.
STARRING
BATMAN
60¢
U.K. 20p
ALL NEW! MORE PAGES!
NO. 508
NOV.
APPROVED BY THE COMICS CODE AUTHORITY
STAND, BATMAN!
--OR KNOW THE FURY OF A PHARAOH REBORN!
APARO

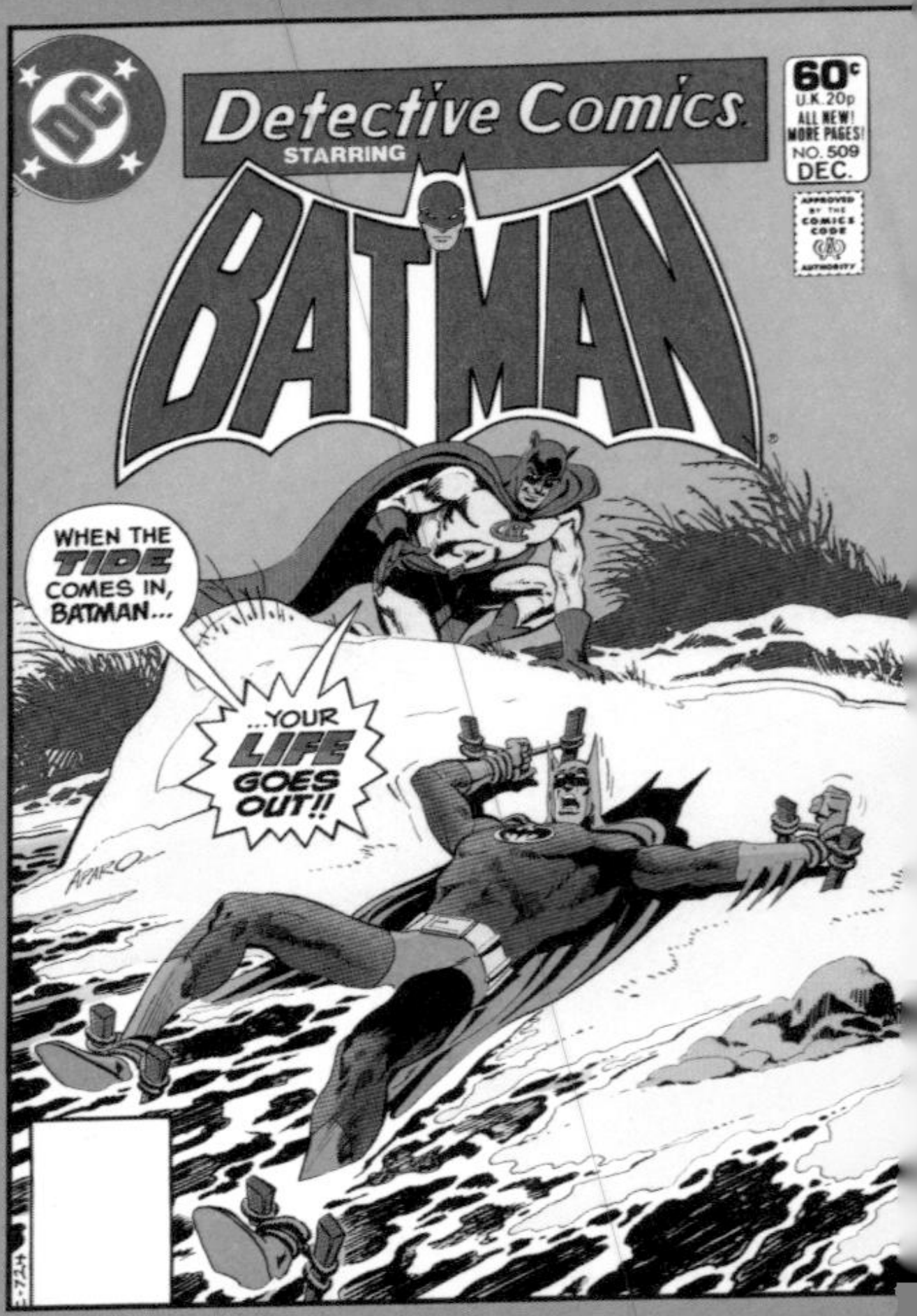
DC
Detective Comics
STARRING
BATMAN
60¢
U.K. 20p
ALL NEW! MORE PAGES!
NO. 509
DEC.
APPROVED BY THE COMICS CODE AUTHORITY
WHEN THE TIDE COMES IN, BATMAN...
...YOUR LIFE GOES OUT!!

DC
Detective Comics
STARRING
BATMAN
ALL NEW!
60c
U.K. 20p
MORE PAGES!
NO. 510
JAN.
APPROVED BY THE COMICS CODE AUTHORITY
THE MAD HATTER USED TO COLLECT HATS...
...BUT NOW HE HUNTS THE HEADS THEY COVER!
COLAN & GIORDANO

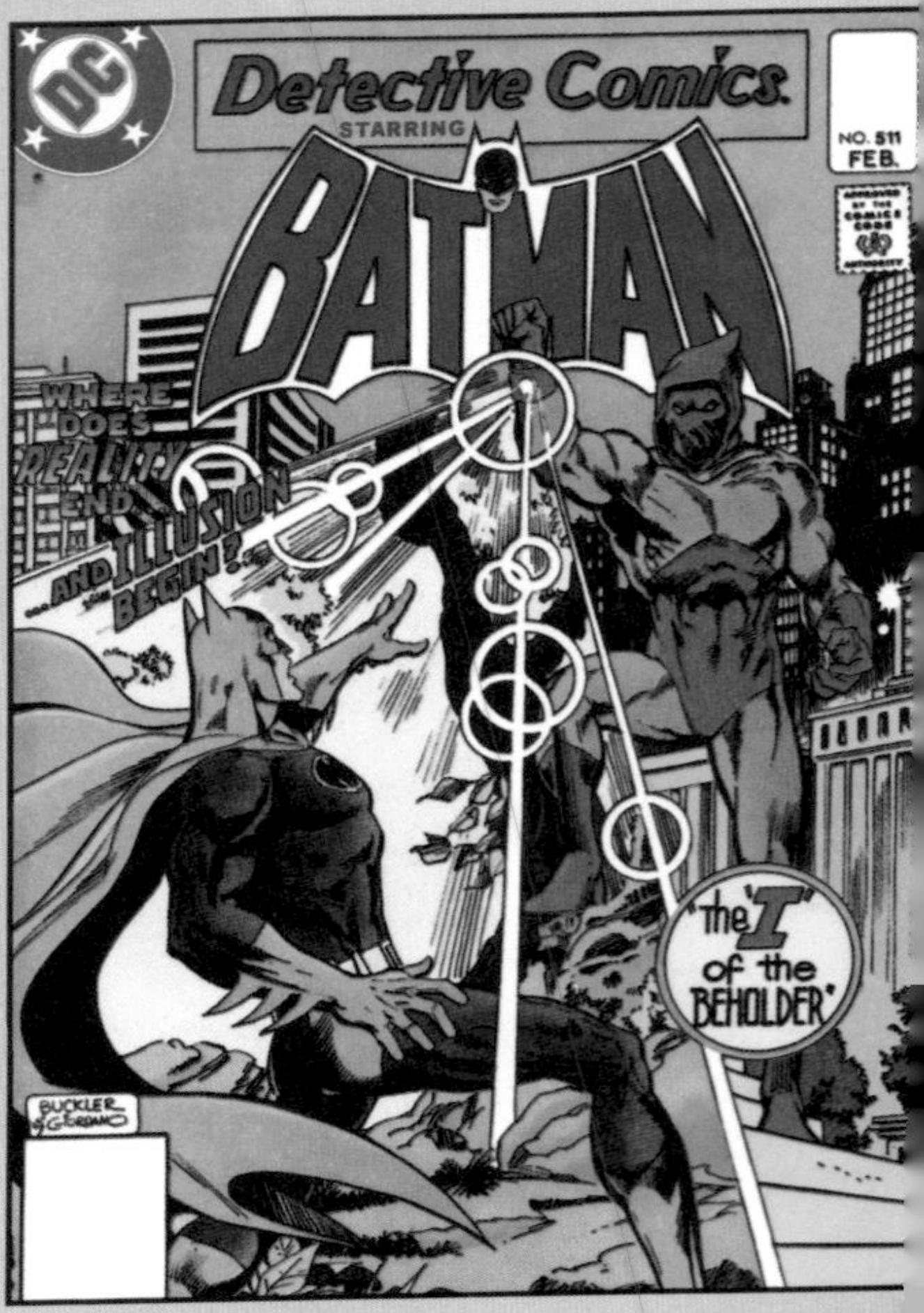
DC
Detective Comics.
STARRING
BATMAN
NO. 511
FEB.
WHERE DOES REALITY END AND ILLUSION BEGIN?
"The 'I' of the BEHOLDER"
BUCKLER & GIORDANO

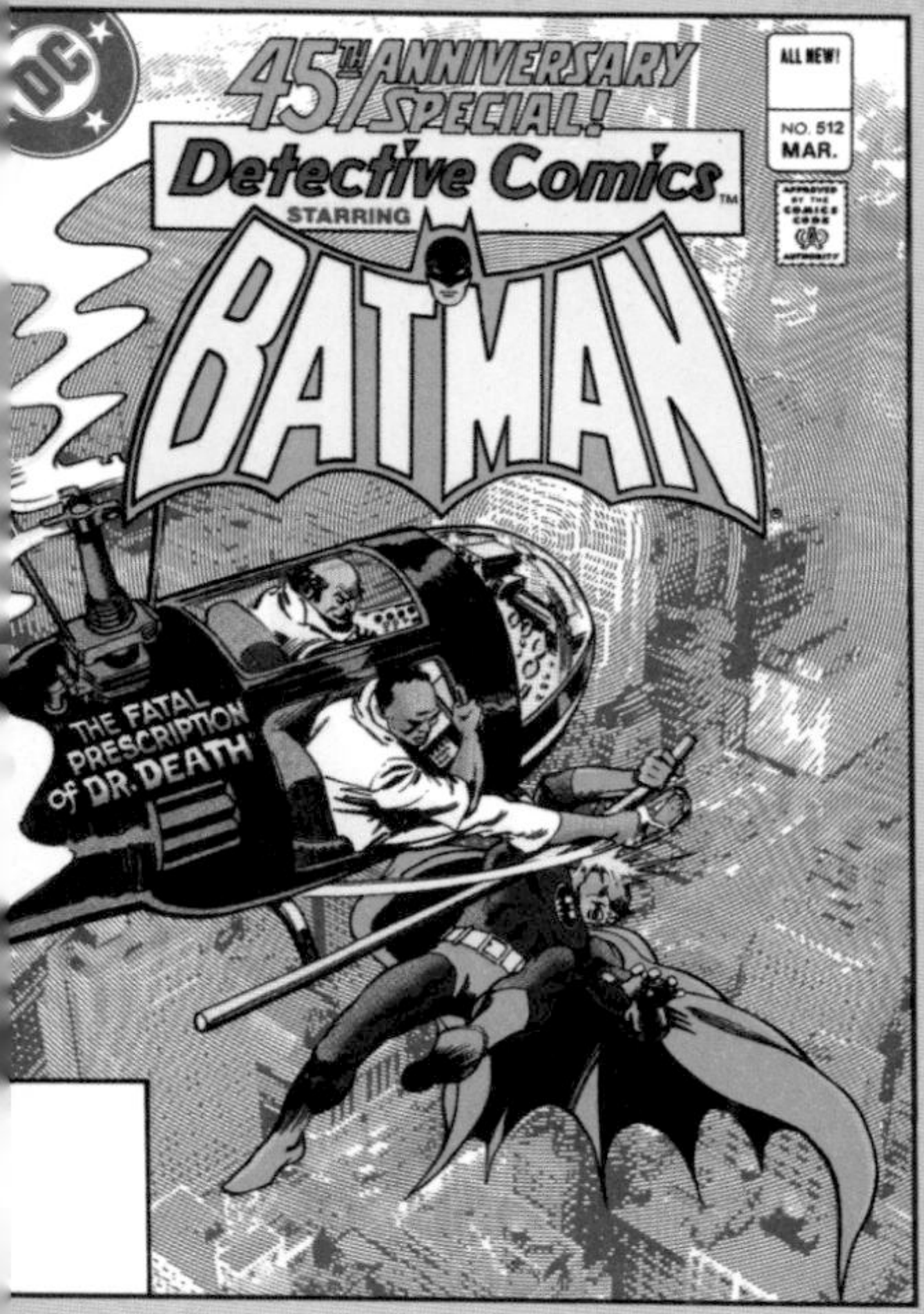
45TH ANNIVERSARY SPECIAL!
Detective Comics
STARRING
BATMAN
ALL NEW!
NO. 512
MAR.
"THE FATAL PRESCRIPTION of DR. DEATH"

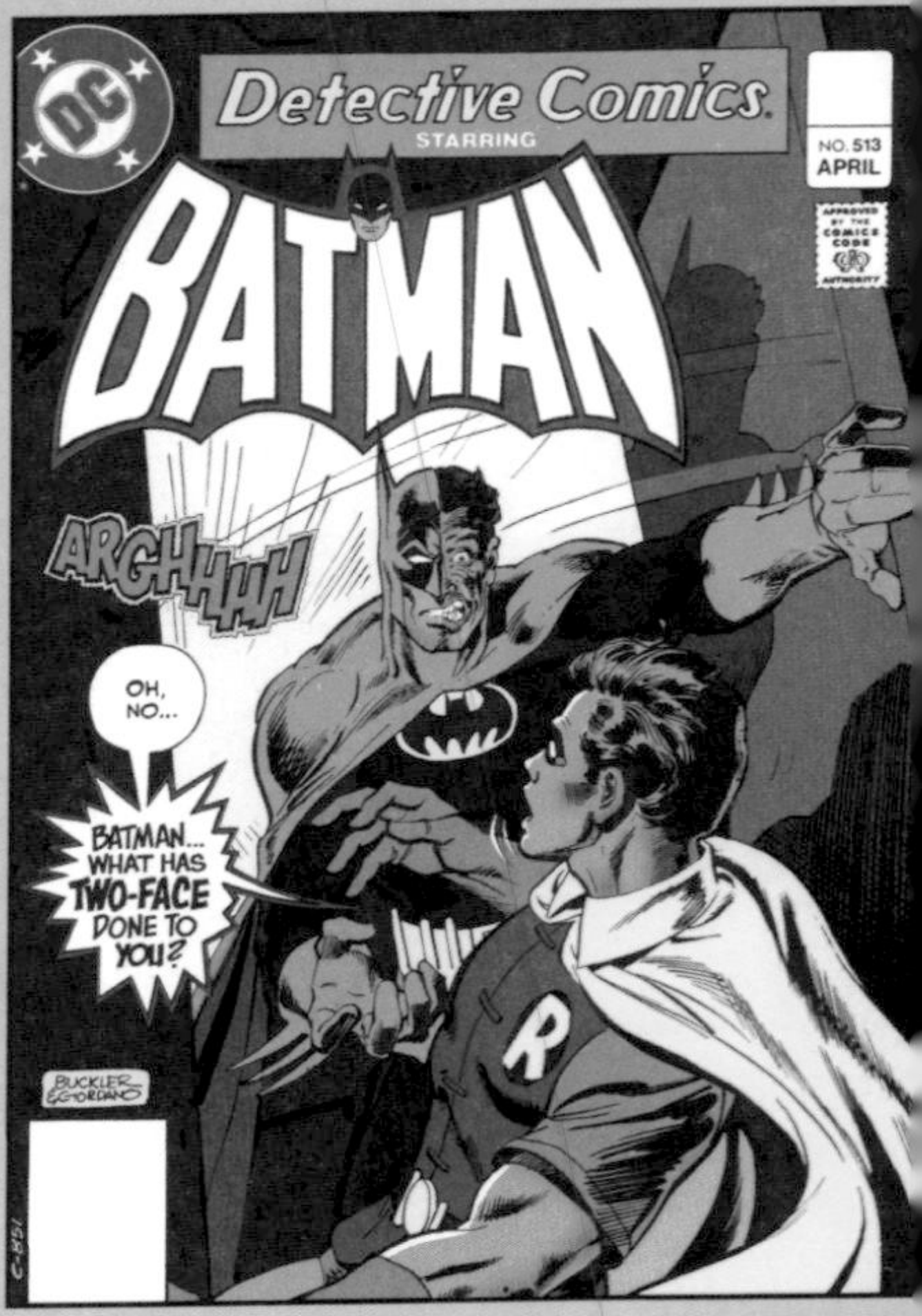
DC
Detective Comics.
STARRING
NO. 513
APRIL
APPROVED BY THE COMICS CODE AUTHORITY
BATMAN
ARGHHHHH
OH, NO...
BATMAN... WHAT HAS TWO-FACE DONE TO YOU?
R
BUCKLER
EGIORDANO

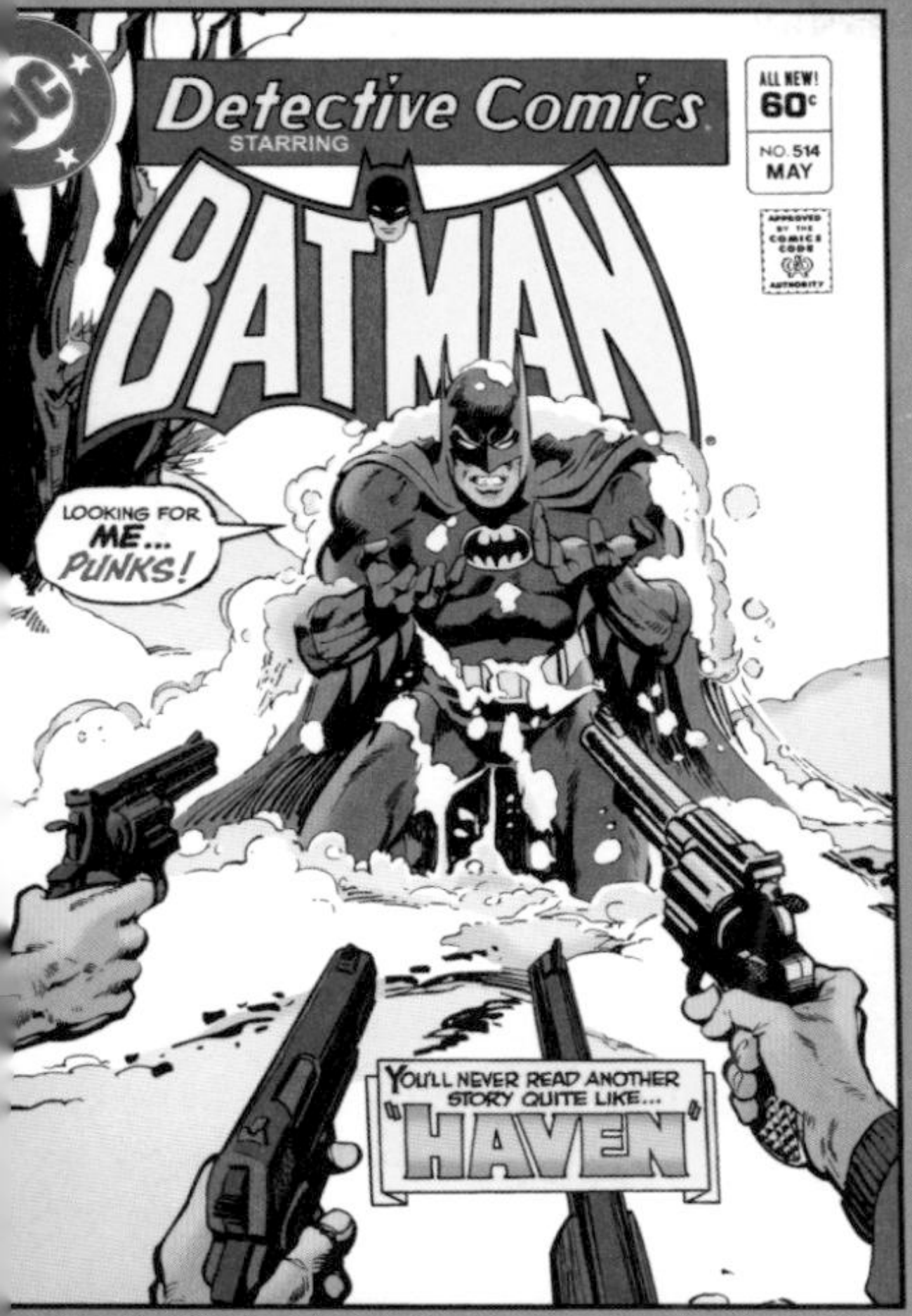
Detective Comics
STARRING
BATMAN
ALL NEW!
60¢
NO. 514
MAY
APPROVED BY THE COMICS CODE AUTHORITY
LOOKING FOR ME... PUNKS!
YOU'LL NEVER READ ANOTHER STORY QUITE LIKE...
"HAVEN"

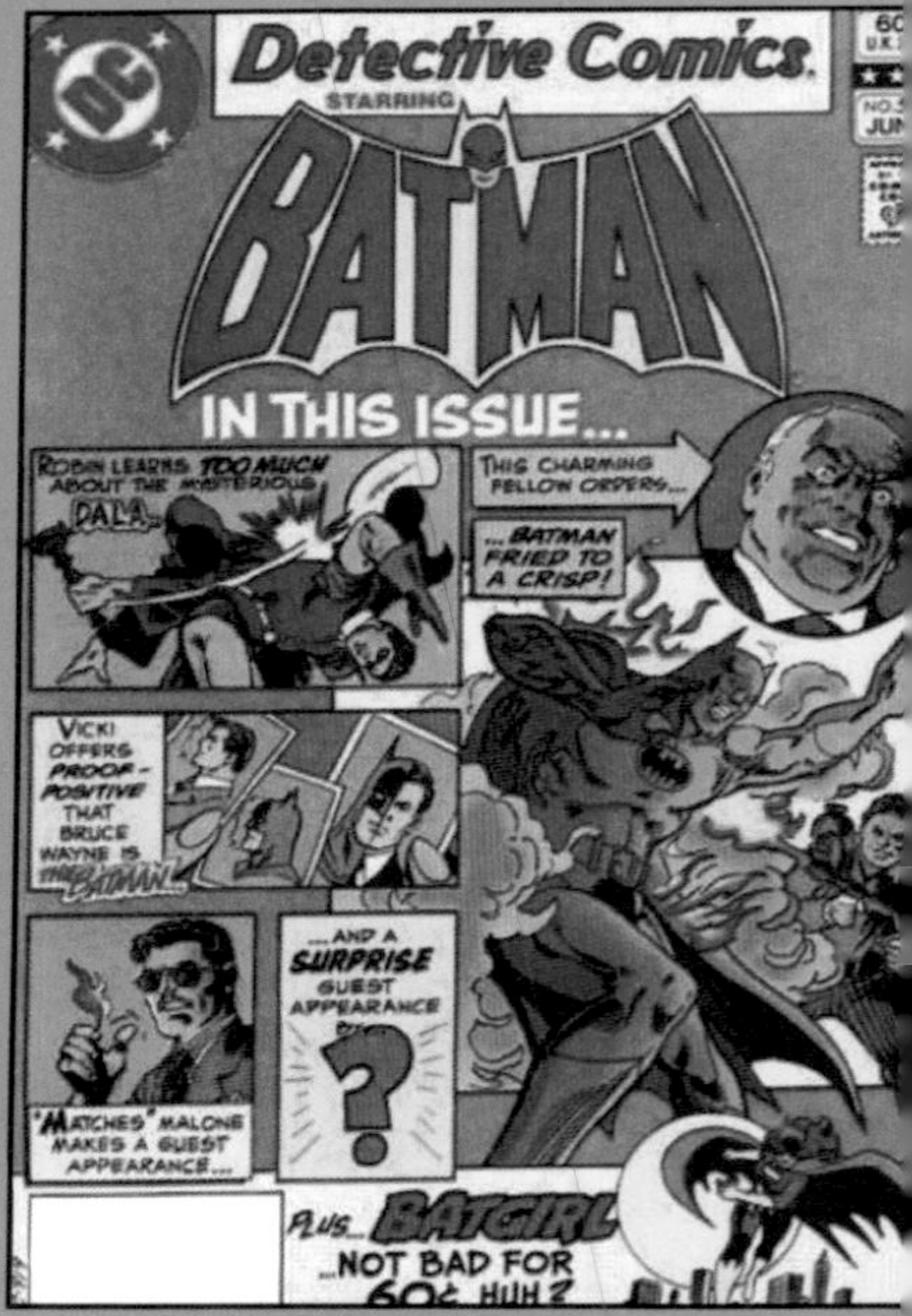
Detective Comics
STARRING
BATMAN
IN THIS ISSUE...
ROBIN LEARNS TOO MUCH ABOUT THE MYSTERIOUS DALA...
THIS CHARMING FELLOW ORDERS...
...BATMAN FRIED TO A CRISP!
VICKI OFFERS PROOF-POSITIVE THAT BRUCE WAYNE IS THE BATMAN!
"MATCHES" MALONE MAKES A GUEST APPEARANCE...
...AND A SURPRISE GUEST APPEARANCE BY...
?
PLUS... BATGIRL
...NOT BAD FOR 60¢ HUH?

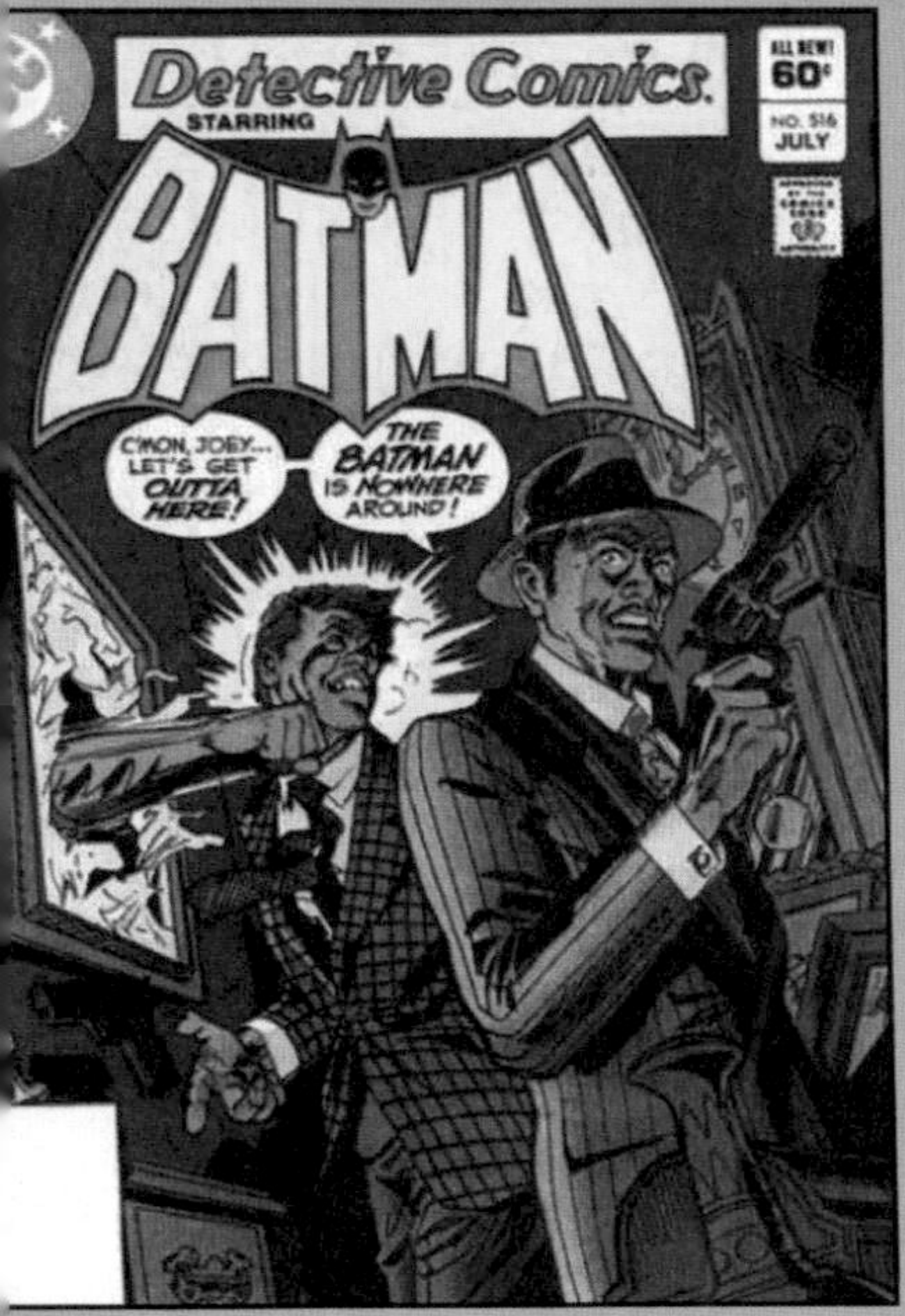
Detective Comics.
STARRING
BATMAN
ALL NEW!
60¢
NO. 516
JULY
C'MON, JOEY... LET'S GET OUTTA HERE!
THE BATMAN IS NOWHERE AROUND!

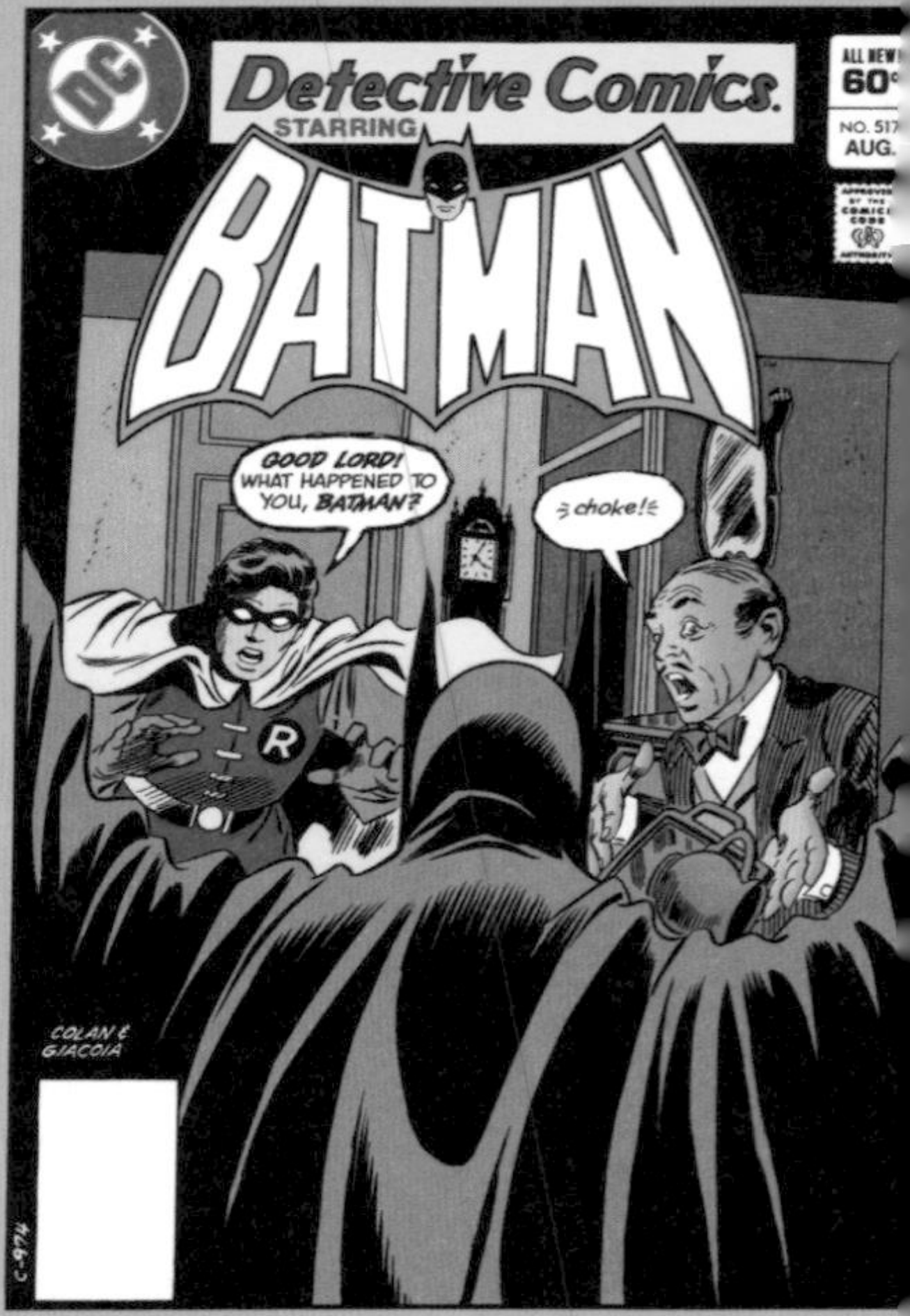
DC
Detective Comics.
STARRING
BATMAN
ALL NEW!
60¢
NO. 517
AUG.
GOOD LORD! WHAT HAPPENED TO YOU, BATMAN?
choke!
COLAN & GIACOIA

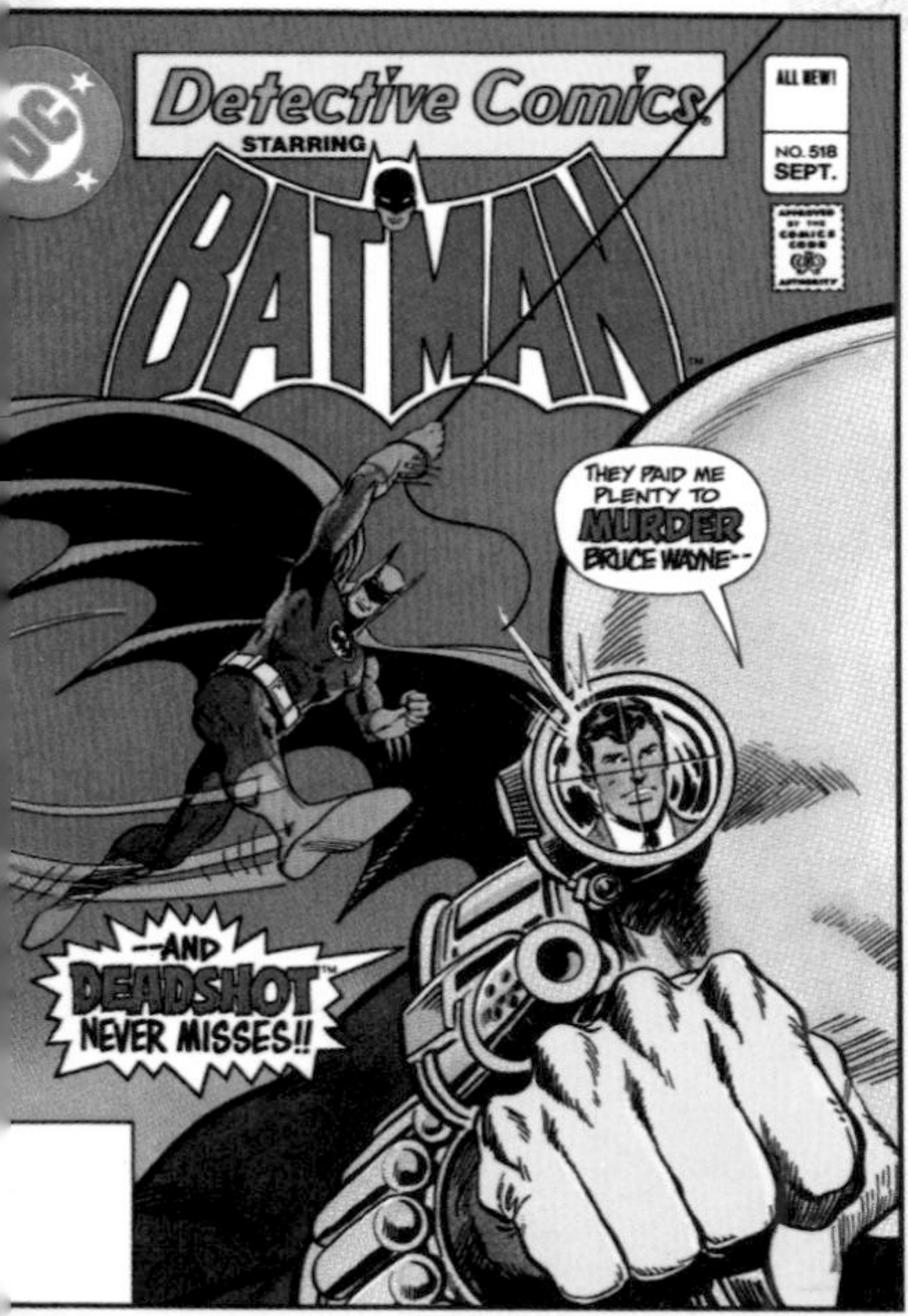
Detective Comics
STARRING
BATMAN
ALL NEW!
NO. 518
SEPT.
THEY PAID ME PLENTY TO MURDER BRUCE WAYNE--
--AND DEADSHOT NEVER MISSES!!

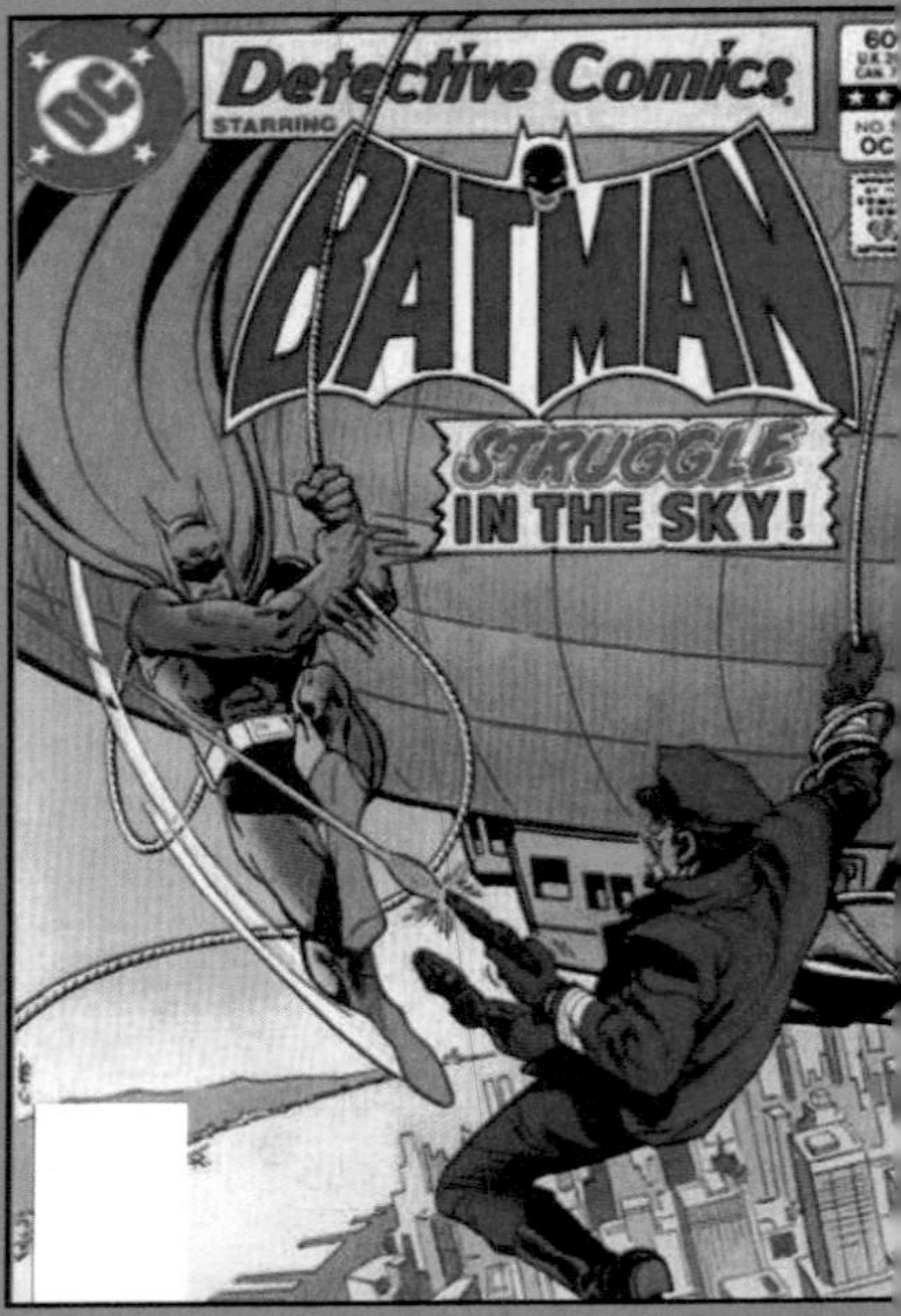
DC
Detective Comics
STARRING
BATMAN
STRUGGLE
IN THE SKY!

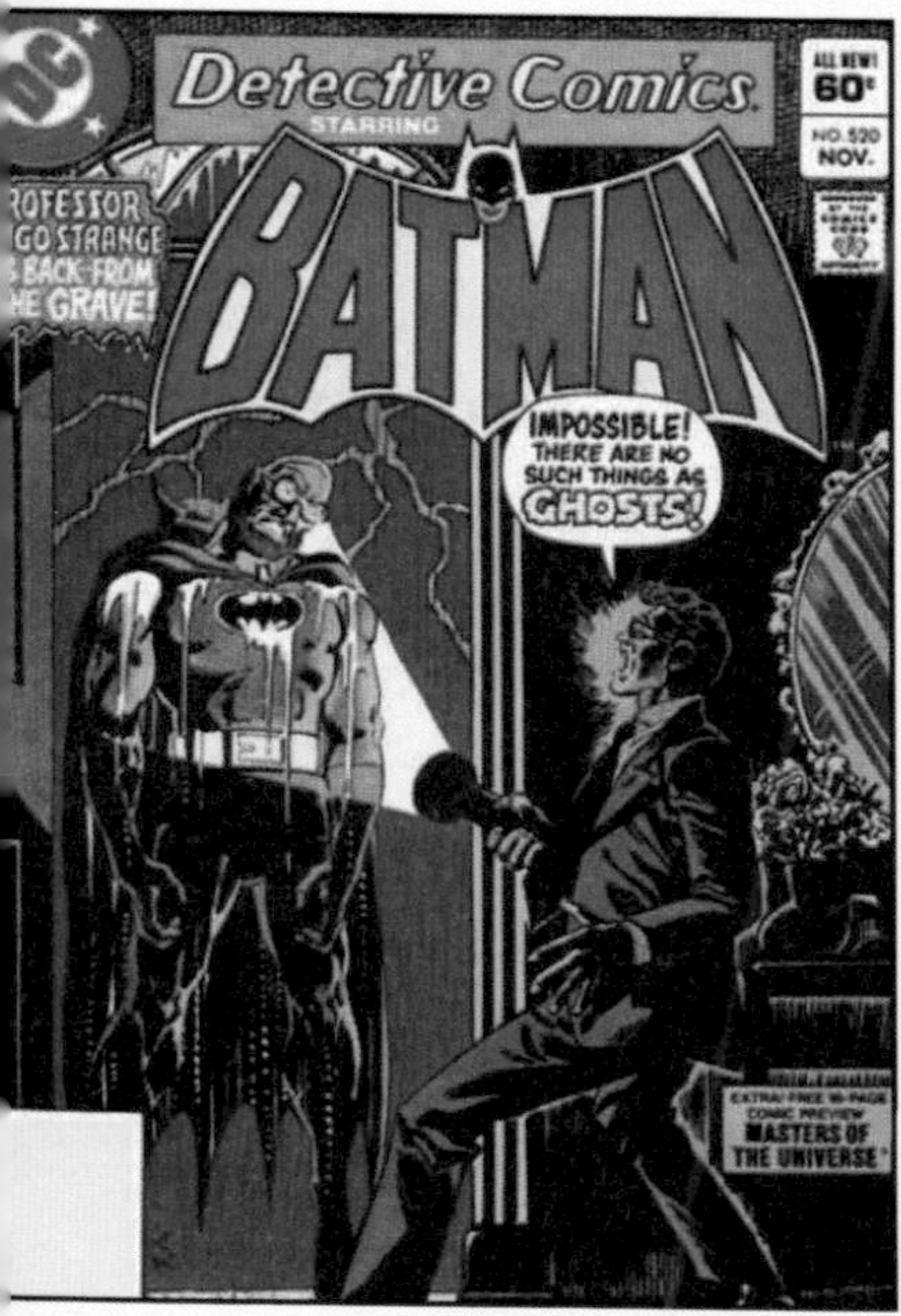
Detective Comics
STARRING
BATMAN
ALL NEW!
60¢
NO. 520
NOV.
PROFESSOR
GO STRANGE
BACK FROM
HE GRAVE!
IMPOSSIBLE! THERE ARE NO SUCH THINGS AS GHOSTS!
EXTRA! FREE 16-PAGE COMIC PREVIEW
MASTERS OF THE UNIVERSE

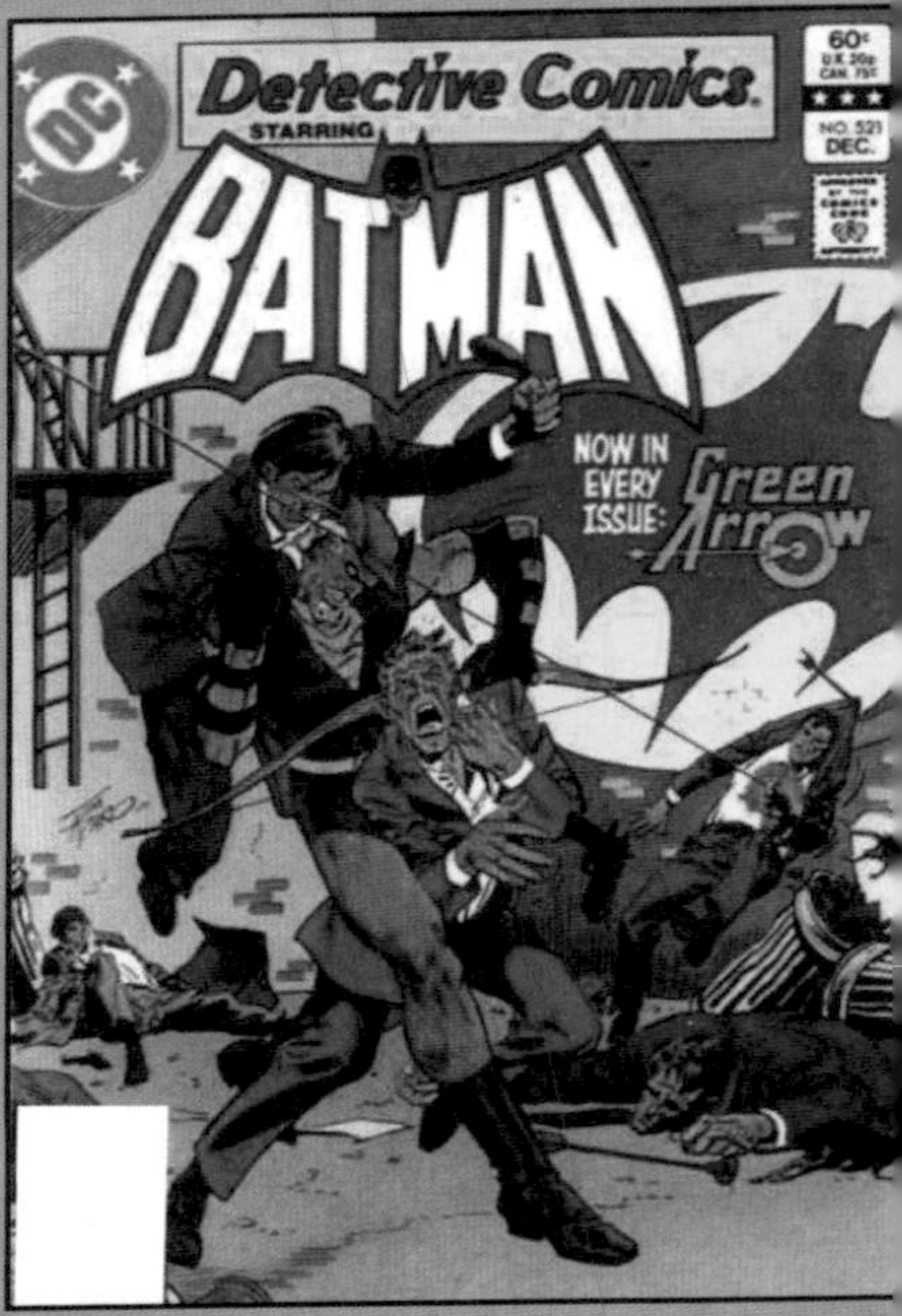
DC
Detective Comics
STARRING
BATMAN
60¢
U.K. 30p
CAN. 75¢
NO. 521
DEC.
NOW IN EVERY ISSUE: Green Arrow

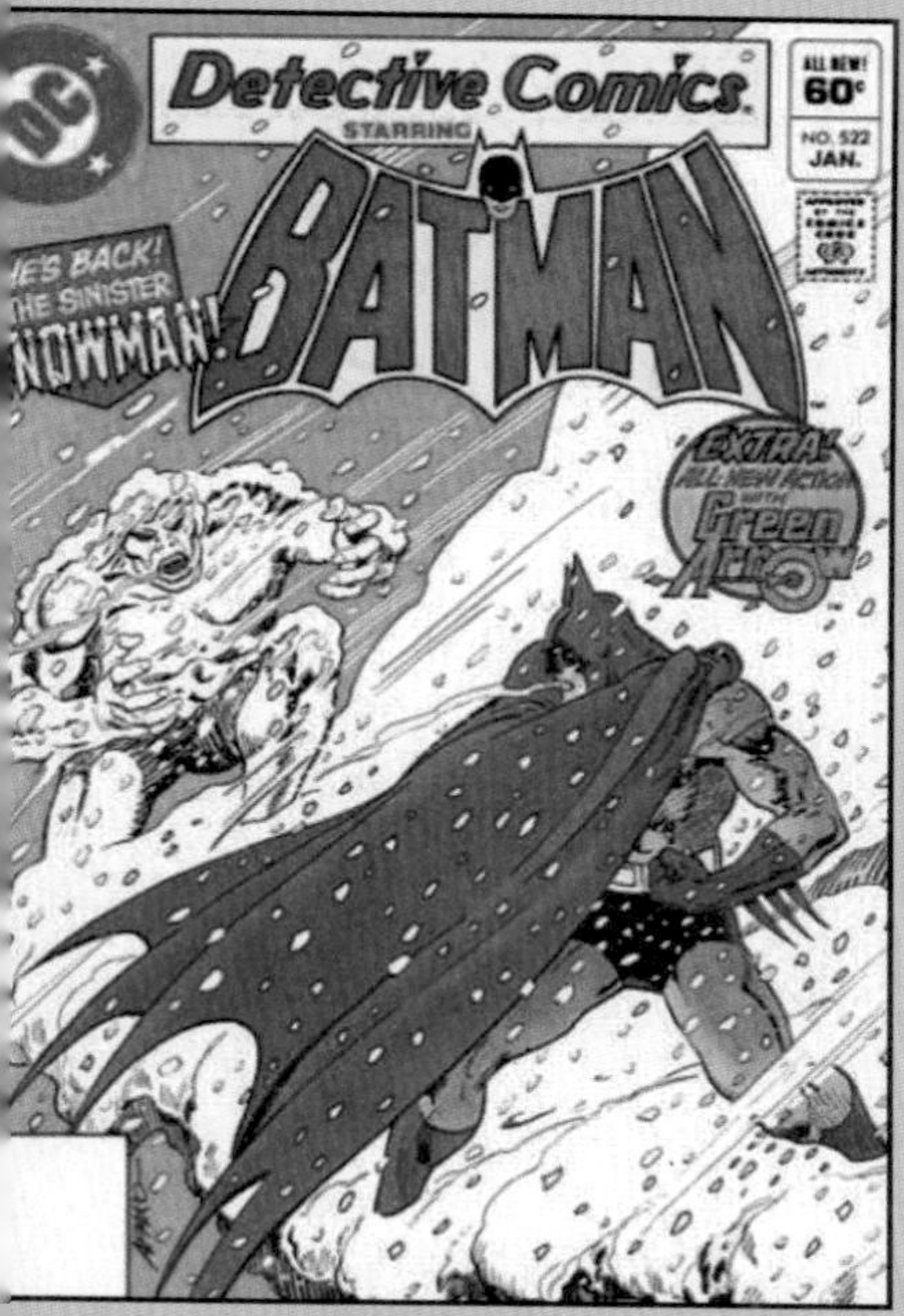
DC
Detective Comics
STARRING
BATMAN
ALL NEW!
60¢
NO. 522
JAN.
HE'S BACK!
THE SINISTER
NOWMAN!
EXTRA!
ALL NEW ACTION
WITH
Green Arrow

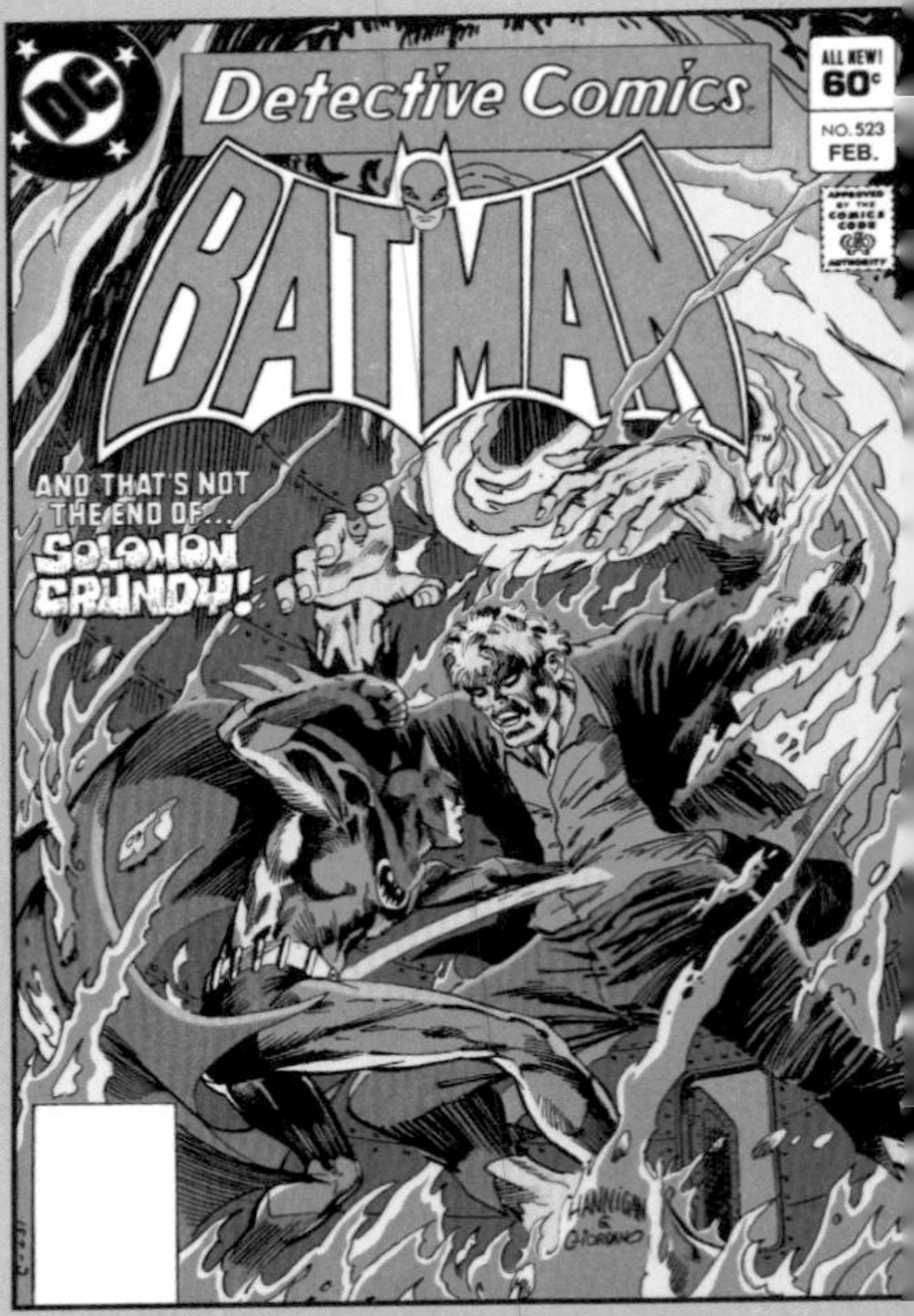
DC
Detective Comics
ALL NEW!
60¢
NO. 523
FEB.
APPROVED BY THE COMICS CODE AUTHORITY
BATMAN
AND THAT'S NOT THE END OF...
SOLOMON GRUNDY!
HANNIGAN & GIORDANO

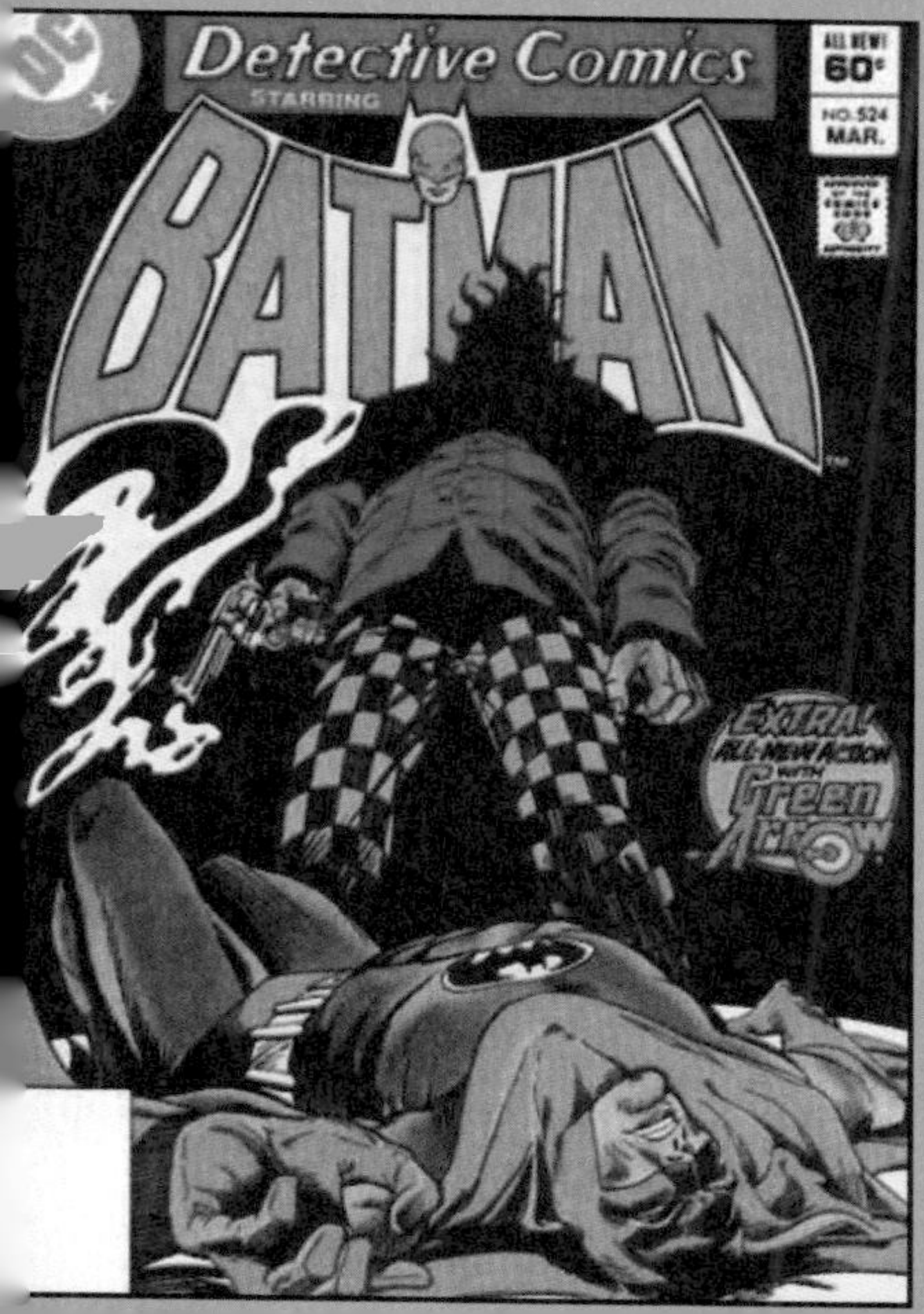
Detective Comics
STARRING
BATMAN
ALL NEW!
60¢
NO. 524
MAR.
EXTRA!
ALL NEW ACTION
WITH
Green Arrow

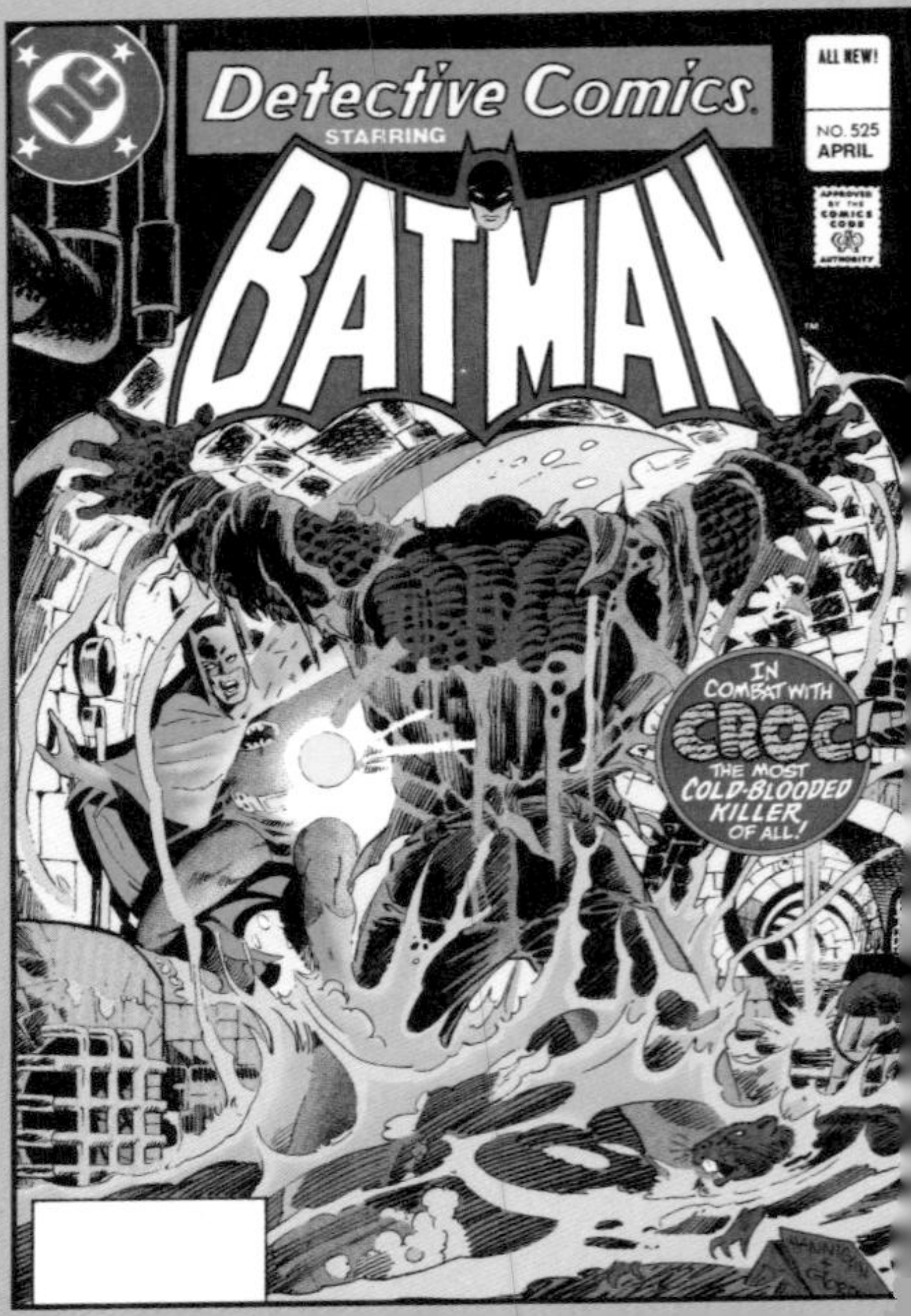
DC
Detective Comics.
STARRING
BATMAN
ALL NEW!
NO. 525
APRIL
APPROVED BY THE COMICS CODE AUTHORITY
IN COMBAT WITH
CROC!
THE MOST COLD-BLOODED KILLER OF ALL!

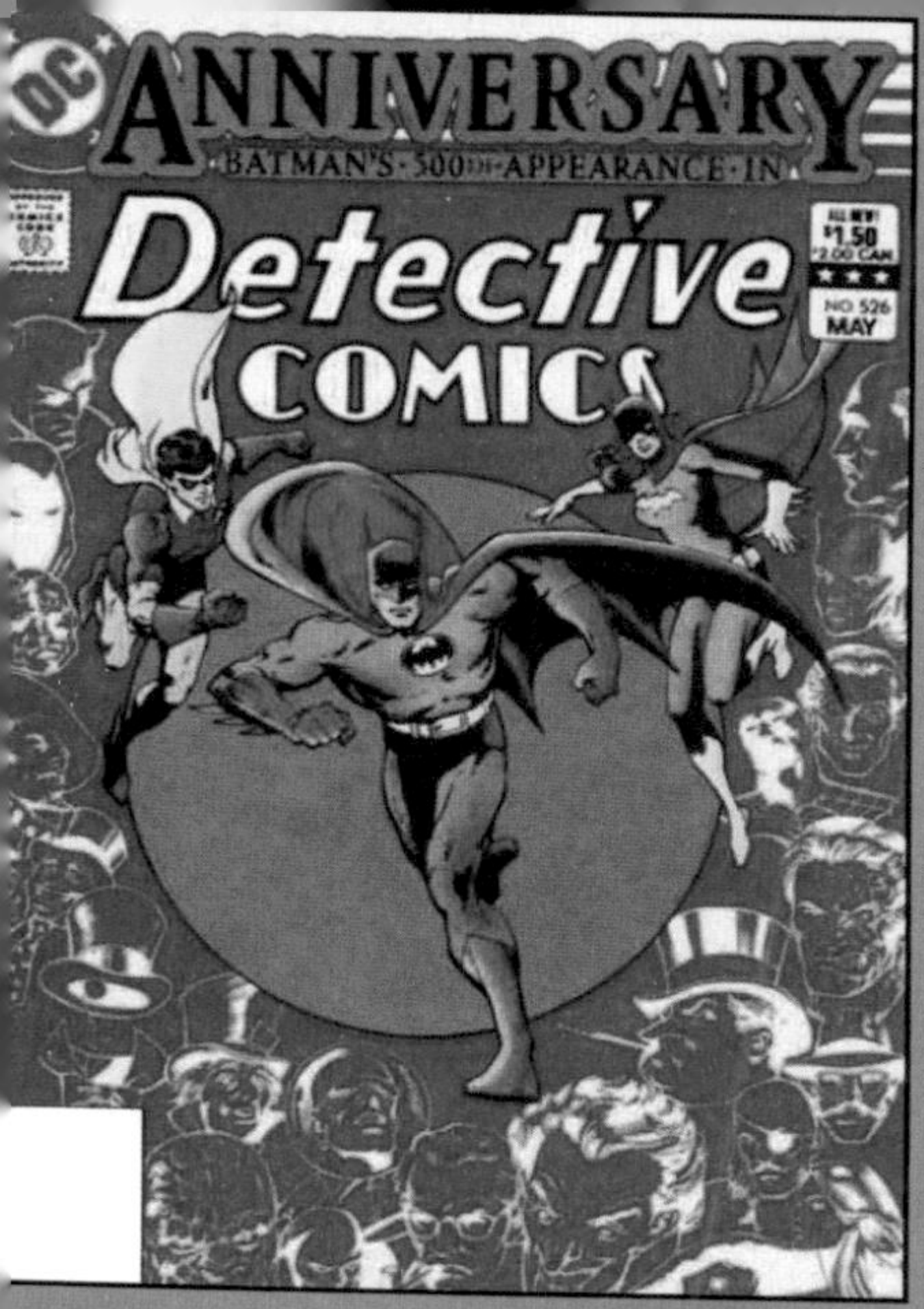
DC
ANNIVERSARY
BATMAN'S 500TH APPEARANCE IN
Detective
COMICS
ALL NEW!
$1.50
$2.00 CAN
NO. 526
MAY

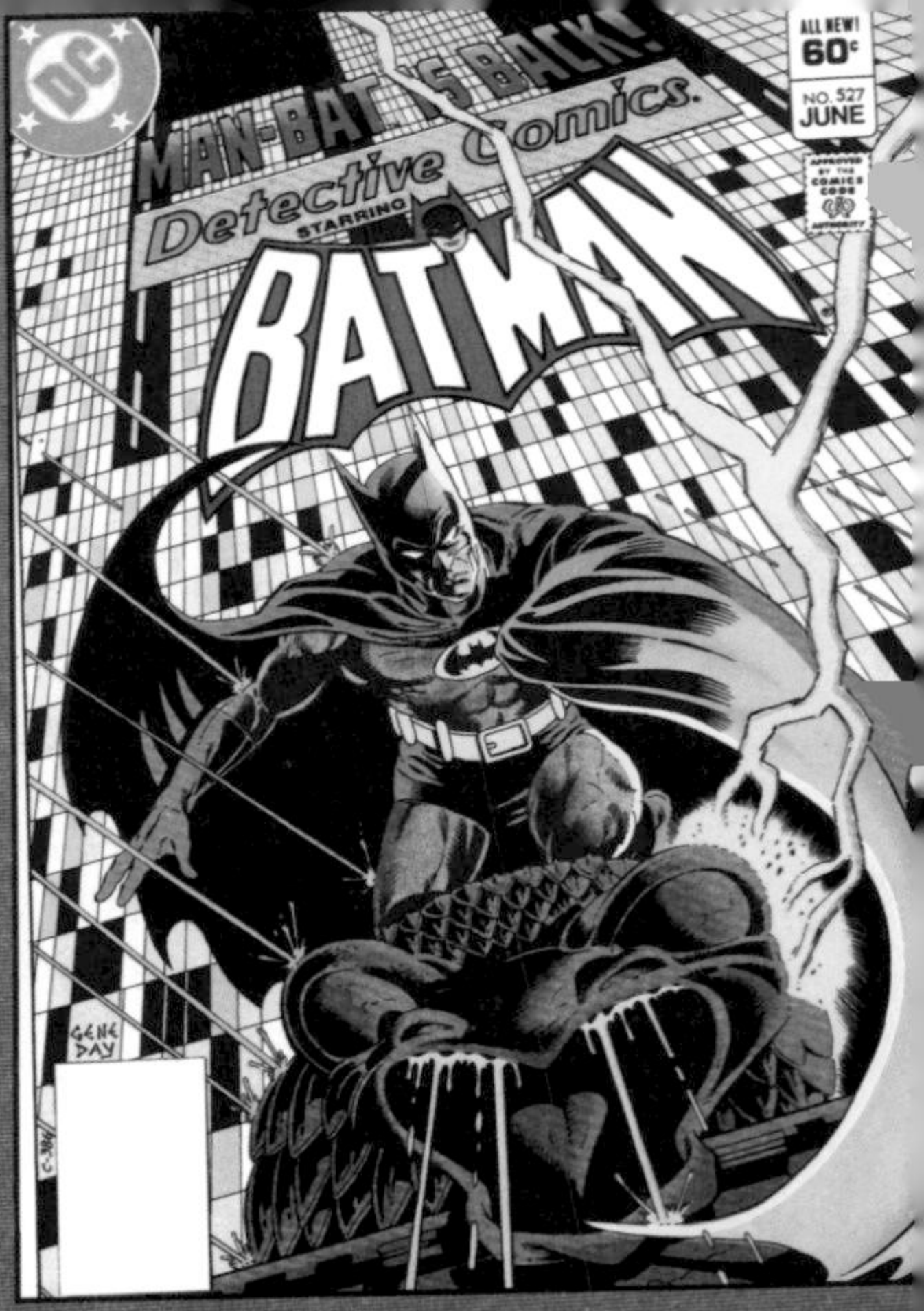
DC
MAN-BAT IS BACK!
Detective Comics.
STARRING
BATMAN
ALL NEW!
60¢
NO. 527
JUNE
APPROVED BY THE COMICS CODE AUTHORITY
GENE DAY
C-304

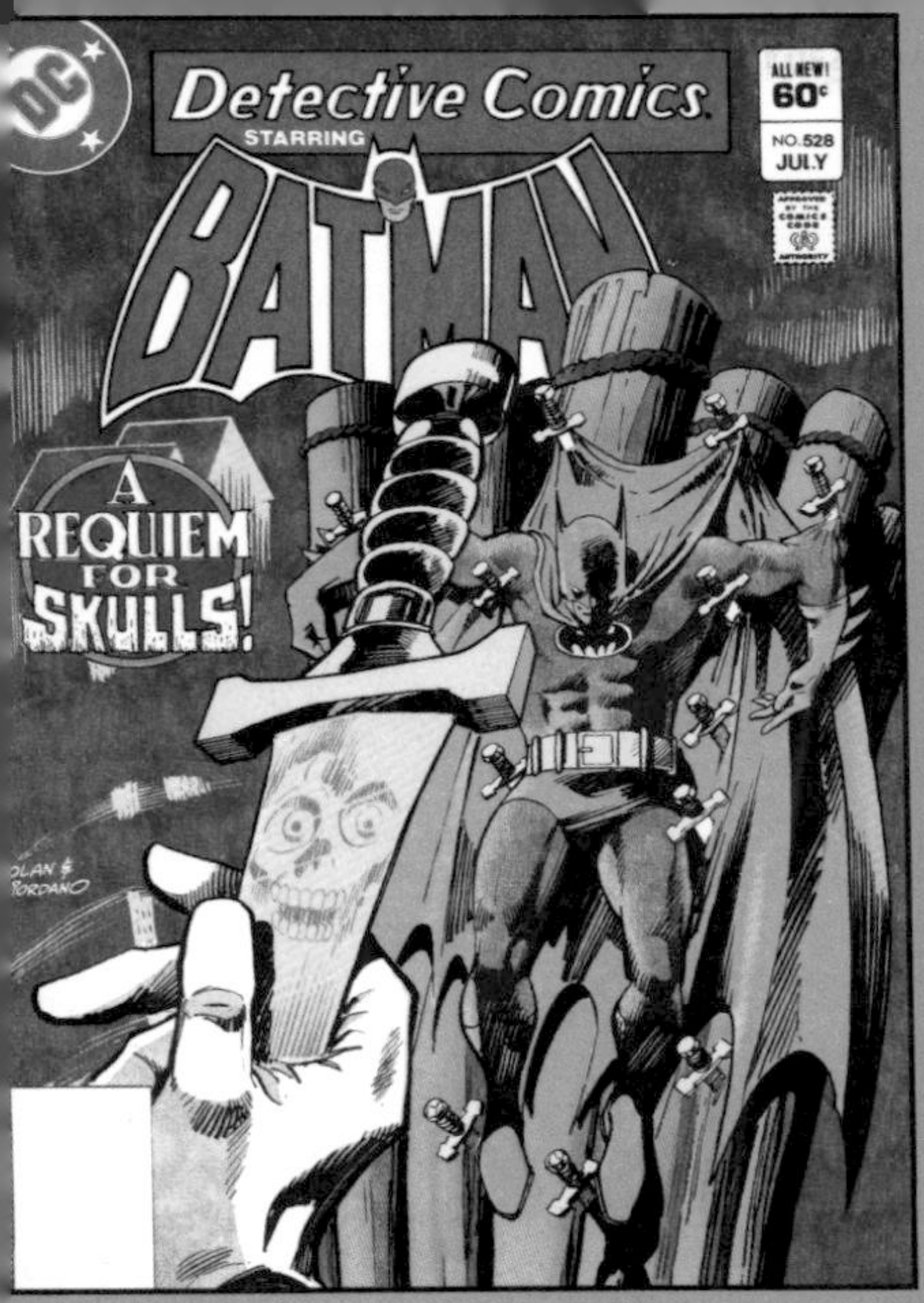
DC
Detective Comics
STARRING
BATMAN
ALL NEW!
60¢
NO. 528
JULY
A REQUIEM FOR SKULLS!
OLAN & RORDANO

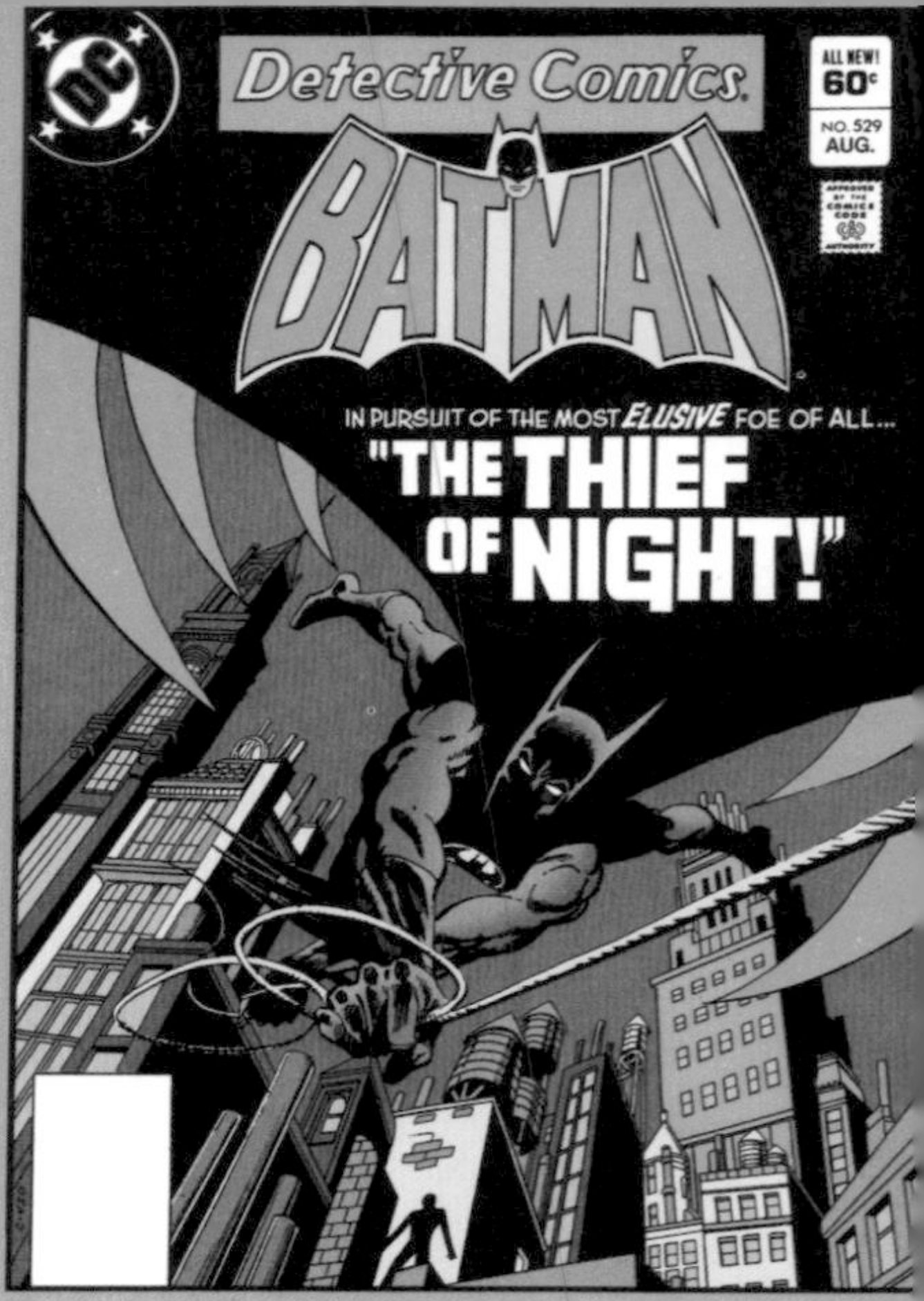
DC
Detective Comics.
ALL NEW!
60¢
NO. 529
AUG.
BATMAN
IN PURSUIT OF THE MOST ELUSIVE FOE OF ALL...
"THE THIEF OF NIGHT!"

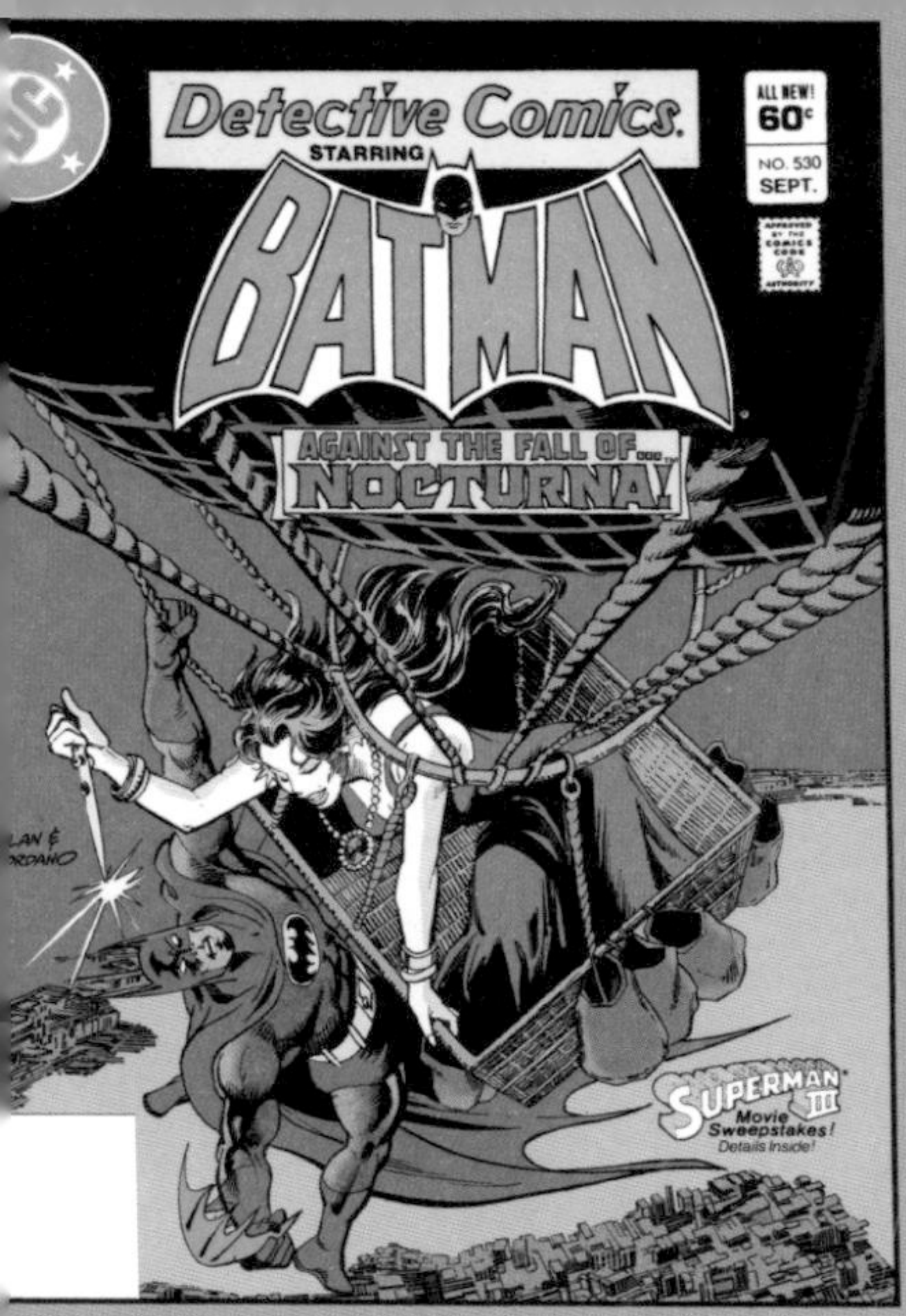
Detective Comics.
STARRING
BATMAN
ALL NEW!
60¢
NO. 530
SEPT.
AGAINST THE FALL OF NOCTURNA!
SUPERMAN III
Movie Sweepstakes!
Details Inside!

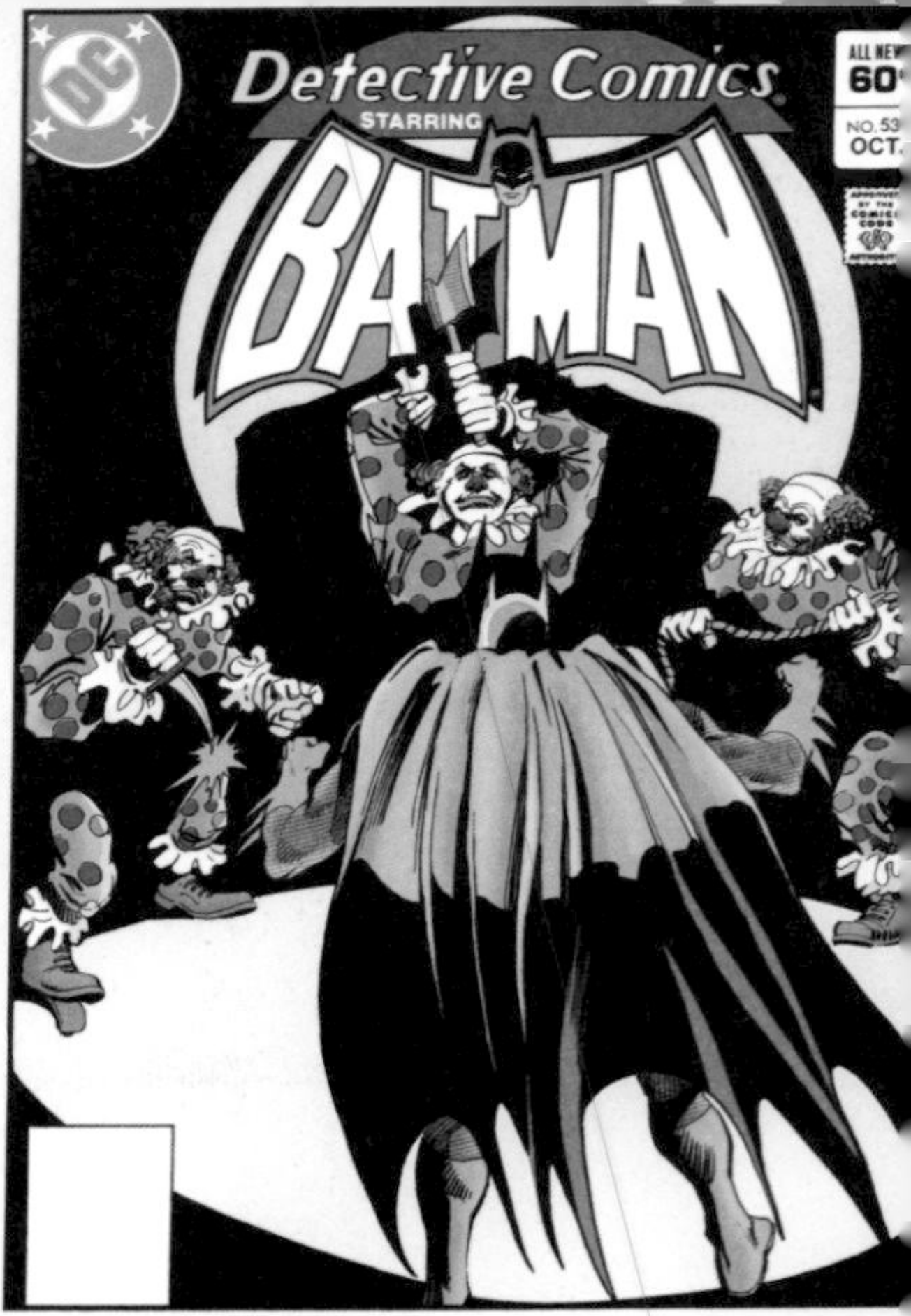
DC
Detective Comics
STARRING
BATMAN
ALL NEW
60
NO. 53
OCT.

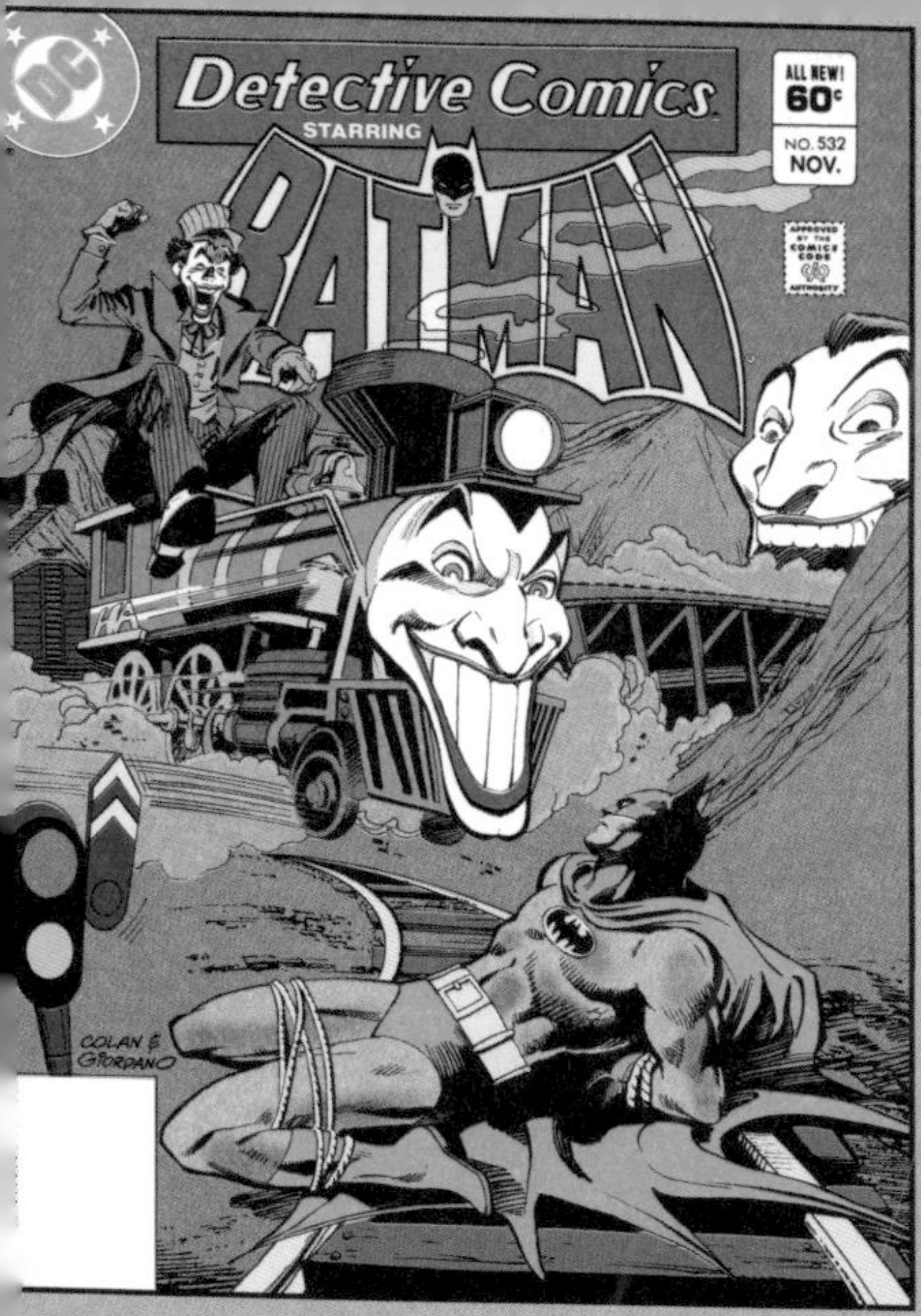
Detective Comics
STARRING
BATMAN
ALL NEW!
60¢
NO. 532
NOV.
APPROVED BY THE COMICS CODE AUTHORITY
COLAN & GIORDANO

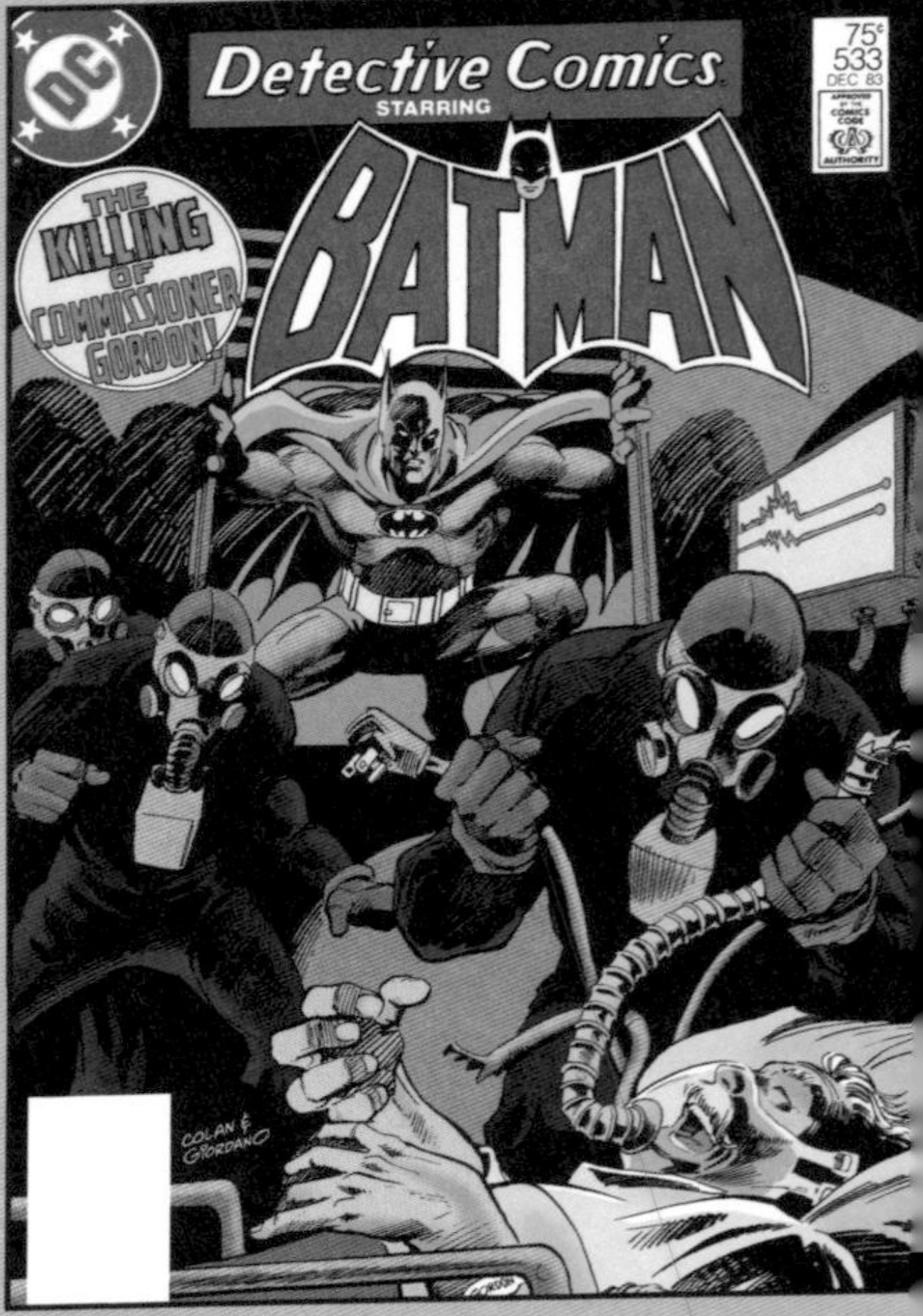
DC
Detective Comics
STARRING
BATMAN
75¢
533
DEC. 83
APPROVED BY THE COMICS CODE AUTHORITY
THE KILLING OF COMMISSIONER GORDON!
COLAN & GIORDANO

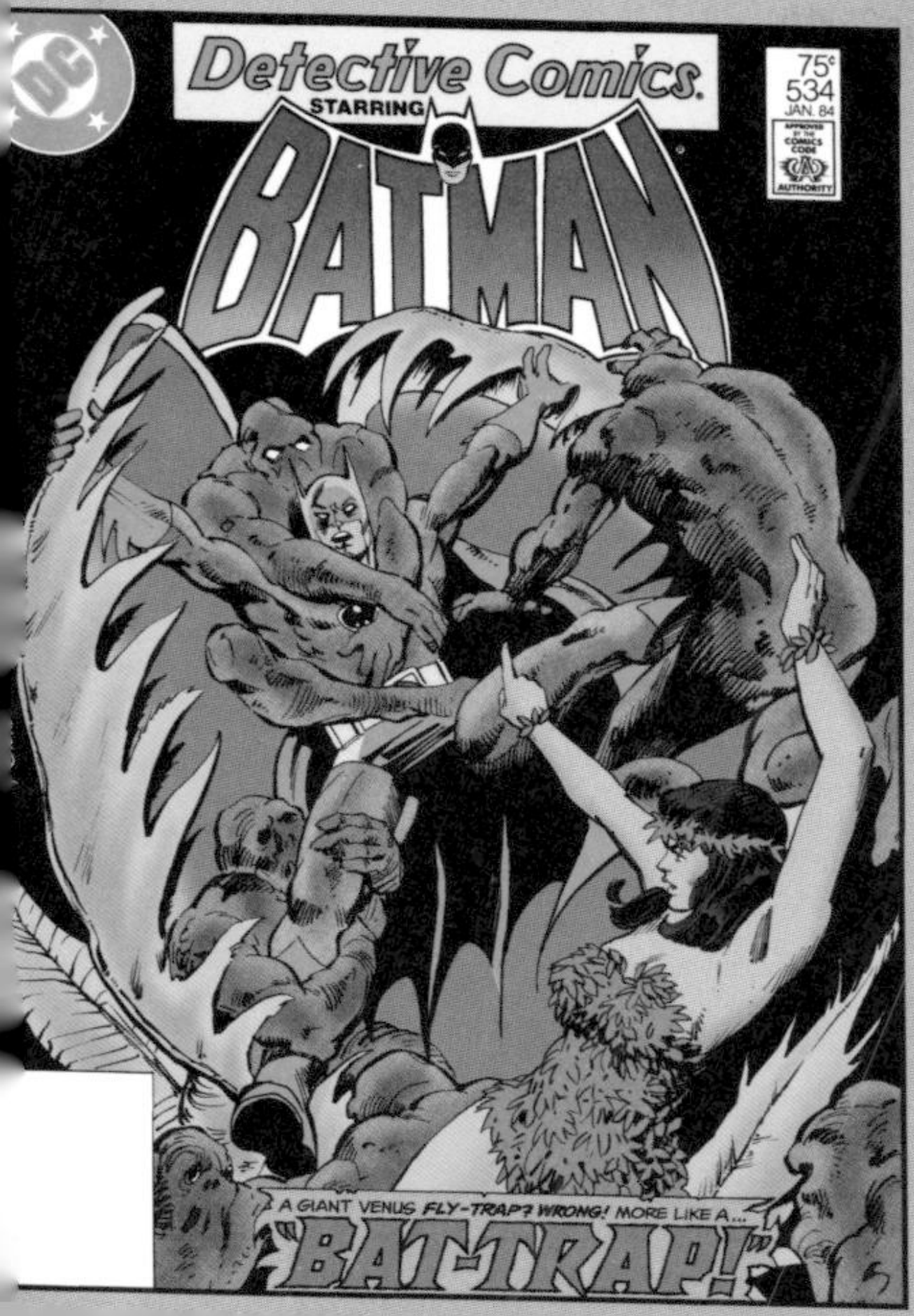
Detective Comics.
STARRING
BATMAN
75¢
534
JAN. 84
APPROVED BY THE COMICS CODE AUTHORITY
A GIANT VENUS FLY-TRAP? WRONG! MORE LIKE A...
BAT-TRAP!

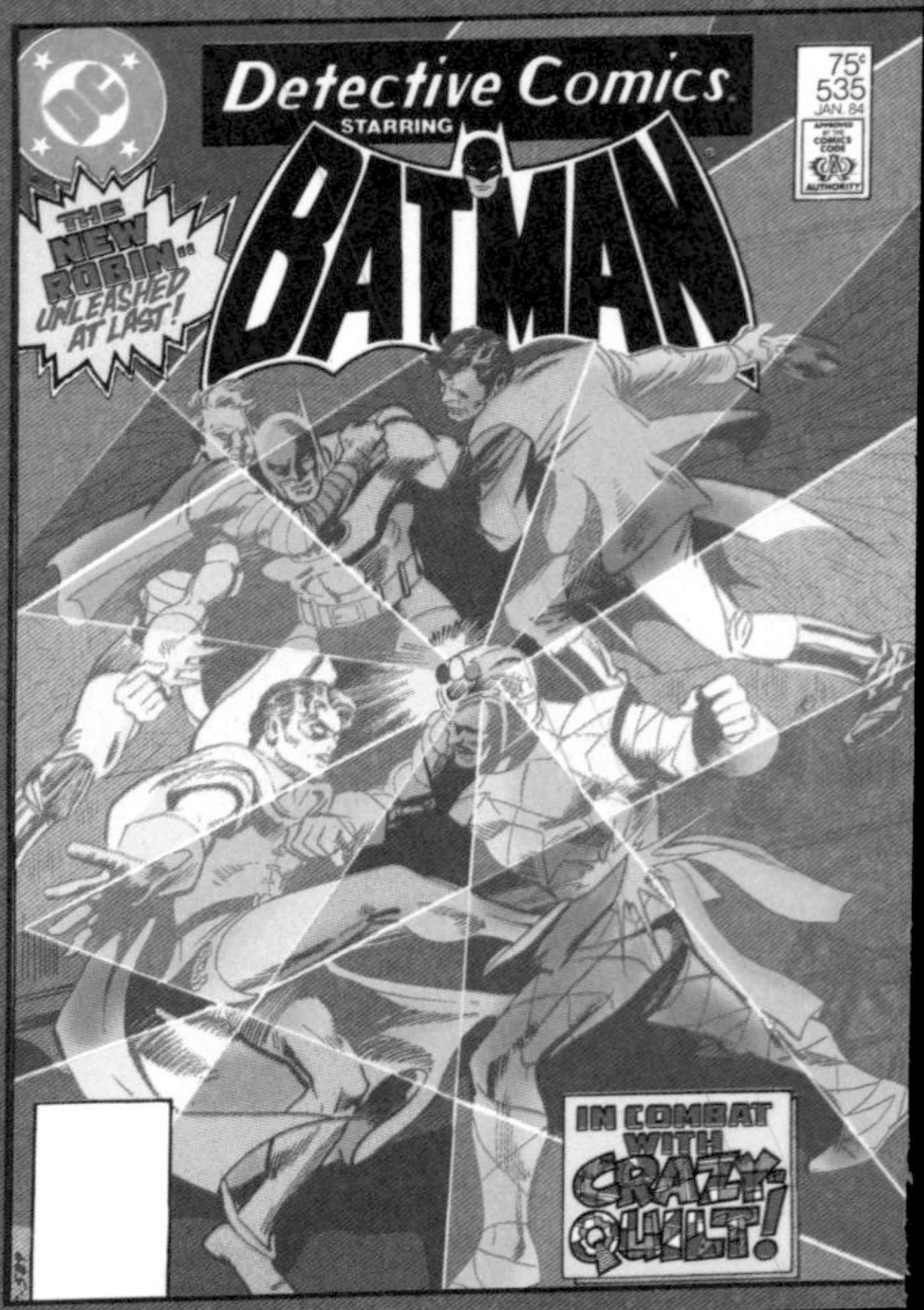
DC
Detective Comics
STARRING
BATMAN
75¢
535
JAN. 84
APPROVED BY THE COMICS CODE AUTHORITY
THE NEW ROBIN UNLEASHED AT LAST!
IN COMBAT WITH CRAZY QUILT!

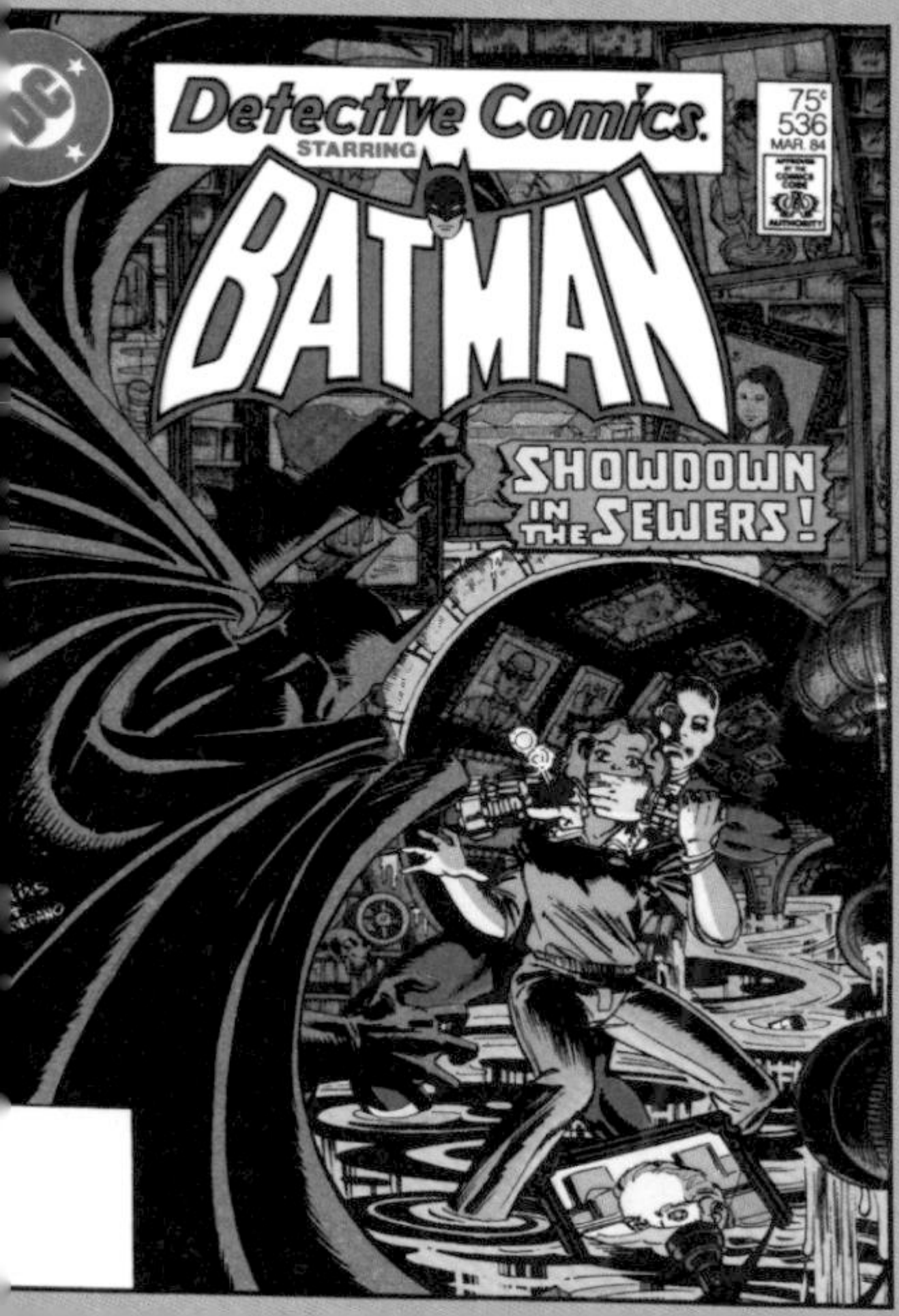
DC
Detective Comics.
STARRING
BATMAN
75¢
536
MAR. 84
SHOWDOWN IN THE SEWERS!

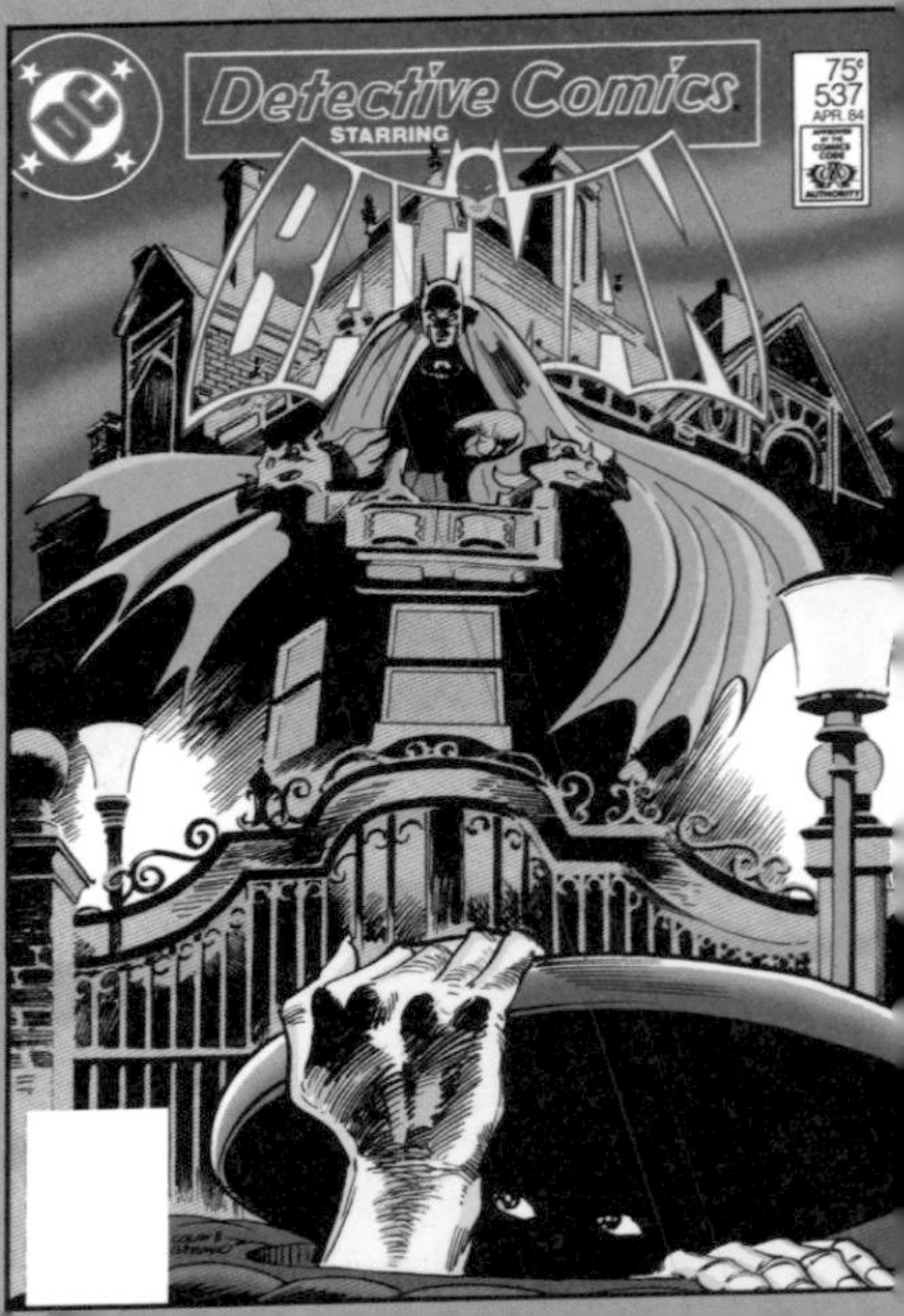
DC
Detective Comics
STARRING
BATMAN
75¢
537
APR. 84

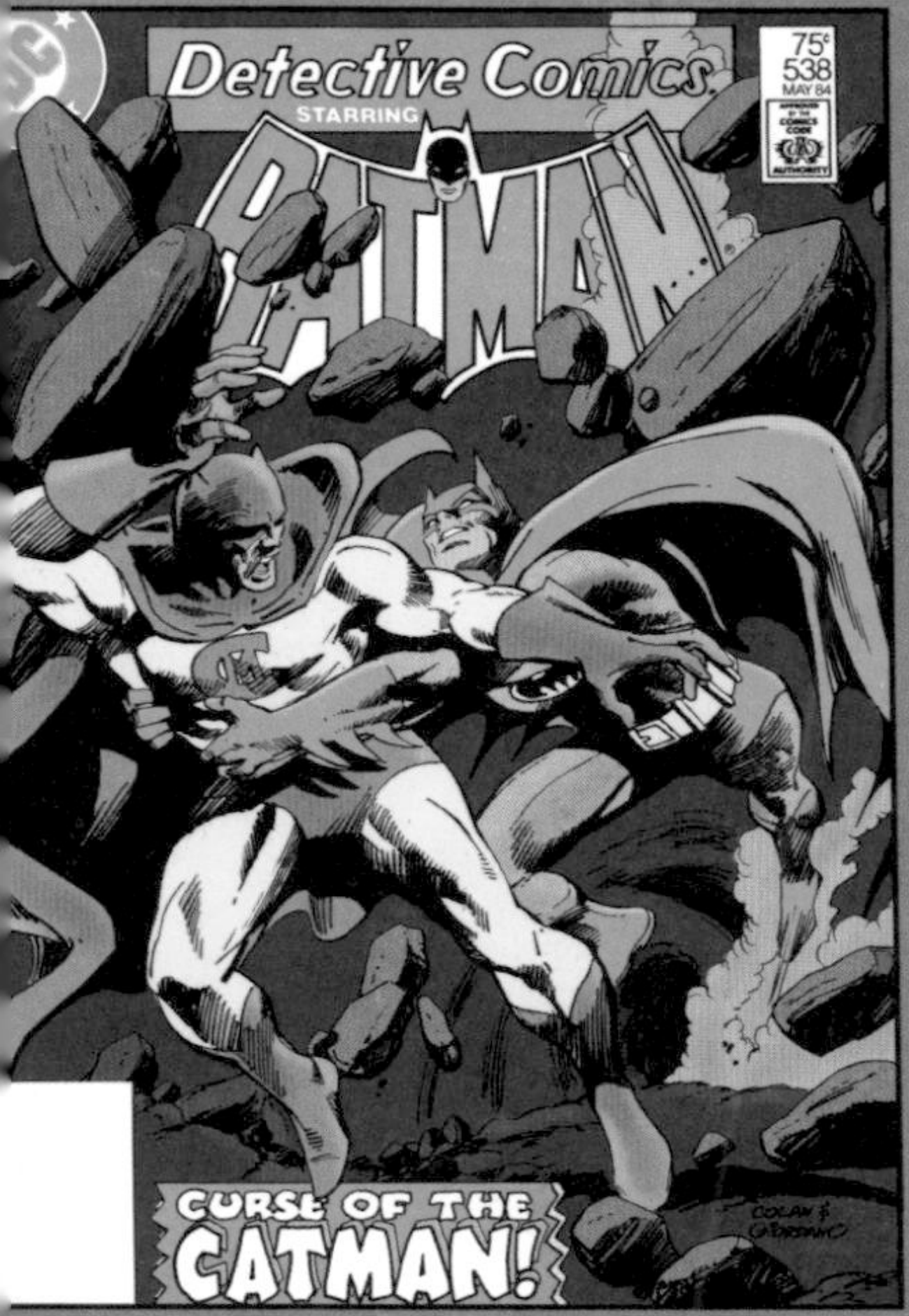
Detective Comics
STARRING
BATMAN...
75¢
538
MAY 84
CURSE OF THE
CATMAN!

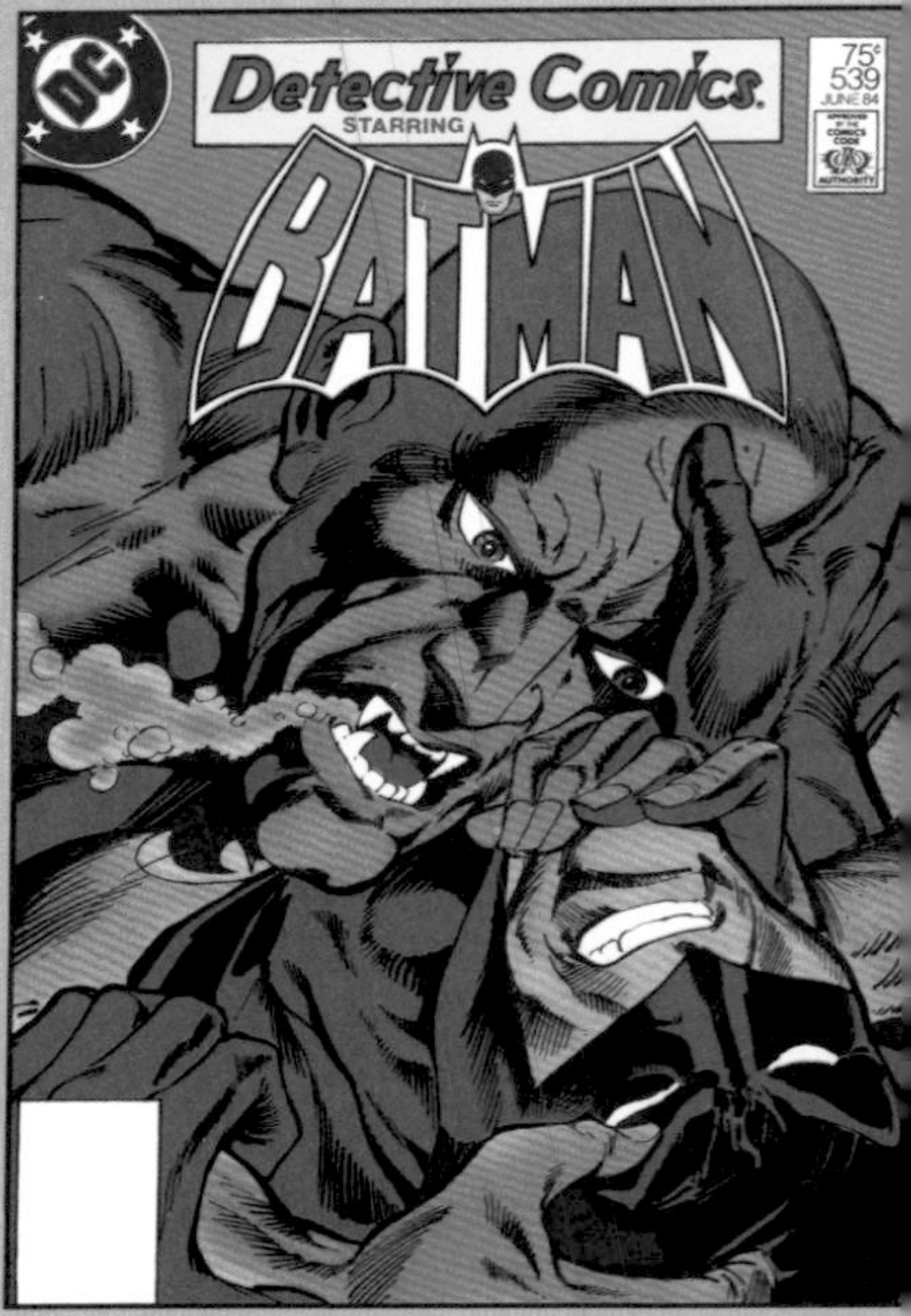
DC
Detective Comics.
STARRING
BATMAN
75¢
539
JUNE 84
APPROVED BY THE COMICS CODE AUTHORITY

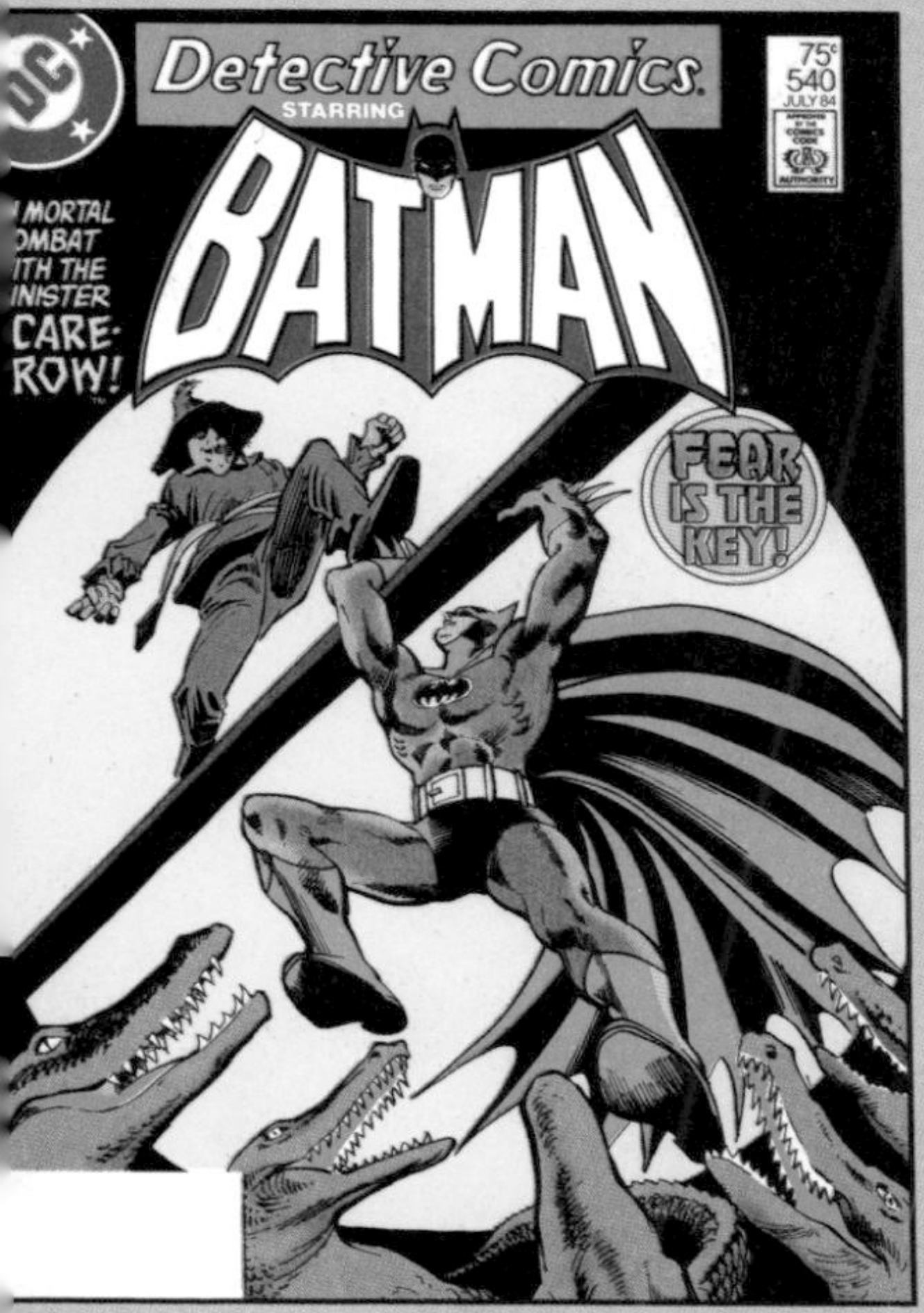
DC
Detective Comics.
STARRING
BATMAN
75¢
540
JULY 84
MORTAL
OMBAT
ITH THE
INISTER
CARE-
ROW!
FEAR IS THE KEY!

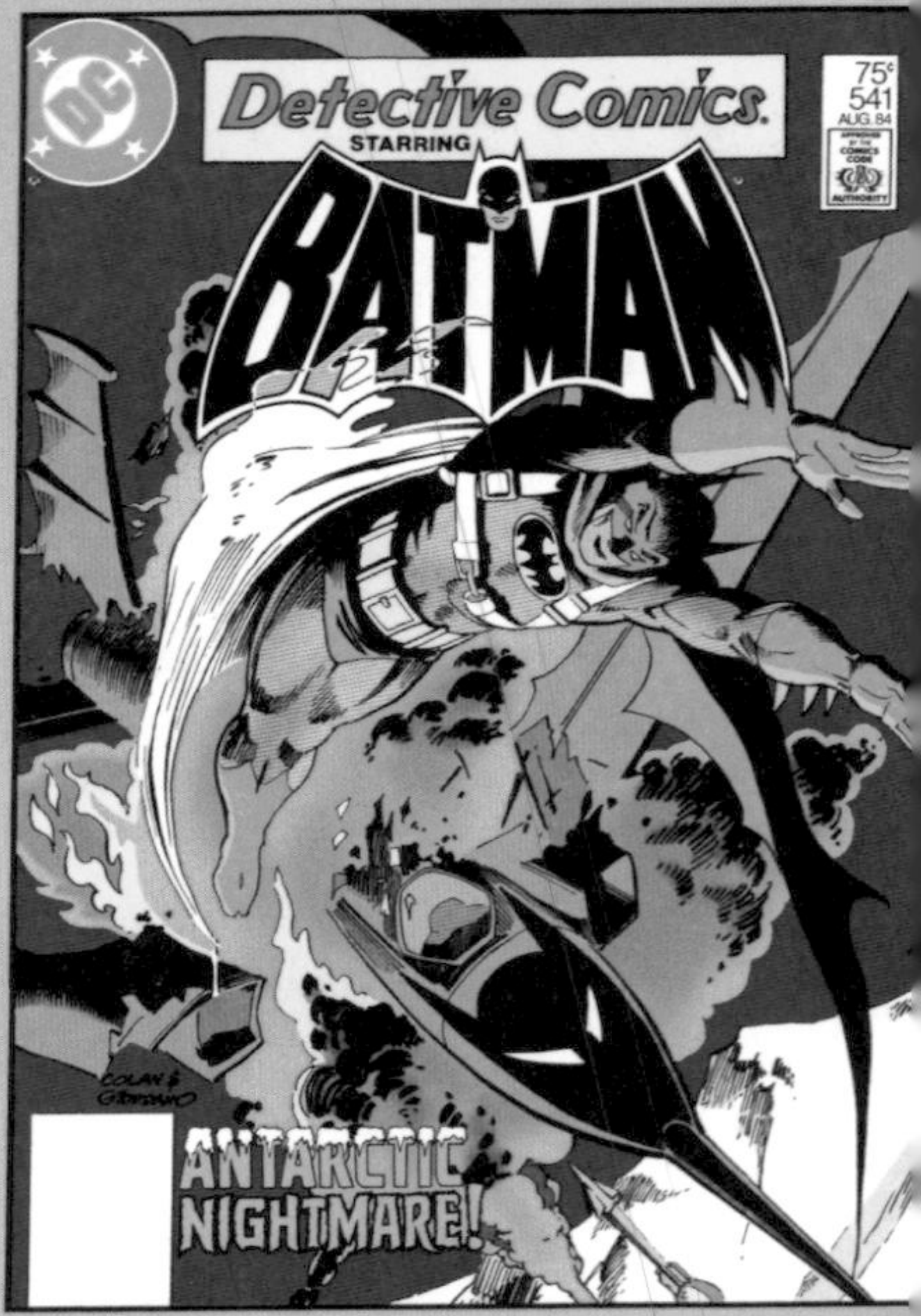
DC
Detective Comics.
STARRING
BATMAN
75¢
541
AUG. 84
COLAN & GIORDANO
ANTARCTIC NIGHTMARE!

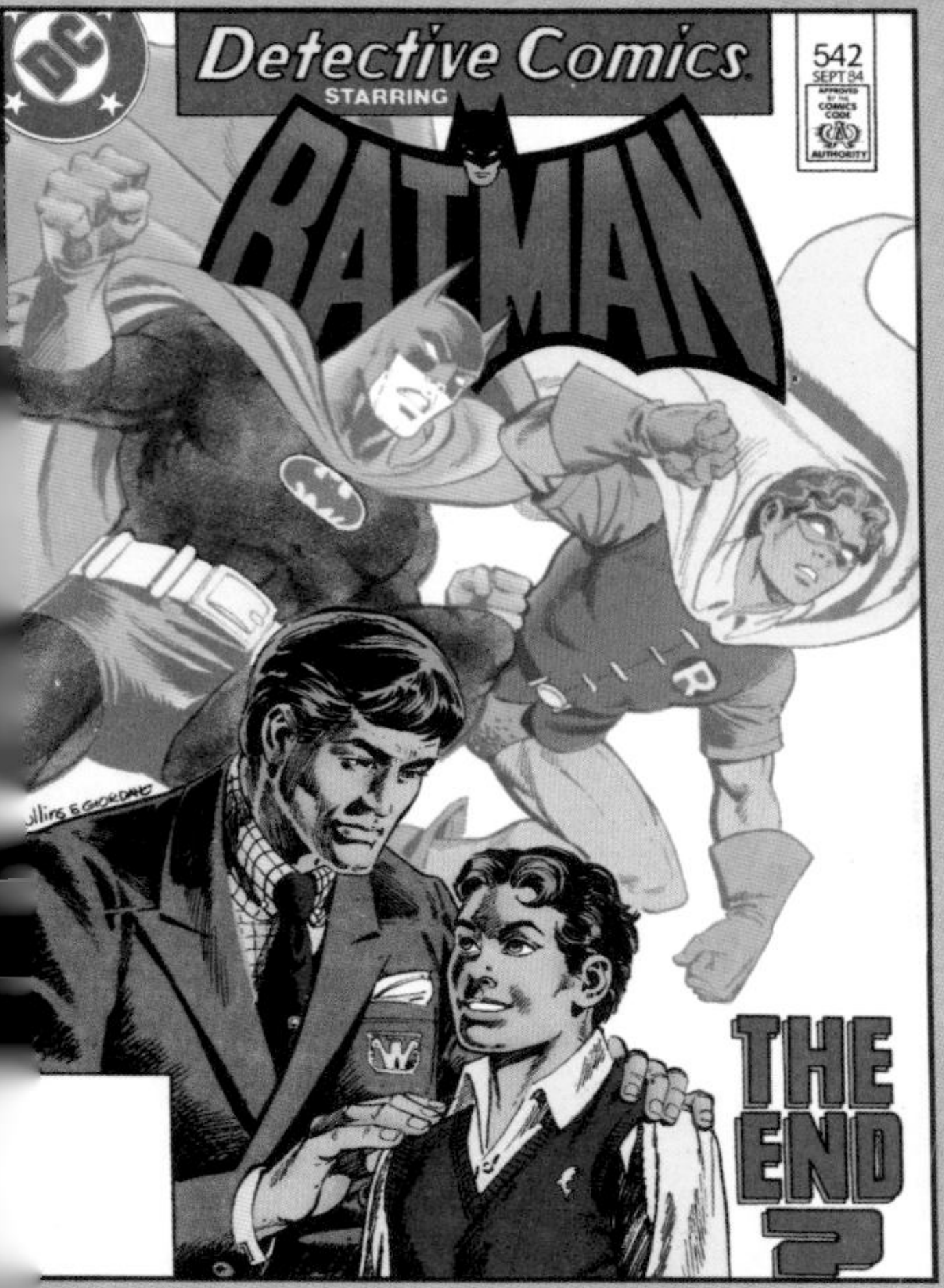
DC
Detective Comics
STARRING
BATMAN
542
SEPT 84
APPROVED BY THE COMICS CODE AUTHORITY
THE END ?

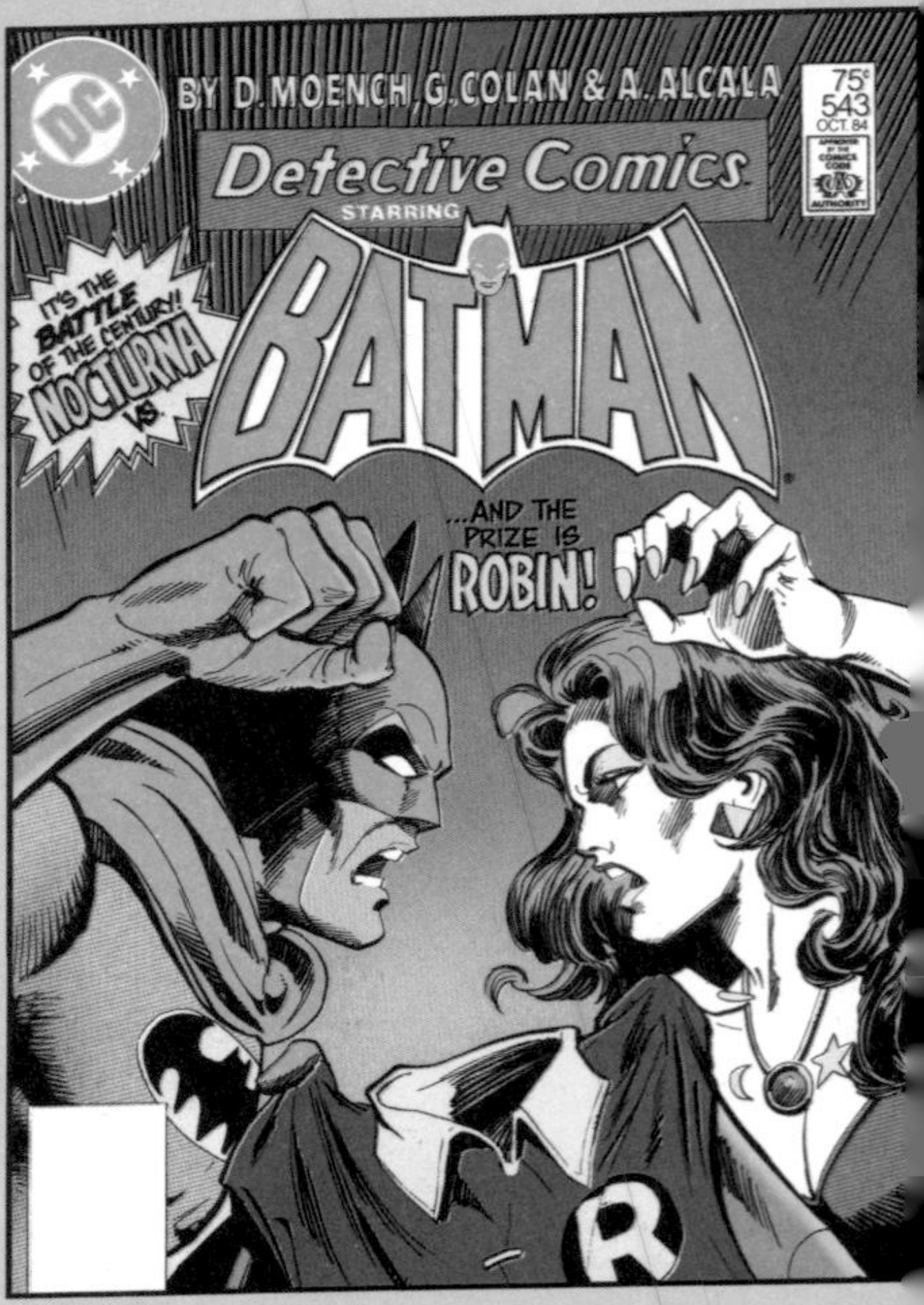
BY D. MOENCH, G. COLAN & A. ALCALA
75¢
543
OCT. 84
Detective Comics
STARRING
BATMAN
IT'S THE BATTLE OF THE CENTURY! NOCTURNA VS.
...AND THE PRIZE IS ROBIN!

BY D.MOENCH, G.COLAN & A.ALCALA
75¢
544
NOV. 84
Detective Comics
STARRING
BATMAN
GOTHAM GAZETTE
POLICE SEEK THIEF OF NIGHT

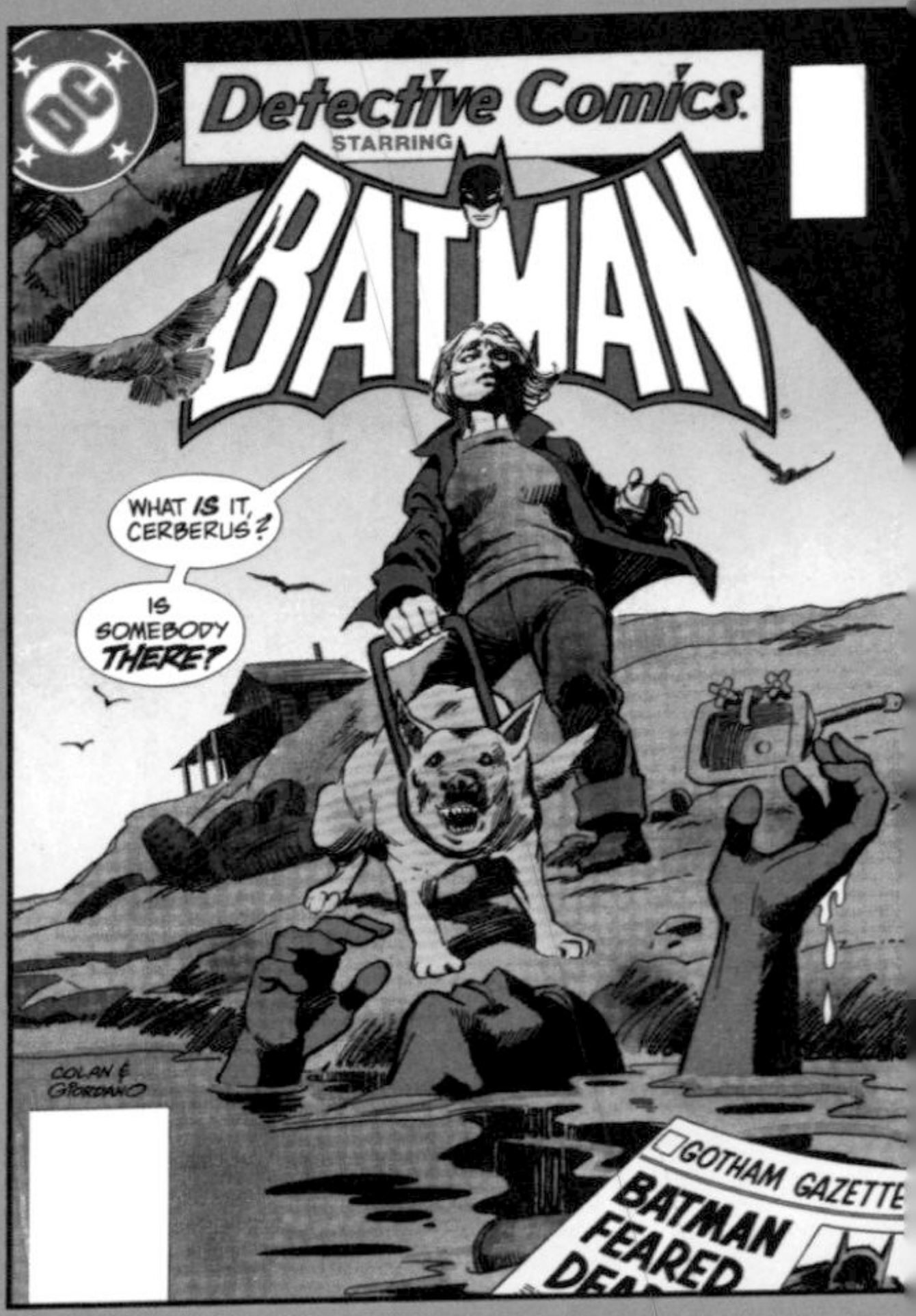
DC
Detective Comics.
STARRING
BATMAN
WHAT IS IT, CERBERUS?
IS SOMEBODY THERE?
COLAN & GIORDANO
GOTHAM GAZETTE
BATMAN FEARED

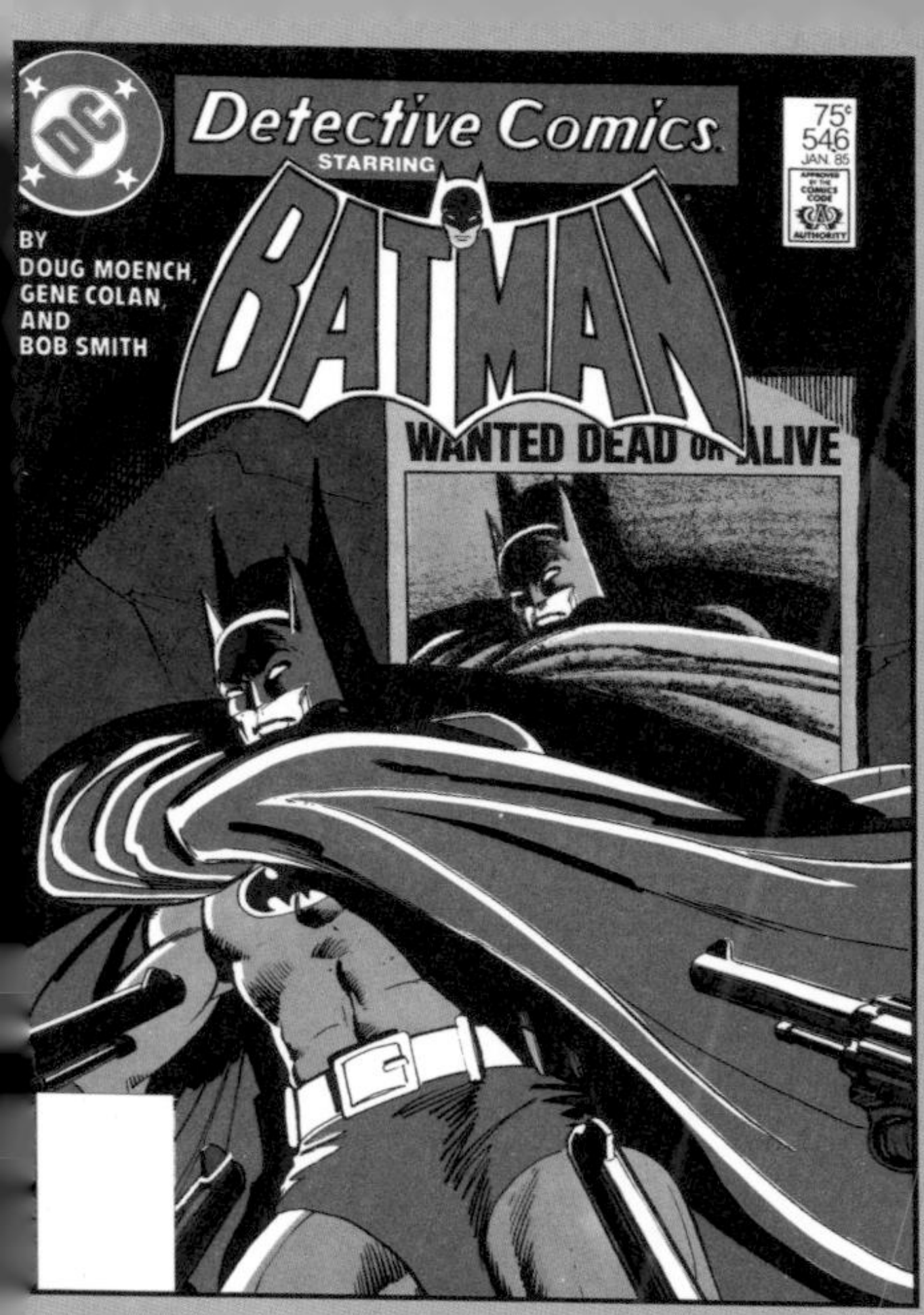
DC
Detective Comics
STARRING
BATMAN
75¢
546
JAN. 85
APPROVED BY THE COMICS CODE AUTHORITY
BY
DOUG MOENCH,
GENE COLAN,
AND
BOB SMITH
WANTED DEAD OR ALIVE

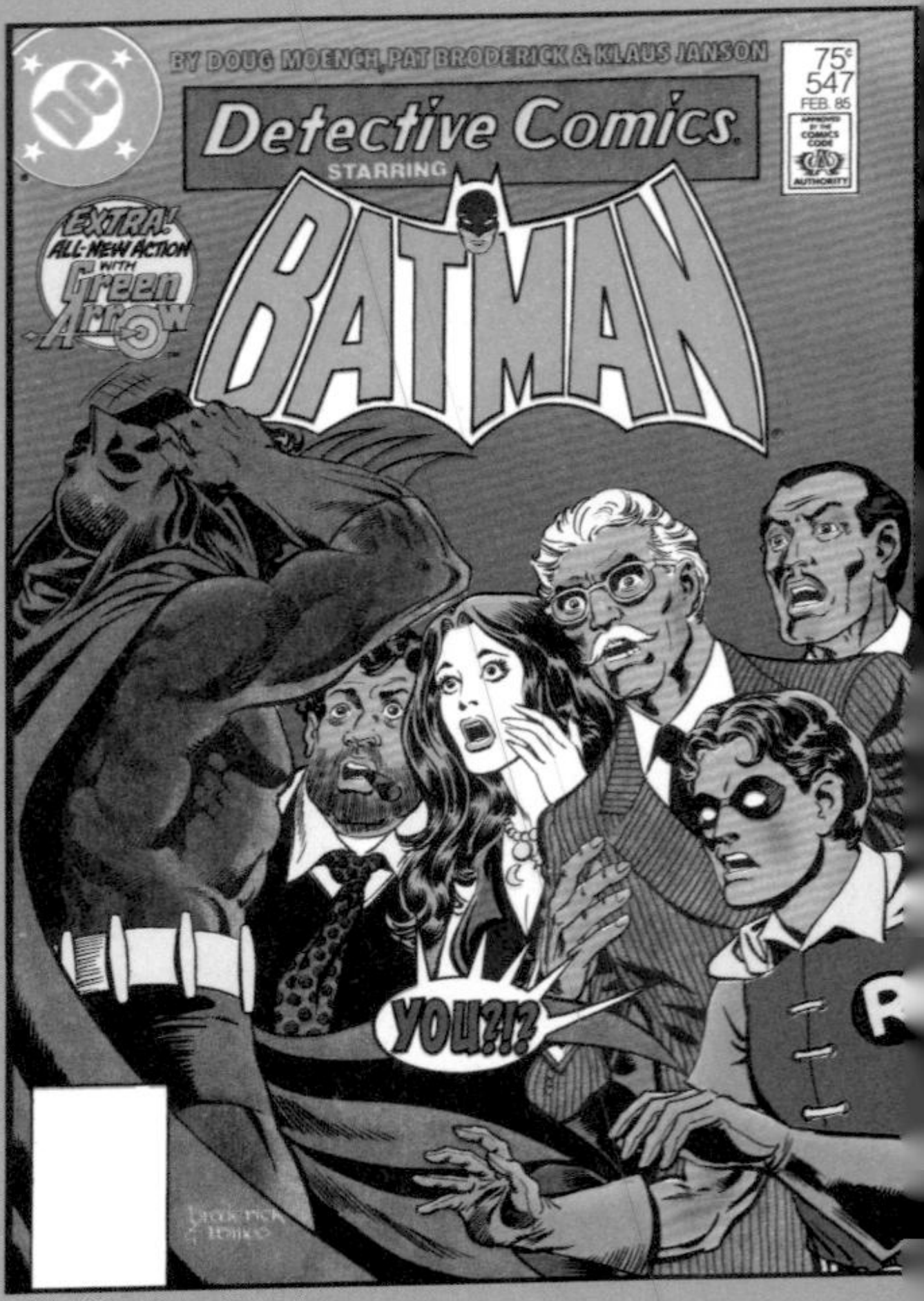
BY DOUG MOENCH, PAT BRODERICK & KLAUS JANSON
75¢
547
FEB. 85
Detective Comics
STARRING
BATMAN
EXTRA! ALL-NEW ACTION WITH Green Arrow
YOU?!?

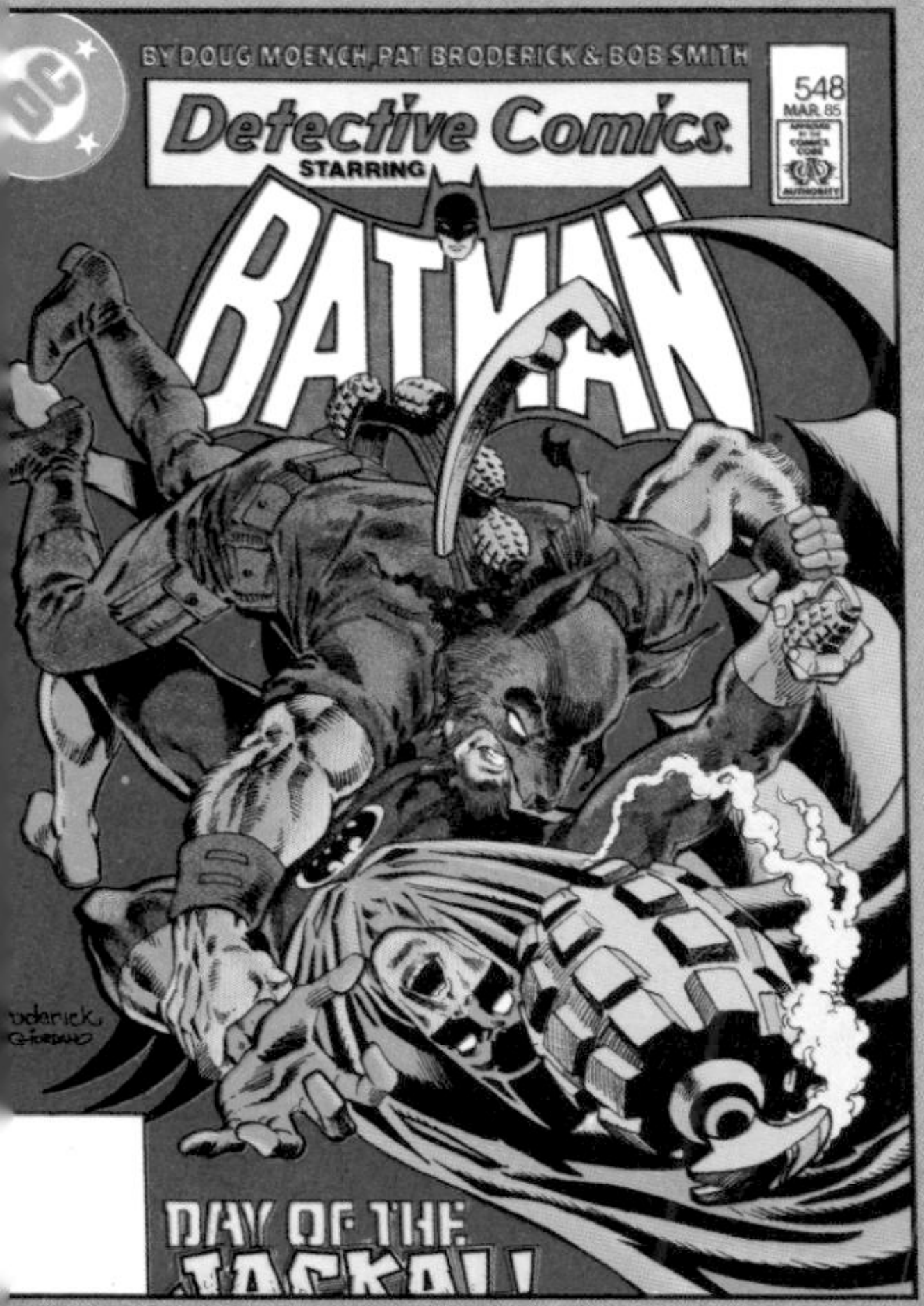
BY DOUG MOENCH, PAT BRODERICK & BOB SMITH
Detective Comics
548
MAR. 85
STARRING
BATMAN
DAY OF THE

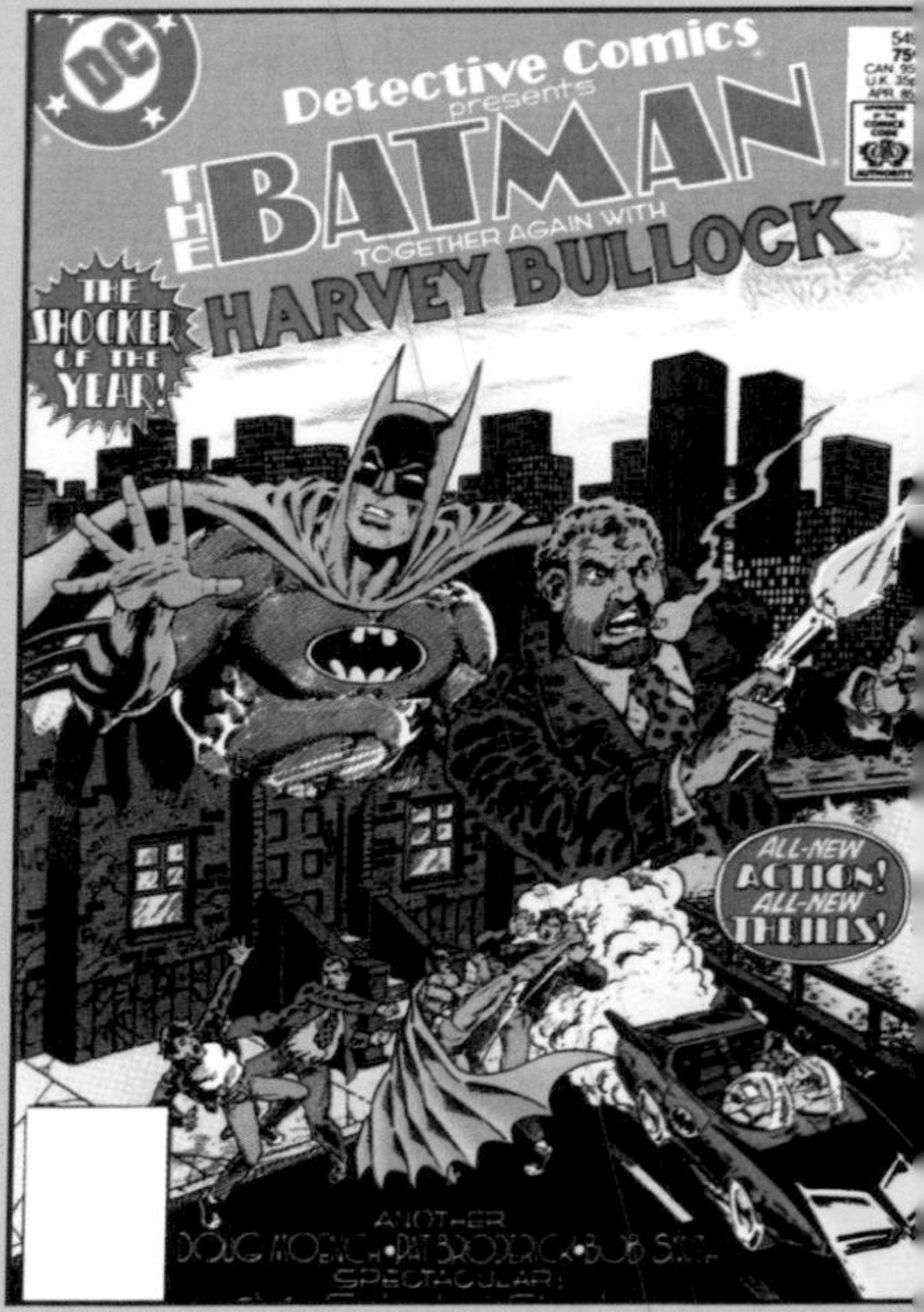
DC
Detective Comics
presents
THE BATMAN
TOGETHER AGAIN WITH
HARVEY BULLOCK
THE SHOCKER OF THE YEAR!
ALL-NEW ACTION! ALL-NEW THRILLS!
ANOTHER
SPECTACULAR!

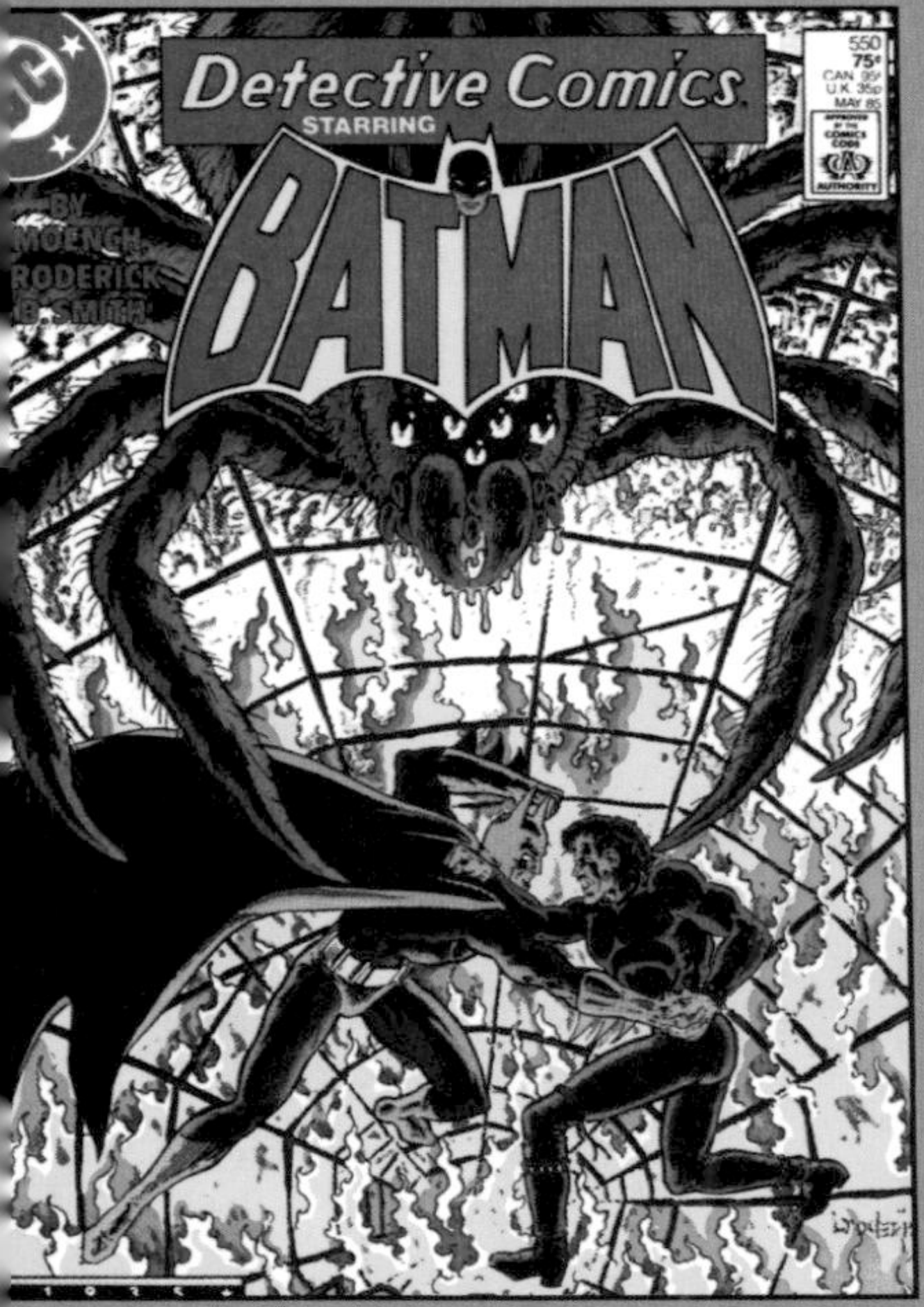
Detective Comics
STARRING
BATMAN
550
75¢
CAN. 95¢
U.K. 35p
MAY 85
BY
MOENGH,
RODERICK
& SMITH

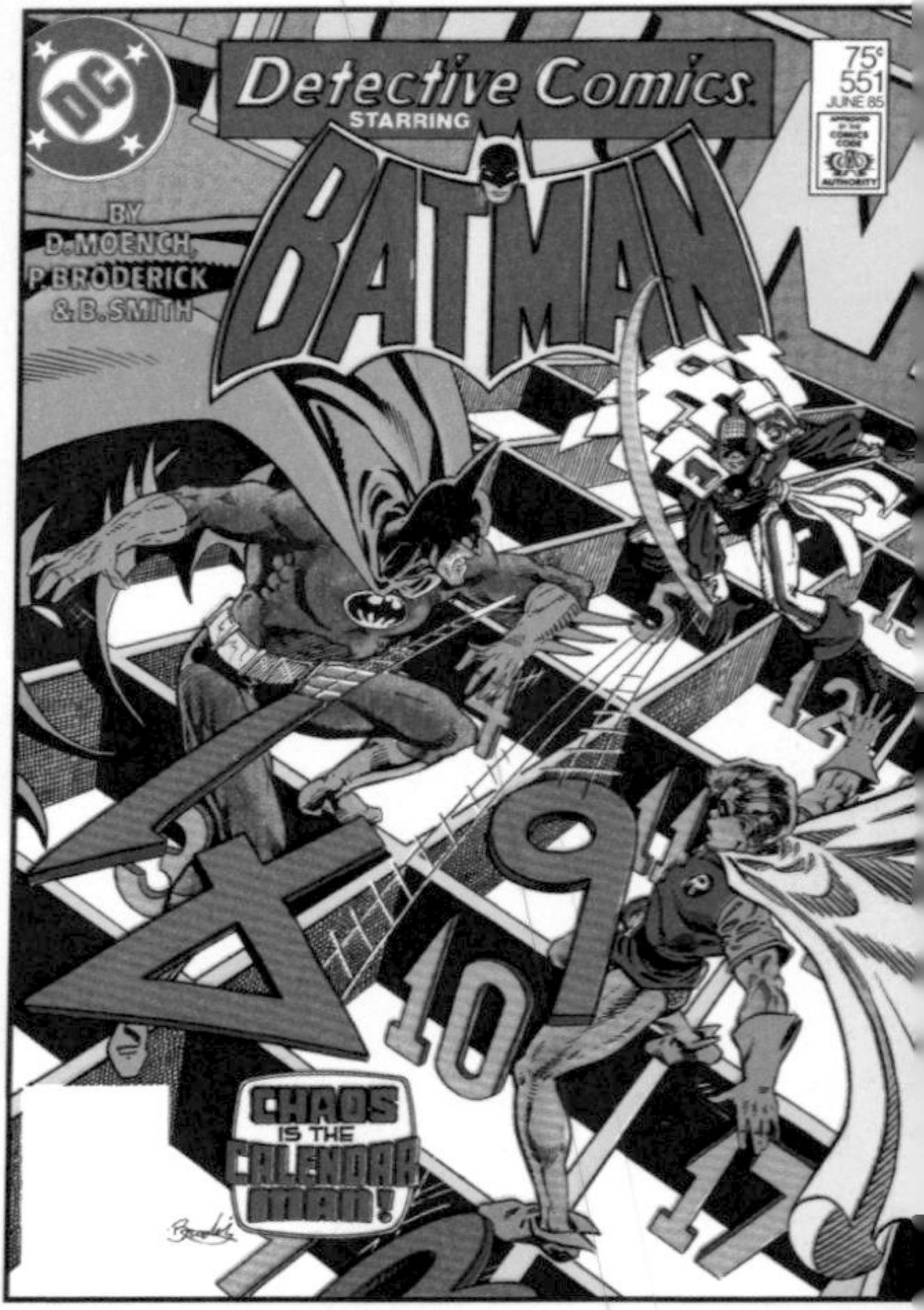
DC
Detective Comics
STARRING
BATMAN
75¢
551
JUNE 85
BY
D. MOENCH,
P. BRODERICK
& B. SMITH
CHAOS IS THE CALENDAR MAN!

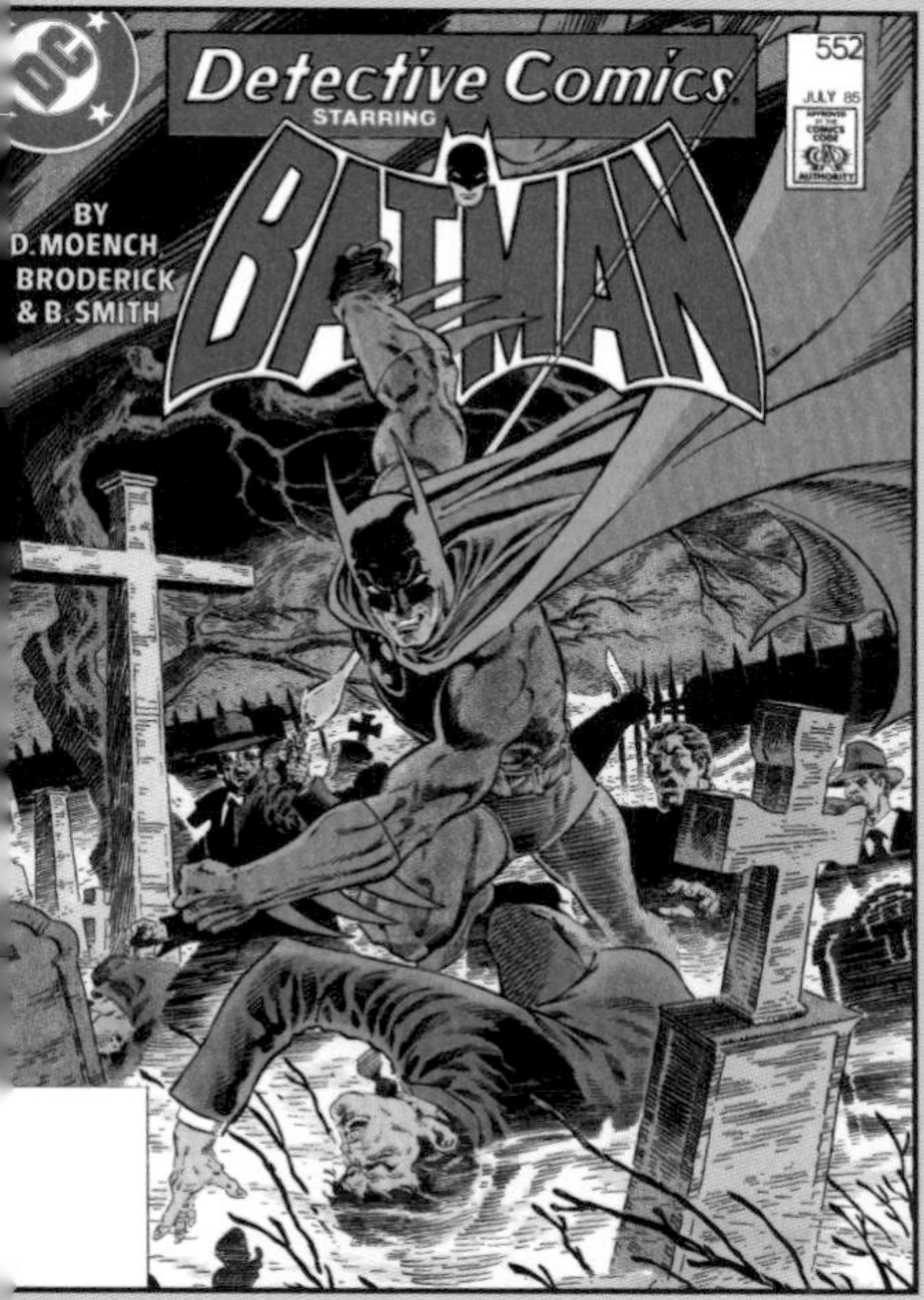
DC
Detective Comics
STARRING
BATMAN
552
JULY 85
BY
D. MOENCH
BRODERICK
& B. SMITH

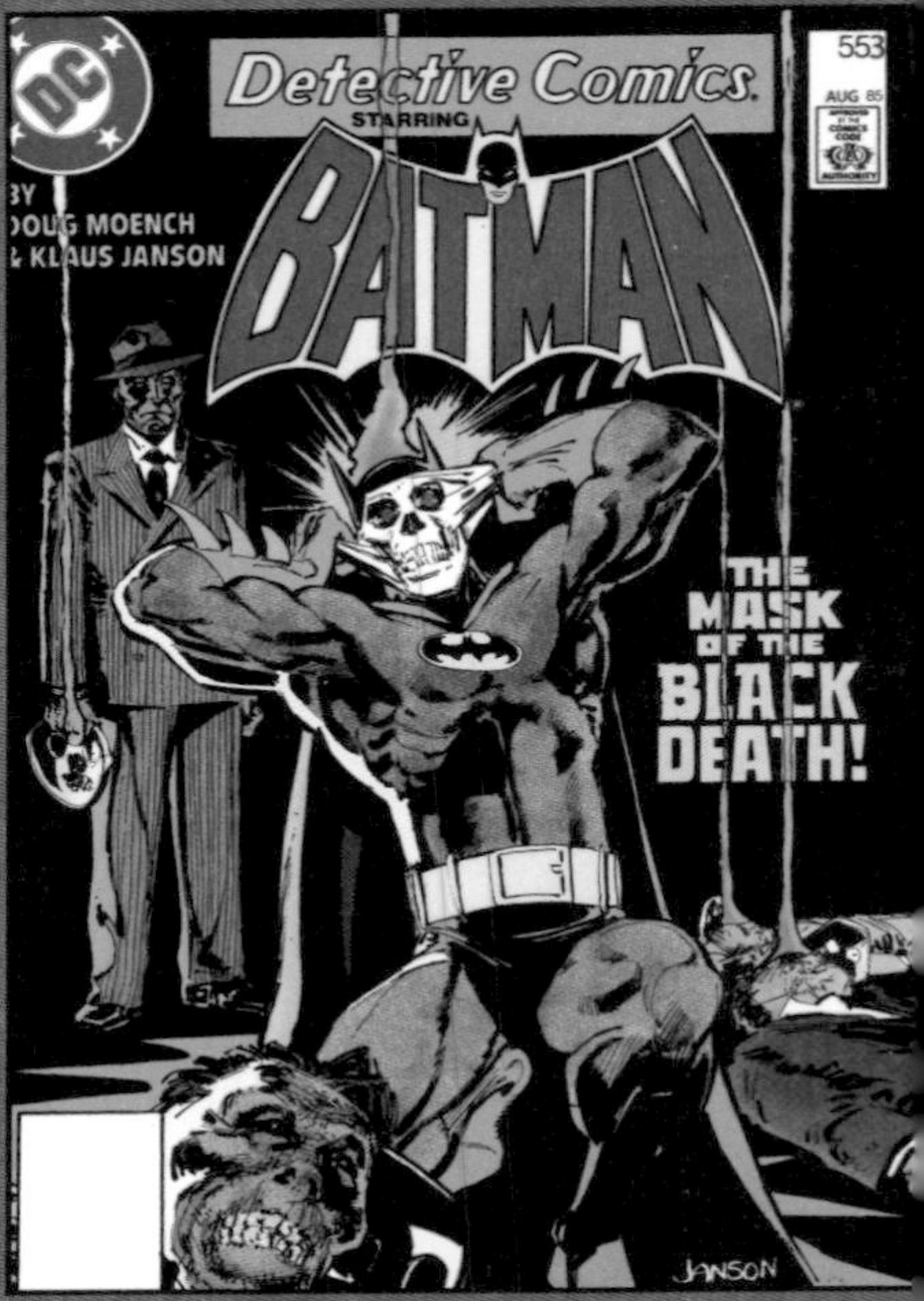
DC
Detective Comics.
STARRING
BATMAN
553
AUG 85
BY
DOUG MOENCH
& KLAUS JANSON
THE MASK OF THE BLACK DEATH!
JANSON

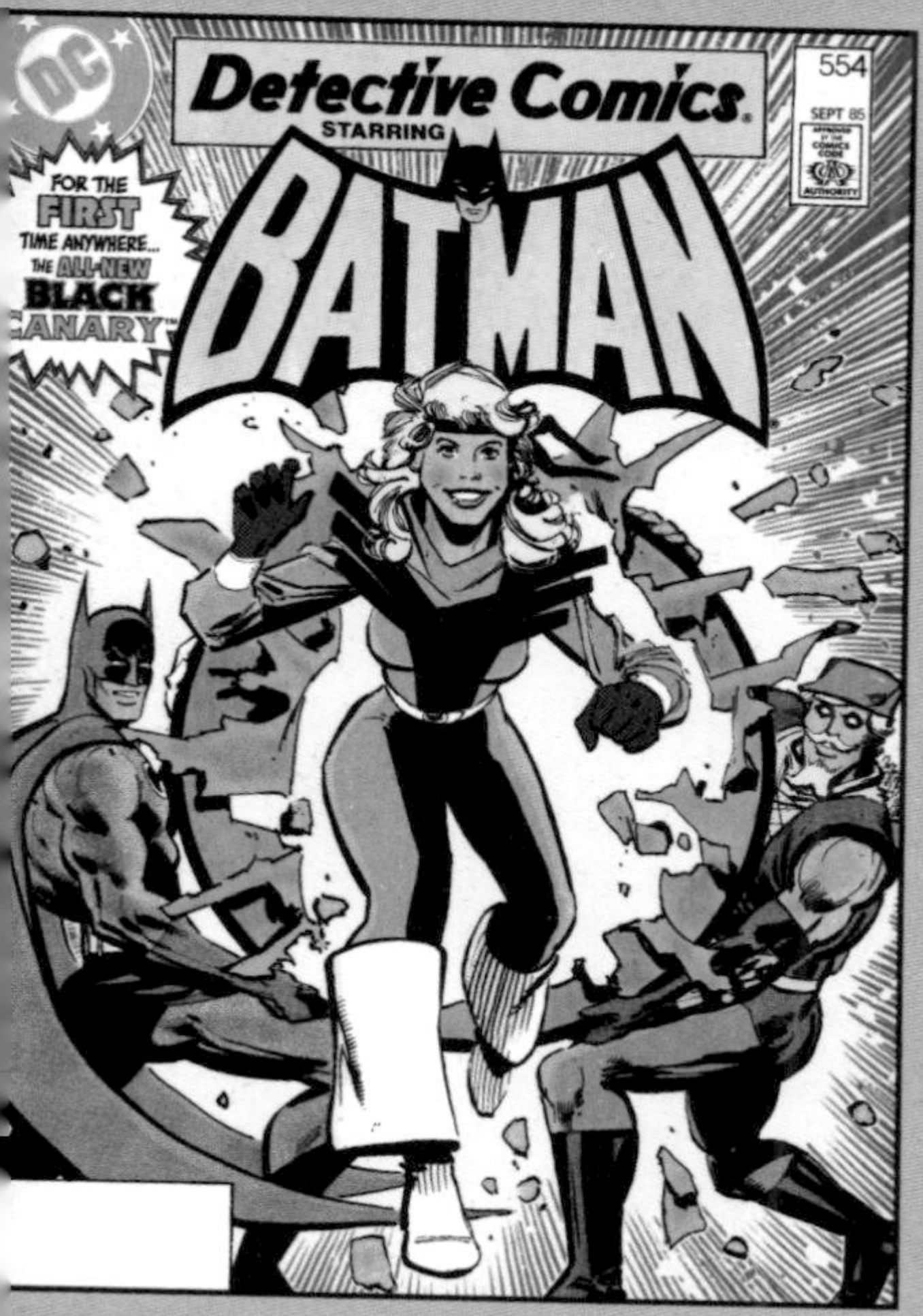
DC
Detective Comics
STARRING
BATMAN
554
SEPT 85
APPROVED BY THE COMICS CODE AUTHORITY
FOR THE FIRST TIME ANYWHERE... THE ALL-NEW BLACK CANARY

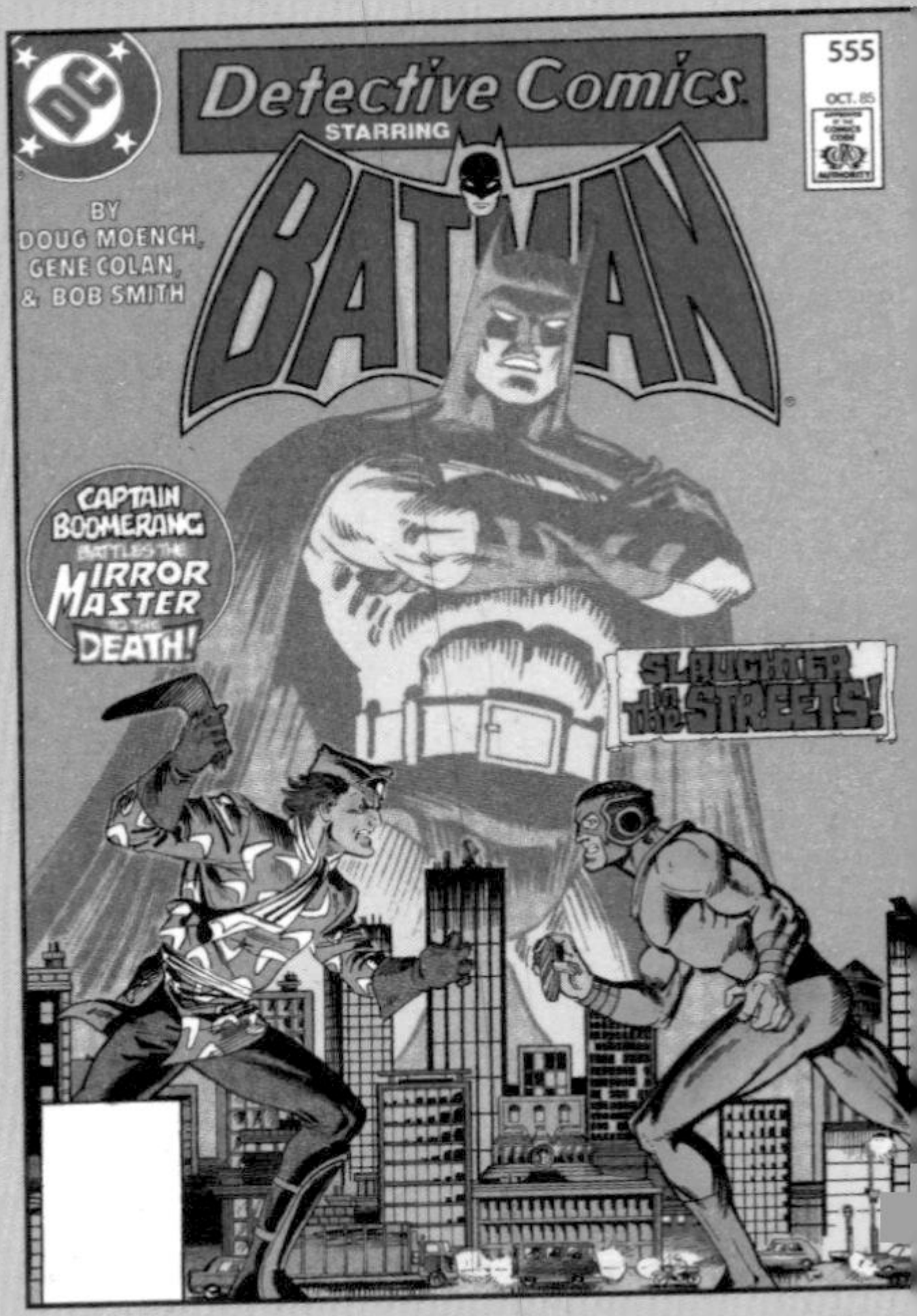
DC
Detective Comics
STARRING
BATMAN
555
OCT. 85
BY
DOUG MOENCH,
GENE COLAN,
& BOB SMITH
CAPTAIN BOOMERANG
BATTLES THE
MIRROR MASTER
TO THE
DEATH!
SLAUGHTER
THE STREETS!

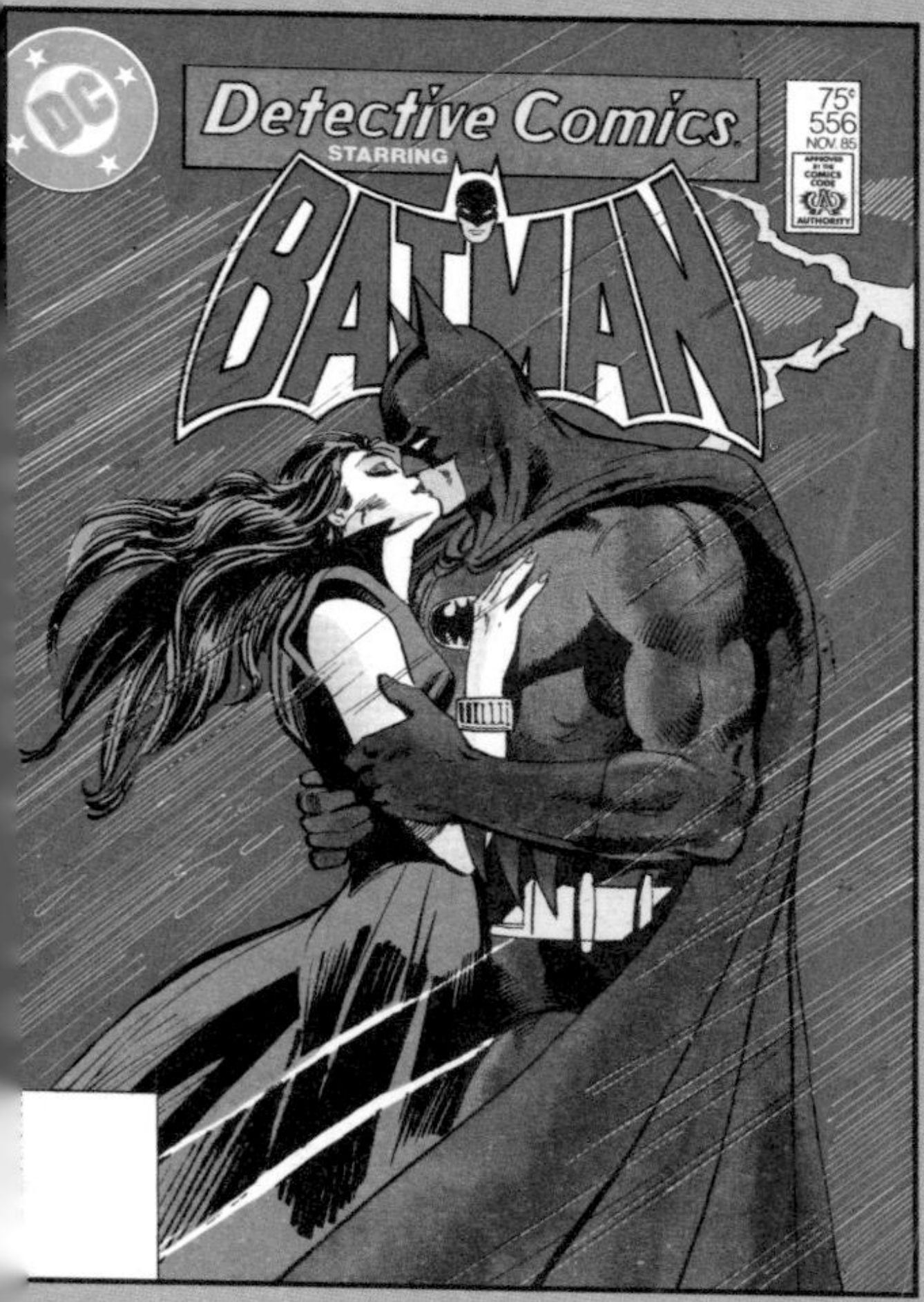
DC
Detective Comics
STARRING
BATMAN
75¢
556
NOV. 85
APPROVED BY THE COMICS CODE
AUTHORITY

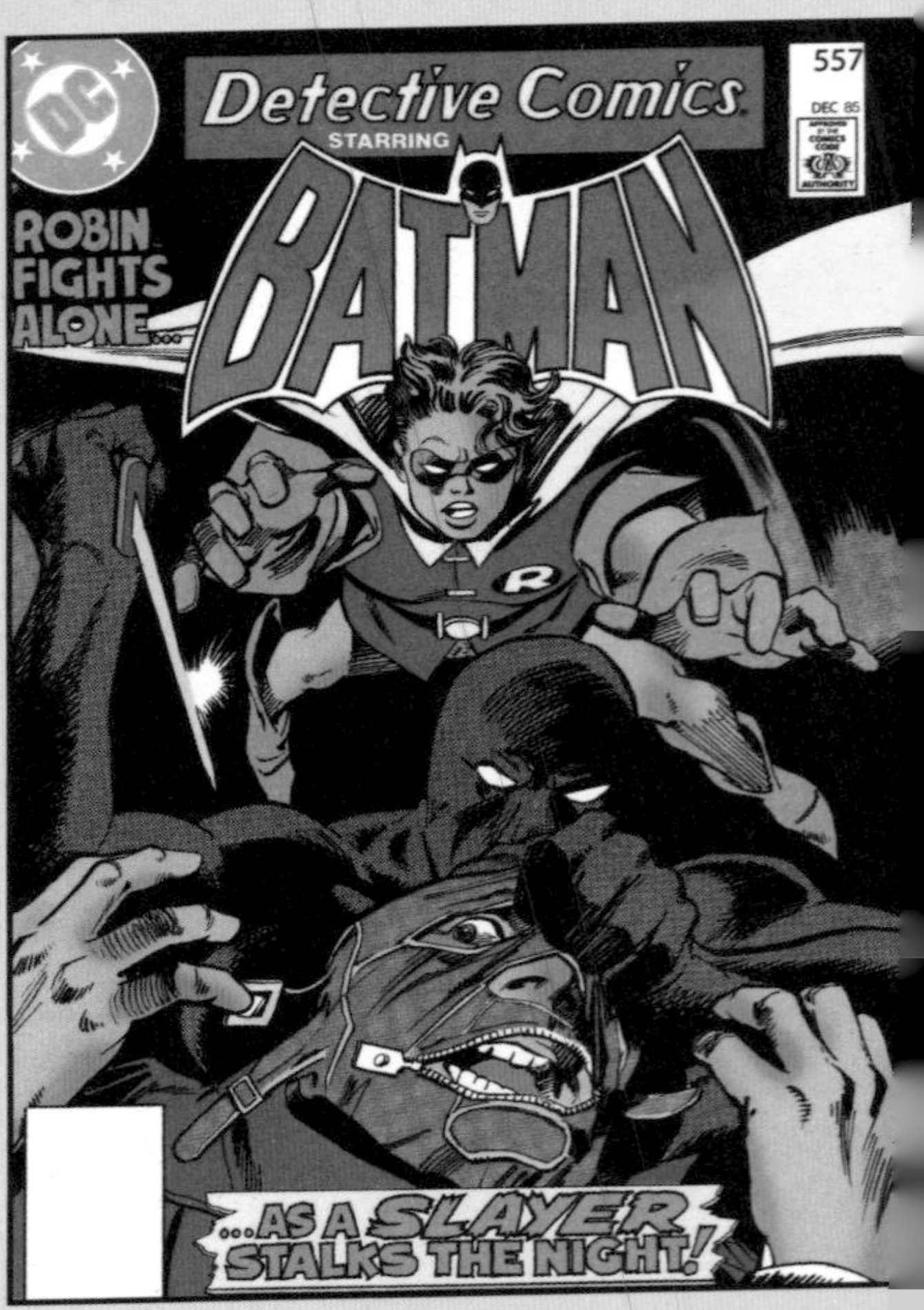
DC
Detective Comics
STARRING
BATMAN
557
DEC 85
ROBIN FIGHTS ALONE...
...AS A SLAYER STALKS THE NIGHT!

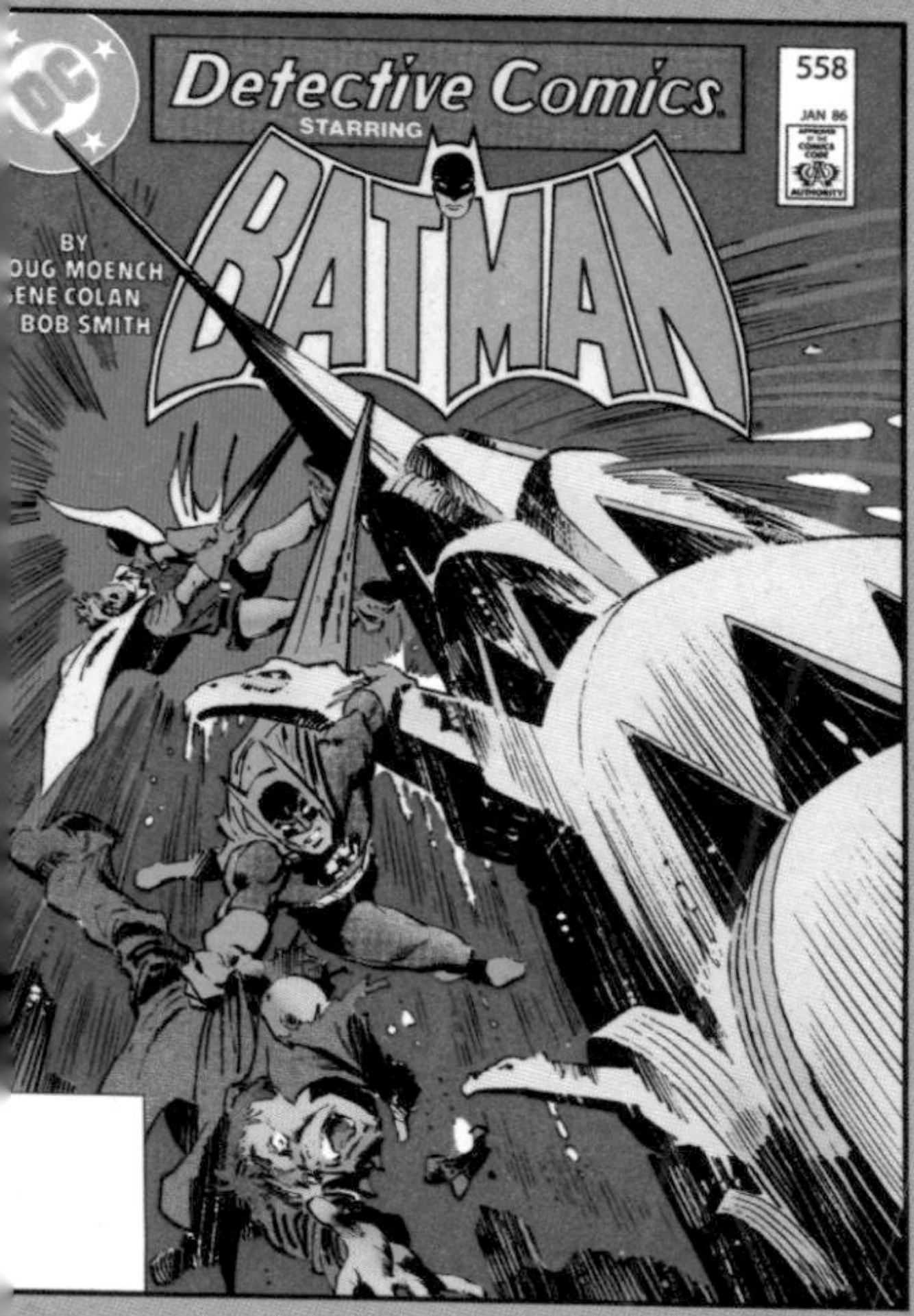
DC
Detective Comics
STARRING
BATMAN
558
JAN 86
BY
OUG MOENCH
ENE COLAN
BOB SMITH

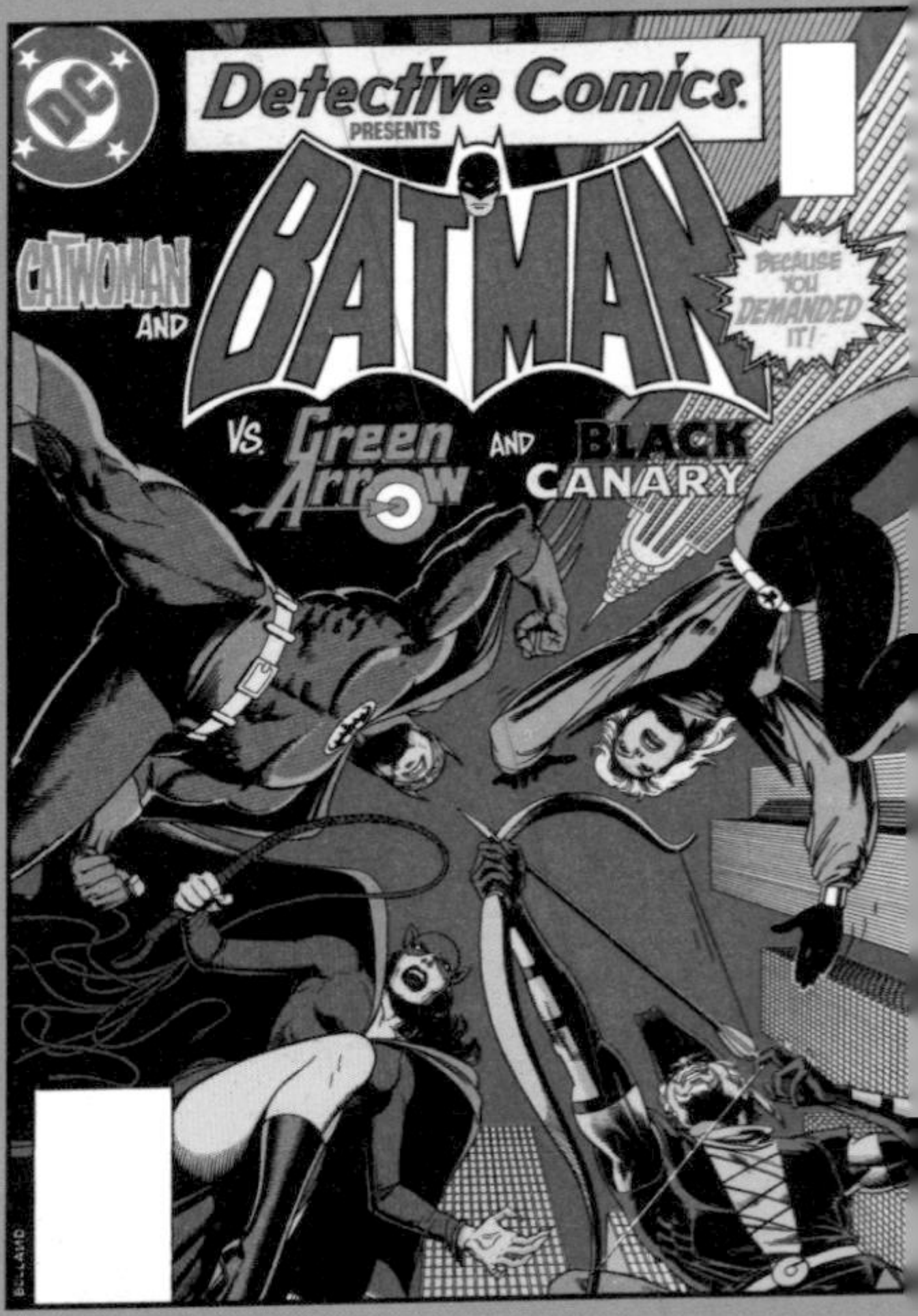
DC
Detective Comics.
PRESENTS
CATWOMAN AND
BATMAN
BECAUSE YOU DEMANDED IT!
VS. Green Arrow AND BLACK CANARY
BILL AND

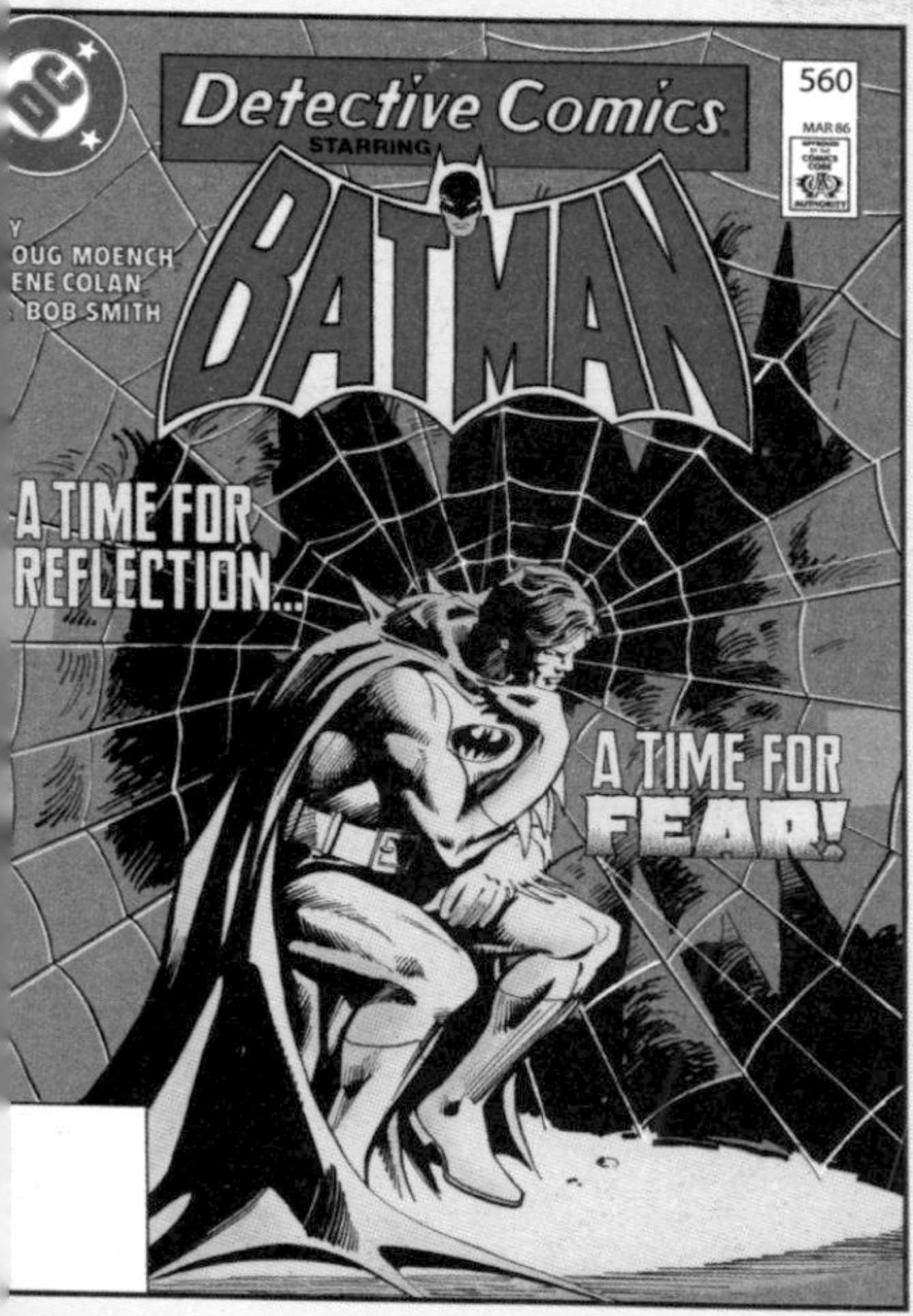
DC
Detective Comics
STARRING
BATMAN
560
MAR 86
Y
OUG MOENCH
ENE COLAN
BOB SMITH
A TIME FOR REFLECTION...
A TIME FOR FEAR!

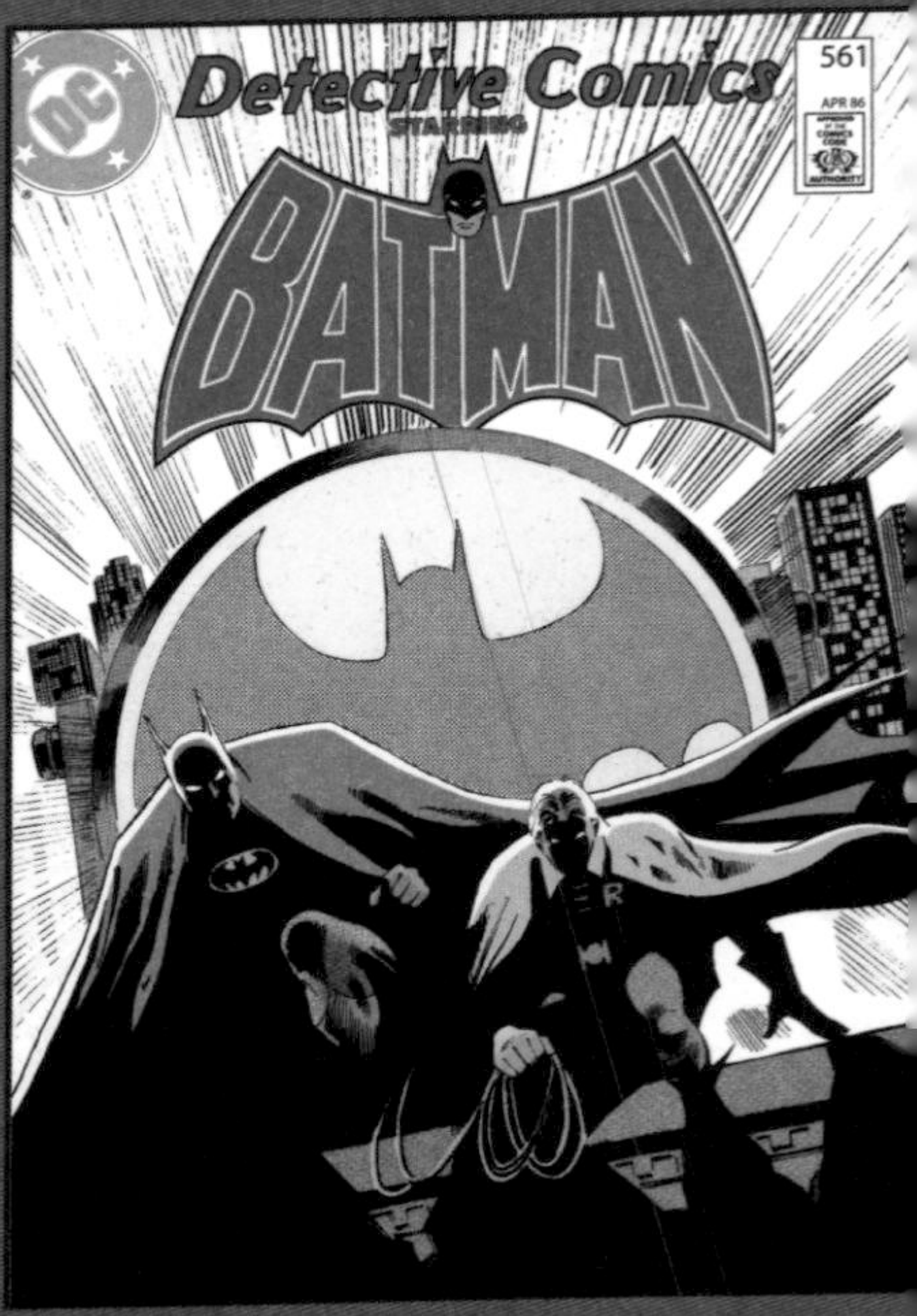
DC
Detective Comics
561
APR 86
STARRING
BATMAN

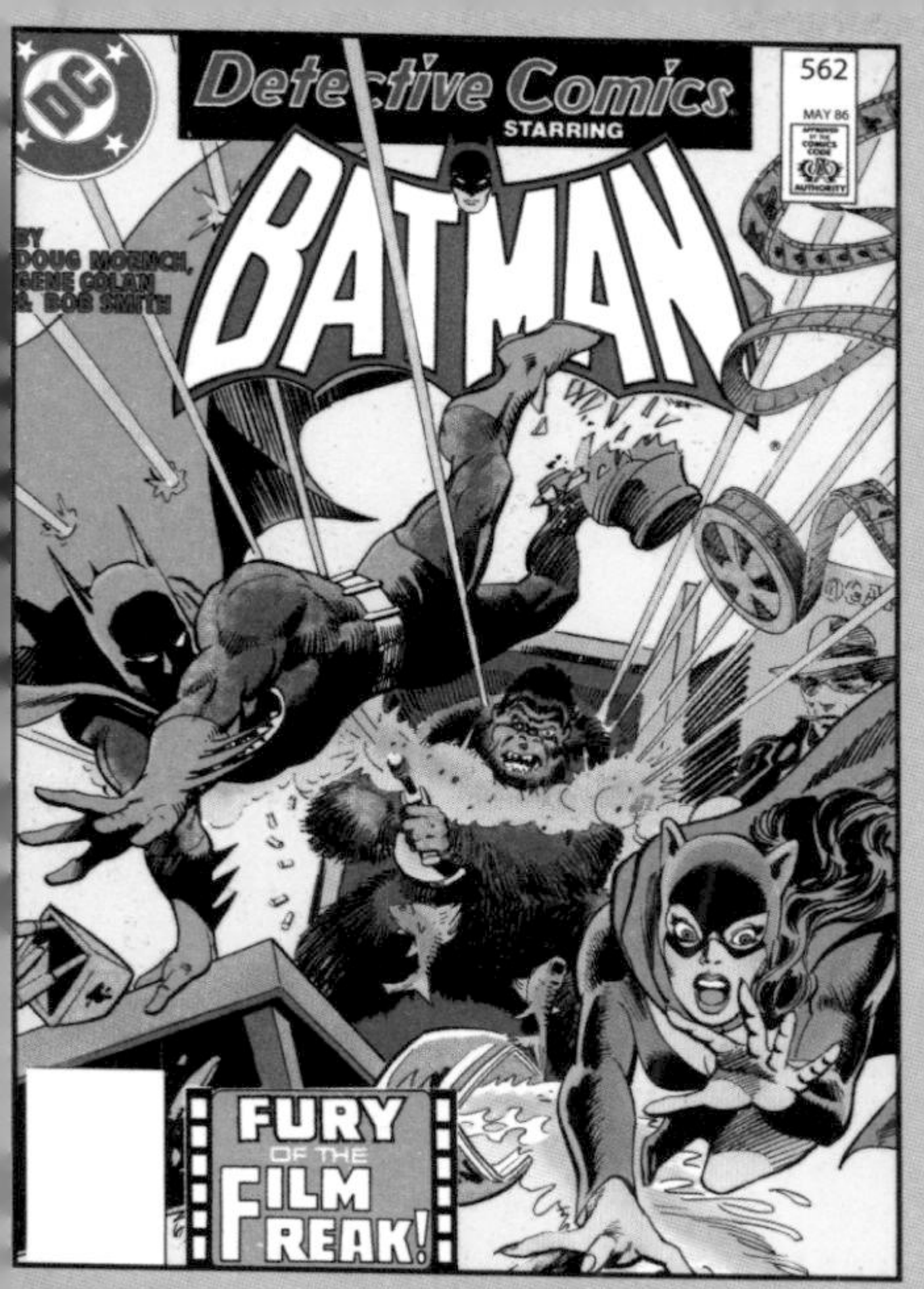
DC
Detective Comics
STARRING
BATMAN
562
MAY 86
BY
DOUG MOENCH,
GENE COLAN
& BOB SMITH
FURY
OF THE
FILM
FREAK!

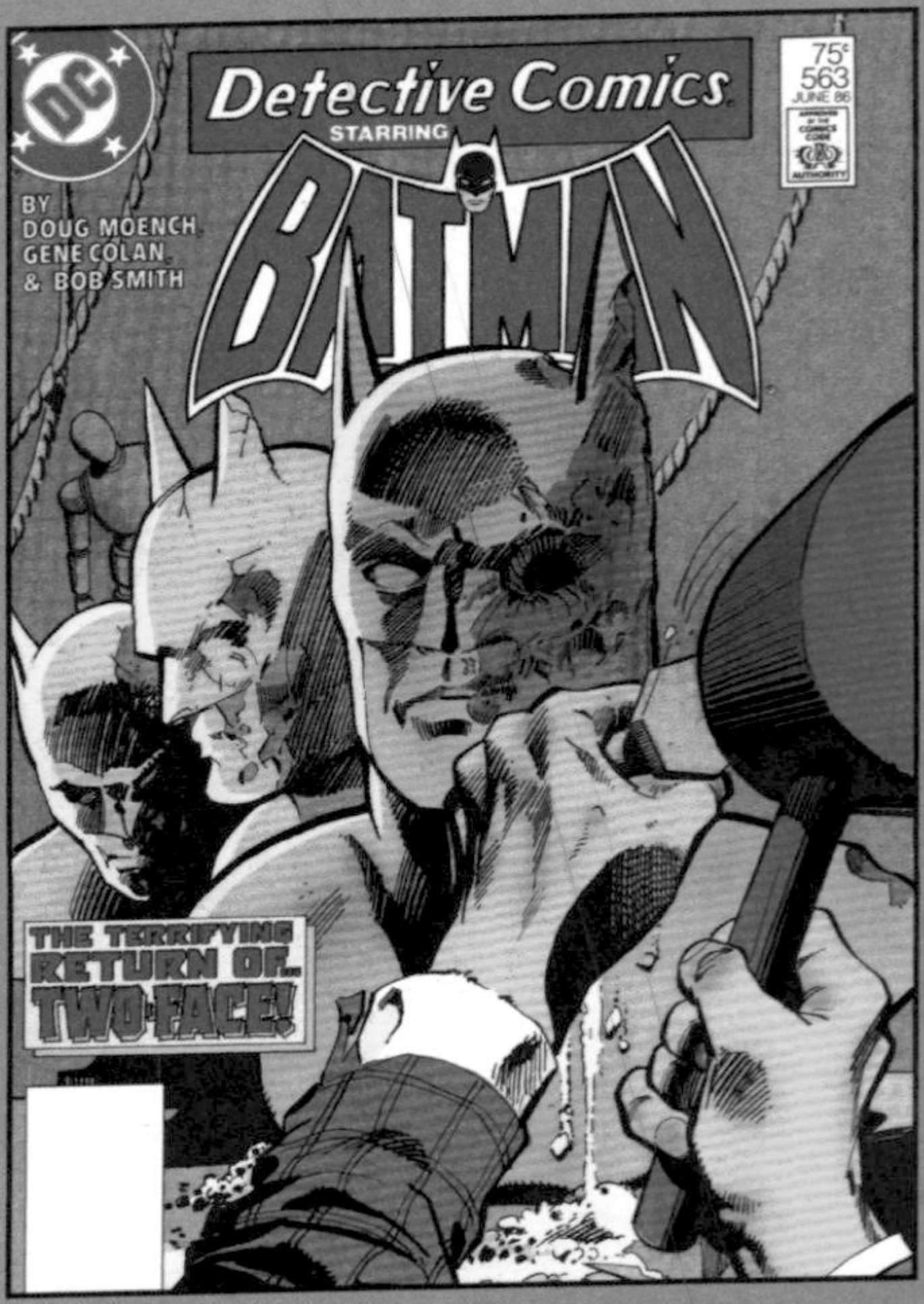
DC
Detective Comics
STARRING
BATMAN
75¢
563
JUNE 86
BY
DOUG MOENCH,
GENE COLAN,
& BOB SMITH
THE TERRIFYING
RETURN OF...
TWO-FACE!

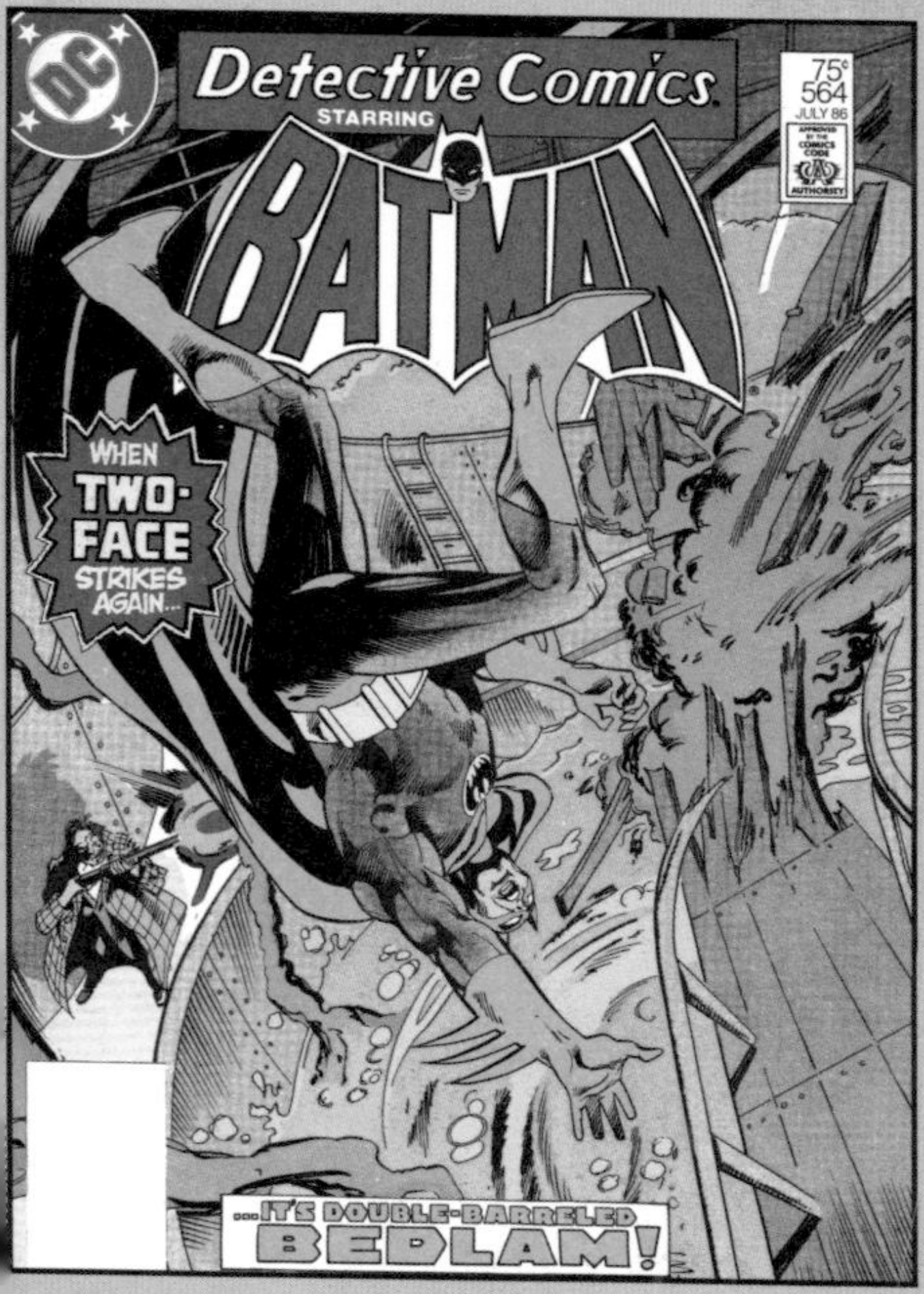
DC
Detective Comics
STARRING
BATMAN
75¢
564
JULY 86
APPROVED BY THE COMICS CODE AUTHORITY
WHEN TWO-FACE STRIKES AGAIN...
...IT'S DOUBLE-BARRELED BEDLAM!

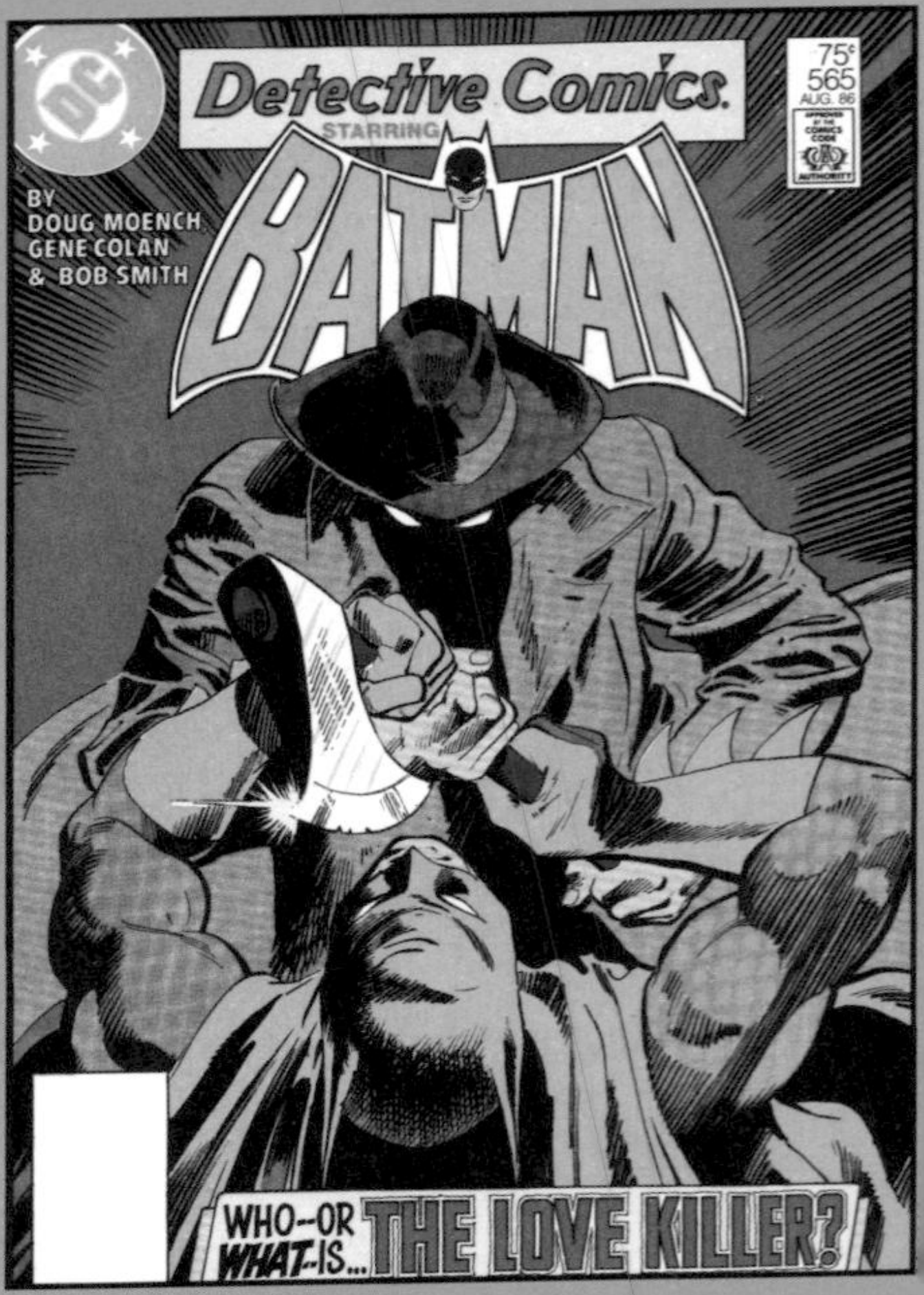
DC
Detective Comics.
STARRING
BATMAN
75¢
565
AUG. 86
BY
DOUG MOENCH
GENE COLAN
& BOB SMITH
WHO--OR WHAT-IS... THE LOVE KILLER?

DC
Detective Comics
STARRING
566
SEPT. 86
BATMAN
BY
DOUG MOENCH,
GENE COLAN
& BOB SMITH
PROWL THE
DARK KNIGHT'S
ROGUES
GALLERY
...IF YOU
DARE!
GIORDANO

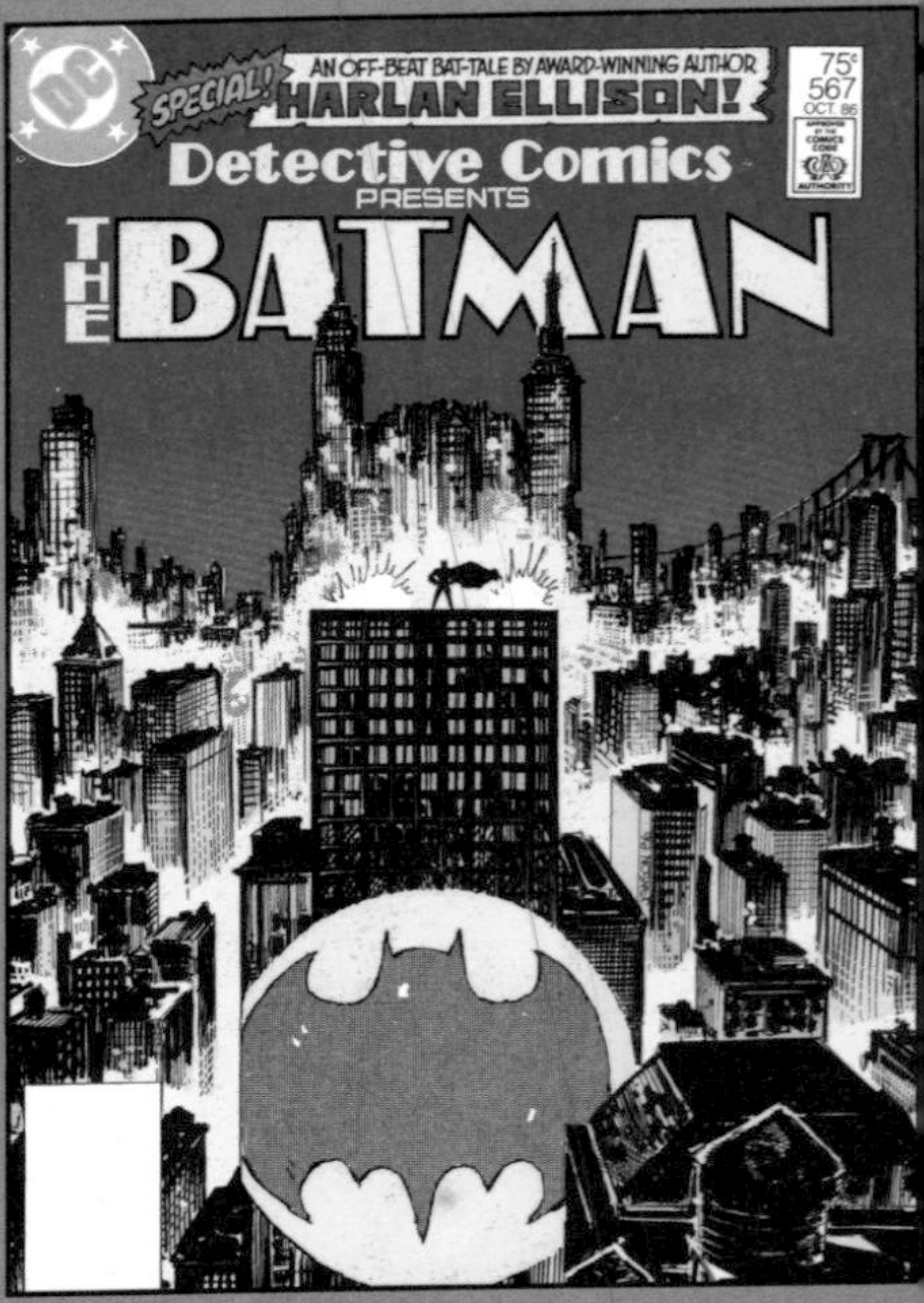
SPECIAL!
AN OFF-BEAT BAT-TALE BY AWARD-WINNING AUTHOR
HARLAN ELLISON!
75¢
567
OCT. 86
Detective Comics
PRESENTS
THE BATMAN

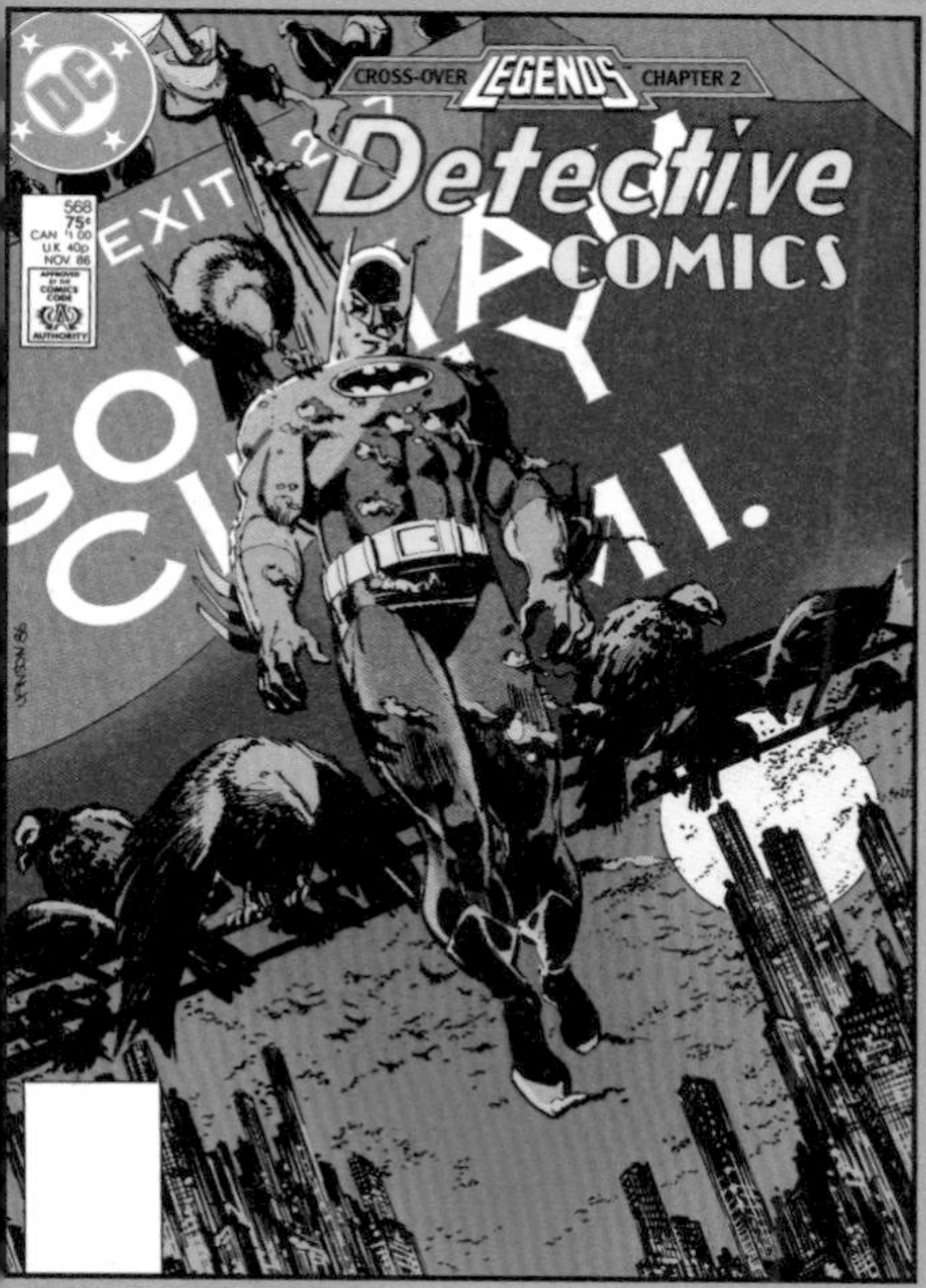
CROSS-OVER LEGENDS CHAPTER 2
Detective COMICS
568
75¢
CAN $1.00
U.K. 40p
NOV 86
APPROVED BY THE COMICS CODE AUTHORITY
EXIT
GOTHAM CITY
JANSON 86

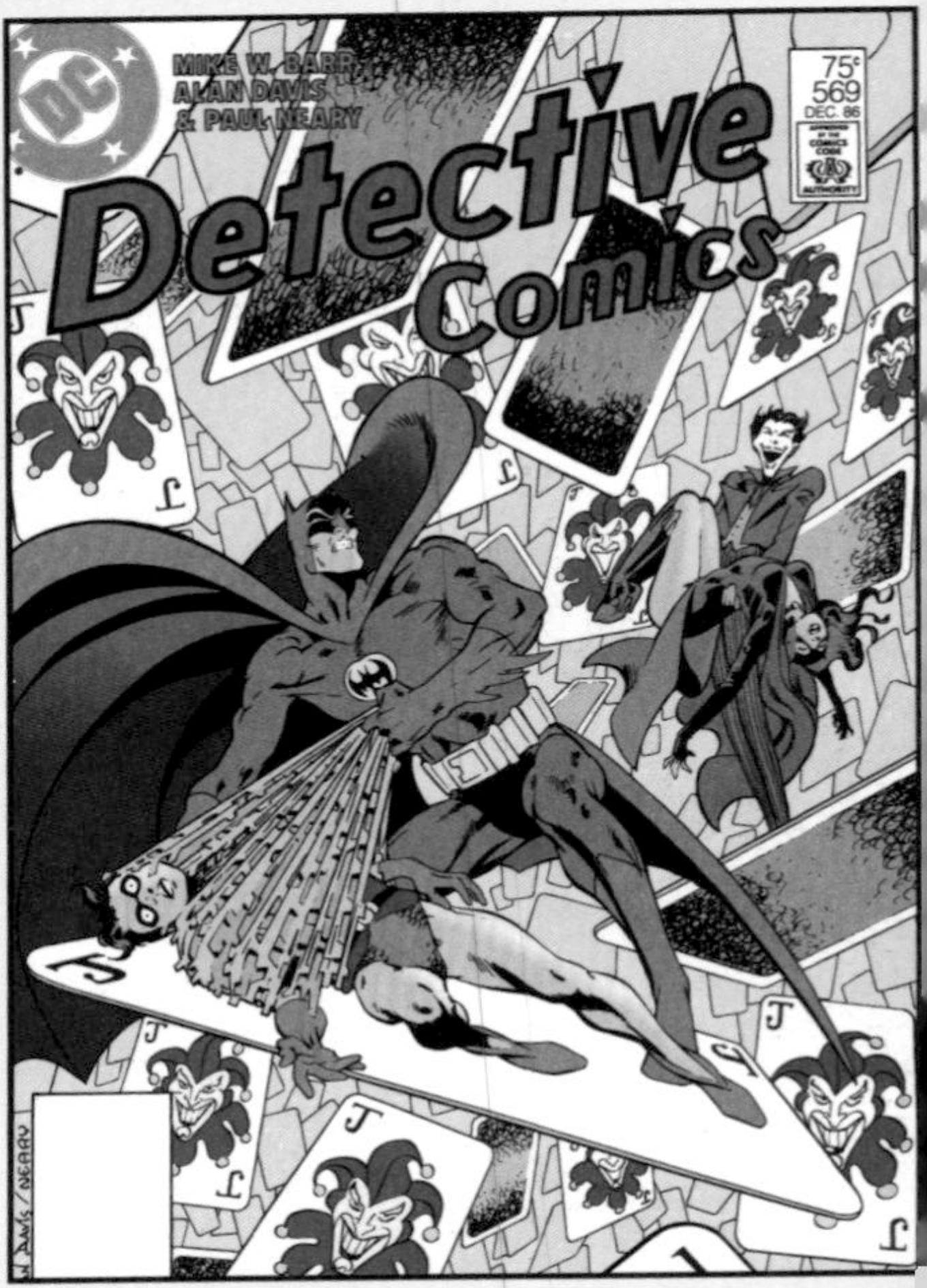
DC
MIKE W. BARR
ALAN DAVIS
& PAUL NEARY
Detective Comics
75¢
569
DEC. 86
W. DAVIS / NEARY

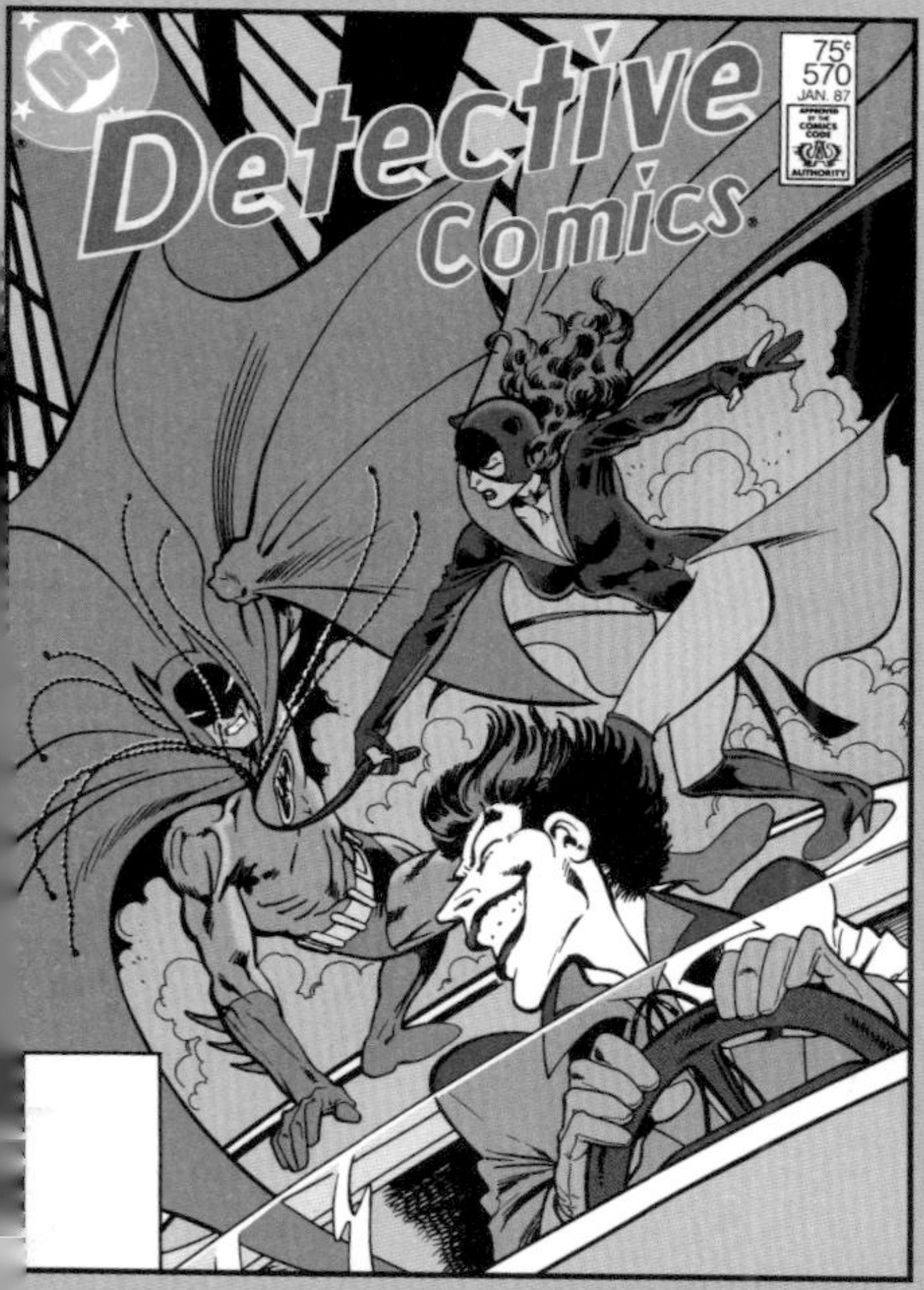
DC
Detective Comics
75¢
570
JAN. 87
APPROVED BY THE COMICS CODE AUTHORITY

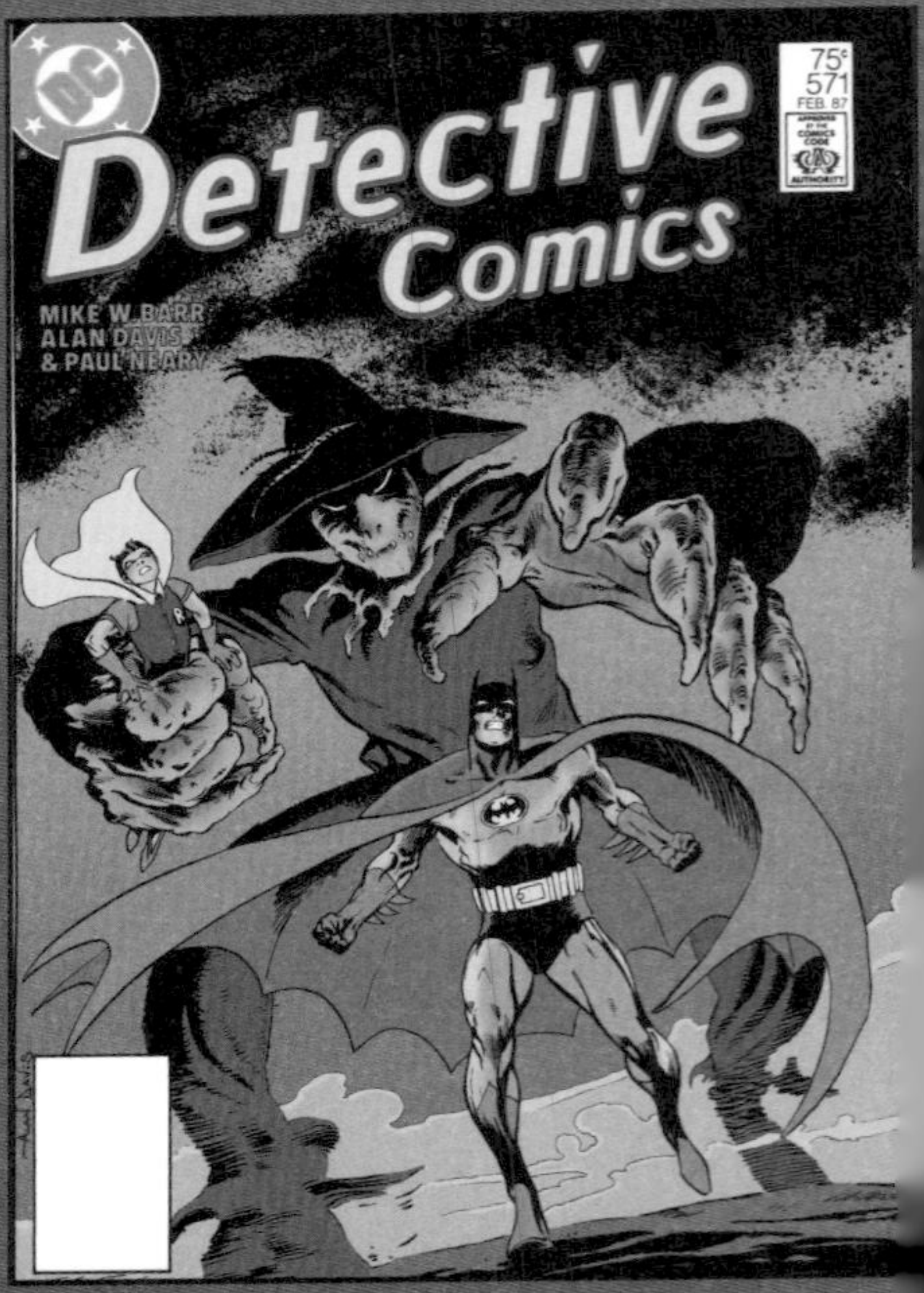
DC
Detective Comics
75¢
571
FEB. 87
APPROVED BY THE COMICS CODE AUTHORITY
MIKE W. BARR
ALAN DAVIS
& PAUL NEARY

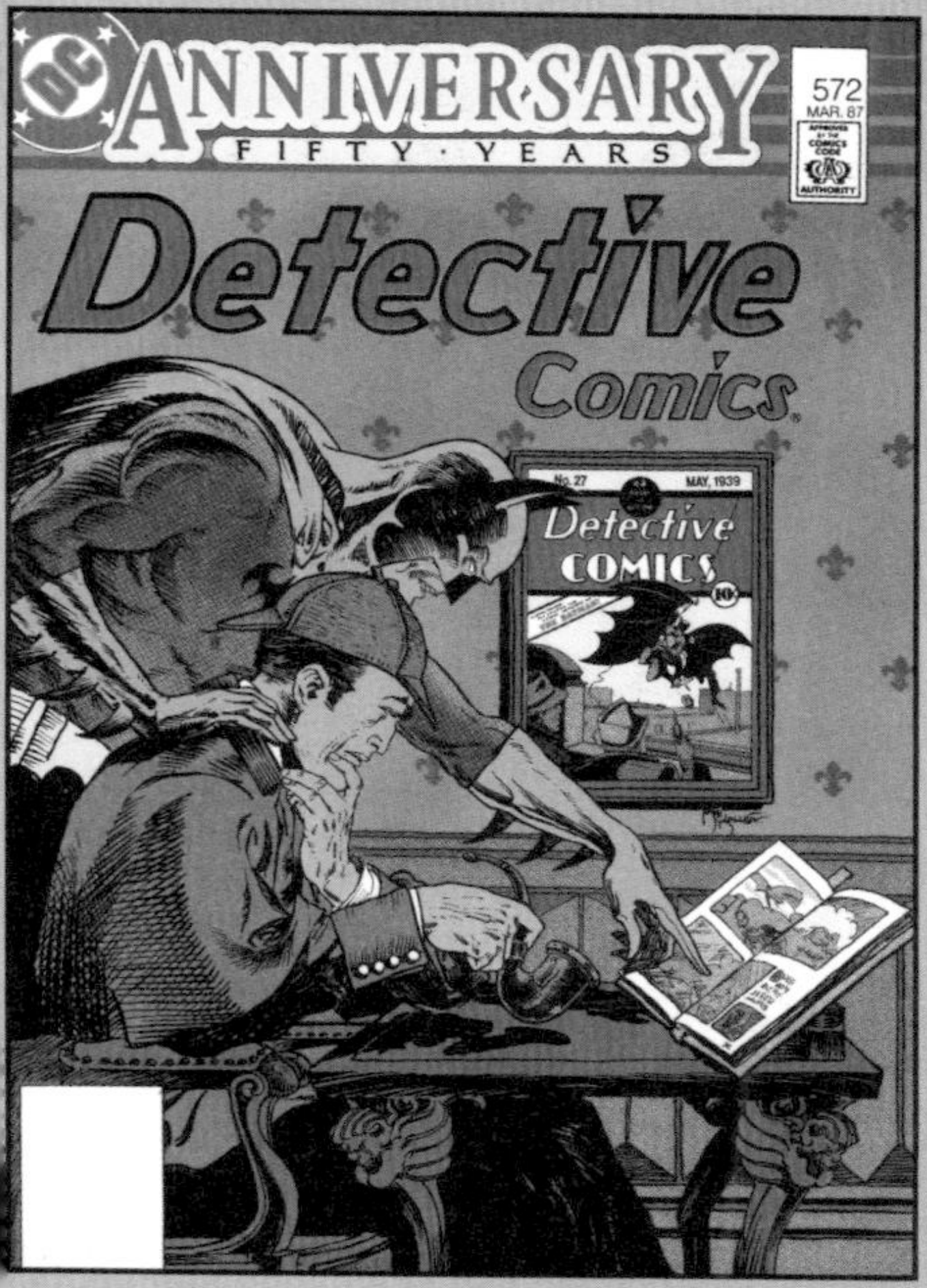
DC
ANNIVERSARY
FIFTY · YEARS
572
MAR. 87
Detective
Comics
No. 27
MAY, 1939
Detective
COMICS

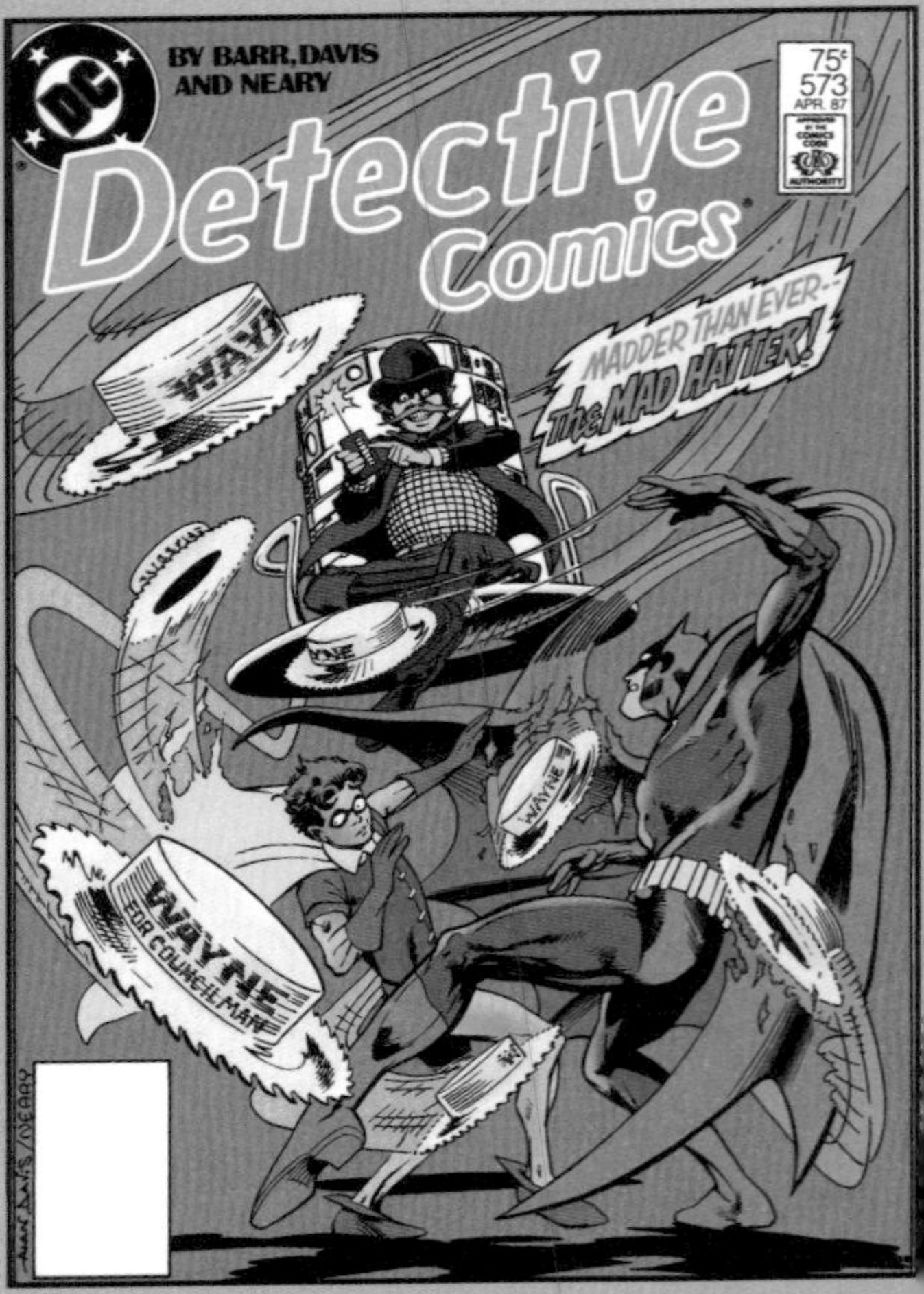
BY BARR, DAVIS AND NEARY
Detective Comics
75¢
573
APR. 87
MADDER THAN EVER--
The MAD HATTER!
WAYNE
WAYNE
WAYNE
WAYNE
FOR COUNCILMAN

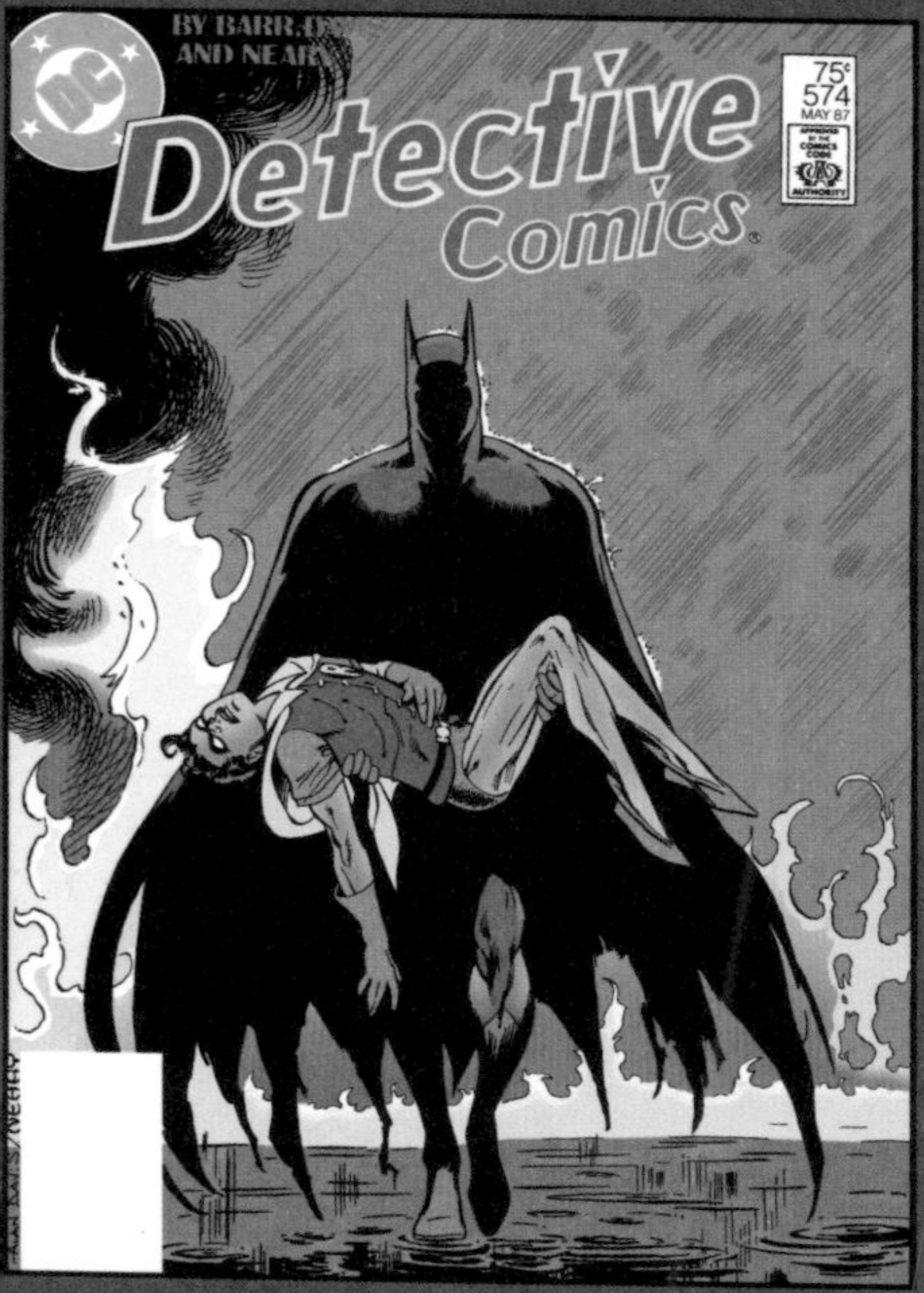
BY BARR, D
AND NEAR
Detective
Comics
75¢
574
MAY 87
APPROVED BY THE COMICS CODE AUTHORITY

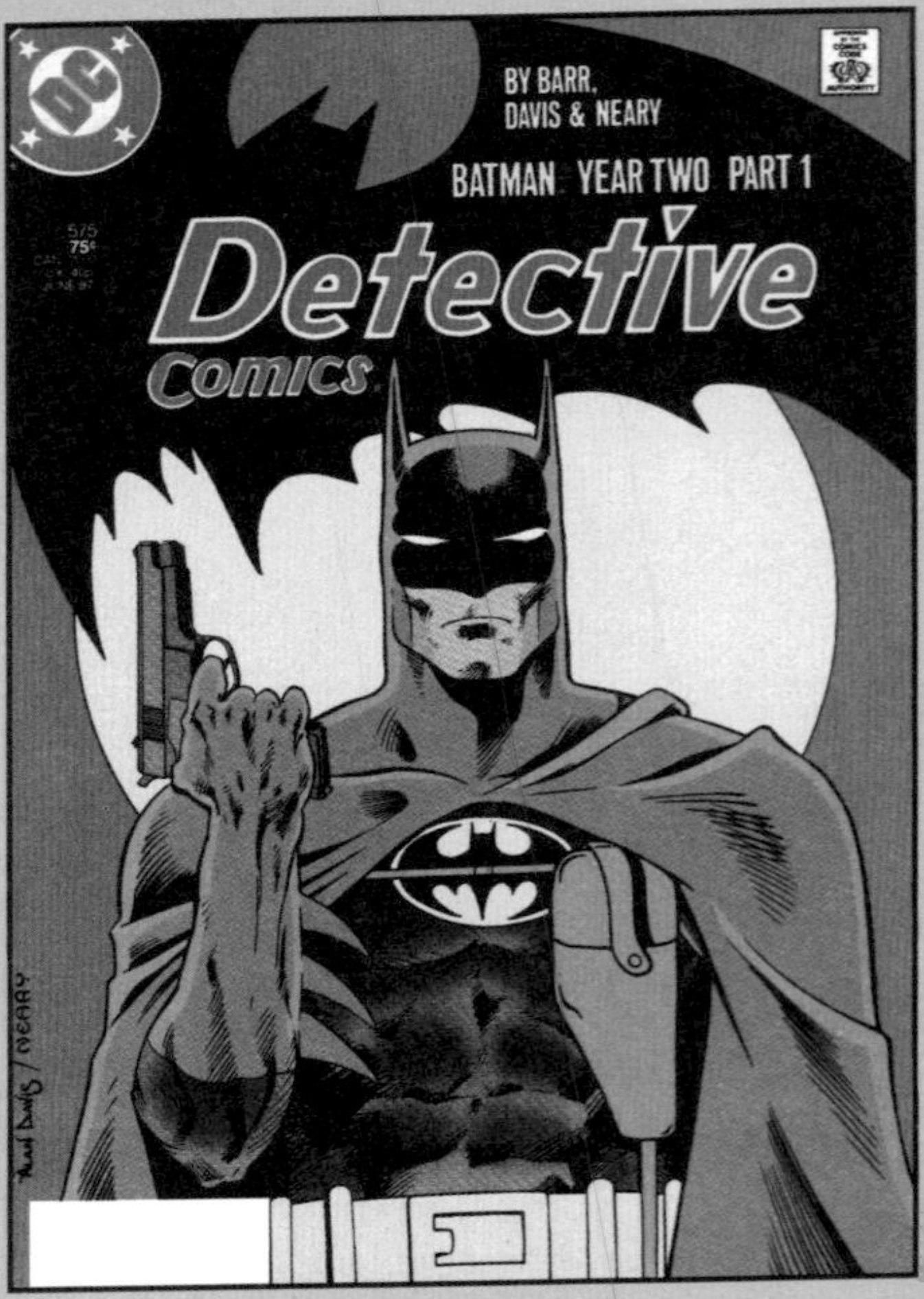
BY BARR,
DAVIS & NEARY
BATMAN: YEAR TWO PART 1
575
75¢
Detective
Comics
Alan Davis / NEARY

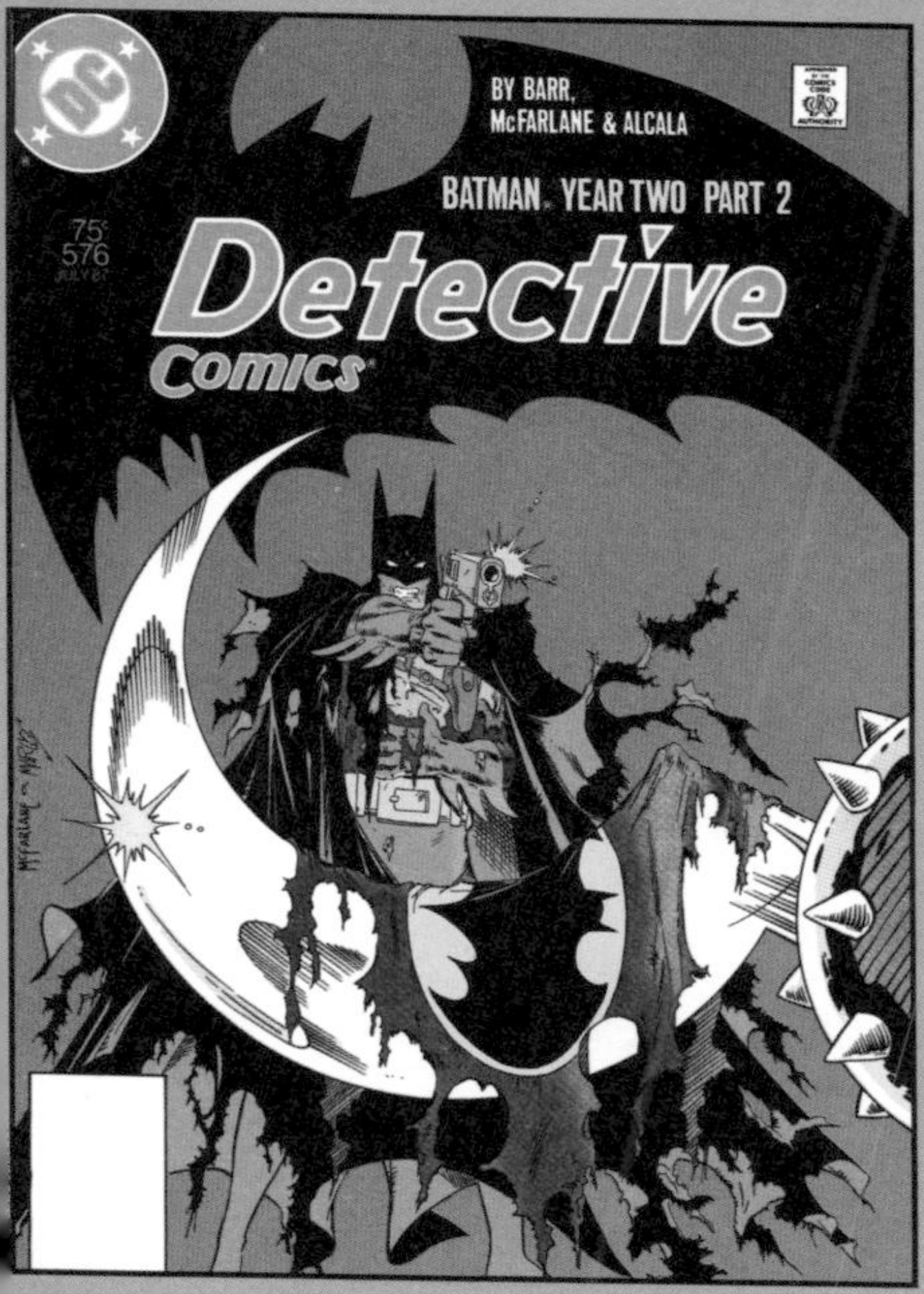
DC
BY BARR,
McFARLANE & ALCALA
BATMAN: YEAR TWO PART 2
75¢
576
JULY
Detective
Comics

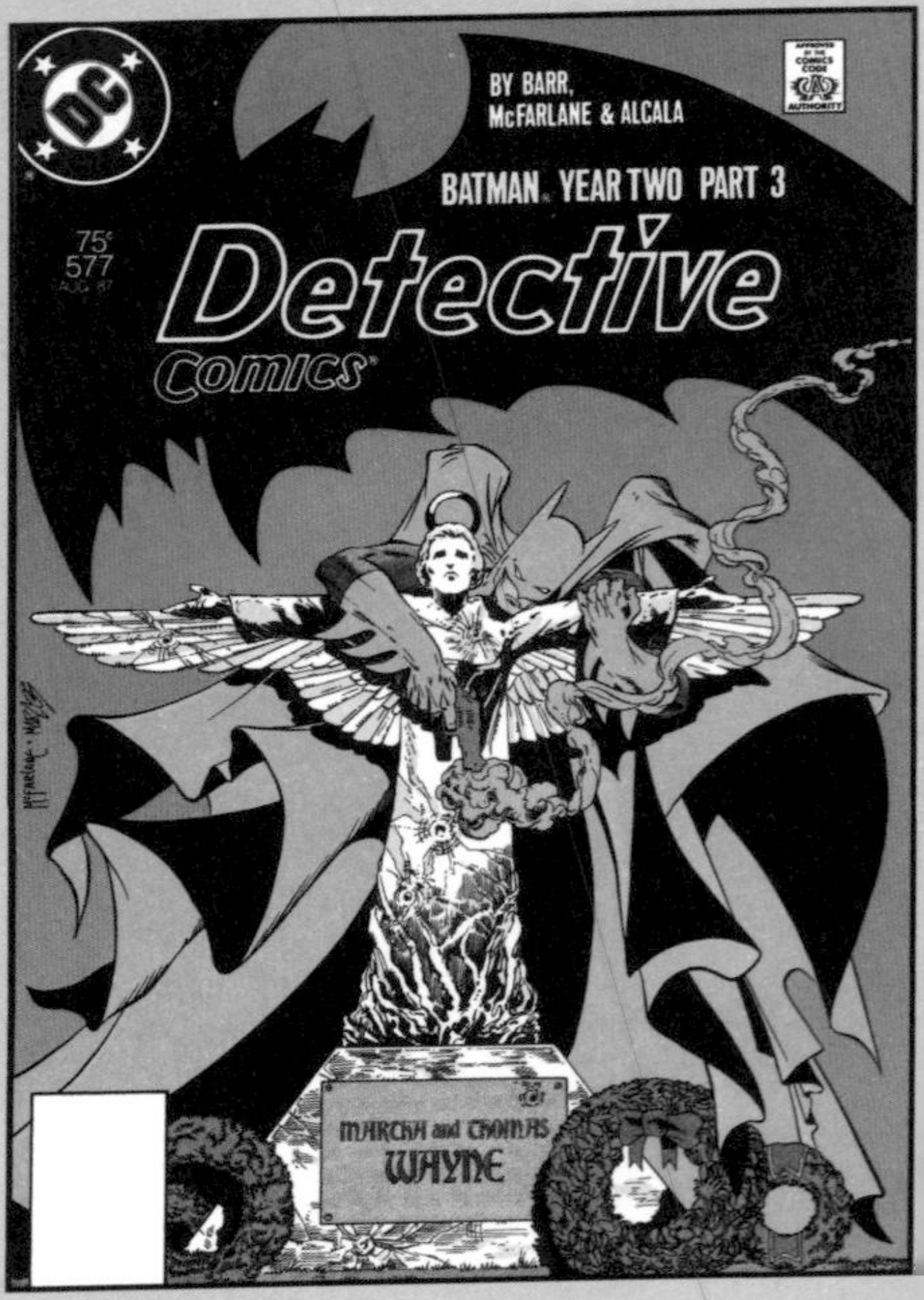
DC
BY BARR,
McFARLANE & ALCALA
BATMAN YEAR TWO PART 3
75¢
577
Detective
Comics
MARTHA and THOMAS
WAYNE

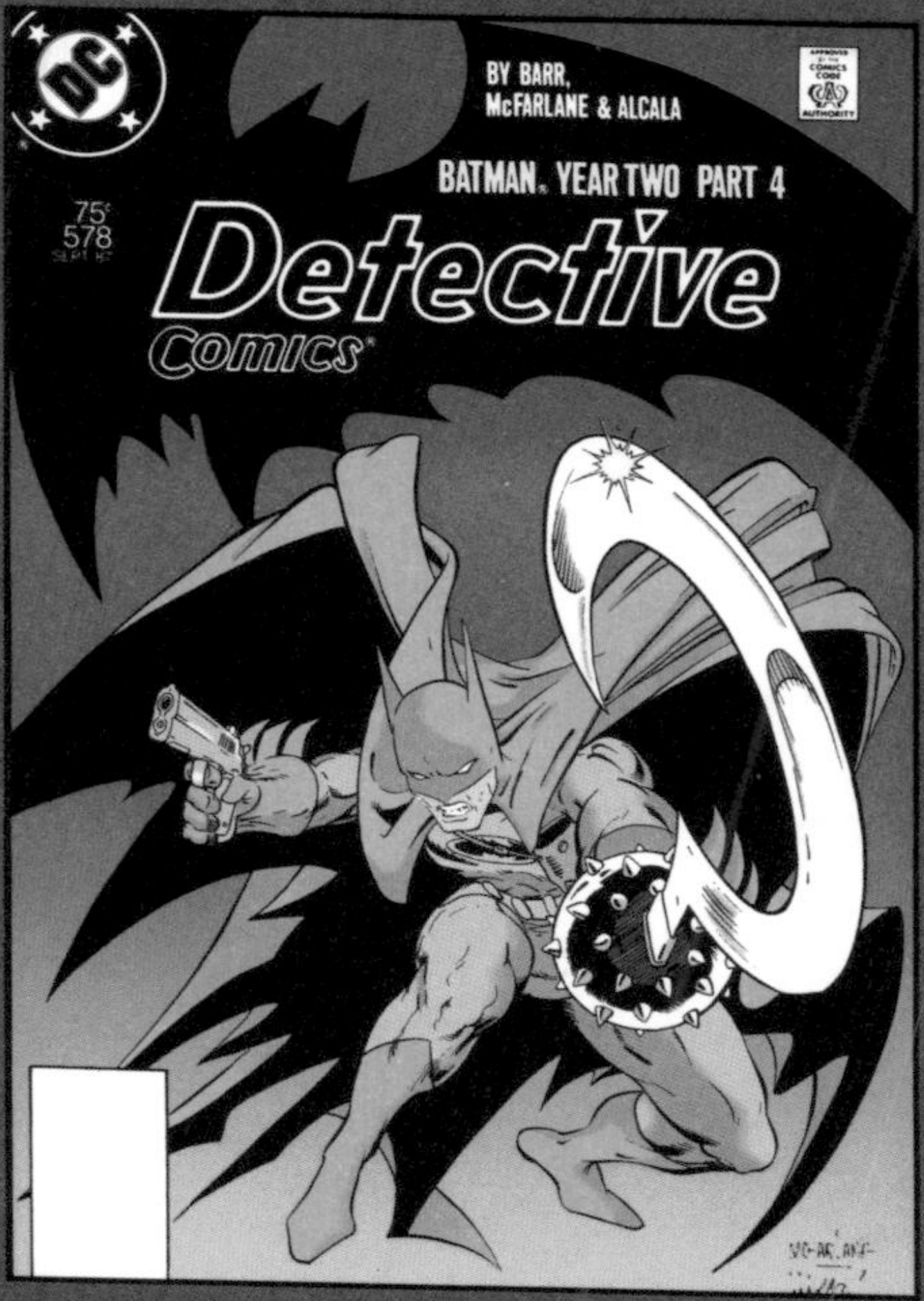
BY BARR,
McFARLANE & ALCALA
BATMAN YEAR TWO PART 4
75¢
578
Detective
Comics

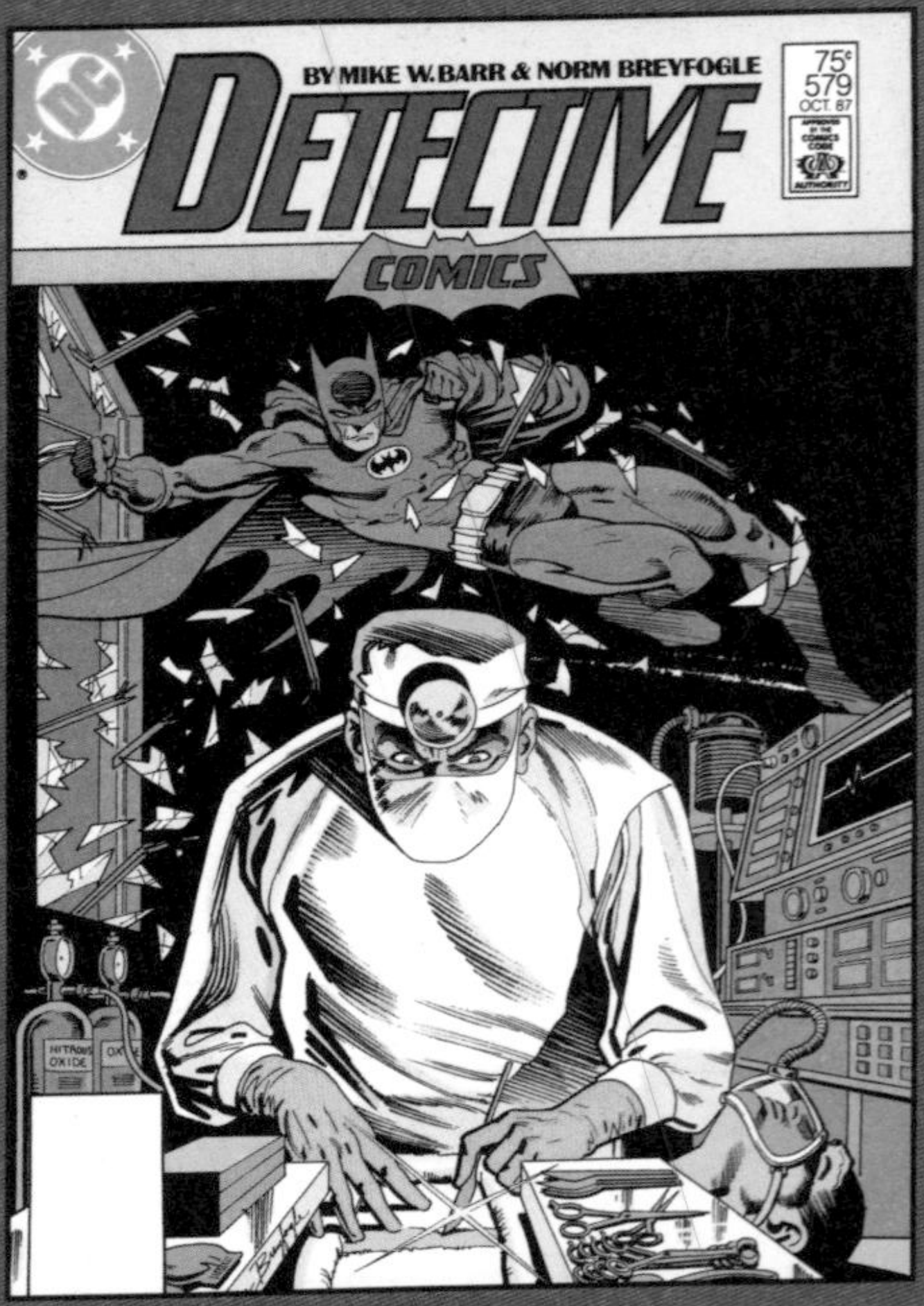
BY MIKE W. BARR & NORM BREYFOGLE
DETECTIVE
COMICS
75¢
579
OCT. 87
NITROUS OXIDE

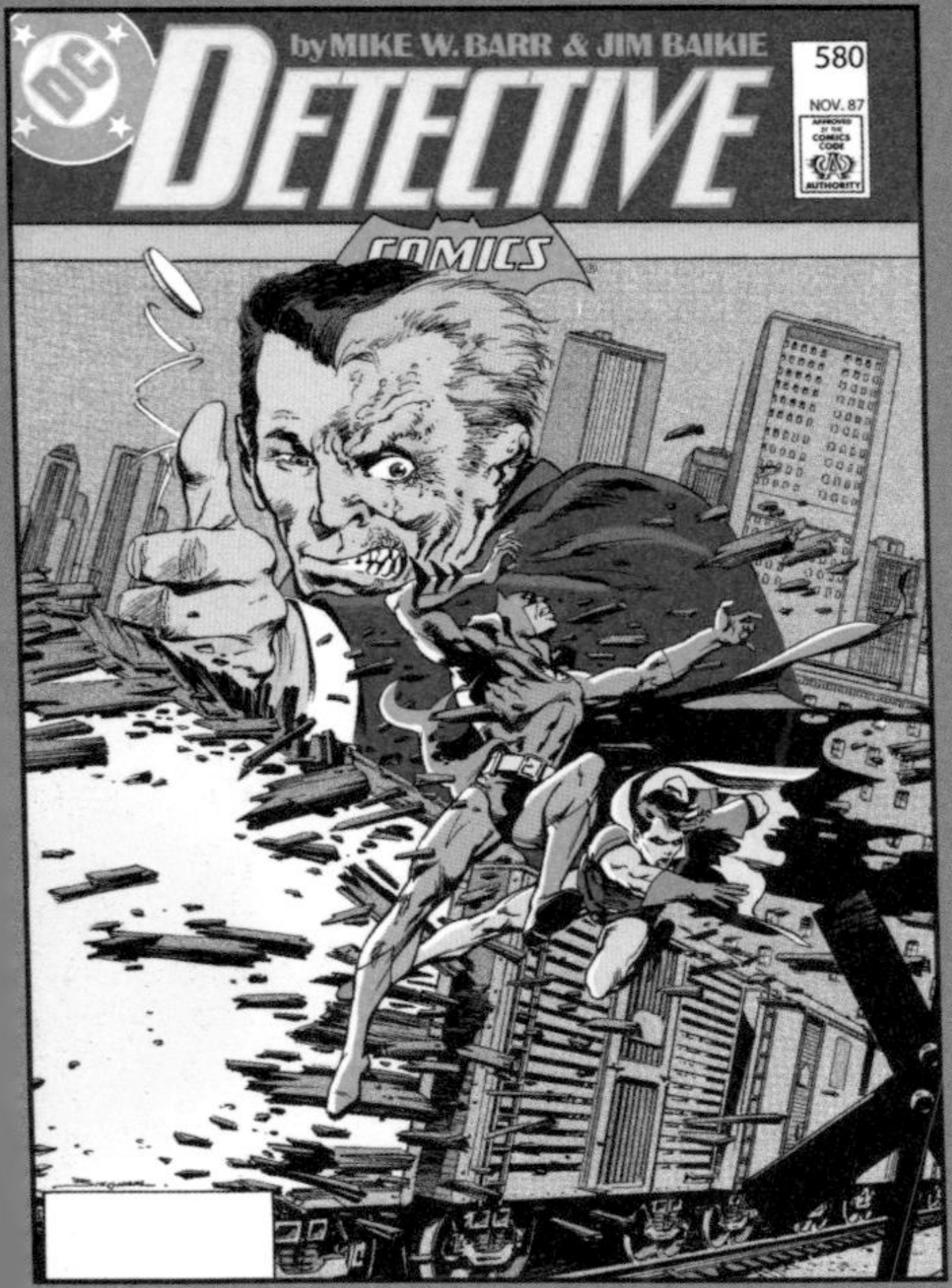
by MIKE W. BARR & JIM BAIKIE
DETECTIVE
580
NOV. 87
APPROVED BY THE COMICS CODE AUTHORITY
COMICS

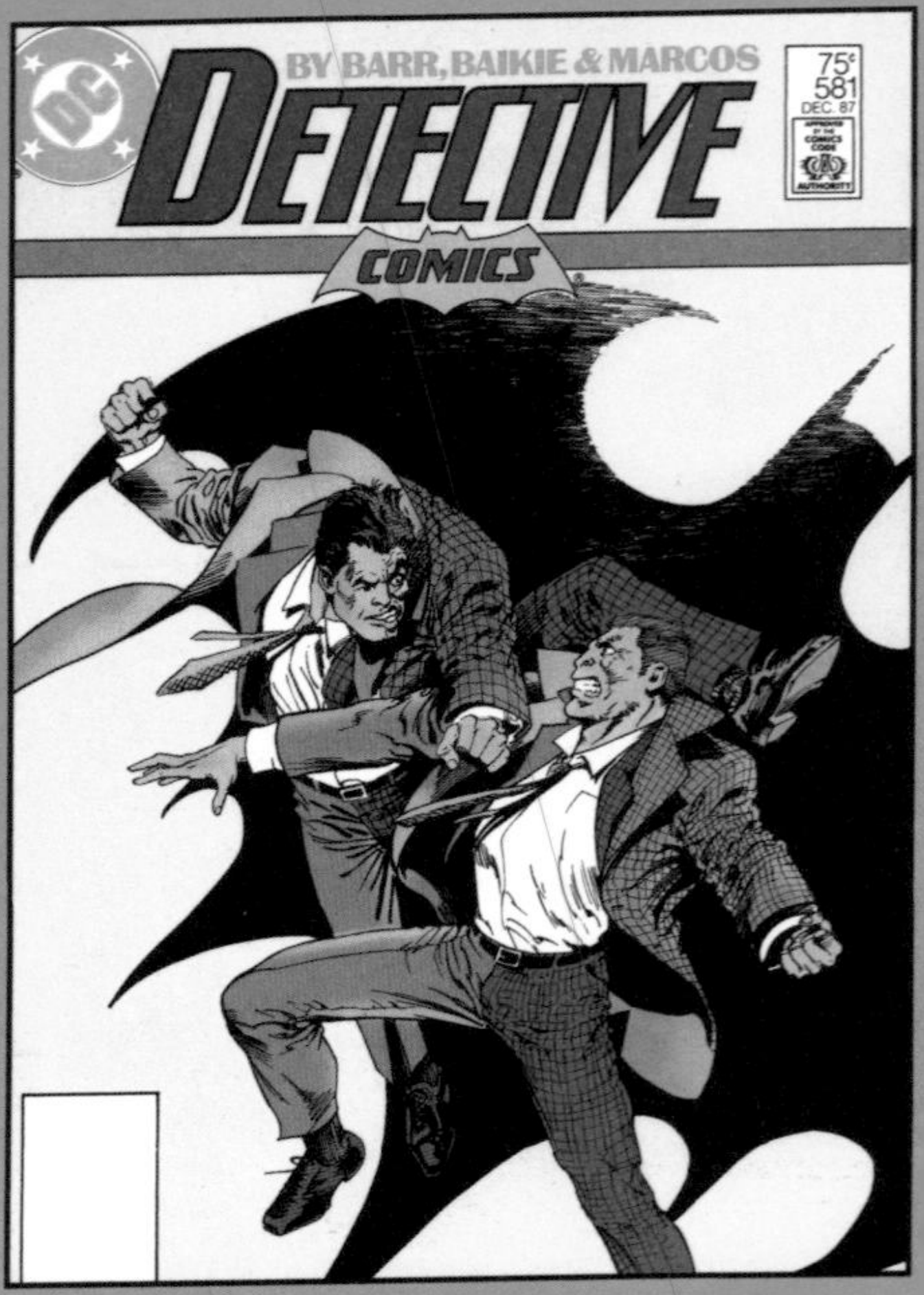
BY BARR, BAIKIE & MARCOS
DETECTIVE
COMICS
75¢
581
DEC. 87

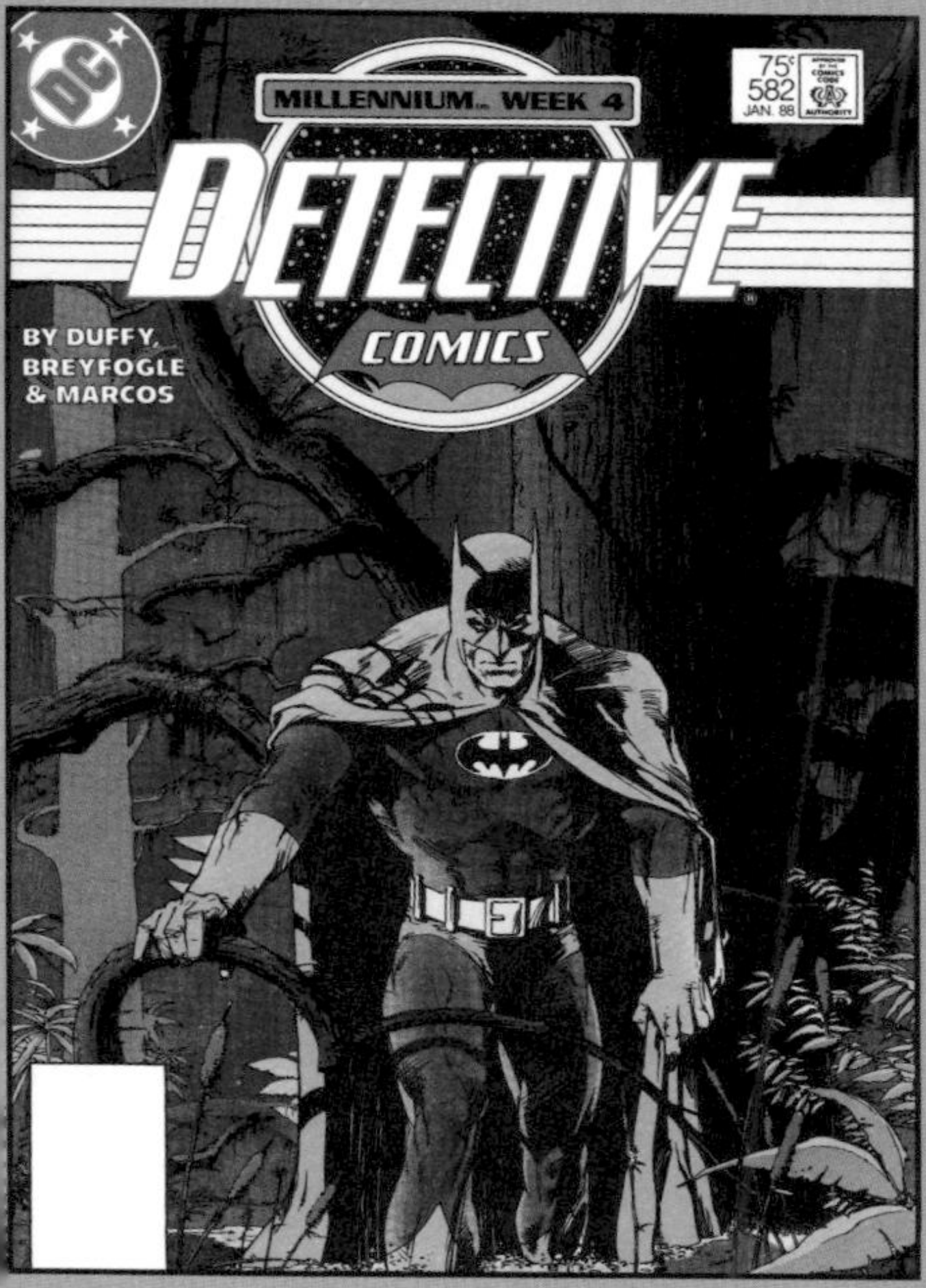
DC
MILLENNIUM... WEEK 4
75¢
582
JAN. 88
DETECTIVE
COMICS
BY DUFFY,
BREYFOGLE
& MARCOS

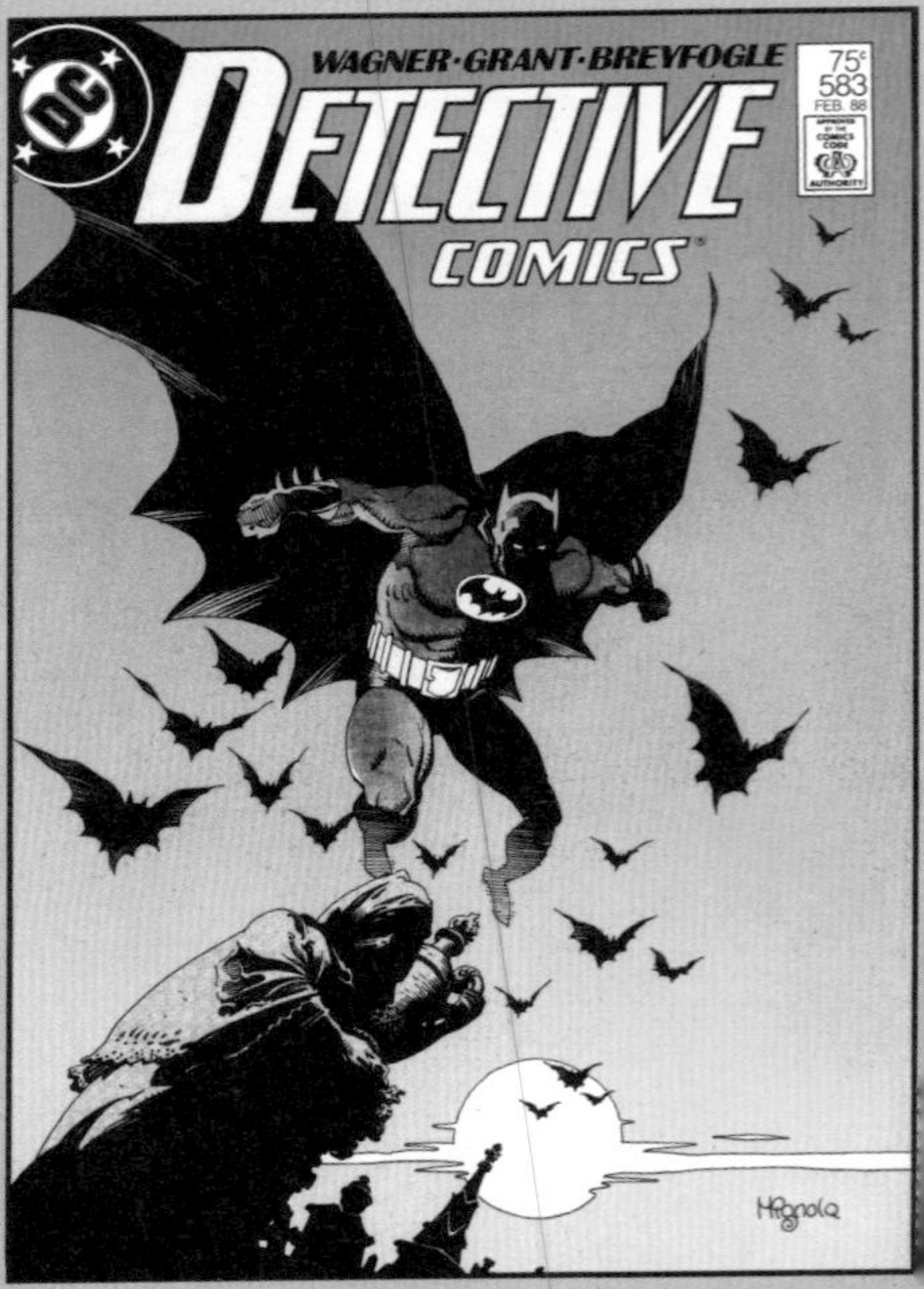
WAGNER · GRANT · BREYFOGLE
DETECTIVE
COMICS
75¢
583
FEB. 88
APPROVED BY THE COMICS CODE AUTHORITY
HRonda

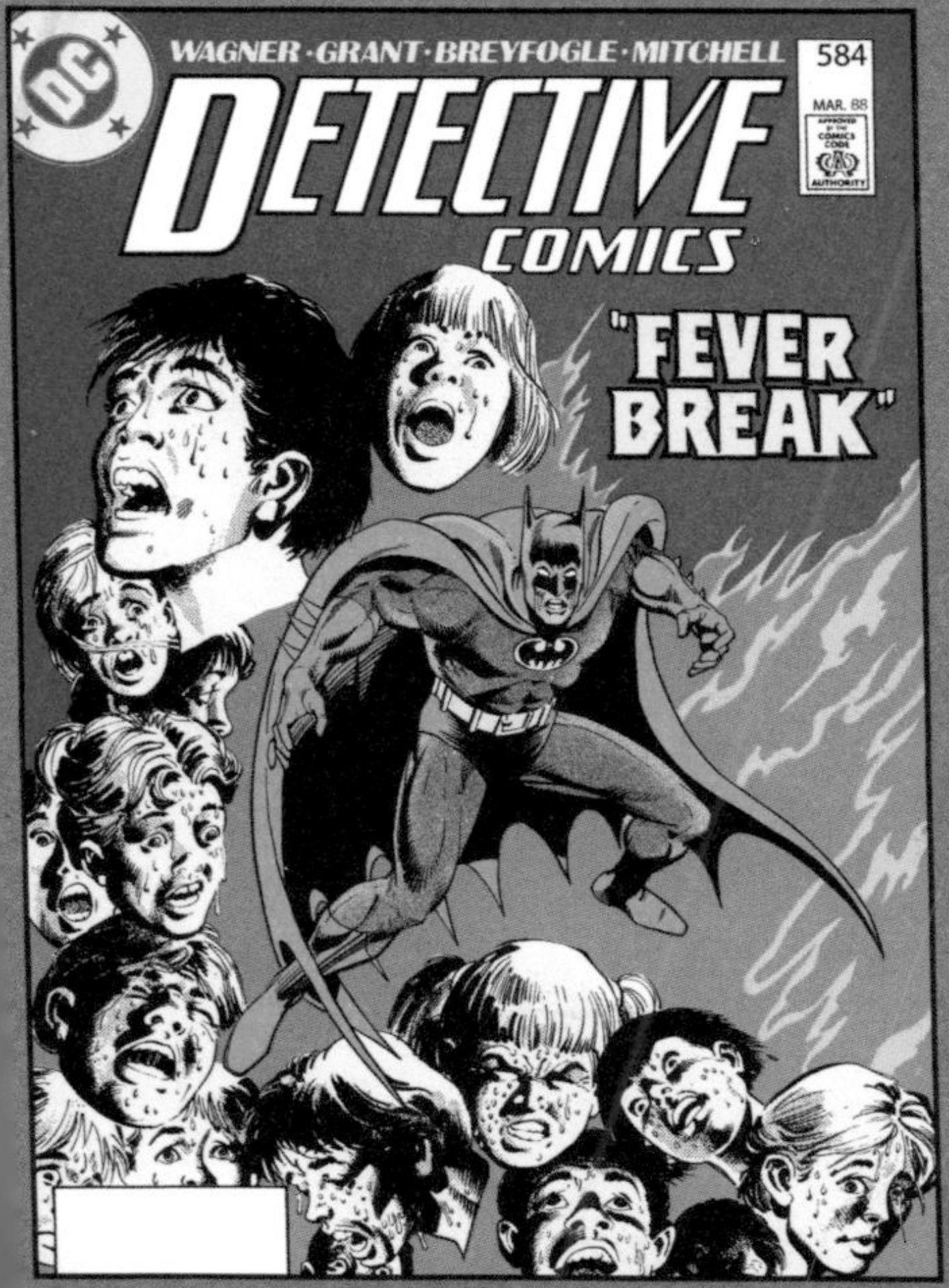
WAGNER · GRANT · BREYFOGLE · MITCHELL
584
MAR. 88
DETECTIVE
COMICS
"FEVER BREAK"

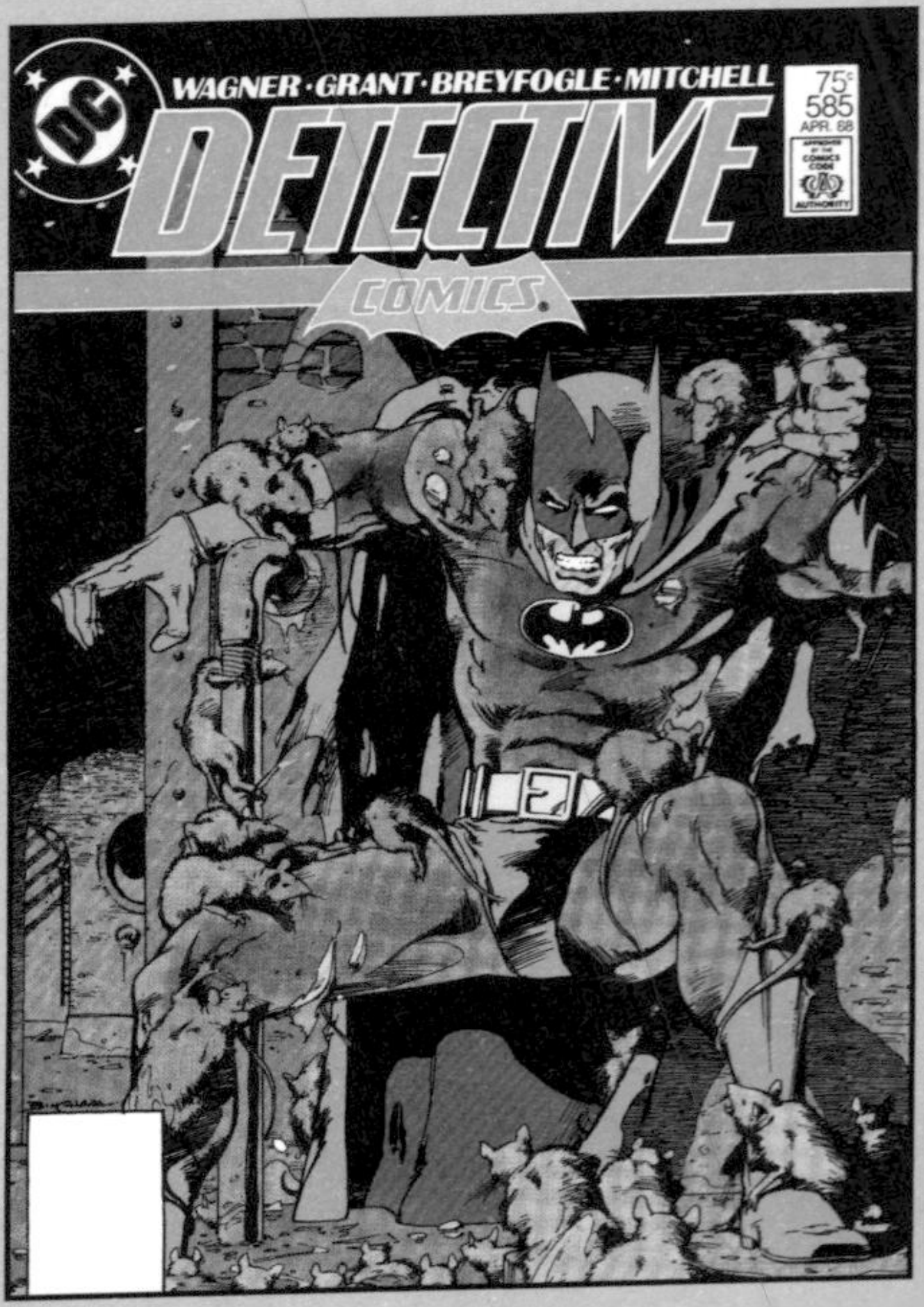
WAGNER · GRANT · BREYFOGLE · MITCHELL
DETECTIVE
COMICS
75¢
585
APR. 88
APPROVED BY THE COMICS CODE AUTHORITY

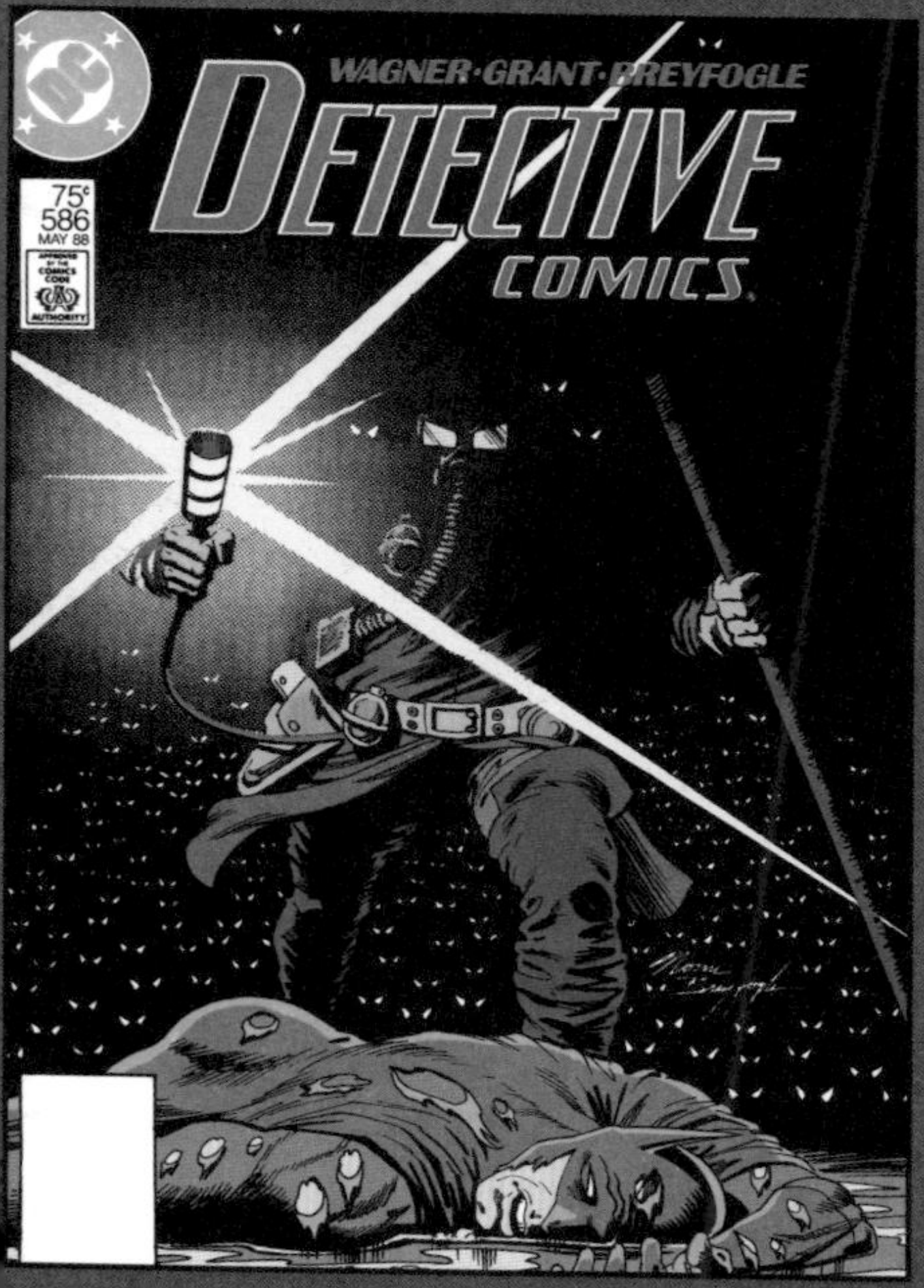
WAGNER·GRANT·BREYFOGLE
DETECTIVE
COMICS
75¢
586
MAY 88
APPROVED BY THE COMICS CODE AUTHORITY

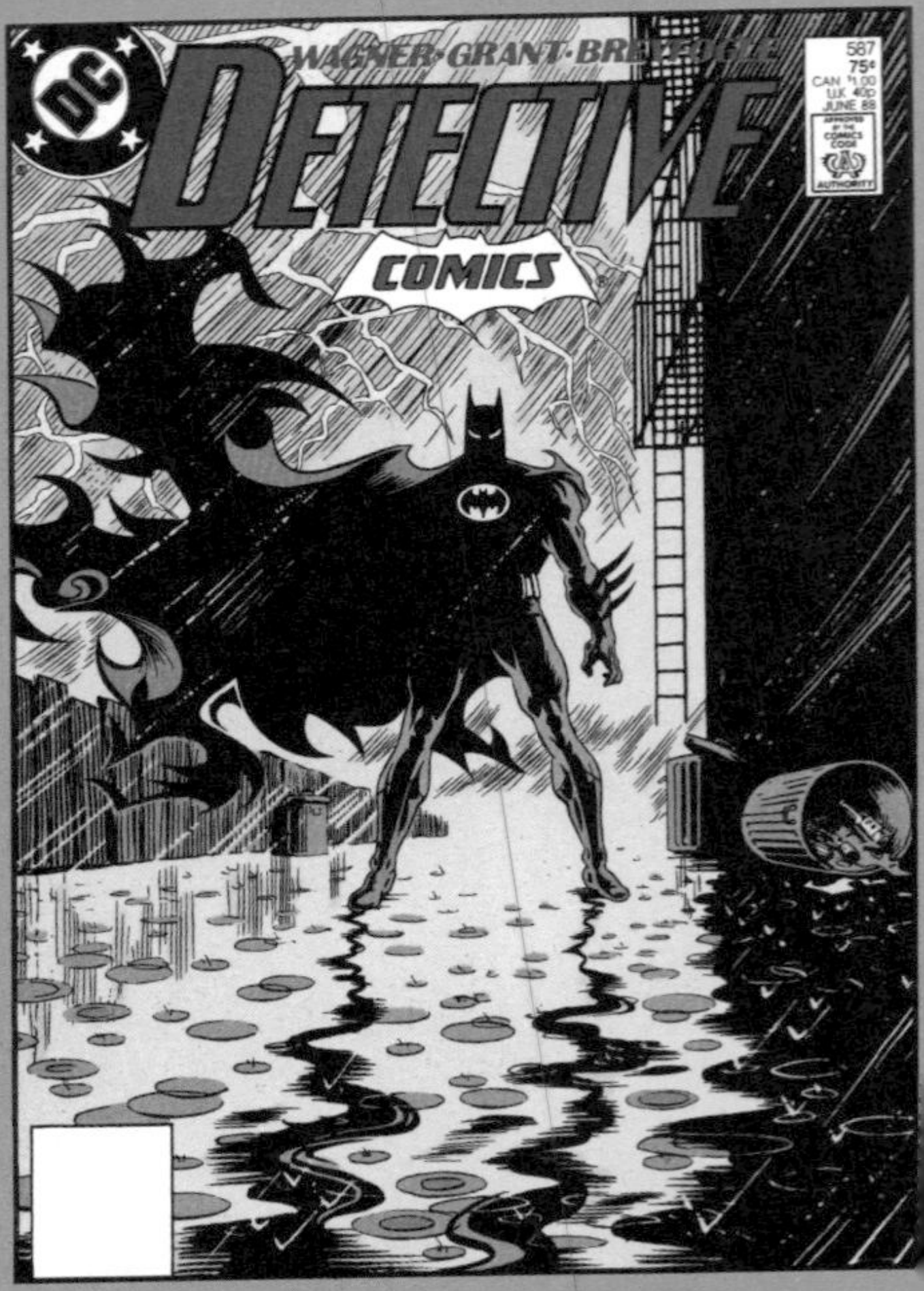
WAGNER·GRANT·BREEDLOVE
DETECTIVE
COMICS
587
75¢
CAN $1.00
U.K. 40p
JUNE 89
APPROVED BY THE COMICS CODE AUTHORITY

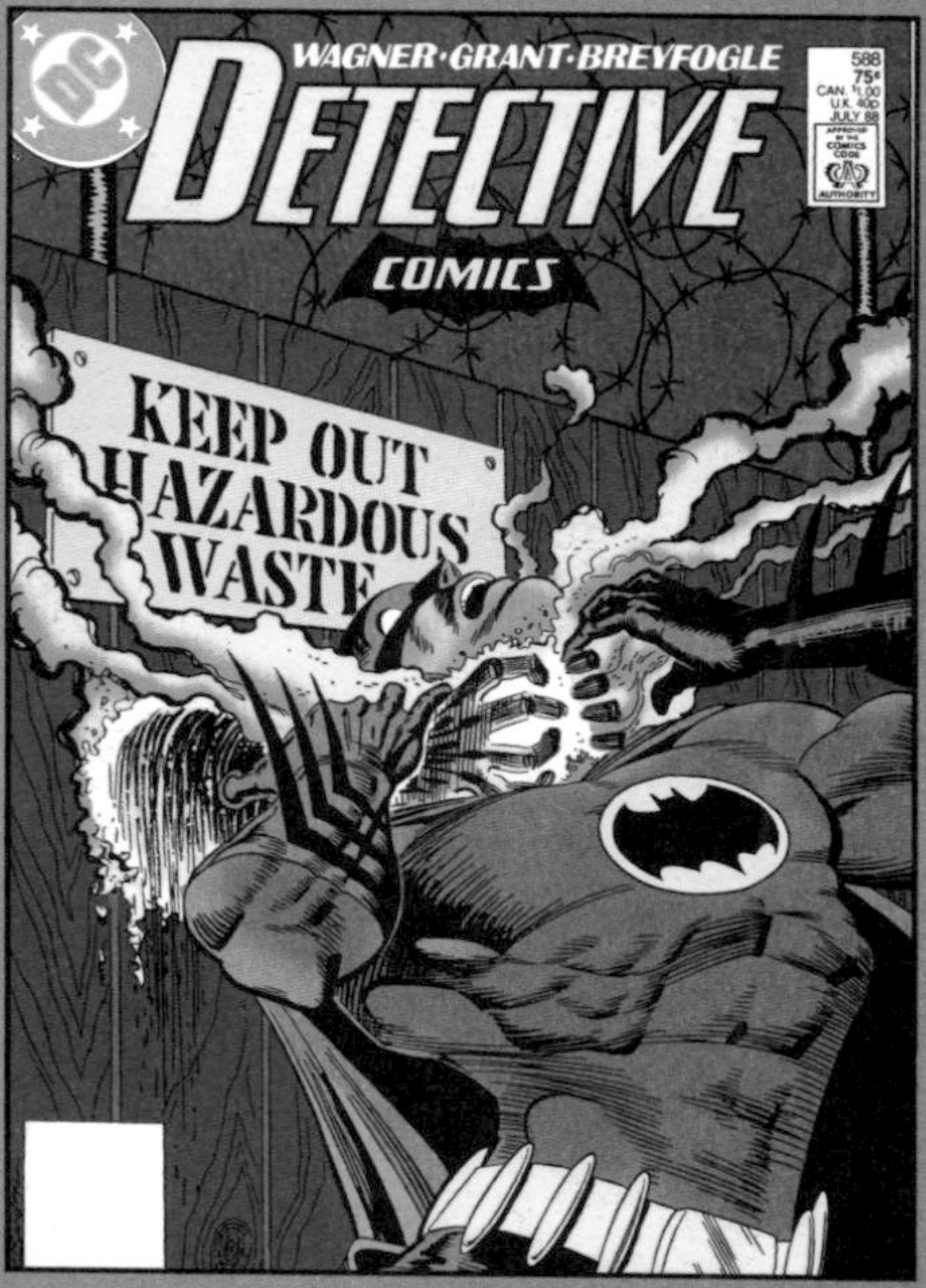
WAGNER·GRANT·BREYFOGLE
DETECTIVE
COMICS
588
75¢
CAN. $1.00
U.K. 40p
JULY 88
APPROVED BY THE COMICS CODE AUTHORITY
KEEP OUT
HAZARDOUS
WASTE

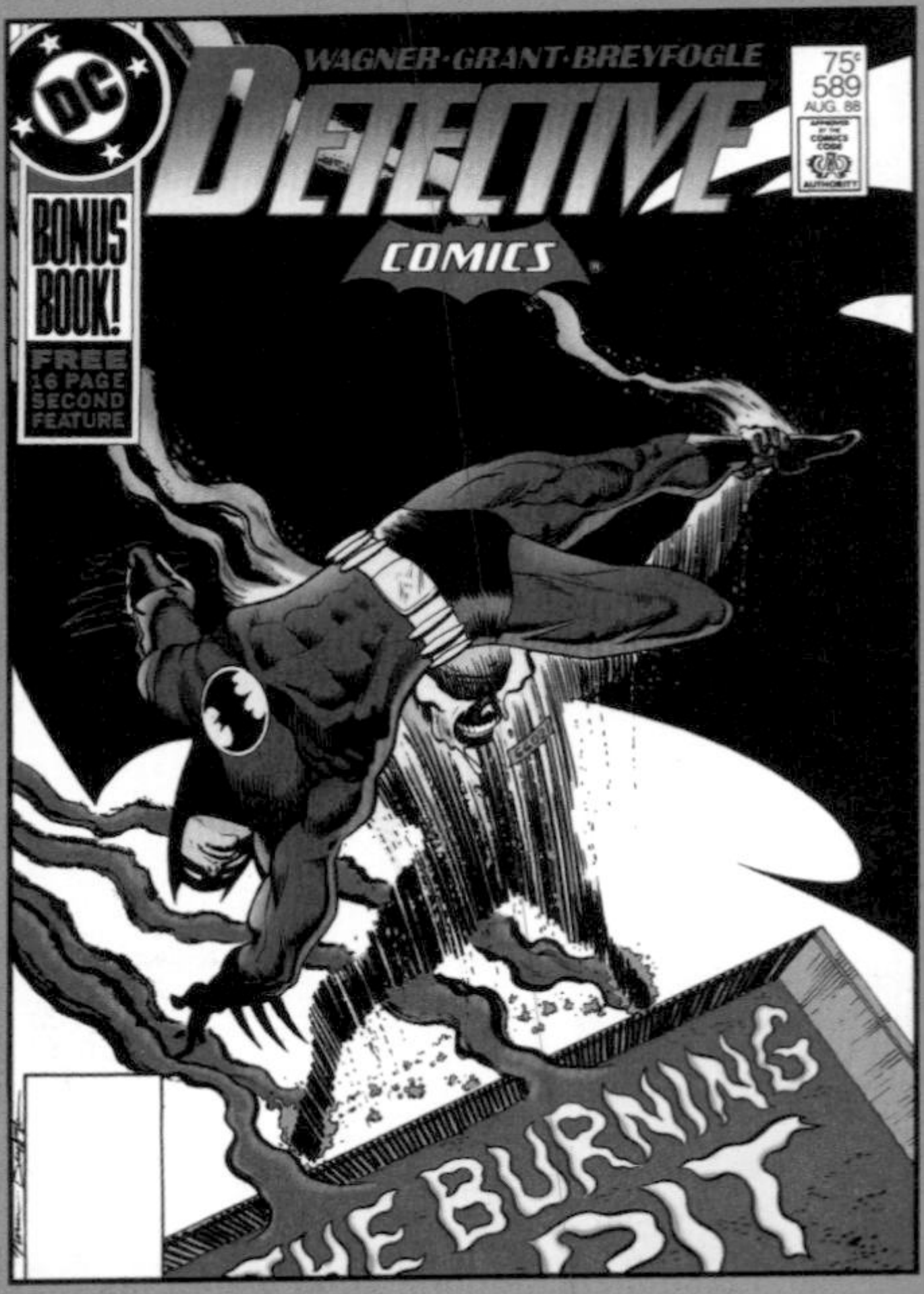
DC
WAGNER · GRANT · BREYFOGLE
DETECTIVE
COMICS
75¢
589
AUG. 88
BONUS BOOK!
FREE 16 PAGE SECOND FEATURE
THE BURNING PIT

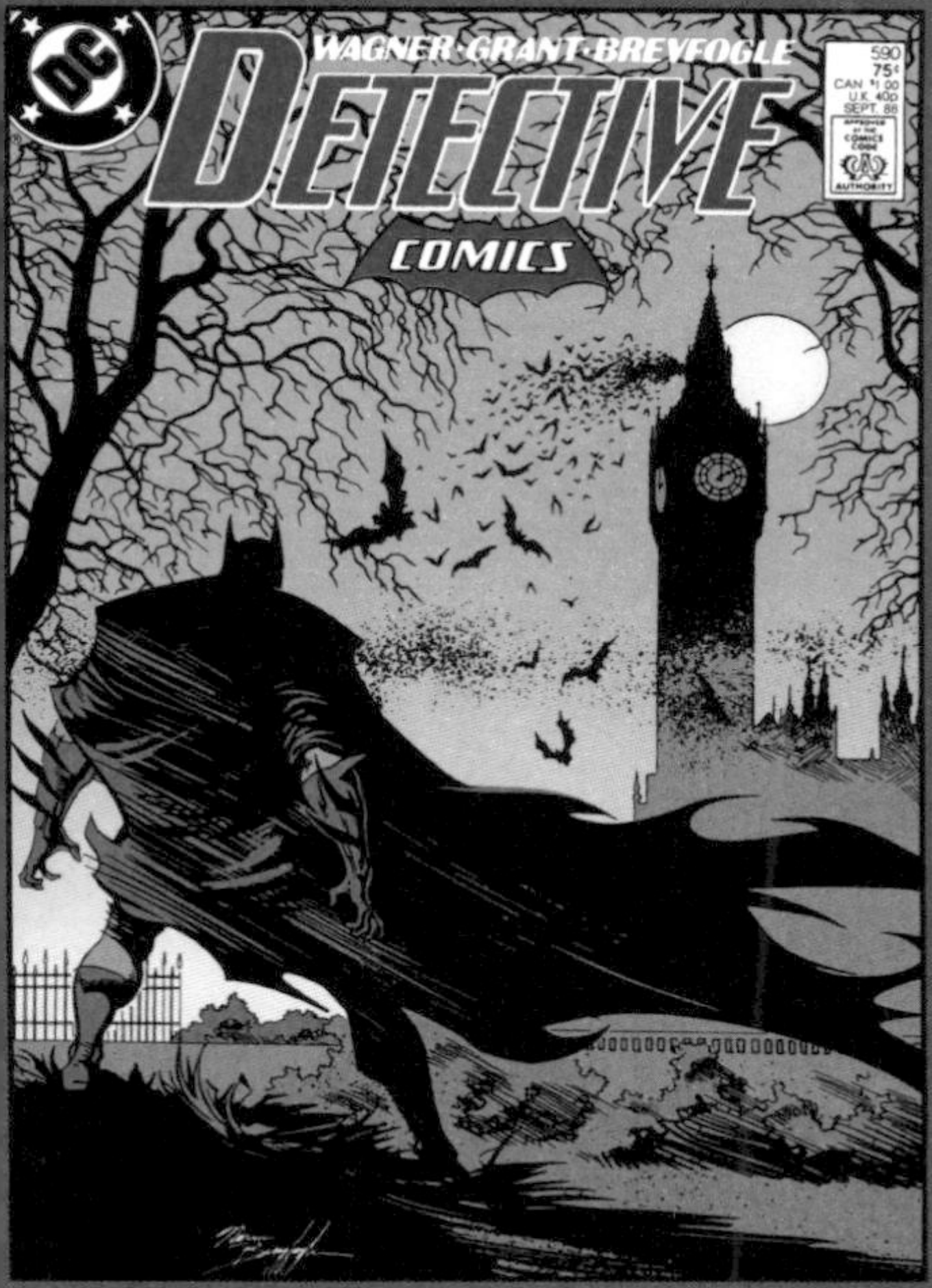
DC
WAGNER·GRANT·BREYFOGLE
DETECTIVE
COMICS
590
75¢
CAN $1.00
U.K. 40p
SEPT. 88
APPROVED BY THE COMICS CODE
CCA
AUTHORITY

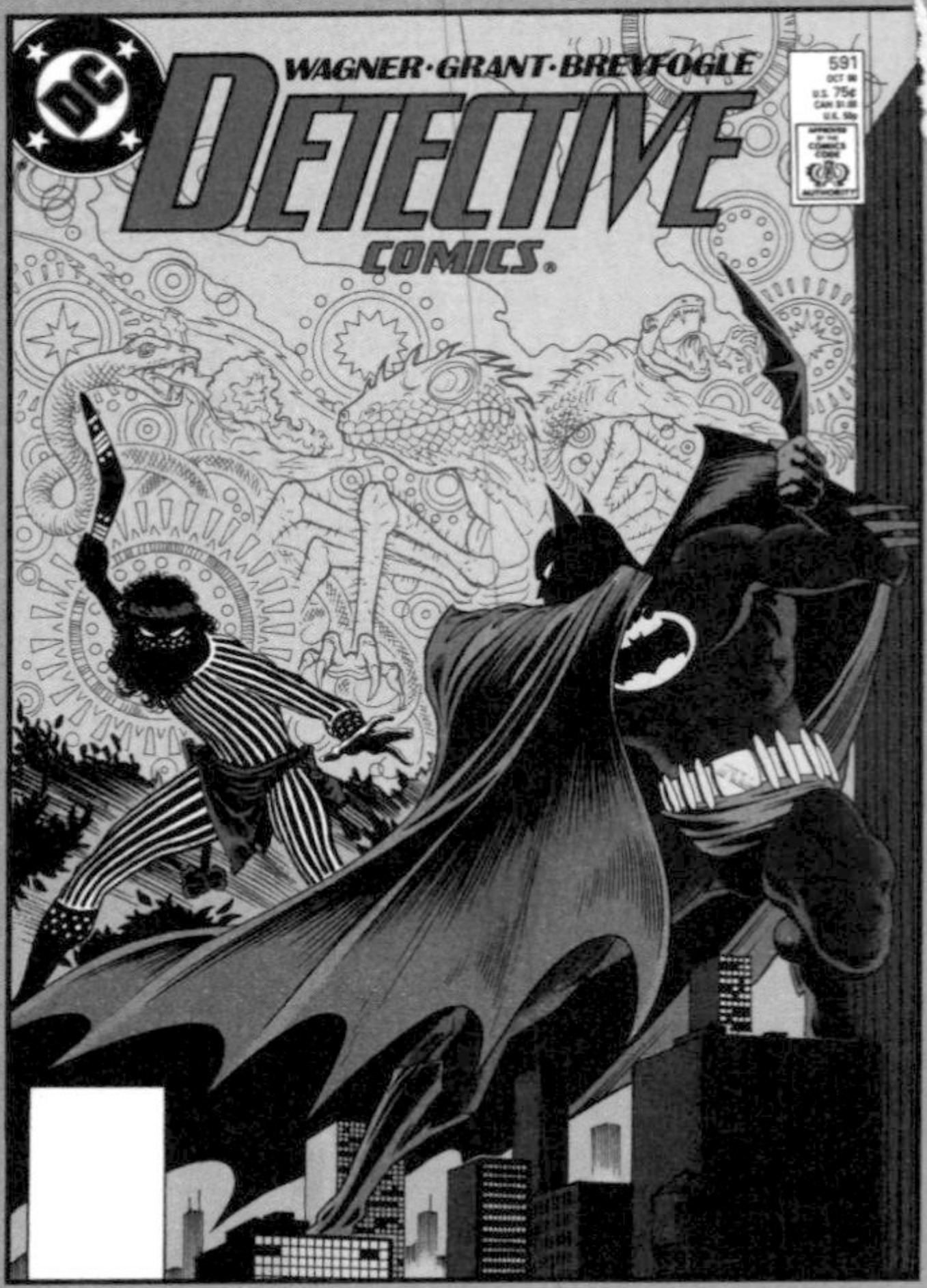
WAGNER · GRANT · BREYFOGLE
DETECTIVE
COMICS
591
OCT 86
U.S. 75¢

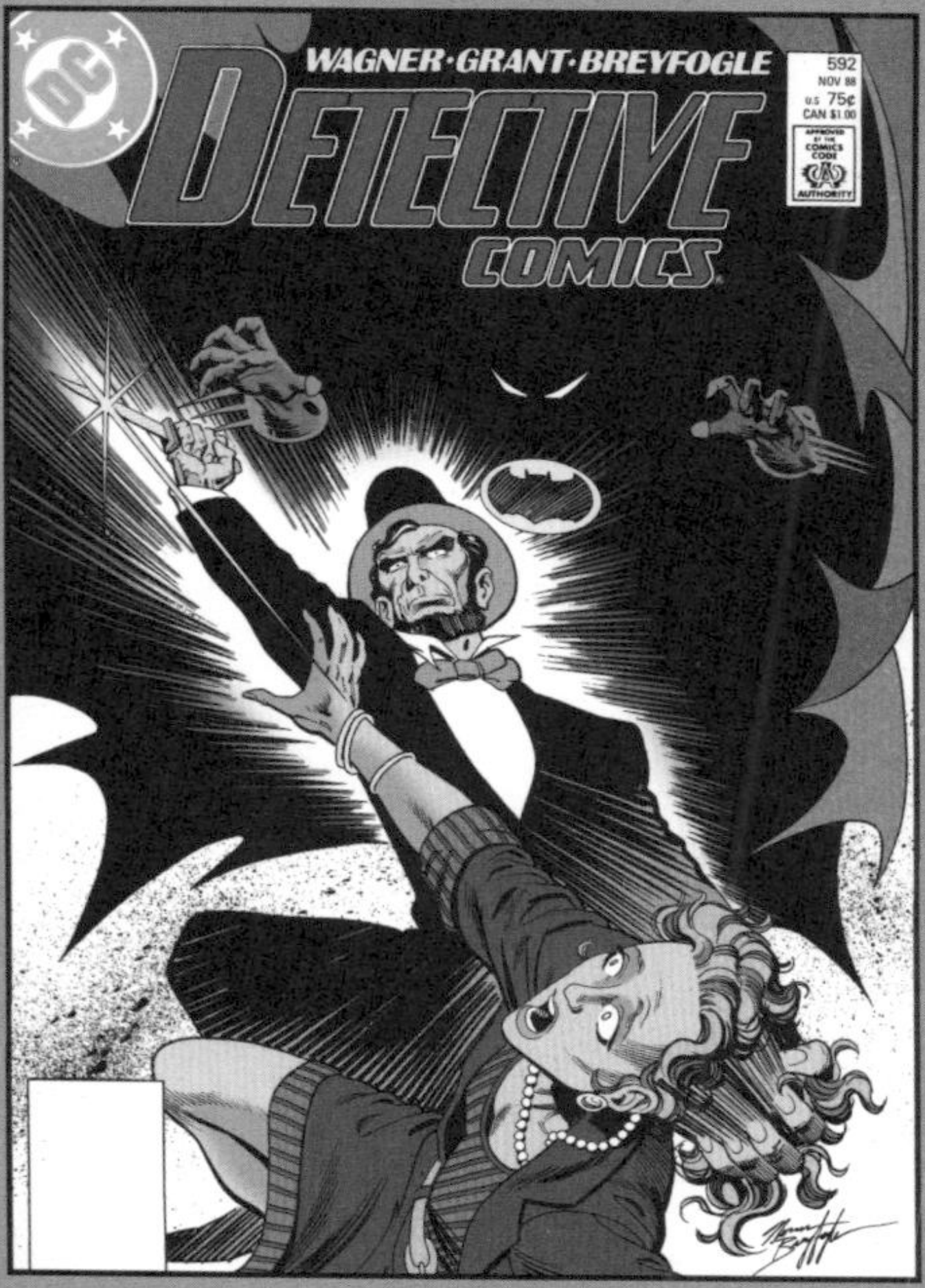
WAGNER·GRANT·BREYFOGLE
DETECTIVE COMICS
592
NOV 88
U.S. 75¢
CAN $1.00
APPROVED BY THE COMICS CODE AUTHORITY

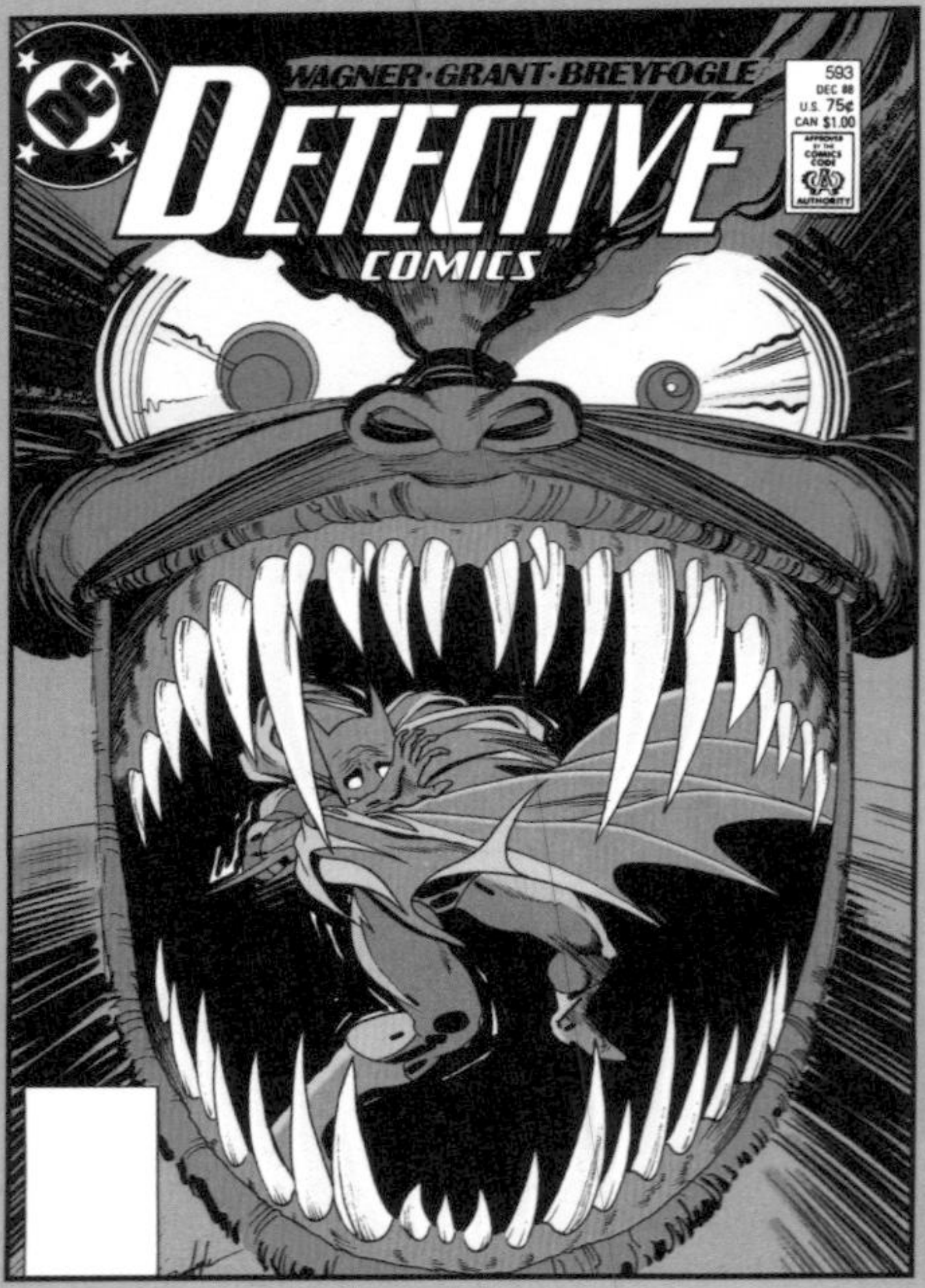
WAGNER · GRANT · BREYFOGLE
DETECTIVE
COMICS
593
DEC 88
U.S. 75¢
CAN $1.00
APPROVED BY THE COMICS CODE AUTHORITY

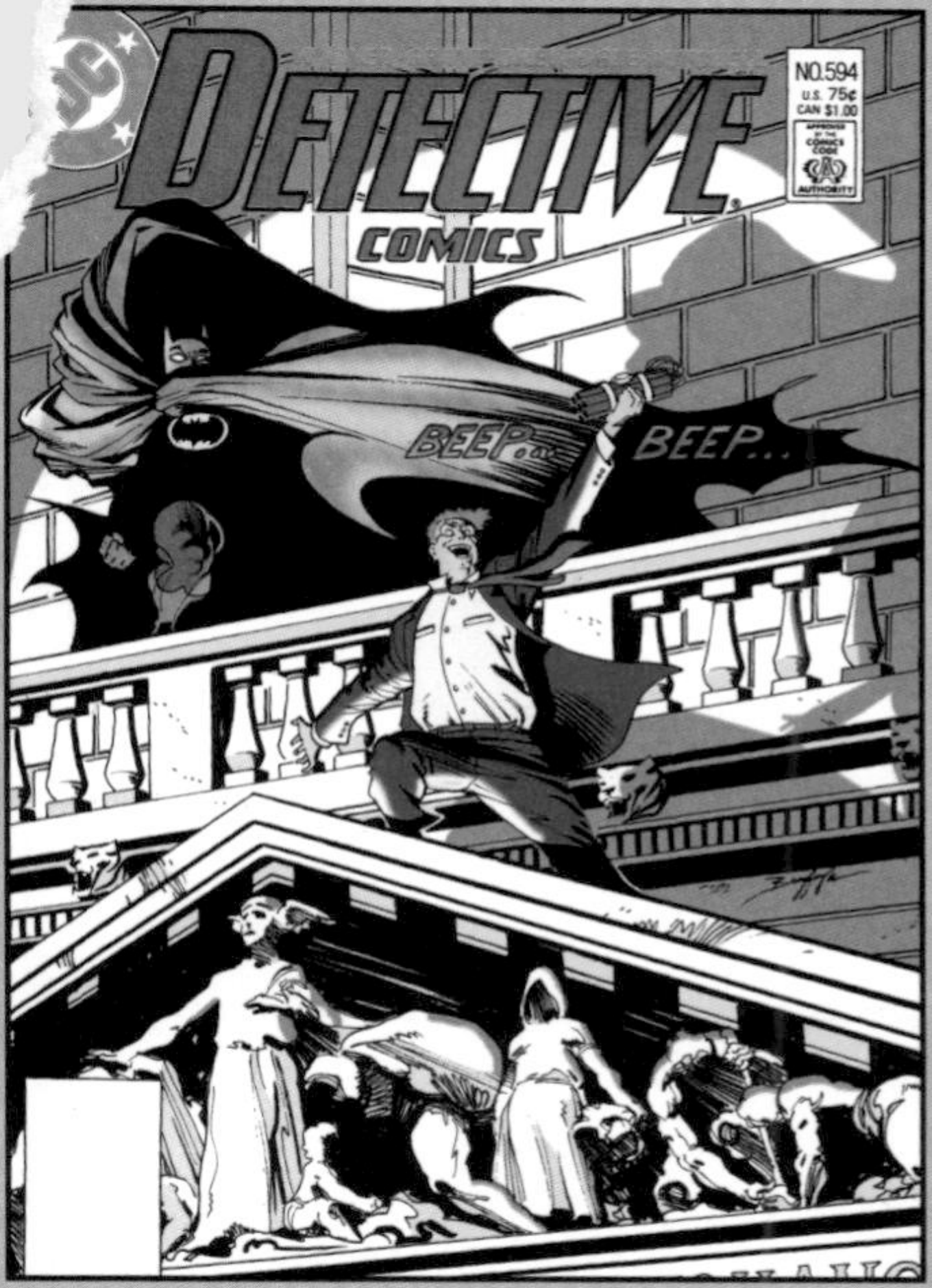
DETECTIVE
COMICS
NO.594
U.S. 75¢
CAN $1.00
BEEP...
BEEP...

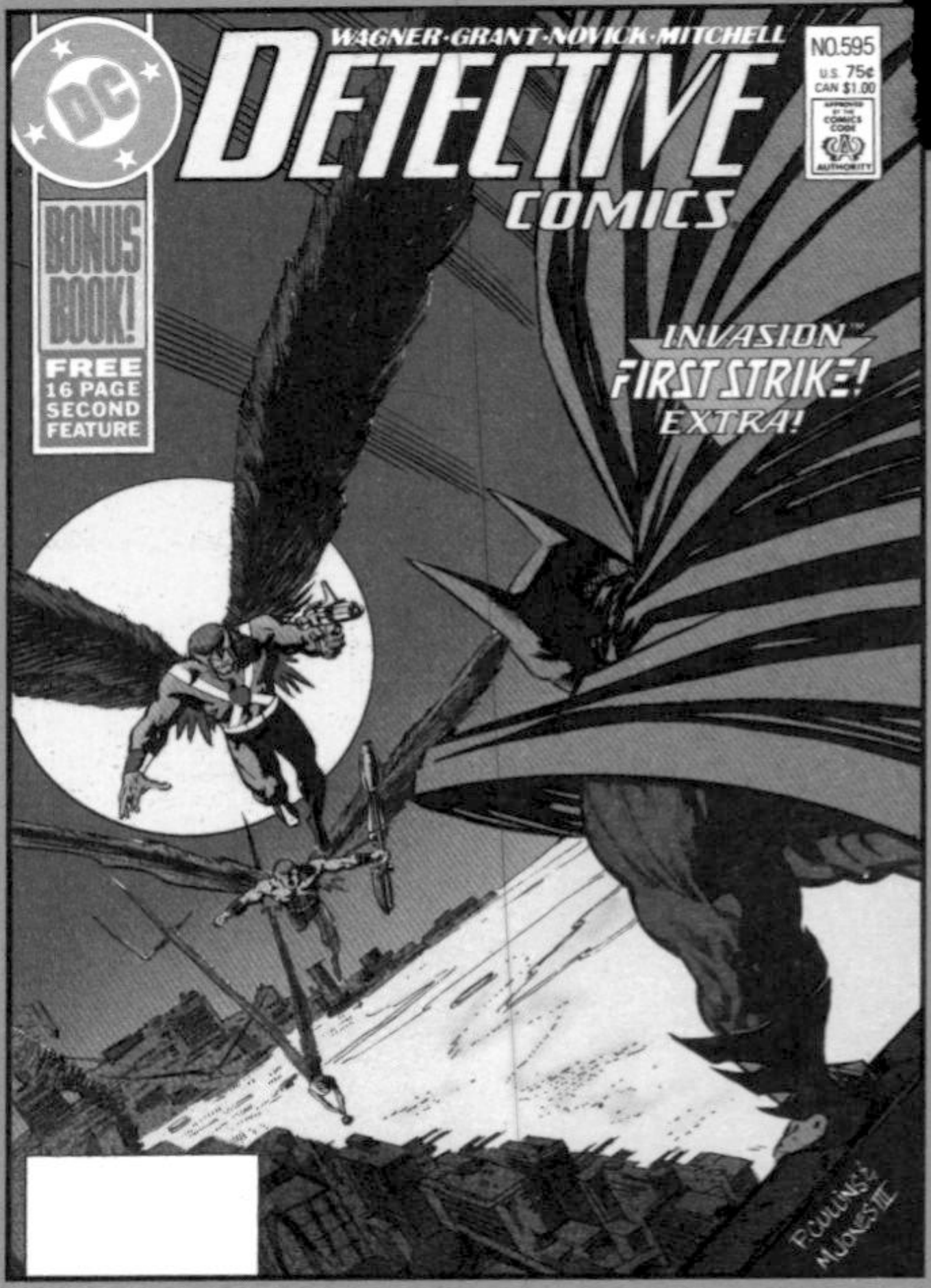
WAGNER·GRANT·NOVICK·MITCHELL
DETECTIVE COMICS
NO.595
U.S. 75¢
CAN $1.00
BONUS BOOK!
FREE 16 PAGE SECOND FEATURE
INVASION™ FIRST STRIKE! EXTRA!
F.COLLINS & M.JONES II

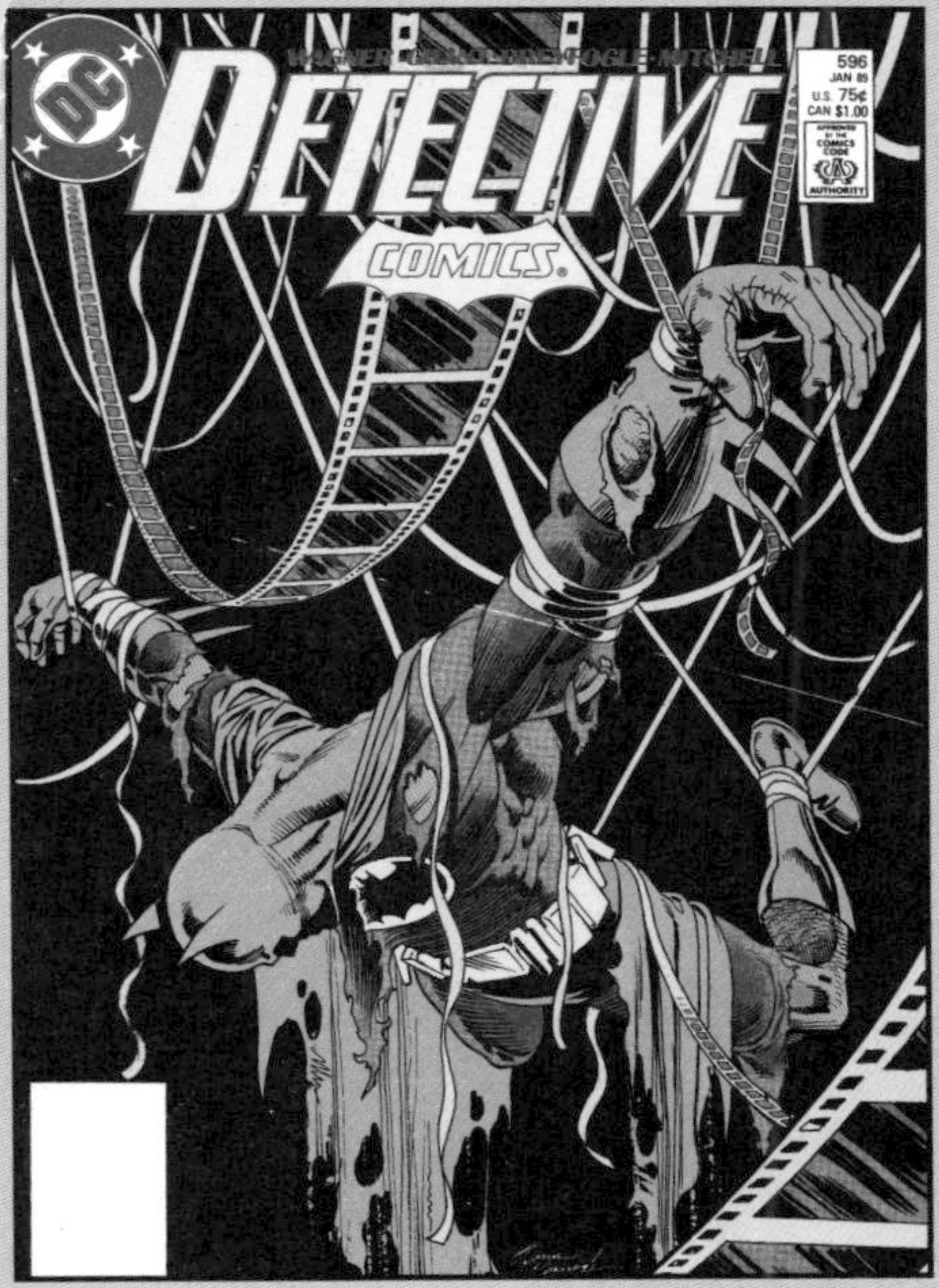
WAGNER · GRENDEL · FOGLIO · MITCHELL
DETECTIVE
COMICS
596
JAN 89
U.S. 75¢
CAN $1.00
APPROVED BY THE COMICS CODE
AUTHORITY

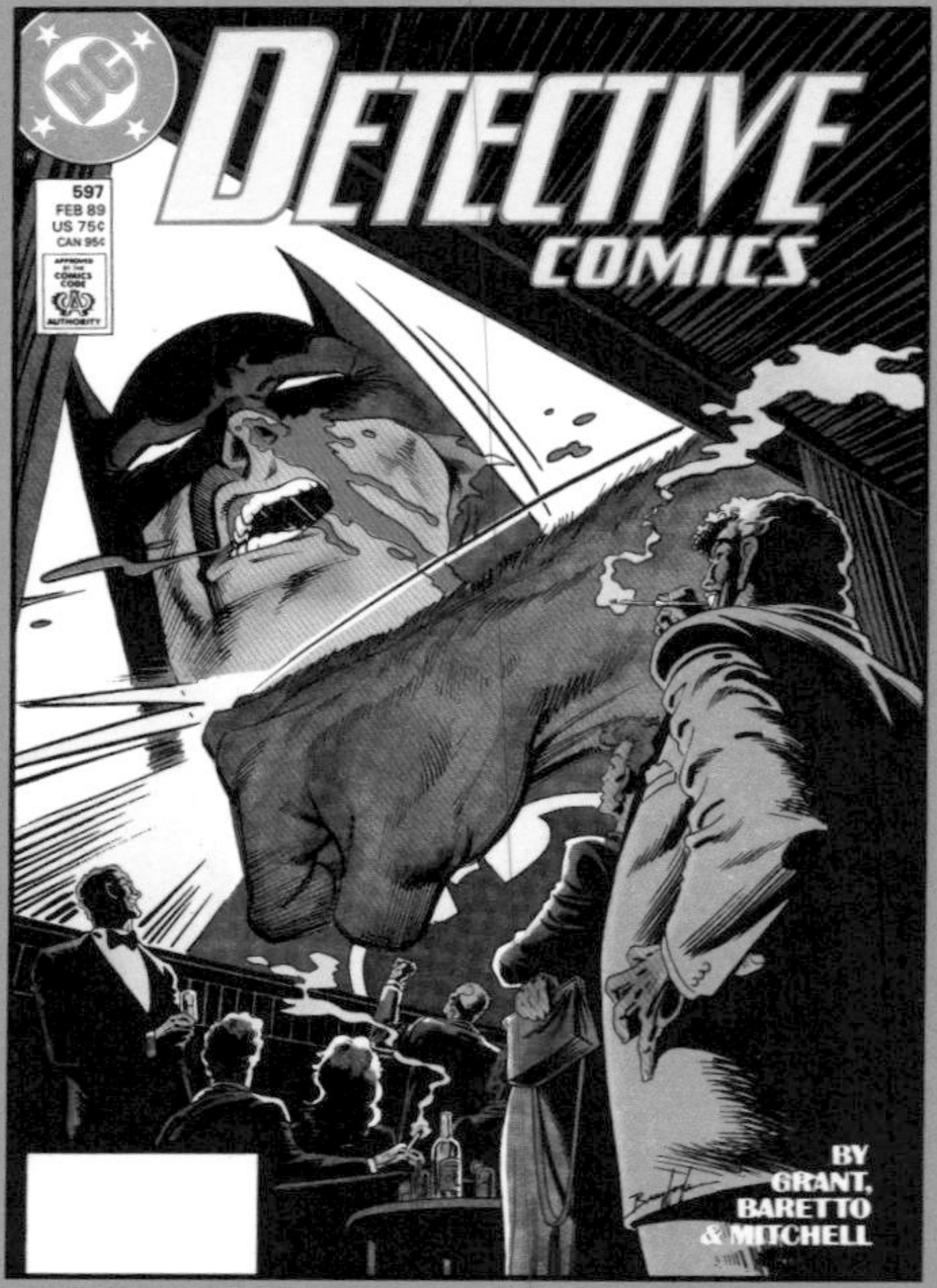
DC
DETECTIVE
COMICS.
597
FEB 89
US 75¢
CAN 95¢
APPROVED BY THE COMICS CODE AUTHORITY
BY
GRANT,
BARETTO
& MITCHELL

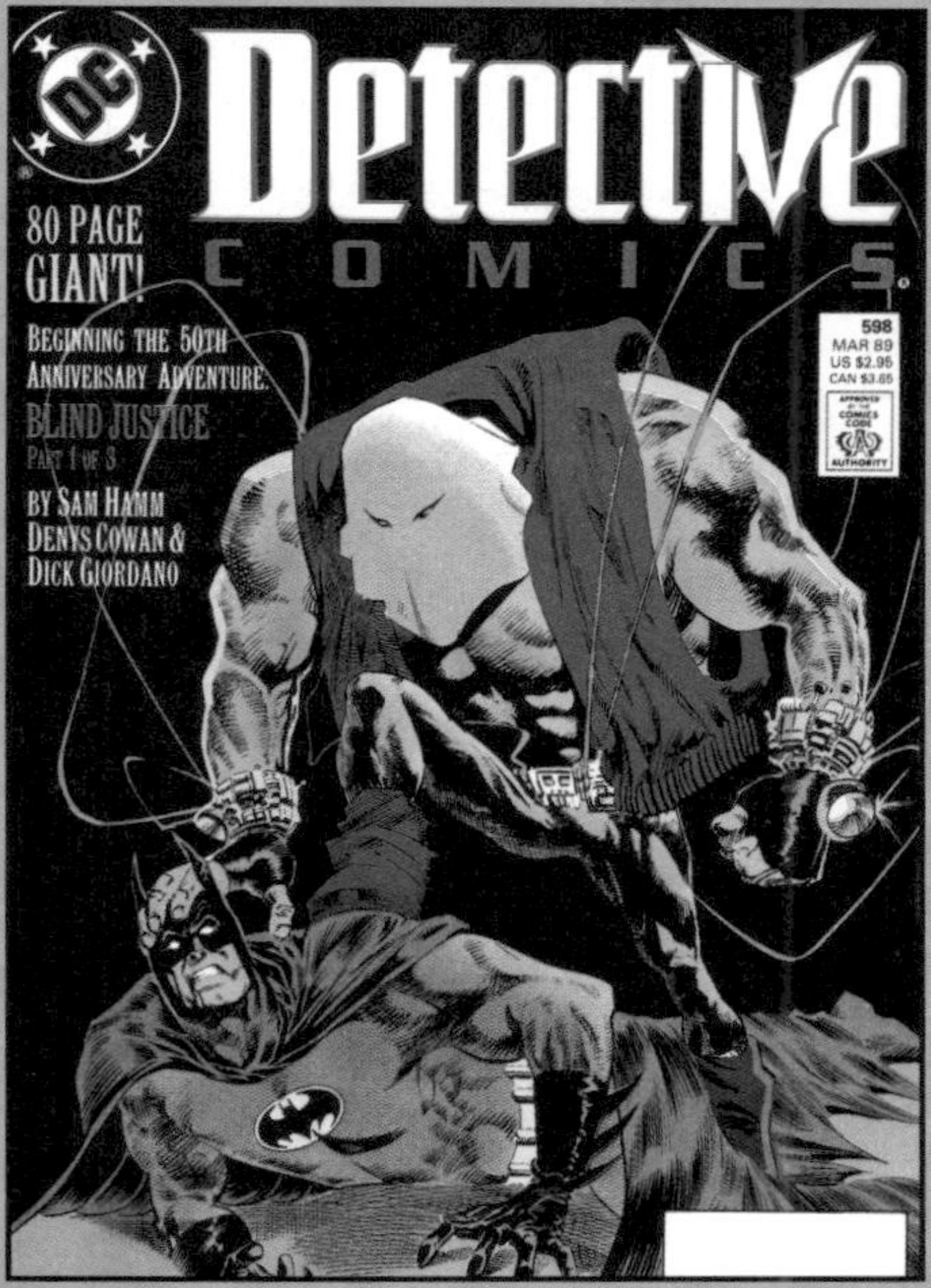
DC
Detective
COMICS
80 PAGE GIANT!
BEGINNING THE 50TH ANNIVERSARY ADVENTURE.
BLIND JUSTICE
PART 1 OF 3
BY SAM HAMM
DENYS COWAN &
DICK GIORDANO
598
MAR 89
US $2.95
CAN $3.65
APPROVED BY THE COMICS CODE
CA
AUTHORITY

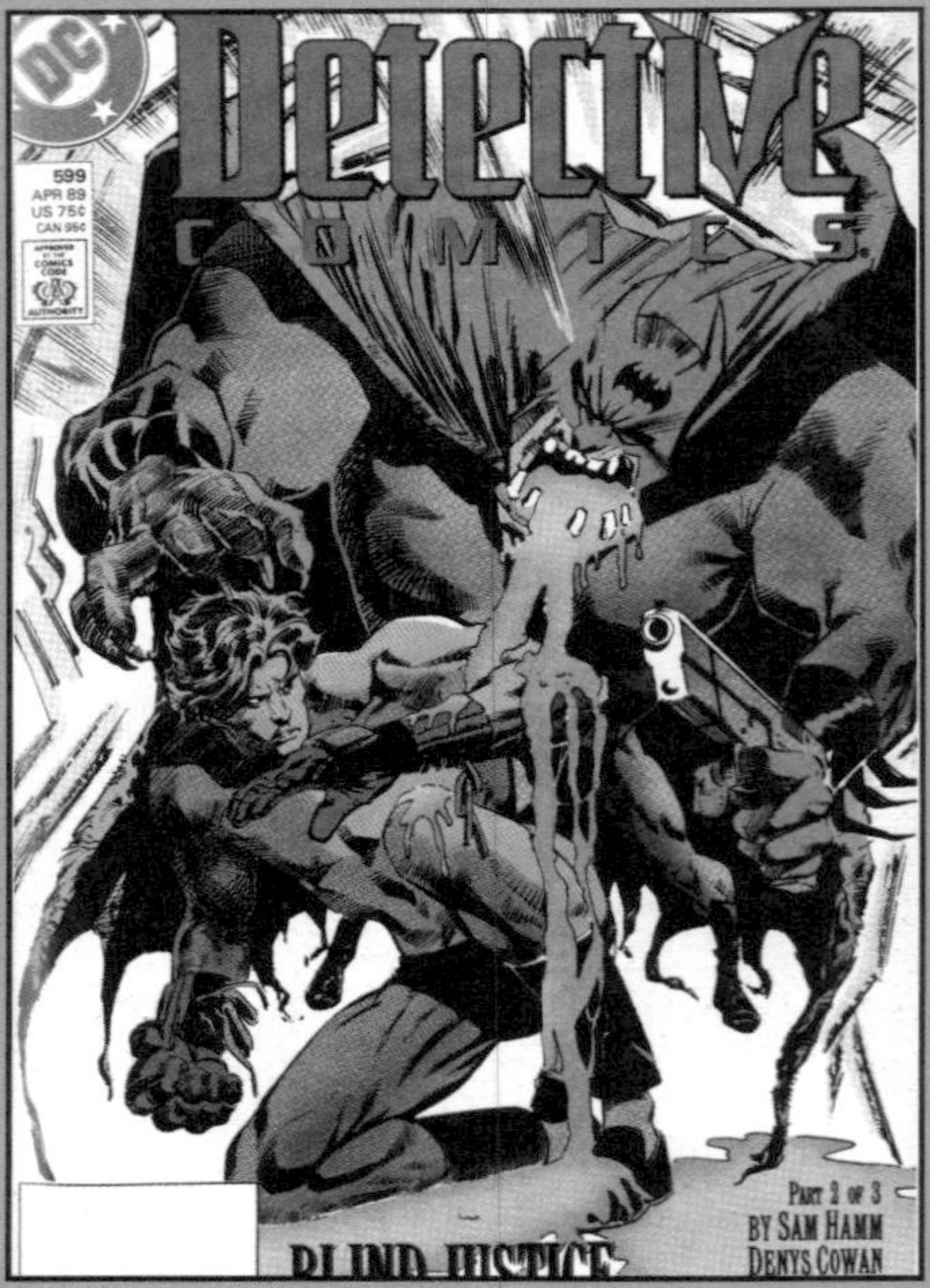
DC
Detective
COMICS
599
APR 89
US 75¢
CAN 95¢
AUTHORITY
PART 2 OF 3
BY SAM HAMM
DENYS COWAN
BLIND JUSTICE

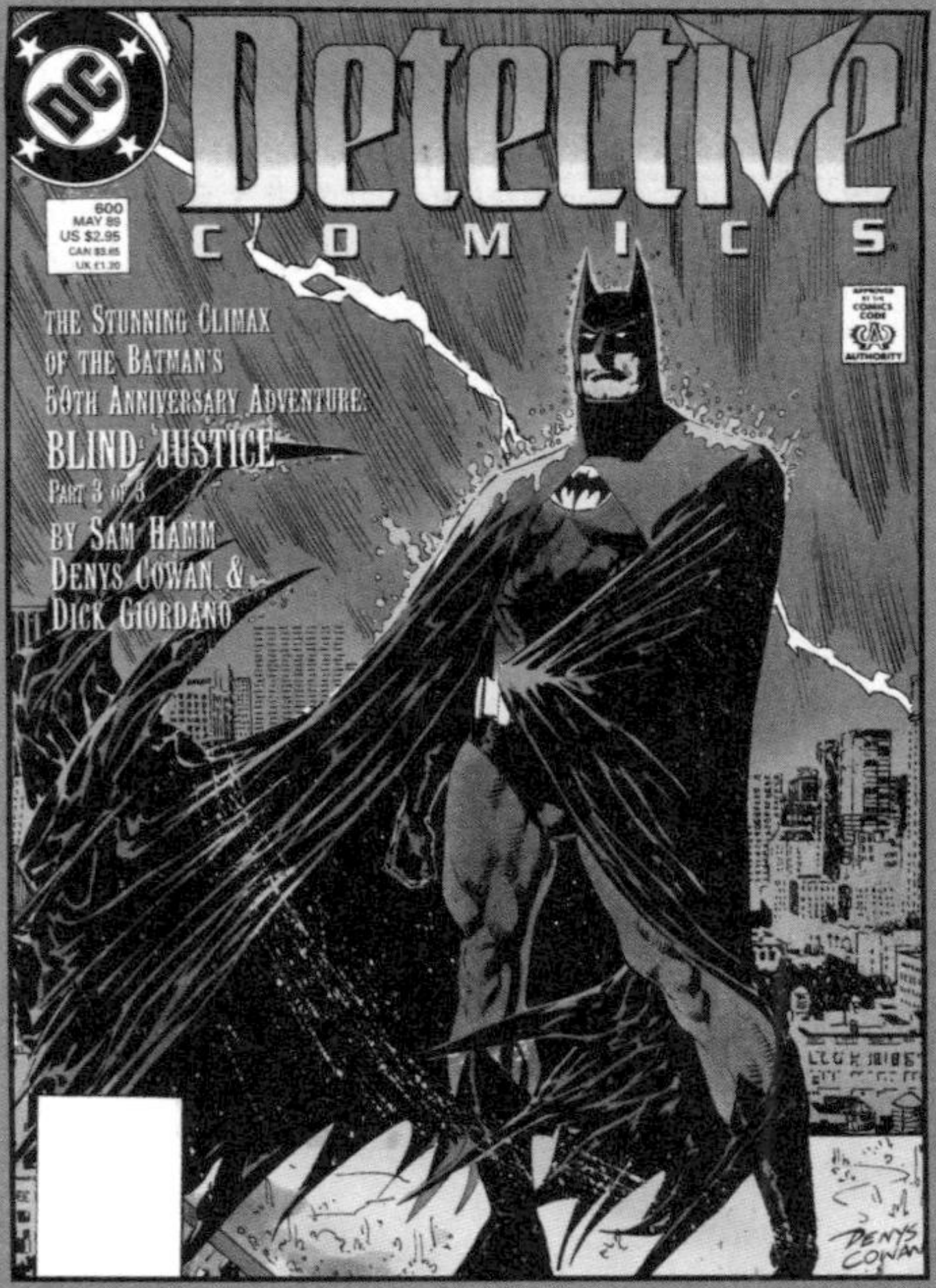
DC
Detective
COMICS
600
MAY 89
US $2.95
CAN $3.95
UK £1.20
THE STUNNING CLIMAX
OF THE BATMAN'S
50TH ANNIVERSARY ADVENTURE:
BLIND JUSTICE
PART 3 OF 8
BY SAM HAMM
DENYS COWAN &
DICK GIORDANO
APPROVED BY THE COMICS CODE
AUTHORITY
DENYS COWAN

INSIGHT
EDITIONS
PO Box 3088
San Rafael, CA 94912
www.insighteditions.com

Find us on Facebook: www.facebook.com/InsightEditions

Follow us on Twitter: @insighteditions

BATMAN and all characters and elements © & ™ DC Comics. WB SHIELD: TM & © Warner Bros. Entertainment Inc. (s19)

INED41435

Published by Insight Editions, San Rafael, California, in 2019.
All rights reserved. No part of this book may be reproduced in any form without written permission from the publisher.

Library of Congress Cataloging-in-Publication Data available.

ISBN: 978-1-68383-484-7

Manufactured in China by Insight Editions

10 9 8 7 6 5 4 3 2 1